Fourteenth Edition

Boating Skills and
Seamanship

 Mc Graw Hill Education

INTERNATIONAL MARINE / McGRAW HILL EDUCATION

Camden, Maine • New York • Chicago • San Francisco • Lisbon • London • Madrid • Mexico City • Milan • New Delhi • San Juan • Seoul • Singapore • Sydney • Toronto

Fourteenth Edition

Boating Skills and
Seamanship

 United States Coast Guard Auxiliary

America's Volunteer Lifesavers℠

1 2 3 4 5 6 7 8 9 0 Q VS Q VS 19 18 17 16 15 14 13

ISBN   978-0-07-182932-8
MHID   0-07-182932-6

e-ISBN   978-0-07-182933-5
e-MHID   0-07-182933-4

Library of Congress Cataloging-in-Publication Data is available.

Questions regarding the content of this book should be addressed to:
www. internationalmarine.com

Questions regarding the ordering of this book should be addressed to:
McGraw Hill Education
Customer Service
P.O. Box 547
Blacklick, OH 43004
Retail Customers: 1-800-262-4729
Bookstores: 1-800-722-4726

The 14th Edition of *Boating Skills and Seamanship* has been edited and revised by Paul DeVita, Division Chief—Course Management, USCGAUX.

The following Coast Guard Auxiliary members have also contributed time, talents, and efforts to *Boating Skills and Seamanship*, 14th Edition:
Ralph W. Fairbanks, USCGAUX
Jay G. McDonald, USCGAUX
Thomas P. Walsh, USCGAUX
John N. Vanosdol, Deputy Department Director, Education, USCGAUX
Photo Corp, Dept. of Public Affairs, USCGAUX
Robin L. Freeman, Vice President, Educational Products Development, CGAuxA

Unless otherwise credited, illustrations by Joseph Comeau.

contents

Part One: Basic Skills and Seamanship

Part Two: More Boating Skills

CONTENTS

Dear Fellow Boater,

The mission of the United States Coast Guard Auxiliary, the uniformed volunteer component of Team Coast Guard, is to assist the Active Duty in the performance of its civil functions – particularly the promotion of recreational boating safety. The Coast Guard Auxiliary does this through its public education, vessel examination, and RBS Outreach.

This book is the text for one of the core public education courses taught by the Coast Guard Auxiliary – Boating Skills and Seamanship (BS&S). This course is a key component of a well-developed educational program that reaches from preschool through adulthood. The Coast Guard Auxiliary Public Education Program is the most comprehensive program available to pleasure boaters of today.

The 14th edition of the BS&S text continues our tradition of providing courses for quality classroom education to boaters. The National Association of State Boating Law Administrators (NASBLA) approves the BS&S course. Information contained herein is consistent with current knowledge and with federal regulations in effect at the time of printing. Your instructor will present supplemental material on applicable state regulations. Many insurance companies provide discounts to graduates of the BS&S course.

This text has been prepared at no cost to the United States government but developed by resources provided by the Coast Guard Auxiliary Association, Inc. Members of the Coast Guard Auxiliary teach this course. Coast Guard Auxiliary members are a well-prepared group of individuals dedicated to saving lives by promoting recreational boating safety. Their pay is the satisfaction of doing a good job and knowing they have helped other people have safe and enjoyable boating experiences.

I hope that you find this course both stimulating and enjoyable. Let me also urge you to take other Coast Guard Auxiliary courses and to consider supporting and even joining the United States Coast Guard Auxiliary. Visit our website at www.cgaux.org to learn more about how you could help others.

Very respectfully,

Thomas C. Mallison
National Commodore
United States Coast Guard Auxiliary

Welcome Aboard!

THE BOOK YOU ARE ABOUT TO READ is designed to help you become a better recreational boater. Through it, we hope to teach you the knowledge and skills that you need to boat safely. With this knowledge, you can avoid problems and enhance your enjoyment of on-the-water activities. We also want to raise your awareness of what bad things might happen to you or others, so that they can be prevented.

Fourth of July gatherings to watch fireworks—like this one on the Charles River, Boston, Massachusetts—often entail numerous boats, some of them rafting together for hours. (PHOTO BY MOLLY MULHERN)

The twin-outboard-powered 22-foot C-Dory cabin cruiser *Sea-life* makes her way down the Sacramento River through wind chop and tidal current. (PHOTO BY MERRILL WALSTAD)

A Growing Recreational Activity

The number of people using recreational boats is increasing rapidly and boating is changing. Today's boating is much different from the yachting of yesterday. Today, most recreational boats are small, less than 20 feet long, and their number is growing rapidly. Boating has become an important recreational activity.

For most of us, boating means a fun way to pass a day or a weekend with our family and friends. We use boats for cruising, sightseeing, waterskiing, hunting, fishing, swimming, diving, waterbiking, and other purposes.

The Need for Boating Safety

For some people boating experiences are not always pleasant. Boating, at times, involves injury, financial loss, and sometimes death. Considering the small amount of time we actually spend on the water, injury and death rates exceed those of many hazardous occupations.

Fortunately, injury and death rates are declining. This has resulted, in part, from the efforts of the United States Coast Guard, the Coast Guard Aux-

iliary, the United States Power Squadrons, and state and local agencies. They have been effective in preventing boating accidents and in saving lives.

Promoting Boating Safety

Among the factors that account for improved boating safety are improved boater safety education, expanded law enforcement, safer boats, and greater awareness of the roles of alcohol and drugs in boating accidents. The purpose of this book is to promote safe boating. In so doing, we have tried to use as little jargon as possible, including only that which we believe is basic to safe boating.

Boating Skills and Seamanship

This book uses a timeline approach. This is a logical line from thinking about boating and buying a boat through equipping it and using it safely and legally. Part One, Basic Skills and Seamanship (Chapters 1 through 8), introduces the basics. In Part Two, More Boating Skills (Chapters 9 through 13), we delve into topics you'll want to explore after your initial boating experiences.

Each chapter has been written to help you achieve important goals. Each chapter starts with stating the objectives, and has practice questions at the end to confirm your understanding. (State and local boating information is not included because of the large variation of requirements between the states. State regulations are available from the National Association of State Boating Law Administrators [NASBLA] at www.nasbla.org.) **CHAPTER 1, WHICH BOAT IS FOR YOU?,** helps you select a boat to fit your needs. You'll learn what uses boats are designed for, how this influences their types and construction, and what you need to know to select one for your particular purposes. In addition, you'll learn what you need to know to talk intelligently about a boat, how to rate a boat before you buy it, and what else should guide your purchase. **CHAPTER 2, EQUIPMENT FOR YOUR BOAT,** teaches you what to have on your boat to satisfy legal requirements. You will also learn what other equipment to carry for your safety and convenience. And you will learn how to find out if your boat and its equipment meet safety and legal requirements.

CHAPTER 3, TRAILERING YOUR BOAT, provides information on how to get your boat safely and legally from your home to where you want to launch it. It will also help you know how to store it to protect it from the weather and from theft.

CHAPTER 4, HANDLING YOUR BOAT, teaches you about handling your boat after it is in the water. What are some of the special circumstances you may meet? What can you do about them? What are some of the more serious safety problems? How can you prevent them?

CHAPTER 5, YOUR "HIGHWAY" SIGNS, teaches you about the aids to navigation provided by federal, state, and local authorities. Knowing about these aids will help you have a safe voyage, and knowing how to locate them on a chart will help you know where you are. These aids to navigation and the Navigation Rules in Chapter 6 are important guides during your outings.

CHAPTER 6, THE RULES OF THE NAUTICAL ROAD, describes the Navigation Rules that govern the conduct of your vessel while it is on the water. These traffic rules help prevent boat collisions. Knowledge of the rules will help you have safe and enjoyable boating experiences.

CHAPTER 7, INLAND BOATING, concentrates on questions such as: What special knowledge do you need to boat safely on rivers, lakes, and canals? What do you need to know to operate safely around dams? What procedures should you use in locks?

CHAPTER 8, BOATING SAFETY, considers a variety of problems such as small boat safety, personal watercraft, hypothermia, conduct of motorboats near sailboats, and carbon monoxide poisoning.

CHAPTER 9, INTRODUCTION TO NAVIGATION, teaches you the basics of how to get from where you are to where you want to be, safely! You will also learn how to read a chart, plot a course, and measure your voyage progress.

CHAPTER 10, POWERING YOUR BOAT, helps you to learn more about how your boat is powered. Its primary focus is on what you need to know to maintain and operate your boat's power plant properly.

CHAPTER 11, LINES AND KNOTS FOR YOUR BOAT, teaches you how to tie some of the more important knots. The chapter centers on what you need to

Two boaters inspect their boat before heading home after a great day on the water. (PHOTO BY BOB DENNIS)

know about handling ropes and lines and working with them to insure their proper use.

CHAPTER 12, WEATHER AND BOATING, provides information on where to find, and how to interpret, weather conditions, and how they affect your boating activities. The goal is to provide you with the knowledge necessary to make informed go, no-go decisions prior to leaving the dock and throughout the voyage.

CHAPTER 13, YOUR BOAT'S RADIO, describes the functions of various radios. Additionally, proper phraseology and etiquette will be stressed. Information gained in this chapter will assist you in the purchase of an appropriate radio for your type of boating, as well as many of its valuable uses.

The Auxiliary's goal is to help you become a better recreational boater. We wish you safe and happy boating!

An approaching thunderstorm with a lead gust front. Rain-cooled air moves out ahead of the storm, plowing under warm, moist air ahead to form a flat shelf cloud. (COURTESY NOAA PHOTO LIBRARY; NOAA CENTRAL LIBRARY; OAR/ERL/NATIONAL SEVERE STORMS LABORATORY)

This 75-foot houseboat on Lake Guntersville is powered by twin Mercruiser inboard/outboard motors. (PHOTO BY DUNCAN WILKINSON)

part I

BASIC SKILLS AND SEAMANSHIP

A pontoon boat powered by an outboard takes this family of five fishing. (COURTESY TRACKER MARINE GROUP)

chapter 1

Which Boat Is for You?

(COURTESY RANGER BOATS)

The objectives of this chapter are to describe:

✔ The importance of boating safety.

✔ The U.S. Coast Guard Auxiliary.

✔ Parts of a boat in proper language.

✔ Types of hulls and means of propulsion.

✔ The variety of boats available to match your needs.

✔ How to get information on possible defects in a vessel.

✔ Considerations in a contract to purchase a boat.

✔ The importance of boat insurance.

A BOAT is anything used for transportation on the water. Huck Finn's raft was a boat. A seaplane is a boat when it is on the water. Canoes, kayaks, rowboats, and other small craft are boats. Boats range in size from personal watercraft (PWC) to large ships, and they might have deep or shallow hulls; flat, round, or V-shaped bottom sections; and tall or short cabin sides and superstructures. They can be slender or stout, and they might have one, two, or even three hulls. They vary, too, in the materials from which they're built. As defined by the Federal Boat Safety Act of 1971, all boats are vessels, but a vessel is not a boat (and therefore exempt from certain commercial safety regulations) unless it was manufactured or is engaged primarily for noncommercial use or is engaged in carrying six or fewer passengers for hire.

Boats come in such a large assortment because they serve many purposes. In this lesson you will learn about these purposes and how vessels are designed for them. You will also learn the basics of boat construction, materials, and uses.

Boaters' Language

Newcomers to any subject usually must learn a new vocabulary. Boating is no exception. The language of mariners has been developing for many centuries. It has the virtues of utility, economy, and an exactitude you need when talking about boats and boating.

As we introduce terms, we will usually define them for you. You can also find some of them in the Glossary at the back of the book. If you do not find a word listed in the Glossary, look for it in the Index. The first time we use a technical term, we will print it in *red*.

Origins of Boaters' Language

Boaters have been around a long time, so the vocabulary has come from many places: ancient Greece, the Roman Empire, Scandinavia, England, and elsewhere.

Some nautical terms have found their way into our everyday vocabulary. The term "blue Monday" came to us from England. The British Navy disciplined sailors on Mondays for infractions over the preceding week. The punishment consisted of lashes with a cat-o'-nine tails, or whip. No wonder Monday was blue. When not in use, the cat stayed in a sack. Of course, the cat was "out of the bag" when used.

Other terms came from Norway. Most vessels are steered by *rudders*. On an ancient sailing boat, the rudder was to the right of center at the rear, or *stern*, of the vessel. There it was protected from damage when the ship was in port. The *tiller*, which turned the rudder, was kept under the *helmsman's* right arm.

In Norway, the rudder was a "stjorn" board or steering board. *Stjorn*, when pronounced, sounds like "starn." So the right side of a vessel when looking *forward* became known as the *stjorn board* or *starboard* side (Figure 1-1).

When a vessel came into port, it was with its left side next to the *wharf*. This was the side most visible to the helmsman. It was also the side for the "load board." No wonder the left side of the vessel became known as the *larboard* side. "Larboard" and "starboard" are more exact terms than "left" and "right" since they do not change if you are facing forward or *aft*.

Because larboard and starboard sound somewhat alike, they are easily confused. Thus, larboard was changed to *port*. This was a logical choice, as this was the side of a vessel next to the wharf when the vessel was in port. Larger vessels load through *ports*, or openings, in their sides.

Remnants of ancient boats made of large, hollowed-out tree trunks or *keels* still exist. These unstable vessels took on water easily. Although they didn't sink, they were of little value when slightly submerged in rough or icy water.

Planks were added later, and the trunk became but one part of the vessel. The name keel re-

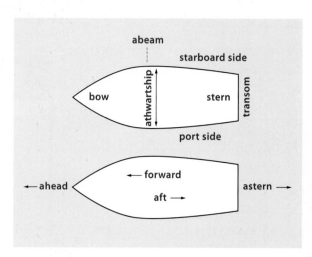

Figure **1-1.** Directions and locations on a boat.

Figure **1-2.** Bass boats underway. This is a purpose-built boat, meant to get you to the fish in a hurry and give you full walkaround fishability once you get there. (COURTESY RANGER BOATS)

mained, however. The body of the vessel, formed by the keel and the planks together, became known as the *hull*.

The aft terminus of many boats is a flat, vertical surface extending from one side of the vessel to the other. This part of a boat became known as a *transom*, from the Latin root "trans," meaning across (Figure 1-3).

The *bow* is the forwardmost portion of a vessel. This term came from the Norwegian word "bov," meaning shoulder, and pronounced "bow." You can almost see the shoulder of a boat pushing its way through the water.

Types of Boats

Boats come in a wide range of sizes and a great variety of types and models, each optimized to serve a specific need. It would be a wonderful boat that could do all things equally well, but in the real world this is not possible. Boat design and construction involve compromise, and a boat developed for one purpose may serve poorly for another. Likewise, a boat that is safe in one set of conditions may not be safe in conditions for which it is not intended. When you select a boat, be sure it will suit your needs. Also, be certain to operate it in appropriate sea and weather conditions.

Bass boats, for example, help their owners get to good fishing holes quickly (Figure 1-2). They are propelled by one or two high-horsepower outboard motors, and many of them have a small electric motor mounted off the bow to maneuver the boat at slow speeds around fishing holes in a manner that does not spook fish. These boats have sharply pointed bows and minimal V-shaped hulls at the bows. Their design permits them to operate safely at high speeds in sheltered water.

A bass boat can be dangerous, though, when used in a tidal inlet, rough water, or the large swells of an open sea. One feature that makes it dangerous is its low *freeboard*, which is the vertical distance from the *gunwales*, or tops of the boat's sides, to the surface of the water. In many boats the freeboard is lowest at the transom, higher amidships, and even higher toward the bow, but a bass boat has low freeboard everywhere so that an angler can play a fish with equal ease anywhere on the boat, moving around as necessary. Bass boat owners place a high emphasis on this "360° fishability."

Another feature that may make some bass boats dangerous in inlets and other rough water is a foredeck that slants downward toward the bow. Such a bow shape can bury or "stuff" itself in a wave, shipping water over the bow and *swamping* the boat. This is not to say that a bass boat is unsafe, which would not be true. What it does say is,

"Operate your boat only under the conditions for which it was designed."

We will explore other boat types later in the chapter. For the moment, let's look at one other type. Suppose you are in a *runabout*, a small, mostly open boat powered by one or two outboard motors. These are the boats that populate lakes, reservoirs, rivers, and sheltered coastal waters on pleasant summer days, engaged in fishing, waterskiing, or simply day cruising. A runabout is at its best in those conditions, but it is not designed for a strong wind and a choppy sea.

Suppose you get caught in rough conditions and your runabout is *dead in the water*, or *adrift*. This means that it is not under power and not *moored*, *anchored*, or *aground*. As with other boats that are higher in the bow than the stern (as most boats are), its bow will be blown away from the wind. This means that the stern, with little freeboard, turns into the waves. Let's further suppose that there is a cutout in the transom where the outboard motor is mounted (see Figure 1-3), and let's assume that there is no self-draining well between the transom and the boat's open cockpit to intercept a boarding wave. It is all too easy for a wave to roll over the transom and swamp the boat. (And by the way, this example is anything but hypothetical; this sort of accident happens frequently, and the victims are usually unaware of the danger until the wave comes aboard.)

Select your boat to suit your needs, and use it only under the conditions for which it was designed. It always pays to check the weather before you go out and while you are on the water. You can get continuous weather information on your VHF-FM radio. (See Chapter 12 for more on predicting the weather.)

Types of Propulsion

Most recreational powerboats less than 25 to 30 feet long have *outboard motors* (Figures 1-2, 1-4, and 1-5) or *stern-drive engines* (see Figure 1-6 opposite). Stern drives are also called *inboard/outboards*, or I/Os. Most boats longer than 35 feet have *inboard engines*, and those from 30 to 35 feet long might have any of the three.

An outboard motor bolts or clamps to the transom. In the past most outboards were *two-cycle* (also known as two-stroke) engines, meaning that the crankshaft requires two revolutions to complete a power stroke. Many small engines, such as lawnmower engines, are two-cycle. These engines operate at high revolutions per minute (rpm) and produce a large amount of power per pound of engine weight, but this higher engine stress usually results in a shorter engine life and higher maintenance costs. Also, in part because their lubricating oil mixes with the fuel rather than recirculating through separate passageways, two-cycle outboards are characterized by incomplete combustion and resultant pollution, although these problems have been greatly decreased by electronic fuel injection and ignition technologies.

For all these reasons, *four-cycle* outboards are increasingly popular. These operate like automobile engines (or like stern-drive and inboard marine engines, for that matter) in that the crankshaft requires four revolutions to complete a power stroke. These engines are heavier and produce less

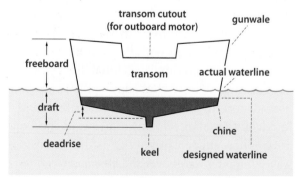

Figure **1-3.** Some terms used to describe a boat.

Figure **1-4.** An inflatable dinghy offers great stability and load-carrying ability. (COURTESY ZODIAC)

Figure **1-6.** A stern-drive engine installation. The out-drive unit rotates for steering and also tilts up (though not enough to emerge from the water) for shallow-water operation or when not in use. (REPRINTED WITH PERMISSION FROM *AMERICA'S BOAT-ING COURSE*, PUBLISHED BY BOAT ED)

Figure **1-5.** This cutaway view of a direct fuel-injected 200-horsepower outboard hints at the complexity of a modern outboard motor. (COURTESY MERCURY MARINE)

power per pound of engine weight, but they are also more fuel efficient, more reliable, and generally quieter.

A stern-drive engine is mounted inside the hull (like the inboard engine of a bigger boat), but the engine is connected to a drive unit through a system of gears. This drive unit, also called the *lower unit* or *outdrive*, protrudes through the boat's transom and functions much like the lower portion of an outboard motor. Outboard and stern-drive boats are steered by turning the lower unit in one direction or the other, thereby directing the stream of water discharged by the propeller (Figure 1-6).

Comparing outboard motors with stern-drive engines, outboards are easier to remove for servicing and easier to replace, take up less space inside the boat, and are lighter than stern drives of the same horsepower. Stern drives, however, are quieter and burn less fuel than two-cycle outboards.

Stern-drive engines have longer service lives than two-cycle outboards, and, like inboard engines,

they are quiet, efficient, and out of sight. Yet like outboards, they derive significant speed, steering, and trim advantages over inboard engines from their adjustable, steerable lower units. They are especially popular on fresh water, where the inability to raise the lower unit out of the water when not in use, as you can by tilting an outboard, is of less consequence. In the water, and especially in rough weather, it is easier to work on a stern-drive engine than an outboard, because the stern-drive engine is in the boat and not behind the transom.

The transom on a boat with an outboard motor usually has a large section cut away (refer back to Figure 1-3). This is done to get the lower unit and propeller deep enough for best performance, but a cutaway transom lowers a boat's freeboard and invites swamping.

To keep boats with transom-mounted outboards from swamping, many have a well forward of the transom into which their motors tilt when raised. The well drains overboard, and its forward wall is made high enough to keep most waves from entering the boat. A well takes up deck space, but the lack of a well can be dangerous when waves approach from astern, as described earlier.

The need for a cutaway transom can be eliminated by attaching an outboard motor to a mount, or bracket, that extends aft of the transom. A bracket-mounted motor is entirely outside the boat, permitting a full transom and unimpeded interior volume. When mounted this way, an outboard will make less noise in the boat, and the full transom will be safer for small children. A bracket-mounted outboard does increase the effective length of the boat slightly, which could be a disadvantage when maneuvering in close quarters (or when renting a marina slip by the foot), and the engine is harder to reach from inside the boat, but these considerations are outweighed by the advantages of such an arrangement (Figure 1-7).

There are three significant disadvantages of a stern drive. The first is the loss of deck space, since the engine is mounted inside the hull near the stern and enclosed under a large hood. Second, the articulated mechanism connecting the engine to the lower unit may be a source of problems. And third, any engine mounted within a boat's hull presents dangers from fire and explosion; these can be controlled with proper ventilation, however, as described in Chapter 2.

Outboard motors and stern-drive engines are rarely found on boats longer than 35 feet, because their smaller props don't develop enough thrust to move heavy boats effectively. That is why big boats usually use inboard engines, which are generally mounted below the deck amidships or slightly aft of amidships. (Stern-drive engines, by contrast, are mounted aft, against the transom, where there is rarely enough belowdeck room to accommodate them. They therefore require a full or partial abovedeck enclosure.) Inboard engines usually drive straight propeller shafts (Figure 1-8). Inboards are simpler in design and generally more reliable than I/Os, but the propeller is fixed below the hull and inaccessible if it becomes fouled.

Outboards and I/Os can be raised to allow easy removal of debris from the propeller or to escape from a shoal, and an outboard or I/O drive on most boats can be adjusted to trim the boat's bow up or down to the optimum running angle.

TYPES OF PROPULSION

Outboard Motor

- Easy to remove from the boat for servicing
- Lighter than a stern-drive engine
- Takes up little room in the boat
- Poses less danger of fire
- Easily maneuverable with engine in forward gear
- Sufficiently maneuverable with engine in reverse gear
- Drive angle can be trimmed up or down to optimize boat trim underway

Stern-Drive Engine

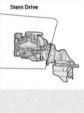

- Quieter than an outboard motor
- Uses less fuel
- Longer engine life
- Easier to service
- Easily maneuverable with engine in forward gear
- Sufficiently maneuverable with engine in reverse gear
- Maneuverability is poor to nonexistent when engine is out of gear
- Drive angle can be trimmed up or down to optimize boat trim underway

Inboard Engine

- Straight driveshaft from engine to propeller
- All machinery except propeller is in the boat
- Single-engine inboard boats are less maneuverable than outboard or stern-drive boats, especially when backing
- Twin-engine inboard boats are the epitome of maneuverability, and can be steered under engine alone if the steering system fails

Jet-Drive Engine

- No external propeller
- Very maneuverable at medium and high throttle settings
- Less maneuverable at low throttle settings and when backing
- Maneuverability nonexistent when engine is out of gear

Figure **1-7.** Mounting an outboard engine on a bracket aft of the transom permits a full transom and unimpeded interior volume. (PHOTO BY ED SWEENEY)

Figure **1-8.** Cutaway view of an inboard engine installation. This boat has twin engines, each with its own driveshaft and propeller, and twin rudders. (REPRINTED WITH PERMISSION FROM *AMERICA'S BOATING COURSE*, PUBLISHED BY BOAT ED)

Jet Drives

Personal watercraft (PWC), as well as some other boats, have a *jet drive*, which is simply an engine-driven pump with an impeller mounted in a tube that jets water out the back end of the tube to serve as a propellant. The advantages of jet drives include fast acceleration, an enhanced ability to operate in shallow water, and enhanced safety for people in the water. The propellers on conventional-drive boats often continue to turn slowly even when their gears are in neutral, and an exposed propeller can cause serious injury. The enclosed impeller of a PWC jet drive does not present the safety hazard to a swimmer that a propeller does (Figure 1-9).

Jet drives are often favored in shallow, rock-strewn waters where propellers are easily damaged. For example, sightseeing boats in the Hell's Canyon area of the Snake River use jet drives. An operator should use caution around rocks even with a jet engine, however. Rocks can puncture a boat's hull.

Although PWCs can operate in shallow, muddy, or sandy water, other jet-propelled boats should not. The difference is in the size of their engines. The engines of runabouts and cruisers equipped with jet drives pump large quantities of water. The mud or sand that is pumped with the

Figure **1-9.** A jet-drive engine installation on a personal watercraft (PWC). Water is sucked up through a grating just forward of the enclosed impeller, then discharged astern through the steerable nozzle. (REPRINTED WITH PERMISSION FROM *AMERICA'S BOATING COURSE*, PUBLISHED BY BOAT ED)

water quickly damages parts in their pumps and propelling mechanisms.

Tunnel Drives

In a tunnel drive configuration, the propeller and part of the driveshaft are partially recessed in a trough in the bottom of the boat. The trough, or tunnel, acts as a shroud to protect the propeller and increase its efficiency. It also provides a more favorable thrust angle for the propeller and a better angle of attachment of the driveshaft to the engine. These drives are advantageous in shallow water.

Hull Design

One way to classify boats is by how they ride in the water. *Displacement* boats move through the water and push it aside or displace it. *Planing* boats move faster and, after gaining speed, ride more nearly on top of the water.

There is no single, all-purpose, perfect hull design. Each design is a compromise, and you must make a choice based on your boat's projected use.

Displacement Hulls

All boats at rest or moving slowly are displacement boats. Each displaces a volume of water equal in weight to its own weight. If the weight of the boat exceeds the weight of the water displaced, it sinks deeper into the water until the two weights are equal. This is true of a planing hull, a semidisplacement hull, and a displacement hull, but only the latter is designed specifically to achieve greatest efficiency at slow speeds.

At slow speeds, it is easy for a displacement boat to push aside the water it displaces. A displacement hull is designed to do just that, and the resultant *bow wave* will likely be less for a displacement hull than a planing hull. As speed increases, however, the effort required to push the water aside increases geometrically, and the bow wave becomes higher. In effect, the boat must try to climb its own ever-steepening bow wave and thereby escape its hole in the water in order to go faster. But a displacement boat is not designed to do this, so there is a practical limit to its speed. The longer its waterline, assuming it is not limited by engine horse-power, the faster it can move, up to a top speed of 1.34 to 1.5 times the square root of its waterline length. (The wave pattern against the hull of a catamaran appears to be sufficiently different from a monohull to exclude cats from these hull speed lim-

HULL TYPES

Displacement Hull

- Displaces a volume of water equal to its weight
- Pushes the water out of the way
- Speed is limited by waterline length, making a top speed of 7 to 8 knots for a boat with a length at the water-line between 25 and 30 feet
- Steady and comfortable
- Economical to operate
- Will carry a large load without a significant performance handicap

Semidisplacement Hull

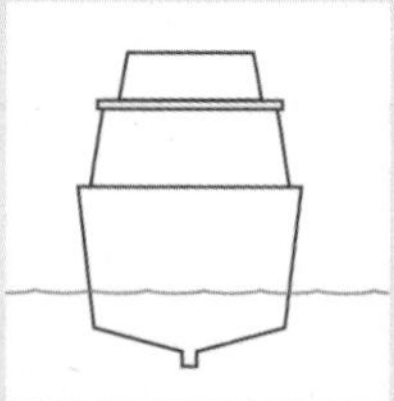

- Rises partly out of the water at cruising speeds
- Can go faster than a displacement hull
- Less efficient than a displacement hull at low speeds
- Less efficient than a planing hull at high speeds
- High fuel consumption at slow speed
- Provides greater cruising range than a displacement hull, with the ability to outrun a storm back to port
- Many trawler yachts and motor cruisers are in this group

Planing Hull

- Fast
- Rides on top of the water at cruising speeds
- Extensive flat surfaces on bottom
- V-shaped cross sections forward of amidships and in some cases all the way aft to the transom
- Stable when planing
- Inefficient at low speeds
- Less comfortable in a seaway than a displacement hull
- Overloading will cause a substantial impairment of performance

itations.) Any attempt to go faster will merely make the stern squat deeper in the water and cause the boat to consume more fuel (Figures 1-10 and 1-11).

This is what limits the top speed of a small trawler yacht to 8 knots or so. It is also one factor making the design of a keel sailboat such an art. All keel sailboats are displacement boats, so the speed potential of similar designs is measured in incre-ments of a tenth of a knot or less. The designer of a racing sailboat must try to increase performance without sacrificing seaworthiness, comfort, or ap-pearance. Again, the top speed for most small dis-placement boats is about 7 to 8 knots, or about 8 to 9 miles per hour (Figure 1-12).

Despite their slow speeds, displacement ves-sels have advantages and special uses. They are steady and comfortable and can handle rougher water than planing boats. They are more econom-ical to operate and can carry a heavy load of gear and provisions without a noticeable impairment of performance. They lend themselves to cruising and living aboard.

Planing Hulls

A planing hull climbs its own bow wave, escaping its hole in the water to ride on the water surface. When a planing boat is moving slowly, it is in effect a displacement vessel, but as its speed increases it derives more and more lift from the water beneath its hull until, at higher speeds, it escapes its bow

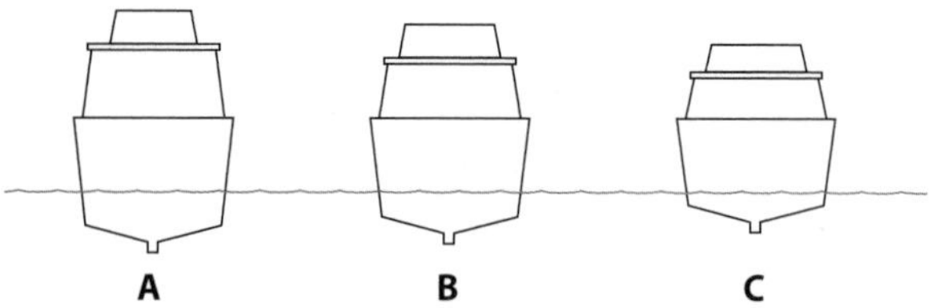

Figure **1-10.** These three hulls show similar freeboard and beam at their midsections, but hull A is clearly much heav-ier, with greater immersed volume. Hull B is intermediate, and hull C is the lightest of the three. Hull A is a displacement hull; hull B, semidisplacement; and hull C, planing. A displacement hull might be round-bottomed, and even a semidisplacement hull might have a tightly radiused round bottom, but shape is-n't the primary determinant. It's weight, as these drawings show. (REPRINTED WITH PERMISSION FROM *GETTING STARTED IN POWERBOAT-ING* BY BOB ARMSTRONG)

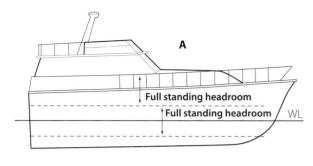

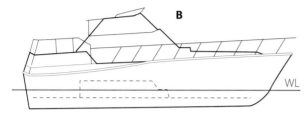

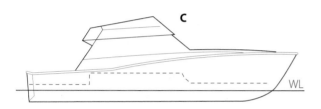

Figure **1-11.** The same hulls as in Figure 1-10, here seen in profile. All are about 50 feet long. Boat A has two full-length decks with full standing headroom, while boats B and C offer less room but greater speeds. (REPRINTED WITH PERMISSION FROM *GETTING STARTED IN POWERBOATING* BY BOB ARMSTRONG)

wave entirely and is said to be *on plane*, at which point it uses most of its power to move forward instead of pushing water aside. When on plane, it displaces a volume of water less than its own weight, which is only possible due to the hydrodynamic lift that supports it. There are many types of planing hulls. Most have extensive flat surfaces on their underbodies, which are angled upward from the centerline to form V-shaped hull sections. The more nearly horizontal these surfaces—the shallower the V—the harder the ride in choppy and rough water. Flat-bottomed boats usually are more stable than round-bottomed or deep-V-shaped hulls, yet deep-V hulls derive hydrodynamic stability at speed along with a much smoother ride through waves. So-called modified-V or variable deadrise boats have deep-V sections forward to cut through waves and shallower sections aft to give a flat surface on which to plane. The design of planing hulls is a rich and ongoing area of development (Figures 1-13, 1-14, and 1-15).

Semidisplacement Hulls

Some hulls are hybrids, falling somewhere between displacement and planing hulls (Figure 1-16). Up

Figure **1-12.** **Left:** This fishing vessel in St. John's, Newfoundland, shows how much water a displacement powerboat pushes aside at cruising speed. Any further incremental speed increase is gained only at the cost of greatly increased fuel consumption. **Right:** A sailboat is also a displacement hull. (LEFT PHOTO BY JIM BARTLETT, COURTESY NATIONAL MARINE MANUFACTURERS ASSOCIATION. RIGHT PHOTO COURTESY SPECTRUM PHOTO/FRAN GREON)

to a certain power and speed they displace water as any boat does. Beyond this point their hulls rise to a partial plane, but they cannot develop enough hydrodynamic lift to come onto a full plane. Increasing the engine size of a semidisplacement ves-

Figures 1-13. **Top and middle:** Two planing powerboats skimming over the water in ideal conditions. (COURTESY U.S. COAST GUARD OFFICE OF BOATING SAFETY) **Bottom:** A commercial vessel with twin jet drives on plane. (COURTESY HAMILTON JET)

Figure 1-14. This approaching powerboat shows two running strakes beneath a chine flat on either side. These features add lift for planing as well as side-to-side stability. (COURTESY BAYLINER)

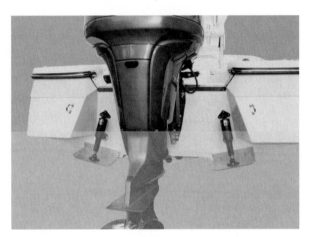

Figure 1-15. A stern-view illustration showing trim tabs slightly lowered to help a powerboat get on plane. For more on trim tabs, see Chapter 4. (COURTESY LENCO MARINE)

sel increases its top-end speed, and so does decreasing its weight. It never gets "on top" like a planing hull, however. Most *cruisers* and many *trawlers* fit into this group. Many sailboats up to about 19 feet in length have semidisplacement hulls as well. In the right conditions, a high-performance sailing dinghy can even get up on a full plane.

Catamaran Hulls

Power catamarans have become popular in recent years, their principal attractions being their intrinsic stability, spacious decks, and a soft ride in choppy water. They are designed both with displacement and with planing hulls, but a 25-foot displacement-hulled catamaran can often cruise at

Figure 1-16. A semidisplacement hull at speed, showing separation of the wake around the transom. (COURTESY CRUISERS YACHTS)

25 knots—a planing speed—because its hulls are so narrow that they escape the normal limitations of a displacement hull (Figure 1-17).

Some anglers prefer trailerable, outboard-powered 20- to 30-foot catamarans for offshore fishing due to their stability, soft ride, and cruising speeds. The principal limitations of a catamaran in this size range include the lack of room in its narrow hulls (although there is plenty of room on deck) and the fact that waves over a certain height and steepness will slap the roof of the tunnel between the hulls,

Figure 1-17. A power catamaran showing a good turn of speed and a comfortable hull. (COURTESY VENTURER)

which can be annoying and uncomfortable. True planing cats, because they ride higher when on plane, have a slight advantage over displacement cats on this point.

Details of hull design will have a significant effect on a catamaran's characteristics. A test drive under a range of conditions is highly recommended before making a purchase.

Sailboats

Sailboats are discussed in this book's companion text, *Sailing Skills and Seamanship.*

Uses of Boats

A common way to classify powerboats is by their uses. Powerboats include *utility boats, runabouts, cruisers, pontoon boats, houseboats, personal watercraft,* and others. Some of these may be available in both monohull and multihull configurations.

Utility Boats

Utility boats include *prams* and *dinghies, inflatables, skiffs,* and *utility outboards.*

Prams and Dinghies

Prams and dinghies are among the smallest of the utility boats. *Dinghies* have a pointed bow, and *prams* have a squared-off bow (Figure 1-18). Both serve as *tenders* for larger craft, transporting people, gear, and supplies to and from the larger craft. They are usually 8 to 10 feet long and have wide *beams,* or widths, relative to their lengths. They usually have oars for rowing, but may also have small outboard motors. On cruises, they are either towed behind a larger boat or carried aboard.

Inflatables

Inflatables are used as dinghies and as sportboats (refer back to Figure 1-4). They are extremely stable, can carry significantly larger loads than rigid boats of the same size, and are usually so buoyant that they will stay afloat even when filled with water. As dinghies, they may be towed astern, hoisted

Figure **1-18.** Two sailing prams underway. The Optimist class of prams, which are very much like these, are raced worldwide. Prams without sailing rigs, built for rowing, serve as stable, inexpensive tenders for larger boats. (COURTESY NATIONAL MARINE MANUFACTURERS ASSOCIATION)

on *davits*, stored on deck, or deflated and stored in a locker.

Generally, inflatables used as sportboats have hard transoms to which outboard motors may be attached. Some, known as *rigid inflatable boats* or RIBs, have fiberglass hulls along the sides of which, above the waterline, are attached inflated (and sometimes foam-filled) tubes (Figure 1-19). RIBs plane and steer more easily than inflatables with nonrigid hulls. Although heavier than other inflatables, RIBs weigh considerably less than all-fiberglass boats of the same size—an advantage for transporting as well as when underway—and their inflated or foam-filled collars give them excellent positive buoyancy.

Skiffs

A skiff is a flat-bottomed utility boat with straight or slightly flared sides. (A boat with flared sides is wider on deck than at the waterline. This describes most boats.) One form of skiff is a *jonboat*—a long, narrow boat with a flat bottom (Figure 1-20). It

Figure **1-19.** A rigid inflatable boat (RIB) provides excellent buoyancy and stability with lower weight than a conventional fiberglass boat of similar size and capacity. (COURTESY ZODIAC)

may be as short as 10 feet or as long as 16 feet. A jonboat has the same width from bow to stern, which means that the bow is square (like a pram's), not pointed, and resembles the transom stern although it might be slightly narrower. Also, the flat bottom turns up slightly near the bow end. A homemade jonboat is most often made of wood, but commercially built ones are usually made of aluminum.

Although skiffs are easy to row, many have small outboard motors. A skiff with a wide beam is stable and ideal for hunting or fishing in sheltered waters.

Utility Outboards

Utility outboards are small boats much like rowboats. They have small outboard motors and are sometimes difficult to row.

Some utility outboards have small decked-over areas in their bows, but most are completely open.

Figure **1-20.** An aluminum jonboat with camouflage paint for duck hunting. (COURTESY U.S. COAST GUARD OFFICE OF BOATING SAFETY)

Figure **1-21.** The qualities valued most in a utility outboard are stability and load-carrying ability, achieved in this boat in part with a blunt, skiff-like bow. (COURTESY BOSTON WHALER)

They are usually 12 to 14 feet long, and can operate in choppier water than skiffs because of their pointed bows. The amount of chop in which they are safe, however, depends on their freeboard and load. They are popular as fishing boats and should be used in sheltered waters (Figure 1-21).

Runabouts

Runabouts are small, sporty craft used for day cruising, waterskiing, and fishing (Figure 1-22). They may be completely open or have decked-over bows, and the roughness of the water in which they can operate depends on their freeboard and the weights of their loads.

Runabouts range from highly polished craft with cushioned seats used primarily for day cruising and ski towing to boats designed primarily for fishing.

Bowriders

One type of runabout has a split dashboard and windshield that gives ready access to the forward part of the boat (Figure 1-23). This is called a *walkthrough* windshield. Usually, the forward area has padded seats that can be used while the vessel is underway. This type of boat is sometimes called a *bowrider*. A bowrider boat should not be confused with *bowriding*, where passengers sit on the raised, forward deck of the vessel. They may or may not have their legs draped over the side, and may or may not be straddling a *stanchion*, an upright post that supports the *bow rail*. Bowriding is a danger-

Figure **1-22.** **Top:** The classic wooden runabout of 50 years ago was a thing of beauty with its varnished wooden hull. The inboard engine of this Hacker Craft is beneath the hatches on the afterdeck. Speedboats in the era of low-powered engines had to be narrow to reduce their resistance through the water. (COURTESY HACKER BOAT COMPANY) **Bottom:** The modern equivalent of a Hacker Craft is perhaps not as beautiful, but it's more durable, more versatile, more affordable (since they are mass produced), and requires less upkeep. (COURTESY BOSTON WHALER)

ous activity. Rails can give way; a person can fall overboard because of an unexpected wave, wake, or sudden turn; or when the boat is docking, legs can be crushed against pilings. Since bowriding is so dangerous, and a fall overboard can be fatal (it is difficult for the person to avoid the boat's propeller), it is illegal in most states and in all federal parks and waters.

Figure **1-23.** A bowrider, showing the walkthrough windshield that is characteristic of the type. (COURTESY BAYLINER)

Cathedral Hulls

Another type of runabout has a *cathedral hull*, which is V-shaped in the middle and has smaller Vs on each side (Figure 1-24). While it is a very stable boat, it is a hard ride in rough or choppy water.

Open Fishermen

Less sporty runabouts are used primarily for fishing. An *open fisherman* (Figure 1-25), for example, has no raised decks. Instead it has a *console*, most often in the center of the boat, and is therefore called a *center console* boat. The console holds the *helm* or steering wheel, the boat's instruments, and the gearshift mechanism.

Center console boats make excellent fishing boats. They are usually powered by outboard motors, and some have dual outboard installations. Many have at least one disadvantage, however—their shallow depth from the gunwale to the deck. This makes it difficult for fishermen who like to stand on the deck and lean their legs against the gunwale for support. Many other small boats have this disadvantage.

Figure **1-25.** A center console fishing boat—the cockpit provides protection from the sun. Rod holders on the hardtop are another feature shown here. (COURTESY COAST GUARD AUXILIARY)

Cuddy Cabin

Trailerable boats with a *cuddy cabin* (Figure 1-26) offer a modest degree of shelter. Although intended for overnight cruises, the cabin is seldom used for this purpose since it is small and difficult to keep insect free. Cuddy cabin boats usually lack sanitary and cooking facilities, although portable *heads* or toilets may be added. A cuddy cabin can serve as dry storage space, and it does provides some security for equipment left aboard or for your children if you're caught on the water by a squall or rainstorm.

It is often difficult to go forward around a cuddy cabin, which means that to anchor, you usually must enter the cabin and crawl up through a *hatch* to

Figure **1-24.** In the Boston Whaler line of boats, the smaller models—13 feet and under—derive much of their stability from the sponsons of a cathedral hull form (top). The 15- to 17-foot models (middle) derive more stability from their greater hull width, so the sponsons can be reduced in favor of a deeper-V central hull that offers smoother rough-water performance. This trend continues in the 18-foot and longer boats (bottom), with the sponsons replaced by chine flats. (COURTESY BOSTON WHALER)

Figure **1-26.** A cuddy cabin offers shelter and creature comforts but impedes access to the foredeck. (COURTESY BOSTON WHALER)

Figure **1-27.** A walkaround cuddy incorporates a narrow side deck for access to the foredeck. (COURTESY BOSTON WHALER)

Figure **1-28.** An outboard-powered pontoon boat. (COURTESY TRACKER MARINE)

reach the forward deck. The novelty of this wears off quickly, especially if you are bottom fishing and are frequently moving from one spot to another.

In some boats, this disadvantage is overcome by "walkaround" cuddy cabins, created when space is taken from the upper areas of the cabin and used for walkways on each side of the vessel (Figure 1-27). In addition to making anchoring easier, this arrangement usually provides a seat forward on which it is legal to ride.

Cruisers

Large runabouts with cuddy cabins are like small cruisers. Strictly speaking, though, cruisers are motorboats with cabins, *galleys* (cooking facilities), plumbing, and other facilities necessary for living aboard comfortably (refer back to Figure 1-16).

Cruisers come in many shapes and sizes and range from small overnight vessels to boats for extended voyages and living aboard. Cruisers, in general, are more *seaworthy* than runabouts. While in the past most cruisers were displacement craft, today most are semidisplacement craft powered by single- or dual-engine installations. Small cruisers may use outboards or stern drives, but those longer than 30 feet or so usually have inboards.

Pontoon Boats

Pontoon boats are popular for use in sheltered waters. In their simplest form, they are platforms mounted on two or more cylindrical floats, but they are often more elaborate.

Most pontoon boats have outboard motors, though stern drives are common on larger boats (Figure 1-28). All pontoon boats have a shallow *draft*, which means they do not require much water in which to operate.

Pontoon boats are popular on rivers and small, inland lakes, where they are used as fishing boats, cruisers, work platforms, and party boats. They tend to be unstable and are not suitable for use in rough water, however. Use them with extreme caution in exposed waters, and do not expose them to severe weather. Pontoon boats with covered tops may blow over when winds are strong so do not use them then or on large bodies of water.

Houseboats

A houseboat is a variation of a cruiser and offers most of the conveniences of home, including hot and cold running water (Figure 1-29). They usually have one or two stern-drive or inboard engines; some have enough speed and power to plane and to tow water-skiers.

Houseboats give their owners a lot of space, but at some cost. Seaworthiness is sacrificed for livability—they are limited to relatively sheltered waters because of their hull designs, low freeboards, and large windows, which are vulnerable in rough water and, if broken, would let waves aboard.

Figure 1-29. A houseboat underway on sheltered waters. (COURTESY U.S. COAST GUARD OFFICE OF BOATING SAFETY)

Canoes

Canoeing is one of the few quiet, restful, yet adventurous boating activities open to all (Figure 1-30). Besides being an excellent physical activity, canoeing affords boaters the opportunity for a peaceful on-the-water experience or a challenging go at a set of rapids.

For those who want a little assist in propulsion, many canoes will support a small outboard engine. Some can even be rigged with a sail.

All of this fun, however, does come with a price. Canoes are not very stable, and to be a safe and competent canoeist requires practice and the development of basic skills. Good balance, good paddling technique, and the ability to steer a boat with little or no keel and no rudder are just a few of the requirements for safe canoeing.

While canoeing looks easy, it is by no means risk free. Remember, a canoe is just as much a water vessel as a large motor or sailing yacht and must adhere to all boating regulations and good practices.

Figure 1-30. Exploring a lakeshore in a solo canoe. (COURTESY U.S. COAST GUARD OFFICE OF BOATING SAFETY)

Due to the risk of inadvertent capsizing, the wearing of a *personal flotation device* (PFD), or life jacket, is highly recommended in a canoe. We discuss life jackets in Chapter 2.

Kayaks

Kayaking is fast becoming widespread. It is not uncommon to see kayaks on lakes, rivers, and streams, and even on oceans and their tributaries (Figure 1-31).

These vessels have the remarkable ability to allow the boater and the boat to act almost as one. The actions of the boat and boater together produce results unlike any other boat/boater relationship. Great physical activity and exciting maneuvering are hallmarks of kayaking.

Getting wet is one of the enjoyments of this sport. It will probably happen often, so knowing how to recover from a rollover is a must, as is wearing proper flotation devices. Kayaks are inherently safe vessels, but have a high accident rate; since kayaks are so simple to operate, kayakers often ignore basic safety precautions.

Figure 1-31. **Top:** Tackling whitewater in a river kayak. **Bottom:** Beached sea kayaks. Note the compasses in the foredecks—you don't need a compass in a river kayak! (COURTESY U.S. COAST GUARD OFFICE OF BOATING SAFETY)

Figure **1-32.** **Top:** A PWC operator maneuvers away from the launch ramp at a Dana Point, California, marina. (PHOTO BY BOB DENNIS) **Bottom:** Early PWCs were solo craft, but that is no longer true, as this Sea-Doo demonstrates. (COURTESY BOMBARDIER RECREATIONAL PRODUCTS)

Remember, kayaks are vessels and therefore subject to all maritime laws, regulations, and good practices.

Personal Watercraft

Personal watercraft (PWC) are highly maneuverable, jet-driven vessels that can operate in very shallow water (Figure 1-32) and carry up to four riders. Most people know these planing vessels as Jet Skis, a registered trademark.

Boatbuilding Materials

The first boats were built of wood. Today, boatbuilders use fiberglass, aluminum, steel, wood with epoxy, and combinations of these materials in addition to wood.

Steel

Steel is an ideal material for shipbuilding. Unfortunately, steel-hulled boats less than 30 to 35 feet long are too heavy for economical operation, but when speed can be sacrificed for strength, steel is an excellent building material, producing a boat that will withstand collisions and groundings to an extraordinary degree.

Aluminum

Aluminum hulls are light, cost less than hulls made of other materials, and can take the hard knocks of canoeing, fishing, groundings, and ice floes. Many canoes, skiffs, jonboats, runabouts, and small cruisers, among other small craft, are built of aluminum, as are larger custom motor yachts and voyaging sailboats (Figure 1-33).

Aluminum has the disadvantage of being noisy; all sea noises are heard through the hull. Noises inside the hull are also transmitted to the water—an important consideration for anglers. And aluminum is a good transmitter of heat, so aluminum hulls tend to sweat considerably.

Another disadvantage of aluminum is that it is easily corroded by *electrolysis*. This is not a disadvantage for canoes and skiffs used in fresh water and stored on land, but it is a serious consideration for boats moored in salt water.

Boats moored in salt water usually have their bottoms painted with *antifouling paint* to reduce plant and animal growth. Most of these paints contain copper. In salt water, copper and aluminum set up an electrolytic action, and the aluminum quickly corrodes. Tin-based antifouling paints,

Figure **1-33.** An aluminum runabout underway. (COURTESY LOWE BOATS)

which do not interact as readily with aluminum, were once used on aluminum hulls but the U.S. Environmental Protection Agency has determined that the tin is poisonous to marine life, so such paints are now banned.

There are presently two alternatives for protecting aluminum. One is to use a layer of non-metallic paint between the hull and the antifouling bottom paint, which works fine unless a scratch exposes the aluminum hull. The other alternative is to use a polymer antifouling paint, which is expensive and difficult to apply.

Wood

Wood, once the primary choice of boatbuilders, is used much less frequently today. This is not because wood is an undesirable construction material; many people would not trade their wooden boats for any other. Wood is attractive and, if properly maintained, lasts a long time. Good wood for boat construction is expensive, however, and demands considerable attention. Owners of traditional plank-on-frame wooden boats spend many hours each year getting them ready for launching. Wood needs scraping, sanding, and repainting annually, and the underwater seams of wooden boats need periodic *caulking* to make them watertight.

These drawbacks have been overcome with newer methods that use wood in combination with reinforcing resins and fabrics to eliminate caulked seams, increase longevity, and reduce maintenance while retaining the distinctive beauty of a wooden boat. In stitch-and-glue boatbuilding, for example, hull panels are cut to prescribed measurements from marine plywood sheets, laid down over tem-

porary station molds cut to the cross-sectional shapes of the boat at various points along its centerline, and then stitched together where their edges meet using temporary wire stitches. The stitches hold the hull together long enough for these joints to be permanently glued with rock-solid epoxy fillets; then the entire structure is covered with fiberglass, Dynel, or another fabric laid in place with epoxy or fiberglass resin. This technique is not only user-friendly for home builders, but it also makes a handsome, long-lasting boat.

Another popular technique—especially suited to canoes and kayaks built in a home workshop—creates a boat from narrow strips of wood coated and attached with epoxy resin. The boats are beautiful and amazingly durable and maintenance free, and the skills required are well within reach of an enthusiastic amateur builder (Figure 1-34).

While methods like these have spurred a renewal of amateur wooden boat building, they are not suitable for commercial production of boats. In production boatbuilding, fiberglass predominates.

Fiberglass

For commercial boatbuilding, fiberglass is the material of choice. Fiberglass boats account, in large part, for the rapidly growing popularity of recreational boating. Our nation's waterways abound with fiberglass runabouts, center consoles, cruisers, and other powerboats, and unless you have special needs that an aluminum skiff, jonboat, or canoe can best meet, your first boat should probably be fiberglass.

Fiberglass is relatively inexpensive and can easily be formed into complex shapes and curves (Figure 1-35). It's ideal for production boatbuilding because a single hull mold can be used to build dozens or even hundreds of copies of the same hull. Furthermore, fiberglass is easily repaired when damaged, lasts seemingly indefinitely, and most importantly for the average boatowner, is easily maintained, requiring much less effort and time than wood. Less time spent on maintenance means more time on the water.

Fiberglass, or more properly, glass-reinforced plastic (GRP), does have disadvantages. It is heavy, for one thing; fiberglass with the strength of steel weighs more than steel. Today's more carefully engi-

Figure **1-34.** A strip-built tandem canoe, suitable for home construction. (COURTESY NICK SCHADE)

Figure 1-35. A fiberglass boat under construction.
(COURTESY NATIONAL MARINE MANUFACTURERS ASSOCIATION)

neered boats are a lot lighter than the fiberglass boats of 30 to 40 years ago, however, simply because early fiberglass boats were built to wooden boat thicknesses (in the absence of better guidance) and thus were way overbuilt. Also, although the glass will not burn, the resins that bind it together will.

How Fiberglass Boats Are Built

To build a production run of fiberglass hulls, the builder needs a mold in which the fiberglass materials can be shaped and adhered. The first step, therefore, is to construct a *plug* in the shape of the hull, and then form a mold over the plug. Imagine carving the shape of the hull from a huge block of wood; if you could do this, you would be creating a plug. The surface of the plug must be flawless so that the inner surface of the female mold formed over the plug will also be flawlessly smooth. When the fiberglass mold has cured and been properly stiffened on the outside, the plug is removed from the mold, which is then ready for building a series of hulls.

Each hull is built from the outside in within the female mold. The gelcoat is sprayed over the mold surface first, which gives the vessel its color and finished, mirror-smooth outer surface. Then follow layers of fiberglass mat (or chopped fiberglass strands sprayed from a hand-operated gun) alternated with layers of finely woven fiberglass cloth and/or coarse woven roving, until the desired thickness of the hull is reached.

The strength and durability of the hull will depend on what fiberglass materials and resins are used, how they are combined, how many layers are laid down, and how much quality control is exercised throughout. When hull thickness is built up

in part with chopped strands sprayed from a chopper gun (which mixes the strands with resin as it sprays), the gun operator must be careful to keep the fiber-to-resin ratio at optimal levels—neither resin starved nor too resin rich. Ask the dealer if the boat you're looking at incorporates chopped strand. If it does, ask what kind of quality control the builder exercises.

A builder will also typically make a hull thicker near the keel and in high-stress areas, and may use special, directionally reinforced materials locally to impart particular strength. After the hull is laminated and cured, it is strengthened with stiffeners, stringers, and other members. Then decks, cabins, and superstructure are added; usually these too are fiberglass, and in production boatbuilding these so-called parts are likewise laminated in molds.

Variations on the Method

Over time, variations on the fundamental method have evolved. In one, known as *sandwich construction*, a core material (usually balsa wood) is sandwiched on either side by layers of fiberglass impregnated with resin. Other core materials are sometimes used, such as Airex foam or other formed plastics. Sandwich construction provides a boat that is strong and buoyant. Should leaks develop in the fiberglass and water reach a balsa core, however, rot will occur.

In another variation called a *matched-die process*, male and female molds, usually made of metal, are clamped together with a fiberglass-and-resin laminate between them. By applying the correct pressure and heat, the hull is made uniform throughout.

The international demand for environmental and worker safety, along with the need for more efficient manufacturing, has resulted in another new process for producing fiberglass products in the marine and aircraft industry called the *Seeman Composite Resin Infusion Molding Process*, or SCRIMP. This process, like the matched-die process, requires a male and female mold between which the fiberglass or other filler material is encapsulated. Then resin is injected with a vacuum assist to ensure that unwanted encapsulated gases are removed. This is an environmentally clean process and results in a laminate with no voids. This process can be used to produce aircraft and even small submarines as well as boats, and is finding increasing favor, in large part because of its environmental benefits.

General Considerations

Fiberglass boats are strong, and since most production-line boats are built of fiberglass, they dominate the market. A fiberglass hull lasts indefinitely—longer, usually, than the engine that powers it and the gear it carries—so the used-boat market is also dominated by fiberglass. For these reasons, as well as for economy and ease of maintenance, your first boat is likely to be fiberglass—along with your second boat and most boats thereafter. The quality of workmanship is not always obvious in a fiberglass boat, so the reputation of the builder should be one important guide for you. Ask around, and browse boat sites on the Internet.

Fiberglass is heavier than water and a fiberglass boat filled with water will sink unless it has built-in flotation. All new boats less than 20 feet long (sailboats, canoes, kayaks, inflatables, multihulls, and raceboats excepted) are legally required to have sufficient built-in flotation to keep a portion of the boat above water even when the boat is flooded. (This would not be feasible on larger boats; however, they are less vulnerable to swamping.) Sometimes the flotation is in the form of a sealed compartment; sometimes it is Styrofoam or another closed-cell foam. Consider adding supplemental flotation to an exempted boat as well. An offshore kayak, for example, could capsize miles offshore, and the boater might have insufficient freeboard even after righting the boat to bail it out.

You can find out more about the boat you wish to buy by reading the literature published by its manufacturer. How complete is the information? Reputable manufacturers want you to know what you are buying, and are usually proud of their quality control programs, which are critical in this industry. If you can visit the manufacturing plant, arrange for a tour. Most factories will be glad to show you boats in various stages of construction.

Your Intended Use

One guideline in selecting a boat is how you will use it. Make certain the boat you intend to buy matches your intended use. People tend to look at boating in one of two ways: some owners take pleasure in knowing that their boats are built for heavy seas, while others enjoy the rush of adrenaline they get from pushing their boats to their limits. The table on pages 28–29 gives you some idea of how the various powerboat types are grouped in terms of intended use and seaworthiness.

Not all boats are designed for the rigors they will endure. Hull failures are common on planing boats driven by would-be ocean racers since most hulls are not designed for jumping wakes and waves and lunging off swells.

Displacement and semidisplacement hulls can also be overstressed. For example, a houseboat used on the ocean may be subjected to stresses for which it was not designed. Even a well-constructed boat hull can be damaged by use in adverse sea conditions.

Marine Surveyors

Marine surveyors make boats their specialty, serving much the same function that home appraisers serve ashore. If you are planning to buy a used boat, it is a

---

BOATBUILDING MATERIALS

Steel
- Strong and heavy
- Better for large boats than small
- Must be painted to avoid rust

Aluminum
- Lightweight
- Relatively inexpensive
- Rather noisy
- Can take hard knocks
- Vulnerable to electrolysis in salt water

Fiberglass
- Today's most popular boatbuilding material
- Strong and heavy
- Easily molded
- Easily repaired
- Relatively easy to maintain

good idea to hire a surveyor. The surveyor will assess the boat's condition and tell you what it needs to bring it to good working condition. He or she will also appraise the boat's value based on condition, builder's reputation, and the local market for the kind of boat in question, so that you can judge the fairness of the asking price. Finally, a surveyor can help you judge to what extent the money you save by buying old versus new will be consumed by the repairs and upgrades you might have to make. With a little knowledge and care you can eliminate many boats from consideration without the expense of a professional survey, but when you get ready to make an offer, you're well advised to get a professional second opinion. Sometimes a surveyor will also suggest that you hire a mechanic to compression-test and otherwise evaluate the boat's engine or engines.

Buying a Boat

When you are buying a boat—new or used—there is no substitute for a written sales agreement that clearly states your intent and that of the seller. This should prevent unpleasant surprises. The sales contract should state the price, delivery date, and method of payment, and should also include an inventory of the boat's equipment and a detailed description of the overall condition of the boat. Any refundable deposit you make should be noted, along with possible limitations on the refund. If a loan is involved, the contract should state whether the sale is subject to the availability of the loan.

The contract should also stipulate that the sale is subject to a satisfactory marine survey. As a buyer, you should take a sea trial, but have the survey done on land. Problems noted during the trial run and the survey should be addressed in the contract. If the boat is not being sold "as is," the contract should say so. It should also state whether the seller is responsible for correcting problems or defects and if so, what the time limit is for making such corrections. The length of time for discovering and correcting new problems after the purchase date should be included as well.

Even if you are having the boat surveyed, you should ask probing questions about its prior use, maintenance record, and history of problems. Has

it had any blistering? Has it had accidental damage? What is its present condition? The seller should be completely honest, but again beware!

Finally, make certain that you have all of the boat's papers. You will need them for state registration or for new documentation with the Coast Guard, as you'll see in Chapter 2.

As a buyer, you should realize that you do not have any rights under the seller's insurance. Arrange to have your own insurance in place at the closing date.

Ways to Learn More

All About Powerboats: Understanding Design and Performance. Roger Marshall. Camden, Maine: International Marine, 2002.

The Boat Buyer's Guide to Motor Yachts and Trawlers. Ed McKnew. Camden, Maine: International Marine, 2006.

The Boat Buyer's Guide to Sportfishing Boats. Ed McKnew. Camden, Maine: International Marine, 2006.

The Boat Buyer's Guide to Trailerable Cruisers and Runabouts. Ed McKnew. Camden, Maine: International Marine, 2006.

The Boat Buyer's Guide to Trailerable Fishing Boats. Ed McKnew. Camden, Maine: International Marine, 2006.

Chapman Piloting & Seamanship. 66th ed. Charles B. Husick. New York: Hearst Books, 2009. Chapter 1.

Getting Started in Powerboating. 3rd ed. Bob Armstrong. Camden, Maine: International Marine, 2005.

Boating Magazine's Insider's Guide to Buying a Powerboat: Featuring Tips and Traps for the Smart Boat Buyer. J. R. Lamy. Camden, Maine: International Marine, 1999.

The Pontoon and Deckboat Handbook. David Brown. Camden, Maine: International Marine, 2007.

Your First Powerboat. Bob Armstrong. Camden, Maine: International Marine, 2008.

Sorensen's Guide to Powerboats. 2nd ed. Eric Sorensen. Camden, Maine: International Marine, 2008.

Seaworthiness Factors

Hull Shape	Most Efficient Hull	Fastest Hull	Inshore Fishing	Water Skiing	Wake Boarding	Trawler-Style Yacht
Boat speed	low to moderate	highest	low to moderate	high	high	low
Sea states	flat water	flat water	moderate seas	flat water	moderate waves	moderate to large seas
Wave height	0–1 feet	none	0–2 feet	0–1 feet	up to 3 feet	sea heights to 30% of length
Hull shape	round hull	3-point hydro	V or round	V hull	V hull	round or V
Hull length	long	moderate	moderate seas	moderate	moderate waves	moderate to long
Draft	shallow	low	shallow	shallow	moderate to deep	moderate to deep
Waterline length	long	low	moderate	moderate	moderate to heavy	moderate to heavy
Beam	narrow	wide for stability	moderate	proportional to length	proportional to length	proportional to length
Displacement	light	as light as possible	light to medium	moderate to light	moderate to heavy	moderate to heavy
Horsepower	low or very low	very high	low to moderate	high for length	high for length	low to moderate
Bow height	low to moderate	low	low to moderate	low to moderate	low to moderate	high
Bow fineness	fine to moderate	fine	fine to moderate	moderate	moderate	moderate to full
Bow flare	moderate	none	minimal	minimal	moderate	moderate to high
Deadrise angle	low	moderate	0–5 degrees	0–5 degrees	5–10 degrees	5–12 degrees
Sea-worthiness	limited	limited	limited	limited	limited	good
Comfort when stopped	tendency to roll	none	moderate	moderate	moderate	some roll
Comfort at cruising speed	comfortable	none	moderate	moderate	moderate	comfortable
Comfort at full speed	comfortable	none	moderate	moderate	moderate	comfortable
Range	moderate	limited	limited	limited	limited	extensive
Construction costs	moderate to high	very high	moderate	moderate to high	moderate	moderate to high
Suitable for use on:						
Estuaries/ salt marshes	yes	no	yes	no	no	no
Small ponds/ small lakes	yes	no	yes	yes	yes	yes
Large lakes	select optimum conditions	select optimum conditions	select optimum conditions	select optimum conditions	select optimum conditions	yes
Coastal shorelines	select optimum conditions	select optimum conditions	select optimum conditions	select optimum conditions	select optimum conditions	yes
Open ocean	select optimum conditions	no	select optimum conditions	select optimum conditions	select optimum conditions	select optimum conditions

Inshore Cruiser	Offshore Cruiser	Offshore Sport-fisherman	Inshore Racer	Offshore Racer	Inshore Catamaran	Offshore Catamaran
moderate	moderate	high	very high	very high	moderate to high	very high
moderate to large seas	moderate to large seas	moderate to large seas	moderate seas	moderate to large seas	moderate seas	moderate to large seas
sea heights to 20% of length	sea heights to 30% of length	sea heights to 30% of length	sea heights to 20% of length	sea heights to 30% of length	sea heights to 20% of length	sea heights to 30% of length
round or V	round or V	V hull	V hull	V hull or catamaran	round or V	mostly V
moderate to long	moderate to long	moderate	long	long	long	long
moderate to deep	moderate to deep	moderate	low to moderate	low to moderate	low	low
moderate	moderate to heavy	moderate	long	long	long	long
proportional to length	proportional to length	proportional to length	proportional to length	narrow for length	narrow hulls/wide overall	narrow hulls/wide overall
moderate to heavy	moderate to heavy	moderate	light to moderate	light to moderate	low to moderate	light to moderate
low to moderate	moderate	moderate to high	high	high	moderate to high	moderate to high
low to moderate	high	moderate to high	low	low	moderate	moderate
moderate to full	moderate to full	moderate	fine to moderate	fine to moderate	moderate	moderate
low to moderate	low to moderate	high	minimum	minimum	moderate	moderate
5–12 degrees	8–15 degrees	10–18 degrees	8–20 degrees	15–25 degrees	10–20 degrees	15–25 degrees
good	excellent	good to excellent	limited	moderate to excellent	good	good
some roll	some roll	good	some roll	some roll	good	good
good	excellent	good to excellent	good	moderate	good	good
good	excellent	good to excellent	good	good	good	good
moderate	extensive	good	limited	good	low to moderate	high
moderate	moderate to high	moderate to high	high	moderate to high	moderate to high	moderate to high
yes	no	no	no	no	no	no
yes	yes	yes	no	no	yes	no
select optimum conditions	yes	yes	yes	yes	yes	yes
select optimum conditions	yes	yes	yes	yes	yes	yes
select optimum conditions	yes	yes	select best conditions	yes	select optimum conditions	yes

Practice Questions

IMPORTANT BOATING TERMS

In the following exercise, match the words in the column on the left with the definitions in the column on the right. In the blank space to the left of each term, write the letter of the item that best matches it. Do not use an item in the right-hand column more than once.

THE ITEMS

1. _____ stanchion
2. _____ starboard
3. _____ aft
4. _____ head
5. _____ transom
6. _____ planing hull
7. _____ outboard
8. _____ tender
9. _____ bowrider
10. _____ PWC

THE RESPONSES

a. toward the back of a boat

b. the stern cross section of a square-stern boat

c. a runabout with seats in the front

d. it transports people and gear

e. it rises up on top of the water when it has enough speed

f. a personal watercraft

g. a marine toilet

h. its engine is mounted on the transom

i. the right side of a boat, looking forward

j. it holds up a rail

Multiple-Choice Items

In the following items, choose the best response:

1-1. The shortest distance from the waterline to the top of a vessel's sides or transom is its

a. freeboard
b. gunwale
c. deadrise
d. draft

1-2. Select your boat to suit your

a. local waters
b. pocketbook
c. needs
d. desires

1-3. A vessel is anything used on the water for

a. skiing
b. transportation
c. fishing
d. cruising

1-4. The part of a stern-drive engine that is outside the vessel is called the

a. outboard
b. propeller
c. upper unit
d. outdrive

1-5. If a boat weighs more than the water it displaces, it

a. sinks
b. floats
c. is sluggish
d. handles easily

1-6. Skiffs, jonboats, houseboats, and pontoon boats should be used only

a. in sheltered waters
b. for pleasure
c. in fresh water
d. for fishing

Multiple-Choice Items (continued)

1-7. The primary responsibility for the safety of all persons on board a boat whether rented or privately owned belongs to

    a. the boat manufacturer
    b. the insurance company
    c. the boat operator
    d. the rental agency

1-8. The means of propulsion often used in rocky, shallow water where propellers are easily damaged is

    a. an inboard
    b. an outboard
    c. an I/O
    d. a jet drive

1-9. When selecting a powerboat, consider

    a. a boat that matches your intended use
    b. the most expensive one you can afford
    c. purchasing only a planing hull
    d. the value of a jet drive

1-10. If you are buying a used boat, have it examined for possible defects by

    a. the Coast Guard
    b. a reliable dealer
    c. a friend
    d. a marine surveyor

1-11. The forward part of a vessel is called the

    a. bow
    b. transom
    c. hull
    d. stern

1-12. Fiberglass is a popular boatbuilding material because it is

    a. strong and heavy
    b. easily molded
    c. easily repaired
    d. all of the above

1-13. From the Norse, we got the term "steering board," which eventually became

    a. starboard
    b. port
    c. larboard
    d. forward

1-14. The keel and the planks of a boat together make the

    a. stringers
    b. hull
    c. bilges
    d. deck

1-15. Which of the following is a vessel?

    a. a raft
    b. an inflatable
    c. a PWC
    d. all of the above

1-16. A bass boat can become dangerous in rough water because of

    a. its low freeboard
    b. its high gunwales
    c. its heavy stern
    d. its large V-shaped hull

1-17. A planing-hulled vessel

    a. is usually round on its bottom
    b. is characteristically slow
    c. rides on top of the water at cruising speeds
    d. pushes its way through the water when underway

1-18. The flat, vertical surface on the aft portion of boats is called the

    a. steering board
    b. loading board
    c. transom
    d. cross member

1-19. The top speed of a displacement-hulled vessel depends primarily on its

    a. draft
    b. length
    c. weight
    d. freeboard

1-20. In the water, and especially when it is rough, the easiest type of engine to work on is

    a. a stern drive
    b. an outboard
    c. a magnetic drive
    d. a pulse drive

Equipment For Your Boat

The objectives of this chapter are to describe:

✔ The safety equipment your boat must have.

✔ Additional recommended safety equipment to have on board.

IN 1971 CONGRESS ordered the U.S. Coast Guard to improve recreational boating safety. In response, the Coast Guard drew up a set of regulations known as the Federal Boat Safety Act. This act governs boating safety regulations in the United States and its territories.

Besides these federal regulations, there are state and local laws you must follow that sometimes exceed the Coast Guard requirements. This chapter discusses only the federal laws. If you're using this book in conjunction with a Coast Guard Auxiliary class, your instructors will cover state and local laws. As with other laws, "Ignorance of the boating laws is no excuse."

The rules fall into two categories: regulations for your boat, and regulations for equipment on your boat. Remember, a personal watercraft (PWC) is a motor vessel governed by these laws and regulations, just like any other motor vessel.

Requirements for Your Boat

Most powerboats must be registered in their state of principal use. Some states exempt documented boats (see below), and some exempt dinghies with small motors (less than 10 horsepower) when these are used solely for transportation to and from a larger registered boat. But with these two exceptions, you can be fairly certain that your powerboat—whether kept on fresh or salt water—must be registered in the state where you use it most.

Documenting of Vessels

A recreational vessel of 5 or more net tons may be *documented* as a yacht with the U.S. Coast Guard. Assuming your boat is less than 79 feet long, you can calculate its possible eligibility for documentation by multiplying its length on deck by its maximum breadth and then by its depth of hull (from the deck amidships to the bottom of the hull, excluding the keel), with all measurements in feet. Divide that result by 100 and multiply it by 0.67 (or 0.5 for a sailboat) to get an estimate of your boat's gross tonnage, then multiply gross tonnage by 0.8 (or by 0.9 for a sailboat with an auxiliary engine) to get net tonnage. If the result is 5 or more net tons, your boat is probably eligible for documentation.

Documentation is a form of national registration, and as such is highly regulated. It is compara-

ble to recording the sale of real estate property, and the record includes a history of all title transfers for the vessel and may include critical associated documentation. Documentation often permits preferential status for obtaining mortgages. The vessel owner must be a U.S. citizen, a partnership of U.S. citizens, or a corporation controlled by U.S. citizens. The captain and other officers must also be U.S. citizens, though the crew need not be. In foreign ports, the vessel is considered part of the United States. The original documentation papers must be carried aboard the vessel.

A documented boat need not display registration numbers, though most states will still require state registration. Most powerboaters do not pursue documentation.

Registration of Boats

Registering a boat is comparable to registering a motor vehicle. All states require registration, though some waive the requirement for a documented boat. (Most also waive the requirement for rowboats, canoes, and small sailboats without mechanical propulsion, and some, as mentioned, waive it for low-power dinghies used exclusively as tenders.) A boat used in multiple states should be registered in the state of principal use. When you change from one state to another, there is generally a grace period before you must re-register your boat. The length of the grace period varies from state to state, and it is your responsibility to ascertain the applicable time period and register in a timely manner.

Numbering of Vessels

You will find a registration number on the registration certificate you receive from your town office or similar authorized registration site. The "number" is, in fact, a sequence of two letters, up to four numerals, and one or two more letters. The first two letters are the code for the state of registration. Unless your boat is documented, you must paint or permanently attach this number to both sides of the forward half of your boat, favoring the bow end. Do not display any other number there (Figure 2-1).

The registration number must be clearly visible. It must not be placed on the obscured underside of a flared bow—i.e., one that, when viewed

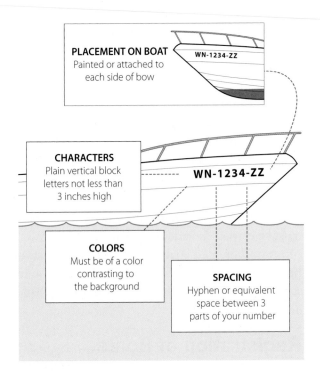

Figure 2-1. The proper display of a boat's registration number.

from ahead, has a pronounced outward curve between the waterline and the deck. If the number will not fit properly directly on the hull, affix it to a plate or to a forward portion of the superstructure (cabin).

The letters and numbers must be plain vertical block characters and must read from left to right. Use a space or a hyphen to separate the prefix and suffix letters from the numerals. The color of the characters must contrast with that of the background, and they must be at least 3 inches high.

In some states the registration is good for only 1 year, and in others, it is good for as long as 3 years. Renew your registration before it expires. At that time you will receive a new decal or decals, which should be placed within 6 inches of the registration number and as required by state law, after removing the old decals. Some states require that you show only the current decal or decals. If your vessel is moored, it must have a current decal even if it is not in use.

If your boat is lost, destroyed, abandoned, stolen, or transferred, you must inform the issuing authority. You should also notify the issuing authority as soon as possible if you lose your certificate of number or change your address.

Sales and Transfers

Your registration number is not transferable to another boat. The number stays with the boat unless the boat is registered with another state.

Hull Identification Number

A *hull identification number* (HIN) is like the vehicle identification number (VIN) on your car. Boats built between November 1, 1972, and July 31, 1984, have HINs like those shown in Figure 2-2A. The letter M in Figure 2-2A means the optional method for showing the date of certification was used. The last four characters show the model year and month when construction started. In the illustration, the 73 means 1973. Model years began in August, which is an A; E stands for December.

Since August 1, 1984, a new format has been used (Figure 2-2B). The first three characters are the manufacturer's ID, and the next five characters are the hull serial number. The ninth character shows the month construction began. In this system, A stands for January. The tenth character is the last digit of the year of manufacture, and the last two characters are the model year.

Your boat's HIN must appear in two places. If the boat has a transom, the primary location is on its starboard side within 2 inches of its top. If it does not have a transom or if it is not practical to use the transom, the number is on the starboard side, within 1 foot of the stern and within 2 inches of the top of the hull side. On pontoon boats, it is on the aft crossbeam within 1 foot of the starboard hull attachment. The secondary location is in an unexposed location determined by the manufacturer. This will be somewhere in the boat's interior or under a fitting or item of hardware.

Figure 2-2A. Hull identification numbers on boats manufactured between November 1, 1972, and July 31, 1984, look like this.

Figure 2-2B. Hull identification numbers on boats manufactured since August 1984 have this format.

Length of Boats

For some purposes, boats are classed by length. Each class has its own requirement for safety equipment.

Manufacturers may measure a boat's length in several ways for marketing purposes. Officially, however, your boat is measured along a straight line from its bow to its stern, parallel to its keel (Figure 2-3), and the length does not include *bowsprits*, *boomkins*, or *pulpits*, rudders, brackets, outboard motors, outdrives, diving platforms, or other hull attachments.

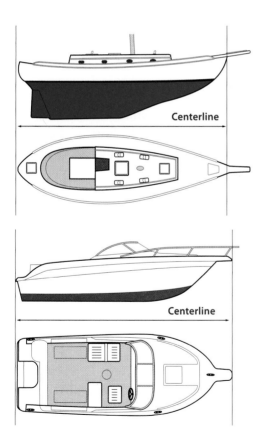

Figure 2-3. Length overall, also known as length on deck, includes a bow platform that is a molded part of the boat (bottom) but does not include a bowsprit (top) or a bow pulpit.

Capacity Information

Manufacturers must put *capacity plates* on most monohull recreational motorboats less than 20 feet long. Sailboats, canoes, kayaks, and inflatable boats are exempt. Outboard boats must display the maximum permitted engine horsepower on their capacity plates (Figure 2-4), but inboards and stern drives need not (Figure 2-5). Plates must also show the allowable maximum combined weight of the people on board and the allowable maximum combined weight of people, motors, and gear. The capacity for boats that were hand made or were manufactured before the requirement for capacity plates was instituted can be calculated using the equation Boat Length X Boat Width divided by 15 = Boat Capacity.

The capacity plate must be placed where it is clearly visible to the operator when getting underway. This information serves to remind you of the capacity of your boat under normal circumstances. You should ask yourself, "Is my boat loaded above its recommended capacity?" and, "Is my boat overloaded for the present sea and wind conditions?" If you are stopped by a legal authority, you may be cited if you are overloaded.

There are also capacity limits on PWCs. Those limits should be obtained from the manufacturer if a capacity plate is not on the PWC.

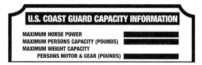

Figure 2-4. A capacity plate for an outboard-powered boat less than 20 feet long.

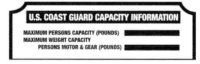

Figure 2-5. Capacity plate for an inboard or stern-drive boat less than 20 feet long.

Figure 2-6. The manufacturer must also affix a compliance plate on any motorboat less than 20 feet long.

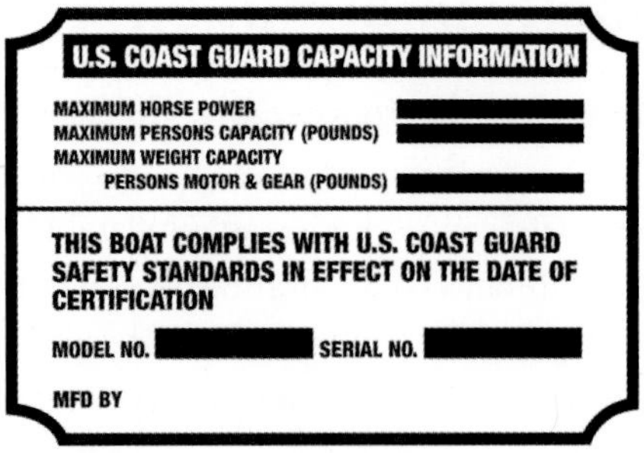

U.S. COAST GUARD CAPACITY INFORMATION

MAXIMUM HORSE POWER
MAXIMUM PERSONS CAPACITY (POUNDS)
MAXIMUM WEIGHT CAPACITY
PERSONS MOTOR & GEAR (POUNDS)

THIS BOAT COMPLIES WITH U.S. COAST GUARD SAFETY STANDARDS IN EFFECT ON THE DATE OF CERTIFICATION

MODEL NO.   SERIAL NO.

MFD BY

Figure **2-7.** A combination capacity and compliance plate.

Figure **2-8.** This boat was destroyed by an electrical fire that started near the batteries and battery charger. (REPRINTED WITH PERMISSION FROM *SEAWORTHY: ESSENTIAL LESSONS FROM BOATU.S.'S 20-YEAR CASE FILE OF THINGS GONE WRONG* BY ROBERT A. ADRIANCE)

Manufacturer's Certificate of Compliance

Manufacturers are required to put a *compliance plate* on a motorboat less than 20 feet long (Figure 2-6) that says, "This boat [or equipment] complies with U.S. Coast Guard Safety Standards in effect on the date of certification." Letters and numbers can be no less than 1/8 inch high. The manufacturer may combine capacity and compliance plates as shown in Figure 2-7.

Fire Prevention and Detection

Your Boat's Ventilation

"A cup of gasoline spilled in the *bilge* has the potential explosive power of 15 sticks of dynamite!" This statement, commonly repeated more than 20 years ago, may be an exaggeration, but it illustrates an important fact. Gasoline fumes in the bilge of a boat are highly explosive and a serious danger. They are heavier than air and will stay in the bilge until vented out.

Because of this danger, Coast Guard regulations require ventilation on many powerboats. There are several ways to supply fresh air to engine and gasoline tank compartments to remove dangerous vapors. Whatever the choice, it must meet Coast Guard standards.

The discussion below does not deal with all regulations, nor does it cover all recreational boats. It deals only with the following:

1. boats built after July 31, 1980
2. vessels made or used for noncommercial purposes
3. vessels leased, rented, or chartered for non-commercial use
4. boats carrying six or fewer passengers for hire

Neither is it intended to be a complete discussion of the regulations. Nevertheless, it covers the majority of recreational vessels.

General Precautions

Ventilation systems will not remove raw gasoline leaking from tanks or fuel lines. If you smell gasoline fumes, you may need immediate repairs. The best device for sensing gasoline fumes is your nose. **Use it!** If you smell gasoline in an engine compartment or elsewhere, **don't start your engine.** The smaller the compartment, the less gasoline it takes to make an explosive mixture.

Ventilation Systems

A ventilation system is required in an enclosed compartment with a permanently installed gasoline engine that has a cranking motor (see Figures 2-9 and 2-12). A compartment is exempt if its engine is open to the atmosphere. Diesel-powered boats are also exempt.

Table 2-1 on page 38 lists the ventilation requirements for a variety of boat configurations.

To be "open," a boat must meet certain conditions. Engine and fuel tank compartments and long, narrow compartments that join them are to

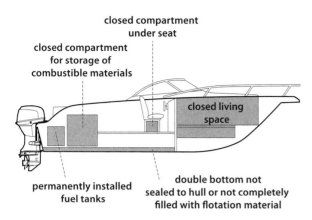

Figure 2-9. A boat with one or more enclosed spaces like these must carry at least one fire extinguisher (see page 39). In addition, this boat requires a ventilation system because of its permanent fuel tank in a closed compartment.

be "open to the atmosphere," which means that at least 15 square inches of open area for each cubic foot of net compartment volume must be open to the atmosphere. Also, there should be no long unventilated spaces open to engine and fuel tank compartments into which flames could extend.

There are two types of ventilation systems. One is *natural ventilation*, in which air circulates through closed spaces due to the boat's motion. The other is *powered ventilation*, in which air is circulated by a motor-driven fan or fans.

Natural Ventilation System Requirements

Natural ventilation is required for each enclosed compartment that includes one or more of the following (refer to Table 2-1):

- a permanently installed gasoline engine
- a sufficiently large opening between it and a compartment that requires ventilation
- a permanently installed fuel tank and an electrical part that is not ignition-protected against producing sparks
- a fuel tank that vents into it
- a nonmetallic fuel tank that exceeds technical requirements for permeability (some plastic tanks "bleed" excessively)

Gasoline tanks with a capacity of less than 7 gallons may be called *portable*. Tanks larger than 7 gallons may sometimes be called portable, but the

Coast Guard considers them permanent and requires that they be permanently secured before a boat can be awarded its safety decal.

A natural ventilation system has an air supply from outside the boat (Figure 2-10) or from a ventilated compartment or a compartment open to the atmosphere. Intake openings are required (Figure 2-11), and intake ducts may also be required to direct the air to appropriate compartments.

The system must have an exhaust duct that starts in the lower third of the compartment and opens into another ventilated compartment or into the atmosphere.

> **WARNING** *Play it safe: Keep your boat free of explosive vapors.* Always sniff the bilge to detect gasoline vapors. On a PWC, remove the seat to check for fuel leaks from the tank, fuel lines, and carburetor.

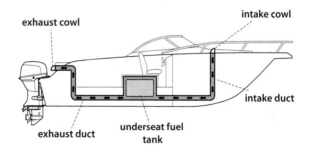

Figure 2-10. An example of natural ventilation through a fuel tank compartment.

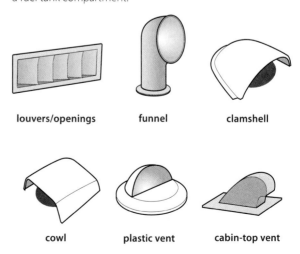

Figure 2-11. A natural ventilation system requires an air intake opening like one of these.

> **WARNING** *Inspect ducts frequently. Ducts can come loose and plastic ducts can break.*

Each air supply opening, exhaust opening, and duct, where present, must be above the usual level of the bilge water. Openings should be at least 3 square inches in area or 2 inches in diameter and placed so that exhaust gases do not enter the fresh-air intake, any cabin, or other enclosed nonventilated space. The carbon monoxide gas in exhaust gases is deadly.

Intake and exhaust openings have to be covered by *cowls* or similar devices to keep out rainwater and water from breaking seas. Most often, intake cowls face forward and exhaust openings face aft, but on boats built after March 1987, intake cowls may face in any direction. Forward-facing intake cowls capture the flow of air when the boat is moving or at anchor, since most boats face into the wind when anchored.

Powered Ventilation System Requirements

Powered ventilation systems must meet the standards of a natural system, but also have one or more

TABLE 2-1	VENTILATION FOR POWERBOATS (VESSELS BUILT AFTER JULY 31, 1980)	
Type of Boat	**Powered Ventilation**	**Natural Ventilation**
Open boat	No	No
Open boat with portable tank	No	No
Portable tank in enclosed compartment	No	Yes*
Permanent tank vented to outside	No	No
Permanent tank and engine compartment	Yes	Yes
Permanent tank and engine compartments**		
Tank compartment	No	No***
Engine compartment	Yes	Yes

* Assumes that portable tanks are not vented to the outside.
** Assumes that permanently installed tanks are vented to the outside.
*** If electrical components are present, they must be ignition-protected.

exhaust blowers (Figure 2-12). The blower duct can serve as the exhaust duct for natural ventilation if fan blades do not obstruct the airflow when not powered.

Openings in engine compartments for carburetion do not count toward satisfying ventilation system requirements.

WARNING LABEL. On boats with powered ventilation, a warning label must be mounted near each ignition switch, in plain view of the operator. It should include at least the information in the warning opposite.

Backfire Flame Arresters

Gasoline engines other than outboards must have an acceptable means of controlling backfires, which occur when flames from an engine exit through the carburetor instead of the exhaust system. A backfire control keeps these flames from entering the engine compartment.

The usual (though not the only) method of controlling backfires is by fitting a backfire flame arrester (Figure 2-13) to the carburetor. A flame arrester works by rapidly dissipating the heat of the flame, thus keeping the flame out of the engine compartment. An acceptable backfire flame arrester will bear either a Coast Guard approval number, a notice of compliance with Underwriters Laboratories standard UL 1111, or a label stating that it complies with the Society of Automotive Engineers (SAE) standard J1928.

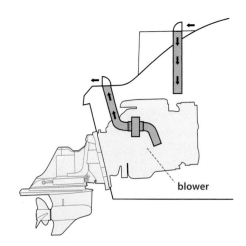

Figure **2-12.** A powered ventilation system requires a blower in the exhaust duct.

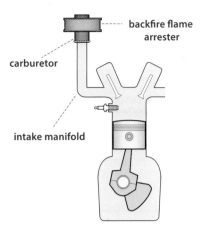

Figure **2-13.** This simplified schematic (not to scale) shows the location of a backfire flame arrester over a carburetor.

> **WARNING** *Gas vapors can explode. Before starting engine, operate blower for 4 minutes and check engine compartment bilge for gas vapors.*

To be effective, flame arresters must be free of oil, grease, and dirt and should therefore be cleaned periodically with grease-dissolving detergent. Otherwise, backfire flame arresters do not need servicing or replacing.

Carbon Monoxide

Carbon monoxide poisoning is a rapidly increasing risk as more and more boatowners are using gasoline generators to power air conditioners. The generator exhaust is commonly located in the transom, which on most boats is a popular area for congregating, swimming, and socializing. Houseboats, in particular, experience this problem due to frequent use of air-conditioning while people are socializing and swimming.

When there is a space between the stern and the swim platform, fumes are funneled up and accumulate, possibly resulting in injury and death. Propulsion engines provide another source of carbon monoxide, one to which all boats are subject.

The best solution for this problem is to turn off all engines when activities are in progress at the stern of the boat, especially on the swim platform or in the water directly under or behind it.

Your Boat's Equipment

Coast Guard regulations require that your boat have certain equipment aboard (see chart next page). These requirements are minimums and should be exceeded whenever possible.

Fire Extinguishers

If your motorboat includes one or more of the following, you must have at least one fire extinguisher aboard (see Table 2-2 and Figure 2-9):

1. inboard or stern-drive engine(s)
2. closed compartments under *thwarts* and seats where portable fuel tanks can be stored
3. double bottoms not sealed together or not completely filled with flotation materials
4. enclosed living spaces
5. closed stowage compartments in which combustible or flammable materials are stored
6. permanently installed fuel tanks
7. a length of 26 feet or more

Types of Fires

Fire extinguishers have labels that tell the types of fires for which they are designed. There are three common classes of fires:

- Class A fires are in ordinary combustible materials such as paper or wood.
- Class B fires involve gasoline, oil, or grease.
- Class C fires are electrical.

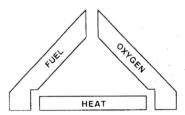

Figure **2-14.** Removing one element of a fire will suppress it. (REPRINTED WITH PERMISSION FROM *SMALL BOAT SEAMANSHIP MANUAL*)

COAST GUARD EQUIPMENT REQUIREMENTS: QUICK REFERENCE CHART

Vessel Length (in feet)				Equipment	Requirement
<16	16<26	26<40	40<65		
X	X	X	X	Certificate of Number (State Registration)	All undocumented vessels equipped with propulsion machinery must be State registered. Certificate of Number must be on board when vessel is in use. Note: some States require all vessels to be registered.
X	X	X	X	State Numbering	(a) Plain Block letters/numbers not less than 3 inches in height must be affixed on each side of the forward half of the vessel (Contrasting color to boat exterior). (b) State validation sticker must be affixed within six inches of the registration number
	X	X	X	Certificate of Documentation	Applies only to "Documented" vessels: (a) Original and current certificate must be on board. (b) Vessel name/hailing port marked on exterior part of hull—letters not less than 4 inches in height. (c) Official Number permanently affixed on interior structure—numbers not less than 3 inches in height.
X	X	X	X	Life Jackets (PFDs)	(a) One Type I, II, III, or V wearable PFD for each person on board. (must be USCG approved)
	X	X	X		(b) In addition to paragraph (a), must carry One Type IV (throwable) PFD.
X				Visual Distress Signal (VDS)	(a) One electric distress light or Three combination (day/night) red flares. Note: only required to be carried on board when operating between sunset and sunrise.
	X	X	X		(b) One orange distress flag or One electric distress light—or—Three handheld or floating orange smoke signals and One electric distress light—or—Three combination (day/night) red flares: handheld, meteor or parachute type.
X	X			Fire Extinguishers	(a) One B-I (when enclosed compartment)
	X				(b) One B-II or Two B-I. Note: fixed system equals One B-I
			X		(c) One B-II and One B-I or Three B-I. Note: fixed system equals One B-I or Two B-II
X	X	X	X	Ventilation	(a) All vessels built after 25 April 1940 that use gasoline as their fuel with enclosed engine and/or fuel tank compartments must have natural ventilation (at least two ducts fitted with cowls). (b) In addition to paragraph (a), a vessel built after 31 July 1980 must have rated power exhaust blower.
X	X	X		Sound Producing Devices	(a) A vessel of less than 39.4 ft. must, at a minimum, have some means of making an efficient sound signal (i.e. handheld air horn, athletic whistle—Human voice/sound not acceptable).
	X	X			(b) A vessel 39.4 ft. (12 meters) or greater, must have a sound signaling appliance capable of producing an efficient sound signal, audible for $1/2$ mile with a 4 to 6 seconds duration. In addition, must carry a bell with a clapper (bell size not less than 7.9" —based on the diameter of the mouth)
X	X	X	X	Backfire Flame Arrester	Required on gasoline engines installed after 25 April 1940, except outboard motors
X	X	X	X	Navigational Lights	Required to be displayed from sunset to sunrise and in or near areas of reduced visibility.
	X	X		Oil Pollution Placard	(a) Placard must be at least 5 by 8 inches, made of durable material. (b) Placard must be posted in the machinery space or at the bilge station.
	X	X		Garbage Placard	(a) Placard must be at least 4 by 9 inches, made of durable material. (b) Displayed in a conspicuous place notifying all on board the discharge restrictions.
X	X	X	X	Marine Sanitation Device	If installed toilet: Vessel must have an operable MSD Type I, II, or III.
	X	X		Navigation Rules (Inland Only)	The operator of a vessel 39.4 ft (12 meters) or greater must have on board a copy of these rules.

The extinguishers on motorboats must be for Class B fires. Never use water on Class B or Class C fires since it spreads Class B fires, and could cause you to be electrocuted if used on a Class C fire.

Sizes of Extinguishers

Fire extinguishers are also classed by the amount of material they contain. Table 2-3 lists the types of Class B extinguishers and their contents.

Contents of Extinguishers

Fire extinguishers use a variety of materials (Figure 2-15). Those used on boats usually contain dry chemicals, aqueous foam, or carbon dioxide (CO_2). Dry chemical extinguishers, which contain chemical powders such as sodium bicarbonate, or baking soda, are the most frequently used extinguishers on recreational boats because they are reasonably inexpensive, convenient, and will put out Class A, B, and C fires.

Figure **2-15.** **Left to right:** Dry chemical, carbon dioxide, and Halon fire extinguishers. For reasons explained in the text, dry chemical extinguishers are the most popular type on recreational boats. (PHOTO BY NORMA LOCOCO)

TABLE 2-2 REQUIRED FIRE EXTINGUISHERS

Minimum number of hand-portable fire extinguishers on a boat with and without a fixed extinguishing system

Length of Vessel	No Fixed System in Machinery Space	Fixed System in Machinery Space
Less than 26 ft.	1 B-I	none
26 ft. to under 40 ft.	2 B-Is or 1 B-II	1 B-I
40 ft. to 65 ft.	3 B-Is or 1 B-I and 1 B-II	2 B-Is or 1 B-II

Carbon dioxide extinguishers leave no residue when discharged and will not damage an engine, and they are therefore sometimes used in an engine compartment's fixed extinguishing system. Portable CO_2 extinguishers are not often found on boats, however, in part because CO_2 is colorless and odorless when released from an extinguisher. It is not poisonous, but caution must be used when entering compartments filled with it since it keeps oxygen from reaching your lungs and is lethal in fire-killing concentrations. If you are in a compartment with a high concentration of CO_2, you will experience no difficulty breathing, but the air you breathe will not contain enough oxygen to support life. Unconsciousness or death can result.

Aqueous foam extinguishers are rarely used because they leave a hard-to-clean residue when discharged and can damage an engine when discharged in the engine compartment.

Halon and FE-241 Extinguishers

Until 1994, Halon gas was commonly used both in portable extinguishers and in fixed or built-in automatic fire extinguishing systems. Although Halon has excellent firefighting properties, it is thought to deplete the earth's ozone layer and has not been manufactured in the United States since

January 1, 1994. In the mid- to late-90s, Halon extinguishers could still be refilled from existing stocks of the gas, but this is no longer possible in most cases. When you dispose of an old Halon extinguisher, take it to a recovery station rather than releasing the gas into the atmosphere.

Alternative gases such as FE-241 have replaced Halon. While appropriate for an engine compartment, FE-241 is toxic and should therefore not be used in occupied spaces.

Obsolete Extinguishers

Some other extinguishers also require caution. Carbon tetrachloride extinguishers have been outlawed for years, so you are unlikely to encounter one of these. If you do, however, it should be safely disposed of. In contact with a flame, it produces phosgene, a poisonous gas used in World War I.

Some obsolete hand-portable extinguishers must be inverted to be activated and are either ineffective on boat fires or dangerous to use. They include soda-acid, foam, and cartridge-operated water extinguishers. Neither the soda-acid nor cartridge-operated ones should be used on gasoline, oil, or grease fires, such as occur on boats, because they contain water. All are potentially dangerous; if their discharge hoses are blocked, they may explode. Dispose of them safely.

TABLE 2-3 CLASS B FIRE EXTINGUISHERS

Coast Guard Classification (type-size)	Underwriters Laboratories Listing	Aqueous Foam (gals.)	Carbon Dioxide (lbs.)	Dry Chemical (lbs.)	FE-241 (lbs.)
B-I	5B	1.25	4	2	5
B-II	10B	2.5	15	10	10

Fire Extinguisher Approval

Fire extinguishers must be Coast Guard–approved and in serviceable condition. Look for the approval number on the nameplate and information such as the following on the label: "Marine Type USCG Approved, Size . . ., Type . . ., 162.208/."

Care and Treatment

Make certain your extinguishers are stowed in their service locations and are not damaged. Replace cracked or broken hoses and be sure nozzles are free of obstructions such as wasps and other insects that sometimes nest inside and render the nozzles inoperable.

Check extinguishers frequently for proper pressure, and check the locking pin with its sealing wire to ensure that it hasn't been used since charging. Don't test an extinguisher by operating it since its valves will not reseat properly, and the remaining gas will leak out. When this happens, the extinguisher is useless.

Weigh and tag carbon dioxide, Halon, or FE-241 extinguishers twice a year (Figure 2-16). If their weight loss exceeds 10% of the weight of the charge, recharge them. You should also check to see that they have not been used. They should be inspected by a qualified person every 6 months, and should carry tags showing all inspection and service dates.

If your dry chemical extinguisher has a pressure indicator, check it frequently. Check the nozzle to see if there is powder in it; if there is or if there is

Figure 2-16. A fire extinguisher should carry a tag showing all inspection and service dates. (PHOTO BY NORMA LOCOCO)

low pressure in the nozzle, replace it or have it serviced. The quality and serviceability of extinguishers varies greatly, so the decision to service or replace them is often best made by a professional.

Occasionally invert your dry chemical extinguisher and hit the base with the palm of your hand. The chemical in these extinguishers packs and cakes due to the boat's vibration and pounding, and while there is a difference of opinion about whether hitting the base helps, it can't hurt. Sometimes the gauge will stick in the full position and give a false reading and jarring the extinguisher will often dislodge the stuck indicator. Caking of the chemical powder is a major cause of failure of dry chemical extinguishers. If you hear a thud when tilting the extinguisher back and forth, suspect caking. Carry spare extinguishers in excess of the minimum requirement.

If you have guests aboard, make certain they know where the extinguishers are and how to use them.

Using a Fire Extinguisher

A fire extinguisher usually has a metal or plastic locking pin or loop to prevent accidental discharge. If you need to use your extinguisher, take it from its bracket, remove the pin or loop, and point the nozzle at the base of the flames. Now squeeze the handle and discharge the extinguisher's contents while sweeping from side to side (Figure 2-17). Recharge or replace a used extinguisher as soon as possible after use.

If you are using a Halon, FE-241, or CO_2 extinguisher, keep your hands away from the discharge, as the rapidly expanding gas will freeze them. If the fire extinguisher has a horn, hold it by its handle.

Legal Requirements for Extinguishers

Carry fire extinguishers as defined by Coast Guard regulations. They must be readily accessible in a secure location, and it is recommended that they be attached to the boat. As summarized in Table 2-2 above, a powerboat less than 26 feet long is required to have at least one approved, hand-portable, Type B-I extinguisher aboard unless the boat either (1) has an approved fixed fire extin-

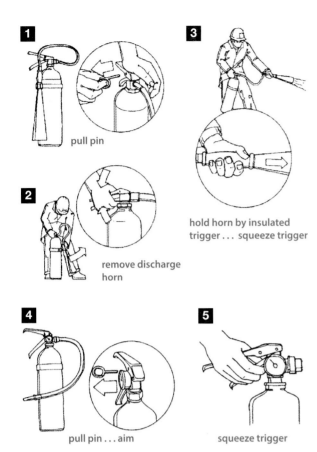

pull pin

remove discharge horn

hold horn by insulated trigger . . . squeeze trigger

pull pin . . . aim

squeeze trigger

Figure **2-17.** How to use a CO$_2$ (**1, 2, 3**) or dry chemical (**4, 5**) extinguisher. (REPRINTED WITH PERMISSION FROM *SMALL BOAT SEAMANSHIP MANUAL*)

A powerboat 26 feet to under 40 feet long must have at least two Type B-I Coast Guard–approved hand-portable extinguishers or one approved Type B-II. If you have an approved fixed fire extinguishing system, only one Type B-I is required.

A powerboat 40 to 65 feet long must have at least three approved portable Type B-Is or at least one Type B-I plus one Type B-II. If the boat has an approved fixed fire extinguishing system, two Type B-Is or one Type B-II extinguisher is required.

Warning System

Various devices such as fire, smoke, gasoline fumes, and carbon monoxide detectors are available to alert you to danger. If your boat has a galley, it should have a smoke detector. Where possible, use wired detectors because household batteries often corrode rapidly on a boat.

You can't see, smell, or taste carbon monoxide gas, but it is lethal. There are many ways in which carbon monoxide can enter your boat, and as little as 1 part in 10,000 parts of air can bring on a headache. The symptoms of carbon monoxide poisoning—headaches, dizziness, and nausea—are like seasickness. By the time you realize what is happening to you, it may be too late to take action. If your boat has enclosed living spaces, protect yourself with a carbon monoxide detector.

Personal Flotation Devices

Personal flotation devices (PFDs) are commonly called life preservers or life jackets and are available in a variety of types and sizes according to intended

guishing system (Figure 2-18), or (2) is propelled by an outboard motor or motors and does not meet any of the criteria listed at the beginning of this section. It's a good idea to carry a portable extinguisher even when not required. If a nearby boat catches fire, or if a fire occurs at a fuel dock, you'll be glad you have it.

✓ WHICH EXTINGUISHER TO USE	
TYPES OF FIRES	**APPROPRIATE EXTINGUISHER**
CLASS A—Ordinary Combustible Material (such as Paper and Wood)	Water, Halon or FE-241, Carbon Dioxide, Dry Chemical
CLASS B—Gasoline, Diesel Fuel, Oil, Grease	Halon or FE-241, Carbon Dioxide, Dry Chemical (NOT WATER)
CLASS C—Electrical	Halon or FE-241, Carbon Dioxide, Dry Chemical (NOT WATER)
Boats with Motors	Must use a CLASS B Extinguisher

use. The term "approved PFD" as used here refers to a PFD type that is approved for a given application. Additionally, each individual PFD must bear a label stating that it is approved by the U.S. Coast Guard.

PFD Characteristics

The most common PFDs are inherently buoyant and do not require inflation. They have been in use for a long time. The relatively new inflatable PFDs, however, are convenient and comfortable to wear. No PFD should be stuffed into storage and forgotten, but inflatable PFDs have mechanisms that require even more regular inspection.

Three inflatable systems are approved by the Coast Guard. One, called a manual inflatable, allows inflation by pulling a lanyard. Another, called a manual inflatable with automatic backup, is inflated the same way but also has a backup automatic inflation system that activates if the PFD becomes immersed in water. A third, called a hybrid, has a small amount of built-in buoyancy that is augmented by a manual or automatic inflatable device. Hybrids are no longer generally available but are still usable if they are serviceable and armed correctly.

All inflatables have an additional backup inflation capability that requires the wearer to blow into a tube. More details are given under the sections on Type III and Type V PFDs below. It's likely that in the near future there will be more inflatable design improvements.

Figure **2-18.** A fixed fire-suppression system should have a status light like this one near the helm.

Types of PFDs

TYPE I PFDs. This type is also called an offshore life jacket and will turn most unconscious people to a faceup position (Figure 2-19). These PFDs come in both inherently buoyant (foam-filled) and inflatable models. The adult size in the inherently buoyant models has at least 22 pounds of buoyancy, while the child's size has at least 11 pounds. An adult inflatable generates up to 34 pounds of buoyancy at maximum inflation.

Type I life jackets are bulkier and less comfortable than other types, although the inflatable models are quite comfortable when not inflated. Type Is keep an individual afloat for extended periods when rescue is delayed, and are therefore especially appropriate for offshore use. Because of their buoy-

Figure **2-19.** Type I PFDs. (COURTESY PERSONAL FLOTATION DEVICE MANUFACTURERS ASSOCIATION)

Inherently Buoyant (Primarily Foam)

❙ The *most* reliable
❙ Adult, Youth, Child, and Infant sizes
❙ For swimmers & non-swimmers
❙ Wearable & throwable styles
❙ Some designed for water sports

Minimum Buoyancy		
Wearable Size	Type	Inherent Buoyancy (Foam)
Adult	I	22 lb.
	II & III	15.5 lb.
	V	15.5 to 22 lb.
Youth	II & III	11 lb.
	V	11 to 15.5 lb.
Child and Infant	II	7 lb.
Throwable:		
Cushion	IV	20 lb.
Ring Buoy		16.5 & 32 lb.

ancy, they will support individuals higher in the water; thus, they are excellent in rough water.

TYPE II PFDs. This type, also called a near-shore buoyant vest, comes in both inherently buoyant and inflatable models (Figure 2-20). Inherently buoyant Type IIs will turn some unconscious individuals to a faceup position, while inflatable models do this as well as Type I foam PFDs do.

While Type IIs are more comfortable than Type Is, they provide less buoyancy. Adult foam models have 15.5 pounds of buoyancy, youth models have 11 pounds, and infant models have 7 pounds (Figure 2-21). Adult inflatable models

offer up to 34 pounds of buoyancy, on a par with Type I inflatables.

Type IIs are recommended for inshore and inland cruising on calm waters where the chances of fast rescue are high.

TYPE III PFDs. A Type III is also called a flotation aid (Figures 2-21 and 2-22), and it too comes in inherently buoyant and inflatable models. The foam vest has the same minimum buoyancy as Type II PFDs, but Type IIIs are designed so that their wearers must turn themselves upright and may have to tilt their heads back to avoid being rolled facedown.

Type IIIs are designed for conscious individuals in calm inland waters where the chance of quick rescue is high. They come in many colors and styles, such as fishing vests and float coats, and are comfortable to wear. Freedom of movement is one of their strong points, which makes them attractive to sport users.

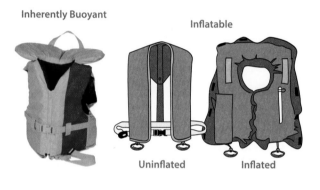

Inherently Buoyant

Inflatable

Uninflated Inflated

Hybrid

Uninflated Inflated

Figure **2-20.** Type II PFDs. (COURTESY PERSONAL FLOTATION DEVICE MANUFACTURERS ASSOCIATION)

Inflatable

▮ The most compact
▮ Sizes only for adults
▮ Only recommended for swimmers
▮ Wearable styles only
▮ Some with the best in-water performance

Minimum Buoyancy		
Wearable Size	Type	Inflatable Buoyancy
Adult	I & II	34 lb.
	III	22.5 lb.
	V	22.5 to 34 lb.

Figure **2-21.** **Top:** These kids are wearing inherently buoyant Type III PFDs, while the adult is wearing a Type III inflatable. **Bottom:** The driver is wearing a Type II inflatable vest. Note the lanyard on his wrist. This leads to a kill switch, which would cut the engine should he be thrown from his helm position. In the stern, a child wearing a Type III inherently buoyant PFD sits between two adults wearing Type III inflatable vests. (COURTESY U.S. COAST GUARD OFFICE OF BOATING SAFETY)

Inherently Buoyant

Inflatable

Hybrid

Hip pack—uninflated

Figure 2-22. Type III PFDs. (COURTESY PERSONAL FLOTATION DEVICE MANUFACTURERS ASSOCIATION AND WEST MARINE)

Hybrid (Foam & Inflation)

❚ Reliable
❚ Adult, Youth, and Child sizes
❚ For swimmers & non-swimmers
❚ Wearable styles only
❚ Some designed for water sports

Minimum Buoyancy			
Wearable Size	Type	Inherent Buoyancy	Inflated Total Buoyancy
Adult	II & III	10 lb.	22 lb.
	V	7.5 lb.	22 lb.
Youth	II & III	9 lb.	15 lb.
	V	7.5 lb.	15 lb.
Child	II	7 lb.	12 lb.

TYPE IV PFDs. A Type IV, also called a throwable device (Figure 2-23), is designed to be thrown to someone in the water who can hold onto it until rescued. This type, which should not be worn, includes rings, horseshoe buoys, and buoyant cushions. There are no inflatable Type IVs.

Most throwables have handles or grab lines for

Ring buoy

Boat cushion

Figure 2-23. Type IV PFDs. (COURTESY PERSONAL FLOTATION DEVICE MANUFACTURERS ASSOCIATION)

the person in the water to hold on to. In addition, while not a requirement, it is a good idea to attach about 60 feet of polypropylene line (which floats) to the throwable to better assist the user in retrieving the device and also assist the rescuer in retrieving the user. If your boat is 16 feet or more in length and is not a canoe or kayak, you must have at least one Type IV aboard.

Be careful when throwing the device so that you don't hit and possibly injure the intended receiver.

TYPE V PFDs. This type, also called a special-use device, is intended for special activities and may be carried instead of another PFD only if used according to the approval conditions on its label (Figure 2-24). The performance of these devices is marked on their labels. If the label says the PFD is "approved only when worn," the device must be worn except in enclosed spaces (i.e., the boat's cabin) and used in accordance with the approval label.

Some Type Vs offer hypothermia protection. The wide range of varieties includes deck suits, work vests, and windsurfing vests.

Legal Requirements

A Coast Guard–approved PFD must show the manufacturer's name and approval number. Most are marked as Type I, II, III, IV, or V. You are required to carry at least one wearable PFD of suitable size for each person on board your boat.

If a person elects to wear a Type V PFD with a "required to be worn" label only at selected times, he or she must have another Type I, II, or III PFD aboard to meet the boat's PFD count requirement. Type Vs don't count toward the requirement when not worn or when worn for other than the labeled use.

If your vessel is 16 feet or more long and is not

Figure **2-24.** Top: A canoeist wearing an inflatable vest. If this is a Type III, the paddler must pull the lanyard to inflate it. If it's a Type V, it will inflate automatically (with manual backup), providing Type II protection. (COURTESY U.S. COAST GUARD OFFICE OF BOATING SAFETY) **Bottom:** This work vest and immersion suit are two examples of Type V special-purpose configurations. (COURTESY PERSONAL FLOTATION DEVICE MANUFACTURERS ASSOCIATION)

a canoe or a kayak, you must also have at least one Type IV PFD on board. These requirements apply to all recreational vessels that are propelled or controlled by machinery, sails, oars, paddles, poles, or another vessel. Sailboards are not required by federal law to carry PFDs, but some states require them.

You can substitute an older Type V hybrid for any required Type I, II, or III PFD provided that its approval label shows that it is all of the following:

1. approved for the activity the vessel is engaged in
2. approved as a substitute for a PFD of the type required on the vessel
3. used as required on the label
4. used in accordance with any requirements in its owner's manual, if the approval label makes reference to such a manual

You are required to keep your PFDs readily accessible. Type IV devices must be immediately at hand so that you can reach out and get them when needed.

Coast Guard–approved inflatable PFDs are authorized only for people at least 16 years old, and it is recommended that nonswimmers wear inherently buoyant PFDs at all times while on board.

General Considerations

The proper use of a PFD requires the wearer to know how it will perform. Because of variances in weather, water conditions, and boat traffic, boating conditions can change rapidly. Boat operators and passengers should wear a properly fitted PFD at all times. It is nearly impossible to put on a PFD while in the water, so merely disclosing the location of PFDs is not sufficient. Boaters should also be aware of state and federal regulations regarding the need for children to wear PFDs while on board. You can gain this knowledge only through experience, and a good place to practice donning a PFD is in a swimming pool.

Each person on your boat should be assigned a PFD. To ensure the proper fit of a PFD, have the wearer put it on and adjust the straps as necessary until it feels snug. Have the wearer raise his or her arms above their head and then cinch the upper straps of the PFD firmly. A properly fitted PFD will not ride higher than the ears or mouth of the wearer. Note that it is very difficult to adjust the straps while in the water. *Note: This fitting procedure is not applicable to inflatable PFDs, which should have their retaining straps adjusted loosely to allow for the inflation of the devices.*

It is wise to follow this advice even if the water is calm and you intend to boat near shore. Most drownings occur in inland waters within a few feet of safety, and most victims have PFDs available but fail to wear them.

Storing PFDs in your cabin in the plastic covers they came wrapped in assures that they will stay clean and unfaded, but this is no way to carry them when you are on the water. A PFD must be readily accessible and adjusted to fit its wearer if it's going to be useful. You can't spend time hunting for it or

RIDING GEAR FOR PWCs

Although not specified in federal requirements, operators and riders of PWCs should consider purchasing and using the following personal items: (1) a wet suit to combat hypothermia, (2) gloves to protect your skin, (3) foot protection to help keep your footing and prevent scrapes, and (4) eye protection, such as tinted glasses or goggles, to prevent spray from getting into your eyes and to minimize the adverse effects of sun.

learning how to put it on in an emergency situation.

There is no substitute for the experience of entering the water while wearing a PFD. Children, especially, need practice. If possible, give your guests this experience. Advise them to keep their arms to their sides when jumping in, in order to keep the PFD from riding up. Then let them jump in and see how the PFD responds. Is it adjusted so it does not ride up? Is it properly sized? Are all the straps snug? Does a child's PFD fit properly, with proper adjustments?

Nonswimmers, children, and the elderly and handicapped should always wear PFDs on a boat, and many states require this. In hazardous waters, rough weather, and at night everyone aboard should wear one. Indeed, it is highly recommended that all passengers wear PFDs at all times. Coast Guard members always wear PFDs on the water, even when it is calm.

Inspect your lifesaving equipment from time to time, and leave any questionable or unsatisfactory equipment ashore. An emergency is no time to conduct an inspection.

Care of Life Jackets

Given reasonable care, PFDs last many years. Thoroughly dry them before putting them away in a well-ventilated place. Avoid the bottoms of lockers and deck storage boxes where moisture may collect, and air and dry them frequently no matter where they are stored.

PFDs should not be tossed about or used as *fenders* or cushions. Many contain kapok or fibrous glass material enclosed in plastic bags, which can rupture and become unserviceable. Squeeze your life jacket gently. Does air leak out? If so, water can leak in, rendering the jacket unsafe to use. Cut it up so no one will use it, and throw it away.

The covers of some PFDs are made of nylon or polyester, which, like many other plastics, will break down after extended exposure to the ultraviolet light in sunlight. This process may be more rapid when the materials are dyed with bright dyes such as neon shades.

Rips and badly faded fabric are clues that the covering of your PFD is deteriorating. A simple test is to pinch the fabric between your thumbs and forefingers and then try to tear it. If it can be torn, it should definitely be destroyed and discarded.

The condition of the straps and hardware used to secure a PFD to a person is also an important consideration. A PFD that cannot be securely fastened is of little value to a person in the water. If any of the metal or plastic hardware or the webbing or straps on a PFD are broken, deformed, ripped, or separated from their attachment points, discard it.

Special Care for Inflatable PFDs

Inflatables require more care than foam-filled PFDs. Users should follow the manufacturer's recommendations. Inflatables should be inspected at least once a year. Each manufacturer has their own checklist that will include inflating the bladder manually—once you have done so ensure that it remains inflated overnight or for at least 10 hours. The inflation cartridge should not be outdated, and it should be replaced if the cartridge weight is below minimum. Check to ensure that the green indicator is showing green, too.

Sound-Producing Devices

All boats, including PWC, are required to carry some means of making an efficient sound signal. A device for making the whistle or horn noises required by the Navigation Rules must be capable of a 4-second blast that is audible for at least ½ mile. Athletic whistles are not acceptable on boats 12 meters (39 feet) or longer and should be used with caution (Figure 2-25). When wet, some of them come apart and lose their "peas," rendering them useless. Consider attaching a whistle to each PFD.

If your vessel is 12 meters (39 feet) long or more, a power whistle (or power horn) is required on board. If your vessel is longer than 20 meters (65

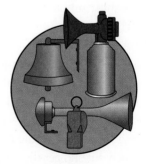

Figure **2-25.** Acceptable sound-signal devices include a bell, a compressed-air horn, a power horn, and a whistle. A boat more than 39 feet long needs both a horn and a bell under the Inland Rules (see Chapter 6).

TABLE 2-4   VISUAL DISTRESS SIGNALS

Pyrotechnic Visual Distress Signals

CG Approval Number	Description	Use
160.021	Handheld flare	Day/night
160.022	Floating orange smoke	Day only
160.024	Pistol parachute red flare	Day/night
160.036	Handheld parachute red flare	Day/night
160.037	Handheld orange smoke	Day only
160.057	Floating orange smoke	Day only
160.066	Red aerial pyrotechnic flare	Day/night

Nonpyrotechnic Visual Distress Signals

160.072	Orange flag	Day only
161.013	Electric distress light	Night only

feet), you will need a bell in addition to the horn. The bell must be in operating condition and have a minimum diameter of at least 200 mm (7.9 inches) at its mouth.

Visual Distress Signals

Visual distress signals (VDS) attract attention to your vessel if you need help. They also help to guide searchers in search-and-rescue situations. Be sure you have the right kinds, and use them properly.

It is illegal to fire flares in a nonemergency unless authorized by the Coast Guard. False distress signals cost the Coast Guard and its Auxiliary many wasted hours in fruitless searches each year. If you signal a distress with flares and subsequently receive the necessary help, please let the Coast Guard or the appropriate search-and-rescue (SAR) agency know so that the distress report can be canceled.

Recreational boats less than 16 feet long are required to carry VDS only when operating on coastal waters between sunset and sunrise. (Coastal waters include oceans and gulfs and the bays or sounds that empty into them; the Great Lakes and their contiguous bays and sounds; and rivers that are more than 2 miles across at their mouths, upstream to where they narrow to 2 miles; Figure 2-28.) All pyrotechnic VDS must be Coast Guard–approved, readily accessible, serviceable, and within their stamped expiration dates.

Recreational boats 16 feet or longer must carry VDS at all times on coastal waters, day or night, and the same requirement applies to boats carry-

ing six or fewer passengers for hire. Open sailboats less than 26 feet long without engines are exempt in the daytime, as are manually propelled boats. Also exempt are boats in organized races, regattas, parades, and other such events. Boats owned in the United States and operating on the high seas must be equipped with VDS.

A wide variety of signaling devices meet Coast Guard regulations (Figure 2-26). If you choose pyrotechnic devices, a minimum of three are required. Any combination can be carried, as long as it adds up to at least three signals for day use and at least three signals for night use. Three day/night signals meet both requirements. If possible, carry more than the legal requirement. These devices are listed in Table 2-4.

Flying the American flag upside down is a commonly recognized distress signal, although it is not recognized in Coast Guard regulations. In an emergency, your efforts would probably be better used in more effective signaling methods.

Types of VDS

All VDS must be Coast Guard–approved, in good serviceable condition, within their stamped expiration dates, and readily accessible to meet federal carriage requirements.

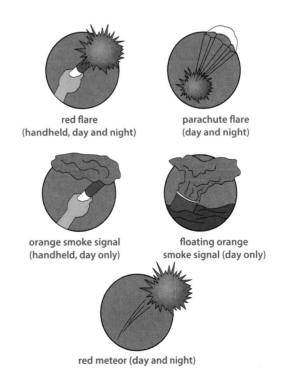

red flare
(handheld, day and night)

parachute flare
(day and night)

orange smoke signal
(handheld, day only)

floating orange
smoke signal (day only)

red meteor (day and night)

Figure **2-26.** Pyrotechnic distress signals.

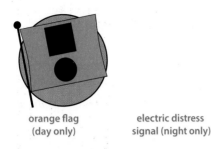

orange flag
(day only)

electric distress
signal (night only)

dye in water

red ribbon
in water

Figure **2-27.** Nonpyrotechnic distress signals.

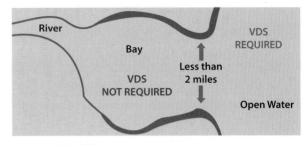

Figure **2-28.** All boats operating on coastal waters, territorial seas, or the Great Lakes must carry visual distress signals. This requirement also applies on any waterway directly connected with these waters, but only to the point, proceeding inland, where the connecting waterway narrows to less than 2 miles wide.

DAYTIME NONPYROTECHNIC SIGNALS. A bright orange flag with a black square above a black circle is the simplest daytime VDS (Figure 2-27), plus it has the advantage of being a continuous signal.

A mirror, while not an approved device, can be used to good advantage on sunny days. Mirrors can attract the attention of other boaters and of aircraft from great distances and are available with holes in their centers to aid in aiming. In the absence of a mirror, any shiny object such as a CD can be used.

When another boat is in sight, an effective VDS is to extend your arms from your sides and move them slowly up and down. Don't do it too fast or observers may think you are just being friendly. This simple gesture is seldom misunderstood and requires no equipment.

DAYTIME PYROTECHNIC DEVICES. Orange smoke is a useful daytime signal. Handheld or floating smoke flares are very effective in attracting attention from aircraft (Figure 2-26). Smoke flares don't last long and are not effective in high wind or poor visibility, however. As with other pyrotechnic devices, use them only when you know there is a possibility that someone will see the display.

To ensure that they remain usable, keep smoke flares in airtight containers and store them in dry places. If the striker is damp, dry it out before trying to ignite the device. Some pyrotechnic devices require a forceful strike to ignite them.

NIGHTTIME NONPYROTECHNIC SIGNALS. An electric distress light is available (Figure 2-27) that automatically flashes the international Morse code SOS distress signal (• • • – – – • • •). Flashed four to six times a minute, it is an unmistakable VDS. The label must show that it is approved by the Coast Guard. Check the batteries to make sure they haven't expired.

Under the Inland Rules, a high-intensity white light flashing fifty to seventy times per minute is a distress signal. Therefore, use strobe lights on inland waters only for distress signals.

NIGHTTIME PYROTECHNIC DEVICES. Aerial and handheld flares can be used at night or in the daytime. Obviously, they are more effective at night.

Currently, the serviceable life of a pyrotechnic device is rated at 42 months from its date of manufacture. Since pyrotechnic devices are expensive, look at their dates before you buy them and choose ones with as much time remaining as possible.

Like smoke flares, aerial and handheld flares may fail to work if they have been damaged or abused. They will not function if they are or have been wet and should therefore be stored in dry, airtight containers in dry but readily accessible places.

Aerial VDS, depending on their type and the conditions in which they are used, may not go very high. Again, use them only when there is a good chance they will be seen.

A serious disadvantage of aerial flares is that most burn for less than 10 seconds. Even parachute flares usually burn for less than 45 seconds.

If you use a VDS in an emergency, do so carefully, even when it is a marine flare designed to lessen risk. Hold handheld flares over the side of the boat and never use a road hazard flare because it can easily start a fire.

WARNING *All handheld pyrotechnic devices may produce hot ashes or slag when burning. Hold them over the side of your boat so that they do not burn your hand or drip into your boat.*

Give aerial flares the same respect as firearms, since they are firearms. Never point them at another person, and don't allow children to play with or around them. When you fire one, face away from the wind and aim it downwind and upward at an angle of about 60° to the horizon. If there is a strong wind, aim it somewhat more vertically, but never fire it straight up. Before you discharge a flare pistol, check for overhead obstructions that could be damaged by the flare or that might redirect it to strike something.

Disposal of VDS

Keep outdated flares when you get new ones. They do not meet legal requirements, but you might need them sometime, and they usually work after their expiration dates. Since it is illegal to fire a VDS on federal navigable waters unless an emergency exists, do not try to dispose of a flare that way. Many states have similar laws. Each state has its own regulations for disposing of unwanted VDS.

Marine Sanitation Devices

All recreational boats with installed toilets must also have an operable marine sanitation device (MSD) that is certified by the Coast Guard. Type I and Type II MSDs are flow-through devices, the most common of which are called macerator-chlorinators. These grind up solids, disinfect the resultant waste, and discharge the treated effluent overboard. Type II MSDs meet more stringent bacterial coliform counts and are rarely installed in small craft. Type I MSDs—the kind you are more likely to see on a boat—are certified to meet a looser bacterial standard. Some bodies of water are designated no-discharge zones by state or federal statute, and it is illegal to discharge even treated waste into such waters, so know your local regulations.

Type III MSDs are holding tanks containing treated or untreated sewage where the waste cannot be discharged overboard. Some vessels have a Y-valve installed between the toilet/head and the holding tank to enable direct discharge of sewage. This is because prior regulations allowed a direct sewage discharge under certain conditions. This device must be locked in the closed position at all times with wire, a lock, or other approved methods.

Portable toilets are not considered installed devices and therefore are not subject to the regulations. Contents of portable toilets may not be dumped in U.S. waters. Contact the state marine police to learn the locations of pumpout stations near you (Figure 2-29). Discharge regulations for garbage are covered in Appendix A.

Emergency Position-Indicating Radio Beacon

An emergency position-indicating radio beacon (EPIRB) is a small (about 6 to 20 inches high), battery-powered radio transmitter that is activated either by immersion in water or by a manual switch (Figure 2-30). It requires no license. You should buy an EPIRB that transmits on 406.025 MHz (commonly called 406s).

Recreational boats are not required to carry EPIRBs; some commercial and fishing vessels must have them if they operate beyond the 3-mile limit, however, and vessels carrying six or fewer passengers for hire must have EPIRBs under some circumstances when operating beyond the 3-mile limit.

Some EPIRBs contain a 121.5 MHz frequency, which was intended to be monitored by commercial aircraft. But its use by recreational boaters is prohibited by the U.S. Coast Guard as of 2007.

Figure 2-29. Look for this symbol to locate a marine toilet pumpout station.

Figure 2-30. A 406 MHz EPIRB.

The Coast Guard highly recommends that recreational vessels carry 406s, whose signals can be received worldwide by satellites. When a satellite receives a 406 signal, it records the signal and retransmits it to the first land-based receiving station the satellite passes over. A 406's signal can be pinpointed anywhere on the earth's surface to within 3 nautical miles on the first pass and within 1 mile on the third.

Newer 406 signals are uniquely coded for each unit. The individual information is recorded in National Oceanic and Atmospheric Administration (NOAA) computers; it aids in search-and-rescue efforts by identifying your vessel's characteristics and also helps reduce false alarms.

Too often, EPIRBs are turned on during designated test periods and then are not turned off. When you test your 406, be certain that it is in the "test" mode.

If you buy a new or used 406 EPIRB (or change your boat, address, or telephone number), you must register it with NOAA. To request and submit 406 MHz EPIRB registration forms, go to www.sarsat.noaa.gov/beacon/html. You can also write to Sarsat Beacon Registration, NOAA, NSOF, E/SPO53, 1315 East-West Highway, Silver Spring, MD 20910; send a fax to 301-817-4565; or call 1-888-212-7283 or 301-817-4515.

The biggest drawback of an EPIRB is its cost, which ranges upward from $400. They are, however, available for leasing. If you are thinking of buying an EPIRB, be sure it has been approved by the Federal Communications Commission (FCC).

Equipment Not Required but Recommended

Although not required by law, there is other equipment that is good to have aboard.

Second Means of Propulsion

All boats less than 16 feet long should carry a second means of propulsion. A paddle or oar can come in handy at times, and for most small boats, a spare trolling or outboard motor is an excellent idea. If you carry a spare motor, it should have its own fuel tank and starting power, and if you use an electric trolling motor, it should have its own battery.

Dewatering Devices

All boats should carry at least one effective manual dewatering device such as a bucket, can, scoop, or hand-operated pump in addition to any installed electric bilge pump. If your battery "goes dead" it will not operate your electric pump.

First-Aid Kit

Your first-aid kit should contain items such as adhesive bandages, gauze, adhesive tape, antiseptic ointment, and aspirin. Check the kit from time to time and replace anything that is outdated. It is also to your advantage to know how to use your kit, and you should consider taking a recognized first-aid course.

Anchors

Anchors are recommended for all boats, although they are not required by the U.S. Coast Guard. Choose one of suitable size for your boat, or better still, have two anchors of different sizes. Use the smaller one—your "lunch hook"—in calm water or when anchoring for a short time such as to fish or eat. Use the larger one when the water is rougher

A REMINDER *This lesson covers only the federal regulations with which you must comply. You must also comply with all applicable state and local laws and regulations. Your instructor will distribute state and local information.*

Figure **2-31.** The aftermath of the collision between a sailboat, *Obsession*, and powerboat *Line Item* seven miles east of Bethany Beach, Delaware, in July 2012. The Coast Guard rescued eight people and one cat. (COURTESY COAST GUARD PETTY OFFICER THIRD CLASS JENNIFER WILLIAMSON)

or for overnight anchoring. See Chapter 4 for more on anchors and anchoring.

Carry enough anchor line of suitable size for your boat and the waters in which you will operate. If your engine fails, the first thing to do is lower your anchor. This is good advice both in shallow water where you may be driven aground by the wind or water and in windy weather or rough water. The anchor will usually hold the bow into the waves.

VHF-FM Radio

Your best means of summoning help in an emergency or in case of a breakdown is a VHF-FM radio, which you can use to get advice or assistance from the Coast Guard (Figure 2-31). In the event of a serious illness or injury aboard your boat, the Coast Guard can have emergency medical equipment meet you ashore. Chapter 13 covers marine communications in greater depth.

Tools and Spare Parts

Carry a few tools and some spare parts, and learn how to make minor repairs. Many search-and-rescue cases are caused by minor breakdowns that boat operators could have repaired. If your engine is a stern drive or inboard, carry spare belts and impellers and the tools to install them.

Legal Considerations

Boating entails a number of legal considerations, most of which involve nothing more than common sense and courtesy. All of them have been enacted to protect you, other people, or the environment. Some have already been mentioned; others are discussed in Appendix A. Please take the time to inform yourself of your responsibilities to the environment in which you operate your boat and the other boaters you meet.

Ways to Learn More

Chapman Piloting & Seamanship. 66th ed. Charles B. Husick. New York: Hearst Books, 2009. Chapter 1. Chapters 2 and 3.
Getting Started in Powerboating. 3rd ed. Bob Armstrong. Camden, Maine: International Marine, 2005.
www.navcen.uscg.gov

Practice Questions

IMPORTANT BOATING TERMS
In the following exercise, match the words in the column on the left with the definitions in the column on the right. In the blank space to the left of each term, write the letter of the item that best matches it. Do not use an item in the right-hand column more than once.

THE ITEMS

1. _____ Vessel Safety Check
2. _____ not inherently buoyant
3. _____ sound signal
4. _____ marine sanitation device
5. _____ throwable PFD
6. _____ VDS
7. _____ HIN
8. _____ near-shore buoyant vest
9. _____ offshore life jacket
10. _____ documentation

THE RESPONSES

a. Type IV life jacket
b. flares, for example
c. all vessels must have the means to make
d. it's on the transom
e. Type II life jacket
f. an inflatable life jacket
g. national registration
h. free; made by the Coast Guard Auxiliary
i. Type I life jacket
j. required on installed toilets that do not have holding tanks

Multiple-Choice Items

In the following items, choose the best response:

2-1. A boat's length is measured in a straight line from its bow to its stern and includes

a. bowsprits
b. boomkins
c. pulpits
d. none of the above

2-2. You must register your powerboat in

a. the state where you keep it
b. the state of principal use
c. either the state where you keep it or the state of principal use
d. registration is not required

2-3. The registration number of a boat

a. may be transferred to a new replacement boat
b. may not be transferred to a new boat-owner
c. will stay with the boat unless the principal state of use is changed
d. may be changed if the number on the boat is damaged

2-4. When purchasing a USCG-approved PFD you should select it based on

a. cost and style
b. use, type, and size
c. the swimming ability of the user
d. color and flexibility

2-5. The letters and numbers you use to put your registration number on the bow of the vessel must

a. be at least 3 inches high
b. contrast in color with the hull
c. be plain block letters
d. all of the above

2-6. Many boats display a capacity plate where it is clearly visible to the operator. It specifies the recommended

a. maximum speed
b. maximum fuel capacity
c. maximum weight-carrying capacity, among other things
d. minimum engine oil capacity

2-7. As their active extinguishing agent, marine-type fire extinguishers usually use

a. water
b. dry chemical
c. carbon tetrachloride
d. soda acid

2-8. Most powerboats in use on federal waters must be

a. seaworthy
b. properly equipped with an anchor
c. registered or documented
d. operated by licensed skippers

2-9. A Class B fire involves

a. paper and wood
b. gasoline, oil, or grease
c. any combustible
d. electrical

2-10. One serious disadvantage of aerial flares is that they

a. are so bright they can blind the operator
b. can be seen from long distances
c. have an expiration date
d. burn for only a short time

2-11. In order to meet federal boating law requirements, life jackets must be approved by the

a. American Red Cross
b. Underwriters Laboratories
c. U.S. Coast Guard
d. Marine Underwriters

2-12. At least one approved life jacket must be aboard each vessel for each

a. person on board
b. available seat
c. paying customer
d. occupied bunk or berth

2-13. Even if your flares are within their dates of expiration, they may not function if they have been

a. wet
b. stored in an airtight container
c. previously used
d. kept aboard the boat in case of emergency

Multiple-Choice Items (continued)

2-14. Which of the following equipment is not re-quired by law but is recommended by the U.S. Coast Guard Auxiliary?

a. life jackets
b. a backfire flame arrester
c. a sound-producing device
d. an anchor

2-15. Exhaust and air supply ducts must be above

a. the gunwales
b. the bilge
c. the usual level of water in the bilge
d. the engine

2-16. Halon extinguishers

a. require an indicator in the engine compartment
b. are no longer manufactured
c. are environmentally friendly
d. have a disagreeable odor

2-17. How many minutes should you operate your ventilation blower before starting your engine?

a. 2
b. 4
c. 6
d. 7

2-18. The most usual means of preventing fires and explosions from backfires is a Coast Guard–approved

a. fire extinguisher
b. life jacket
c. gasoline vapor detector
d. backfire flame arrester

2-19. Never test your extinguisher by

a. filling it
b. weighing it
c. firing it
d. shaking it

2-20. Which type of life jacket affords the greatest protection for its wearer?

a. Type I
b. Type II

c. Type III
d. Type IV

2-21. Inboard motorboats less than 26 feet long must have at least

a. one semi-portable Class B extinguisher
b. at least one approved hand-portable Type B-I extinguisher
c. at least one soda-acid extinguisher
d. at least two approved hand-portable Type B-I extinguishers

2-22. Type III life jackets are designed for

a. calm, inland water
b. offshore use
c. near-shore use
d. vessels carrying paid passengers

2-23. Although not legally required, the Coast Guard Auxiliary recommends that you have which of the following equipment aboard in addition to other equipment?

a. a second means of propulsion
b. a first-aid kit
c. an anchor
d. all of the above

2-24. When using a fire extinguisher, you should first remove the pin or loop and

a. shake the container
b. position yourself directly in front of the flames
c. point the nozzle at the base of the flames
d. work from the top of the flames to the base of the fire

2-25. It is important to maintain and regularly inspect PFDs for

a. ripped and badly faded fabric
b. straps and hardware that cannot be secured
c. air that leaks out when the PFD is squeezed
d. all of the above

chapter 3

Trailering Your Boat

The objectives of this chapter are to describe:

✔ The essential safety considerations for boat trailering.

✔ Important factors to consider when selecting a trailer.

✔ Available safety equipment.

✔ The fundamentals of trailer care and maintenance.

✔ Some of the legal requirements for trailering.

✔ How to ready a boat and trailer for traveling.

✔ Considerations for storing a boat and trailer.

✔ Preventing theft.

✔ The importance of filing and canceling a float plan.

IN CHAPTER 1 you selected a boat, and in Chapter 2 you learned how to equip it. In this chapter you will learn how to get a trailerable boat to where you will use it.

The place where you keep your boat may limit its use. The average small sailing cruiser goes about 4 knots (4.6 miles per hour). On a weekend cruise, with two days of sailing and

Thoroughly check your out board and ensure all drain plugs are secure before you launch. (COURTESY BOMBARDIER RECREATIONAL PRODUCTS)

5 or 6 hours underway each day, your cruising range is limited to 25 miles or so.

If you dock your boat in a marina for the summer, you probably will cruise in the immediate area of the marina. But you may not be able to find space in a convenient marina, and even if you can, its hours may not be convenient for you or the price of storage may be beyond your means. So where does this leave you?

Trailering a boat has its good and bad points. If your boat is trailerable, you can start your vacation many miles from your usual cruising area and then visit places you don't normally see, while avoiding the costs and hazards of marinas. At season's end, you can store your boat at home and work on it at your convenience through the winter months.

This scenario also has a negative side, and the potential problems of trailering are many. This chapter deals with the most common ones. Once you're comfortable with trailering, however, the good points outweigh the bad, which is why boat trailering has become increasingly popular in recent years. More than 95% of the recreational boats in the United States are trailerable.

Legal Considerations

There are several legal considerations that affect boat trailering.

Width

One of the few absolute limits for trailering a boat is its width. Without a special permit, the widest boat you can trailer on most state roads is 8 feet. On interstate highways, some access roads, and federally supported highways with 12-foot-wide lanes, the maximum width is 8.5 feet. These widths include both the boat and the trailer.

This width limitation indirectly limits the length of your boat. Practically speaking, a boat with an 8-foot beam is unlikely to be longer than 25 feet.

Brakes

Legal requirements for brakes vary from state to state. Most states require brakes on a trailer if it is designed for a *gross vehicle weight rating* (GVWR—the weight of the trailer and its load) of 3,000 or more pounds. In a few states that requirement is relaxed to 4,000 pounds or higher, and in others it's more stringent—1,500 or 2,000 pounds. The American Boat and Yacht Council recommends trailer brakes for a trailer with a GVWR of 1,500 or more pounds, and this conservative standard is our recommendation as well.

There are three legal brake systems: electrical, hydraulic (surge), and air. The trailer's brakes should activate automatically when the car's brakes are applied, and should continue to operate even if the trailer separates from your car. Since electrical brakes are vulnerable to immersion of the trailer's wheels, hydraulic surge brakes are by far the most popular.

Surge brakes work from the trailer's momentum (Figures 3-1 and 3-2). When you apply your car's brakes, the trailer surges forward, depressing a piston in a hydraulic cylinder in its tongue and thereby activating its brakes through a closed hydraulic system. Part of the beauty of this system is that the braking response of the trailer is automatically proportional to the intensity of braking in the tow vehicle. If you have surge brakes, make sure the emergency brake cable that exits from the trailer's coupler is fastened by means of its S-hook to the tow vehicle or the hitch. That way, if the trailer breaks loose, this lightweight cable (sometimes it's a light chain rather than a cable) will come taut and engage the trailer brakes.

Figure **3-1.** A surge brake actuator mounted on a trailer tongue. Note the light breakaway chain exiting the trailer coupling above the heavier, crisscrossed safety chains above. Should the trailer jump off the hitch and the safety chains fail, the breakaway chain will activate the trailer's brakes. (PHOTO BY BOB DENNIS)

2012 TOWING LAWS*

STATE	Max. Towing Speed	Max. Trailer Length	Max. Trailer Width	Max. Trailer Height	Max. Overall Length	Weight Requiring Trailer Brakes
Alabama	70	40'	8'	13'6"	65'	3,000
Alaska	55	40'	8'6"	14'	75'	5,000
Arizona	75	40'	8'	13'6"	65'	3,000
Arkansas	70	53'6"	8'6"	13'6"	65'	3,000
California	55	N/A	8'6"	14'	65'	1,500
Colorado	75	N/A	8'6"	13'	70'	3,000
Connecticut	65	45'	8'6"	13'6"	60'	3,000
Delaware	55	40'	8'6"	13'6"	55'	4,000
Dist. of Columbia	55	60'	8'	13'	55'	3,000
Florida	70	40'	8'6"	13'6"	65'	3,000
Georgia	55	N/A	8'	13'6"	60'	3,000
Hawaii	55	40'	9'	13'6"	65'	3,000
Idaho	65	48'	8'6"	14'	75'	1,500
Illinois	55	60'	8'	13'6"	60'	3,000
Indiana	65	40'	8'	13'6"	60'	3,000
Iowa	70	48'	9'	14'	70'	3,000
Kansas	70	45'	9'	14'	65'	N/A
Kentucky	65	N/A	8'	13'6"	65'	N/A
Louisiana	70	30'	8'	13'6"	65'	3,000
Maine	55	48'	8'6"	13'6"	65'	3,000
Maryland	65	33'	8'	13'6"	55'	3,000
Massachusetts	65	40'	8'6"	13'6"	60'	10,000
Michigan	55	53'	8'	13'6"	65'	3,000
Minnesota	70	45'	8'6"	13'6"	75'	3,000
Mississippi	55	N/A	8'6"	13'6"	53'	2,000
Missouri	70	N/A	8'6"	13'6"	N/A	N/A
Montana	65	N/A	8'6"	13'6"	N/A	3,000
Nebraska	75	40'	8'6"	14'6"	65'	3,000
Nevada	75	N/A	8'6"	13'6"	70'	3,000
New Hampshire	55	48'	8'	13'6"	N/A	1,500
New Jersey	65	40'	8'	13'6"	62'	3,000
New Mexico	75	N/A	8'	14'	65'	3,000
New York	65	48'	8'6"	13'6"	65'	3,000
North Carolina	55	35'	8'6"	13'6"	60'	1,000
North Dakota	70	53'	8'6"	14'	75'	N/A
Ohio	55	N/A	8'6"	13'6"	65'	2,000
Oklahoma	65	N/A	8'6"	13'6"	65'	3,000
Oregon	55	N/A	8'6"	14'	65'	N/A
Pennsylvania	55	N/A	8'6"	13'6"	60'	3,000
Rhode Island	65	48'	8'6"	13'6"	60'	4,000
South Carolina	55	48'	8'6"	13'6"	N/A	3,000
South Dakota	75	53'	8'6"	14'	80'	3,000
Tennessee	70	40'	8'	13'6"	65'	3,000
Texas	70	N/A	8'6"	14'	65'	4,500
Utah	75	40'	8'6"	14'	65'	2,000
Vermont	65	53'	8'6"	13'6"	68'	3,000
Virginia	55	45'	8'6"	13'6"	65'	3,000
Washington	65	N/A	8'6"	14'	60'	3,000
West Virginia	65	40'	8'	13'6"	55'	3,000
Wisconsin	65	48'	8'6"	13'6"	60'	3,000
Wyoming	75	60'	8'6"	14'	85'	3,000

* Subject to change; check with your state for updates.
SOURCE: *NSA RV PRODUCTS INC.*

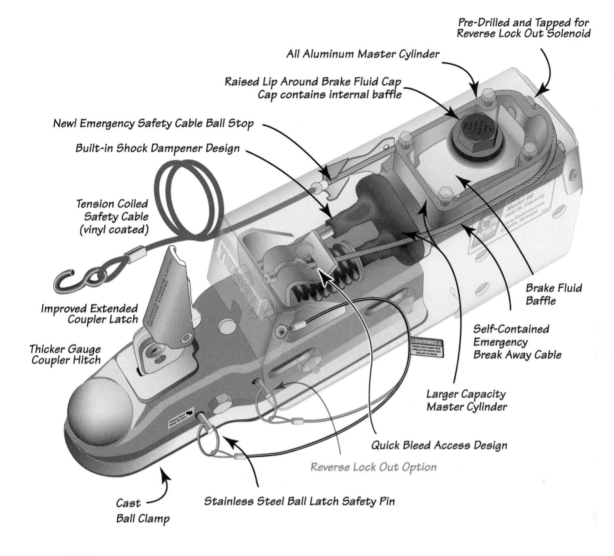

Pre-Drilled and Tapped for
Reverse Lock Out Solenoid

All Aluminum Master Cylinder

Raised Lip Around Brake Fluid Cap
Cap contains internal baffle

New! Emergency Safety Cable Ball Stop

Built-in Shock Dampener Design

Tension Coiled
Safety Cable
(vinyl coated)

Improved Extended
Coupler Latch

Thicker Gauge
Coupler Hitch

Brake Fluid
Baffle

Self-Contained
Emergency
Break Away Cable

Larger Capacity
Master Cylinder

Quick Bleed Access Design

Reverse Lock Out Option

Cast
Ball Clamp

Stainless Steel Ball Latch Safety Pin

Figure **3-2.** Cutaway view of a surge brake actuator. (COURTESY TIE-DOWN ENGINEERING)

Lights

Lights may be required on trailers in your state. Some states do not require trailer lights if the tail-lights, stoplights, and turn signals of the tow vehicle are not obscured by the trailer or the boat. Other states require trailers to have sidelights, taillights, stoplights, and turn signals under all conditions (Figure 3-3). Check with your automobile registration authority.

Pay special attention to the plug and socket that connect the car's lighting system to the trailer (Figure 3-4). The wiring should be under no stress, or tension, and should be as weather-proof as possible. It should not sag or loop so it can catch on anything, nor drag along the road. Use stranded wire because it reduces vibration damage. A good ground is necessary, so a ground wire may be needed between the car and trailer. The most frequent cause of trailer light failure is a poor ground.

You may want to add reflectors and taillights on your boat or trailer beyond those required by law since they increase safety at night. A heavy-duty flasher to control the turn signals when towing is also better than a normal flasher, which operates too fast under a heavy electrical load. If you have a heavy-duty flasher, though, you will not know if you have a burned-out turn signal bulb since the flash inside the car will continue to show. So check your bulbs from time to time. Flashers are easy to install.

A vehicle with separate turn signals and brake lights needs an adapter to match the car's lights to the trailer.

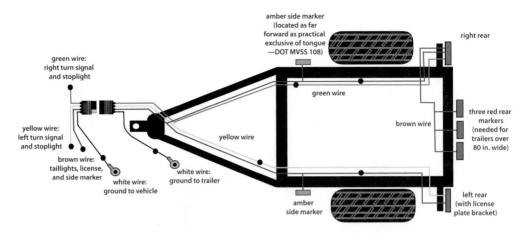

green wire:
right turn signal
and stoplight

amber side marker
(located as far
forward as practical
exclusive of tongue
—DOT MVSS 108)

right rear

green wire

yellow wire:
left turn signal
and stoplight

brown wire

three red rear
markers
(needed for
trailers over
80 in. wide)

brown wire:
taillights, license,
and side marker

yellow wire

white wire:
ground to vehicle

white wire:
ground to trailer

amber
side marker

left rear
(with license
plate bracket)

Figure **3-3.** Typical (four-prong plug) trailer wiring setup. (COURTESY CEQUENT TOWING PRODUCTS)

Figure **3-4.** A five-prong connector with the fifth wire (color varies) goes to the towing vehicle's backup lights to deactivate the trailer's brakes. (PHOTO BY BOB DENNIS)

Licenses

Most states require licenses for trailers. Check with your local authorities.

Mirrors

Your state may require extended side-view mirrors if the view through your vehicle's standard side mirrors is obscured (Figure 3-5). Even when not required, consider getting these mirrors to make your driving easier and safer.

Safety Chains

Safety chains, which run from the tongue of the trailer to the towing hitch, are a legal requirement in most states. The chains should be just long enough to permit free turning and should be crossed under the hitch to form a cradle and then secured to the hitch. If the coupler fails, the cradle may keep the tongue from hitting the pavement and digging in, which could cause the trailer to cartwheel over the back of your vehicle.

If the chains have S-hooks, pass them through the eyes in the hitch from underneath. This way they will be less apt to jump out. Better still, use *shackles* as shown in Figure 3-6. These will not jiggle loose. If you use S-hooks, fasten them on with a piece of wire.

Other Legal Requirements

There are other legal requirements, such as the type of trailer hitch used. These are discussed in the sections that follow.

Figure **3-5.** This extended side-view mirror shows the reflection of the boat trailer behind. (PHOTO BY LEN SCHULTE)

Practical Considerations

In trailering your boat, you should be guided by several practical considerations.

Hull Shape

Your boat's hull shape is a major factor in trailering. The ideal hull for trailering is flat-bottomed, though most small powerboats are easy enough to trailer and to launch. Deep-V powerboats; displacement powerboats with skegs and fixed running gear (i.e., with propellers, shafts, and rudders beneath the hull); and sailboats with fixed keels are the most difficult to support adequately on a trailer and require deeper water for launching (Figures 3-7, 3-8, and 3-9). If your boat has any of these characteristics, you'll quickly tire of trailering it. Whatever the hull shape, support it evenly on the trailer.

Consider the problem of fitting your boat to a trailer before buying the boat. Fortunately, most small boat designers have standard brands of trailers in mind when they design their hulls. Ask your dealer.

You may also want to keep launching considerations in mind when you buy your boat. Considering the size and shape of the boat, are there facilities for launching it where you probably will use it? For example, large boats and sailboats are difficult to launch from a beach. Sailboats are most easily

Figure **3-6.** Safety chains attached to a trailer hitch with shackles rather than the standard S-hooks impart an added measure of safety. (PHOTO BY RAY PAGES)

Figure **3-7.** Hull support for a deep-V powerboat on a trailer. (PHOTO BY JUNE ESPARZA)

Figure **3-8.** A V-bottomed rigid inflatable boat (RIB) on a trailer. (PHOTO BY BOB DENNIS)

Figure **3-9.** Trailering a fixed-keel sailboat represents the greatest challenge of all. (PHOTO BY BOB DENNIS)

launched from a lift. Is the water deep enough at the launch site so a particular boat can be launched?

Selecting Your Trailer

There are also important considerations in selecting a trailer.

Your Trailer's Size

A trailer's class depends on its own weight and the weight of its load. When considering the load, remember the weight you will add to the boat, including the weight of things such as the gasoline, trolling motor, equipment, and gear. Trailer classes are given in Table 3-1.

Federal law requires that trailers show their GVWR. Add the weight of the boat, its contents, and its motor to that of the trailer. If the sum is within 15% of the GVWR of the trailer, select the next larger class of trailer. On multiaxle trailers, the combined *gross axle weight rating* (GAWR) of all axles must be at least equal to the GVWR.

If you are planning to pull a load of 4,000 pounds or more, you will want a multiaxle, tandem trailer, which has four wheels rather than two. A powerful towing vehicle, most likely with a special towing package (see below), will also be needed.

Types of Trailers

The three types of boat trailers in common use are skid, roller-supporting, and float-on.

SKID TRAILERS. These trailers, also called bunker trailers, have carpet-covered rails, usually 2 x 4s (Figures 3-10 and 3-11), that are called *bunkers*. The boat skids along these (or floats off or onto them) when you launch or retrieve it. The simplest type has only two bunkers and is used for small boats with flat or slightly rounded bottoms. Large skid trailers have multiple skids. You can adjust the height of these skids to conform to the slope of your boat bottom and offer maximum support to the hull.

Boat hulls can sag or warp if stored on trailers that are not adjusted to give them maximum support. This can cause serious problems such as poor engine alignment, broken *bulkheads*, and broken stringers. Poor engine alignment on a stern-drive (I/O) or inboard engine can have serious consequences.

The main support from the trailer should be along the boat's keel (Figure 3-12). Support of the transom and localized heavier weights is also important. Weight may be concentrated under fuel tanks, holding tanks, and engines. Remember, when you adjust one support, there is a matching support on the opposite side.

It is a good idea to have the dealer fit the trailer to the boat. Adjusting skids and rollers with a boat on the trailer is next to impossible, and the dealer will have a hoist to raise and lower the boat while fitting it to its trailer. Check the trailer's fitting bolts from time to time. Are they tight? Take appropriate wrenches with you when towing the boat. **ROLLER-SUPPORTING TRAILERS.** On a roller-supporting trailer (Figure 3-13), the rollers give maxi-

Figure **3-10.** The vertical posts on the rear quarters of this skid- or bunker-type trailer help guide the boat onto the trailer when the trailer is submerged. Some boaters mount their trailer's taillights and brake lights on posts like these to keep them out of the water. (PHOTO BY BOB DENNIS)

Figure **3-11.** A skid trailer emerging from the water after launch. (COURTESY NATIONAL MARINE MANUFACTURERS ASSOCIATION)

TABLE 3-1	TRAILER CLASSES
Class	**Gross Weight of Trailer and Load (lbs.)**
1	No more than 2,000
2	2,001–3,500
3	3,501–5,000
4	More than 5,000

mum support to the vessel and aid in launching and retrieving it. Some of these trailers, called tilt trailers, are hinged somewhere along their tongues, and unlocking the hinge allows the trailer to tilt up or down. When it's time to launch the boat, releasing a pin tilts the trailer up, and the boat slides into the water. To retrieve the boat, you tilt up the trailer. As the boat is pulled up on the trailer, the trailer returns to its original position and locks shut. If your trailer has this mechanism, check to see that the pin is in place before pulling your boat up the ramp.

One advantage of a tilt trailer is that you do not have to get your automobile close to the water. A float-on trailer sometimes requires you to back your car's tailpipe into the water, which is good to avoid if you can. In fact, with a tilt trailer, you often do not even have to back the trailer wheels into the water. This is helpful when a ramp stops at the water's edge, as it sometimes does at deep-water launching sites. It is also good when launching in salt water. Wheel rims immersed in salt water can rust, and when they do, tubeless tires will not hold air.

Figure **3-12.** A basic skid trailer for a small flat-bottomed boat. (COURTESY KING TRAILERS)

Figure **3-13.** A roller-supporting trailer. (COURTESY SHORE-LANDER)

FLOAT-ON TRAILERS. Although we're treating them separately, float-on trailers are really skid or roller-supporting trailers used with boats more than 20 feet long. Some have both skids and rollers. In use, they are immersed in the water and the boat is floated off or on, simply because a boat longer than 20 feet is too big to wrestle on or off a nonimmersed trailer. These trailers are easy to use, but brakes immersed in water will not "hold" until they dry out. Also, iron or steel immersed in salt water will rust, even if washed down frequently. Maintenance of wheel bearings and electrical connections (see below) is especially important for a trailer that's frequently immersed.

Care of Your Trailer

Your trailer will last longer and serve you better if you care for it properly.

Wheel Bearings

Tilt trailers offer the advantage of keeping your trailer's wheel bearings and brakes out of the water on most launch ramps. Bearings exposed to water, especially salt water, soon seize up, and when they do they are useless. If they seize up on the road, they create a dangerous situation.

A device called a wheel-bearing protector, or Bearing Buddy (Figure 3-14), is designed to keep water out of the bearings. This plastic cylinder, which you push into place on the wheel hub where the dustcap would otherwise be, contains a spring-loaded piston and has a grease fitting on its end similar to those used for lubricating automobiles (often called a zerk fitting). Using a small grease gun (that you should carry in your tow vehicle), fill the bearing protectors with grease just before you launch.

Why should you do this? Because when riding down the highway, even well-lubricated bearings warm up. Sometimes they get hot. When immersed in cold water, the hubs cool rapidly and a partial vacuum results. Were it not for the bearing protectors, water would rush into the wheel hubs. With protectors in place, however, the hub will pull in grease instead of water—at least in theory. Even so, some water may enter the hub. It makes good sense to use a good-quality marine wheel bearing grease on your bearings and to keep the hubs out of the water whenever possible, even if you have wheel-

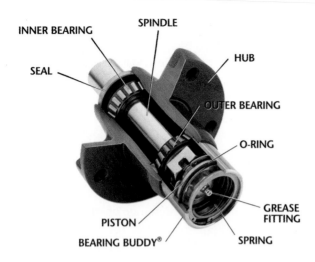

Figure 3-14. Cutaway view of a Bearing Buddy pushed into place on a wheel hub. (COURTESY BEARING BUDDY, INC.)

Figure 3-15. Two boaters clamp removable trailer lights to their boat's transom. (PHOTO BY KIM JOHNS)

bearing protectors. If you must immerse your bearings, let them cool off first. Always carry spare bearings, grease, and tools for replacing bearings when trailering on a highway. It may be impossible on a Sunday afternoon to find bearings to fit your trailer.

Trailer Lights

If possible, mount the trailer lights on a removable board, and remove it before backing the trailer into the water (Figure 3-15). Boards such as these usually clamp on the boat's transom. No lighting system can tolerate repeated immersion, even lights that supposedly keep water out. "Waterproof" trailer lights are more water-resistant than waterproof, and this goes double for salt water.

If your trailer lights are not on a removable board, disconnect them before backing down a ramp. Applying the brakes heats the bulbs and they may crack when they contact cold water.

Always carry spare bulbs. Lights on trailers receive rougher treatment than lights on automobiles. If your lights fail and the bulbs seem okay, polish the terminals with a piece of fine sandpaper. Even a small amount of corrosion will keep bulbs from lighting. The same thing applies to the boat's lights.

Always carry highway safety flares, a trouble flag, and trouble lights for use along the road. It is not advisable to store highway flares aboard your boat, however, as they represent a fire hazard there.

Trailer Tires

Trailer tires require special attention. The chances are good that they will rot of old age before their treads are gone. This comes partially from the conditions under which trailers are stored, and partially from overheating. The number one enemy of tires is heat. Watch for spiderweb cracking on the sidewalls, which is a sign of old age.

TIRE PRESSURE AND TIRE LIFE. The portion of a tire in contact with the road surface is continually flexing. Trailer tires are often smaller than those used on automobiles, which means that they spin and flex many more times per mile than a tow vehicle's tires do. When tires flex, they get hot, and eventually they may blow. Therefore, it is important when trailering your boat to check the temperature of the trailer's tires and wheel hubs at rest stops. A hot or excessively warm tire or hub may indicate an impending problem.

Reduce excessive tire wear by keeping trailer tires properly inflated according to the manufacturer's recommendation. Small trailer tires carry high air pressures (60 pounds per square inch is common), which reduces flexing and heating.

The correct pressure for tires is usually stamped on their sidewalls. Inflate them correctly; above all, do not underinflate them. Carry a pressure gauge and check tire pressures often, but be careful. Each time you check a tire's pressure, some air escapes, and you don't have to let much air out of a small tire to reduce its pressure significantly.

Trailer tires normally do not require balancing. If your trailer bounces when being pulled, however, either with or without a load, consider having them balanced.

Your tow vehicle's tires may also need to be inflated for the added load of the boat and trailer. Your vehicle owner's manual should state the correct tire pressure for tires when carrying a heavy load; if it doesn't, the trailer owner's manual may. **CHANGING A TIRE.** Regardless of how well you care for your trailer tires, sooner or later you may have to change a flat tire. Chances are that this will occur on a weekend when the stores are closed, which is when most people trailer their boats. Be prepared! Always carry a mounted spare tire and wheel, and check to see that it is properly inflated.

A spare tire will not do you any good if you do not have a lug wrench that fits the trailer's lugs. Get one of the correct size with a handle long enough and sturdy enough to loosen the lugs. Since the lugs were probably put on with a pneumatic wrench, they may be more than hand-tight.

In most cases, your car's jack will not work on your trailer. Buy a special jack to take with you and don't forget its handle. You should also carry a strong board or something similar to give the jack support on a soft shoulder.

A scissors-type jack will probably work (Figure 3-16), but make sure that it can be lowered enough to fit under the trailer's axle when a tire is flat.

If you have a flat tire, drive completely off the road if possible, but not onto soft ground. Gather all your tools, including the mounted spare tire, and check to see that you will not have a problem jacking the trailer. Then, before jacking up the trailer, use the wrench to loosen the lugs slightly since you may find it impossible to loosen them when the wheel is up in the air. Jack up the trailer, put on the new tire and tighten the lugs moderately, and lower the trailer. Then make certain that the lugs are tightened securely.

If you can't get your jack under the trailer's axle for any reason, consider putting the spare tire flat on the ground in front of the blown tire; then pull the trailer up on the spare with your car. You should now have enough room to put the jack under the axle.

Other Practical Considerations

There are other factors you must consider for your safety and the protection of your load.

Figure **3-16.** A scissors-type jack in use to change a trailer tire. (PHOTO BY RAY PAGES)

Fire Extinguishers

Keep a fire extinguisher readily available when trailering. Overheated bearings can catch fire, or someone might carelessly throw a cigarette in your boat and cause a fire. If the boat is covered with a tarpaulin, a cigarette could land on it and you would not be able to get to the boat's extinguisher.

Consider mounting an extinguisher on the winch stem or in your car's trunk. Wherever it is, be certain it is readily accessible.

Winches

A winch is an invaluable aid when retrieving a boat. Two types are available: a manually operated one, which is usually standard equipment (Figure 3-17); and an electrically powered one, which is optional and recommended for boats longer than 16 feet. An electrically powered winch operates off the automobile battery and often requires special wiring. The cables to complete this wiring are usually packed with a new winch.

The line on a winch is generally either polypropylene or steel wire, though sometimes it is a web belt. If you have an electric winch, the line will be steel wire. Steel wire is also recommended for any vessel 16 feet or longer, since polypropylene deteriorates in sunlight and may not hold your boat. Nylon stretches too much and is therefore not used on winches.

The primary point of attachment of the boat to the trailer is at the winch. Be certain the winch has a good antireverse mechanism and keep it in good working order. But don't rely on it; after your boat is on the trailer, you should also tie the boat's towing eye to the stem of the winch. The usual ratchet-type antireverse mechanism is small enough that you don't want to trust your boat's security to it.

If you are using a manually operated winch, be careful when you launch your boat. As the boat slides off the trailer, the winch handle will turn forcefully and could seriously injure your hand or arm.

Tie-Downs

Use a *tie-down* from the towing eye of your boat to the tongue of the trailer (Figure 3-18) to secure it firmly to the trailer. This way the bow of the boat will still be secure even if the winch stem comes loose. Also use tie-downs at or near the stern of the boat.

If there are *lifting rings* on the transom, tie lines

Figure **3-17.** The winch cable is hooked to the boat's towing eye, and the boat has been pulled onto the trailer until its bow rests against the rubber stop on the winch stand. Note that the towing eye is at this point tied or hooked to the winch stand, so that you are not depending entirely on the winch ratchet mechanism to hold the boat snug against the bow stop. (PHOTO BY BOB DENNIS)

Figure **3-18.** Cinching a strap from the towing eye to the trailer frame to prevent sway. Note that the winch cable has already been backed up with a line or strap to the base of the winch stand. (PHOTO BY BOB DENNIS)

from each ring to the trailer (Figures 3-19 and 3-20). If you can't get these lines tight enough, consider buying winching straps made for this purpose.

You can buy tie-down straps made of webbing that stretch across the boat and hook to either side of the trailer. If you use straps, place cushioning material under them to keep from marring the boat's varnish or gelcoat.

Straps that reach across the vessel are acceptable for small boats, but larger boats should be tied down at the stern. Should you be in an accident, you will want the boat to stop when you do.

Rust and Breakdowns

If your trailer isn't galvanized, you need to be on the lookout for rust. Iron and steel are subject to rusting, which can be especially heavy if they are exposed to salt water or air. Touch up rust spots as they occur by sanding off the rust with emery cloth and spraying the areas with galvanizing paint or another rust-resistant paint.

Pay special attention to keeping the springs and axles on the trailer rust free (Figure 3-21). If they become rusted, replace the springs or reinforce the axles. Both are subject to heavy strains on the highway and may break, causing serious damage to you, your tow vehicle, and your boat. As with other

Figure **3-19.** Transom tie-down strap. (PHOTO BY BOB DENNIS)

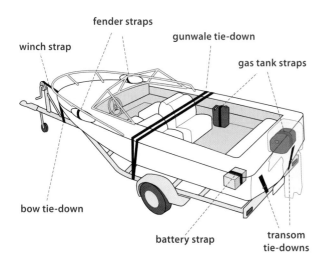

Figure **3-20.** Recommended tie-down locations for a trailered boat.

Figure **3-21.** A trailer's axle and leaf springs are prime places for rust to form. (PHOTO BY JUNE ESPARZA)

aspects of trailering, an ounce of prevention is worth a pound of cure.

The Towing Vehicle

Your vehicle is an important part of the towing package. Most vehicles are not designed, however, to trailer a boat. If yours has front-wheel drive, it is even less capable of trailering.

To steer properly, a vehicle must have enough weight on its front axles, but when weight is added to the rear of a vehicle, the front end lifts, which makes it difficult to control. Weight in the rear also affects the traction of a front-wheel-drive vehicle, as well as the focus of the headlights and the driver's view. In addition, it places a strain on the vehicle's rear tires, shocks, and springs.

The typical front-wheel-drive compact car has a gross weight of about 2,800 pounds. The owner's manual for such a vehicle typically says that it should not pull a trailer weighing more than 800 to 1,000 pounds unless the trailer has brakes. (This maximum tow weight is typically twice as high for a medium-sized car and five or more times higher for a large car, SUV, or pickup.) With trailer brakes and a manual transmission, a compact car can pull 2,200 pounds up hills with less than a 12% slope. It can pull the same 2,200 pounds up a 16% slope if it has an automatic transmission.

Your tow vehicle needs enough power to merge safely with highway traffic when towing its maximum load. It must also be able to climb hills without loss of speed. This usually justifies choosing the largest power package possible when you're buying a vehicle that will be used for towing.

Towing Package

Unless the vehicle is specially equipped, do not tow a trailer that weighs more than the vehicle. Many manufacturers sell towing packages, which are not expensive if ordered with the car. If ordered later, their cost may be prohibitive. Towing packages include several modifications for your car.

Cooling

When a car is pulling a boat, it uses more energy than usual, which produces more heat. You will need a heavy-duty, high-capacity radiator that has more core tubes to aid heat release. It may also have a special fan shroud. A thermostat-controlled spraying unit may also be available to spray cool water on the radiator if the coolant temperature goes too high.

Transmission

Towing a trailer places an extra load on a car's transmission. This may thin out its fluid and damage it. A small supplemental radiator to cool the transmission fluid is often available. Be alert to transmission leaks, slippage, or rough shifting.

Brakes

A towing package also includes oversized brake drums and/or special heavy-duty brake linings for the tow vehicle. Standard auto brakes are too small for towing all but very light trailers. Premium brake linings are essential.

Suspension System

A tongue weight of 100 pounds has the same effect as putting 400 pounds in the trunk of a car. To avoid sagging and bottoming out, you need heavy-duty springs and extra-large or air-adjustable shock absorbers. These allow the tow vehicle to ride nearly level, which also improves visibility and handling.

Other Equipment

The trailering package may also contain a larger battery, and a larger alternator for charging it. The tow vehicle probably will have oversized tires and a lower gear ratio in its differential.

Trailer Hitches

Three types of trailer hitches are available. The first two hold the entire tongue weight of the trailer, while the third distributes the load to all four wheels of the tow vehicle.

Bumper Hitches

Bumper hitches are the simplest trailer hitches, merely clamping on the bumper of the tow vehicle. They are illegal in many states, however, because they don't offer enough support for a boat trailer. Modern bumpers, usually made of a lightweight aluminum alloy, are not strong enough for this purpose and may twist out of shape. Most molded bumpers will not accept a bumper hitch in any event, and even if one could, a bumper hitch is not recommended.

Step-bumper hitches, which are mounted on many light trucks (Figure 3-22), are something else again; if your vehicle has one of these, it may be acceptable for towing a boat. Check the tow rating in your owner's manual. Some step bumpers are for light duty only and—despite having a hole to accept a hitch ball—do not have tow ratings.

Weight-Carrying Hitches

Weight-carrying hitches are available for most vehicle models. They bolt to the vehicle's frame and are rated in parallel with trailer ratings (Figure 3-23). Most are stamped with the total weight they can pull and the tongue weight they can support.

A Class I, or light-duty hitch, attaches to at least two points on the vehicle's frame and may also attach to the bumper, though this is not recommended. The maximum tongue weight on a Class I hitch should not exceed 150 pounds, and for many cars it should not be more than 100 pounds. Its maximum load is 2,000 pounds, which means that the longest boat that can be trailered with it is less than 16 feet long unless the boat is very light. A 16-foot fiberglass boat may weigh 1,600 pounds or more without a motor.

A Class II, or regular-duty hitch, is entirely frame mounted at multiple attachment points and should be professionally installed. This hitch can pull up to 3,500 pounds and support a tongue weight up to 300 or so pounds. Class II hitches are available with the ball mount built into the hitch frame or as receiver-type models, in which the ball mount is inserted into a square receiver and secured with a pin.

A Class III, or heavy-duty hitch, can tow up to 5,000 pounds and support a tongue weight up to 500 pounds, and will almost certainly need to be mated with a truck or heavy-duty SUV.

A Class IV, or extra-heavy-duty hitch, can tow up to 10,000 pounds of towing weight and support 1,000 pounds of tongue weight.

Figure **3-22.** A step bumper hitch on a pickup truck.
(PHOTO BY JIM FRIJOUF)

Weight-Distributing Hitches

A *weight-distributing hitch*, also sometimes known as a load-equalizing hitch, shifts some of the trailer's tongue weight from the rear axle to the front axle of the tow vehicle, which reduces tow vehicle wear and gives the driver more stability and better handling.

In a weight-distributing system, the standard ball-mount platform is replaced in the hitch receiver by a ball-mount assembly that includes two sockets. Each socket receives the hitch end of a steel bar; the other end of the bar rides beneath the trailer tongue, to which it is attached by a chain (Figure 3-24). Shortening the chain puts tension on the bar, which provides lift at the hitch frame and corresponding downward pressure on the front axle. Many Class III and IV hitch receivers will accept a weight-distributing ball-mount assembly, as will some Class II hitches. If your trailer is depressing the back end of your tow vehicle and noticeably impairing its handling, this may be the solution. Note that a weight-distributing hitch sometimes interferes with surge brake operation. The hitch manufacturer or the manufacturer of your trailer's surge coupler can advise you on this.

Some hitches come with antisway bars that help control trailer sway and further improve control. Be aware that these too can sometimes interfere with the normal operation of a surge brake coupler.

Trailer Ball and Coupler

The trailer hitch has a ball-mount platform that the trailer coupler attaches to (Figure 3-25). Balls come in several different diameters; the most common are 1⅞ inches, 2 inches, and 2⁵⁄₁₆ inches. A 1⅞-inch ball is used only with Class I (tow weight up to 2,000 pounds) hitches and trailers. A 2-inch ball is limited to Class II (up to 3,500 pounds) or Class III (up to 5,000 pounds) hitches and trailers, depending on the capacity stamped on the ball. Class IV setups require a 2⁵⁄₁₆-inch ball.

You should always use the correct ball for your trailer's load and its coupler. A trailer coupler designed for a larger ball may seem to fit on a smaller one, but it is dangerous to do this since the coupler might come loose on the highway.

It is sometimes possible to put a coupler on a larger ball than it is designed for, but again, don't do this. It will bind, and the trailer will not track

Figure **3-23.** An array of frame-mounted hitches. **Top to bottom:** Class I, Class II, Class III, and Class IV. (COURTESY CEQUENT TOWING PRODUCTS)

Figure **3-24.** This weight-distributing (or load-equalizing) hitch from Draw-Tite also has antisway bars. The steel spring bars are sometimes called equalizing bars. Note that both the spring bars and antisway bars can interfere with surge brake operation. Do not use a weight-distributing and/or antisway hitch without manufacturer or dealer advice and installation. (COURTESY CEQUENT TOWING PRODUCTS)

correctly. The threaded shanks of balls vary with the size of the ball. If a smaller ball than required is used, you are also using an undersized shank that could shear.

The trailer's coupler determines the size of the ball, which in turn is determined by the GVWR of the trailer. All couplers manufactured after 1973 have the GVWR they can support stamped on them.

Carry an extra ball with you, and a wrench to install it with, as wear and turning stresses may force a ball out of round. Secure the ball with a lock washer and nut, and then grease it before coupling the trailer to it.

There are two types of couplers—latch or screw (Figure 3-26). If you have a latch coupler, secure it with a padlock or a pin to keep it from coming loose. A padlock also protects your trailer against theft, an important consideration when leaving your car and trailer at a public ramp.

Balancing the Load

Balancing the load on your trailer is an important factor in successful towing; 10% to 15% of the total weight of the tow (boat + motor + contents + trailer) should be on the tongue. If you have much more than this, the front end of your tow vehicle may lift up while the rear squats, making the vehicle hard to handle. If you have less than this, the trailer is likely to fishtail, which is dangerous and difficult to control. The wind from a large truck could then cause you to have a serious accident.

Compact cars, and some midsize cars, will not accept more than 100 pounds of tongue weight. Any additional weight will overload the car. Since tongue weight is roughly 10% to 15% of trailer weight, this means that a gross weight of 1,000 pounds is the maximum such a car should tow. Remember that this 1,000 pounds includes the weight of the trailer, boat, motor, and the boat's contents (Figure 3-27). As already mentioned, larger cars, pickups, and SUVs can tow heavier loads.

To measure tongue weight, load your boat with the gear it usually carries. Then stack a couple of cinder blocks in the driveway and put your bathroom scale on the stack. On top of this put something to protect the scale. The total height should be the same as the height of the trailer ball above the ground. Now lower the trailer tongue onto the scale.

You can adjust the weight on the tongue in two ways. The simpler way is to move the load inside the boat. If too little weight is on the tongue, move the equipment forward in the boat. If you have too much weight, move the equipment aft.

More serious weight adjustments entail shifting the boat forward or back on the trailer. The winch

Figure **3-25.** A ball-mount platform being slid into its hitch receiver. (PHOTO BY BOB DENNIS)

Figure **3-26.** Screw-type (top) and latch-type (bottom) trailer couplers. (PHOTOS BY NORMA LOCOCO AND BOB DENNIS)

stems of most trailers can be moved forward or backward on the tongue if necessary.

Determine the trailer's GVWR by adding the weight of the trailer, the boat and motor, and the equipment. Your dealer can tell you the weight of the trailer, boat, and motor. Estimate the weight of your equipment.

To get a more accurate measure, take the rig to the nearest platform scale, which can be found at highway weighing stations, building supply companies, trucking companies, or junkyards. As a last resort, the local moving company will know where scales are located.

If the tongue weight of the trailer is 70 to 75 pounds or more, consider fixing an accessory jack and dolly wheel to it (Figure 3-28). It will be easier to move the boat, and the jack can be used to raise or lower the tongue to couple it to your car. You can also raise the jack to its highest point to allow the boat to drain when stored.

Handling Your Trailer

If you have never handled a trailer before, drive it to a large, empty parking lot some Sunday afternoon and practice backing and parking.

On the way to the parking lot, accelerate slowly from stops and take your vehicle smoothly and gently through gear changes. This will help you get used to your reduced acceleration and longer stopping distances. Think twice before passing another car. If you decide to pass, pick a spot and go. Don't hesitate. Remember that when you turn a corner your trailer will turn inside the arc of your tow vehicle, so be sure to swing wide enough that you don't hit curbs or other cars waiting in

the cross street (Figure 3-29). When turning, check traffic behind and alongside and give others plenty of warning with your turn signal.

Underway, remember that you have a long, heavy, awkward "tail" behind you. This is easy to forget, especially when returning to your lane after passing another vehicle.

Remain sensitive to any unusual sounds. If you notice anything at all out of the ordinary, pull over and check. On the highway, check out the entire rig every hour or so. Check the temperature of the wheel hubs and tires by touching them, and check tie-downs, wheel lugs, and trailer bolts. If you are using a heavy-duty flasher, check for burned-out bulbs by turning them on and walking around the car and trailer.

When you reach the parking lot, practice turning. Light poles are excellent for learning how to judge your swing at corners. But be careful—you don't want to buy one!

The main thing to practice is backing up. This can be difficult, especially if you have a short trailer. In fact, the shorter the trailer, the more difficult it is to back. If your trailer is shorter than your automobile, you have a very difficult problem. The

Figure **3-27.** A rusted trailer tongue broke, causing this mishap. (PHOTO BY BARBARA ESTES)

Figure **3-28.** A trailer tongue supported above the pavement by a jack and dolly wheel. (PHOTO BY JUNE ESPARZA)

trick is to back slowly and not allow the trailer to get much out of line with the towing vehicle.

It is easier to back if you place your hand on the bottom of the steering wheel instead of its top. Then turn your head and watch where you are going. When you want the trailer to go to the left, move your hand on the wheel to the left. To make the trailer go to the right, move your hand to the right (see Figure 3-32).

Work out a set of hand signals with your partner for things such as "continue," "stop," "left," and "right," and rely on these rather than oral directions, which can be hard to hear. The driver can lose sight of the trailer as it starts down many ramps, making a partner indispensable.

Predeparture Checks

Some things should be done before the day you go. These pertain to the trailer, the boat and its motor, and the tow vehicle.

Check Your Trailer

The two most important items in a predeparture check of your trailer are its wheel bearings and the amount of air in its tires. Have a regular schedule of maintenance for wheel bearings, and clean and repack them at regular intervals or after they have been immersed in water. Before departing, check the air pressure in the trailer's tires.

Figure **3-29.** When pulling a trailer, swing wide in order to take a tight corner. (PHOTO BY BOB DENNIS)

Assemble the emergency equipment, parts, and tools to take with you. You might want to make a checklist to remind you to do things such as inflate your spare tire and take it along, and to take your jack, lug wrench, spare bearings and grease, spare bulbs, spare fuses, wrenches, trouble flag, and trouble lights.

Before setting out, see that items in your boat are secured, and make certain that no one has tossed in last-minute items that may significantly alter your trailer's balance.

Did you grease the ball before coupling? Is the coupler locked? Are electrical connections made and are the lights and electric brakes, if you have them, working? Are the turn signals working? Are the safety chains in place—crisscrossed under the trailer tongue and hooked securely into the hitch with enough slack to permit turning, but no excess? If your trailer has surge brakes, is the breakaway cable hooked up with enough slack for turns but not so much that it would fail to engage before the safety chains came taut? Have you installed the heavy-duty flasher?

Have you raised your boat's motor or outdrive (Figure 3-30)? Is it secured in its "up" position with something other than its hydraulic cylinders? Are your tie-downs secured? If your trailer has a tilt bed, is the pivot point properly locked? If the trailer has a dolly wheel or tongue jack, is it locked in the "up" position? Is the boat's bow held firmly to the bow stop on the winch stem not just by the winch cable, but also with a line from the boat's towing eye to the winch stem and another from the towing eye down to the trailer tongue?

If you are trailering a sailboat, did you secure the rigging to the mast? Are the mast and boom padded and tied down? Does the mast protrude beyond the trailer? If so, does it have a red flag on it? If the rudder is removable, did you remove it? If not, did you fasten it in its "up" position? After you put the boat on the trailer, did you lower its centerboard or daggerboard to a secure position on a cross member of the trailer? (If there is no cross member that the centerboard or daggerboard can rest on, leave it in its "up" position.)

You may wish to add items to the checklist. Whatever you do, review it thoroughly before you go.

Check Your Boat's Engine

Proper maintenance of your boat's engine is the best thing you can do to help it give trouble-free performance. Study the manual that came with your engine and follow its recommended maintenance schedule. Lubricate the engine and change its spark plugs at proper intervals, and clean its filters on a regular schedule. If it has a hydraulic lift, check its oil reservoir and fill it as necessary.

Preparing to Launch

At the ramp, pull to one side and let your bearings cool down. While waiting, prepare your boat for launching; this way you will hold up other people as little as possible once you've moved to the ramp. Here, again, it is good to have a checklist.

If there is a cover on your boat, remove it and store it in the tow vehicle. Next, undo the tie-downs and put in the drain plug. It is surprising how easy it is to overlook this important item—until your boat slowly sinks into the water after you launch!

If you're launching a sailboat, you must step its mast. Before doing so, check to see what is overhead. Are there any low power lines? Many municipal ramps were designed for skiffs, not masted vessels. If your mast should fall, are there overhead obstructions it could hit? This is especially important if electrical wires are present, since an aluminum mast and electrified wires are a dangerous

Figure **3-30.** A stern-drive boat with its outdrive in the raised position for trailering. (PHOTO BY BOB DENNIS)

✓ TRAILERING CHECKLIST

- ☐ Is boat securely attached to trailer?
- ☐ Is ball locked in socket?
- ☐ Are safety chains in place?
- ☐ Is dolly wheel retracted?
- ☐ Is electrical connection secure?
- ☐ Are brake lights and turn signals working?
- ☐ Are trailer tires properly inflated?
- ☐ Is trailer load properly balanced?
- ☐ Is motor/stern-drive unit in the "up" position?
- ☐ Are antennas lowered?
- ☐ Have wheel bearings been checked recently?

mixture. Also check to see that you have a clear overhead path from where you are to the ramp and beyond.

If there is a finger pier, and if your mast is difficult to raise, you may prefer to wait to raise it until you are tied up to the pier, where it will be easier.

Check to see that nothing is protruding from the boat to snag on the trailer frame. Is the daggerboard or centerboard pulled all the way into the well and is the pendant lashed down? Is the rudder fastened in the "up" position if it is not removable?

Next, undo the trailering support for your outboard or outdrive, but wait until the boat is in the water to lower either of them (Figure 3-31). Also wait to lower the centerboard or daggerboard and to install the rudder.

Unplug the trailer's lights, and put the connector from the car where it will not dangle into the water. You are now ready to launch your boat.

Launching

Some recent videos have shown an operator in a boat with its motor running during launching. This practice is not recommended. Most likely your boat's engine will be cooled by ambient water, and most outboard, stern-drive, and inboard engines pump this water by means of *impellers*. If an impeller runs without water, it will be damaged or destroyed. Even inboard and stern-drive engines that have closed, recirculating coolant systems must pump ambient water through a heat exchanger to draw the heat from the engine's coolant.

Staying in a boat during launching is also unsafe, since boats can tip over when launched. PWC are the exception; it is common to be aboard a personal watercraft during launch.

Make sure you have a line or lines running from your boat to the shore before launching. If the boat weighs 2,500 or more pounds, tie the shore end of one line to some object onshore. The boat may come off the trailer rapidly and be difficult to control.

Make certain everyone is out of the way before backing down the ramp, and know where children are at all times. Back the trailer slowly until the boat's stern is in the water (Figure 3-32). There is no prize for backing rapidly, but if you run off the ramp, you may find that there is a penalty! Some people remove the winch line before they are on the launch ramp, but this practice sometimes re-

Figure 3-31. A boatowner backs his trailer down a launch ramp. Fenders are in place, and this boater probably knows from local experience that he can leave the outboard motors lowered for launch without risking damage to props or lower units. It is usually better, however, not to lower an outboard motor or out-drive until after the boat is afloat. (PHOTO BY RAY PAGES)

sults in an early launch onto the ramp rather than into the water. Don't remove the winch line until you reach the launch point.

Ramps can be dangerous, and this is particularly true of ramps in tidal waters. Algae grows on ramp surfaces, which can become extremely slick, making it a challenge to walk and sometimes even to prevent your vehicle from following your boat into the water. The steeper the ramp, the more of an issue this can be.

Some bodies of water such as impounded lakes experience periodic changes in their water levels. If the level is low, be careful that you do not back your trailer off the end of the ramp's hard surface into rocks or mud. If you do, you may have a serious problem.

If at all possible, stay in your vehicle while launching your boat and have someone else remove the winch cable when you request it. That way, you can keep your foot on the brake pedal, thus applying the brakes to all four wheels of your vehicle. If you leave the vehicle and engage the parking or hand brake, you are applying brakes only to the rear wheels.

If you put an automatic transmission in Park, you have even less braking power than with the parking brake set. In Park the transmission and driveshaft lock, but the vehicle has a differential on its rear axle that allows the rear wheels to turn in-

If you must leave the vehicle, put the transmission in Park, set the hand brake, and then turn off the engine. If you have a manual transmission, put it in reverse to obtain the lowest gear ratio. Carry wheel chocks with you and have someone put them behind your wheels before you take your foot off the brake.

After launching, pull the trailer up the ramp to the parking area. Don't take unnecessary time and keep others waiting.

While you are parking your vehicle, your crew can pull the boat to the pier and tie it up (Figure 3-33). Now you are ready to lower the outboard or stern-drive engine's lower unit into the water. Remember that starting the engine without the water intake immersed can damage the impeller in the engine's cooling-water pump in a very short time.

Retrieving

Recovering a boat is the inverse of launching it (Figure 3-34). While it is in the water, raise the outdrive or outboard. If it is a sailboat, raise its daggerboard or centerboard and secure it, and remove its rudder or raise it to the traveling position. Then get your trailer and back it down the ramp.

If your trailer is a float-on type, back it into the water and pull your boat up on it. Connect the winch cable to the towing eye of your boat to secure it.

If your trailer is not a float-on type, back it far enough into the water to reach the bow of your boat, but keep the trailer's wheel hubs above water if possible. Connect the winch cable to the towing eye of your boat and pull it up on the trailer. Make certain the boat is centered on the trailer. Unless it is very light, you will not be able to move it once it is on the trailer. The use of significant boat engine power to drive a boat onto the trailer or to pull it off the trailer is called "power loading" and should be avoided. This disturbs the lake or sea bottom immediately beyond the ramp and causes ground holes or pockets. This in turn causes trailer wheels to become trapped in these pockets.

With the boat firmly on the trailer, drive up the ramp to the parking area, park, and secure the motor or outdrive for trailering. If your boat is a sailboat, lower the mast, and secure it and the boom. Lower its

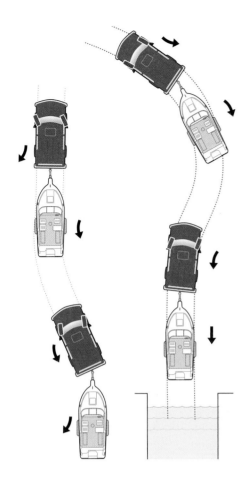

Figure **3-32.** When backing a trailer, turn the back end of your vehicle to the right in order to make the trailer turn left, and vice versa. Do not oversteer, and begin to straighten your tires somewhat *before* a turn is completed. If the trailer starts to turn too sharply, pull ahead far enough to straighten it out, then try again. Don't get flustered. You'll get the hang of it soon enough.

dependently of each other when cornering. Thus, one wheel or the other can turn at any time. This means, in effect, that you are sitting on a steep, slippery ramp depending on the braking power of one wheel. Also, with the engine running and under the strain of the trailered load, the transmission can slip out of Park. It is a horrible feeling to watch your boat, trailer, and vehicle launch themselves. It's even worse if they run you over in the process.

However, don't rely too heavily on your parking brake either. It's not that good. How many times have you backed out of your driveway and then discovered that you hadn't released the brake? In addition to the weight of the vehicle, you have the weight of the trailer, the boat, and its contents to help pull you down the ramp.

Figure **3-33.** After a boat is launched, a line handler guides it to the dock. (PHOTO BY BOB DENNIS)

Figure **3-34.** A boat being jockeyed onto a trailer at the launch ramp. Note that this boater has had to submerge his trailer's wheel hubs. Presumably there are bearing protectors on the wheel hubs, and he will hose the trailer with fresh water when he gets home. (PHOTO BY BOB DENNIS)

centerboard or daggerboard so that it isn't suspended. Tie the boat's towing eye to the winch stem. Then tie down everything that is loose, pull the drain plug, tie down the boat, and replace its cover.

Finally, plug the trailer's electrical connection into the tow vehicle's outlet. After checking to see that everything is secure, you are ready to roll.

Storing Your Boat and Trailer

A few simple measures can extend the life of your boat and trailer. If you are going to store your boat on its trailer for an extended period, jack up the trailer and put cinder blocks under its axles. Then check to see that the boat is still evenly supported, since jacking up a trailer can twist it out of shape. Make certain that the whole rig is stable, especially if your boat is a sailboat; this will help prevent strong winds from blowing it over.

Removing the wheels will extend tire life. Put them inside, where they aren't exposed to the sun. Jack up the trailer's tongue so the boat will drain, and make sure the drain plug is removed. Keep the interior of your boat dry to prevent mildew and dry rot.

Cover the boat to keep rainwater out, but let air circulate under the cover to keep it ventilated. Ready-made covers are available, or you can have one custom-made. Be certain that it is secure and will not blow away. Remember, too, that you must prevent puddling of water. Water weighs about 8.3 pounds per gallon and the weight of collected water stretches the cover, allowing the puddle to grow larger. Eventually, the cover will split and the water will get into the boat. Supporting the cover from below can help prevent puddles.

Before leaving your boat on its trailer for an extended time, check to see that it is still firmly supported. If any rollers or skids have come loose, adjust and tighten them.

If you have an inboard or stern-drive engine, or if you plan to leave your outboard motor on your boat while it is stored, be certain to flush it and then drain all the water from it. To drain a stern drive or outboard, move the lower unit or the motor to a vertical (operating) position and leave it there until all the water has drained. An inboard engine can be drained by opening its sea valves.

If you plan to leave your outboard motor attached to the boat during the winter, leave it in its vertical position. Do the same thing for a stern drive's lower unit. Otherwise, rainwater will enter its exhaust and may crack its housing during freezing weather. If you plan to store your boat for an extended period, follow the layup procedures recommended in your owner's manual.

One final thought. Replace the heavy-duty flasher on your vehicle with a standard-duty flasher, so that you will be able to tell if a bulb burns out.

Theft Prevention

Pleasure boats of all sizes, small outboard motors, radios, compasses, binoculars, and other items of boating gear are stolen every year. A few simple measures and some forethought can prevent such thefts. Some of these are things to do at home, and others apply at the launch site.

Before Trailering Your Boat

Permanently mark your boat's hull identification number (HIN) at a second hidden location on your boat. It's already marked on the stern and in another, hidden location, but these numbers can be defaced or altered. Put the HIN in a spot only you know about so that you can identify your boat if it is stolen and recovered.

Propellers are expensive items and are often stolen. Inexpensive locks are available to keep them from being removed from a boat.

Mark all your valuable equipment with an identification number. Most police departments recommend using your driver's license number, which is available on most police computers, and can provide an engraving tool for inscribing ID numbers on hard surfaces. Soft materials such as cloth covers, sleeping bags, blankets, and tents can be marked with paint, indelible markers, or invisible ink that shows up under ultraviolet light. Visible markings discourage theft and help law enforcement authorities recover your belongings.

Keep an up-to-date inventory of your boating and fishing equipment that includes the name of each piece of equipment and its description and serial number, if any. This will help document any loss. Video or digital recordings, color photographs, or slides can also help identify your equipment and document its condition and that of your boat.

Make sure your insurance covers theft of your boat or its equipment. Homeowners' policies may not provide adequate coverage of marine equipment. Marine coverage for your boat, trailer, outboard motor(s), and equipment is usually worth the low premium charged. Shop around for a reliable company and for the lowest premium.

Stolen vessels can be used for illegal activities that range from reckless joyriding to use in the drug trade. Or your boat may be resold to an unsuspecting victim. Do what you can to protect it and prevent its illegal use.

At the Launch Site

Keep your valuables out of sight but not in a glove compartment. Don't leave anything in bags or cartons inside the vehicle; a thief may damage your vehicle while trying to see what's inside them. Instead put your gear in the trunk and lock it and the vehicle. It is not difficult to force entry into a locked trunk, but few thieves will do it just on the chance of finding something of value.

Leave your vehicle in a well-lighted area if you expect to be gone until after dark. This enhances personal safety and reduces theft. Do not leave your keys in the vehicle.

Use a trailer-hitch lock, which is difficult to cut loose, to secure your trailer to your vehicle. If you don't lock the trailer to your vehicle, it may disappear at the launch site.

Back Home

At home, secure your trailer by removing a wheel or chaining the trailer to a large tree. Alternatively, you can sink a case-hardened steel eyebolt in concrete and either chain the boat or attach a trailer ball to that. If the latter, lock your trailer on the secured ball with its hitch lock.

But don't be lulled into a false sense of security simply because you have a good hitch lock. Professional thieves carry coupler devices that can be quickly attached to your trailer.

If possible, store your boat in the backyard or in a garage so it won't be seen by passersby. If you have to store it in the driveway, don't leave the hitch facing the street.

If you plan to remove the propeller, do it now. You should remove it every few months anyway and grease its shaft with a high-grade marine grease. This keeps the propeller from freezing on the shaft. If you remove it, don't forget to put it back on before you go boating the next time. (Your boat will run better with it attached.)

Remove all valuable portable equipment from your boat and lock it in a safe place; just don't forget to put it back aboard when you next take out your boat. Above all, don't leave the boat's keys or registration certificate on the boat.

If you have a small outboard motor, remove it from the boat when not in use. This will protect it from the weather as well as from thieves. If you don't remove it, fasten it with a motor lock across its clamps or a case-hardened chain securely fastened to the boat. On larger, less portable, permanently mounted outboards, use special transom retainer bolts that can be removed only with special sockets.

If you keep your boat at a dock or on a mooring buoy, secure it with a case-hardened chain and lock. Remove portable fuel tanks and a vital engine part such as a distributor rotor or ignition wire(s). A hidden switch in the electrical system between the motor and the ignition switch can be a useful deterrent.

Work with your neighbors and fellow boaters to watch for strangers or suspicious activity. Call local law enforcement if you have any doubt whether someone is authorized to work on a boat or trailer. Write down a description of any suspicious people and get their license numbers or the registration numbers and descriptions of their boats.

Aquatic Nuisance Species

Foreign plants and animals, often called *aquatic nuisance species* (ANS), are invading our waters. Most are thought to come from the ballast water of ships, but once here, the invaders are spread by recreational boaters whenever boats are moved from one body of water to another.

Zebra mussels were accidentally introduced into the Great Lakes region around 1986. Since then, they have spread into the Hudson, Susquehanna, Ohio, Illinois, Tennessee, and Mississippi rivers and many lakes. The economic damage the

Figure **3-35.** Milfoil aquatic weed on Lake Guntersville, Alabama, in August. (PHOTO BY DUNCAN WILKINSON)

mussels have caused by fouling power plants and industrial and public drinking water systems, and their damage to boat hulls, engine cooling systems, docks, and navigation buoys, underscore the need to prevent their further spread.

The Japanese tsunami on March 11, 2011, generated an estimated 5 million tons of ocean debris. The Japanese government estimated that about 1.5 million tons remained afloat, some of which has washed ashore on the western coastlines of the United States, including Hawaii. NOAA expects this process to continue throughout 2013. Some of the debris, such as docks, buoys, or vessels, could have nonnative, potentially invasive organisms attached to them. If you find debris that you think is from the tsunami, especially if it contains unfamiliar living organisms, remove it from the water and move above the high-tide line. Take photos of the debris, if possible, and send them—along with as much detail as you can provide, including the location, the date and time you found it, and a description of the item(s)—to www.DisasterDebris@noaa.gov. This information will be shared with a marine debris response team and invasive species experts to determine what action needs to be taken. For more information, go to http://marinedebris.noaa.gov/tsunamidebris/faqs.html and www.anstaskforce.gov/tsunami.html.

Eurasian water milfoil invades North American lakes so aggressively that, once introduced into a new water body, it quickly outcompetes all indigenous species and spreads across the lake or pond in dense mats that make boating impossible and may even choke all other life out of the lake (Figure 3-35). Milfoil is readily transported on a boat bottom from one lake to another.

The following are steps boaters can take before moving from one body of fresh water to another to keep zebra mussels and other ANS from spreading to uninfested waters:

- Paint your boat's hull with an environmentally acceptable antifouling paint.
- After boating, flush your boat's engine, hull, and outdrive and your trailer's frame, preferably with hot water (140°F or hotter).
- Empty your bilge, bait wells, and bait buckets and flush them with water containing chlorine bleach.

- Do not take bait from one body of water to another.
- Remove any plants, mud, or animals from equipment before leaving all waters.

After flushing, allow your boat and trailer to dry at least two to four days in the sun before moving to another body of fresh water. If you do not follow the above precautions, drain your engine, bait wells, and bilge, and allow them to dry for at least two weeks before launching them in a different body of fresh water.

Float Plan

Before setting out, file a *float plan*. A copy of a suggested float plan is in Appendix B. Copy it and fill in the descriptive facts about you and your boat.

File your float plan with a friend, relative, or neighbor. The plan tells where you are going, the route you will take, when you will be back, and whom to call if you don't return on time. Most often you will ask that the Coast Guard be notified if you are overdue. The Coast Guard does not accept float plans but will mount a search as soon as you are reported overdue.

When trailering, if you can't find someone to accept your float plan, leave a copy under your windshield wiper. Some police authority will find it, probably soon after dark.

Be sure to cancel your float plan when you return. Otherwise the person with whom you left it, not knowing you have returned, may initiate a needless search.

Ways to Learn More

Chapman Piloting & Seamanship. 66th ed. Charles B. Husick. New York: Hearst Books, 2009. Chapter 7.

The Complete Guide to Trailering Your Boat: How to Select, Use, Maintain, and Improve Boat Trailers. Bruce W. Smith. Camden, Maine: International Marine, 2007.

Getting Started in Powerboating. 3rd ed. Bob Armstrong. Camden, Maine: International Marine, 2005.

www.readybrake.com/state_laws.html

Practice Questions

IMPORTANT BOATING TERMS

In the following exercise, match the words in the column on the left with the definitions in the column on the right. In the blank space to the left of each term, write the letter of the item that best matches it. Do not use an item in the right-hand column more than once.

THE ITEMS

1. _____ surge brakes
2. _____ Bearing Buddy
3. _____ seize
4. _____ lifting rings
5. _____ bumper hitch
6. _____ tie-downs
7. _____ fishtails
8. _____ impeller
9. _____ float plan
10. _____ flasher

THE RESPONSES

a. secure your boat to its trailer

b. on a boat's transom

c. bearings immersed in salt water

d. less than 5% of weight on tongue

e. wheel bearing protector

f. automatically applied when towing vehicle stops

g. circulates water

h. controls turn signals

i. completed prior to cruising

j. usually illegal

Multiple-Choice Items

In the following items, choose the best response:

3-1. The widest boat you can trailer on most state roads is

a. 6 feet
b. 7 feet
c. 8 feet
d. 9 feet

3-2. The safety chains of your trailer, under the hitch, should always be

a. crossed
b. of open link construction
c. attached to the towing vehicle's bumper
d. short

3-3. A bumper hitch is

a. recommended
b. legal in all states
c. the best available
d. illegal in many states

3-4. The ball of a trailer hitch and the coupler on the trailer must

a. be free of grease
b. be matched for size
c. be insulated from each other
d. be made of the same material

3-5. You should have brakes on your trailer if it is designed for a gross weight of

a. 1,500 or more pounds
b. 2,000 or more pounds
c. 2,500 or more pounds
d. 3,000 or more pounds

3-6. Many states require that boat trailers have

a. safety chains
b. licenses
c. lights and turn signals
d. all of the above

3-7. Trailer light failure can be reduced by

a. using waterproof lights
b. mounting lights on a high bracket or board
c. unplugging the trailer electrical system before launching or recovering the boat
d. all of the above

3-8. Which brakes work from a trailer's momentum?

a. compressed air
b. surge
c. electric
d. none of the above

3-9. When trailering, always take along

a. an inflated spare tire
b. a jack
c. spare bearings
d. all of the above

3-10. How much of the load should be on the hitch to avoid fishtailing?

a. 2% to 4%
b. 7% to 10%
c. 10% to 15%
d. 12% to 14%

3-11. Small trailer tires

a. cost more
b. turn faster and need more air pressure
c. are made with solid cores
d. turn slower and need less air pressure

3-12. Winch lines for retrieving boats are made of

a. steel
b. polypropylene
c. webbing
d. all of the above

3-13. Dry rot forms most often in

a. salt water
b. fresh water
c. brackish water
d. potable water

3-14. It is easier to back a trailer if you place your hand on the bottom of the steering wheel and then move your hand

a. in the direction you want the trailer to go
b. in the opposite direction from where you want the trailer to go
c. clockwise so the trailer will go to the right
d. counterclockwise so the trailer will go to the left

Multiple-Choice Items (continued)

3-15. You can increase the life of your trailer's lights if you

a. mount them on a removable board
b. keep them out of the water
c. disconnect them before immersing them in water
d. all of the above

3-16. Before you step the mast of a sailboat

a. launch the boat
b. check to see what is overhead
c. take it to the launching ramp
d. moor it securely

3-17. Before leaving the dock

a. check to see that you have enough bait
b. file a float plan with a friend or relative
c. be sure you have enough ice
d. make certain you have the water skis

3-18. If you have too much weight on the hitch, it will cause

a. the front end of your automobile to lift up
b. you to lose some steering control
c. the automobile's rear end to squat
d. all of the above

3-19. An advantage of tilt trailers is

a. they are cheaper
b. they can carry a heavier load
c. you can usually keep the trailer's wheels out of the water
d. it's easier to balance the load on them

3-20. When you buy a boat

a. buy an inexpensive one
b. keep launching problems in mind
c. remember how much trouble it is to maintain it
d. buy a trailer

3-21. A flat-bottomed boat fits best on

a. a roller-supported trailer
b. a tilt trailer
c. a skid-type trailer
d. a float-on trailer

3-22. While launching a boat

a. have someone stay in it to guide you
b. put the transmission in Park to ensure that your car does not roll down the ramp
c. if at all possible, stay in your car with your foot on the brake
d. set the hand brake to ensure that your car does not roll down the ramp

3-23. Zebra mussels have been found in

a. the Great Lakes
b. the Mississippi River
c. the Hudson River
d. all of the above

3-24. When filing a float plan, you should

a. take it with you on the boat
b. file your plan with a friend, relative, or neighbor
c. send a copy to the Coast Guard
d. file it with the local police

chapter 4

Handling Your Boat

The objectives of this chapter are to describe:

- ✔ The principles of handling a boat.
- ✔ Safety precautions for handling a boat.
- ✔ The One-Third Rule for fuel, and why it is important to follow.
- ✔ Precautions for fueling your boat.
- ✔ What to do if you find gasoline in your bilge.
- ✔ The fundamentals of propeller selection and operation.
- ✔ How your boat steers and turns.
- ✔ The fundamentals of trim adjustment for outboards and stern drives.
- ✔ How to load your boat safely.
- ✔ Safe conduct in a small boat.
- ✔ How to retrieve an overboard person.
- ✔ The importance of pretrip routine checks.
- ✔ How to depart from and return to a pier or mooring.
- ✔ Your responsibility for damage you may cause others.
- ✔ Characteristics and limitations of anchors.
- ✔ How to anchor safely.
- ✔ Safety practices for towing a skier.
- ✔ How to handle your boat in adverse weather and seas.

(COURTESY U. S. COAST GUARD)

HANDLING A POWERBOAT is a skill that comes through practice and experience. You will find that each boat handles differently, depending on its weight, hull shape, type of power, and load. Even two boats that look the same may handle differently, and it's up to you to learn the unique characteristics of your boat.

Leave with a Full Fuel Tank

Refuel whenever possible. This policy will help guard against running out of fuel and will reduce condensation that can occur when a partially empty tank cools, causing the water vapor in the air to condense. Filling the tank eliminates this possibility.

It's a horrible feeling to look at an empty fuel gauge after your motor sputters and quits. While leaving with a full tank is one way to safeguard against this, another is to follow the One-Third Rule, which says that you should use one-third of your fuel on your trip out, save another third for the trip back, and keep one-third in reserve. If this seems overly cautious, remember that the return trip may take more fuel than you expect. When you go out, the wind and waves may be calm or from astern, or you may be going downriver or with a tidal current. But when you turn around, you may find yourself headed into the wind, waves, current, or all three, in which case your return progress will be slower and your fuel consumption higher. The One-Third Rule can save you from a lot of inconvenience or even serious trouble in unexpected emergencies or heavy weather.

Fueling Your Boat

With a few simple precautions, fueling a boat's gas tank is a safe task.

Know What You Are Doing!

When fueling, it pays to know what you are doing. For example, people have pumped gasoline into water tanks and even into fishing rod holders. Both of these errors, on occasion, have resulted in explosions and serious injuries. Be certain that you are pumping gas into your gas tank and not into your bilge.

The law requires electrical parts in an enclosed engine space to be ignition-protected. This means that the parts will not produce sparks that can ignite gasoline fumes. Unfortunately, rebuilt or replaced parts may not be ignition-protected. You may, for example, inadvertently replace a marine alternator with one built for an automobile.

Keep Fumes Out!

Gasoline vapors are much heavier than air and flow to the lowest spot on your boat. Avoid trapping them, since there are many sources of sparks and flames aboard a boat that can ignite such fumes.

Close all cabin doors, hatches, and ports before fueling. This will help keep gasoline vapors from

---

✓ FUELING SAFETY CHECKLIST

PRIOR TO FUELING

☐ Turn off all engines.

☐ Close all doors, hatches, and ports.

☐ Turn off all electrical equipment.

☐ Extinguish all open flames.

☐ Turn off galley stove and heaters.

☐ Don't smoke.

☐ Instruct crew and passengers on safe practices. (Consider having passengers go ashore during refueling.)

AFTER FUELING

☐ Open doors, hatches, and ports.

☐ On gas-powered boats, operate blowers for at least 4 to 5 minutes.

☐ Clean up all fuel spills.

☐ Check all compartments by sniffing for fuel fumes.

☐ Have a fire extinguisher at hand for engine start.

TIP *Reserve Fuel Tank Management*
The reserve fuel tank should always be full. It should only be drawn on in an emergency (when the regular tanks are dry), so be sure that the reserve fuel switch hasn't been turned on inadvertently. You should "test" the reserve supply periodically by checking for contaminants in the fuel and running the engine from the reserve tank for a short time.

> **TIP** **Monitor Your Fuel Reserves**
>
> *Unlike our highways, our waterways are not lined with gas stations every few miles or so. Boaters need to pay careful attention to fuel management. In addition to leaving with a full tank, you should check the amount of fuel on board periodically and change your plans if fuel consumption appears to be significantly greater than originally estimated. Know your boat's approximate fuel consumption rates at various speeds. Not all boats and tanks are equipped with fuel gauges. For example, many PWC do not have fuel gauges. Instead, they have reserve tanks. When the engine quits from fuel starvation, the operator needs to switch to the reserve tank and refuel as soon as possible.*

entering your boat. Also, turn off all electrical devices such as ventilating fans, radios, bilge pumps, navigational devices, generators, and lights. Extinguish all open flames, turn off the galley stove, and don't smoke.

To be on the safe side, operate your blower for at least 4 to 5 minutes after fueling. Then, before starting your engine, check all compartments and engine spaces for gas fumes by sniffing. If you have a problem smelling odors, get an electronic fume detector. Bear in mind, though, that an electronic device is not always as sensitive as your nose.

The need to thoroughly air out your bilge and other compartments after fueling cannot be overemphasized. It is possible for trapped gasoline vapors to be so rich that a spark will cause an explosion. When you open a hatch, port, or door, or when your vessel begins to move, you may introduce enough air to make the vapors combustible. Many vessels have exploded and caught fire after leaving a fueling dock.

Built-In Tanks

The filler pipe for the gasoline tank should be located so spills do not enter your boat and become dangerous. Clean up any spill that does occur immediately and get the dirty rags off your boat right away. Spills should be avoided both for the dangers they pose and for environmental protection (Figure 4-1). Any spill that makes a sheen on the water is a violation of federal pollution laws. When you see one, report it immediately to the nearest Coast Guard station or facility. You can also report a spill to the National Response Center in Washington, D.C., by calling 1-800-424-8802.

Your boat's fuel filler pipe should be connected (grounded) to your boat's electrical grounding system (Figure 4-2). Gasoline passing through the hose line from a pump can generate static electricity, and a spark between the hose nozzle and the filler pipe might then cause an explosion. To prevent this, always keep the hose nozzle in contact with the metal of the fuel filler pipe.

Fuel Tank Vents

A built-in fuel tank must be vented outside your boat's hull (Figure 4-3). This provides an outlet for gasoline vapors and air so you can fill your tank. It also allows air to enter the tank as you use the gasoline. Without a vent, you could not draw gas from the tank without collapsing it.

Figure **4-1.** Refueling at the marine dock. Note the use of an absorbent pad to prevent spills. (PHOTO BY BOB DENNIS)

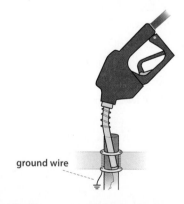

ground wire

Figure **4-2.** When refueling, keep the nozzle in contact with the filler pipe to prevent static electricity buildup.

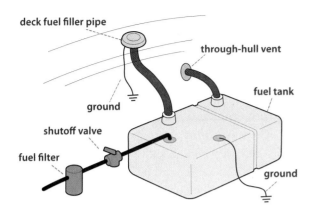

Figure **4-3.** The fuel filler deck plate and the tank's air vent must be located outside the hull's enclosed spaces so that fumes do not accumulate in the bilge.

Vents are covered with a wire mesh that may become clogged from corrosion, insect nests, etc. When this happens, poor engine performance results.

Unfortunately, both the filler pipe and the vent can cause environmental problems. If you overfill your tank, some of the fuel may spurt out of the filler pipe and into the water, and some may leak out of the vent. You can avoid either of these sources of environmental pollution by knowing the capacity of your fuel tank and never filling it to more than 95% of capacity.

There are also devices available that collect fuel spilling from the fuel vent outlet. They attach with a suction cup and can be removed easily.

If you completely fill the tank and then leave your boat in the sun, the fuel will expand and some will leak out of the vent. Any fuel spill, no matter how small or how it occurs, is illegal and can result in a fine from a state regulatory agency or the U.S. Environmental Protection Agency (EPA).

The EPA statute on oil spills is unambiguous. Note in what follows that the term "general rule" gives the EPA leeway to impose even higher penalties under special conditions such as not cooperating with the responsible official:

"If your recreational vessel discharges oil into the navigable waters or adjoining shorelines (or what is referred to as the 'exclusive economic zone') of the U.S., then, as a general rule, you are liable for all oil removal costs and certain specified damages resulting from that discharge up to $500,000 or $600 per gross ton, whichever amount is greater."

If a spill occurs and you are in federal waters, it is your responsibility to report it immediately to the Coast Guard. For more information on oil spill liability or compensation questions, contact the National Pollution Funds Center at 202-493-6999, or visit www.uscg.mil/hq/npfc.

Gasoline in Your Bilge

If you find raw gasoline in your bilge, don't operate anything electrical and don't disconnect your battery. Turn off all power by using the enclosed, marine-type battery switch. (If you have an open, "knife" switch, do not use it!) A marine-type battery switch is ignition-protected and should not produce a spark.

If a sizable bilge spill occurs at a gas dock, call the fire department. You can clean up small amounts of spilled gasoline with a sponge and a plastic bucket. Put the bucket and the sponge ashore. After that, leave the boat open until you can no longer smell fumes. Then use your blower for at least 4 minutes.

When you don't know where raw gasoline in your bilge has come from, look for its source. But do it after you have cleaned up the mess and before you try to start your engine. A leaking fuel line, for example, could be an invitation to disaster.

Portable Tanks

Remove portable tanks from your boat before filling them. When filling a portable tank, keep the hose nozzle in contact with the tank to reduce the chance of sparking from static electricity.

Your Boat's Propeller

Most recreational powerboats use propellers, with jet-drive boats being the principal exception. When viewed from aft, most props turn in a clockwise direction when the boat is moving forward, and are thus said to be right-handed (Figure 4-4). Left-handed propellers also exist, particularly on *twin-screw* boats (boats with two engines driving two propellers), where pairing a left-handed prop with a right-handed one cancels the unwanted side thrust of each and makes the boat efficient and well-mannered (Figure 4-5).

Propeller Characteristics

In addition to the direction it spins, a propeller is described by its diameter and pitch, the number of its blades, and the material used to make it.

Propeller Diameter

The diameter of the circle described by a propeller's blade tips when they spin is the propeller's diameter. The bigger the diameter, the more shaft power a propeller can absorb and the more thrust it will deliver, up to a point. Most powerboats get greater efficiency from a larger propeller, though this is not true of high-speed powerboats (faster than 35 knots or so), in which the drag created by a large propeller becomes excessive.

Propeller Pitch

Propeller blades fasten to their hubs at angles (Figure 4-6). Thus, as a blade spins, its leading edge is canted forward. The degree of cant, or twist, determines the pitch of the propeller. Looked at another way, *pitch* is the distance the propeller would screw itself forward into the water in one rotation if there were no slippage (Figure 4-7). A propeller with a pitch of 10 inches would, in the absence of slippage, screw itself forward 10 inches through the water with each complete revolution.

Although a propeller does not work like a wood screw, you can think of it as one to understand what is meant by pitch. The pitch of a wood screw is the distance it penetrates the wood with each complete turn.

Unlike a wood screw, however, a propeller slips when turning in water. *Slip* is the difference between the distance the propeller moves forward in one turn and the distance it would move if it were in a solid medium.

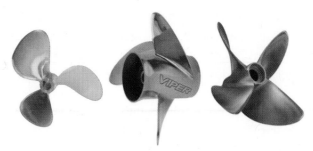

Figure **4-6.** **Left to right:** A three-bladed propeller for an inboard engine. (COURTESY MICHIGAN WHEEL) A three-bladed stern-drive or outboard propeller. (COURTESY JOHNSON) A four-bladed prop can deliver less vibration and more blade area in a given diameter than a two- or three-bladed propeller, though with some loss of efficiency. (COURTESY BOMBARDIER RECREATIONAL PRODUCTS)

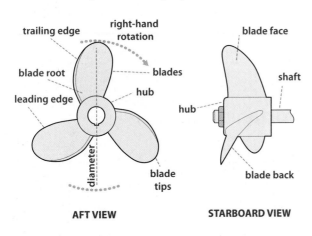

Figure **4-4.** Propeller anatomy.

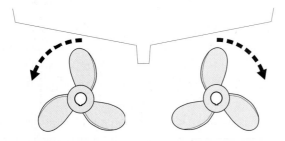

Figure **4-5.** In a twin-screw installation, the starboard propeller is typically right-handed, and the port prop is left-handed. With this configuration, the two props cancel each other's unwanted side thrust.

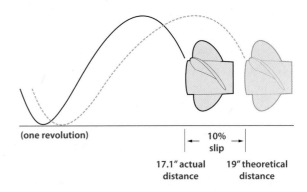

Figure **4-7.** Propeller pitch and slip. A prop with a pitch of 19 inches would move the boat forward 19 inches with each complete revolution were it not for slip. With 10% slip, as here, each revolution moves the boat forward 17.1 inches. (COURTESY MACH PERFORMANCE INC.)

Propeller Size

A propeller's size is described by its diameter and pitch. A 14 x 12 prop, for example, has a diameter of 14 inches and a pitch of 12 inches. The size markings on a propeller hub are not standardized, however, and may include only the manufacturer's part number. You may have to contact the manufacturer to determine a propeller's characteristics. Propellers used on inboards are usually well marked.

Propeller Safeguards

Most drive mechanisms include one or more parts that are designed to fail under stress before the propeller itself or some other equally expensive part is severely damaged. In a small outboard motor this function is served by a *shear pin*, which is a soft metal pin that looks like a nail without a head. One end of the pin fits into a hole in the propeller shaft and the other end slips into a matching hole on the inside face of the propeller hub, thus transmitting the shaft torque to the propeller. When the propeller hits an object that keeps it from turning, however, the pin shears, thus decoupling the propeller from the still-turning driveshaft. If you're lucky, this will happen before you damage either the propeller or its shaft.

Replacing a shear pin is relatively easy unless the boat is in deep water. If the motor is small enough, you can dismount it to change the pin. In shallow water, you can pull the boat ashore or get in the water to replace the pin. Usually, all you have to do is remove a cotter pin and a nut, and the propeller will slide off its shaft. After you replace the pin, put the propeller back on the shaft, tighten the nut, and replace the cotter pin.

Unfortunately, a pin will sometimes shear even without the propeller hitting anything. Normal engine operation in forward or reverse puts a strain on the pin, and eventually, through metal fatigue, it will fail. *If your propeller uses a shear pin, never leave home without a spare and the tools to install it.*

Larger outboard motors have propellers held in place by the friction of a slip hub, which is designed to release, or spin, when the prop hits an object, thus minimizing damage to the prop or the shaft. The hub of a spun propeller can be replaced at a propeller repair shop.

You may be able to use a spun prop to return home. If you proceed very slowly, there may be enough remaining friction to turn the propeller.

It's a good idea to take a spare propeller with you, since when you spin a hub, you may need to replace the propeller to get home. Also, when you hit a rock or some other hard object, the propeller may be damaged before the hub spins. A badly damaged prop vibrates excessively and should be replaced before you damage your motor or its driveshaft.

Cavitation

Cavitation refers to the bubbles of partial vacuum that may appear around the blades of a propeller that is spinning at excessive speed or under an excessive load. A propeller that is too small or carries too much pitch for its application is susceptible to cavitation, which will cause vibrations similar to those of unbalanced blades and can eventually pit and destroy the blades. Boats with properly sized engines and propellers will usually experience cavitation only under very high engine speeds. If your propeller is cavitating, be sure it has a large enough diameter for its application and that its pitch is not excessive. There are also special blade designs that will reduce cavitation with some compromise in efficiency.

Note that the flat side of a propeller blade faces toward the bow and is the suction surface when the boat is moving forward, whereas the cupped, after surface is the pressure surface. Cavitation occurs when the propeller is moving so fast that water cannot move into the suction side of the blade, producing a partial vacuum.

Ventilation

When a propeller is too close to the water surface, it sucks air down into the blades; this *ventilation* can lead to vibration and a loss of thrust. If the propeller can't be lowered, there are special blade designs that will reduce ventilation (Figure 4-8).

Selecting Your Propeller

The propeller must be the right size for your boat if it is to operate efficiently. Too large a propeller will result in a large amount of slippage. If it is too small, it will lose energy through cavitation.

The selection of a propeller is a complex decision. Most boat dealers and propeller retailers have access to a computer analysis service that can recommend a propeller based on input information about the boat, the engine, and the intended use. If you suspect a propeller issue, remember, too, that marine growth on your boat's hull will slow down your engine and boat. Before you change propellers, get advice from a reliable dealer.

Steering

Steering a boat is quite different from steering an automobile. When you turn a car's steering wheel, the front wheels turn the front of the car, and the rest of the car follows. When you turn a boat's wheel, on the other hand, you're turning either the propeller(s) of an outboard or stern-drive boat or the rudder(s) of an inboard boat, so that the turn is initiated from the stern of the boat (Figures 4-9 and 4-10) rather than its bow.

When you turn the wheel to the right, the stern moves to port, which causes the bow to move to starboard, and the boat turns on its *pivot point*, which is located about one-third of the way back from the forward end of the waterline.

The result is that even as your bow is swinging toward the direction you want to go, your stern is swinging to the other side of your previous track, and by a wider amount.

A boat turns differently from a car in another respect too. A car doesn't skid around a turn unless it's going too fast for the road conditions, but a boat always slides somewhat sideways through a turn. This is the inevitable result of the momentum the boat still carries from its previous track and the fact that it operates on a fluid surface, not a hard one. The tendency can be controlled with proper speed and steering, and it can be anticipated and compensated for—sometimes even turned to advantage—but it can't be eliminated. The net result of these factors is that your stern will swing to port when you're turning to starboard, and vice versa. The way a boat pivots is not particularly important in open water, but alongside a pier or another boat it becomes critical. If you operate your boat like a car while in "close quarters," you will drive its stern into the pier or another boat (Figure 4-11).

While the ability to direct the propeller thrust

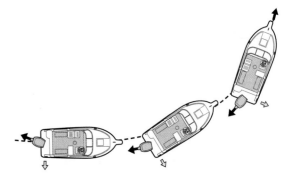
Figure **4-9.** The directed thrust of an outboard or stern drive in forward gear moves the stern of the boat into a turn.

Figure **4-8.** This stern-drive lower unit shows an antiventilation plate just above the prop and a small rudder below it. The rudder conveys some steerage to the boat even when the engine is not in gear. Note the five-bladed prop, permitting more power and smoother operation from a small-diameter prop, albeit with some loss of efficiency. (COURTESY MERCURY MARINE)

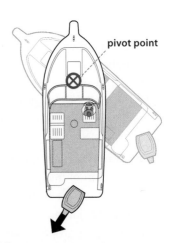
Figure **4-10.** A turning boat pivots about a point a third of the way back from the bow.

gives an outboard or a stern-drive boat a lot of maneuverability, it is also possible to turn too sharply, causing the boat to turn over or *capsize*.

Steering a personal watercraft (PWC) or other jet-drive boat is considerably different, and is discussed below in the Jet Drives section.

Stopping

Boats also differ from cars in that they have no brakes. Boats slow gradually when you remove power and will eventually stop, but they don't respond the way a car responds to its brake pedal. In an emergency, you can stop your boat's forward motion quickly by slamming the engine from forward to reverse, but most boaters avoid doing this in ordinary circumstances, as it stresses the gears and shafts of a motor. Preferably, when going from forward to reverse or vice versa, you first shift to neutral. Then, when the engine has slowed to idle speed, you can again shift gears.

If you have a choice when docking, you should choose to dock with your boat facing *into* the wind or current (whichever is the more significant factor). That way the wind or current (or both) will help you slow down instead of speeding you up, and you'll be able to adjust your engine throttle in forward gear so that your boat moves very slowly ahead while maintaining steerageway, permitting a smooth, gentle landing.

Steering with a Single Inboard Engine

A boat with a single inboard engine requires special care when maneuvering. The engine is for-

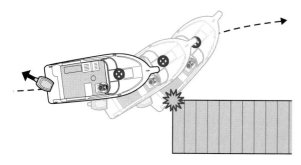

Figure **4-11.** In tight quarters, turning away from an obstacle may actually induce your boat's stern to swing into the very thing you are trying to avoid.

ward of the boat's stern and transmits its torque to the propeller through a long, rigid shaft. Because of this, you cannot direct the prop's thrust from side to side as you can with a stern drive or an outboard. Instead, steering is done by means of a rudder.

A *rudder* is a blade attached to a rotating shaft (the *rudderpost*) that extends down into the water beneath the boat's stern. In most inboard-powered boats, the rudder is directly behind the propeller. It is controlled by a tiller (rarely) or by a wheel (usually) that turns the rudderpost via a mechanical or hydraulic linkage. When the boat is moving ahead, turning the rudder left or right causes it to deflect the water discharged from the propeller and streaming past the boat, which pushes the stern in the direction opposite the deflection (Figure 4-12). If you turn the wheel right, for example, the rudder turns right, which forces the stern to the left and the bow to the right (Figure 4-13).

Inboard-powered boats, in general, operate more efficiently and more economically than outboards and stern drives. (This is not true at high speeds—say, more than 30 knots—at which point the drag of an inboard boat's rudder, propeller shaft, and other running gear makes it less efficient than

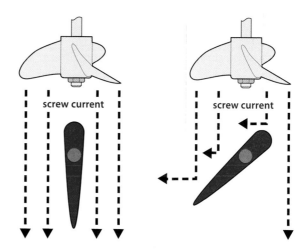

Figure **4-12.** The steering forces in play aboard a single-engine inboard boat. When the engine is in forward gear, the propeller discharge (i.e., the screw current) washes over the rudder blade, making the rudder more effective. When the engine is reversed, the screw current no longer impinges on the rudder, which is therefore less effective in reverse gear than in forward.

an outboard or stern drive.) As long as an inboard boat is moving, its rudder will exert directional control even when the engine is out of gear, though that control is reduced when no prop wash impinges on the rudder. Because outboard and stern-drive boats have no rudder except the small fin at the bottom of the lower unit, they do not respond well to the wheel when the engine is in neutral. Also, since an inboard engine is mounted farther forward, inboard boats usually ride on a level keel, whether on or off plane. This level attitude, plus the presence of a rudder, makes them good choices for waterskiing. They are less easily pulled one way or the other by a skier.

Nevertheless, because inboard engines are limited mainly to larger yachts and commercial craft, we won't devote much space to them here. Later in this chapter we'll focus more on outboard and stern-drive engines, since these are what most "weekend" boats use.

Twin Screws

Outboard, inboard, and stern-drive boats may have two engines, and sometimes (but not commonly) even more. Twin engines confer greater reliability, since it is unlikely that both engines will fail at the same time (especially if each engine has its own fuel tank), but the best reason for installing twin engines is improved maneuverability.

Turning with Twin Screws

With twin screws, the starboard propeller is usually right-handed, and the port prop is left-handed. When you increase the power on the starboard prop while going ahead, the boat will turn to port in a large arc. Conversely, increasing power on the port prop causes the boat to turn to starboard. You can, if need be, steer a twin engine boat by its

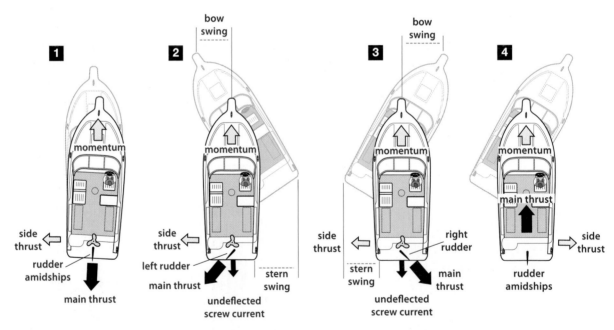

Figure **4-13.** The turning characteristics of a single-engine inboard boat with a right-handed propeller. When you power ahead with the rudder amidships, the side thrust from the prop will tend to push the stern to starboard (**1**). This phenomenon is known as prop walk, and must be counteracted with slight right rudder in order to keep the boat moving in a straight line. When you apply left rudder, the rudder deflects the water through which the boat is traveling as well as the discharge current from the propeller to the left, which causes the stern to swing right (**2**). The boat's natural prop walk enhances this left turn. When you apply right rudder, the rudder forces the stern to the left but is partially counteracted by prop walk, meaning that the boat will take longer to turn right than to turn left (**3**). When you reverse the engine with the rudder amidships, the direction of prop walk is reversed and the stern swings to port (**4**). In this illustration the engine has just been reversed and the boat is still moving ahead, but the stern would be swinging the same way even if the boat were actually backing, unless counteracted by rudder action. When driving a single-engine inboard, you must anticipate these factors and turn them to advantage—for example, by approaching a dock port-side-to so that reversing the engine will cause your stern to swing toward rather than away from the dock.

throttles alone, leaving the steering wheel centered (Figure 4-14).

Tighter turns can be made by going ahead on one engine and reversing the other (Figure 4-15). Going forward on the starboard engine and reversing the port engine, for example, causes your boat to turn sharply to port, but don't attempt this when you have much *headway*, or forward motion through the water, because doing so might induce a capsize. With adequate throttle management, your boat can be made to turn without going forward or backward—essentially spinning on a dime (Figure 4-16). This can be a huge advantage in a narrow channel or while docking.

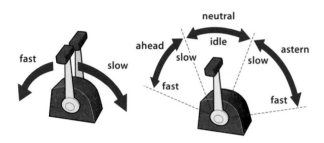

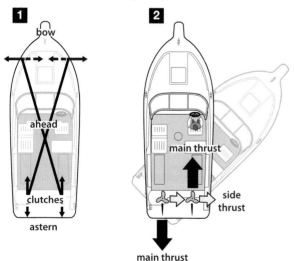

Figure **4-14.** Some boats have separate controls for the gearshift and throttle (left), whereas on others these are combined into a single lever (right), which limits you to a shorter throttle range but is perfectly adequate on most boats.

Twin versus Single Engines

Twin engines do have disadvantages, the biggest of which is initial cost. The average cost of twin engines is about double the cost of a single large engine. In addition, twin engines require more expensive and complex control systems. Furthermore, they add weight to your boat. Twin engines are about 50% heavier than a single large engine of equivalent horsepower.

Twin screws also cause additional underwater drag and thus greater fuel consumption, using one-third to one-half more fuel than a single large engine. When the twin engines are outboards or stern drives, they place additional weight at the boat's stern, adversely affecting the boat's attitude in the water.

Engine Reliability

The old argument that twin engines offer greater reliability is less compelling than it used to be thanks to the greater reliability of newer outboards. Modern outboard motors are highly dependable as well as highly efficient. Four-stroke outboard engines are, in effect, automobile engines stood on end, and are just as reliable as the engines that

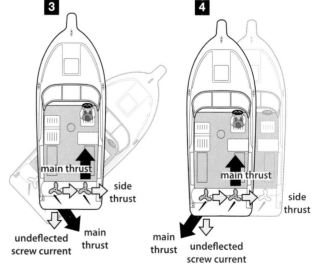

Figure **4-15.** Turning with twin screws. To picture the cause and effect, imagine a huge X superimposed on your boat **(1)**. Engaging the starboard engine in forward gear while the port engine is in neutral or reverse will cause the bow to swing left, and vice versa. Reversing the starboard engine while the port engine is in forward gear swings the bow to starboard **(2)**. Note that the side thrust from the right-handed starboard prop in reverse will accentuate this turn, as will the side thrust from the left-handed port prop in forward gear. The turn can be made even sharper by bringing the rudders into play **(3)**. Here the rudders are countering the turning action of the engines and prop walk **(4)**. The result, if you experiment, is a dynamic balance in which the boat will actually "walk" sideways—a pretty clever way of sidling into a berth.

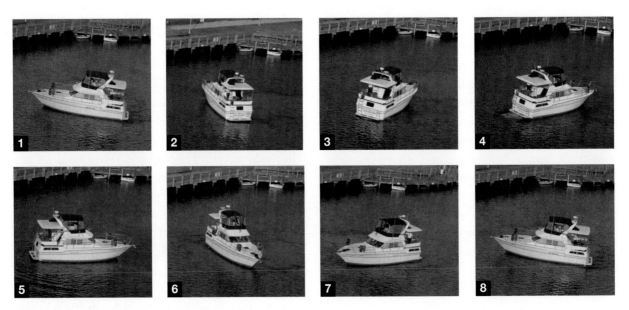

Figure **4-16.** In this series of photographs, a twin-screw boat turns in its own length. (REPRODUCED WITH PERMISSION FROM *GETTING STARTED IN POWERBOATING* BY BOB ARMSTRONG)

power our cars. Modern two-strokes, too, are dependable and efficient thanks to technological developments over the past 10 years. Newer models feature electronic fuel injection and electronically metered lubricating oil. Many have dual carburetion, and most have solid-state electronic ignition for each cylinder. Should one carburetor or one cylinder's ignition system fail, you can usually get home. If you run out of gas, however, or if the black box computer module fails, or if you should blow a powerhead, you are out of luck.

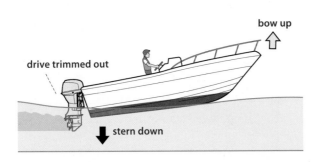

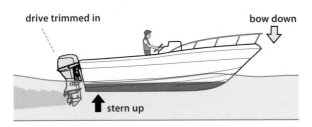

Figure **4-17.** The effect of outboard motor tilt adjustment on the trim of a boat.

Auxiliary Motors

A small auxiliary outboard motor can protect you in case of engine failure. Mount it on a spring-loaded bracket on your boat's transom and then when needed, lower it into the water. It is important to care for your auxiliary motor faithfully if you want it to be ready for an emergency. If you use your boat for fishing, this smaller motor will come in handy for trolling as well, which will ensure that it gets some use.

The auxiliary motor will probably need its own gasoline source. The gasoline in this tank should either be stabilized by using a gasoline additive or changed at least every 6 months, as old gasoline can gum up the carburetor.

Outboard and Stern-Drive Installation and Tilt Adjustment

If your boat has an outboard motor of 25 horsepower or more, it is probably permanently installed on your boat's transom. Of course, all stern-drive engines are permanently installed.

Installing a Small Outboard

If you have a portable outboard motor, you will probably take it off at home and store it to prevent theft. Reinstalling it is a simple task. When you mount the motor, be certain that its center is on the boat's centerline. It is not unusual for clamps to loosen over time; if they do, the motor may fall off. Chaining and locking prevents this and is also a good security precaution.

Tilt Adjustment

Outboard engines and stern-drive lower units tilt up for trailering and can be trimmed up or down while the boat is underway in order to fine-tune the plane of the propeller thrust, which will alter the boat's trim (Figures 4-17 and 4-18). Stern drives and larger outboards usually have hydraulic tilting mechanisms, while small outboards are adjusted manually. For best performance, the thrust of the propeller should be horizontal when the boat is at its most efficient operating angle. Tilting the motor or outdrive so the propeller is farther forward is called tucking it in, or lowering it; this will direct the propeller discharge below the horizontal plane, forcing the boat's stern up and its bow down. Tilting the motor or outdrive farther aft is called raising it, which tends to lower the stern and raise the bow.

When the propeller is too close to the transom, it lifts your boat's stern too high and causes the bow to plow into the water. When the prop is tilted too far back, it forces the stern down too far and the bow up too high. Boats operate inefficiently with improper thrust angles.

You may need to adjust the tilt angle to match water conditions. In calm, smooth water, raise the prop slightly for a faster and more fuel-efficient ride. In this position, a smaller amount of the boat's hull surface is in contact with the water. In rough water, you may want to lower the prop to bring the bow down and give a smoother ride. When the bow is up in choppy water, you get excessive pounding. But don't tilt it so far forward that the boat plows into waves.

Underway, when the propeller becomes fouled with weeds, it is possible to stop an outboard or stern-drive engine, raise the motor or the outdrive, and remove the obstruction. If your motor begins

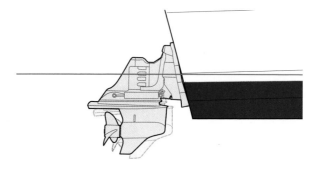

Figure **4-18.** Tilt adjustment on a stern-drive lower unit.

to run hot, stop the boat and raise the motor or the outdrive. Weeds or discarded plastic may have clogged the water intake. Don't forget to lower the motor or outdrive before restarting your engine.

You can also raise your motor or outdrive to clear shoals or to run in shallow water. Be careful, though. Keep the water intake below the surface of the water, or you may damage the engine. When the propeller cavitates, lower it farther into the water.

Some people believe that the best way to cross shallow water is to partially raise the outdrive or outboard and pass over the shallows on a plane at high speed. This is risky and probably not the best procedure. The safest approach is to keep the boat as high in the water as possible by partially raising the propellers and proceeding at a very slow speed. Paradoxically, the worst way to cross a shoal is at a moderate speed. When a planing or semidisplacement hull starts slowly and gradually gains speed, it goes through a transition phase during which it is trying to go on a plane but has not yet developed sufficient hydrodynamic lift to do so. The stern sinks lower and lower during this transition before the boat develops enough speed to climb its own bow wave and reach a plane. Then, and only then, will the stern rise. Therefore, traveling over a shoal at a moderate speed, with your boat's stern squatting deep in the water, is the worst choice.

Jet Drives

Jet-drive boats less than 16 feet long are often called personal watercraft (PWC), but there are larger jet-drive boats as well. A jet-drive propulsion package includes an inboard engine(s) but no propeller(s). Instead, the engine operates a powerful

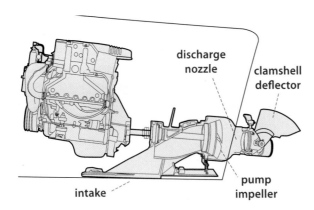

Figure **4-19.** A jet-drive propulsion unit.

> **WARNING** OPERATING PWC IN RE-VERSE *Some PWC are equipped with a reverse gear. This is intended to be used for low-speed maneuvering, not for emergency stopping. Consult the owner's manual for your PWC.*

PWC SAFETY

Man-Overboard Safety with PWC

Riders frequently fall off personal watercraft. Therefore, PWC operators should know how to swim and how to reboard their craft. When reboarding a PWC, swim to the rear and place both hands on the gunwale. Pull yourself up on the footrest deck (boarding pad) and kneel. Move forward to the seat and sit astride. Reattach the kill-switch lanyard if your PWC is equipped with this feature. If the PWC has capsized, follow the righting directions provided in the owner's manual and on warning placards mounted on the PWC. If capsized, many (but not all) models should only be righted by rotating in a clockwise direction when viewed from aft. Righting the craft in the wrong direction can cause water to enter the engine and damage it.

PWC Off-Throttle Steering

With jet-drive propulsion, there is little or no steering capability when the throttle is off or at idle. Turning the handlebars changes the angle of the water exiting the jet drive, but there is no directional thrust unless there is power to the pump. Riders unfamiliar with this phenomenon, called off-throttle steering, can get into accidents. This can happen in a possible collision situation when a novice rider's intuition is to close down the throttle (to avoid high rates of closure) and steer away to avoid the collision. Without throttle there is no steering, and the PWC continues in its original direction, resulting in a collision. It is necessary to make a controlled-speed turn to avoid danger.

water pump (Figure 4-19) that sucks in and ejects water at high speed and volume through a special nozzle. This forceful ejection of water powers the boat, and the nozzle turns to one side or the other to steer the boat. These boats can travel at very high speeds.

An important jet-drive feature is its rapid response to acceleration, stopping, or turning. To stop some jet-drive boats, a barrier called a clamshell is lowered into the discharge stream, which deflects the stream of water forward. These vessels can stop very quickly if reversed with high power. All jet-driven vessels have poor maneuverability at low speeds, however, and this is especially important in tight spaces.

Since jet-drive boats, including PWC, steer by turning their jet nozzles, they do not have rudders. This means they must have pump power to have steering control. If you throttle back or shut off a PWC's engine, or have a power failure during a turn, you lose steering control. The PWC will not continue to turn, but will instead continue forward in the direction it was traveling before the loss of power. This causes many PWC accidents. For example, if the PWC is close to a pier or another vessel when power is reduced, it may crash into the pier or vessel.

Jet drives do not have gearboxes (i.e., transmissions). The pump impeller turns in the same direction when the vessel is going ahead or astern, and it is the lowering of the clamshell deflector that reverses the discharge stream. Thus, you can shift directly from full ahead to full astern without straining the engine. Just be sure to warn your passengers before you do this!

Jet drives are popular for watersports, since their propeller-free engines are safer to operate around swimmers and skiers. The impeller is housed inside the nozzle and thus does not represent a major hazard to swimmers. Jet-drive boats can also run in shallow water without fear of damaging a prop. They may suck up mud, sand, or debris, however, which will damage their impellers.

The engine of a jet-propelled boat is mounted amidships or farther astern. The boat's pivot point is about 14 to 20 inches forward of the engine, which makes sharp turns possible. These boats can reverse their courses in less distance than their lengths.

Loading Your Boat

Most monohulled powerboats less than 20 feet long must have capacity plates, which (as discussed in Chapter 2) displays the maximum load a boat should carry.

When loading your boat, distribute weight evenly, forward and aft and *athwartships* (side to side). The more weight you put into a boat, the deeper it will sink into the water, reducing its freeboard, and the less freeboard a boat has, the greater its tendency to swamp or capsize. An overloaded or improperly loaded boat is unstable and dangerous.

Passengers are often unaware of the need to balance the load forward, aft, and athwartships. Too many may seat themselves forward, causing the boat to plow through the water. Some may seat themselves on a gunwale, causing the boat to *list* to one side, and passengers who perch on the transom may cause the boat to be stern-heavy. All of these conditions can make the vessel difficult to handle, and most of these seating positions are also violations of the law. The skipper should place the passengers so as to be safely inboard and to trim the craft.

Whether you should carry the maximum weight shown on the capacity plate depends on several factors. First, consider the sea state or water conditions. When you expect rough water, carry less weight. A heavily laden boat will *ship water* more easily than one riding higher in the water. When a boat ships water, water comes in over the gunwales or the transom. Once this happens, conditions become dangerous quickly, because the water in the bilge is so heavy and because it flows to the low side, accentuating the boat's roll and pitch.

Second, as you load the boat, consider the activity you expect to engage in underway. When fishing, someone will want to stand. Standing in a small boat is dangerous and becomes more so in choppy water or when the boat is heavily laden. Standing in a boat raises its *center of gravity*—the point where its mass is centered—thus increasing the chances of falling overboard or capsizing.

Learning and practicing the techniques for reboarding a small boat from the water and for recovering a person overboard are absolutely crucial. Reenter a small boat by climbing over its bow or its stern, since attempting to climb over its side may cause it to swamp or capsize. Practice reducing your boat's speed and coming about to recover a person in the water, because you never know when you will need to do it. We'll return to man overboard procedures later in this chapter.

Falling overboard is even more dangerous in cold water, which carries with it the danger of hypothermia and cold shock even after a short period of immersion. Hypothermia occurs whenever a person's body loses large amounts of heat and is unable to maintain its core temperature. Immersion in cold water or exposure to strong, cold winds, especially when you are wet or under the influence of drugs or alcohol, greatly increases the chance of hypothermia.

The best approach to hypothermia is to prevent it by taking steps to see that you do not fall overboard. If you do fall overboard, get back in the boat and out of the wind as soon as possible. Eating a good meal provides energy reserves you can draw on when you're exposed to extreme cold. Wear warm clothing and avoid long periods in cold winds.

Another factor to consider when deciding how many guests to invite on board is the weight of the equipment, fuel, tools, food, and other gear you're carrying. The more gear you have on board, the less capacity you'll have for carrying passengers.

Even when you have loaded your boat correctly, you may have problems under adverse conditions. Running too fast in choppy water can buffet a boat excessively, causing damage and increasing the possibility that you will lose control. Hitting a wave too fast or turning very hard can also cause a boat to capsize.

Getting Started

Before getting underway, always check the weather and review your vessel's systems and gear, using your checklist. Make sure your boat's registration is aboard.

Before Starting Your Engine

BRIEF YOUR GUESTS. Your guests should be familiar with your boat and its safety equipment. Show them how to start and stop the engine and how to operate the radio. Passengers need to be informed of the location of flares and first-aid kits, anchoring procedures, rough-weather procedures, line handling, and emergency boat operations.

Also, show them where the fire extinguishers are kept and how to operate them. While you are orienting your guests, let them know that no trash is to be thrown overboard.

GET A WEATHER CHECK. Before you cast off, get an up-to-date marine weather forecast and be guided by it. When stormy weather or rough water is predicted, you may want to cancel your trip. Always load the boat according to the weather conditions you expect to meet.

The most readily accessible and accurate forecasts are those given by the National Weather Service (NWS), a division of the National Oceanic and Atmospheric Administration (NOAA). You can get these on your VHF-FM radio, where they are broadcast on a continuous basis and updated as new information is received. Listen to them from time to time as you cruise to see if there have been adverse developments. These predictions are also available online at www.nws.noaa.gov, and local newspapers and radio and television broadcasters develop their own forecasts from NOAA data.

EMERGENCY NEEDS. Preparing for an emergency is essential, considering how isolated the boat may be from all services. When you leave, the day may be warm and sunny, and you may plan to be back well before sundown. But trouble can develop, so be prepared for it. Number one on your list should be a reserve supply of drinking water. Include warm clothes, too, as it can get cold on the water after sundown. It's also a good idea to have a warm blanket or two aboard, and insect repellent.

Sunscreen is a requirement, too. On the water, direct and reflected sunlight can combine to give you a bad sunburn, which can be further exacerbated when a strong breeze sensitizes the skin.

Take your PFDs (life jackets) out of the locker and put them where they are readily accessible. Before you leave the dock, make sure each person is assigned a PFD that fits and knows how to put it on. Better still, have everyone wear a PFD at all times. It is always difficult to don a PFD in the water, and in cold water it may be impossible. In many places, the law requires nonswimmers and persons under a certain age to wear a PFD.

THROTTLE AND STEERING. Take the time to check your throttle, gearshift lever, and steering mecha-

nisms. This is especially important when using your boat in salt water, since these mechanisms can corrode and freeze.

OTHER EQUIPMENT. Have you brought all the equipment on board that you will need? This includes electronic equipment such as global positioning system (GPS), radar, and a portable depth finder, if you have them. If you removed your radio, did you remember to install it again? Do you have your anchor and enough line? In an emergency you may have to anchor in deeper water than you had originally planned.

Do you have your whistle or horn aboard? Is it in working condition? Permanently installed horns may corrode, and when they do, they no longer work.

You should also have a heaving line and a boathook available. A *heaving line*, which is a light line weighted at one end, is useful when you need to throw a line to another vessel or to a person on the pier should you have trouble docking. The *boathook* can aid in mooring and docking as well as in retrieving objects dropped in the water.

CHECK YOUR GAS, OIL, AND LIGHTS. Check the fuel supply to determine if it's sufficient, and remember the One-Third Rule of fuel management. It is rare to start a trip in stormy weather, but bad weather may develop, and the fuel requirements to get home may become high. This is the worst time to run out of fuel. When you have a stern-drive or inboard engine, check its oil level. If you have an outboard motor that automatically mixes oil with the gasoline, check to see that this oil reservoir is full.

Following this, check all lights, including the running lights. You never know when you will encounter rain or fog, or when an unexpected situation will keep you out late. Should the lights not be working properly, fix them before you go.

Starting Your Engine

Check enclosed spaces, including the cabin and engine compartment, for gas fumes. Even when you don't smell fumes, run your blower for 4 to 5 minutes before starting your engine. (It is not necessary to vent fumes from a diesel engine, since those fumes are much less combustible.) You are ready now to start your engine.

After you start your engine, allow time for it to warm up. This will prevent stalling as you shift

Figure **4-20.** The telltale cooling water streams coming from these idling outboard motors show that the cooling water flow is normal. (PHOTO BY BOB DENNIS)

into gear to leave the pier. Avoid excessive idling, however, since the engine's lubrication is usually poorest while idling.

While waiting, check the telltale of your outboard motor to confirm cooling water flow. The *telltale* (also called the tracer) is a jet of cooling water that sprays from a relief valve under the outboard's powerhead (Figure 4-20). Most of the cooling water is exhausted through the propeller hub or a nearby underwater valve, but a good spray from the telltale indicates that the cooling system is working normally. If the telltale is *not* spraying, the problem may be nothing more than a blockage in the telltale orifice. Try working the end of a paper clip into the orifice; if the spray resumes, all is well.

If your motor lacks a telltale but the cooling water exits through the exhaust, check to see that it is flowing freely. For any engine, keep an eye on the temperature gauge to see that the engine is not overheating.

If your outboard motor has a warning signal, heed it and immediately shut down your engine upon hearing it. Then check the water intake. Floating plastic debris is a frequent source of intake problems. If you have a stern drive or an outboard, shut off the engine, then raise the motor or the outdrive to see if anything is clogging its intake ports.

Also, while waiting for the engine to warm up, check all gauges to see that everything is functioning properly. Is your alternator charging correctly? Does your voltmeter show problems with your battery? If you have a stern-drive, inboard, or four-stroke outboard engine, do you have enough oil pressure?

Getting Underway

With the engine warm and all gauge readings satisfactory, it is time to get underway. Secure all loose gear about the deck, and after you have cleared the pier, take in all fenders.

Before casting off, pay special attention to the direction and strength of the wind and water current. You will need to work with these as you leave and when you return. Also, note all hazards and obstructions in the area.

To cast off, untie all lines not needed in maneuvering away from the pier, and bring aboard those you will take with you. Stow them where they are readily available and where they will not be a hazard. Some skippers leave their lines at the pier so they will be there to tie up with when they return. Take at least a bow and a stern line with you. You may want to stop for fuel or for lunch, and you will need them at that time.

Figure 4-21 shows lines that will safely moor your boat to a pier or a seawall. If you have tied these lines with appropriate knots, they will be easy to untie and cast off. The best knots for mooring purposes are clove hitches, half hitches, and belaying to a cleat (see Chapter 11).

As you leave the dock, move at idle speed. Most marinas have a 5-knot or 5-mile-per-hour speed limit. You are liable for any damage caused by your wake or wash, and may also be cited for negligent operation.

In open water, avoid cruising at top engine speed. Top speed is hard on an engine and can be dangerous. Many boats become unstable at top

BEFORE YOU GO

A "pre-underway" checklist will ensure that your boat's systems are running smoothly before you go. Don't leave the dock only to discover that your steering doesn't work. Take the time to start the engine(s) and check the steering and gears, cooling water flow, oil, electrical systems, and through-hull fittings. Like a pilot making pre-flight checks, you should inspect your boat and its systems before every trip. Brief your passengers, too, as discussed in the accompanying text.

Routine maintenance of your boat and systems will save time and money on repairs later. See Appendix I for a sample preventive maintenance checklist you can modify for your boat.

speeds, and serious—even fatal—accidents may result. Vessels that are particularly unstable at top speeds include those with deep-V hulls, those with single-cable steering, and those that are overpowered. Bass boats operated at high speeds should be equipped with dual-cable steering to reduce the amount of play inherent in a single-cable system.

As a vessel's speed increases, the amount of its hull surface in contact with the water decreases. The less hull contact there is, the less control you have over the vessel. If you feel your boat becoming unstable, immediately slow down, lower your outdrive or outboard farther into the water (i.e., toward the transom), and/or lower your boat's trim tabs, if present. *Trim tabs*, also known as flaps, are a pair of hinged plates mounted on either side of the transom's bottom edge. In the raised, horizontal position, they have little effect on trim, but when lowered they lift the stern and force the bow down (Figures 4-22, 4-23, and 4-24). The tabs are usually controlled hydraulically by means of rocker switches mounted at the helm, so that they can be adjusted underway. They can also be adjusted independently, so that you can lower the flap on the side of the boat that's heeling into a crosswind or due to uneven weight distribution (Figure 4-25).

No Wind/Current

When there is no current and the wind is not strong, the easiest way to leave a pier in a boat less than 30 feet long is to push off from it. Once your boat is far enough away from the pier, you can proceed in forward or reverse gear.

If you try to leave the pier merely by powering forward without pushing off first, you may find

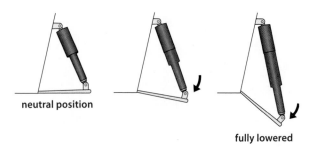

Figure **4-22. Left to right:** Trim tab adjustments. In their neutral, raised position, trim tabs have little impact on boat trim, but when fully lowered they lift the stern and force the bow down.

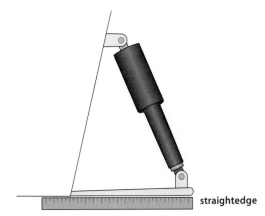

Figure **4-23.** Checking a trim tab with a straightedge. The tab should align with the hull when the indicator dial at the helm position reads zero.

yourself bumping along its entire length. Remember that when you turn away from the pier while moving forward, your stern swings into the pier.

A simple way to leave a dock is by backing out. Turn the outboard or stern-drive lower unit in the direction you want the stern to move, then back out slowly. Once you are clear, go forward. (This technique also works for twin-screw inboards.)

Wind and Current

Wind and current have different effects on different boats. Using the following generalizations, experiment to gauge their impacts on your boat.

Deep-draft boats with comparatively low above-the-water profiles are less affected by wind than by current. There is less boat above the water upon which wind can act, and more boat in the water on which current can act.

Generally, the bow of a powerboat is higher than its stern and is considerably lighter. Thus, the

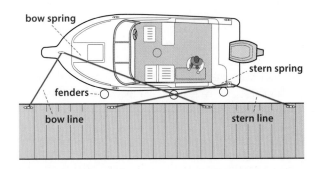

Figure **4-21.** A typical dockline configuration.

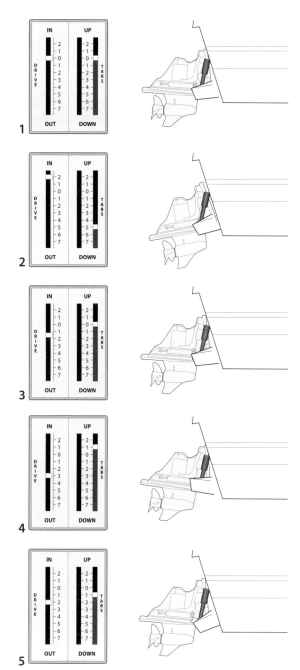

Figure **4-24.** The use of drive trim and trim tabs in tandem to control the trim of a stern-drive boat. **1. Zeroing in:** To create a reference point, use a straightedge such as a yardstick to line up the tabs and drive so they are parallel with the bottom. **2. Getting on plane:** To get on plane faster, use the drive and tabs to raise the stern and keep the bow down. **3. 20–30 knots (smooth water):** The tabs are now aligned with the bottom, and the drive is up. **4. 50 knots or more (smooth water):** The tabs are lifted out of the water stream and the drive is trimmed up to a point just before the prop ventilates. **5. 50 knots or more (rough water):** To keep more of the boat in contact with the water for a smoother ride, bring the drive down from its maximum position and lower the tabs slightly. (REPRINTED WITH PERMISSION FROM *FAST POWERBOAT SEAMANSHIP* BY DAG PIKE)

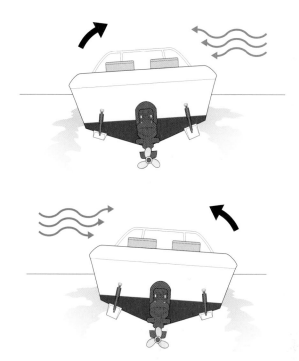

Figure **4-25.** Trim tabs can be adjusted individually to counter the tendency of a boat to lean into a strong crosswind from starboard (top) or port (bottom).

bow almost always turns away from the wind. This leaves the stern, with its lower freeboard, pointed toward the wind and waves when the boat is not anchored by the bow.

Wind/Current Off the Pier

When the wind or current (whichever predominates) is coming from the direction of the pier (Figure 4-26), getting underway is simple. Cast off all lines and let the current or wind carry you far enough away from the pier to allow safe maneuvering.

Wind/Current On the Pier

When the wind or current is pushing you toward the pier, the problem is more difficult. If there are no boats behind you and your boat has a stern-drive or outboard engine, it is easiest to back away. With all lines cast off, turn your helm away from the pier and back out slowly. When you are far enough away from the pier, you can turn and go forward.

If there is insufficient room behind you for that maneuver, however, you may need to perform an additional step (Figure 4-27). In this case, use your bow line to assist in pulling the stern away from the pier. Fasten one end to your bow and pass the line

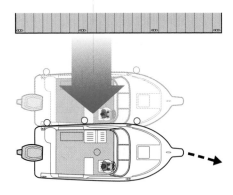

Figure **4-26.** Leaving a dock with the wind blowing off the pier.

once around a **bollard** (post) or a **cleat** on the pier. Bring the other end of the line back to the boat and make one or two simple turns around the bow cleat. Now turn your helm away from the pier and back out slowly. The stern will swing out while the bow line prevents you from backing down on your neighbors. You can then straighten your helm, retrieve your line, and back out.

Alternatively, power forward gently against your bow spring line with your helm turned toward the dock (Figure 4-28). The spring line will prevent forward movement while your stern swings out. When your stern has swung sufficiently, retrieve your spring line and back clear. (This method also works with an inboard engine.)

Wind/Current On the Bow

Leaving a pier with the wind or current on the bow is simple. Push the bow away from the pier and go

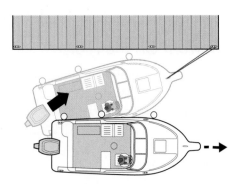

Figure **4-27.** Backing against a bow line enables you to kick the stern away from the pier without backing down on the boat behind you. Loop the bow line around the bollard or cleat on the dock so that you can recover it from the boat as you back away from the pier.

forward at idle speed. The wind or current will swing your bow out and you can go straight forward. This works even in close quarters.

In very tight conditions, a stern spring line can be used to prevent backward movement of the boat as the bow swings out (Figure 4-29). Run a temporary line from the boat's stern cleat around a pier cleat or piling and back to your boat. Secure it with one or two simple turns around the stern cleat. In this way, you can easily retrieve your line after the boat is free of the pier—but be sure to get it back aboard quickly after you release one end before it wraps itself around your prop.

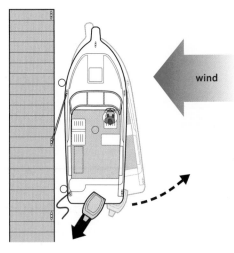

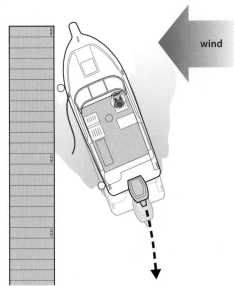

Figure **4-28.** Another way to kick the stern away from a pier is by powering ahead against a bow spring line with the propeller discharge (or rudder) turned toward the pier (top). Once the stern is sufficiently clear, you can back away from the pier, recovering the spring line as you go (bottom).

Wind/Current On the Stern

Having the wind or current on your stern is only a little trickier. If you are not in close quarters, simply push away from the pier and go slowly forward or back until you're clear. In close quarters, you can use a bow spring line to temporarily secure the bow while pulling the stern out with the propellers. Run the line back from a bow cleat and around a cleat or piling on the pier, then back to the bow, making one or two wraps on the bow cleat. Turn the wheel away from the pier and back out the boat's stern as in Figure 4-27. When the boat is clear, retrieve the temporary bow spring. Alternatively, turn the wheel *toward* the pier and power gently *ahead* against the bow spring until the stern swings out (as in Figure 4-28), then shift into reverse to back clear. (This latter technique also works with an inboard boat.)

Turning in a Narrow Channel

You may find it necessary to turn 180° in a channel that is too narrow for your boat's turning radius. A twin-screw boat will have no problem, nor is this maneuver much of a problem for an outboard or stern-drive boat when the wind is on the bow. In this case, simply hug one side of the channel and make a sharp turn toward the other side (Figure

4-30) while reducing your engine speed and shifting to neutral. The wind will bring the bow around and you will be on your way.

If the channel is too narrow for a complete turn, start the turn as in Figure 4-30, but when your boat approaches the far side of the channel, shift into neutral while you turn the helm all the way in the opposite direction, then shift into reverse. Now apply power to back up while pulling the stern in the desired direction. When you once more approach the original side of the channel, shift into neutral and turn the helm the opposite way again, then go forward again to complete the turn (Figure 4-31).

Things get a little trickier when the wind is blowing on your stern in a narrow channel. When your boat turns sideways, the wind will bear directly on one side, and this will cause your boat to resist completing a full turn (Figure 4-32). Also, the boat will continue to be blown up the channel. In this case, it is advisable to hug one side of the channel, then shift into reverse, turn your wheel toward the far side of the channel, and apply throttle so as to drive your stern backward toward the far side (Figure 4-33). After crossing the channel, reverse the helm again and power forward. In a very narrow channel such as a marina approach, it may be necessary to repeat this procedure several times to complete the full turn.

When the wind is strong and blowing from your stern, you may not be able to turn even by backing. In this case, lower your anchor. The wind will cause you to fall back on the anchor, bringing your bow into the wind. Now as you head into the wind, retrieve your anchor line and anchor. This maneuver requires quick action by the person tending the anchor and should be used only in extreme cases.

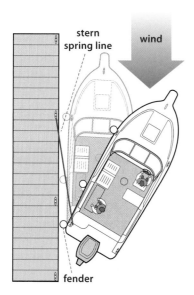

Figure **4-29.** Powering astern against a stern spring line will kick out the bow. You can then leave the dock in forward gear. This technique is useful when the wind or current is on your bow as well as when the wind is blowing toward the dock.

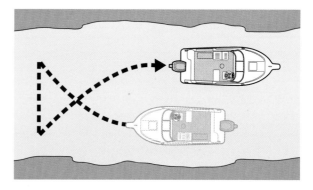

Figure **4-30.** Turning a boat in a narrow channel.

Watch Your Wake!

A variety of speed signs are posted by state, county, and municipal authorities (Figure 4-34), and you have the responsibility of knowing the signs in your area. The terminology varies. The slowest zone may be marked "idle speed zone" or "no wake zone," or it may specify a top speed. This is often defined as the slowest speed you can possibly go

and still maintain steerage, sometimes referred to as clutch speed.

The intermediate zone may be called a "slow speed zone" or "no damaging wake zone." This may be defined as the maximum speed where the boat remains level, or a boat speed that will produce a wake no larger than a certain height.

A planing vessel goes through three stages as it increases its speed (Figure 4-35). At slow speeds, it is a displacement boat, but as it accelerates, its stern sinks and its bow rises. When this happens, you cannot see the water immediately in front of you, and a

Figure **4-31.** A stern-drive boat making a controlled turn in a narrow channel. (PHOTOS BY BOB DENNIS)

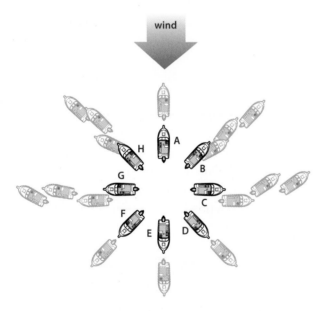

Figure **4-32.** The influence of wind on a boat powering ahead. Boat A will of course be slowed somewhat, and any turn to port or starboard will be exaggerated when the wind begins to push on one side or the other of the bow. Boats B and H will have their bows pushed away from the wind, a tendency that must be countered with steering. This is likewise true of boats C and G. Boats D, E, and F are least affected. (ADAPTED WITH PERMISSION FROM *GETTING STARTED IN POWERBOATING* BY BOB ARMSTRONG)

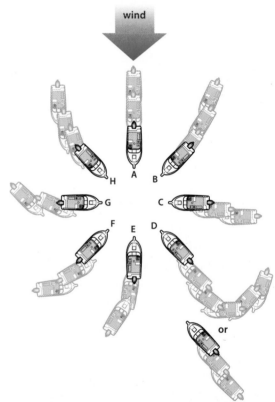

Figure **4-33.** The influence of wind on a boat going astern. We'll assume that the boat has a right-handed propeller, and therefore tends to turn toward port when backing in an absence of wind. Since most boats will swing their bows away from the wind if left unattended, boat A will back straight into a fresh breeze even if it backs to port in the absence of wind. Boats E, F, G, and H, on the other hand, will veer to port in an exaggerated fashion due to the wind on their bows. Boats B, C, and D can be made to back to starboard in a strong breeze even if they refuse to do so at other times, or they can be backed straight, albeit with offset as shown. These effects are most pronounced for single-screw inboard boats, but even a twin-screw boat or a properly trimmed stern-drive or outboard boat will tend to swing its stern into the wind when backing upwind as in boats A, B, and H. (ADAPTED WITH PERMISSION FROM *GETTING STARTED IN POWERBOATING* BY BOB ARMSTRONG)

Figure 4-34. A speed limit and no-wake sign at a marina entrance. (PHOTO BY BOB DENNIS)

large wake follows your boat as water rushes in to fill the "hole" made by your squatting stern.

In this stage, your boat is dangerous to other boats and to property and is also most costly to operate. Its wake can rock other boats and swamp smaller ones, and people in nearby vessels may fall and injure themselves or even be knocked overboard. Your wake can damage seawalls by undercutting them and harm immature sea life in nearby wetlands. It is advisable to run your boat slower or faster than this intermediate speed when there are no speed restrictions. When there are, slow down enough to avoid this second stage (Figure 4-36).

Eventually, as you increase your power, a planing boat rides up over its bow wave and gets on plane. When this happens, both its bow and its fuel consumption drop, and the boat again feels comfortable. There is still a wake, but it is lower than the second-stage wake. When you pass other people, stay far enough away that your wake does not disturb them. Should you be unable to avoid other boats, slow down until you are off plane and back on a level keel—i.e., below the second stage of the speed curve.

As a planing vessel slows down, it passes through the above stages in reverse order. The hull usually settles quickly once you reduce power, stopping in a relatively short distance. In fact, you must avoid slowing down too quickly, or your wake will overtake your boat and may even roll in over the transom, swamping the boat.

Man Overboard

Underway, there is always a risk that someone will fall overboard. That's one of the reasons you wear a PFD. When someone does go overboard, every moment is important, and you and your crew

Figure 4-35. Top to bottom: A powerboat traveling at slow speed, getting up on plane (note squatting stern and bigger wake), and planing (level keel, smaller wake). (PHOTOS BY BOB DENNIS)

should therefore rehearse ahead of time how to react. If you have guests aboard, explain your procedures to them before you go.

The actual recovery of a person from the water requires the skipper to exercise extreme care. The object is to recover the person in the water as quickly as possible while avoiding undue risk to the crew on board. In short, don't make a bad situation even worse.

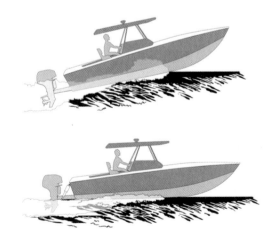

Figure 4-36. Trim tabs can keep a boat on plane at lower speeds. The top boat is squatting dangerously, creating a large wake and running the risk of submerging the bracket-mounted outboard or even taking a wave over the transom. The bottom boat, with trim tabs deployed, is traveling at the same speed but in much better trim. (COURTESY LENCO MARINE)

Sound the Alarm

What is done in the first moments after someone falls overboard may well determine the success or failure of the recovery. The first person to realize that someone has fallen overboard should immediately shout an alarm and point to location of the victim. You should shout loudly and indicate on which side of the boat the person fell. For example, yell "Man overboard, port side!" and keep shouting until the skipper hears and understands.

The skipper should immediately get the engine or engines into neutral and assign someone to keep the victim constantly in sight. If you have a GPS, punch in the coordinates of the accident location; most GPS receivers have a man overboard (MOB) button for just this purpose.

If your boat has a life ring buoy or similar device assigned for this purpose—as it certainly should—throw it to the victim, but wait until there is a reasonable expectation of the victim reaching the life buoy. If the boat has moved out of throwing range from the victim, you will have to get back to the victim as quickly as possible (see below). It is advisable to tie a **polypropylene** retrieval line to the life buoy, because polypropylene floats (Figure 4-37). The person in the water can then either grab the line or the buoy, at which point your crew should

MAN-OVERBOARD PROCEDURES

1. Instruct crew and passengers to:

   A. Keep a close watch for people falling overboard. (A buddy system works well, especially with small children.)

   B. If someone does fall overboard, announce in a loud voice, "MAN [or CREW] OVERBOARD!" point to the MOB, and do nothing except watch the MOB, pointing continuously, while the captain turns the boat and returns to the MOB.

   C. While the boat is returning to the MOB, prepare a throwable PFD and line that should be available for just this circumstance. As soon as the MOB is close enough (or, even better, before he or she is too far away), throw the PFD or buoy close enough for the MOB to grasp.

2. Have an MOB recovery plan for your boat, and practice its implementation.

pull gently but firmly on the line to pull the person toward the boat. If a life ring or buoy is not immediately available, however, throw anything that floats.

Returning to the Victim

If your boat travels well past the person overboard before you can get it stopped, your first priority is to get back to the victim. After making absolutely certain that the victim is nowhere near your propeller or propellers, make a short, hard turn to return to him or her, following the instructions and the pointing finger of the person you have assigned to keep the victim in constant sight. If you have lost visual contact, return to the MOB coordinates you should have punched into your GPS. If the victim is not located after a short search, make a Mayday call to the Coast Guard on Channel 16, and brief them on the situation.

As you approach the victim, do so very slowly and with your bow pointing directly into the wind, waves, or current, whichever is predominant. Throw a life ring or anything that floats as soon as the victim can reasonably reach the flotation aid or its line. Your final approach should be very slow, and be sure to turn off your engine. Even in neutral, propellers may continue to spin and are dangerous. A propeller can cause serious injury and/or death to anyone in the water. Because of this, turn off the engine whenever someone is in the water.

If the victim cannot grab the line or can't keep his or her head above water, make every attempt to recover the person from aboard the boat before allowing someone to go overboard to assist. Anyone who does go into the water to assist should be trained in rescue techniques and should be wearing a PFD with a lifeline. It is common for an MOB to panic and try to climb on top of the rescuer, increasing the chance that they will both drown. The boat captain has the responsibility to weigh the risks of every decision and to prevent an emotional crew from taking unwise actions.

Figure **4-37.** Throwable PFDs. Ideally, the attached retrieval line should be polypropylene.

Retrieving the Victim

Retrieving someone from the water, even someone who can help him- or herself, is difficult when there is no boarding ladder or special device to assist, especially when your boat's freeboard is higher than about 12 inches. If the victim cannot assist his own recovery, there is a good chance that even strong people aboard the boat may not be able to get him aboard.

If your boat is very small, it is usually advisable to recover a person over the bow or stern to keep from capsizing. On larger boats, the stern is the best recovery point because the victim can grab the outboard or outdrive for assistance, using it as a makeshift ladder. When a boarding ladder is available, it can be deployed anywhere, although the stern is the most common location. A secured loop of line extending about 2 feet below the waterline can be used as a "step" to assist a person who has the ability to use it.

If the victim is wearing or can put on a PFD, the recovery crew can try dunking him just before pulling him up. The inertia from bobbing up after being dunked will assist in the recovery. The victim should be facing the boat so that if the initial recovery attempt gets him or her only partway on board, he or she can be held by the torso until the crew can get a new purchase on the victim's legs or belt.

If this fails, turn the victim's back toward the boat and attach a line around his chest and under his armpits, with both parts of the line leading up over his back to the crew on deck to assist in the pulling action (Figure 4-38). The natural roll of the boat may also assist the recovery. Failing this, the only option may be to secure the person so that his or her head is above water, and await additional aid.

Larger sailboats have the advantage of having winches aboard, and can use the boom as a lift point. A *preventer* (a line from the boom to a cleat, toe rail, or other attachment point) should be used to lock the boom in a stationary overboard position.

Propeller Safety

Man overboard accidents have a high potential of leading to propeller strikes; these are extremely harmful and often life threatening. Following some

Figure **4-38.** Using a line under the arms to help get a person back on board.

commonsense rules will help avoid these accidents: never start a boat with the engine in gear; don't allow anyone to ride on a gunwale, transom, or bow; insist that everyone in the boat is seated properly; appoint a lookout whose sole job is to watch for anyone who is not positioned safely and to sound an alarm if someone falls overboard; be on the alert for people in the water, especially when you're in areas where swimmers may be present. As a boat operator, you should investigate some of the new technologies for preventing propeller strikes: guards that prevent contact with a propeller, interlocks that automatically turn off the engine to prevent a strike, and wireless sensors should all be considered.

Docking

Docking a boat can be a source of pride or embarrassment. Some skippers approach a pier at breakneck speed and throw their engines into reverse at the last moment. If they don't go into the pier, they pull alongside just in time to be pounded against the pilings by their own wakes.

Don't be a hot rodder. Make your approach cautiously and slowly. All you need is enough speed to steer your boat. A slow approach doesn't look as spectacular, but it is better seamanship. It is also good seamanship to have fenders, docking lines, a heaving line, and at least one long line ready in advance of docking.

Given a choice, approach a pier or mooring with your bow headed into the wind or the current, whichever is the dominant influence. It is harder to make the boat stop where you want it to when you are heading downwind or downstream. Downwind docking requires more skill than docking into the wind.

Plan your approach carefully. A bad approach can cause your boat to slam into the wharf or another boat, with costly results. Leave yourself an escape route as you make your approach, and if you see a problem developing—such as a gust of wind, a misjudged angle, a swinging boat, or an inattentive boater invading your path—just start over. It is much better seamanship to bail out and try again than to persist in a bad, perhaps even dangerous, approach. Prudent skippers try to foresee and prevent problems before they happen.

Docking with No Wind or Current

In the absence of wind and current, an approach angle of about 20° is ideal (Figure 4-39). Simply bring your bow slowly into the wharf, pier, or float, and just before touching, turn parallel with the dock and reverse your engine or engines to stop the boat. Your fenders should be in place, and you should have your bow and stern lines ready to deploy, their inboard ends secured to the boat's bow and stern cleats. Have your crew *step*—not leap— onto the dock with docklines in hand.

If your boat is a single-engine inboard with a right-handed prop, a port-side-to landing is ideal. That way, when you put the engine in reverse, the propeller's side thrust (sometimes called propeller walk) will nudge the stern into—rather than away from—the dock.

Wind Blowing Off the Pier

When the wind is blowing off the pier toward you, as in Figure 4-40, head into it at a steeper-than-normal angle. The stronger the wind, the greater will be the angle of your approach. In a very strong wind, your approach may even have to be straight in or perpendicular to the pier.

When close to the pier, send the bow line ashore and tie it off. Then put your helm hard over toward the pier and reverse your engine slowly. Backing against the bow line will bring your stern around to the pier. Place a fender between the pier and your boat as you reverse.

As an alternative, after you have a bow line secured, send a stern line ashore and let the line handler on the dock warp in your stern. This only works when you can throw the stern line to a waiting line handler, however. You do not want an anxious crew jumping 2 to 3 feet from the deck to the pier to secure the boat.

Figure **4-39.** Docking on a calm day with no current. The approach is made at an angle of roughly 20° with the dock face. Fenders are in place, and crewmembers have the bow and stern lines ready. (PHOTO BY BOB DENNIS)

Yet another alternative is especially useful for a single-engine inboard boat. In this variation, when you're close to or nudging the pier, send a bow spring line rather than a bow line ashore to be secured near the aft end of the available dock space. Then power gently forward against the spring with your helm hard over away from the dock. This should cause your stern to swing into the dock.

Wind Blowing On the Pier

When the wind is blowing toward the pier, approach as you would in the absence of wind and current but turn parallel with the dock farther out than usual (Figure 4-41). Then simply let the wind blow you in. Since the bow will fall off more quickly than the stern, turn your helm away from the pier. Then, should it be necessary, ease your boat forward to bring the stern in.

Always have fenders deployed in advance to cushion the impact of a landing. When the wind is strong, the impact may be considerable. No one should **EVER** use their arms or legs to fend off as a boat approaches the pier. Arms and legs have been broken or even crushed in this manner. A heavy boat, even when moving slowly, carries a lot of momentum and is difficult to stop.

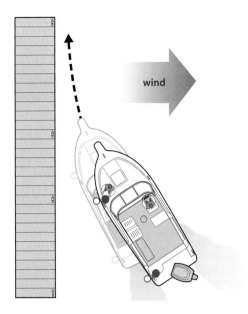

Figure 4-40. With the wind blowing off the dock, this boat approaches at a steeper-than-normal angle before turning more parallel with the dock face at the last moment. The stronger the wind, the steeper the approach angle must be, and the more critical it becomes to get the bow line made fast quickly. Then you can back against the bow line to bring the stern in.

Mooring to a Permanent Anchor

Mooring buoys fasten to permanent anchors sunk deeply into the bottom (Figure 4-42). You will find

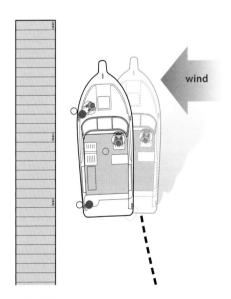

Figure 4-41. When the wind is blowing toward the dock, make your approach to an imaginary dock a few feet seaward of the real dock, then let the wind blow you in.

them near yacht clubs and in some harbors, where they have been placed for the convenience of boaters. In the Florida Keys, you can find them near favorite diving spots so that you can tie up to them instead of anchoring on a coral reef and damaging it.

Mooring buoys are the only ones boaters may tie up to legally. Mooring to any aids to navigation, including buoys, is illegal. Many mooring buoys are privately owned, so get permission before you use them.

As you approach a buoy, remember that some boats are more sensitive to wind while others are more sensitive to current. Approach the buoy against the stronger force, wind or current. When other boats are moored in the vicinity, see how they are heading and then adjust your approach to parallel them. Shift into neutral when you see that you have enough forward momentum to reach the buoy.

There should be a pickup float attached to the buoy (or to the chain beneath it) by a long rope, or *pendant*. Have your crew snag the pickup float and bring it aboard. (Sometimes the float will have a wand to facilitate pickup; other times, you will have to snag it with a boathook—Figure 4-43.) Secure the pendant to your *bitt* (a post on the foredeck) or a bow cleat. After you have tied to the pendant, stop your engine and let your boat drift back.

If you misjudge your approach, simply continue around, line up your approach once more, and try again. This is better seamanship than trying to back down to the buoy.

Some boaters moor both forward and aft, or they might moor forward and anchor aft. Both these practices are discouraged and could cause your boat to swamp or capsize as tides and winds change.

Leaving a mooring is easier than leaving a dock. About the only problem is keeping the pendant out of your prop. You can do this by backing up slowly and dropping the pendant only when there is no longer any danger that it will foul the prop.

Anchoring

Every skipper should master the art of anchoring. You need this ability not just for protection, but for the enjoyment of boating.

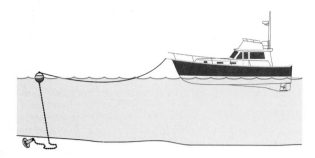

Figure **4-42.** A typical mooring rig.

Figure **4-43.** A crewmember on a cabin cruiser using a boathook to pick up a mooring. (PHOTO BY BOB DENNIS)

Equipment

Anchoring equipment is called *ground tackle*. The kind of ground tackle a boat should carry depends on several factors, including the type, weight, and length of your vessel. Also important are the characteristics of the bottom sediment and the depth of the water in which you will anchor, as well as the strengths of the wind and current. To be adequate, your ground tackle must hold your boat securely under the most adverse conditions.

Anchor Rode

The *rode* of an anchor is its line and chain. An effective combination consists of 4 to 6 feet of heavy chain, a shackle, a thimble, and a nylon line (Figure 4-44). The chain helps the rode lie flat on the bottom, thus enabling the anchor to dig in. It also protects the line against chafing on rocky bottoms.

The *shackle* is a U-shaped piece of hardware, commonly made of galvanized steel, with a pin or bolt across its open end. It connects the chain to the line. Secure the pin or bolt with a length of wire so it won't work loose, causing you to lose your anchor.

The *thimble* is a horse collar–shaped metal or plastic device that is inserted in the eye splice at the end of the anchor line. Its outer surface has a

shallow, U-shaped cross section so that the eye splice will not slip off it. The thimble keeps the eye splice from chafing on the shackle.

Nylon makes an excellent anchor line because of its elasticity, which eases the shock of the boat's movements on the anchor. The anchor chain serves the same purpose. As your boat surges, the chain rises and falls, thus easing the strain on the anchor.

Types of Anchors

There are several types of anchors, and the choice of one over another depends mainly on the type of bottom in which you will anchor (Figure 4-45). Some have greater holding power than others.

DANFORTH/FLUKE. The most popular anchor for recreational craft is the Danforth (Figure 4-46). This is a lightweight anchor with long, narrow, twin flukes that pivot about the stock and dig into the bottom when the anchor is pulled by the rode. A Danforth anchor is of little use on a grassy bottom, however, because the flukes slide across the grass rather than digging in. The anchor works well in mud and sand but may get hung up on a rocky bottom.

To attach a **trip line** to a Danforth, drill a hole in the crown, tie one end of the line there, and place a small buoy on the surface end of the line. If the flukes snag on a cable or rock, you can retrieve the anchor with this line.

Alternatively, you can shackle the anchor chain itself to a hole in the crown, then lash it to the anchor ring with a relatively weak line. If the anchor hangs up, tie off the anchor rode to a cleat

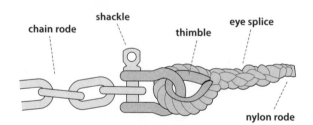

Figure **4-44.** A combination of chain and nylon rode is a popular choice for anchor ground tackle. The chain at the anchor end of the rode resists chafe on the bottom and provides a more nearly horizontal lead from the anchor, enabling the anchor to dig into the bottom more firmly. The nylon rode acts as a shock absorber and is lighter and easier to handle than chain. The connection between the two is best made with a shackle through a thimbled eye splice in the nylon rode, with the thimble protecting the nylon from chafe.

or bitt and power ahead slowly, being careful not to foul the line in your prop. When you have gone far enough, the line fastening the anchor chain to the ring will break. Going farther forward will usually pull the anchor loose.

In one modified Danforth design, the anchor has a slotted shank containing a movable ring to which the anchor chain attaches. If the anchor hangs up, running back across it with a slack rode will usually pull the ring down to the crown, and a slight pull will then free it.

Anchoring with this modified Danforth requires some care. As you lower the anchor, keep the rode taut, and when the anchor hits bottom, back the boat down while keeping slight pressure on the rode until the anchor digs in. If you don't follow this procedure, the ring may slide to the crown and cause the anchor to skip across the bottom instead of digging in.

MUSHROOM ANCHOR. A mushroom anchor is stockless (Figure 4-47) and has a cast-iron bowl at the end of its shank. In large sizes, it is used for permanent moorings. Mushroom anchors gradually dig deeply into a mud bottom, and when embedded, they have tremendous holding power. They do not, however, provide the instant holding power of other anchor types, and are therefore less appropriate for anchoring than for mooring. Small mushroom anchors are used by recreational fishermen when angling, but should not be used to secure a boat left unattended. They do not work well in grassy and rocky bottoms.

GRAPNEL. A grapnel anchor has a straight shank with four or five curved, claw-like arms and no stock

(Figure 4-48). This anchor lacks the strength for regular use on a boat of any size, but on a small boat you can use it to anchor above rocks, the idea being to hook one or more of the arms under a rock. It's a good idea to tie a buoyed trip line to one of the arms at the crown, so that you can retrieve the anchor when (not if) it hangs up under a rock.

NORTHILL ANCHOR. The Northill anchor has a stock at its crown instead of its head, and its arm is at a right angle to its shank. The angle of its broad flukes assures a quick bite and penetration, and the bills' sharp points cause the anchor to dig into the bottom as soon as there is a pull on the anchor line. This is a difficult design to store and carry on board, however, and is not commonly used.

PLOW. The plow anchor, a British design (Figure 4-49), takes its name from the shape of its fluke, which resembles a plow. The fluke digs in quickly and deeply in response to a pull on the anchor line. This is an efficient anchor but clumsy to handle and

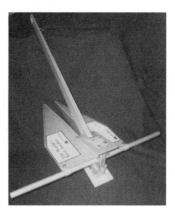

Figure **4-46.** A Danforth anchor.

Figure **4-47.** Small mushroom anchors like this one are sometimes used by anglers, but larger mushrooms are used mainly for permanent moorings, as they must sink into the sediment before they are effective.

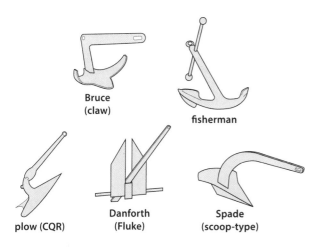

Bruce (claw)

fisherman

plow (CQR)

Danforth (Fluke)

Spade (scoop-type)

Figure **4-45.** The most common anchor types.

stow, and is used most often on large boats, where it stows outboard, on an anchor platform at the bow. Plow anchors are marketed under various names, including CQR and Delta.

SCOOP-TYPE/SPADE. There is a relatively new anchor that's marketed under different names, including Spade, Sword, Ultra, and Raya, shaped like a shovel with a concave fluke. There is a version of these with a roll-bar on the top, marketed under the names of Buegel, Rocna, Manson Supreme. There is no consensus on whether these various scoop-type designs are superior to other anchor designs such as the plow or Danforth/fluke.

Your Boat's Anchors

Your boat should carry at least two anchors. One anchor may be small and light for easy handling. Use this *lunch hook* in good weather, when anchoring in protected areas, or for short stops while fishing. The second anchor should be larger and heavier for overnight anchoring or for use when the smaller anchor might drag.

Cruisers should consider carrying a third anchor as well, for use in heavy weather. Use this storm anchor in winds of 30 knots (34 miles per hour) or higher.

Marine dealers and some marine catalogs have tables and formulas to guide you in the selection of anchors, chain, and lines appropriate for the size of your vessel.

Anchor Line Scope

An anchor holds best when the pull of its rode is as nearly horizontal as possible. For this reason, holding power increases as you increase the length of the rode (Figure 4-50). The *scope* of an anchor rode is the ratio of its length to the vertical distance from your bow chock to the seabed (i.e., the depth of the water plus the distance from the water surface to the bow chock).

Normally, a scope of 7:1 is adequate for holding a boat. Thus, if the water is 10 feet deep and your bow chock is 4 feet above the water, you need an anchor rode of 98 feet. This means you need a lot of line even for a small boat in calm weather and seas. Remember, too, to account for tidal variations when determining how much scope you will need.

A scope of 5:1 is marginal, and a scope of 3:1 is poor unless the weather is excellent and the bottom is good for anchoring. A 3:1 scope may be enough if you have stopped to eat or to fish and you are not leaving the boat, but you should still watch your anchor at all times with this scope.

When anchoring in heavy weather, you should have a scope of at least 10:1, preferably with a good length of stout chain leading from the anchor. You also should maintain an anchor watch in stormy weather.

Anchoring

The first step in anchoring is to check the nature of the bottom and its depth. If you can't do this visually, look at the chart. It may note the bottom type—whether sand, rocks, clay, or mud. You can also tell the type of bottom and its depth by using a lead (pronounced "led") line, which is simply a light line with depth indicators (frequently bits of cloth sewn into the line at 6-foot, or 1-fathom, intervals) and a weight at its end. The end of the weight will usually be hollowed out, and if you place tallow, wax, chewing gum, or bedding compound in the hollow before "casting the lead," you'll bring up a sample of the bottom when you re-

Figure **4-48.** The grapnel anchor on the bow roller of this dinghy is perfect for a short lunch stop. (COURTESY ZODIAC)

Figure **4-49.** A plow anchor.

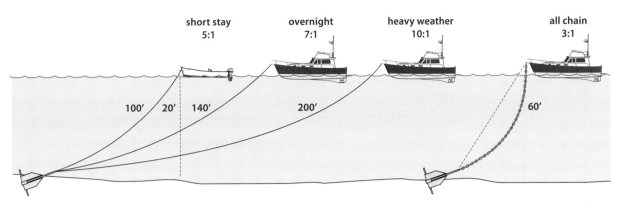

Figure 4-50. Be sure to pay out sufficient scope on your anchor rode. Boats using an all-chain rode can pay out less scope, but all-chain rodes are usually too heavy for small boats to carry.

trieve it. Not many boats carry lead lines in this age of electronic depth sounders, but they remain highly useful tools, and they rarely break!

When anchoring, be certain that you have tied the end of the rode securely to the boat. In larger boats it is usually secured below the deck in the chain locker.

If the anchorage you select is pleasant and well protected—perhaps with convenient access to a town, restaurant, or other shoreside attractions—it also is likely to be popular and therefore crowded. If you arrive late in the day, a first glance may convince you that there is no room left to anchor, and you may be right. Don't be hasty, though. If your boat is small and floats in very little water, you may find a site close to shore that won't interfere with other boats.

Having chosen a site, note the position of nearby boats to determine where your boat will settle after it falls back on its anchor in response to wind and current. Make sure your anchor rode will not cross the rodes of other boats, and that you will not be within uncomfortable swinging distance of nearby boats.

If the bottom is satisfactory and the water is not too deep or shallow, head your boat into the wind or current, moving very slowly toward your chosen site. Go far enough beyond the site to allow for the anchor rode length, then stop your forward movement and have someone lower the anchor (he or she shouldn't drop or throw it), being careful not to stand on or get caught in the rode. If the boat does not drift astern of its own volition, gently reverse the engine to keep the boat on course. After about one-third of the planned scope is paid out, the line should be temporarily secured to determine whether

the anchor is holding. Then the remainder of the rode should be paid out and secured.

An anchor rode should never be tied off to the side or only the stern of your boat. Side or stern anchoring may be convenient but is also dangerous. Large wakes or waves could swamp the boat when you are anchored from the side or stern rather than the bow, and in a current, the stern could be pushed under by the force of the moving water. A secondary anchor from the stern, on the other hand, is sometimes required in very crowded anchorages where there is no room for the boat to swing.

By keeping a hand on the line as it is paid out, you can tell if the anchor has dug in. When it vibrates, the anchor is sliding across the bottom. When it digs in and then skips, or when it just skips, pay out more rode until the anchor digs in firmly. You will feel a definite halt in the drift of the boat when it digs in. When there is a current or a breeze, you will see the bow turn into it. After you have a good bite on your anchor, turn off the engine.

When you have finished anchoring, take sights on two or three stationary objects onshore (Figure 4-51), lining them up with more distant objects behind them. A church steeple rising up behind a red barn, for example, makes a good sight. Should your anchor drag, you can tell by checking these *ranges*. Most GPS receivers also have an anchor alarm feature that notes your anchored position and sounds an alarm if you drift from this location.

Anchors hold best in mud, clay, or sandy mud. While hard sand is good with some anchors, soft, loose sand is poor, and in soft mud your anchor may not hold at all. Rocks can give good holding power but may hold your anchor permanently!

Avoid anchoring in grassy areas and coral reefs, both of which are habitats for immature marine life. If you anchor in seagrass, you uproot it, and obviously, you should not damage a coral reef.

Be careful how much line you pay out. If the wind or the tide changes, will you swing into another boat, a buoy, a wharf, or onto the shore? If wind or sea conditions deteriorate, check your position frequently to see that you are not dragging anchor. If you are, let out more line. When this is not practical, *weigh* (raise) anchor and set it again in a better location. Be mindful of the change in direction of a tidal current. When the current reverses, your anchor may become fouled in its own rode or may lose its hold on the bottom.

Should your boat lose power in shallow water or a narrow channel, lower your anchor immediately. It may keep you from going aground.

Weighing Anchor

When ready to depart an anchorage, go through your departure checklist, then start the engine and make sure it is operating properly. Power ahead slowly to a position directly above the anchor, taking up the rode as you proceed. Usually, the anchor will break free of the bottom when you are over it. It can then be raised and stored.

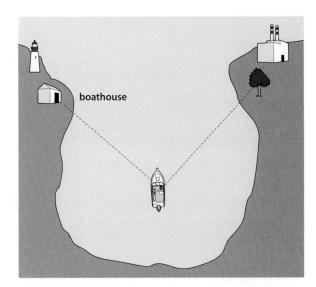

Figure **4-51.** After anchoring, establish ranges onshore such as those shown to keep track of your position. As long as the boathouse remains in front of the lighthouse on one shore, and the tree remains in front of the power plant on the other, this boat has not dragged its anchor.

If the anchor does not break free, it is probably fouled. Take in as much line as possible, and then make the rode fast to a bow bitt or bow cleat and run your boat slowly in circles with the line taut, which will hopefully break out the anchor.

Towing a Skier

Tightrope walkers traversing tall building encounter great risks, but they rarely have serious accidents because they are knowledgeable and they plan accordingly. Water skiers certainly aren't in the same risk category, but the principles of being knowledgeable and acting accordingly are the same. Water skiers rank very high in boating fatalities in the last ten years, so an emphasis on safety is well placed.

Water skiers are exposed to large forces that put the skier and the people surrounding them at risk. For example, a fall at high speed can cause water to enter a body orifice with enough penetration to cause death. Most of the responsibility for safety falls upon the towboat operator. A PWC may be used as a towboat, but the responsibilities are the same. The skier may use other than water skis such as kneeboards or a tube, but the precautions remain the same. The following precautions have been derived from evaluating studies of accidents. Some of these precautions are required by state regulations—check your own state regulations before you head out:

- Assign a second person on board as a skier observer.
- Assure that the skier is wearing a U.S. Coast Guard–approved life jacket. A high-impact jacket is often required.
- Confirm that the operator and skier agree on hand signals (see Figure 4-53).
- Confirm that the towline is at least 60 feet, and that dual towlines are the same length.
- Assure that people and towlines are away from the running propellers. Engine should be off during the dispatch or recovery of the skier.
- The towboat and skier should stay clear of obstructions and areas designated for people; that is, a 100-foot corridor either side of the towboat.

- Anticipate the potential danger from an airborne ski device.
- Always keep the skier in view the entire time that they are in the water.
- Anticipate a PWC towboat being properly rated to tow; that is, 3 people.
- Never ski at night. Some states allow a small leeway to terminate skiing at nightfall.

Heavy Weather

Recreational boating should be a fair-weather activity. The best advice for someone considering going out in a boat in rough weather is, "Don't." Sometimes, though, boaters do get caught out in adverse conditions. Some understanding of the principles of heavy-weather seamanship will be helpful if this happens to you.

Heavy weather, in itself, does not place a small craft in danger. It is comforting to note that a well-found boat operated by a knowledgeable skipper and an able crew is usually equal to the task. Your boat can probably handle adverse conditions better than you can.

Running into a Sea

If you try to power directly into a strong wind and heavy seas, the bow of your boat will plow into the waves instead of lifting over them (Figure 4-54), causing your boat to take a tremendous pounding. Your propeller alternately rises out of the water and falls back in, making your engine load one moment and race wildly the next.

Slow your boat so that the bow can lift with the waves, and don't try to run directly into them. Instead, take them at an angle of about 45°. This will reduce the pounding. Your boat will *pitch* and *roll*—that is, it will go up and down on the long axis and will roll from side to side—but this motion will be easier on your boat and crew than a head-on pounding. Do not let your bow fall off to an angle much beyond 45°, however, because at that point the wind and seas might throw the bow even farther off, causing you to broach. A *broach* is a sudden, unplanned, and unwanted turn that leaves your boat beam-on to the seas, which is dangerous for the reasons explained next.

Running in a Beam Sea

When your desired course is parallel to the wave crests, you'll find yourself running in a *beam sea*. When the seas are high and steep, this is not a course you want to attempt (Figure 4-55). Your boat will roll deeply and uncomfortably, and there's the chance of a wave that is steeper and higher than others rolling your boat sufficiently to capsize it. You can avoid this condition by zigzagging around the steeper crests or by taking the seas at an angle, as described above, rather than beam-to, thus transferring some of the wave-induced motion from rolling to pitching (Figure 4-56).

Figure **4-52.** This water-skier's tow rope is fastened to a towing pylon on the boat. (COURTESY NATIONAL MARINE MANUFACTURERS ASSOCIATION)

| turn | skier in water | back to dock | cut motor |

| slower | faster | speed OK | stop |

| right turn | left turn | skier OK after fall |

Figure **4-53.** Waterskiing hand signals. (COURTESY NATIONAL MARINE MANUFACTURERS ASSOCIATION)

If you cannot make headway under these conditions, it is advisable to *heave-to*, or lie-to. Use enough power to keep your bow into the wind, and adjust your speed so you are making neither headway nor sternway. Commercial fishermen call this tactic *jogging*, and it will give you plenty of time to wonder why you didn't listen more closely to the weather forecast before heading out.

Running in a Following Sea

In a following sea, the waves roll in from astern. When the waves are high and have a short *period* (i.e., when the crests are close together, as happens in shallow waters), following seas are dangerous, in part because most powerboats have more freeboard at the bow than the stern.

When your boat speed exceeds the wave speed, your boat will crest the wave you're overtaking and careen down the front of the wave. This is danger-

Figure 4-54. Running directly into a head sea subjects your boat and your crew to a very rough ride.

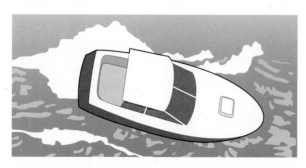

Figure 4-55. On the other hand, taking the seas on the beam will subject your boat to uncomfortable rolling, and may even put it at risk of capsizing if the seas are steep and high enough.

ous in high seas, first because the boat can easily broach on the wave front, and second because it may, upon reaching the trough, bury, or stuff, its bow in the back of the next wave ahead, shipping water over the bow and possibly broaching (Figure 4-57). Running fast in very high seas might even cause the boat to fall off the front of a wave and *pitchpole*, or somersault back over front.

On the other hand, when you travel too slowly in a big following sea, you risk having an overtaking wave roll in over your transom and swamp the boat. Your boat will be especially vulnerable in this attitude if it has a low transom and is overloaded.

If you must run down sea in heavy weather, it's best to travel at the same speed as the waves. In very rough weather, you'll have to speed up when a wave approaches from behind and slow down when your boat is threatening to break through a wave crest and careen down the wave front. This is tricky, tiring work, and you'd probably do better to take the waves at an angle over the bow as described above. Pick a relatively flat spot between waves to turn the boat up sea.

In more moderate conditions, it will be enough when running down sea to limit your boat speed and watch your stern wave to ensure that it stays within safe limits and does not reinforce an approaching wave crest. Counter any *yawing* (unintended course changes caused by wind and sea) by steering and controlling the throttle. When you correct a yaw early, you prevent it from developing into a full-scale broach.

Impaired Visibility

Fog is the most common cause of impaired visibility, but heavy rain, sleet, hail, snow, or dust is also possible. The proper responses are the same for all such conditions.

The first rule for safe boat operation in impaired visibility is, "Don't go." Fog will burn off. Rain, sleet, hail, or snow will stop. Be patient. Being out on the water when the weather closes in puts you in a whole new world that you want to avoid if possible.

Visibility never changes instantly and without warning. Be sensitive to changing conditions. Use the time before the fog or rain closes in to determine your position. If you don't know where you are when the weather closes in, you will not know later.

As the weather closes in, do slow down. Adjust your speed by gauging the distance you can see ahead of you. The Navigation Rules require you to be able to avoid a collision and to travel at a safe speed. It is your responsibility to determine what a safe speed is based on the conditions around you.

The law requires that you always maintain a proper lookout when you are underway, regardless of the weather. The most frequent cause of collisions is a failure to maintain a proper lookout. In poor visibility, post your lookout as far forward as possible. This keeps the lookout as far from the engine noise as possible and makes it easier to hear sounds from other vessels.

In poor visibility, if possible, get clear of channels and shipping lanes. A small boat can frequently operate safely outside the shipping channels; your navigation chart will tell you whether the water depth is sufficient there. If in doubt, drop anchor outside the channel. In the chapters that follow, we'll look at aids to navigation and discuss the navigation rules. Chapter 9 covers navigation in greater depth.

Narrow Inlets

Many rivers and coves connect to the sea by narrow inlets. Although no two are alike, they have a lot in common. Where the tidal range is large, there is usually rapid water flow into or out of the inlet at the height of the flood or ebb tide. These tidal currents often deposit silt and sand in the mouth of an inlet, and the resultant shoals and sandbars shift constantly, which makes it difficult to mark channels with buoys. Seas may break in the mouths of these inlets, especially when waves rolling in from seaward meet an ebb current there. Shoals may also cause unusual currents that run sideways. Many dangerous inlets do not *look* bad until you're actually in them, at which point it may be too late to turn back.

Prudent skippers will research the inlets that they intend to run. Some are known to be benign, and some are a little tricky but manageable with local knowledge and a little forewarning. Some are safe on the flood tide but not on the ebb, and some should be attempted only at high-water slack tide.

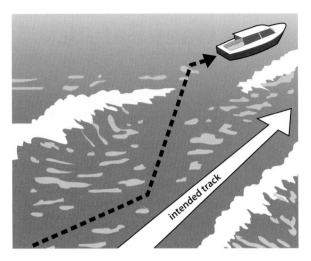

Figure **4-56.** Zigzagging around steep crests and breaking seas is both safer and more comfortable.

Figure **4-57.** Running with a following sea is tricky, tiring work. The boat shown here is careening down the steep front of the wave it has just overtaken, and may bury its bow in the back of the next wave ahead, which could cause it to ship water, broach, or both.

When approaching from seaward, wait for slack or flood tide if possible. Locate the approach channel and make sure everyone aboard is wearing a PFD. Then, if there is a sea running, wait for a set of comparatively small waves, then ride a wave crest in, adjusting your throttle so that you neither outrun the wave nor drop behind it. To exit an inlet, line up your boat in midchannel and point your bow more or less straight into the oncoming waves, playing your throttle so that you have enough power to surmount the crests but not enough to bury your bow in the troughs.

Some inlets are so treacherous that it is prudent to have a local pilot aboard, or to follow the boat of an experienced skipper, or to avoid the inlet altogether.

Small Boat Safety

If judged by the number of accidents and fatalities reported each year, and the limited time that boaters actually spend on the water, boating would seem like a dangerous sport. But boating is exciting, refreshing, and a lot of fun when proper precautions are taken.

Contrary to popular belief, boating accidents do not always occur on large bodies of open water, nor do they always happen to people who consider themselves boaters. The victim of a boating accident is most often a man between the ages of 24 and 34, fishing on a quiet lake on a Saturday afternoon. Often the victim is a hunter. These people may not consider themselves to be boaters, but they should.

People who fish or hunt frequently use small boats of 12 to 14 feet or less in length. Such boats are generally safe but can be unstable and may be dangerous under some circumstances. If you stand up in one, it may capsize. If it is overloaded, it may easily swamp, especially in adverse weather and water conditions.

Although the boat may be unstable, its occupants may stand up and move about to land a fish, shoot a duck, exchange positions in the boat, relieve themselves, or for other reasons. One of them may fall overboard, or their movements may cause the boat to capsize and everyone may end up in the water. If these boaters are not wearing PFDs, they may find themselves in serious trouble.

Many people who drown under such circumstances are good swimmers, but a sudden plunge into cold water is disorienting. Sometimes an injury occurs during the fall—a head is hit on the side of the boat, or a hand is caught in the propeller. These sorts of accidents are always unexpected, so a PFD should be worn at all times. The smaller the boat, the more important it is to observe this rule.

Hunters often overload their boats and fail to get weather checks to learn water and wind conditions. A safe load in favorable weather may not be safe with approaching poor weather, and hunting seasons often coincide with periods of changing weather that may turn suddenly violent.

In a fatal accident that occurred several years ago, two duck hunters launched a small aluminum boat at a ramp in a sheltered cove about an hour before sunrise, when the wind was calm. They carried two shotguns, ammunition, twenty decoys with lead weights, lunches, a thermos of hot coffee, a 50-pound Labrador retriever, two PFDs (which they were not wearing), extra fuel, and a 15-horsepower outboard. Each man weighed about 180 pounds.

Although heavily loaded, the boat was not overloaded for the water and wind conditions in the cove. As the men turned into the river and headed upstream, however, they met a brisk breeze. Since this stretch of the river was short and the wind was blowing across it, surface conditions were fairly calm.

At the first bend in the river, they headed directly into the wind. The combination of the river current and the wind blowing downstream raised considerable spray. Suddenly, they found themselves in a dangerous situation. They turned the boat to return to the cove. Unfortunately, when the boat's beam turned to the waves and the wind, it swamped. One man drowned.

Many other incidents could be cited, but they all teach the same lessons:

- If you move about in a small boat, keep as low as possible; better still, avoid moving about.
- Wear your PFD under all conditions.
- Get a weather report before you launch your boat.
- Keep a weather eye peeled for changing conditions.
- Load your boat with current and anticipated weather conditions in mind, but never overload it.

Running Aground

A soft grounding occurs when a boat runs aground a short distance while going at low speed onto a soft surface of mud or sand. A hard grounding results from grounding a large distance at high speed, or grounding onto a hard rough surface like rocks. The actions and priorities to recover the boat vary according to the conditions—however, there are several critical steps to take:

- Assess and treat any personal injuries.
- Put on life jackets.

- Notify the Coast Guard on your VHF radio, Channel 16. This can be a simple notice of the grounding, or it can be a request for help. Also, hail for assistance from other boaters, either on the VHF or manually.
- Assess whether the hull has been damaged and is leaking. If so, it is most likely safer to remain grounded rather than move the boat off the rocks.
- Assess wind and current to determine strategy for pulling free.
- Consider the effects of the tide.
- Lift the motor drive or tilt your outboard into the "up" position to reduce the draft of your boat's transom.
- Tip sailboats on their side to reduce draft, but make sure all hatches and deck openings are closed tight.
- Rock the boat fore/aft and side to side.
- Remove portable weight to the dinghy, or move crew weight to stern.
- Kedge the anchor by carrying the anchor to deep water and pulling the boat away, either from a dinghy, or by foot, if shallow enough.
- Consider the risk of slingshot recoil from a broken tow line if a winch is employed.

Not all of the conditions encountered when going aground can be addressed here, so expand your skills and knowledge from other sources. The risks of grounding can vary between simple embarrassment to loss of life.

Environmental Concerns

Boating continues to be a popular pastime, and with the ever-increasing number of boats on the water, the small environmental damage caused by each boat is accumulating fast. Also, the public sensitivity arising from major oil spills has resulted in federal and state legislation that imposes heavy penalties for harming the environment. As a boater, it is prudent to be mindful of these environmental risks—and besides, what boater would want to harm the environment that attracts him or her to this activity in the first place?

These are some of the practices that boaters can adopt to reduce pollution and damage to the marine environment:

- Follow channel markers. This assures the safety of your boat, reduces the risk of boat damage from churning shallow bottoms, and leaves bottom-dwelling organisms undisturbed.
- If your boat becomes grounded, try to move into safe water using paddles or by pushing, or wait for a higher tide. Churning your way out is not friendly, and in some cases is not safe.
- Use proper anchoring techniques. This minimizes anchor dragging, thus reducing damage to the sea bottom.
- Maintain good engine performance with regular maintenance checks. This will improve engine longevity and fuel economy. It also reduces the risk of engine failure and will reduce the emission of hydrocarbons.
- Maintain your boat's bottom coating, which improves efficiency and reduces water churning.
- Observe speed limits. This will avoid speed fines and reduce wave action, which in turn reduces shore damage.
- Properly dispose of untreated sewage, plastics, and garbage, as outlined in Appendix A.
- Be careful not to spill fuel or oil during refueling.

Ways to Learn More

Anchoring: A Captain's Quick Guide. Peter Nielsen. Camden, Maine: International Marine, 2007.

Boat Handling Under Power: A Captain's Quick Guide. Bob Sweet. Camden, Maine, International Marine, 2005.

Boating 101: Essential Lessons for Boaters. Roger Siminoff. Camden, Maine: International Marine, 1999.

Boat Maintenance: The Essential Guide to Cleaning, Painting, and Cosmetics. William Burr. Camden, Maine: International Marine, 2000.

Chapman Piloting & Seamanship. 66th ed. Charles B. Husick. New York: Hearst Books, 2009. Chapters 6 and 9.

The Complete Anchoring Handbook: Stay Put on Any Bottom in Any Weather. Alain Poiraud, Achim Ginsberg-Klemmt, and Erica Ginsberg-Klemmt. Camden, Maine: International Marine, 2007.

Confident Powerboating: Mastering Skills and Avoiding Trouble Afloat. Stu Reininger. Camden, Maine: International Marine, 2008.

Fast Powerboat Seamanship: The Complete Guide to Boat Handling, Navigation, and Safety. Dag Pike. Camden, Maine: International Marine, 2004.

Getting Started in Powerboating. 3rd ed. Bob Armstrong. Camden, Maine: International Marine, 2005.

Outboard Engines: Maintenance, Troubleshooting, and Repair. 2nd ed. Edwin Sherman. Camden, Maine: International Marine, 2008.

Powerboat Care and Repair: How to Keep Your Outboard, Sterndrive, or Gas-Inboard Boat Alive and Well. Allen Berrien. Camden, Maine: International Marine, 2003.

Powerboat Handling Illustrated: How to Make Your Boat Do Exactly What You Want It to Do. Bob Sweet. Camden, Maine: International Marine, 2006.

The Practical Encyclopedia of Boating: An A–Z Compendium of Navigation, Seamanship, Boat Maintenance, and Nautical Wisdom. John Vigor. Camden, Maine: International Marine, 2007.

The Practical Mariner's Book of Knowledge: 460 Sea-Tested Rules of Thumb for Almost Every Boating Situation. 2nd ed. John Vigor. Camden, Maine: International Marine, 2013.

The Propeller Handbook: The Complete Reference for Choosing, Installing, and Understanding Boat Propellers. Dave Gerr. Camden, Maine: International Marine, 2001.

Reed's Skipper's Handbook for Sail and Power. 4th ed. Malcolm Pearson. Camden, Maine: International Marine, 2005.

Seamanship Secrets: 185 Tips and Techniques for Better Navigation, Cruise Planning, and Boat Handling Under Power or Sail. John Jamieson. Camden, Maine: International Marine, 2009.

Practice Questions

IMPORTANT BOATING TERMS

In the following exercise, match the words in the column on the left with the definitions in the column on the right. In the blank space to the left of each term, write the letter of the item that best matches it. Do not use an item in the right-hand column more than once.

THE ITEMS

1. _____ propeller size
2. _____ ground tackle
3. _____ bilge
4. _____ headway
5. _____ bollard
6. _____ cavitation
7. _____ bitt
8. _____ shackle
9. _____ yaw
10. _____ pitchpole

THE RESPONSES

a. place where fumes are most likely to accumulate

b. post or piling

c. device to which an anchor line is secured

d. forward motion through water

e. anchoring equipment

f. turn end over end

g. diameter and pitch

h. swing from side to side about a vertical axis

i. rapid boiling of water

j. device for attaching a rode to an anchor

Multiple-Choice Items

In the following items, choose the best response:

4-1. An exhaust blower should be run for 4 minutes before starting an engine to

a. warm up the engine
b. remove carbon dioxide fumes
c. remove fuel vapors
d. remove debris in the bilge

4-2. The propellers of small outboard motors are protected from damage by

a. their warranties
b. shear pins
c. shrouds
d. slip hubs

4-3. Check gasoline fuel lines for leaks

a. during the winter
b. before each use of the boat
c. in the morning
d. every June

4-4. While fueling a boat with a built-in tank

a. close all cabin doors, hatches, and ports before you begin
b. shut off the fuel tank air vent
c. run the blower
d. open all compartments

4-5. After fueling the boat, you should always

a. check for fuel fumes in the engine and tank compartments
b. clean up any spills and put the rags in the bilge
c. wash the deck to remove spilled fuel
d. fill the fuel tank to air vent level

4-6. When you start your outboard motor, check to see that water is coming out of

a. the tattletale
b. the telltale
c. the vent pipe
d. the propeller shaft

4-7. When you refuel a portable tank

a. do it quickly and don't hold up other people at the fueling dock
b. use the best grade of gasoline available
c. close off all compartments
d. do it with the tank on the fueling dock

4-8. When loading your boat, consider

a. sea state and weather
b. the activity you expect to engage in
c. the weight of equipment, fuel, food, and other gear
d. all of the above

4-9. The best way to go through shallow water with a stern drive or outboard is to

a. raise your motor or lower unit slightly and proceed at idle speed
b. lower your motor or lower unit
c. raise your motor or lower unit and increase your speed
d. lower your motor or lower unit and go through at idle speed

4-10. If you tuck your outboard or outdrive in too much, your boat may

a. cavitate
b. be stern-heavy
c. bounce
d. plow

4-11. When viewed from aft, most boat propellers

a. are left-handed
b. are right-handed
c. turn counterclockwise
d. are counterbalanced

4-12. When the pressure on the flat side of a propeller's blades is reduced, the water boils and may damage your propeller. This is called

a. transmission
b. plowing
c. cavitation
d. surging

4-13. An outboard or a stern drive tilts up or down to adjust its

a. steering ability
b. direction of thrust
c. tendency to steer to port or to starboard
d. turning ability

Multiple-Choice Items (continued)

4-14. When leaving a pier in a boat with an outboard or stern-drive engine with a wind or current pushing you toward the pier

a. it is usually easier to back out slowly until you are far enough away from the pier to turn and go forward

b. turn your helm as far away from the pier as possible and go forward

c. release all lines and allow the wind to move the boat

d. run a stern line from your boat around a bollard and back to your boat and then back out

4-15. If you are turning in a narrow channel and have a strong wind on your stern

a. hug the right side of the channel, turn your helm all the way to starboard, and go forward

b. hug the right side of the channel, turn your helm all the way to the opposite shore and back down

c. hug the left side of the channel and go forward

d. hug the left side of the channel, turn your helm all the way to port, and back around

4-16. For normal scope, the length of the anchor rode should be

a. two times the depth of the water

b. three times the depth of the water

c. five times the depth of the water

d. seven times the depth of the water

4-17. To minimize the violent pitching motion when running into a heavy sea, point your bow

a. directly into the waves

b. about 20° to either side of the direction from which the waves are coming

c. about 45° to either side of the direction from which the waves are coming

d. directly away from the direction of the waves

4-18. When caught in severe weather, you should

a. head toward the storm

b. increase speed and run parallel to the waves

c. reduce speed and head for the nearest safe shore

d. tie up to the closest navigational aid

4-19. If your vessel runs aground, you should

a. check for leaks

b. call the Coast Guard

c. gun the engines in reverse

d. check the depth of the water

4-20. The size of a propeller is

a. the diameter of the circle it makes when it turns

b. the theoretical distance it moves forward in one turn

c. its pitch and diameter

d. none of the above

4-21. To improve the efficiency and speed of your outboard or stern drive in smooth water

a. use a high-grade lubricating oil

b. use the highest grade of gasoline available

c. lower your outboard or outdrive

d. raise your outboard or outdrive slightly

4-22. Deep-draft boats are affected most by

a. the wind

b. the size of their engines

c. the current

d. the size of their superstructures

4-23. The primary responsibility for informing crew or passengers about the location and use of safety equipment such as PFDs, fire extinguishers, and docklines belongs to

a. the marina owner

b. USCG personnel

c. the insurance agent

d. the boatowner or operator

chapter 5

Your "Highway" Signs

The objectives of this chapter are to describe:

✔ Aids to navigation (ATONs).

✔ Cautions in the use of ATONs.

✔ The meaning of chart symbols.

✔ The availability of electronic ATONs.

✔ Reference materials that alert you to changes in ATONs.

THE FIRST SAILORS rarely left sight of land, and their only navigational aids were familiar landmarks. Later mariners began taking long voyages out of sight of land with only the sun, stars, and crude instruments to guide them. To this day

Buoy tenders, like *Spar* shown here in Alaska, monitor the position of aids to navigation. (COURTESY U.S. COAST GUARD/SEAMAN JUSTIN HERGERT)

121

we still depend on visible landmarks and points of reference, but we also enjoy many more sophisticated aids to navigation.

An *aid to navigation*, or ATON, is any man-made device designed to help you determine your location on the water and plot a safe course to your destination. Short-range ATONs include *buoys*, *beacons*, *major lights*, *directional* or *sector lights*, *ranges*, *racons*, and *sound signals*. Long-range electronic aids include *satellite beacons* and *GPS*.

ATONs are shown on nautical charts. With a good chart, a knowledge of ATONs, and proper caution, your boating can be safe and enjoyable.

Although they are not ATONs, prominent structures and natural objects—including church spires, radio towers, water tanks, mountain peaks, promontories, and other landmarks—can also help you navigate. To be useful, landmarks must be visible from the water and appear on charts of the area.

All ATONs are protected by law. It is a criminal offense to damage an ATON or hinder its proper operation. Do not alter, deface, destroy, or move an ATON. Never tie up to one, and avoid anchoring so close to one that it is obscured from the sight of passing boaters.

Buoyage Systems

Most ATONs are grouped in *buoyage systems*. The United States uses five principal buoyage systems:

1. U.S. Aids to Navigation System
2. Intracoastal Waterway Marking System (ICWMS)
3. Western Rivers System
4. Uniform State Waterway Marking System (USWMS)
5. Private Aids to Navigation (PATONs)

We'll discuss each in turn.

U.S. Aids to Navigation System

The *U.S. ATON System* is the principal buoyage system used in the United States, and it conforms to the Region B standards of the International Association of Lighthouse Authorities (IALA). The IALA-B system applies throughout North and South America, including Canada, in the Caribbean Sea, and in Japan, Korea, and the Philippines. The rest of the world, however, uses the IALA-A system, which is conceptually similar and uses marks of the same shape but with their colors reversed.

The U.S. ATON System uses buoys, beacons, and lights as marks. These mark obstructions, dangers such as wrecks, the edges of navigable channels, and other things of importance to mariners. The U.S. Coast Guard maintains the marks in the system.

There are nine types of marks, or ATONs:

1. **Lateral marks**, including **preferred channel marks**
2. **Isolated danger marks**
3. **Safe water marks**
4. **Special marks**
5. **Information** and **regulatory marks**
6. **Mooring buoys**
7. **Inland waters obstruction marks**
8. **Cardinal marks**
9. **Other marks**

The first six are summarized with their chart symbols in Figure 5-1.

Intracoastal Waterway

The *Intracoastal Waterway* (ICW), which is maintained by the U.S. Army Corps of Engineers, runs south from Manasquan Inlet in New Jersey to the Florida Keys. It then runs north along the west coast of Florida and west along the Gulf Coast to Brownsville, Texas. Wherever possible, the ICW runs through protected bays, sounds, and canals, and it also takes maximum advantage of the protection given by offshore islands.

Marks on the ICW, which are maintained by the U.S. Coast Guard, are similar to those of the U.S. ATON System, and are used to show the limits of navigable channels, preferred channels, safe water, and ranges. The system also includes marks with no lateral significance. The aids look the same as the lateral system shown in Figure 5-1, but each includes an additional small yellow symbol (a square for "green" aids, a triangle for "red" aids) designating the ICW markings, as shown in the up-

U.S. AIDS TO NAVIGATION SYSTEM
on navigable waters except Western Rivers

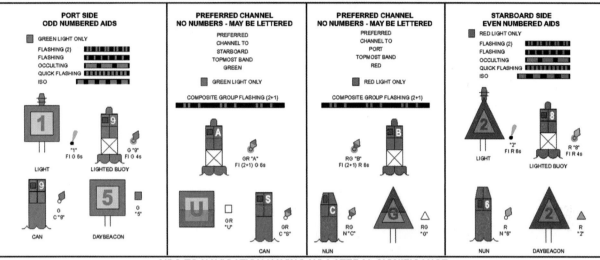

LATERAL SYSTEM AS SEEN ENTERING FROM SEAWARD

AIDS TO NAVIGATION HAVING NO LATERAL SIGNIFICANCE

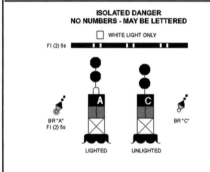

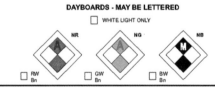

Aids to Navigation marking the Intracoastal Waterway (ICW) display unique yellow symbols to distinguish them from aids marking other waters. Yellow triangles △ indicate aids should be passed by keeping them on the starboard (right) hand of the vessel. Yellow squares ⬜ indicate aids should be passed by keeping them on the port (left) hand of the vessel. A yellow horizontal band ⬜ provides no lateral information, but simply identifies aids as marking the ICW.

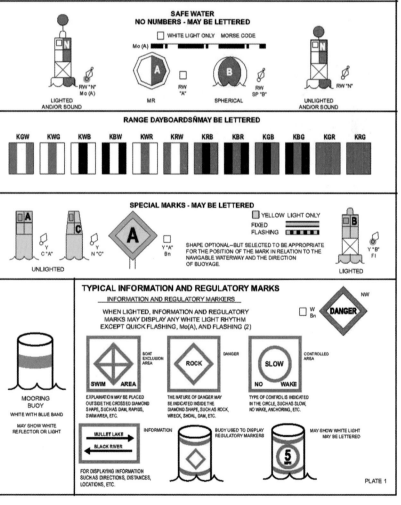

Figure **5-1.**

per portion of Figure 5-2. There are books and charts available specifically to guide you through the ICW.

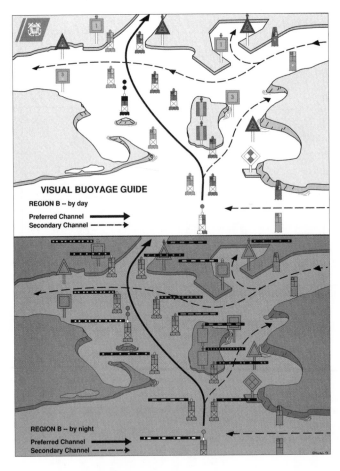

Figure **5-2.**

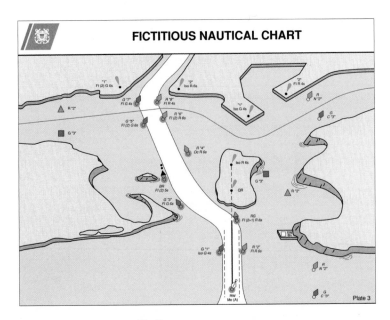

Figure **5-3.**

Western Rivers

Officially, the designation *Western Rivers* includes the Mississippi River, its tributaries, South Pass, Southwest Pass, and the Port Allen–Morgan City Alternate Route. It also includes the Atchafalaya River above its junction with the Port Allen–Morgan City Alternate Route, the Old River, and the Red River.

Fortunately, you do not need to know all this unless you are boating along the lower Mississippi River. Otherwise, all you need to know is that the Western Rivers include the Mississippi, its tributaries, and other rivers.

The U.S. Coast Guard maintains the marks on the Western Rivers, and these aids are shown in Figure 5-4.

Uniform State Waterway Marking System

The marks of the *Uniform State Waterway Marking System* (USWMS) were similar to those of the U.S. ATON System. However, in 2003, all states have adopted the U.S. ATON System.

Private Aids to Navigation

Private Aids to Navigations (PATONs) are those not established and maintained by the U.S. Coast Guard. PATONs may be established by local and state agencies, commercial establishments, or individuals. They include permanent and temporary aids that are in use less than 6 months. They are required to be placed, operated, and maintained in accordance with the U.S. Coast Guard authorizing permit.

Waterway Marks

Waterways are marked by a variety of buoys, daybeacons, and fixed structures serving a variety of purposes.

WARNING   *Give buoys an adequate berth. Boaters attempting to pass a buoy close aboard risk collision with a yawing buoy or with the obstruction marked by the buoy.*

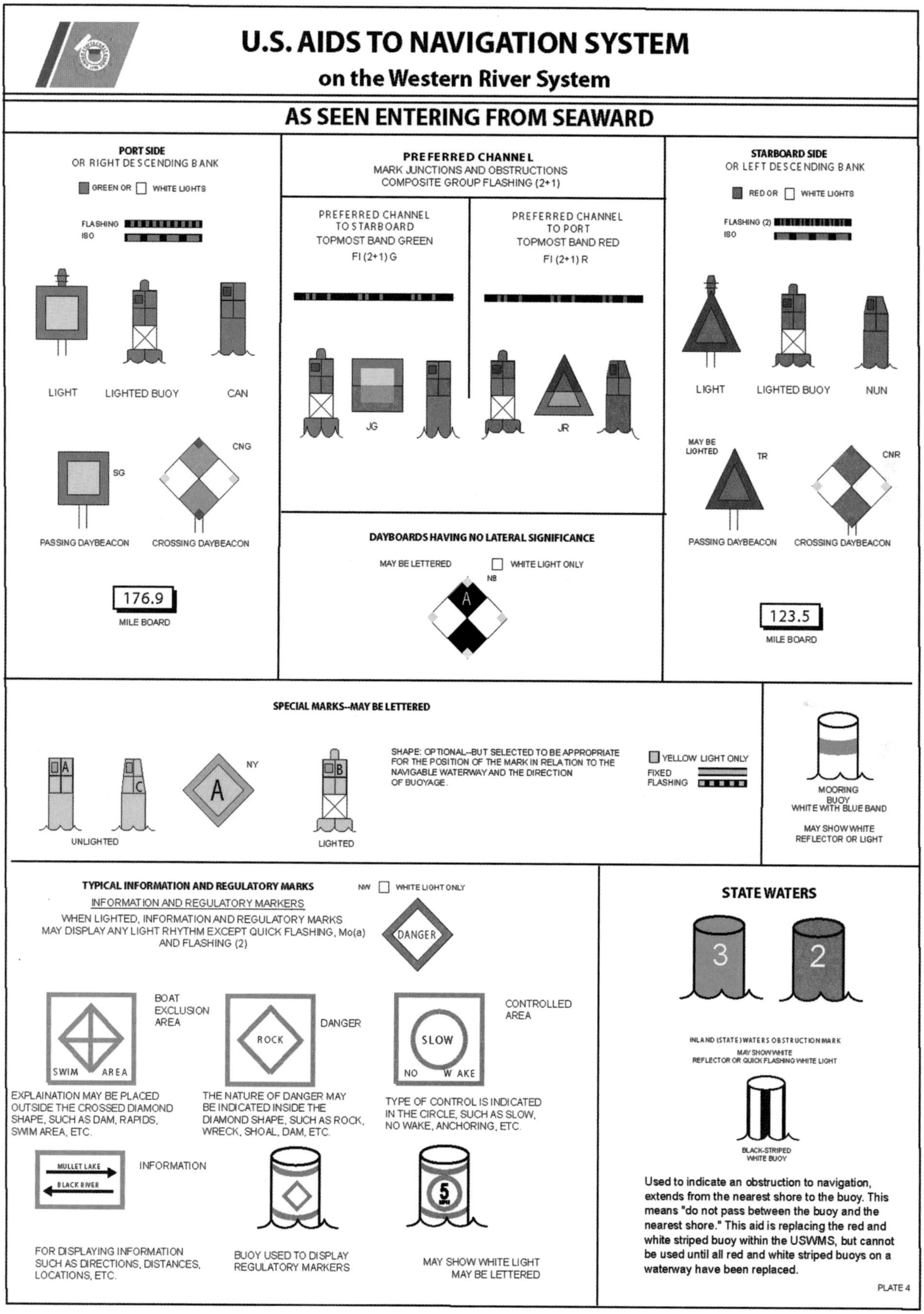

U.S. AIDS TO NAVIGATION SYSTEM
on the Western River System

AS SEEN ENTERING FROM SEAWARD

PORT SIDE
OR RIGHT DESCENDING BANK

GREEN OR ☐ WHITE LIGHTS

FLASHING
ISO

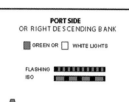

LIGHT   LIGHTED BUOY   CAN

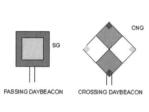

CNG

SG

PASSING DAYBEACON   CROSSING DAYBEACON

176.9
MILE BOARD

PREFERRED CHANNEL
MARK JUNCTIONS AND OBSTRUCTIONS
COMPOSITE GROUP FLASHING (2+1)

PREFERRED CHANNEL TO STARBOARD
TOPMOST BAND GREEN
Fl (2+1) G

PREFERRED CHANNEL TO PORT
TOPMOST BAND RED
Fl (2+1) R

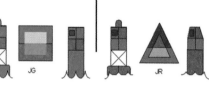

JG   JR

DAYBOARDS HAVING NO LATERAL SIGNIFICANCE

MAY BE LETTERED   ☐ WHITE LIGHT ONLY
NB

A

STARBOARD SIDE
OR LEFT DESCENDING BANK

RED OR ☐ WHITE LIGHTS

FLASHING (2)
ISO

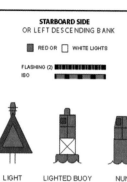

LIGHT   LIGHTED BUOY   NUN

MAY BE LIGHTED

TR   CNR

PASSING DAYBEACON   CROSSING DAYBEACON

123.5
MILE BOARD

SPECIAL MARKS--MAY BE LETTERED

A   C

NY
A

B

SHAPE: OPTIONAL--BUT SELECTED TO BE APPROPRIATE FOR THE POSITION OF THE MARK IN RELATION TO THE NAVIGABLE WATERWAY AND THE DIRECTION OF BUOYAGE.

☐ YELLOW LIGHT ONLY
FIXED
FLASHING

MOORING BUOY
WHITE WITH BLUE BAND

MAY SHOW WHITE REFLECTOR OR LIGHT

UNLIGHTED   LIGHTED

TYPICAL INFORMATION AND REGULATORY MARKS

NW ☐ WHITE LIGHT ONLY

INFORMATION AND REGULATORY MARKERS
WHEN LIGHTED, INFORMATION AND REGULATORY MARKS MAY DISPLAY ANY LIGHT RHYTHM EXCEPT QUICK FLASHING, Mo(a) AND FLASHING (2)

DANGER

BOAT EXCLUSION AREA

SWIM AREA

EXPLAINATION MAY BE PLACED OUTSIDE THE CROSSED DIAMOND SHAPE, SUCH AS DAM, RAPIDS, SWIM AREA, ETC.

ROCK   DANGER

THE NATURE OF DANGER MAY BE INDICATED INSIDE THE DIAMOND SHAPE, SUCH AS ROCK, WRECK, SHOAL, DAM, ETC.

SLOW
NO   WAKE

CONTROLLED AREA

TYPE OF CONTROL IS INDICATED IN THE CIRCLE, SUCH AS SLOW, NO WAKE, ANCHORING, ETC.

MULLET LAKE
BLACK RIVER
INFORMATION

FOR DISPLAYING INFORMATION SUCH AS DIRECTIONS, DISTANCES, LOCATIONS, ETC.

BUOY USED TO DISPLAY REGULATORY MARKERS

5
MAY SHOW WHITE LIGHT MAY BE LETTERED

STATE WATERS

3   2

INLAND (STATE) WATERS OBSTRUCTION MARK
MAY SHOW WHITE REFLECTOR OR QUICK FLASHING WHITE LIGHT

BLACK-STRIPED WHITE BUOY

Used to indicate an obstruction to navigation, extends from the nearest shore to the buoy. This means "do not pass between the buoy and the nearest shore." This aid is replacing the red and white striped buoy within the USWMS, but cannot be used until all red and white striped buoys on a waterway have been replaced.

PLATE 4

Figure **5-4.**

Buoys

Floating ATONs, or *buoys*, come in various sizes and shapes and may or may not have lights (Figure 5-5). They mark navigable channels, isolated dangers, obstructions, or shoals. The light, when present, turns on automatically and shines from dusk to dawn. Solar energy charges many of the batteries that power these lights. There are four common types of buoys.

Pillar Buoys

Pillar buoys vary considerably in shape and function, but most consist of a steel lattice erected on a flat base. The lighted green buoy "3" and the lighted red-and-white bell "LC" in Figure 5-6 are both pillar buoys. The chart symbols for both buoys are also shown in the illustration, and from these we learn that buoy "3" flashes green every 4 sec-

onds, while buoy "LC" flashes the Morse code letter A (one short flash followed by one long flash) that is characteristic of a red-and-white safe water buoy. (We'll discuss light signals later in the chapter.) Pillar buoys range in size from small ones to large, floating lighthouses, and in addition to lights, they may have bells, gongs, whistles, foghorns, or a combination of a light and a sound-producing device. The larger structures are multifunctional (Figure 5-7) and may have weather recording and transmitting equipment in addition to lights.

Spherical Buoys

Spherical buoys are red-and-white striped (Figure 5-8) and are used to mark a *fairway*, or the middle of a channel in *traffic separation schemes* (TSS), which are one-way traffic lanes used in some harbors and other congested areas.

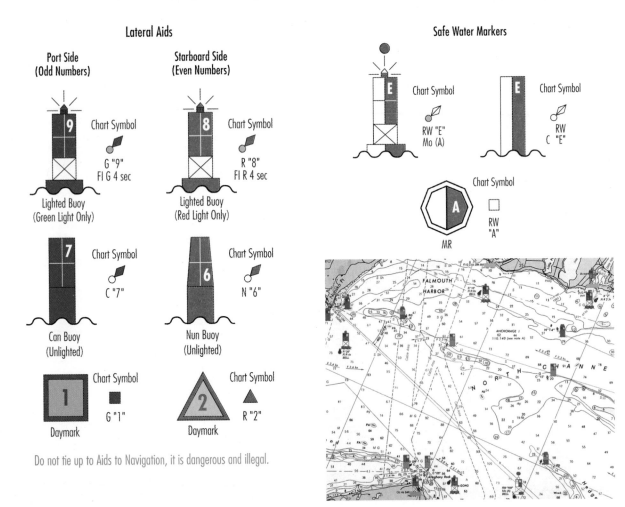

Figure 5-5. Left and top right: Buoy shapes and their chart symbols. (REPRINTED WITH PERMISSION FROM "FEDERAL REQUIREMENTS & SAFETY TIPS FOR RECREATIONAL BOATS," U.S. COAST GUARD OFFICE OF BOATING SAFETY) **Bottom right:** Illustrations of selected navigation buoys are superimposed on this chart segment next to their corresponding chart symbols. (REPRINTED WITH PERMISSION FROM *THE WEEKEND NAVIGATOR* BY BOB SWEET)

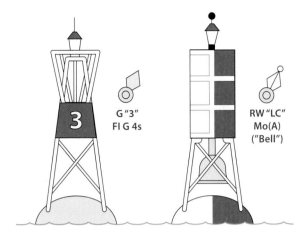

Figure **5-6.** **Top:** Pillar buoys and their chart symbols. **Bottom left:** A midchannel bell buoy with its single spherical topmark. (PHOTO BY USCG PA3 ROBIN REISLER) **Bottom right:** Two crewmembers from the U.S. Coast Guard cutter *Sycamore*, home port Cordova, Alaska, repair the extinguished light atop a pillar buoy near Spruce Cape on a January day. In the distance, a fishing vessel heads out to sea from Kodiak. (PHOTO BY PETTY OFFICER PAUL ROSZKOWSKI)

Figure **5-7.** Inspecting a large, multifunctional pillar buoy. (COURTESY NOAA)

Nun and Can Buoys

The two most common buoys are *cans* (cylindrical shape) and *nuns* (conical shape; Figures 5-9 and 5-10). In the U.S. ATON System, a can is most often green and bears an odd number, while a nun

is most frequently red and bears an even number. Nun and can buoys mark the edges of navigable channels.

Be Cautious Around Buoys!

When navigating near buoys, use caution. They are at anchor and, like an anchored vessel, they drift around their anchor with wind or current in what is called a *watch circle*. For this reason, the location of a buoy on a chart is sometimes marked "PA," which stands for position approximate. A buoy may even drag its anchor out of its charted position due to wind, ice, flooding, or being run down by a vessel. Such a buoy is said to be **off-station**, a condition that may go unreported for some days. In extreme cases a buoy may go missing altogether.

Occasionally the lights on normally lighted buoys will fail for one reason or another, or sound-

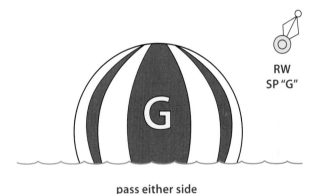

pass either side

Figure **5-8.** A red-and-white vertically striped spherical buoy serves as a fairway or midchannel marker in a traffic separation scheme.

Figure **5-9.** A red nun buoy being serviced by a Coast Guard buoy tender. (PHOTO BY USCG PA1 JERRY L. SNYDER)

Figure **5-10.** Can buoys being serviced by the U.S. Coast Guard. (PHOTOS BY USCG AND JONATHAN MCCOOL)

producing buoys will fail to sound their signals. Waves and swells activate the many whistles, gongs, and bells, but often in a fog the sea is gentle or calm, which means the buoys may be silent.

Daybeacons

Daymarks are colored geometrical shapes such as triangles, squares, octagons, diamonds, or rectangles. They are often called **dayboards**, a term in such wide use that it is now accepted. A *daybeacon* is a daymark plus the pile or *dolphin* (a group of three or more piles, usually fastened together with a wire rope) that holds it.

Triangular Daymarks

A triangular daymark is an equilateral triangle (Figure 5-11) resting on its base. Generally, these daymarks are red and, when numbered, have even numbers—which means that a daymark with an odd number of sides displays an even number.

Square Daymarks

Generally, square daymarks are green and, when numbered, have odd numbers (Figures 5-12 and 5-13). Thus, a daymark with an even number of sides displays an odd number.

Diamond-Shaped Daymarks

There are two kinds of diamond-shaped daymarks. The first is used in the U.S. ATON System and on the ICW, the Western Rivers, and other navigable waters. In this type, two smaller diamonds—which may be red, green, or black—are contained within the outline of the principal diamond (Figure 5-14). These daymarks have no lateral significance—i.e., they do not direct you to pass them on one side or the other. Rather, they are like the Xs on shopping mall maps that show "You are here." When you find the daymark on a chart, you will know where you are. Sometimes, too, they mark underwater hazards; as always, consult your chart to be sure.

The second type of diamond-shaped daymark is called a **crossing daymark** and is found on the Western Rivers and other navigable rivers. These daymarks indicate to upbound and downbound

Figure **5-11.** A red daymark on a piling. (PHOTO BY USCG)

traffic when the channel crosses from one bank of the river to the other.

Light Structures

Lighted ATONs, or *light structures*, vary greatly in size, from simple battery-powered lights on wooden piles or dolphins to tall lighthouses with powerful lights (Figure 5-15). Light structures have the same functions as lighted buoys but are used where they are more appropriate.

A beacon, for example, may mark the mouth of a channel. *Beacons* are stationary daymarks equipped with lights, and are either red, green, or white (Figure 5-16). If the beacon is red, the daymark is a red triangle with an even number. If the light is green, its daymark is a green square with an odd number. And if the light is white, its daymark is diamond or octagonal shaped and may have a letter.

Informational and Regulatory Marks

Informational and *regulatory marks* are white buoys or white daymarks with orange markings, as seen in Figures 5-1, 5-4, and 5-17, top. The buoys are white cylinders, each with an orange band near its top, a

second orange band just above its waterline, and an orange diamond or circle between these.

An open diamond on a board or buoy warns of "Danger." If the diamond has lines connecting its opposite corners, it marks an exclusion area for boats. Stay out! This mark frequently guards a swimming area. An open circle on a board or buoy marks an area of restricted operations, such as "slow," "idle speed," or "no wake." The warning is usually printed within the circle.

One informational mark that needs special em-

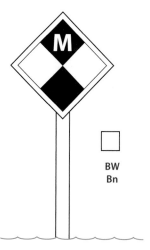

Figure **5-14.** **Left:** A diamond-shaped daybeacon together with its chart symbol. This mark has no lateral significance, but exists to mark a hazard or to help you locate your position on the water. **Right:** A diamond-shaped daybeacon. (PHOTO BY USCG PA1 RON MENCH)

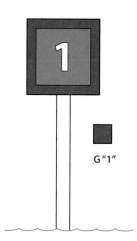

Figure **5-12.** A green daymark together with its chart symbol.

Figure **5-13.** This green daybeacon is equipped with a battery-powered light (the battery is recharged by solar panels) and is therefore more properly considered a minor light. The light, like the daymark, is green. (PHOTO BY USCG PA1 TELFAIR H. BROWN)

Figure **5-15.** The Angel's Gate (Los Angeles Harbor) Lighthouse, built in 1913, is the only lighthouse in the world that emits an emerald-colored light. (PHOTO BY JUNE ESPARZA)

phasis is a sign that says "Caution, Manatee Area." South Florida has many such marks (Figure 5-17, bottom), which seek to protect the manatee, an endangered mammal that is especially vulnerable to injury by small boats. If you see the sign, slow to idle speed.

Although other marine mammals do not enjoy the privilege of special informational markers, they are nonetheless endangered and deserving of our protection. Thirty-five species of mammals live near the Atlantic, Pacific, and Gulf coasts, including thirty-two species of whales, dolphins and porpoises, seals, and manatees. At last estimate, there were fewer than 500 northern right whales—the most endangered of the marine mammals—still alive.

The Marine Mammal Protection Act was passed by Congress in an effort to prevent the extinction of these animals. The act, for example, prohibits vessels from approaching within 500 yards of a right whale. If you sight a right whale, you must change your course and leave the area.

Marks for Special Purposes

Special-purpose marks are yellow and may have letters and amber (yellow) lights. They may be can or nun buoys, diamond daymarks, or small floating structures.

Special-purpose ATONs mark things such as fishnet and anchorage areas, spoil grounds, water intakes, and military exercise zones. They also mark traffic separation schemes when conventional

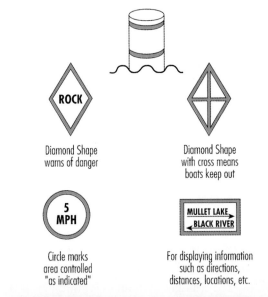

Figure **5-17.** **Top:** Representative information and regulatory marks. (REPRINTED WITH PERMISSION FROM "FEDERAL REQUIREMENTS & SAFETY TIPS FOR RECREATIONAL BOATS," U.S. COAST GUARD OFFICE OF BOATING SAFETY) **Bottom:** A "Manatee Zone" sign on the Intracoastal Waterway in Florida. (PHOTO BY GENE HAMILTON)

channel marking would be confusing. You can find examples of these special marks in the lower right portion of Figure 5-1.

How Waterways Are Marked

Waterway marks fall into two groups: marks that help you operate in navigable channels, and marks that show special conditions.

Marks on Navigable Waters

Marks on the navigable waters of the United States (except Western Rivers and the Intracoastal

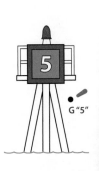

Figure **5-16.** **Left:** A beacon with a daymark on a dolphin, together with its chart symbol. **Middle:** This beacon has a red daymark, so the light itself is also red. (PHOTO BY USCG PA1 PETE MILNES) **Right:** A beacon erected on a more elaborate shore platform. (PHOTO BY USCG PA1 RON MENCH)

Waterway) appear in Figure 5-1. Those ATONs that help guide you along channels—i.e., those with **lateral significance**—are shown in the upper half of the illustration. To understand their use, you need to know the principle of "returning from sea," or "red, right, returning."

Red, Right, Returning

A basic convention of ATON usage is the concept of returning from sea, which is handily summarized in the phrase "red, right, returning." This means that in North America you should always keep red buoys and marks on your starboard side as you return from the sea, while green ones should be on your port side. (In regions of the world where the IALA-A system of lateral buoyage is used, these colors would be reversed.)

When entering a channel that leads from the sea, the meaning of "returning from sea" is obvious. In other cases, however, it is not. By convention, therefore, when traveling in a clockwise direction around the coasts of the United States and Canada, you are returning from sea (Figure 5-18). Thus, traveling south along the east coast of Canada and the United States, north along the west coast of Florida, west along the Gulf Coast, and north along the west coast of the United States and Canada is considered returning from sea.

The situation in the St. Lawrence River and the Great Lakes is less arbitrary. Traveling up the St. Lawrence from its mouth toward its source is considered returning from sea, as is traveling up any river. Similarly, the outlet ends of the Great Lakes are the seaward ends.

Within a body of water such as a bay or sound, channels leading to docking or mooring areas follow the same convention. When returning to a docking or mooring area, you are returning from sea, so you don't even need to have been "to sea" to be considered as returning from it.

> **WARNING** *Give beacons and other fixed structures a wide berth.* Boaters should not pass fixed ATONs close aboard due to the danger of collision with rip-rap or structure foundations, or with the obstruction or danger that is being marked.

Still, in complicated waters with many branching channels, it can be difficult or impossible to determine when you are returning from seaward. Your navigation chart (see Chapter 9) is always the final arbiter; consult it wherever you go.

Lateral Marks on Navigable Waters

The ATONs that mark the sides of navigable channels are called *lateral marks*. They consist of lighted and unlighted buoys, daybeacons, and minor lights, and they have distinctive colors and numbers as already discussed.

Again, you should leave the red marks with even numbers to starboard when returning from sea. Those you keep to port are green and have odd numbers. When you are going to sea, keep green marks to starboard and red ones to port. When lighted, red marks have red lights and green marks have green lights. The upper half of Figure 5-2 is a channel system as seen entering from seaward.

NUMBERS ON LATERAL MARKS. The numbers on lateral aids are in sequence, which means that when entering a waterway from seaward, you will see the buoy, daybeacon, or minor light with the lowest number on the waterway. Usually, this is number 1 and it will be a green lighted structure, a green buoy, or a green daybeacon. Keep this mark on your port side as you pass it. Sometimes, however, the first mark is a red ATON with an even number, to be kept to starboard when returning.

Red and green marks occur in pairs only when needed, and such pairs are usually numbered in sequence. Green beacon "5," for example, will stand across the channel from red beacon "6." Though the numbers increase sequentially from seaward, numbers may be missing. For example, a channel

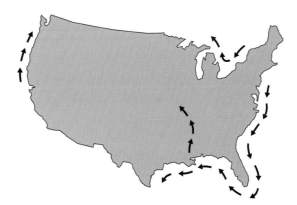

Figure **5-18.** The "red, right, returning" convention.

may have a long sequence of green marks with no corresponding red marks, simply because there are fewer hazards to mark on the starboard side of the channel. Sometimes a mark will have a letter after its number, such as "5A"; this indicates that the mark was added after the original sequence was established. At other times the number may have a one- or two-letter prefix denoting the name of the waterway. "MB6," for example, is mark 6 on Mobjack Bay. Your chart will show which numbers mark the waterway and the location of the ATONS.

> **WARNING** *If a daybeacon appears on your chart but you cannot see it at its charted location, be careful! A collision may have broken it off, and its remains, especially its stump, may still be there. If so, it is a hazard.*

Regulatory Markers

There are two kinds of *regulatory markers*: signs and buoys. As mentioned above, both are white with orange markings, and the signs have orange borders. Where letters or numbers appear on the signs or buoys, the lettering is black. Regulatory markers show boat exclusion, danger, and controlled areas and give information or directions.

Safe Water ATONs

Safe water ATONs are spherical buoys, floating structures with balls attached to their tops, or octagonal daymarks. They are red-and-white vertically striped (Figure 5-19) and when lighted, have white lights. Safe water ATONs may have letters, but they never have numbers. The middle portion of Figure 5-1 shows the safe water marks seen in fairways or midchannel.

Preferred Channel Marks

Preferred channel marks (sometimes called "junction buoys"), which are found at junctions of navigable channels (Figure 5-20), show the main or preferred channel, as in Figure 5-2. They may also mark wrecks or obstructions. You may pass on either side, but consult your chart to find the location of the obstruction.

Preferred channel marks include daymarks, nun and can buoys, and floating structures. Their special features are their red and green horizontal color bands. As with safe water marks, these ATONs may have letters but do not have numbers.

The color bands on a preferred channel mark help you know which is the main or preferred channel. The main channel may have the deeper water. When the top band of the mark is red, treat it as if it were a red mark in order to stay in the preferred channel, and leave it to starboard when returning from sea. When the top band is green, treat it like a green mark in order to stay in the preferred channel.

If the preferred channel mark is a can buoy, its top color band will always be green, and if it is a nun buoy, its top color will always be red. So if at a junction point you see the shape of the buoy, you don't even need to see the color of its top band. If it is a can, keep it to port when returning from the sea. If it is a nun, keep it to starboard when you return.

Ranges

A *range* is a pair of ATONs (Figure 5-21) placed a suitable distance apart. When the more distant one, which is always higher, is directly behind the lower, nearer one from your position, your vessel is in the center of a navigable channel. If you veer to the left of the channel's center, the forward mark will move to the right of the rear one. If you wander to the right of center, the forward one will move to the left of the rear one. To correct your course, steer in the direction of the closer (lower) mark.

Ranges are established to keep a vessel on a course that avoids dangers on either side. While they are most often used by large vessels, they can also be useful to small boats trying to run very narrow channels.

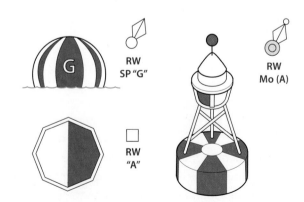

Figure **5-19.** Vertically striped safe water buoys and their chart symbols.

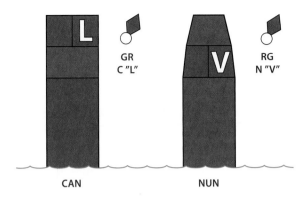

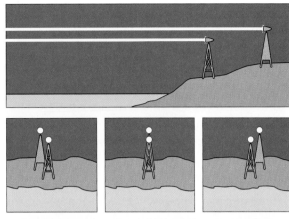

Figure 5-20. Buoys marking preferred channels and their chart symbols.

Ranges appear in a variety of colors (see Figure 5-1) and may have letters, but they never have numbers. They often have red, green, or white lights to serve as guides at night. You use the lights in the same manner as the range. Keep them in line and you will be in the middle of the channel.

Always consult your chart when using a range. The marks help you stay in midchannel but do not tell how far you can follow the range before the channel ends or turns. Range marks are often on land, a poor medium in which to operate your boat.

Directional Lights

A *directional light* may be used where it is impractical to install range lights. A single light is placed at one end of a straight section of a channel, high enough to be seen the full length of the channel. It produces a narrow, intense beam of white light, bordered by broader red and green sectors on the red-buoyed and green-buoyed sides of the channel, respectively. Your chart will show the arcs covered by each sector.

When you see only the white light, you are in the center of the channel. If the red light is visible while you are returning from sea, you are to the right of the channel's center. If the green light is visible, you are to the left of the channel's center.

Even though a channel is marked with ranges or directional lights, it may not always be necessary or advisable for you to follow them. In harbors, for example, the water is usually deep enough outside marked channels for small boats to navigate safely. If there is commercial traffic in the channel, or if the channel or harbor is congested, consult the chart to see if you can safely navigate outside the channel.

Figure 5-21. Top: Range lights. **Bottom:** Range marks like this pair on the Intracoastal Waterway keep boats and ships in hard-to-follow channels. When the marks get out of alignment, as here, you are wandering toward the edge of the channel. In this case, to get back to the center of the channel, you would steer to port if sighting the range over your bow, or to starboard if sighting it over your stern. (PHOTO BY GENE HAMILTON)

Intracoastal Waterway Marks

ATONs on the Intracoastal Waterway are the same as those elsewhere on the navigable waters of North America, with one exception.

Yellow Triangles, Squares, and Bands

All lateral marks on the ICW have yellow, reflective triangles or squares on them. Generally, red daymarks, buoys, and minor lights have yellow triangles, while yellow squares appear on green marks (Figure 5-22).

When you follow the ICW south from Manasquan, New Jersey, around Florida, and west along the Gulf Coast, keep daybeacons, buoys, and minor lights with yellow triangles to starboard, while leaving ATONs with yellow squares to port.

Nonlateral ICW ATONs, such as safe water marks and ranges, have yellow bands. ICW ATONs can be seen in the upper half of Figure 5-2.

Dual-Purpose Marks

There are possible points of confusion where the ICW joins or crosses another waterway. There you will find the yellow ICW triangles and squares on the marks of the crossing waterway. Thus, it is possible to see a yellow triangle on a green, square daymark, a green buoy, or a structure with a green light, and you can find a yellow square on a red, triangular daymark, a red buoy, or a structure with a red light. This is done to avoid duplication of daymarks, which would be even more confusing. When you do encounter this condition, interpret the meaning of these dual-purpose marks as follows: be guided by the yellow markings if you are traveling the ICW; if you are traveling the cross-ing waterway, ignore the yellow marks and be guided by the colors, shapes, and numbers of the original ATONS.

The upper portion of Figure 5-2 illustrates how you should interpret dual-purpose marks. Note that the ICW is the dashed line going from the upper right to the upper left corner of Figure 5-2. The crossing waterway is shown by the heavy black line.

When traveling on the ICW from right to left in the illustration, you are considered to be returning from sea. As you would expect, red nun buoy "2" has a yellow triangle on it and should be kept to starboard. Green can "3" has a yellow square on it and should be kept to port.

When returning from sea, you might expect to keep red buoy "6" to starboard. Since you are on the ICW, though, and returning from seaward, you are guided by its yellow square and should keep the buoy on the port side. Red buoy "8" has a yellow triangle and should be kept to starboard.

Light Characteristics

Red ATONs, when lighted, have red lights, and green marks have green lights. ATONs with white lights rarely have lateral significance except on the Western Rivers System above Baton Rouge (see

Figure 5-22. A can (top) and a red daybeacon (bottom) on the Intracoastal Waterway show the yellow square and yellow triangle, respectively, that are characteristic of ICW ATONs—although, on the red daybeacon, the yellow triangle is mostly obscured by an osprey nest. (PHOTOS BY GENE HAMILTON)

Figure 5-4). Elsewhere, white-lighted ATONS mark safe water (as in midchannel buoys) and ranges, and informational, regulatory, and diamond-shaped marks also have white lights when lighted.

Light Patterns

Most lights on ATONs have flashing patterns of illumination to help identify them. Some lights, though, are *fixed*, which mean they shine continuously from sundown to sunup.

Lights flash in a variety of ways. They may flash at regular intervals; a light that flashes every 4 seconds, for example, is said to have a period of 4 seconds. Alternatively, a light may show groups of flashes. It might, for example, flash twice and then remain off for a short period of time. A *quick light* flashes 60 times per minute, making its period 1 second. The lower range light in the middle of Figure 5-2 is a quick light. Figures 5-1 and 5-23 show several of the light patterns in use.

Occulting Lights

A *flashing light* flashes on while an *occulting light* blinks off. Put another way, a flashing light is off more than on, and an occulting light is on more than off. Lights can occult with regular patterns. An *isophase*, or iso, light is on for an interval equal to the time it is off. (**Iso** is from the Greek *isos*, which means equal.) The upper range light in the middle of Figure 5-2 is an isophase light. Red buoy "4" in the middle of Figure 5-2 has an occulting light.

Safe Water ATON Lights

The white lights on safe water marks flash a regular pattern of a short flash followed by a longer one. A period of darkness follows these two flashes. The light is flashing the Morse code letter A (• –) and any light with such a flash is a safe water mark. The light on the red-and-white striped buoy at the bottom of Figure 5-2 is an example.

Preferred Channel Lights

The light on a preferred channel mark is either red or green; its color matches the color of the top band on the ATON. Whatever its color, it always flashes in a set pattern—two flashes followed by a brief period of darkness, then a single flash—that means "I am a preferred channel light." The period of darkness after the single flash is longer than the one following the two flashes. After this period of darkness, the pattern repeats. Lights that flash in this manner are called *composite group flashing lights*. The particular sequence described here is 2 + 1—that is, two flashes followed by one flash. Note the preferred channel light on Figure 5-2.

Articulated Lights

An *articulated light* is a combination of a beacon and a buoy. It is a sealed hollow cylinder, up to 50 or more feet long, that attaches directly to the seabed by means of an articulated sinker rather than being anchored with ground tackle. The light remains in a vertical, nearly stationary position, moving only in small circles, thus providing a more precise location than an anchored buoy. The length of the cylinder is equal to the water depth plus the tidal range plus 10 to 15 feet of height above the surface. At its top are daymarks and an appropriate light.

Articulated lights mark positions where more precision is needed than buoys can give, and where water is too deep for a pile or dolphin structure. Since they do not have chains, they are almost always directly over their sinkers and have very small watch circles.

> **TIP** On the ICW, you should be guided by the yellow square or triangle, not by the colors or shapes of the ATONs on which they are placed.

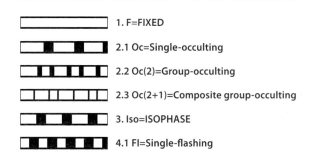

1. F=FIXED

2.1 Oc=Single-occulting

2.2 Oc(2)=Group-occulting

2.3 Oc(2+1)=Composite group-occulting

3. Iso=ISOPHASE

4.1 Fl=Single-flashing

Figure **5-23.** A selection of light patterns.

Chart Symbols

Chart symbols help you identify ATONs. The symbol for a buoy, for example, is a diamond with a small watch circle at its tip. If the buoy is lighted, the watch circle is overprinted with a larger, magenta-colored disk. Magenta is used because it is visible under the red lights used in many cockpits and on ships' bridges at night.

When the diamond symbol is green, it represents a green buoy; when red, it represents a red buoy. Letters and figures printed next to the diamond tell you more about the buoy. For example, in the notation G "9" *Fl G 4s*, "G" means green and "9" is the number on the buoy. The buoy has a light that flashes green every 4 seconds, and the italic type indicates that it's a buoy and not a fixed mark. This buoy appears at the left of Figure 5-1.

Suppose a preferred channel buoy has a green top band and its green light flashes in a composite group every 6 seconds. On a chart it would appear as a buoy symbol with the top half green and the bottom half red. It would have a magenta disk overprinted on the watch circle and the notation *Fl (2 + 1) G 6s* such as that for buoy "A" on the left side of Figure 5-1.

Fixed Structure Lights

Lights on fixed structures, including minor lights, also have their characteristic chart symbols. These are magenta exclamation marks with black dots that show the locations of the structures. In addition, each light's period, color, number, height, and the distance from which it may be seen appear on the chart. If the position is only an approximation, it is marked PA. The chart symbol and description shown in Figure 5-24 indicate a minor light that flashes green every 6 seconds. It is 12 feet above mean high water and can be seen for 3 miles in clear weather. Note that the printing is roman (not italic), which confirms that it is a minor light, not a buoy.

Symbols for Buoys

The chart symbol for a can buoy is a green diamond with a small watch circle, with the green color indicating a can. If the buoy is not overprinted in magenta, you know that it has no light. If G C "7" was printed next to the diamond, you would know that it is green can number 7. Red nun buoys have symbols that follow a similar pattern. Figure 5-1 shows a complete description of a green can ("9") and a red nun ("6").

Symbols for Daymarks

A green daymark appears on a chart as a green square. If the description on the chart is G "1," you know that it is daymark number 1. The symbol for a red daymark is a red triangle, as in Figure 5-1.

You can also tell from a chart if an ATON is a buoy or a fixed structure by the type in which its description is printed. The symbols and descriptions of fixed ATONs are printed in "straight-up" roman type, while symbols and descriptions of floating structures and buoys are printed in italic. You can find additional chart symbols on Figure 5-3.

Light Structures

Lighted aids to navigation may be as small as minor lights on wooden piles in small creeks or as large as tall lighthouses on the coasts. Their intensities also vary from weak to brilliant. They may be small, battery-powered minor lights or powerful lights with millions of candlepower, such as those in coastal lighthouses. Regardless of their sizes or intensities, they serve the same functions as buoys and daybeacons. Except for lighthouses, they have the same numbering, coloring, light, and sound characteristics as buoys.

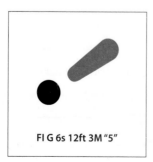

Fl G 6s 12ft 3M "5"

Figure **5-24.** Chart symbol and description for a light.

Lighthouses

Lighthouses are **short-range aids** (SRAs) and are not a part of any buoyage system. Rather, they are built where they will give the most help. While their primary purpose is to mark prominent headlands, harbor entrances, isolated danger areas, and other points, they also serve to support lights at considerable heights above the water. Some have quarters for personnel.

Lighthouse structures vary considerably in appearance, with their designs depending upon their needed heights, their locations, and the geological structures that support them (Figure 5-25). The *Light List*, a Coast Guard publication that lists all aids to navigation, gives a brief description of each lighthouse. For example, the description given for Alligator Reef Light in the Florida Keys says, "White octagonal pyramid skeleton tower enclosing stair cylinder and square dwelling; black pile foundation."

Cylindrical or conical towers may have distinctive color combinations painted on them. The Cape Hatteras Light in North Carolina, for example, has black and white spirals. Each structure and its distinctive colors make up a lighthouse "daymark" to help navigators identify it during the day since its lights usually shine only at night.

The distance a lighthouse light must be seen is a major consideration in its height and location and the intensity of its light. The higher and the more brilliant the light, the farther away it is visible.

Lighthouse Sectors

Some lighthouse lights have *red sectors*, which indicate danger. These are created by placing red glass in the beams of light from the lighthouses so that when viewed from areas of shallow water, rocks, or other dangers, the normally white lights appear red. Such red sectors are shown on charts of the area.

The red sectors of Alligator Reef Light are shown in Figure 5-26. The light is normally white, but to a boat between the dotted lines it appears red. The spaces between the dotted lines are the red sectors.

The teardrop-shaped magenta symbol for Alligator Reef Light indicates that it is a light. The light flashes in groups of four flashes every 40 seconds. It is 136 feet above mean high water, and can

be seen for 8 miles on a clear night. From its height you can tell it is a major light, one you would expect to be white, which it is except in its red sectors. Charts often include pictures of major lights to aid in identifying them.

Classes of Light Structures

Lights on fixed structures include primary seacoast lights, secondary lights, river or harbor lights, and

Figure **5-25.** **Top:** Marblehead Light. (PHOTO BY USCG PA3 ALLYSON TAYLOR) **Bottom:** Cape Disappointment Light, Ilwaco, Washington, on a stormy day. (PHOTO BY LARRY KELLIS)

beacons. The *Light List* gives a description of each light, which include the following:

- name and light rhythm
- location (latitude and longitude)
- nominal range (distance the light can be seen under optimal conditions)
- height above mean high water
- type and appearance of the structure, including height above ground and daymark, if any
- characteristics of sound devices present
- year built

Light Structure Sound Signals

Most lighthouses and major lights, and some minor light structures, have foghorns or other sound-producing devices that warn mariners of danger in periods of poor visibility. On some floating structures, the signals operate either mechanically or electrically, with electrical operation being the most dependable since mechanical operation may depend on wave action.

You can identify a particular structure by the timing of its signals, the silent period between signals, and the tone of the signal, all of which are given on nautical charts. When the number of blasts and the time for a complete cycle are not enough to identify the structure, you may refer to the *Light List*, where the exact length of each blast and silent interval is described.

In some boating areas there may be several active foghorns, each with its own period and tone. When you boat in such an area, you need to be able to recognize each foghorn to help assure safe passage.

Lights on Bridges

Nautical charts show bridges and describe them and their characteristics. Bridges are described as "fixed" or "draw." Also listed are their horizontal and vertical clearances when closed, the latter given as feet above mean high water. A *bascule*

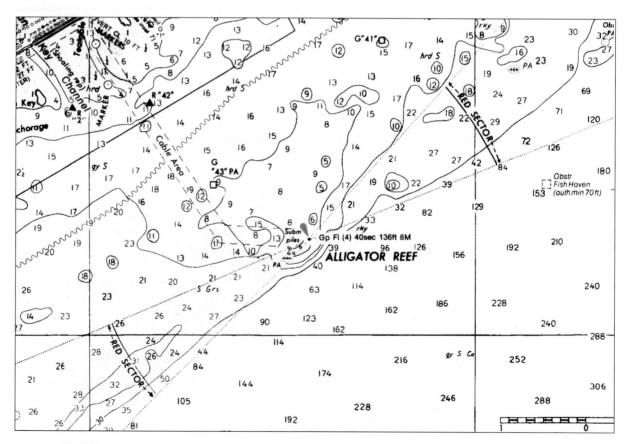

Figure **5-26.** The red sectors of Alligator Reef Light.

bridge is a type of drawbridge that has a counter-weight on one side.

The lights on bridges do not conform to any buoyage system. Red lights mark piers and other parts of bridges and also show that a drawbridge is in the closed position. A corresponding green light on a drawbridge shows that it is open. A green light on a fixed bridge marks the centerline of the channel, while the red lights mark the pilings on the sides.

Sometimes there is more than one safe channel under a bridge, in which case the preferred channel has three white lights in a vertical line above its green light.

Electronic Aids to Navigation

An array of sophisticated electronic navigational aids is available to assist you. These include GPS, satellite navigation systems, radar, and others.

Loran

Loran (long range navigation) was an electronic navigation system implemented more than 50 years ago. The United States, Canada, Russia, and Europe

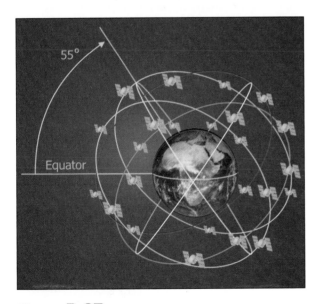

Figure **5-27.** The GPS satellite constellation covers the earth, deployed in six orbital planes inclined at 55 degrees from the equator. The U.S. Air Force controls the satellites. (U.S. AIR FORCE)

stopped using loran in 2010. However, some nautical charts have not been updated and continue to show loran overlay information. Loran has been replaced by the global positioning system (GPS).

Global Positioning System

The *global positioning system* (GPS) employs a constellation of earth-orbiting satellites. Each satellite completes an orbit around the earth every 12 hours. As a result, satellites move across the sky slowly as viewed by an observer on earth. The constellation is designed to always provide a number of satellites to be in view at virtually every place on earth (Figure 5-27). There are typically 30 satellites in orbit of which 24 are active at any one time. A minimum of three satellites must be in view at the same time in order for a GPS receiver to determine position on the earth's surface. Nominal accuracy is 30 feet (9.1 meters).

A supplementary system called *Differential GPS* (DGPS) was created for mariners by the U.S. Coast Guard to work in conjunction with GPS. This system uses precisely located land-based receivers to correct GPS signals for slight distortions due to atmospheric and other factors, then transmits these corrections to appropriately equipped shipboard GPS receivers. This allows users within about 100 miles of a DGPS radiobeacon to realize an accuracy of 5 meters (16.4 feet) or better. These radiobeacons are located at most U.S. harbors, including the U.S. Virgin Islands, Puerto Rico, and most of Alaska. You must have a DGPS antenna and receiver to realize this enhanced precision.

Basic GPS accuracy is further improved by the *wide area augmentation system* (WAAS). WAAS was developed by the Federal Aviation Agency for aircraft, although all GPS users benefit from it. WAAS improves a GPS receiver's three-dimensional accuracy to better than 10 feet (3 meters). All GPS units manufactured in recent years are WAAS capable. WAAS satellites are geostationary, meaning they are always at the same place in the sky (Figure 5-28). Part of WAAS includes ground stations that have highly accurate known positions called geodetic markers. The ground stations provide reference data allowing WAAS to determine regional positional errors caused by conditions in space. That correctional information is eventually sent to GPS receivers.

Traditional chart navigation fixes are established during prevoyage planning based on latitude and longitude. With GPS, these fixes, called *waypoints*, can be entered into an onboard or handheld receiving unit. Multiple waypoints can then be grouped into a *route* for navigational purposes. Some advanced units also incorporate chart information utilizing depth measurements to determine safe routes. If wind, current, or inattention causes you to drift off your course line, GPS will report this to you as *cross-track error*. GPS has truly revolutionized navigation, but it does not relieve you from the need for careful chartwork and "dead reckoning," as discussed in Chapter 9. This subject is covered more thoroughly in more advanced Auxiliary courses like the "The Weekend Navigator" or "GPS for Mariners."

Coast Guard *Local Notices to Mariners*, and the website www.navcen.uscg.gov, inform users of forecasted long-term outages of GPS. This website also offers general information about all the navigation systems supported by the U.S. Coast Guard. The mailing address is: Commanding Officer, USCG NAVCEN, 7323 Telegraph Road, Alexandria, VA 20598. The Coast Guard also broadcasts information regarding the systems, as needed, on VHF-FM Channels 16 and 22A.

Shortwave radio station WWV, in Fort Collins, Colorado, also reports the status of GPS at 14 to 15 minutes after the hour. WWVH in Kekaha, Hawaii, reports the same information at 43 to 44 minutes after the hour.

RACONS

A *racon* is a **ra**dar bea**con** device typically attached to a buoy. The racon will automatically return a radar signal coming from a nearby vessel. It will include directional and other coded information. They are used by the U.S. Coast Guard and private users to alert vessels to critical nearby structures such as bridges, offshore oil rigs, or critical turning points used by large vessels. They are operated on a timed schedule.

Navigation Publications

There are a number of publications and charts to aid you (Figure 5-29). Since the location, characteristics, and maintenance status of ATONs change from time to time, obsolete charts can be dangerous and you should be sure yours are up to date.

There are several government and commercial sources of charts, but most of these rely on charts produced by the National Oceanic and Atmospheric Administration's (NOAA) Office of Coast Survey (OCS). In addition, charts of major river systems such as the Mississippi and Ohio are produced by the U.S. Army Corps of Engineers, and charts for the high seas and foreign waters are produced by the National Imagery and Mapping Agency (NIMA), which was recently renamed the National Geospatial-Intelligence Agency (NGA). You can buy charts at marinas, boat stores, and other chart dealers. Reproductions of government

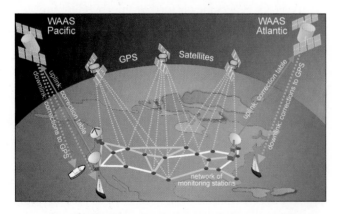

Figure **5-28.** The WAAS includes satellites and ground stations that transmit and receive signals in order to improve the accuracy of GPS. (COURTESY BOB SWEET/*GPS FOR MARINERS*)

Figure **5-29.** Assorted navigation publications, including a *Coast Pilot*, *Chart No. 1*, a *Light List* (PHOTO BY RAY PAGES), and *How to Read a Nautical Chart*.

charts on waterproof paper or reformatted in bound volumes to cover defined regions are also available from commercial sources, and these will sometimes represent a significant savings or gain in convenience over the government charts. You can also obtain the latest edition of a chart from online print-on-demand services, and download free electronic charts in raster format (for use on a laptop computer or chartplotter) from the Office of Coast Survey website. (This web address, www.nauticalcharts.noaa.gov, will also direct you to print-on-demand charts, *Notices to Mariners*, and *Coast Pilots* in print or digital downloadable form.) Note that the latest editions of charts can be several years old and in need of updating.

Each district of the Coast Guard publishes a weekly *Local Notice to Mariners*. Free copies are available online at www.nauticalcharts.noaa.gov or www.navcen.uscg. Use the information in the *Local Notice* to keep your charts and light lists up to date. This publication also includes other important information such as bridge conditions, proposed military operations, and special marine events.

Chart No. 1, Nautical Chart Symbols, Abbreviations, and Terms, published jointly by NOAA and the Defense Mapping Agency, is useful in interpreting nautical charts. Though it is no longer available from the government for distribution through commercial chart agents, you can still obtain a print copy of *Chart No. 1* from the U.S. Government Printing Office, or view and download a digital version at www.nauticalcharts.noaa.gov. In addition, various commercial publishers offer *Chart No. 1* for sale.

Light Lists help you identify aids to navigation, as discussed earlier in this chapter. The Coast Guard publishes it in several volumes as follows:

Volume I, Atlantic Coast, describes ATONs in U.S. waters from the St. Croix River, Maine, to Shrewsbury River, New Jersey.

Volume II, Atlantic Coast, describes ATONs from Shrewsbury River, New Jersey, to Little River, South Carolina.

Volume III, Atlantic and Gulf Coasts, describes ATONs in U.S. waters from Little River, South Carolina, to Econfina River, Florida, including Puerto Rico and the U.S. Virgin Islands.

Volume IV, Gulf of Mexico, describes ATONs from Econfina River, Florida, to the Rio Grande, Texas.

Volume V, Mississippi River System, describes ATONs on the Mississippi and its navigable tributaries.

Volume VI, Pacific Coast and Pacific Islands, describes the ATONs in U.S. waters on the Pacific Coast and Pacific islands. For the convenience of mariners, it includes some of the lighted aids on the British Columbia coast.

Volume VII, Great Lakes, describes ATONs maintained by the Coast Guard and some of the aids maintained by Canada on the Great Lakes and the St. Lawrence River above the St. Regis River.

You can order *Light Lists* by calling 1-866-512-1800, or go to http://bookstore.gpo.gov. You can download the *Lists* and get the latest information at www.navcen.cg.gov/. They are also available from branch offices of the GPO, located in many cities, and from sales agents in most major ports. You can find a sales agent by going to www.aeronav.faa.gov/agents.asp, or get a free catalog by contacting the FAA Mission Support Services AJV-372, AeroNav Products Logistics Group, 10201 Good Luck Road, Glenn Dale, MD 20769-9700, 1-800-638-8972.

Ways to Learn More

Chapman Piloting & Seamanship. 66th ed. Charles B. Husick. New York: Hearst Books, 2009. Chapter 14.

GPS for Mariners. 2nd ed. Bob Sweet. Camden, Maine: International Marine, 2011.

How to Read a Nautical Chart: A Captain's Quick Guide. Nigel Calder. Camden, Maine: International Marine, 2008.

How to Read a Nautical Chart: A Complete Guide to Using and Understanding Electronic and Paper Charts. 2nd ed. Nigel Calder. Camden, Maine: International Marine, 2012.

Using GPS: A Captain's Quick Guide. Bob Sweet. Camden, Maine: International Marine, 2004.

http://en.wikipedia.org/wiki/Global_Positioning_System

www.boatus.com/foundation/guide/navigation_29.html

www.gps.gov/systems/gps/performance/accuracy/

Practice Questions

IMPORTANT BOATING TERMS
In the following exercise, match the words in the column on the left with the definitions in the column on the right. In the blank space to the left of each term, write the letter of the item that best matches it. Do not use an item in the right-hand column more than once.

THE ITEMS

1. _____ daymark
2. _____ lateral marks
3. _____ red markers and buoys
4. _____ safe water marks
5. _____ occulting light
6. _____ fixed light
7. _____ green markers and buoys
8. _____ nun
9. _____ can
10. _____ flashing light

THE RESPONSES

a. mark midchannel
b. even numbers
c. blinks off
d. on from sunset to sunrise
e. mark sides of navigable channels
f. odd numbers
g. cylindrical buoy
h. flashes on
i. has a geometrical shape
j. red buoy, conical top

Multiple-Choice Items

In the following items, choose the best response:

5-1. To be useful to a boater, landmarks must be visible and

a. appear on a chart of the area
b. well known
c. blend with the background
d. historical in nature

5-2. You are "returning from sea" when going

a. counterclockwise around the United States
b. clockwise around the United States
c. downstream on a river
d. east in Lake Erie

5-3. Spherical buoys mark fairways and the middles of navigable channels and are

a. green above red
b. all black
c. red above green
d. red-and-white striped

5-4. The red buoys used to mark the right side of a channel

a. have white lights
b. have green lights
c. have even numbers
d. are can shaped

5-5. Lighted safe water buoys have

a. white lights
b. red lights
c. green lights
d. yellow lights

5-6. Going from Manasquan Inlet in New Jersey on the ICW, down the East Coast, up the west coast of Florida, and west across the Gulf of Mexico is considered

a. returning from sea
b. going to sea
c. cruising
d. going counterclockwise

Multiple-Choice Items (continued)

5-7. A preferred channel marker has

a. green and red lights
b. green and red horizontal bands
c. white lights
d. vertical red-and-white stripes

5-8. In the U.S. ATON System, a can is

a. white
b. red
c. black
d. green

5-9. A nun buoy has

a. a flat top
b. a conical-shaped top
c. no letter or number
d. an odd number

5-10. A square daymark with an odd number is the same as

a. a green can buoy
b. a red lateral marker
c. a no-wake zone marker
d. a midchannel marker

5-11. The following special markings are used in the ICW system:

a. yellow triangles
b. yellow squares
c. yellow bands
d. all of the above

5-12. Daymarks on the sides of channels usually have

a. letters
b. yellow triangles or squares
c. numbers
d. neither letters or numbers

5-13. An occulting light is

a. on more than off
b. yellow
c. off more than on
d. on at all times

5-14. On a chart you can tell if an ATON is a buoy from its

a. gothic type
b. italic (slanting) type
c. boldfaced type
d. large print

5-15. You can find a brief description of each lighthouse in the

a. *Local Notice to Mariners*
b. *Chart No. 1*
c. *Light List*
d. *Notice to Mariners*

5-16. A fixed light is one that

a. is on from dusk to dawn
b. has been repaired
c. shines brightly
d. is on from sunrise to sunset

5-17. The centerline of the navigable channel under a fixed bridge is marked by

a. amber lights
b. red lights
c. green lights
d. red and green lights

5-18. Red daymarks have

a. three sides and odd numbers
b. four sides and even numbers
c. diamond shapes
d. three sides and even numbers

5-19. On a chart, a magenta disk means

a. a buoy
b. a lighted aid to navigation
c. a triangular daymark
d. a square daymark

5-20. A special-purpose mark, such as a yellow buoy, is used to designate

a. an anchorage
b. a dredge pipeline
c. a triangular daymark
d. a square daymark

5-21. If you see a white buoy with an orange diamond, two orange horizontal stripes, and a white center, you should

a. keep the buoy to your starboard
b. keep the buoy to your port
c. keep a safe distance away
d. slow your speed

chapter 6

The Rules of the Nautical Road

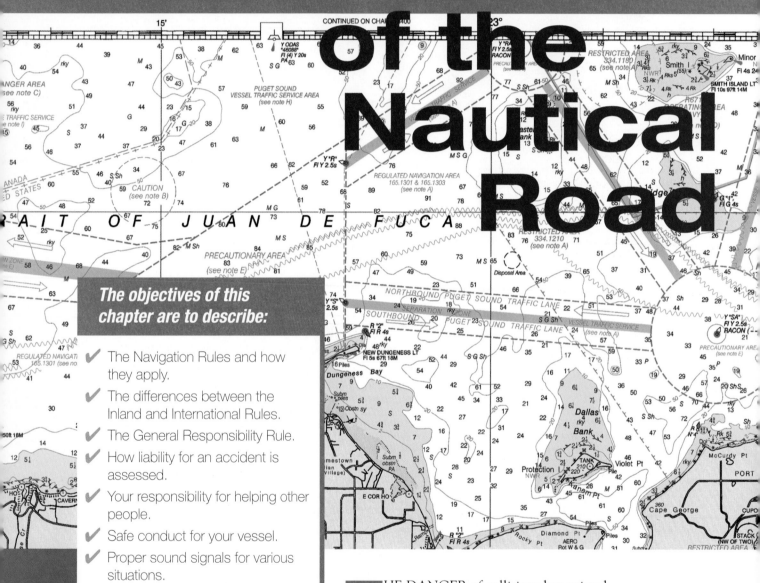

(COURTESY NOAA)

The objectives of this chapter are to describe:

- ✔ The Navigation Rules and how they apply.
- ✔ The differences between the Inland and International Rules.
- ✔ The General Responsibility Rule.
- ✔ How liability for an accident is assessed.
- ✔ Your responsibility for helping other people.
- ✔ Safe conduct for your vessel.
- ✔ Proper sound signals for various situations.
- ✔ The proper light configuration for your vessel.
- ✔ The rules of operation in restricted visibility.
- ✔ What lights and shapes tell you.
- ✔ Legal distress signals.

THE DANGER of collisions has existed since the second vessel was built. Navigation rules exist to help prevent such mishaps. These rules are to vessels what "rules of the road" are to automobiles, and it is the responsibility of a boat operator to know and follow the Navigation Rules.

Two Sets of Rules

There are two sets of Navigation Rules in force in U.S. waters—the *International Rules* and the *U.S. Inland Rules*. The two are for the most part identical, but the U.S. Inland Rules diverge from international standards in those few instances where necessary to meet the unique needs for safe navigation on U.S. rivers, bays, and other inland waters.

Taken together, the Navigation Rules apply to all vessels on the *navigable waters* of the United States, meaning all U.S. territorial waters (up to 12 miles offshore, generally speaking) and any waters that provide a transportation route between two or more states or to the sea. Further, the International Rules apply to all U.S. vessels on the high seas when not subject to another nation's jurisdiction.

The International Rules

Rules to prevent collisions have been evolving for the past 150 years. We now use the 1972 International Regulations for Prevention of Collisions at Sea, other names for which are the International Rules and the **72 COLREGS**. These rules were established by international treaty to secure consistency of standards throughout the world.

The Inland Rules

The Inland Navigational Rules Act of 1980, passed by Congress to align U.S. rules with the International Rules, became effective in 1981. Before that time, vessels on inland waters followed several sets of rules, including an older set of Inland Rules, the Western Rivers Rules, the Great Lakes Rules, and parts of the Motorboat Act of 1940. If you think it is confusing to operate under two sets of rules as we do today, imagine what it was like before 1981!

Both sets of Rules appear in *Navigation Rules, International–Inland* published by the U.S. Government Printing Office. You can order a copy by calling 202-512-1800, go to www.navcen.uscg.gov, or find it at most marine supply stores (Figure 6-1). You can also view them online or download them in PDF format at www.navcen.uscg.gov/. Any

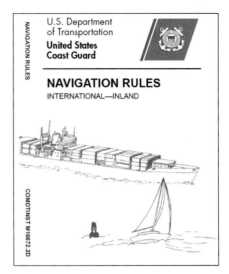

Figure 6-1. *The Navigation Rules, International–Inland.*

boat 12 or more meters long must have a copy of the Inland Rules aboard. The penalty for failure to carry one can be as much as $5,000.

Your Local Waters

The Inland or International Rules may not regulate boating on your local lake or other body of water that does not provide a route across a state line or to the sea. Instead, local ordinances or state laws may apply. Nevertheless, when you boat on such waters, you should use the same standards of common sense that underlie the Inland and International Rules.

Demarcation Lines

Demarcation lines separate waters on which the Inland Rules apply from those regulated by the International Rules. The Commandant of the U.S. Coast Guard draws these lines, which can be seen as a dashed magenta line on some navigational charts.

In general, the demarcation lines follow the coasts. Across bays and other inlets, they go from one easily described point of land or landmark to another. Seaward of these lines, the International Rules apply (Figure 6-2); landward, the Inland Rules apply. In some areas—along the coast of New England, for example—the line is drawn well into bays and rivers, and a local chart is the best arbiter of where the transition occurs. Exact descriptions of the demarcation lines also appear in the *Navigation Rules*.

To Whom Do the Rules Apply?

Rule 1 of both the International and Inland Rules answers this question: The International Rules ". . . apply to all vessels upon the high seas" and on all connecting waters such as rivers and bays that are navigable by seagoing vessels. The Inland Rules ". . . apply to all vessels on the inland waters of the United States." They apply also to U.S. vessels on the Canadian waters of the Great Lakes unless they conflict with Canadian law.

Vessel Definitions

Rule 3 tells us that a *vessel* is any type of watercraft, including seaplanes, that can be used for transporta-

tion on the water. *Seaplanes* are considered ". . . aircraft designed to maneuver on the water."

The rule further defines *power-driven vessels* as vessels propelled by machinery, and *sailing vessels* as vessels under sail, not using propulsion machinery. When a sailing vessel is using engine power instead of or in addition to sails, it is legally classed as a power-driven vessel. Rule 3 also makes the following distinctions.

Vessel Underway

Some of the Rules require an understanding of the term "underway." A vessel *underway* is not at anchor, nor made fast to a shore or pier, nor aground (Figure 6-3). A vessel *making way* is being pro-

Figure **6-3.** These vessels are all classified as not underway by the rules. **Top to bottom:** Docked, anchored, and aground. (TOP AND MIDDLE PHOTOS BY BOB DENNIS; BOTTOM PHOTO REPRINTED WITH PERMISSION FROM *SEAWORTHY: ESSENTIAL LESSONS FROM BOAT U.S.'S 20-YEAR CASE FILE OF THINGS GONE WRONG* BY ROBERT A. ADRIANCE)

Figure **6-2.** Seaward of the dashed magenta demarcation line (circled in yellow) on this chart, the International Rules apply. Upriver of the line, the Inland Rules apply. (REPRINTED WITH PERMISSION FROM *THE WEEKEND NAVIGATOR* BY BOB SWEET)

pelled through the water. It is **adrift** when it is not being propelled, not at anchor, not made fast to the shore, or aground (Figure 6-4). A **drifting vessel** is underway but not making way.

Fishing Vessel

A *fishing vessel* is any vessel fishing with nets, lines, trawls, or other fishing apparatus that restricts its ability to maneuver under the Rules. Vessels fishing with trolling lines are not fishing vessels, and your vessel is not a fishing vessel if you are sportfishing.

Vessel Restricted in Ability to Maneuver

Some vessels are *restricted in their ability to maneuver*, meaning that their work keeps them from abiding by the Rules and staying out of the way of other vessels. Dredges, cable- and pipe-laying vessels, and other such vessels are restricted in their ability to maneuver.

Vessels in Sight of Another

A vessel is *in sight of another* when it can observe the other vessel or the other vessel's lights visually, without mechanical or optical aids. Other rules apply when one vessel has another in "sight" with radar.

Vessel Not Under Command

A vessel is *not under command* when some exceptional circumstance keeps it from maneuvering as required by the Rules. This means that it can't keep out of the way of other vessels. A drifting boat with an inoperative engine or steering system is not under command.

Vessel Constrained by Draft

The International Rules describe a vessel *constrained by draft* as a power-driven vessel that is severely restricted in its ability to change course because of its draft relative to the depth of water (Figure 6-5). The Inland Rules do not contain such a definition.

The General Responsibility Rule

Rule 2 is the General Responsibility Rule, which has two principal aspects.

The Rule of Good Seamanship

Part (a) of the General Responsibility Rule has been called the Rule of Good Seamanship. It says, sim-

Figure **6-4.** The 90-foot tall ship *Irving Johnson* lies hard aground only yards from shore near the entrance to Channel Islands Harbor, Oxnard, California. Until it can be refloated, this vessel will be classified under the rules as not underway! (PHOTO BY MIKE BRODEY)

Figure **6-5.** The Law of Gross Tonnage is not listed in the COLREGS, but prudence and common sense dictate that you should keep away from large vessels. Even when not constrained by draft, a ship like this takes a mile or two to stop or turn, and it's moving a lot faster than it may appear to be. (REPRINTED WITH PERMISSION FROM *SEAWORTHY: ESSENTIAL LESSONS FROM BOAT U.S.'S 20-YEAR CASE FILE OF THINGS GONE WRONG* BY ROBERT A. ADRIANCE)

ply, that nothing in the Rules excuses you from failure to follow the Rules or to practice good seamanship. In situations not covered by the Rules, take the action required by the special circumstances.

The General Prudential Rule

Part (b) of the General Responsibility Rule is sometimes called the General Prudential Rule. It directs you to consider all the dangers to navigation when applying the Rules, evaluating and responding to any special circumstances that may make you depart from the Rules to avoid immediate danger. "Immediate danger" means more than just the mere perception of a risk of collision. It means, rather, that a collision is imminent unless you act immediately to avoid it. In such a circumstance, Rule 2(b) says, you *must* depart from the Rules to avoid the collision.

Assessing Legal Liability

There are important differences in legal liability between maritime and civil law. Because each skipper must act to prevent a collision and must depart from the Navigation Rules when necessary, all parties usually share responsibility for a marine accident. This does not mean that the shares are equal, however. That is a matter for a court to decide.

If you have a collision, you may be at least partially responsible no matter what the other skipper does. Likewise, skippers operating under the influence of alcohol or drugs are usually held at least partially responsible for an accident no matter what the other skipper may have done. It is not unusual for all parties to be responsible for some act they did or did not do. Only rarely do marine accidents produce a finding of fault on only one skipper.

Assisting Boaters in Distress

Federal law requires you to give assistance to another vessel in peril if doing so will not greatly endanger you, your vessel, and your crew. However, maritime courts have also decided that Good Samaritans who render service to those in distress may be liable for injuries or death caused by their

failure to exercise reasonable care. These legal conditions make it difficult to decide where to start and where to stop when rendering assistance. The stress of an emergency only complicates the situation. Individuals must make their own decisions about rendering assistance, but here are some guidelines:

- Get early guidance from the U.S. Coast Guard because they have well-thought-out protocols for most conditions.
- Doing less rather than more is usually wise, especially if you have no special training or knowledge. For example, moving an injured person to a more comfortable place might seem compassionate, but could also cause further injury. See also Appendix A.

General Considerations

The Rules make several important generalizations.

Vessel Size and the Rules

All vessels from the smallest personal watercraft (PWC) to the largest supertanker must obey the Rules. It would be foolhardy, though, for you to demand your "rights" under all circumstances. There are practical limitations on that right. Large vessels are not as maneuverable as small ones. A supertanker, for example, may take several miles to stop even with its engines in reverse. Large freighters throw up high wakes that can swamp or capsize small boats, and you should keep away from them.

You should also keep clear of deep-draft tugs, which can create dangerous currents, especially in shallow water, and sweep small vessels into these currents with serious results.

When a tug is pushing a long line of barges, its operator has a blind spot immediately ahead of the barges. The longer the line of barges, the larger the blind spot. The operator can't see you if you pass in front of the barges, and even when you are seen, the operator can't do anything to avoid hitting you if you come too close.

All vessels, and PWC in particular, should use extreme caution to avoid passing in front of other vessels, including barges and other large vessels. Large vessels move faster than you may think. A deep-draft vessel traveling at a speed of 10 knots covers about 1,000 feet in 1 minute.

It is tempting to jump the wake of another vessel with your PWC, but this can be an extremely dangerous practice, not only because you or a passenger can be thrown off the craft, but also because large vessels operating in shallow waters can often churn up submerged debris, which poses a collision hazard. Various states have passed laws to limit this practice (e.g., no wake jumping within a specified number of feet from the vessel causing the wake).

Maintain a Lookout

Both sets of Rules require every vessel to maintain a proper *lookout*. The lookout must listen for danger as well as look for it (Figure 6-6), and must also

Figure **6-6.** Always maintain a lookout. (PHOTO BY DUNCAN WILKINSON)

use all means available for watching, including radar, if available. Even if the Rules did not require a lookout, common sense would suggest such a need. **The principal cause of vessel collisions is failure to maintain a lookout!**

Lookouts should have nothing else to do, so don't divide their attention. If you are alone on a vessel and it is underway, serve as your own lookout. Otherwise, appoint someone as lookout who is not responsible for anything else, and change lookouts frequently.

Safe Speed

The Rules require all vessels to proceed at safe speeds so they can stop or take proper and effective action to avoid collisions.

The Rules do not say what a safe speed is, but they do say that a safe speed depends on visibility, traffic density, and maneuverability of your vessel,

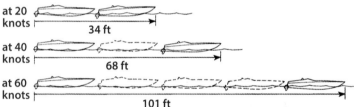

Figure **6-7.** Given a 1-second reaction time, this is how far your boat would travel at various speeds before you could react to danger ahead—and your boat would go a lot farther still before your reaction could produce its desired effect. In poor visibility, even 10 knots might be an unsafe speed. (ADAPTED FROM *FAST POWERBOAT SEAMANSHIP* BY DAG PIKE)

WARNING ***Speed and the need for constant vigilance.*** *Many boats are capable of operating at high speeds. PWC, for example, can operate at speeds greater than 60 miles per hour. As speeds increase, the time available to react decreases. According to a recent report by the National Transportation Safety Board, "Operators of two PWC traveling at 40 mph on a head-on course will have a response time of 1.3 seconds to travel 50 yards. Even when the vessels are converging on a 45° angle, the response time is less than 2 seconds. The response time must accommodate perceiving the other vessel, deciding . . . [how] . . . to comply with the rules of the road, determining the risk of collision, and executing a response to alter course." Speed is particularly a problem with small and unstable craft. When these craft are operated at high speeds in other than very calm seas, the operator's attention tends to be focused on the nearest upcoming waves—to the exclusion of other vessels. This tunnel vision may mean that the operator fails to see other traffic and react accordingly. Operators of all fast boats need to adjust their speeds to fit the conditions.*

sea state, current, wind, and other factors. If you were to have a collision, you probably would be judged to have been traveling at an unsafe speed. This can happen even if you were maintaining a proper lookout.

In restricted visibility, you must slow down (Figure 6-7). Fog, mist, falling snow, sleet, heavy rainstorms, sandstorms, smoke, and other conditions restrict visibility. A clear night is not considered an instance of restricted visibility, since navigation lights should be clearly visible at night, but slowing down at night is recommended under the standards of prudent seamanship promoted by the Rules.

Do You Have Radar?

Even if your vessel is fitted with operational radar, you must maintain a lookout and travel at a safe speed. Having radar may actually increase your responsibility. You must use it whenever it can help you avoid a collision. With it, you may be able to detect another vessel before it sees you. Thus, you may be the first to see that a collision is possible and that evasive action is necessary.

Assess radar information carefully, and do not reach hasty conclusions. Consider your radar's efficiency and limitations. Carefully evaluate the effects of sea state, weather, and other interference on radar reception, and remember that your radar may not be able to detect small vessels or floating objects. Also evaluate the number, location, and movement of vessels shown by your radar. You have responsibility for your radar's proper use and interpretation.

Figure **6-8.** Looking forward from the bridge of a big container ship approaching Port Everglades, Florida. This photo was taken with a telephoto lens. Stick to the edges of a narrow channel and do not impede a vessel like this one. (REPRINTED WITH PERMISSION FROM *SEAWORTHY: ESSENTIAL LESSONS FROM BOAT U.S.'S 20-YEAR CASE FILE OF THINGS GONE WRONG* BY ROBERT A. ADRIANCE)

Conduct in Narrow Channels

All vessels less than 20 meters long and all sailing vessels are required by both the International and Inland Rules to keep to the right in a narrow channel or fairway, and not to impede the passage of a vessel that can navigate safely only within the channel. This means, for example, that you should not cross a narrow channel or fairway when it will impede a vessel that can travel safely only in the channel, nor should you anchor in a narrow channel except in an emergency (Figure 6-8).

The Inland Rules have an additional requirement for narrow channels subject to currents. Vessels traveling with the current (downbound) in narrow channels or fairways have the right of way. (Note: This is the only place in the Rules where the term **right of way** appears.) This rule is in effect on the Great Lakes, Western Rivers, and other specified waters. The upbound vessel must yield and allow the downbound vessel to pass. The rule exists because it is easier to control your vessel when you are traveling against the current than when traveling with it.

Traffic Separation Schemes

The International Rules make provision for *traffic separation schemes* (TSS), a system of one-way lanes used in congested traffic areas, and regulate traffic in them.

Normally, vessels join or leave a TSS at either end. If you enter obliquely, do so at a small angle. You should avoid crossing traffic lanes, but if you must cross, do so as nearly at right angles to the traffic flow as you can. Don't anchor in a TSS unless you have an emergency.

Vessel Traffic Services

The Coast Guard maintains *vessel traffic services* (VTS) in several U.S. ports (Figure 6-9). When you are boating in waters subject to a VTS, learn its location and whether it uses TSS lanes. If so, you must be able to recognize the buoys that mark the lanes. Never travel the "wrong way" or anchor in a lane.

Stand-On or Give-Way?

To interpret the Rules, you must understand the terms "stand-on" and "give-way." The Navigation Rules require that a *stand-on vessel* maintain its course and speed unless a danger of collision is apparent. A *give-way vessel* must take whatever action is necessary to avoid a collision. A stand-on vessel maintains course and speed so that a give-way vessel can predict what the stand-on vessel will do. Conversely, the give-way vessel should show good seamanship and make a significant course change so that the stand-on vessel can easily see that he is responding properly.

It is also important for you to know that the Rules grant no vessel the right of way except when downbound in certain narrow channels of the inland waters, as mentioned above. Instead, when vessels meet, one is usually stand-on while the other is give-way. The fact that no vessel has the right of way explains, in part, the sharing of liability in marine collisions. When driving, one automobile often has the legal right of way over another, but this is not so for watercraft.

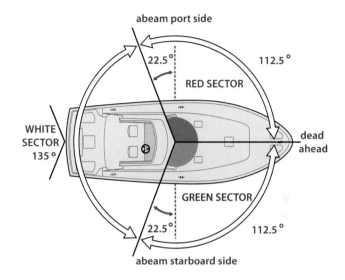

Figure **6-10.** The red, green, and white sectors of a vessel.

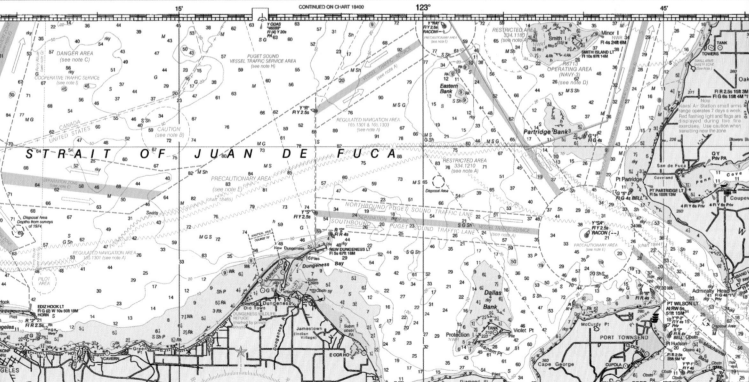

Figure **6-9.** The lanes of the VTS are clearly shown on this chart of Port Townsend, Washington. (COURTESY NOAA)

The Danger Zone

Determination of who is stand-on or give-way requires an understanding of how vessels are **sectored**.

On a vessel, three sectors account for the 360° of a circle. As you can see from Figure 6-10, one sector is from dead ahead to 22.5° abaft (behind) the vessel's starboard beam. A second sector is from dead ahead to 22.5° abaft its port beam. Each of these two sectors is 90° + 22.5° or 112.5°. These two sectors account for 2 x 112.5° or 225°. This leaves 360° – 225° or 135° for the third, or stern, sector.

At night, the three sectors are easy to see if a boat's lights are correct. The sector on the starboard side from dead ahead to 22.5° abaft the starboard beam shows a green navigation light and is called the green sector. When an approaching vessel sees your green light, it is required by the Rules to stand on. This sector is your *danger zone* because you are required to give way to any vessel approaching in that sector. The sector on the port side shows a red navigation light and is called the red sector. Together, the red and green lights are the **sidelights**.

Most boats have white **sternlights** with arcs of 135° to cover the stern (white) sector. They also have white **masthead lights** that shine forward over an arc of 225°, covering the red and green sectors combined. Together, masthead lights and sternlights cover 360°. Some small boats have all-round (360°) masthead lights instead of 225° masthead lights and separate sternlights.

Who Is Stand-On?

There are three situations in which the risk of collision exists. First, when you see both the red and green lights of another vessel dead ahead, you know you are on a collision course, meeting **head-on** (Figure 6-11). When the vessels are power-driven, both are give-way, and each must alter its course to starboard. If you have any doubt about whether a head-on situation exists, you must assume that it does and act accordingly.

Second, when another vessel's sternlight draws steadily closer, you are **overtaking** it. You are the give-way vessel and must avoid the other vessel.

Third, when your power-driven vessel ap-

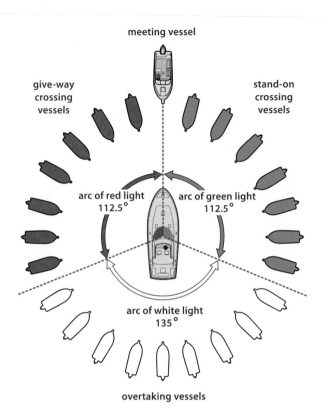

Figure **6-11.** The three situations.

proaches another vessel and you see its red light, you know it is in your danger zone and you are the give-way vessel. The other vessel sees your green light and is required to stand on. Alter your course to pass astern of the other vessel. This is a **crossing situation**, and speeding up to pass in front of a stand-on vessel is dangerous.

Whenever a danger of collision exists, be cautious. The other skipper may not see your lights or know what they mean. If the other vessel does not treat you as stand-on and does not alter its course, you must give the *danger signal*—at least five short and rapid blasts on your whistle—and change your course to prevent a collision. (See Chapter 2 for a description of a boat's whistle.) The change in course is usually to your starboard. When the other vessel is forward of your port beam and you are not overtaking it, do not turn to port. When the other vessel is abeam or abaft the beam on either side of your vessel, do not turn toward it.

In the Daytime

In the daytime, although you will not see lights on the other boat, the same three zones exist. The danger zone is still your "green light" zone. When your vessel is power-driven and another vessel approaches you from starboard, you are give-way. You are also give-way if you approach the stern sector of another vessel.

Courtesy and Common Sense

Remember, courtesy and common sense are as important as the Rules. Don't use your boat to argue with another skipper. If the other skipper is rude, don't use it as an excuse for rudeness on your part. If the other skipper does not treat you as stand-on, sound the danger signal and yield. The other skipper may not know the Navigation Rules, but winning the argument could ruin your whole day.

Constant Bearing

If the direction to another vessel stays the same, or nearly so, as you get closer to it, you are on a *collision course* (Figure 6-12). When this happens, take evasive action. Slow down to permit the other vessel to pass in front of you, or change your course, or both.

When you act to avoid a collision, make your change in course or speed large enough that it can be readily seen by the other vessel, either visually or on radar. A change in course should be at least 60°. Even this may not be enough when approaching a large vessel or a tow or when you are close to another vessel.

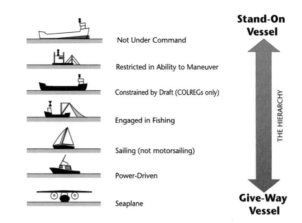

Figure **6-13.** The "pecking order" for stand-on and give-way vessels. (REPRINTED WITH PERMISSION FROM *RULES OF THE ROAD AND RUNNNING LIGHT PATTERNS: A CAPTAIN'S QUICK GUIDE* BY CHARLIE WING)

Rules for Special Vessels

Some vessels are less maneuverable than others. Because of this, the Navigation Rules give them special stand-on status (Figure 6-13).

Overtaking and Overtaken Vessels

For recreational boaters, three special provisions deserve attention. First, an overtaken vessel is stand-on to all other vessels. A sailing vessel that is

Figure **6-12.** When the bearing to an approaching vessel remains constant as its distance off decreases, you are on a collision course. (REPRINTED WITH PERMISSION FROM *SEAWORTHY: ESSENTIAL LESSONS FROM BOAT U.S.'S 20-YEAR CASE FILE OF THINGS GONE WRONG* BY ROBERT A. ADRIANCE)

overtaking another vessel must give way to it even when the overtaken vessel is power-driven.

Second, except when overtaken, a power-driven vessel must give way to a sailing vessel. When a power-driven vessel meets a sailing vessel head-on, the power-driven vessel is the give-way vessel. The same is true in a crossing situation—the power-driven vessel is give-way even if it sees the green sidelight of the sailing vessel.

Third, when on the water, seaplanes are vessels, and should give way to all other vessels except when they are being overtaken.

Sailing Vessels

Because of a sailboat's reduced maneuverability, both the Inland and International Rules make special provisions for sailboats in sight of one another. These provisions are the same in both sets of Rules, and apply whenever there is a risk of collision.

In overtaking situations, the overtaken vessel is stand-on, while in meeting and crossing situations, the wind is the deciding factor. When each sailing vessel has the wind on a different side, the vessel with the wind on its port side is give-way (Figure 6-14), and the vessel with the wind on its starboard side is stand-on.

The *windward* side of a vessel is the side from which the wind is blowing. The *leeward* side is the

side away from the wind, which is also the side on which the sails are trimmed. For example, when the wind is blowing from the port side of a vessel, this is its windward side, which makes its starboard side its leeward side (sailors pronounce this "loo • ard"). When both sailing vessels have the wind on the same side, the vessel to windward is give-way.

Sometimes you cannot tell if the wind is on the port or starboard side of another sailing vessel. If your sailing vessel has the wind on its port side and you cannot tell if a sailing vessel to windward has the wind on its port or starboard side, you must assume that it has the wind on its starboard side and is the stand-on vessel. Keep out of the way of this other vessel.

Again, for the purposes of the Rules, the leeward side of a sailing vessel is the side on which the mainsail is carried. The windward side is deemed to be the opposite side.

Risk of Collision

A risk of collision can exist in head-on, crossing, or overtaking situations. The Navigation Rules prescribe the behavior of vessels in these situations and the signals that power-driven vessels exchange.

Head-On Situations

Vessels that approach each other on reciprocal (opposite) or nearly reciprocal courses are meeting head-on. At night each vessel sees both the red and green sidelights of the other vessel, and should also see its masthead light or lights if it has them. When it is under sail and without power, a sailboat does not use a white masthead light.

When there are two masthead lights on a vessel and you are meeting head-on, they will be in a vertical line, with the forward one lower than the aft one. Two masthead lights mean that the vessel is 50 or more meters long. Get out of its way!

A small vessel yaws in a heavy chop or in ground swells, which means that another vessel meeting it sees alternating red and green sidelights. When you see this pattern of sidelights, assume that you are meeting another vessel head-on.

It is not as easy to determine when a head-on situation exists in the daytime. If you have any

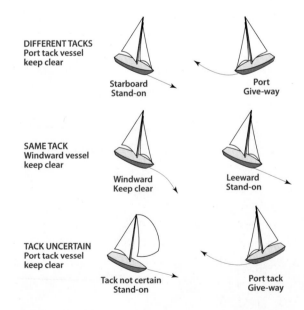

DIFFERENT TACKS
Port tack vessel keep clear

Starboard Stand-on

Port Give-way

SAME TACK
Windward vessel keep clear

Windward Keep clear

Leeward Stand-on

TACK UNCERTAIN
Port tack vessel keep clear

Tack not certain Stand-on

Port tack Give-way

Figure **6-14.** The International and Inland Rules for sailing vessels. (REPRINTED WITH PERMISSION FROM *RULES OF THE ROAD AND RUNNNING LIGHT PATTERNS: A CAPTAIN'S QUICK GUIDE* BY CHARLIE WING)

doubt, assume it is a head-on situation. In a head-on or meeting situation involving power-driven vessels, neither vessel is stand-on. Both are give-way.

Head-On Sound Signals

The usual course of action when two power-driven vessels are meeting head-on is for each vessel to alter its course to starboard. Sound signals are also given, with a **short blast** of a whistle being a blast of 1 second's duration and a **prolonged blast** lasting 4 to 6 seconds. The term "long blast" is not used in the Navigation Rules.

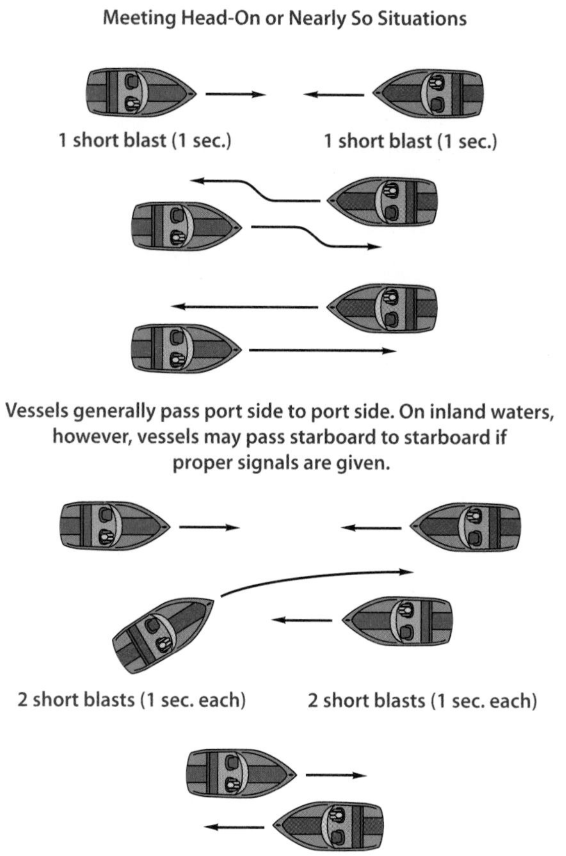

Meeting Head-On or Nearly So Situations

1 short blast (1 sec.)   1 short blast (1 sec.)

Vessels generally pass port side to port side. On inland waters, however, vessels may pass starboard to starboard if proper signals are given.

2 short blasts (1 sec. each)   2 short blasts (1 sec. each)

Figure **6-15.** When power-driven vessels meet, neither vessel is stand-on. Both the International and Inland Rules specify port side to port side passing, and a turn to starboard to accomplish this is signaled with a single short blast (top). On international waters the signal need not be acknowledged before the signaling vessel turns, but on inland waters it must be. On inland waters only, starboard side to starboard side passing is permissible after the proper signal (two short blasts) is made and acknowledged. (REPRINTED WITH PERMISSION FROM "FEDERAL REQUIREMENTS & SAFETY TIPS FOR RECREATIONAL BOATS," U.S. COAST GUARD OFFICE OF BOATING SAFETY)

Whistle signals can be confusing to learn. To make it easier, think of yourself as a vessel's skipper and associate one short blast with the word "port," which has one syllable, and two short blasts with the word "starboard," which has two syllables. Thus, in the head-on meeting situation described above, the other vessel will be on your port side as you pass it so you should sound one short blast. Under the Inland Rules, you may pass another vessel starboard to starboard, in which case you should sound two short blasts.

This rule of thumb is correct in most instances, but as with most rules, there are exceptions. Refer to the *Navigation Rules, International–Inland* for further guidance.

In a meeting situation under International or Inland Rules, when either vessel believes a collision is imminent it must take evasive action. This may consist of trying to stop, signaled by three short blasts. The blasts mean, "I am operating astern propulsion," not "I am backing up." A heavy vessel can operate astern propulsion for some time before it overcomes its headway.

International Meeting Signals

Under the International Rules, when power-driven vessels meet head-on or nearly so and a risk of collision exists, each vessel turns to starboard as in Figure 6-15. At the same time, one vessel gives a short blast. Thus the vessels pass port to port. Note that under the International Rules, one vessel gives a blast to indicate its intentions, but the other vessel is not required to respond with a signal if it agrees.

Inland Meeting Signals

Inland meeting signals for power-driven vessels are similar to those used in international waters, but there are significant differences (see Figure 6-15), one of which is that inland signals announce only your *intention* to act—they require a response before you can act. (Except in overtaking situations in narrow channels and near obscured bends in a channel, the International Rules do not require a response from the other vessel.)

A second difference is that in inland waters, when power-driven vessels in sight of each other meet head-on or cross within $\frac{1}{2}$ mile, they exchange sound signals even if neither vessel has to change course.

On inland waters in a head-on situation, one short blast means, "I intend to pass you on my port side," and two short blasts mean, "I intend to pass you on my starboard side."

If the other vessel agrees to your intended maneuver, it signals its agreement by returning the same signal. For example, if you sound one short blast and the other vessel agrees, it also sounds one short blast. Each vessel, if necessary, alters its course to starboard and the vessels pass port side to port side.

The other vessel answers a two-blast signal with two short blasts. When necessary, each vessel then alters its course to port and the vessels pass starboard to starboard. When there is no danger of collision, neither vessel changes course.

If the second vessel disagrees or does not understand your intention, it should answer with the **doubt** or **danger signal**, at least five short, rapid blasts.

Crossing Situations

When two vessels meet and each sees either a red or a green light, they are crossing. One vessel is coming toward the other in an area from almost dead ahead to 22.5° abaft either beam. When you are not sure whether you are in a meeting or a crossing situation, assume you are meeting and take appropriate action.

When you are power driven and see a green sidelight on another power-driven vessel, you are stand-on and the other vessel, which sees your red sidelight, is give-way. When a crossing vessel is on your starboard side, you are give-way and must stay out of its way. You can do this by slowing down and letting the other vessel pass in front of you, or by altering your course to starboard and passing astern of it, or both.

Crossing Signals

Suppose that in inland waters, you meet another power-driven vessel head-on and wish to pass port side to port side. You will sound one short blast. Suppose, however, that the other vessel believes it would be better for your vessels to pass starboard to starboard. It cannot answer your one blast sig-

nal with two blasts, because doing so would be to **cross signals**.

Instead, the second vessel must respond with the doubt or danger signal. You can then sound two short blasts to announce your intention to pass starboard to starboard. When this is acceptable to the other vessel, it responds with two blasts. So, the other vessel must respond only with the signal you give or with the danger signal.

Crossing in International Waters

In international waters, power-driven vessels do not have to give sound signals in crossing situations unless action is needed by the give-way vessel. Of course, either you or the other skipper can give the doubt or danger signal if necessary.

When the give-way vessel finds it necessary to alter course, it sounds one short blast to show it is altering its course to starboard. It will then pass astern of the stand-on vessel, and the stand-on vessel will be on the give-way vessel's port side. The stand-on vessel does not respond. This is a rule in international waters that is generally true; that is, when one vessel gives a signal, and the other vessel agrees with the action, there is no return signal.

Crossing in Inland Waters

In inland waters, the give-way power-driven vessel announces its intention to pass astern of the stand-on vessel by one short blast (Figure 6-16).

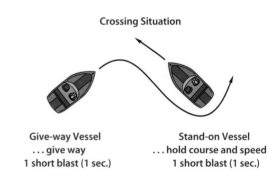

Crossing Situation

Give-way Vessel
...give way
1 short blast (1 sec.)

Stand-on Vessel
...hold course and speed
1 short blast (1 sec.)

Figure **6-16.** When power-driven vessels cross on inland waters, the give-way vessel announces its intention to pass astern of the stand-on vessel, and the latter responds. On international waters no response from the stand-on vessel is required. (REPRINTED WITH PERMISSION FROM "FEDERAL REQUIREMENTS & SAFETY TIPS FOR RECREATIONAL BOATS," U.S. COAST GUARD OFFICE OF BOATING SAFETY)

Overtaking Situations

When you approach another vessel and see only its sternlight, you are overtaking it. This means you are approaching the other vessel from a direction more than 22.5° abaft either of its beams. Whether you are power driven or sailing, you are give-way and must stay clear of the overtaken vessel. If you can't tell if you are overtaking another vessel or crossing its path, assume that you are overtaking and that you are the give-way vessel.

Overtaking in Inland Waters

In inland waters when you intend to overtake a vessel, you announce your intention to pass it on your port side with one short blast. If this is acceptable to the other vessel, it responds with the same signal—one short blast. You then pass the overtaken vessel on your port side (Figure 6-17).

You state your intention to pass the overtaken vessel on your starboard side with two short blasts. Again, if agreeable to the vessel you are overtaking, it responds with the same signal—two short blasts. It can reject your intention by using the danger signal. Don't give cross signals.

Overtaking in International Waters

In open waters under International Rules, if one vessel overtakes another from dead astern, the overtaking vessel must alter course. It sounds one short blast to show it is altering its course to starboard, and two short blasts if it alters its course to port.

Under either set of Rules, you remain an overtaking vessel until you are finally past and clear of the overtaken vessel. Any change in bearing of the two vessels does not change your status. Thus, when you are an overtaking vessel, you cannot become a crossing vessel.

Overtaking in Narrow Channels

The International Rules require sound signals when you are overtaking another vessel in a narrow channel or fairway and the overtaken vessel has to take action to permit safe passage. Sound two prolonged blasts and one short blast to say that you intend to pass the other vessel on your port side.

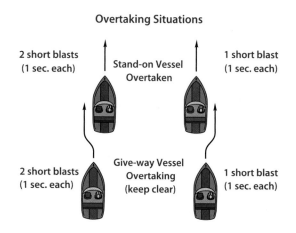

Overtaking Situations

2 short blasts (1 sec. each) — **Stand-on Vessel Overtaken** — 1 short blast (1 sec. each)

2 short blasts (1 sec. each) — **Give-way Vessel Overtaking (keep clear)** — 1 short blast (1 sec. each)

Figure **6-17.** When one vessel overtakes another, it is the give-way vessel and must signal its intentions as shown. No response from the overtaken vessel is required on international waters. See the accompanying text for the rules that apply when one vessel overtakes another in a narrow channel on international waters. (REPRINTED WITH PERMISSION FROM "FEDERAL REQUIREMENTS & SAFETY TIPS FOR RECREATIONAL BOATS," U.S. COAST GUARD OFFICE OF BOATING SAFETY)

When the other vessel agrees, it should sound one prolonged, one short, one prolonged, and one short blast. If it disagrees, it sounds the danger signal. You cannot pass until there is agreement.

Note that this situation is an exception to the general rule governing sound signals in international waters. In this case, your signal announces intent, not action. It is also an exception in that it requires a response from the overtaken vessel.

When, in a narrow channel or fairway, you intend to pass the other vessel on your starboard side, sound two prolonged and two short blasts. If the overtaken vessel agrees, it responds with one prolonged, one short, one prolonged, and one short blast. It can, of course, respond with the danger signal. You can pass only after there is agreement and should not give cross signals.

The one- or two-short-blast rule still holds: when you overtake a vessel on your port side, sound one short blast, and when you overtake on your starboard side, sound two short blasts. The difference in the rule, as applied here, is that you sound two prolonged blasts before either the one- or two-short-blast signal.

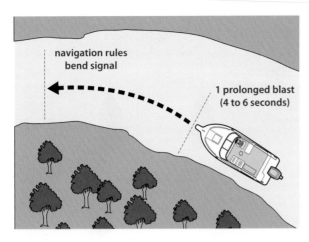

Figure **6-18.** Approaching a bend.

Bend Signals

In a narrow channel or when nearing a bend, your view may be obscured. Both sets of Rules require you to navigate with "alertness and caution," and to sound one prolonged blast (Figure 6-18). An approaching vessel that hears your signal answers with one prolonged blast.

Restricted Visibility

Most of the Rules relate to vessels in sight of each other. The rule for bend signals is an exception, and so are the rules that regulate the conduct of vessels in or near an area of restricted visibility. When vessels are not in sight of one another, no vessel is stand-on to any other vessel. Both vessels should have their engines ready for immediate maneuver in order to avoid a collision. Vessels should proceed at a safe speed, adapting to the conditions while continuing to observe the rules for meeting, crossing, and overtaking that pertain to all conditions of visibility. You must take action to avoid a vessel detected by radar, but use of radar is not a justification for operating at an unsafe speed in conditions of reduced visibility, nor is radar an acceptable substitute for a proper lookout. Reduce your speed or take off all way when you hear a vessel forward of your beam, until you deem the danger of collision to be over.

Sound signals in restricted visibility are the same in both sets of Rules. They may be hand-timed and mechanically produced, or automatically produced by electronic means.

Sound Signals Underway

In or near an area of restricted visibility, use the following sound signals when underway:

- When you are power driven and making way, sound one prolonged blast at least every 2 minutes.

- When you are power driven and adrift, sound two prolonged blasts at least every 2 minutes. There should be an interval of about 2 seconds between your blasts.

- Some vessels underway sound one prolonged blast followed by two short blasts at least every 2 minutes. These include vessels not under command, those restricted in ability to maneuver, sailing vessels, vessels towing or pushing other vessels, and fishing vessels.

Sound Signals Not Underway

When not underway, give the following sound signals in restricted visibility:

- When you are at anchor in open water and your vessel is 12 meters long or longer, ring your bell rapidly for about 5 seconds at least every minute. In a vessel less than 12 meters long, you do not have to give signals with a bell. If you don't, you must make some other efficient sound signal at least every 2 minutes. A vessel 100 meters or more in length sounds a bell in its forepart. Immediately afterward, it sounds a gong for about 5 seconds in its after part. When you hear a bell and a gong, you know you are near a large anchored vessel.

- At anchor you may also sound one short, one

WARNING *Since PWC are not equipped with lights, it follows that they must not operate at night. To do so violates the Navigation Rules. In addition, many states and localities have laws and ordinances specifically prohibiting the operation of PWC during nighttime hours.*

prolonged, and one short blast of your whistle. This tells an approaching vessel of your position and warns of the chance of collision. When at anchor, you make more noise than when underway; you can afford to. When underway, you need to listen for sounds from other vessels. Should your vessel be aground, you must give the bell signal given by a vessel at anchor. In addition, give three separate and distinct strokes on your bell immediately before and after the rapid ringing of the bell.

- In special anchorage areas, vessels less than 20 meters long do not need to give sound signals. Nautical charts show these areas. In restricted visibility, if you hear a whistle or a horn, you know it is usually coming from a vessel underway. That vessel may or may not be making way, however. A bell or a gong tells you the vessel is stationary, either anchored or aground.

Vessel Lights and Shapes

At night, your vessel must have proper navigation lights. Show them from sunset to sunrise and in restricted visibility, and don't show other lights at the same time that might appear to be navigation lights. Also, don't show other lights if they interfere with the vision of your lookout.

Except for searchlights, lights on boats serve different purposes from lights on automobiles. Boat lights do not help you see ahead, but are there to be seen and to communicate vital information to other vessels. Figure 6-20 shows that navigation lights have sectors where they can or cannot be seen, and tells you which way another vessel is facing.

Range of Visibility

The required intensities of your navigation lights are given in terms of their minimum required ranges of visibility. These required intensities vary with

Figure **6-19.** An at-a-glance summary of the Steering and Sailing Rules (Rules 9–18). (REPRINTED WITH PERMISSION FROM *RULES OF THE ROAD AND RUNNING LIGHT PATTERNS: A CAPTAIN'S QUICK GUIDE* BY CHARLIE WING)

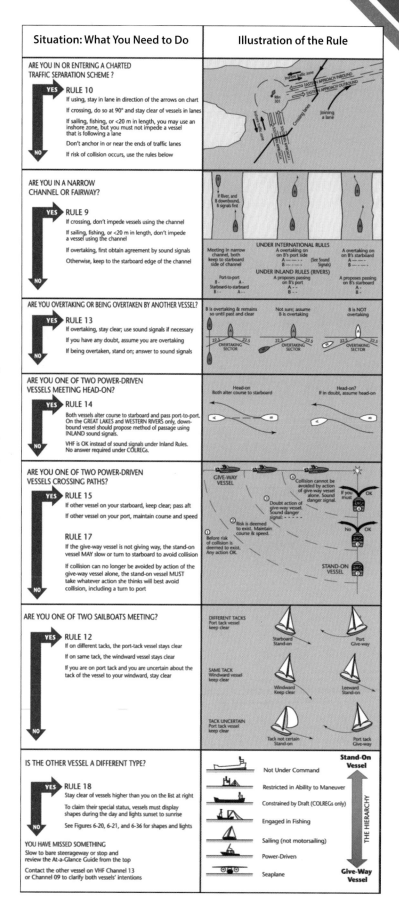

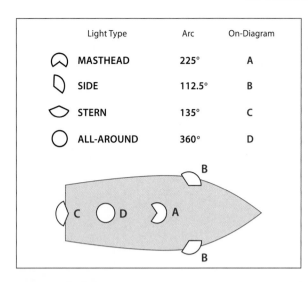

Light Type		Arc	On-Diagram
	MASTHEAD	225°	A
	SIDE	112.5°	B
	STERN	135°	C
	ALL-AROUND	360°	D

Figure **6-20.** Navigation lights and their sectors.

Light Type	Visibility Min. Distance—Nautical Miles			
	1	2	3	5
MASTHEAD		●	▲	◆
SIDE	●	▲◆		
STERN		●▲◆		
ALL-AROUND		●▲◆		
TOWING		●▲◆		
SPECIAL FLASHING (Inland Rules Only)		●▲◆		

● Less than 12 Meters
▲ 12 Meters but Less than 20 Meters
◆ 20 Meters but Less than 50 Meters

Figure **6-21.** Required light visibilities.

colors and purposes. See Figure 6-21 for the intensities of lights required on your boat. If your vessel is less than 12 meters long, its lights should be visible as follows: masthead, 2 miles; sidelights, 1 mile; all-round lights, 2 miles. (An all-round light shines through an arc of 360°.) Your boat manufacturer probably used properly sized bulbs, so if you need to replace them, use comparable bulbs.

What Lights Tell You

You already know something about vessel lights. You know what sidelights, masthead lights, and sternlights are, and also know how to tell who is stand-on and who is give-way by looking at a vessel's lights.

The lights on another boat answer several questions for you: Is the other boat headed toward you? Is it crossing your course? Are you overtaking it?

The lights on vessels also help you to know something about their size, with larger vessels having more navigation lights than smaller ones. In general, the more navigation lights a vessel has, the greater the danger it poses. Stay clear of vessels with navigation lights you do not understand and vessels with many navigation lights.

As you will see, the special navigation lights of a vessel often tell something about its condition or activity.

Shapes on Vessels

In addition to lights, vessels show *shapes* to alert you to their special conditions or activities. Shapes are also called "day shapes," since they are the daytime equivalent of special navigation lights. One of the annexes (appendices) to the Navigation Rules describes these shapes, all of which are black. They may be *balls*, *cones*, *diamonds*, or *cylinders*.

Lights and Shapes on Sailing Vessels Underway

At night, a sailing vessel underway must show sidelights and a sternlight as in Figures 6-22 and 6-23, but it does not have a lighted masthead light. Thus, when you see a sidelight but no white light, you are looking at a sailing vessel underway (unless the vessel is improperly lighted). The lights on sailing vessels are the same under either set of Rules.

The sidelights and sternlight of a sailing vessel less than 20 meters long may be combined in one device or fixture carried at or near the masthead, where it is most visible (Figure 6-24). Don't use this light on a sailboat under power. In that case, show the lights of a power-driven vessel (Figure 6-25).

A sailing vessel underway may show, in addition to its sidelights and sternlight, two all-round lights in a vertical line as in Figure 6-26. The upper light is red and the lower is green, and both lights

Figure 6-22. A sailing vessel underway with separate sidelights.

Figure 6-23. A sailing vessel underway with combined sidelights.

Figure 6-24. Alternative light configuration for a sailing vessel less than 20 meters long.

Figure 6-25. A sailing vessel under 20 meters long using both sail and power.

Figure 6-26. Optional all-round mast-lights for a vessel under sail.

(REPRINTED WITH PERMISSION FROM "FEDERAL REQUIREMENTS & SAFETY TIPS FOR RECREATIONAL BOATS," U.S. COAST GUARD OFFICE OF BOATING SAFETY)

are at or near the top of its mast, where they are most visible. These optional additional lights are not to be used with the three-color light shown in Figure 6-24.

During daylight hours, a sailing vessel that is also under power must show a conical shape with its apex pointed downward (Figure 6-27), and must show this cone where it is most visible. Under the Inland Rules, a sailing vessel less than 12 meters long need not display this day shape.

A sailing vessel less than 7 meters long must, if practicable, show the same lights as larger sailing vessels. If it doesn't have lights, it must have an electric torch (flashlight) or lighted lantern with a white light readily available (Figure 6-28), and this light must be shown in time to prevent a collision. Usually, the skipper directs the flashlight against the sail so it is easier to see.

A rowboat may show the same lights as those used on sailboats, including a white flashlight or lantern (Figure 6-29).

Lights for Power-Driven Vessels Underway

Navigation lights on a power-driven vessel underway depend on the vessel's length and whether it is operating on international or inland waters. For small, recreational vessels, the two sets of Rules are practically identical.

There are many rules regulating navigation lights on power-driven vessels. Only those which

Figure 6-27. (Left) Day shape displayed by a sailing vessel under both power and sail.

Figure 6-28. (Middle) Light for a sailing vessel less than 7 meters long.

Figure 6-29. (Right) Light for a rowboat.

(REPRINTED WITH PERMISSION FROM "FEDERAL REQUIREMENTS & SAFETY TIPS FOR RECREATIONAL BOATS," U.S. COAST GUARD OFFICE OF BOATING SAFETY)

bear on recreational boating are described here. If you want to learn more about navigation lights, consult the *Navigation Rules*.

Under either set of Rules, a power-driven vessel less than 20 meters long must have sidelights, a masthead light, and a sternlight when underway at night. Its sidelights may be separate or combined in one lantern (Figure 6-30). The masthead light of a vessel 12 meters or more long should be at least 2.5 meters above its gunwale. A power-driven vessel 50 meters or more long is to have a second masthead light abaft and above the first one. In the Great Lakes, however, a power-driven vessel may carry an all-round light in lieu of the second masthead light stated above.

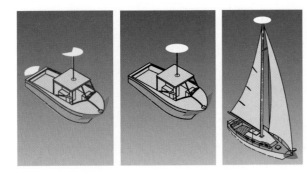

Figure **6-30.** **(Left)** Navigation lights on a power-driven vessel under 20 meters long.

Figure **6-31.** **(Middle and right)** Lights on a power-driven (or power- plus sail-driven) vessel under 12 meters long. (REPRINTED WITH PERMISSION FROM "FEDERAL REQUIREMENTS & SAFETY TIPS FOR RECREATIONAL BOATS," U.S. COAST GUARD OFFICE OF BOATING SAFETY)

The masthead light of a vessel less than 12 meters long must be at least 1 meter above its sidelights. It may have an all-round light in place of the masthead light and sternlight (Figure 6-31). On either international or inland waters, if you see a white light and a sidelight on a vessel, the vessel is power driven. At night, you should never see a white navigation light on a sailing vessel when you see a sidelight.

Many small vessels with all-round lights in place of masthead lights carry the lights too low. They are to be at least 1 meter higher than the sidelights and according to the Rules, must ". . . be placed as to be above and clear of all other lights and obstructions." If the light on your vessel is not high enough, raise it.

In international waters, a power-driven vessel less than 7 meters long needs only an all-round light if its maximum speed is not more than 7 knots (8 miles per hour). Where practicable, it should also have sidelights.

Special Lights and Shapes

Special lights and shapes announce certain activities or conditions of vessels, and are in addition to the masthead, stern, and sidelights required by the two sets of Rules. Except for towing lights and lights on vessels constrained by draft, the lights are the same in the two sets of Rules, as are the special shapes. Vessels show these special shapes in the daytime, while at night they show their special lights.

WARNING *Remember, the more lights a vessel has, the larger it is and the more important it is for you to avoid it.*

Fishing Vessels

A vessel trawling—that is, dragging a net or some other apparatus—shows two all-round lights in a vertical line, with the upper one being green and the lower one being white. In the daytime, it shows a shape comprising two cones in a vertical line with their apexes touching. In silhouette, these appear as two triangles apex to apex.

A fishing vessel other than one trawling shows two all-round lights in a vertical line, the upper of which is red, and the lower one white. It shows the same day shape as a trawler. This type of fishing vessel may have long lines extending from it. If fishing gear extends more than 150 meters from the vessel, it must show an additional all-round white light on the side with the gear at night, and an additional cone with its apex upward on the side with the gear by day.

Vessels Constrained by Draft

A vessel constrained by draft is recognized only in the International Rules. It shows its condition at night by three red all-round lights stacked vertically. In daylight hours, it displays a black cylinder, which, in silhouette, will appear to be a rectangle.

Towing Vessels

A towing light is the same as a sternlight except that it is yellow. A power-driven vessel, when towing astern, shows two masthead lights in a vertical line and the yellow towing light above its white sternlight. When the tow is more than 200 meters long, the vessel shows three vertical masthead lights at night and a diamond shape in the daytime.

A sailing vessel could be confused with a vessel being towed at night. Like a sailboat, a boat or barge under tow shows a sternlight and sidelights. Be careful—you may not be able to see the towing cable. Many boats have been destroyed and lives lost when skippers have steered between

Figure **6-33.** Vessels less than 50 meters long, anchored at night. (REPRINTED WITH PERMISSION FROM "FEDERAL REQUIREMENTS & SAFETY TIPS FOR RECREATIONAL BOATS," U.S. COAST GUARD OFFICE OF BOATING SAFETY)

Figure **6-32.** **Top:** A dredge is restricted in its ability to manuever. **Bottom:** Dredge spoils being deposited on a riverbank to build up the shoreline. (PHOTOS BY LEN SCHULTE)

towboats and their tows. The towing hawsers are not always visible, so be alert for two vessels moving in the same direction and staying the same distance apart. Watch for the two stacked masthead lights and yellow towlight of a towboat at night or the diamond day shape of a vessel with a tow more than 200 meters long.

Other Special Vessels

Other vessels with special lights include those restricted in their ability to maneuver, those not under command, those engaged in dredging (Figure 6-32) or underwater operations, and those aground.

There are two kinds of vessels with special lights that you should recognize. Law enforcement vessels when engaged in law enforcement or public safety activities have flashing blue lights. These vessels include those operated by the Coast Guard, marine police, national and state park rangers, conservation officers, and others with police functions.

A vessel engaged in public safety activities may have a flashing red-and-yellow light. The light serves only to identify the vessel as participating in such activities, and does not confer special privileges. Be aware that this vessel may be towing another vessel, and don't cut behind it.

Vessels at Anchor

A vessel less than 50 meters long will show an all-round white light at night in its forepart, where it can best be seen when anchored (Figure 6-33). In the daytime, it will show a ball, which will appear to be a black disk. When it is 50 meters long or longer, it will show an additional all-round white light near its stern. This light is lower than the forward light. All anchored vessels may show lights to illuminate their decks, and a vessel 100 meters or more long *must* show these lights.

Under either set of Rules, an anchored vessel less than 7 meters long does not have to show an anchor light or shape. However, when it is in or near a narrow channel, a fairway, an anchorage, or where other vessels normally navigate, it must show a light at appropriate times.

Under the Inland Rules, vessels less than 20 meters long do not need to show anchor lights or shapes when anchored in special anchoring areas. A list of these special anchorage areas appears in Title 33, *Code of Federal Regulations*, Part 110, and they are also shown on nautical charts. This exemption addresses the impracticality of leaving an anchor light burning on an unattended small boat in a designated mooring/anchorage area.

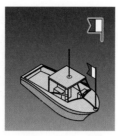

Figure **6-34.** Night and day displays for a vessel engaged in diving operations. (REPRINTED WITH PERMISSION FROM "FEDERAL RE-QUIREMENTS & SAFETY TIPS FOR RECREATIONAL BOATS," U.S. COAST GUARD OF-FICE OF BOATING SAFETY)

Figure **6-35.** Diver-in-the-water flag.

Diving Operations

Under either set of Rules, vessels engaged in underwater operations should show the lights and shapes of vessels restricted in their ability to maneuver, but a vessel has an alternative if its size makes the showing of these lights and shapes impractical. It can, instead, show three all-round lights in a vertical line. The top and bottom lights are red, and the middle one is white (Figure 6-34, left). By day, the boat should fly a rigid replica of the code flag A to show that a diver is down. This **alpha flag** is a white-and-blue swallowtail flag (Figure 6-34, right) and must be at least 1 meter high and visible from any angle (a requirement that can usually be fulfilled only by displaying multiple flags).

The rules about the alpha flag cover "underwater operations," which has left scuba divers and snorkelers confused about which flag to use. As a result, they have informally adopted a red flag with a white diagonal stripe (Figure 6-35). While this flag has legal status in some states, in most places it does not. To be on the safe side, some people use both the red-and-white and the alpha

flags. If you see either of these flags, give them a wide berth.

Do not paint or permanently affix a diving flag to your vessel; it should only be used when there is a diver in the water. All vessels should stay clear of diving operations under the rules of good seamanship.

RULE/VESSEL	GROUPS	SHAPES	BOW	STERN
BOTH INTERNATIONAL AND INLAND **Rule 23(a)** Power-driven ≥50 m	2 Mastheads Sidelights Sternlight	None		
INLAND (GREAT LAKES ONLY) **Rule 23(a)** Power-driven ≥50 m	Masthead Sidelights All-around for 2nd masthead + stern	None		
BOTH INTERNATIONAL AND INLAND **Rule 23(a)** Power-driven <50 m	Masthead Sidelights Sternlight	None		
Rule 23(c) Power-driven optional <12 m	Sidelights All-around in lieu of masthead and stern	None		
INTERNATIONAL ONLY **Rule 23(c)(ii)** Power-driven <7 m & <7 kn max.	Sidelights if practical All-around	None		
BOTH INTERNATIONAL AND INLAND **Rule 23(b)** Submarine	2 Mastheads Sidelights Sternlight Flashing Yellow, 1/sec. for 3 sec., followed by 3 sec. off	None		
Rule 23(b) Hovercraft in displacement mode <50 m	Masthead Sidelights Sternlight	None		
Rule 23(b) Hovercraft non-displacement mode <50 m	Masthead Sidelights Sternlight Flashing Yellow	None		
INLAND ONLY **Rule 23(a)** Law Enforcement <50 m	Masthead Sidelights Sternlight Flashing Blue	None		

Figure **6-36.** A summary of navigation lights and day shapes. (REPRINTED WITH PERMISSION FROM *RULES OF THE ROAD AND RUN-NING LIGHT PATTERNS: A CAPTAIN'S QUICK GUIDE* BY CHARLIE WING)

Distress Signals

Distress signals are described in Rule 37 and in Annex IV. They include (Figure 6-37):

- A gun fired at intervals of 1 minute
- Continuous sounding of a foghorn
- Red star shells

- A Morse code SOS signal (• • • – – – • • •) sent by radiotelegraphy, flashing light, or other means
- A radio signal consisting of the spoken word "Mayday"
- Flying international code flags N and C ("November" and "Charlie" in the phonetic alphabet)

RULE/VESSEL	GROUPS	SHAPES	BOW	STERN
BOTH INTERNATIONAL AND INLAND				
24(a)/Towing astern (Tow 200 m)	2 vert. Mastheads Sidelights Sternlight Towlight	None		
If vessel 50 m, add	Masthead aft			
24(a)/Towing astern (Tow > 200 m)	3 vert. Mastheads Sidelights Sternlight Towlight	◆		
If vessel 50 m, add	Masthead aft			
24(b)/Composite (treated as single power vessel)	Masthead Sidelights Sternlight	None		
If composite 50 m, add	Masthead aft			
24(c)/Pushing ahead or towing alongside (not composite)	2 vert. Mastheads Sidelights Sternlight	None		
If vessel 50 m, add	Masthead aft			
24(e)/Vessel/object being towed astern (other than 24(g)) (Tow 200 m)	Sidelights fwd Sternlight	None		
24(e)/Vessel/object being towed astern (other than 24(g)) (Tow >200 m)	Sidelights fwd Sternlight	◆		
24(g)/Partly submerged 100 m long (<25 m wide)	All-arounds forward & aft	◆		
(25 m wide)	Add all-arounds on beams			
Partly submerged >100 m long (<25 m wide)	All-arounds forward & aft and every 100 m	◆ ◆ aft fwd		
(25 m wide)	All-arounds forward & aft Add beam all-arounds every 100 m	If tow >200 m		
INTERNATIONAL ONLY				
24(f)/Multiple vessels/objects being pushed ahead	Sidelights fwd	None		
24(f)/Multiple vessels/objects being towed alongside	Sidelights Sternlight	None		
INLAND ONLY				
24(f)/Multiple vessels/objects being pushed ahead	Sidelights fwd Special flashing	None		
24(f)/Multiple vessels/objects being towed alongside	Sidelights Sternlight Special flashing	None		
24(f)/Multiple vessels/objects being towed alongside BOTH sides	Sidelights 2 Sternlights Special flashing	None		
INLAND Western Rivers except below Huey Long Bridge				
24(i)/Pushing ahead or towing alongside (not composite)	Sidelights 2 Towing lights NO mastheads NO sternlight	None		

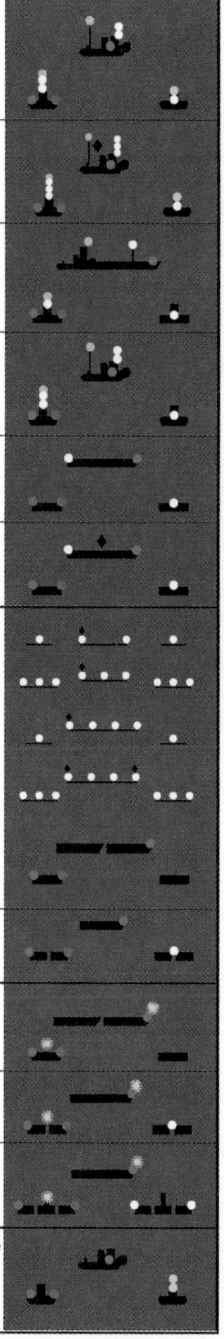

RULE/VESSEL	GROUPS	SHAPES	BOW	STERN
BOTH INTERNATIONAL AND INLAND				
Rule 25(a) Sailing only any length	Sidelights Sternlight	None		
Rule 25(b) Sailing only <20 m option	Tri-color	None		
Rule 25(c) Sailing only optional any length	Sidelights Sternlight R/G all-around	None		
Rule 25(d)(i) Sailing or Rowing <7 m	Sidelights Sternlight	None		
Rule 25(d)(ii) Sailing or Rowing <7 m option	All-around or show only to prevent collision	None		
Rule 25(e) Motorsailing ≥50 m	2 Mastheads Sidelights Sternlight	▼		
Rule 25(e) Motorsailing <50 m	Masthead Sidelights Sternlight	▼		
Rule 25(e) Motorsailing <12 m	Masthead Sidelights Sternlight	▽ Optional under Inland Rules		

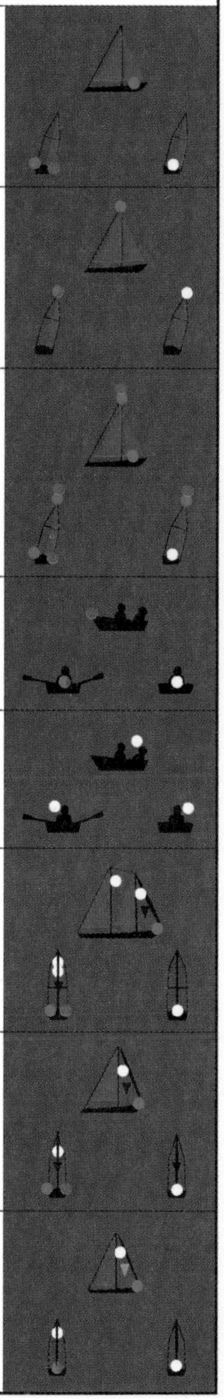

Figure 6-36. (continued on next page)

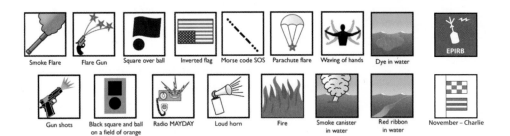

Figure **6-37.** Distress signals. (REPRINTED WITH PERMISSION FROM *EMERGENCIES ON BOARD: A CAPTAIN'S QUICK GUIDE* BY JOHN ROUSMANIERE)

RULE/VESSEL	GROUPS	SHAPES	BOW	STERN
BOTH INTERNATIONAL AND INLAND				
Rule 26(b) Trawling, making way ≥50 m	Masthead Sidelights Sternlight G/W all-around			
Rule 26(b) Trawling, making way <50 m	Sidelights Sternlight G/W all-around			
Rule 26(b) Trawling, not making way	G/W all-around			
Rule 26(c) Fishing other than trawling, making way Any length	Sidelights Sternlight R/W all-around			
Rule 26(c) Fishing other than trawling, not making way Any length	R/W all-around			
Rule 26(c) Fishing other than trawling, making way Gear out >150 m	Sidelights Sternlight R/W all-around All-around	gear side		
Rule 26(c) Fishing other than trawling, not making way Gear out >150 m	R/W all-around All-around	gear side		

RULE/VESSEL	GROUPS	SHAPES	BOW	STERN
BOTH INTERNATIONAL AND INLAND				
Rule 27(a) Not Under Command Making way	Sidelights Sternlight R/R all-around			
Rule 27(a) Not Under Command Not making way	R/R all-around			
Rule 27(b) Restricted in Ability to Maneuver Making way <50 m	Masthead Sidelights Sternlight R/W/R all-around			
Rule 27(b) Restricted in Ability to Maneuver Making way ≥50 m	2 Mastheads Sidelights Sternlight R/W/R all-around			
Rule 27(b) Restricted in Ability to Maneuver Not making way	R/W/R all-around			
Rule 27(b) Restricted in Ability to Maneuver Anchored <50 m	R/W/R all-around W all-around			
Rule 27(b) Restricted in Ability to Maneuver Anchored ≥50 m	R/W/R all-around 2 W all-around			
Rule 27(d) Dredging or Underwater Operations Not making way	R/W/R all-around R/R all-arnd obstr. side G/G all-arnd clear side	obstr. side clear side		
Rule 27(e) Diving, but unable to display Underwater Operations lights	R/W/R all-around	Int'l Code Flag "A"		
Rule 27(f) Mine-clearing Making way ≥50 m	2 Mastheads Sidelights Sternlight G △ all-around			
Rule 27(f) Mine-clearing Making way <50 m	Masthead Sidelights Sternlight G △ all-around			

Figure **6-36.** (continued)

- A black square and ball on an orange background
- Flames on the vessel (as from burning tar or oil in a barrel)
- A rocket parachute flare or a hand flare showing a red light
- A smoke signal giving off orange-colored smoke
- Slowly and repeatedly raising and lowering your arms outstretched to each side

- An automatic radiotelephone alarm signal
- Signals sent by emergency position-indicating radio beacons (EPIRBs)

In addition, on inland waters, a high-intensity white light flashing at regular intervals of fifty to seventy times per minute is a distress signal. Finally, a searchlight may be directed toward a danger to warn other boaters provided it doesn't cause confusion or embarrassment.

Homeland Security Measures

All boats must keep a safe distance away from certain locations that are considered by the U.S. Department of Homeland Security to be at risk to sabotage. The list of these locations is available at local Coast Guard facilities. These locations are typically military installations, commercial port operations, dams, bridges, or any place where massive damage can be inflicted with an explosion or lethal substances. Boaters should call 911 to report any suspicious behavior or call the Coast Guard on VHF-FM Channel 16.

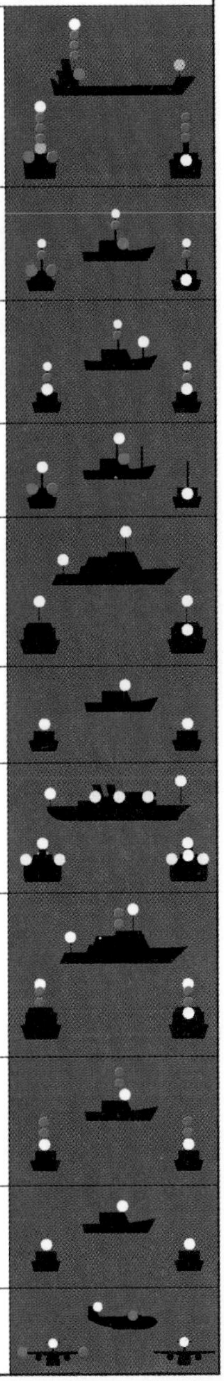

Courtesy and Safety

Common courtesy and respect for other boaters underlie most of the Navigation Rules. As one example of this, the person in charge of a vessel is required to give assistance to another vessel that is in immediate danger, though this Good Samaritan obligation does not require you to place your own vessel in danger. Further, you should be sure that the vessel in apparent trouble is willing to accept your assistance. Most states have laws defining proper assistance. Be very cautious about giving assistance where it is not invited.

Sound signals likewise illustrate the spirit of the Rules. A major purpose of sound signals is to alert other vessel operators to the action you are taking or are about to take. The rules concerning the stand-on status of sailboats in relationship to each other and to power vessels serve the same purpose. The rules at first glance seem many and varied, but this spirit of courtesy and common sense

RULE/VESSEL	GROUPS	SHAPES	BOW	STERN
INTERNATIONAL ONLY				
Rule 28 Constrained by Draft Making way	Masthead Sidelights Sternlight R/R/R all-around	cylinder		
If 50 m, add	2nd Masthead			
BOTH INTERNATIONAL AND INLAND				
Rule 29(a) Pilot Vessel on Duty Underway	Sidelights Sternlight W/R all-around	Int'l Code Flag "H"		
Rule 29(a) Pilot Vessel on Duty Anchored	W/R all-around Anchor Light	Int'l Code Flag "H"		
Rule 29(b) Pilot Vessel off Duty Making way <50 m	Masthead Sidelights Sternlight	None		
Rule 30(a) Anchored 50–100 m	2 W all-around			
Rule 30(b) Anchored 7 m and <50 m	W all-around			
Rule 30(c) Anchored 100 m	2 W all-around All deck lights			
Rule 30(d) Aground 50 m	W all-around forward Lower W all-around aft R/R all-around (if practicable INLAND)			
Rule 30(d) Aground <50 m and 12 m	W all-around R/R all-around (if practicable INLAND)			
Rule 30(f) Aground <12 m	W all-around			
Rule 31 Seaplane Underway	Masthead Sidelights Sternlight	None		

Figure **6-36.**

informs all of them. If you conduct your boating in this spirit, you will rarely run afoul of the Rules.

Because of courtesy violations, many ordinances and laws have been enacted limiting PWC operations, and the public's reaction to discourteous operators threatens to lead to further curtailments. Weaving in and out of a congested area at high speeds; operating too close to shorelines near residential areas; running too close to people who are fishing; making sharp, unpredictable turns; following water-skiers too closely; cutting behind other vessels when vision is obstructed; failing to respect swimming and other restricted areas; steering toward another vessel or person; and other such actions constitute reckless operation. These actions are also a violation of common courtesy and threaten to give rise to further restrictive legislation.

Drawbridges

Most drawbridges are normally closed, but they open to permit the passage of vessels. These bridges have bridge tenders. Other bridges—for example, some railroad bridges on infrequently used lines—are usually open, closing only when needed for land transportation. Some drawbridges are always closed and unattended. If you need to pass through an unattended, normally closed bridge, give advance notice of your intention. Nautical charts describe bridges over navigable waterways and tell their horizontal and vertical clearances.

Get information regarding local bridges at a Coast Guard Station or at a marina. If you are planning a cruise and there are drawbridges along the way, you can get information in advance of your trip from a Coast Guard Station in the area. Title 33 of the *Code of Federal Regulations*, Part 117, includes a brief description and the operating regulations for each drawbridge in the United States. Many libraries have the *Code of Federal Regulations*, or you can view it online at www.gpo.gov/fdsys.

Because of heavy highway traffic, some drawbridges have scheduled opening times, which are posted on signs near the bridges. Changes in the opening schedules of bridges are published in the *Local Notices to Mariners* (Figure 6-38).

Figure **6-38.** A commercial vessel can request that a drawbridge open outside its scheduled opening times, and if you're nearby you can follow it through.

Some bridges do not open during severe weather, such as hurricanes, so they can help provide evacuation routes. Be aware of this and plan ahead if severe weather is approaching.

When bridges have special conditions, such as opening only at specified times, remaining closed during severe weather, or requiring advance notice for opening, a sign announcing the conditions is posted near the bridge. If advance notice must be given, the name, address, and telephone number of the person to contact will be on the sign.

Limitations on Drawbridge Openings

Federal regulations provide penalties of up to $1,000 for causing a bridge to open unnecessarily. Do not request that a bridge be opened for any purpose other than for you to pass through its opening.

If your vessel can pass under a drawbridge with appurtenances such as antennas and outriggers lowered, and if these are not needed for navigation, you must lower them. Most antennas above the highest fixed point on a vessel are collapsible. Examples of appurtenances not considered lowerable are radar antennas, flying bridges, and sailboat masts.

Drawbridge Signals

Signals for requesting the opening of a drawbridge include sound, visual, and radiotelephone. Sound signals are made by whistle, horn, megaphone, hailer, or other device capable of being heard by the bridge tender. When signaling at a bridge with a bridge tender, your signal must be acknowledged, so repeat it until you get an acknowledgment.

If you approach an open draw, give the opening signal. If it is not acknowledged in 30 seconds, proceed, with caution, through the open draw.

Sound Signals

A whistle or horn sound signal is one prolonged blast of 4 to 6 seconds followed no later than 3 seconds by a 1-second short blast. If the bridge can be opened, the bridge tender will respond with a prolonged blast followed by a short blast no later than 30 seconds after your request. When the draw cannot be opened immediately or must be closed after it has been opened, the bridge tender will signal with 5 short blasts in rapid succession.

Visual Signals

To request the opening of a drawbridge by a visual signal, vertically raise and lower a white flag. If the draw can be opened immediately, the acknowledgment signal is a white flag raised and lowered vertically; a white, amber, or green light raised and lowered vertically; or a fixed or flashing white, amber, or green light or lights. If the draw cannot be opened immediately, the acknowledgment signal is a red flag or light swung back and forth horizontally or a fixed or flashing red light or lights.

Radiotelephone

If a drawbridge is equipped with a radiotelephone, there will be a sign on each side of the bridge giving its calling and working channels. This sign will be written or will show a symbol of a telephone handset that is often like the symbol at a service station that has a public telephone. In addition to the handset symbol, the sign will show a three-legged lightning slash above the symbol. The preferred calling channel will be shown in the lower left and the working channel in the lower right.

Usually, you call a bridge tender on Channel 16 and then switch to Channel 13 to request the bridge opening, but there are many exceptions to this general rule. In Florida, for example, you call the bridge tender and make your request on Channel 9. At bridges in other states, you may need to call the bridge tenders on other VHF-FM channels. When planning a cruise, you may want to consult bridge tenders via telephone before departing. (Inland waterway charts frequently note who operates a bridge.) Knowing the calling and working channels in advance will prevent delays. When you make a radiotelephone request that a bridge be opened, stay tuned to the working channel until you have cleared the bridge.

Penalties

If you operate a vessel in violation of the International or Inland Rules, you are liable for a civil penalty of up to $5,000 for each violation. Both the operator and the owner may be held responsible when they are not the same person. When you charter a boat you are liable—not the chartering firm that owns the boat.

If you operate a vessel on U.S. waters in a negligent manner and endanger the "life, limb, or property of a person," you may be liable for a fine of up to $1,000. If you operate a vessel in a grossly negligent manner, you are liable for a fine of up to $5,000 and imprisonment for as long as one year.

Boating accidents occurring in international waters must be reported to the U.S. Coast Guard when the estimated damage is greater than $25,000. This report should be done verbally as soon as possible. There are significant penalties for failing to report.

Accidents occurring in inland waters defer to state reporting requirements, and are reported to the state agency that issued the registration certificate for the vessel. The loss or disappearance of a person must be reported. Also, report any injury that requires medical care beyond first aid. Damage to a vessel estimated to exceed $2,000 should also be reported. The Marine Accident form in Appendix C is a federal form but represents the information that is typically required by state agencies. Damage to any buoy or daymark should be reported as soon as possible to the U.S. Coast Guard.

There are penalties, also, for failure to give help in marine casualties. When you give help, the Good Samaritan clause protects you.

Nothing in the Rules ever requires you to place your own vessel in danger.

Ways to Learn More

Chapman Piloting & Seamanship. 66th ed. Charles B. Husick. New York: Hearst Books, 2009. Chapter 5.

The One-Minute Guide to the Nautical Rules of the Road. Charlie Wing. Camden, Maine: International Marine, 2006.

Rules of the Road and Running Light Patterns: A Captain's Quick Guide. Charlie Wing. Camden, Maine: International Marine, 2004.

Practice Questions

IMPORTANT BOATING TERMS

In the following exercise, match the words in the column on the left with the definitions in the column on the right. In the blank space to the left of each term, write the letter of the item that best matches it. Do not use an item in the right-hand column more than once.

THE ITEMS

1. _____ head-on situation
2. _____ lookout
3. _____ overtaking
4. _____ stay clear of diver
5. _____ sternlight
6. _____ stand-on vessel
7. _____ navigation lights
8. _____ sailing vessel underway at night
9. _____ sailing vessel operating propelling machinery
10. _____ danger zone

THE RESPONSES

a. has an arc of visibility of 135°

b. black conical shape, apex down

c. applies to all boaters at all hours

d. at night you see a red or a green light

e. red flag with white diagonal stripe

f. you see another vessel's sternlight

g. at night you see both sidelights

h. maintains course and speed

i. all vessels must display between sunset and sunrise and in restricted visibility

j. dead ahead to 22.5° abaft the starboard beam

Multiple-Choice Items

In the following items, choose the best response:

6-1. The give-way vessel is responsible
   a. to maintain course and speed
   b. to keep astern of all other vessels
   c. to take early and substantial action to keep clear of the stand-on vessel
   d. to use hand signals when ready to pass

6-2. The primary purpose of the Navigation Rules is
   a. to establish racing rules
   b. to reduce the number of personal injury suits
   c. to prevent collisions between vessels
   d. to tell you how your boat should be equipped

Multiple-Choice Items (continued)

6-3. You may depart from the Navigation Rules when
 a. you are in a marina
 b. you are being overtaken by another vessel
 c. you do not see any other boats
 d. it is necessary to avoid a collision

6-4. When underway, every vessel must proceed at a safe speed and maintain a
 a. proper lookout
 b. constant engine watch
 c. straight course
 d. all of the above

6-5. When you act to avoid a collision, make your changes in course and speed
 a. at right angles to the course you are steering
 b. to port
 c. to starboard
 d. large enough that they are readily seen

6-6. The single white light on a vessel means you are seeing
 a. its sternlight
 b. a power-driven vessel less than 12 meters long
 c. a vessel under oars
 d. any of the above

6-7. Which vessel is stand-on to all others?
 a. a crossing vessel
 b. an overtaken vessel
 c. an overtaking vessel
 d. none of the above

6-8. Lines that mark the boundaries between waters governed by the International Rules and those governed by the Inland Rules are
 a. lines of position
 b. demarcation lines
 c. pickup lines
 d. shorelines

6-9. In an overtaking situation under Inland Rules, you would never expect the other vessel to sound
 a. one short blast
 b. two short blasts
 c. five short blasts
 d. one prolonged blast

6-10. When in a congested area, you should watch your wake because
 a. it should not be more than 3 feet high
 b. it could cause personal injury or damage
 c. it may be used to estimate speed
 d. it can be used to judge clearance from other boats

6-11. The sidelight on the starboard side of a vessel is
 a. red
 b. yellow
 c. green
 d. white

6-12. The color of a sternlight is always
 a. red
 b. yellow
 c. green
 d. white

6-13. To be environmentally responsible and courteous to other boaters, you should
 a. run your boat at slow speeds when close to shore
 b. top off the fuel tank to the air vents
 c. clean the hull with phosphates
 d. empty marine sanitation devices in deep water

6-14. Five or more short blasts of the horn is a signal for
 a. operating astern propulsion
 b. anchoring
 c. danger
 d. a drawbridge

6-15. The appropriate signal for you to give in a head-on, crossing, or overtaking situation when you pass another boat on your port side is almost always
 a. one short blast
 b. two short blasts
 c. one prolonged blast
 d. two prolonged blasts

6-16. If you are at anchor in restricted visibility and in open water, ring your bell rapidly for about 5 seconds at intervals of no more than
 a. 1 minute
 b. 2 minutes
 c. 3 minutes
 d. whenever you think of it

Multiple-Choice Items (continued)

6-17. The basic configuration of lights for power vessels less than 20 meters is

a. sidelights and a sternlight
b. masthead light and sternlight
c. sidelights, sternlight, and masthead light
d. a combination lantern at the masthead

6-18. In the Navigation Rules, the term "right of way" applies only to a vessel that is

a. being overtaken on coastal waters
b. overtaking another on international waters
c. crossing ahead of your vessel from right to left on the Gulf of Mexico
d. downbound in a narrow channel or fairway with a following current

6-19. If you are overtaking another vessel, you remain an overtaking vessel until

a. you are abreast of the other vessel
b. it is obvious one of you must change course
c. you are past and clear of the other vessel
d. until the other vessel signals you are clear

6-20. If you see both sidelights of another vessel, assume that you are in

a. a crossing situation
b. a head-on or meeting situation
c. an overtaking situation
d. none of the above

6-21. Inland meeting sound signals announce

a. action you are taking
b. action you have taken
c. action you intend to take
d. to the other vessel that you are near

6-22. When boating in an unfamiliar channel you should

a. maintain speed and stay on plane
b. keep to the port side of the channel
c. stay in the middle of the channel
d. obtain local knowledge

6-23. In a crossing situation, the give-way vessel

a. alters course to pass in front of the other vessel
b. increases speed
c. sounds the danger signal
d. turns to starboard and passes astern of the stand-on vessel

6-24. In a narrow channel at the entrance to a harbor, which vessel has priority?

a. a deep-draft freighter
b. a kayak
c. a 30-foot sailing vessel
d. a commercial fishing vessel

Inland Boating

chapter 7

(Courtesy U.S. Army Corps of Engineers)

The objectives of this chapter are to describe:

- ✔ The nature of inland waters.
- ✔ The navigation rules that pertain on these waters and the aids to navigation used there.
- ✔ The nature and meaning of crossing and passing daymarks.
- ✔ Some of the hazards of inland waters—including commercial traffic, locks, lowhead and high dams, river currents, dikes, and dredges—and how to avoid them.
- ✔ How to read and understand river charts and navigate inland waters.

The face of the water, in time, became a wonderful book—a book that was a dead language to the uneducated passenger, but which told its mind to me without reserve, delivering its most cherished secrets as clearly as if it uttered them with a voice. And it was not a book to be read once and thrown aside, for it had a new story to tell every day. Throughout the long twelve hundred miles there was never a page that was void of interest, never one that you could leave unread without loss, never one that you would want to skip, thinking you could find higher enjoyment in some other thing.

—Mark Twain, *Life on the Mississippi*

MANY BOATERS spend their time on the open seas, the gulfs, and other tidal waters. Even more are inland boaters.

Inland Waters

Inland waters include rivers, lakes, and canals, each of which offers unique experiences and challenges.

Rivers

There are more than 30,000 miles of *navigable rivers* in the United States, meaning rivers that are subject to tidal influence or are used for interstate or international commerce. These include the Western Rivers and the Tennessee-Tombigbee Waterway (the Tenn-Tom), the Black Warrior, Alabama, Coosa, Mobile, Flint, and Chattahoochee rivers, and the Apalachicola River above its confluence with the Jackson River. The Western Rivers include most of the Mississippi and all its tributaries, including the Missouri, Ohio, Wabash, Green, and Barren rivers. *Navigable waterways* include all navigable rivers as well as the Great Lakes and the Intracoastal Waterway (Figure 7-1).

Figure **7-1.** Inland waterways provide some of the most beautiful boating areas to be found anywhere. **Top:** Sunset on the Mississippi River at St. Louis, Missouri. (PHOTO BY KITTY NICOLAI) **Bottom:** Sunrise at Strawberry Reservoir, Utah. (PHOTO BY BILL SETZER)

Besides the navigable waterways, many other rivers are used by pleasure boaters, hunters, and anglers. Thus, rivers used for boating range in size and character from the wide Missouri and the muddy Mississippi to small, meandering streams such as the Sipsey and the Cahaba in Alabama. They range also from fast-moving streams such as the Snake River between Idaho and Oregon to slow ones such as the Illinois. Each offers its pleasures and challenges.

Lakes

Lakes present as much variety for boaters as rivers do. There are large, natural lakes such as the Great Lakes and Lake Okeechobee. There are also large artificial lakes such as Lake Mead between Nevada and Arizona and Lake Sidney Lanier in north Georgia. In between are long, artificial "lakes" made by damming streams for commerce, generation of electricity, irrigation, water supply, and flood control. Besides the large natural and artificial lakes, small lakes and farm ponds are used by boaters, including those who fish and hunt.

Canals

Canals are also inland waterways and serve important navigational purposes (Figure 7-2). For example, the Sault Sainte Marie canals connect Lakes Superior and Ontario, bypassing the rapids on St. Marys River. The New York State Barge Canal system is 525 miles long and connects the Great Lakes, Lake Champlain, and the Hudson River.

Figure **7-2.** The Albemarle and Chesapeake Canal, in Virginia, is part of the Intracoastal Waterway on the U.S. East Coast. (PHOTO BY KEN STANLEY)

The Chesapeake and Delaware Canal is 19 miles long and runs between the head of the Chesapeake Bay and the Delaware River. The Tenn-Tom makes it possible to go from the Tenneessee River to the Gulf of Mexico by way of the Tombigbee and Mobile rivers (Figure 7-3).

Watch Your Speed

Artificial waterways are usually narrow. This means that boaters must be especially aware of the effects of their boats' wakes on other boats and on the waterways' shores. Although the Tenn-Tom opened only in the 1980s, wakes have caused serious erosion of its banks and partial blocking of its channel.

Many canals post restricted speeds to reduce wakes. Heavy wakes in narrow waterways echo from the shores several times and create considerable turbulence. Reduced speed is also necessary because of heavy commercial traffic. If you use one of these waterways, yield to barges and other commercial traffic. They can be dangerous, and they have very little ability to avoid you.

Inland Navigation

Although inland waters are diverse, they require many of the same skills and knowledge needed for boating on tidal waters. Knowledge of radio communication, marlinespike seamanship, boat construction, engines, boat handling, and other subjects can serve you as well on inland waters as on tidal waters.

There are important differences between river and coastal piloting, however. For example, you seldom need to plot a compass course or maintain a

dead-reckoning (DR) plot on a river. You can tell where you are by using a chart of the river and noting the mile markers.

Besides local knowledge and a chart of the river, the river navigator will find that the most useful piloting tool is a good binocular, which is useful for reading mile markers and locating aids to navigation (ATONs).

Inland Navigation Rules

The Inland Navigation Rules discussed in Chapter 6 are in force on all navigable waterways. They do not apply on nonnavigable lakes and streams that are entirely within a single state, although state and local regulations may be in effect. Even if the Inland Rules are not in force on a body of water, common sense dictates that you follow them whenever possible. They reflect a large body of experience in avoiding collisions, and you will find that conforming to these rules will usually keep you on the right side of state and local regulations as well.

The need for a lookout, for example, is as great on a lake as on any other body of water. Meeting, crossing, and passing situations are as dangerous on lakes as elsewhere, and proper lighting of vessels at night is equally important wherever boating occurs. The Rules help boaters avoid collisions and you should do your best to observe them.

Where the Inland Navigation Rules apply, the equipment requirements listed in Chapter 2 also apply. Safety practices apply equally on inland and international waters. On large bodies of water such as the Great Lakes and Lake Okeechobee, piloting principles also apply.

Inland ATONs

Two ATON systems are in use on inland waters: one marks navigable rivers and is similar to the U.S. ATON System; the other marks waters solely within the control of a state.

Western Rivers ATONs

The ATONs that appear in the upper part of Figure 5-4 are used on the Western Rivers and other navigable rivers, and are installed and maintained by the Coast Guard. Inland river ATONs differ little

Figure **7-3.** The *Southern Belle* on the Tennessee River in Chattanooga, Tennessee. (PHOTO BY WILLIAM MASON)

from those used in the U.S. ATON System, as described in Chapter 5. Red daybeacons, lights, and buoys mark the starboard banks and limits of channels as vessels "return from sea" or proceed upstream, and green daybeacons, lights, and buoys mark the port banks and limits of navigable channels when going upstream.

RIVERBANK NAMES. The banks of rivers are referred to as "left" and "right" from the perspective of a vessel traveling downstream. Thus, the right bank has green ATONs and the left bank has red ATONs. The west bank of the Mississippi is its right bank and has green ATONs.

To avoid confusion, commercial river traffic often calls the right bank the *right descending bank* and the left bank the *left descending bank*. Expressed in this way, it leaves no room for doubt in your mind.

PASSING DAYMARKS. In the Western Rivers System, triangular and square *passing daymarks* mark the rivers' banks (Figure 7-4). If you see a triangular red or square green daymark on the bank, you

know that the channel is on that side of the river. You continue past it, since it is a passing daymark.

CROSSING DAYMARKS. Because the navigable channels of rivers swing from bank to bank as the rivers bend, the Western Rivers System uses *crossing daymarks* to assist river traffic (Figure 7-5). Crossing daymarks help you know when the channel is changing from one side of the river to the other, and daymarks, buoys, and minor lights help you know where the channel is.

USING CROSSING DAYMARKS. The diamond-shaped crossing daymarks, which are always on the opposite side of the river from the channel you have been following, show that the channel is about to cross over to the other side. Thus, you should head for the diamonds!

As you pass a daymark, look back at it. If it has a crossing daymark on its back, you know that the next daymark in your direction of travel will be a crossing daymark on the opposite side of the river. The crossing daymark that you see on the back of a passing daymark is there to guide a vessel travel-

Figure **7-4.** Passing daymarks on inland waterways are like those on coastal waters. **Top:** This green passing daymark marks the right descending bank of the Ohio River. Note the mile marker. **Bottom:** A red passing daymark on the left descending bank of the Cumberland River. (PHOTOS BY JERRY TURLEY)

Figure **7-5. Top:** A crossing daymark with a mile marker on the right descending bank of the Ohio River. **Bottom:** A crossing daymark on the left descending bank of the Cumberland River. (PHOTOS BY JERRY TURLEY)

ing in the opposite direction. Looking back at a passing daymark to see a crossing daymark is particularly helpful at night or in reduced visibility, when the bend in the river may not be visible. It is also easier to spot a green crossing daymark on the opposite bank when you are expecting to see it there.

When you see a crossing daymark, it tells you nothing about what the next daymark will be. It could be a passing daymark or it could be another crossing daymark on the opposite side of the river. Again, look at the back of the crossing daymark you are passing.

In the past, the Western Rivers System has used red or green diamond-shaped dayboards as crossing daymarks. The former has small, darker red diamonds in each of its four corners, and the latter has a small, darker green diamond in each corner.

These older crossing daymarks are being replaced with green-and-white, or red-and-white, diamond-shaped, checkered daymarks like those in the U.S. ATON System (refer back to Figure 5-4). As in that system, the new crossing daymarks have no lateral significance, and indicate only that the channel has crossed over to the other side of the river.

The green-and-white crossing daymarks are easier to see against a background of green foliage, and both the red-and-white and green-and-white ones will be easier to see in dim light. Green passing and crossing daymarks are always on the right descending bank, while red ones are on the left descending bank.

When you look back and see a green crossing daymark, you know that the next daymark will be a red crossing daymark on the left descending bank of the river. Similarly, when you look back and see a red crossing daymark, you know the next daymark is a green crossing daymark on the right descending bank of the river.

RIVER BUOYS. Changes in river channels caused by fluctuations in water level, current speed, and shifting shoals make buoy maintenance a continuous task for the Coast Guard. Shifting shoals frequently require adding buoys or taking them out of the system. In wintertime where rivers freeze, river buoys are lost or moved from position, and because of this somewhat temporary nature, do not have letters or numbers and are not usually shown on river charts.

MILE MARKERS. Among the most useful markers on a river are the *mile markers*, which are placards attached to daymarks or displayed in other easily seen places. They show distances in statute rather than nautical miles.

With the exception of the Ohio River, mile markers tell you how far it is to the mouth of the river. Ohio River markers start at its headwaters and tell you how far downstream you are. Mile markers help locate your position on a river chart, and also help identify which passing and crossing daymarks you are looking at.

Uniform State Waterway Marking System

Until recently, states have marked some of their exclusively state waters with markers from the Uniform State Waterway Marking System (USWMS). Due to the confusion this caused, the states agreed to adopt the U.S. ATON System, and the Coast Guard initiated the plan to replace ATONs in state waters in 1998. Until the conversion is complete, however, you will have to find out which system is used on local state waters. See also Chapter 5.

REGULATORY MARKERS. Markers that show boat exclusion, danger, and controlled areas, and also give information or directions are called *regulatory markers*. There are two types: signs and buoys, both of which have white backgrounds. The signs have orange borders and orange symbols, while the buoys are white with an orange band near the top and a second band near the water's surface, between which orange symbols appear. Where letters or numbers appear on regulatory signs or buoys, the lettering is black.

Exclusion areas are, for example, areas near dams, rapids, and swimming places, and the markers for such areas have orange diamonds with diagonal marks. They also show the nature of the area in black letters.

Danger area markers have open diamonds, with the nature of the danger often written in black letters.

Controlled area markers have orange circles with the nature of the warnings printed in black letters.

On waters marked with the USWMS, a red-striped white buoy was used to tell you not to pass between it and the nearest shore. Since the states have adopted the U.S ATON System, however, that color combination is used to denote safe water on all sides. Therefore, the states have created a white buoy with black stripes to tell you not to pass between it and the nearest shore.

Inland Seamanship

One difference between inland and saltwater boating is the constantly changing nature of inland waterways. Saltwater boaters expect the tidal changes that come with predictable regularity. There may be changes due to gradual shoaling near shore, but it is usually not a surprise to local mariners, who prepare for the changes and take them into account while maneuvering and mooring.

Changing Water Depths

Although some inland waters differ little from day to day, they are the exception rather than the rule. In his book *Life on the Mississippi*, Mark Twain emphasizes the point that rivers are ever-changing. One important feature of this change is the wide range in water depth that occurs in some streams, and another is the speed of their currents.

Rivers and impounded (dammed) waters vary in depth from season to season and day to day, according to the amount of rainfall or melting snow in the area or upstream. Rivers can rise up overnight and overflow their banks, experience droughts and sink to mere rivulets, and even turn from sluggish streams to torrents after rain or snow melts.

The Mississippi River depth at Memphis varies almost 50 feet during an average year; daily changes may be well over a foot. This means that, at times, navigators must use narrow channels, while at other times they have considerable freedom of movement. Continuous monitoring of a river channel's depths is necessary to aid commercial traffic. In many locales, newspapers give daily reports on river and lake levels.

Many rivers have depth gauges posted at important points such as bridges and locks, and a few of these gauges note whether the river is rising or falling. Figure 7-6 depicts two such gauges.

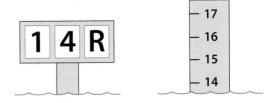

Figure 7-6. River stages are noted on gauges (right) up and down many rivers. The river's level and whether the river is rising or falling may also be displayed on signboards (left).

Lake Hazards

Much of what this chapter says about river boating and its hazards also applies to lakes, especially if the lakes are impounded waters. While all water levels vary from season to season and with local precipitation, the levels of some impounded lakes also vary in response to flood control efforts upstream and to needs for electrical power, irrigation, and community water supplies.

During very high water, boaters need to be aware of overhead power lines that have abnormally low clearance. Sailboaters should be especially cautious.

Underwater Hazards

If a lake's purpose is to control flooding, engineers may have cleared vegetation only from the shoreline of the normal pool. Entire trees may remain standing, some with their tops close to the water's surface, and in agricultural areas, fences and the remains of farm buildings may be just below the surface, especially when the water level is low.

High water may submerge picnic tables and barbecue grills in recreational areas, making it difficult to get to the shoreline for a landing. And in low water, rocks and shoals, which are not problems during normal water levels, may become hazardous.

In some small reservoirs, and especially downstream of dams, water levels can vary with dangerous speed and little warning. It is important to learn about local conditions and then heed posted warning signs and use extra caution when boating in these areas.

Other Lake Hazards

The water in spring-fed lakes can be very cold, even in summer, and hypothermia can develop rapidly if you fall overboard. Also, you may not notice that severe weather is approaching, as tree-lined shorelines or high cliffs and hillsides can block the horizon.

The long, narrow profiles of many lakes serve to channel wind down the lakes, and in ones that are shallow, high wind can create severe water turbulence. Be prepared when you round a bend or cross the mouth of a tributary—wind speed and direction may change abruptly.

Anchoring may be a problem in lakes due to debris on the bottom, such as submerged logs and rocks, which can easily foul your anchor. A trip line is good insurance where there is much debris. Because water levels change rapidly in some lakes, it is possible to anchor in a small cove overnight and find yourself aground the next morning. On the other hand, if you beach your boat for the night, you may find it downstream the next morning.

Services and Facilities

The byword for any trip is planning. If possible, get the telephone numbers of facilities along your route and learn what services they offer ahead of time. You may need to deal with a local service station for fuel and repairs or visit a grocery store ashore for supplies.

Many lakes are far from towns, and emergency responses may be slow. The Coast Guard and the Auxiliary often do not have search-and-rescue capabilities on remote lakes, which means boaters will need to rely on park ranger or sheriff's department rescue teams in such areas. Learn before you go how to contact emergency services, and take a cellular telephone with you if possible.

River Currents

Most rivers have currents—sometimes powerful ones. These can pose major problems for both recreational and commercial boats.

River Channels

The river channel is the deepest part of a river. In a way, it is a river within the river. When a river basin floods, either naturally or because of dams, the channel may be lost under the broader river.

Since the river may be shallow outside the channel, vessel traffic must know where the channel lies. This is not easy to do, since the channel may meander from bank to bank.

Where charts are available, they can help you locate the channel. ATONs mark the channels on inland rivers where traffic must stay within them.

The river's channel is also the point of concentration of the river's current, which can be a concern for riverboaters. Currents in the Mississippi and other rivers reach velocities of 8 to 10 or more miles per hour. Vessels moving upstream against the current may be making considerable speed through the water while making little progress over the ground, and some low-powered motorboats and sailboats may be unable to make any headway at all upstream.

The current aids movement downstream, boosting both speed and fuel economy, but this economy has its drawback. A vessel carried downstream by a strong current loses some control and is more at the mercy of the current. For this reason, the Navigation Rules give the right of way to vessels headed downstream—the only instance in the Rules where one vessel is accorded right of way over another, as opposed to being designated the stand-on vessel (see Chapter 6).

Behavior of Currents

River currents can be complex, as the flow of the river responds to changes in channel direction and the shape of the bottom. The current at one depth may run counter to that at another depth, which means deep-draft vessels may experience a current moving in one direction while shallow-draft vessels are experiencing a current moving in the opposite direction. Knowledge of these currents, which you can gain through experience and by consulting knowledgeable boaters, is very useful.

River Bends

The current usually flows around the outside of a river bend, causing water to pile up there. This deeper water flows faster than water on the inside of the bend, and if it moves fast enough, it scours the channel and sweeps silt downstream. Thus, the water usually moves most rapidly and is deepest on the outside of a bend (Figure 7-7).

On the inside of a bend, where the current moves more slowly, the river deposits silt, and shoaling may occur. Because of the difference in the speed of flow on the inside and outside of a bend, eddies and slack water often occur.

Vessels headed upstream sometimes move to the inside of a bend where the current is weaker or where it may reverse itself and head upstream. If you do this, be careful to avoid running aground. It is good practice to swing wide around points, since they may extend farther out into the streambed than you know.

If you round a bend that obscures your view, sound the bend signal: one prolonged blast (4 to 6 seconds) on your whistle. Any vessel that is entering the bend from the opposite direction should return your signal.

Entering a Current

The effect of a current may be considerable when you enter the main channel from a secondary one. Larger vessels and commercial traffic, such as tows of barges, must anticipate the impact of the change in current. When rounding a bend, tows need to use the current as an aid in maneuvering, so you should be ready to respond to the radical and rapid heading changes tows make as they negotiate such a bend or channel crossing. Tows are like trucks that carry signs saying "This vehicle makes wide turns," and you may suddenly find yourself in the path of the tow (Figures 7-8 and 7-9).

If you run into trouble, try to maneuver out of the channel and away from commercial traffic. Then set an anchor and maintain a lookout until help arrives. If you can't get out of the channel, be prepared

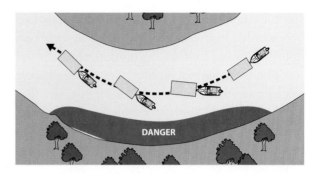

Figure **7-8.** Do not pass a tow on the outside of a bend. The tow will swing to the outside, and its actual path of travel may be very different from the apparent heading of the tow

Figure **7-9.** Rounding a bend on the Black River in Louisiana below the Columbia Lock and Dam. (PHOTO BY JAY J. BRANDINGER)

to warn commercial traffic of your plight by your VHF-FM radio or by visual signals (see Chapter 6).

River Debris

During periods of high water, debris that has collected on riverbanks, such as brush, tree stumps, entire trees, and discarded trash, floats off. You can usually tell if a river is rising by observing the amount of debris that is floating downstream. As a river crests and the water level begins to lower, less debris will be present. While the debris is moving and after it is deposited, it is a danger to water traffic and can seriously damage small recreational vessels.

In the spring of the year, rising water may break apart sheets of ice that have formed on the northern reaches of rivers. These ice floes, which may travel hundreds of miles downstream before melting, constitute a threat to boat traffic, both moving and moored.

When the water level in a river drops, it leaves debris in the path of boating traffic, and that debris is often just below the surface. Boaters should heed

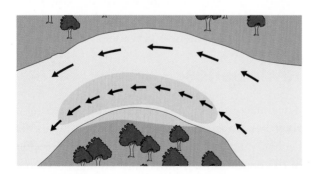

Figure **7-7.** Currents flow more swiftly along the outside of a river bend. Slower-moving water on the inside of a bend allows silting and the formation of bars there.

Mark Twain's advice and watch for subtle disturbances on the water's surface that may show hazards below. Learn to "read" the water.

Maintaining Inland Waterways

Rivers, like living organisms, are constantly changing. Channels may change in depth and location, and during flood periods, a river may even change its course in some places. Because of this, channels need to be monitored and controlled continuously.

Maintenance of navigable waterways is the responsibility of the U.S. Army Corps of Engineers (the Corps), whose charge includes containing the wayward streams of the system, maintaining navigable channels, and ensuring channel depths wherever possible. This last charge is a difficult one in some waterways, especially in times of severe drought.

Levees

Rivers flood and may change their courses. This can cause serious problems on many rivers, including the Mississippi, which cuts across bends and shortens its length when unconstrained. Unless some rivers are controlled, river towns can find themselves far from their rivers and without riverfronts following a flood. To control flooding and wandering, and to provide a navigable channel, the Corps maintains systems of levees on major rivers.

At bends in a river, the Corps uses revetments to protect its embankments. A *revetment* is a facing of stone, concrete, or other material that keeps a river from cutting through its embankments and shortening its course.

Other Devices

For recreational boaters, a more important function of the Corps is its maintenance of navigable channels, which it does by using **dikes** or **wing dams** built out from the shore toward a river channel (Figure 7-10). These dikes, sometimes called "the works" or some other local name, slow the water flow outside the channels, causing silt and sand to accumulate around the dams rather than in the channels.

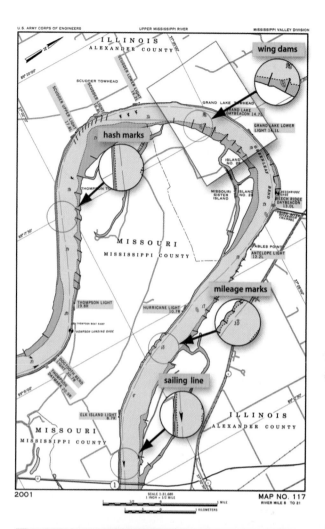

Figure **7-10.** **Top:** U.S. Army Corps of Engineers Map No. 117 covers a 13-mile meander of the Mississippi River beginning just 8 miles upriver from the Ohio River confluence. Note the labeled mileage hash marks (statute miles), the sailing line denoted on the map (with arrows pointing downstream), and the numerous wing dams to control silting and erosion and direct the channel. (COURTESY U.S. ARMY CORPS OF ENGINEERS) **Bottom:** This aerial photo shows two of the wing dams quite clearly. The tow at lower left in the photo is headed upriver. He looks perilously close to the Illinois shore, but from the map you can see that he's right on the sailing line. (COURTESY U.S. GEOLOGICAL SURVEY)

Directing a River's Flow

Wing dams and dikes also direct the flow of a river to the center of a channel. This speeds up the flow in the channel and cleanses it of silt and sand, which helps maintain its depth.

On some navigable rivers, the tops of some wing dams are above water, but many are not. While most tops are above water when constructed, older wing dams can be submerged as dams built later raise surrounding water levels. About 95% of the wing dams in the Rock Island, Illinois, District of the Mississippi are below the water's surface all the time. Today, some wing dams have tops about 3 feet below the water's surface at normal water depth.

There are about 1,200 wing dam structures on the Mississippi. Most were built between 1900 and 1927 to maintain 4.5- to 6-foot channels, but today these depths are too shallow for much commercial traffic, so higher dams have been built. The old wing dams are still there and are often hazards for boaters.

Other Underwater Structures

Wing dams are not the only underwater structures that you must avoid. In many cases the Corps removed only the channel sections of low dams when it built higher ones, meaning the peripheral portions of the low dams remain as hazards.

Wing dams provide calm overnight anchorages downstream, but submerged ones present problems for boaters, as there may not be enough clearance over them to permit the passage of even a small recreational boat. While turbulence may reveal their presence in the daylight, they disappear at night. If river charts are available where you're boating, consult them. Otherwise, get some local knowledge.

Dredging

Wing dams seek to "train" the river into channels and control the amount of silt and sand that a river deposits. Even so, silt and sand deposits can make it necessary to dredge the channels (Figure 7-11). For example, in an area below Keithsburg, Illinois, it was necessary for the Corps to dredge the river twenty-seven times in 25 years, a period in which the channel was lost several times and closed once. In 1985, however, the Corps built wing dams, and

Figure **7-11.** The Memphis District dredge *Hurley* at work dredging the channel along the lower Mississippi River. (COURTESY U.S. ARMY CORPS OF ENGINEERS)

since then, the area has needed dredging only once.

Dredges present problems for boaters. A dredge pumps large volumes of water containing silt and sand, which is then carried through a long pipe and discharged ashore on a **spoil bank**, or into a barge. In the daytime it is easy to see the dredge as well as the pipeline if it is floating or supported on a trestle.

Lights on Dredge Pipelines

At night, pipelines that are floating or supported must have a row of yellow lights that flash fifty to seventy times per minute. These lights are from 1 meter to 3.5 meters above the water and clearly mark the length and course of the pipeline. Where the pipeline crosses a navigable channel, the lights should be equally spaced and not more than 10 meters apart. There should be two red lights at each end of the pipeline, including the ends in a channel where the pipeline is separated to allow vessels to pass.

Dredge Lights and Shapes

Knowing on which side of a dredge to pass is not a problem when it is properly marked (Figure 7-12). The Inland Navigation Rules require dredges to carry three shapes in a vertical line during the daytime; the highest and lowest are balls, and the middle one is a diamond. At night a dredge must carry three all-round lights in a vertical line; the highest and lowest are red, and the middle one is white. These lights and shapes tell you that the dredge is restricted in its ability to maneuver.

The dredge also carries shapes and lights to tell

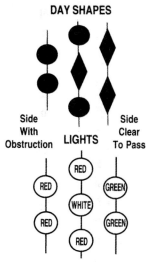

DAY SHAPES

Side With Obstruction — LIGHTS — Side Clear To Pass

RED
RED

RED
WHITE
RED

GREEN
GREEN

Figure **7-12.** This dredge boat working in the Sacramento River (top) displays the day shapes prescribed by the Navigation Rules (bottom). (COURTESY U.S. ARMY CORPS OF ENGINEERS)

where the discharge pipe is. Two balls in a vertical line in the daytime, or two red lights at night, show that the pipe is on that side. The side on which you should pass has two green lights or two diamonds in a vertical line. In the daytime, "Go for the diamonds."

Dams

Over the years, many dams have been built on inland waterways. Some serve to maintain navigable water depths for commercial boating traffic, while others provide water for communities, irrigation, mills, and electrical generation. Some are for flood control.

Dams are seldom, if ever, constructed for recreational boating. While the resulting lakes are often

used for this activity, the dams' imposing powerhouses, spillways, and locks are intimidating to many boaters.

Lowhead Dams

On many small rivers, dams are simply low walls of concrete or stone that remain submerged most of the time. Officially they are "fixed-crest, low-level dams" but they are often called *lowhead dams*. They may be the most dangerous type of dam for boaters, and have been described as "efficient, self-operating drowning machines."

Lowhead dams vary in height from about a foot to several feet and occur frequently in some areas. There are, for example, about 2,000 lowhead dams in the Commonwealth of Pennsylvania. Many serve to impound water for mills, while others provide minimum upstream water levels for water supply systems (Figure 7-13).

Passing Over Lowhead Dams

Because the drops over some of these dams may appear small, some boaters assume that they can safely pass over them, while others do not know that they are near one of these dams and may accidentally pass over it. If the water level is high enough, this is possible, but boaters should realize that **these dams are extremely dangerous.**

Lowhead Dam Dangers

There are hazards both in going over a lowhead dam and in the backwash below the dam (Figures

Figure **7-13.** A drilling rig at work on Dam #2 on the Allegheny River. From upstream, a lowhead dam like this can be hard to see. (COURTESY U.S. ARMY CORPS OF ENGINEERS)

7-14 and 7-15). Anything caught in the backwash circulates around and around, making escape or rescue difficult. A dam does not have to be high to create a backwash, which gets worse during periods of high water and reaches farther downstream.

A person caught in a backwash first encounters tires and logs on the water's surface and rocks and steel bars on the bottom. If you escape these hazards, the backwash will pull you under and recirculate you back to the dam, where it will catch you

again. You can then escape by swimming underwater as far downstream as possible, with the hope of coming up beyond the boil.

Another way to escape is to swim laterally across the stream as you emerge from each cycle. This requires exceptional breathing control and endurance, and your chances of survival are greater if you are wearing a life jacket.

High Dams

Conventional dams, with their large structures, present more easily recognized dangers than do lowhead dams. Furthermore, there is usually a greater effort to warn unwary boaters of the presence and dangers of the dams.

Most high dams have "keep out" buoys above them and "danger dam" buoys below them.

Restricted Areas

Areas immediately upstream and downstream of high dams are restricted and are marked by signs and buoys and, perhaps, by flashing red lights installed in conspicuous places (Figure 7-16). On the upstream side of many high dams there are strong undertows resulting from the rush of water through open gate sections below the water's surface. If a boat approaches the upper side of a high dam too closely, the undertow may pin it against the dam or capsize it.

Dams have gates that open to allow the release of water to the downstream pool, and to control the flow of water during flooding periods or to generate electricity. Most dam operators sound horns or sirens before the gates open, so if you hear such a sound, get out of the way quickly.

Figure **7-14.** **Top:** An "upstream" view of the lowhead dam adjacent to the Ballard Locks, which connect Lake Union with Puget Sound in Seattle. The vertical drop from Lake Union to the saltwater entrance channel is anywhere from 6 to 26 feet, depending on the tide. **Bottom:** The turbulence below the spillway at the Ballard Locks is clearly visible in this photo from the saltwater side. (PHOTOS COURTESY BOB DENNIS)

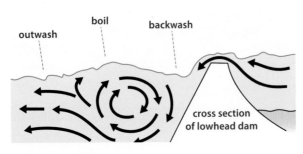

Figure **7-15.** The hydraulic backwash below a lowhead dam.

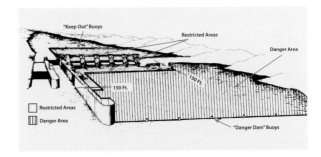

Figure **7-16.** Dams are dangerous. Stay out of restricted areas. This illustration shows the gravity locks that typically permit upstream and downstream traffic past a dam.

Dam Gates

There are several types of dam gates in use. *Wicket gates* lower to lie along the bottom of the waterway so that water passes above them, and their principal advantage is that in times of high water, river traffic can pass over the dam. The height of the dam controls the type of wickets used. Wicket dams present potential hazards to small boats, which can be swept over a partially open wicket.

More often, high dams use *tainter gates* (Figure 7-17), which allow water to flow downstream from the bottom of the dam. The advantage of the flow from the bottom is that it flushes sediment downstream. Since the openings are at the base of the dam, boaters cannot tell by looking if the dam gates are open. Open gates mean turbulent water, and this means a dangerous situation for small boats, which can be caught up against the wall of a tainter dam and be held there until rescued if they do not capsize or swamp first.

Fishing Below Dams

The *tailrace*, or whitewater below a dam (Figure 7-18), is an enticing place to fish, since the moving water churns up food on which fish feed, making them abundant in such an area. Don't succumb to the temptation, however. You may lose your boat and your life.

Many accidents occur when small vessels enter restricted areas, especially those below high dams. If a hydroelectric turbine is turned on, it can send a wall of water 6 feet high that can swamp a boat tied to a short anchor line.

Figure **7-18. Top:** The tailrace below a high dam is an exceptionally dangerous place for small boats. (PHOTO BY JAY J. BRANDINGER) **Bottom:** The tailrace of the Bonneville Dam on the Columbia River in Oregon. (COURTESY U.S. ARMY CORPS OF ENGINEERS)

As with a lowhead dam, the water coming from a high dam creates a boil and a backwash, with the only difference being that the boil and backwash of a high dam are many times stronger. At the water's surface, a strong current moves toward the dam, and if you get into this current and have an engine failure, the current will push you to the face of the dam and swamp your boat. While getting out of the boil below a lowhead dam is difficult, getting out of the boil below a high dam is probably impossible.

Even if you don't experience engine failure, you may have a problem in the tailrace below a dam. From time to time, dams open for power generation or to lower the water level in the pools behind them. Sirens or horns sound before this happens, but your engine may not start and you may be stuck and swamped when the dam opens. Raise your anchor and hope to be carried downstream, but beware that if you are close enough to the dam, the current may push you to the dam's face.

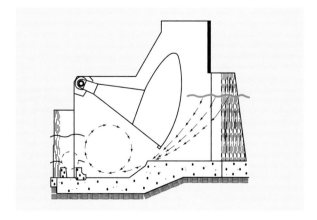

Figure **7-17.** A tainter gate.

Locks

Dams built on navigable streams must have some means of passing vessel traffic through them. Locks serve this purpose by raising or lowering vessels to the level of the next pool of water. A lock on a navigable river is a large chamber, most often about 800 to 1,200 feet long and 100 to 120 feet wide, with gates at each end (Figure 7-19). Locks on canals are often smaller.

Lock Operation

A vessel headed upstream enters the lock chamber through the downstream gates, which then close behind it. Valves in the lock then open to permit water from the upstream pool to enter the chamber, and as the water level rises, the vessel rises with it. When the water level in the lock is even with the level of the upstream pool, the flow of water stops, the upstream gates open, and the vessel moves out of the chamber and continues on its way.

A vessel headed downstream enters the full chamber and the gates close behind it, as in Figure 7-20. The water from the chamber then drains into the lower pool, and this lowers the vessel to the level of the lower pool. When the water inside the lock is at the same level as the water in the lower pool, the lower gates open and the vessel moves on.

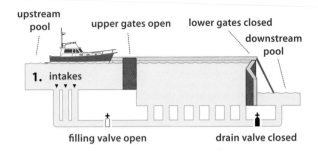

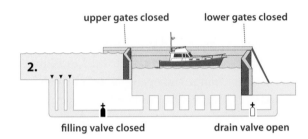

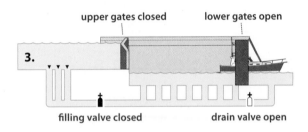

Figure **7-20.** Lock operations for a vessel headed downstream: 1. Preparing to lower the vessel. 2. Lowering the vessel. 3. Leaving the lock.

Figure **7-19.** This aerial view of Lock and Dam #25 on the Mississippi River near Winfield, Missouri, shows a string of barges being locked through in sections while other tows wait their turns. (COURTESY U.S. ARMY CORPS OF ENGINEERS)

While gravity powers the entire operation of lifting or lowering a vessel in a lock, electrical power opens and closes most gates. In some small locks, the gates are manually opened and closed.

Priorities for Use

Federal regulations establish priorities for vessels using locks. Military vessels and mail packets have the highest priority, followed by commercial vessels; recreational vessels have the lowest priority.

This is not as bad as it may sound, as there are only a few naval and military vessels on the waterways, mail packets are rare, and passenger-carrying vessels are not common. Usually, the "competition" for lockage is commercial barge traffic.

Coexisting with Commercial Traffic

On occasion, it is possible to lock through with barges. This depends on the available space in the lock, the nature of the cargo, and the wishes of the towboat operator, whose first responsibility is the safety of the tow. If you do lock through with a tow, use extra caution, as quarters may be tight and you may be moving close to the tow or the lock gates.

Sometimes, when a string of barges is too large to fit into a lock chamber, the operator breaks the tow into two or more parts and locks through in sections. Recreational boats sometimes can lock through in the opposite direction as the chamber is being filled or drained.

Plan on some delay at locks, as long as several hours if commercial traffic is heavy and several tows are waiting. Be patient, but also rest assured that the lockmaster will take you as soon as possible, since few lockmasters want recreational boats loitering near their locks.

The Lockmaster

While the building, maintenance, and operation of river locks are the responsibility of the Corps, each lock is under the control of a lockmaster, who is entirely responsible for its operation. Whenever possible, a lockmaster will lock you through immediately, but there may be more pressing needs that will cause you to have to wait.

Communicating with the Lockmaster

You can reach the lockmaster on Channel 16 of your VHF-FM radio; you will then probably be asked to switch to Channel 13. Contacting the lockmaster in advance by radio can be helpful for both of you. When lockmasters know what traffic to expect, they can plan their moves and make more efficient use of their facilities, and if you know what is going on, you can adjust your speed and plans accordingly. Perhaps you can speed up and get into a group locking through, or take a lunch break while a barge or a restricted tow locks through.

Understand that if you are locking through with a tow or several recreational boats, the lockmaster may not be able to respond immediately to your radio call. You may be able to avoid calling the lockmaster by listening to radio traffic and learning what is going on.

Corps-operated locks are equipped with a manual "Small Craft Signal," usually a chain or pull rope located at the outermost end of the lock wall. It will have an explanatory sign, and you should give this signal one pull if you do not have a VHF-FM radio. You may not be able to hear the signal from your location, so stay where you are and wait for the lockmaster to give you instructions.

Traffic Signals

Light or whistle signals may advise you how to proceed in entering or leaving a lock. Light signals typically resemble traffic signals (Figure 7-21), and you respond to them in much the same way. A red light means "do not approach," and a yellow light, often flashing, means that you should prepare to move

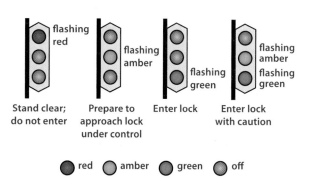

Figure **7-21.** Light signals at a lock.

into the lock. Don't start toward the lock while the light is yellow; instead wait for the green light to signal that the lock is ready to receive vessels.

Sound signals are of two types: one prolonged blast (4 to 6 seconds) means enter the lock; one short blast (1 second) means leave the lock.

Be careful when you see or hear the signals, since they may not apply to you. If there are other vessels waiting for lockage, the signal could be for them if they have a higher priority than you do.

Locking Through

As you approach the lock chamber, move without a wake, which usually means a fast idle speed. There is a conflict between the need to move quickly and the need to keep your wake down, but avoiding wakes takes priority. A lock is a long, narrow chamber with flat concrete walls, and wakes of boats bounce off these walls. When several boats are moving near each other, be extra careful to avoid damaging boats or gate mechanisms.

All crewmembers should wear life jackets during the locking operation. The lock chamber can be turbulent when filling or emptying, and you and your crewmembers will be moving around, tending lines. It is a dangerous time to fall overboard.

As a precaution against fire, you may be asked to stop your engine and extinguish all flames. Smoking is not allowed. With several boats in close quarters in a closed chamber, a fire could be a disaster.

Tying Up in the Lock

Prepare to tie up to bitts or bollards in the lock using your own lines. Since the walls of locks are often rough and dirty and may have sharp, exposed metal pieces, you will want to make liberal use of fenders. Use boathooks or poles, rather than hands and feet, to keep your boat away from the lock wall. While small boats usually use only one line, boats larger than 25 to 30 feet need lines both forward and aft.

Lock bollards are of two types, fixed and floating. Fixed bollards are usually at the top of the lock wall and require lines more than twice the depth of the lock. On a small boat, tie one end of a line to a bow cleat, loop the line around the bollard, and tend the other end around a stern cleat. If you are

being lowered, let out line from the stern cleat as you progress. If you are being raised, take up line.

In other locks, there is a series of fixed bitts in the lock wall. Ladders sometimes serve the same purpose (Figure 7-22), and in such locks, you should move your line from attachment point to attachment point as you are raised or lowered.

Some larger locks have floating bollards (Figures 7-23 and 7-24), and in these you should secure your line to a bow cleat, take a turn around the bollard, and tend the other end of the line at a stern cleat. With this type of bollard, you neither have to

Figure 7-22. A ladder and fixed bitts in a lock wall. (PHOTO BY DEBBIE NEWMAN)

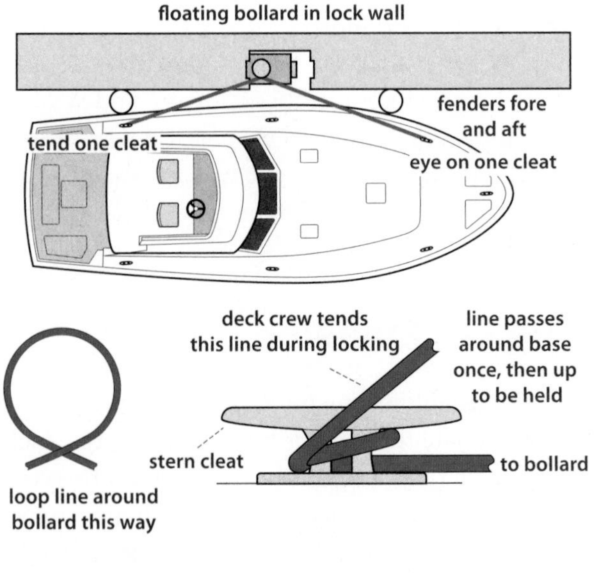

floating bollard in lock wall

tend one cleat

fenders fore and aft

eye on one cleat

deck crew tends this line during locking

line passes around base once, then up to be held

loop line around bollard this way

stern cleat

to bollard

Figure 7-23. Tying up to a floating bollard.

Figure **7-24.** Tending a line on a floating bollard. (PHOTO BY BRIAN DENNIS)

Figure **7-25.** Rafting up in the Ballard Locks, Lake Union, Seattle. (PHOTO BY BRIAN DENNIS)

take up nor pay out line. Tend the line carefully, though, and take action in the unlikely event that the bollard jams and does not move up or down, in which case you may need your long line.

Floating bollards can jam from debris snagged in them. If this happens, take your line from the bollard and fasten it to a ladder or to a fixed bitt in the wall. When you retrieve your line from a jammed bollard, be careful, as the bollard may free itself and float to the surface with considerable force.

Rafting Up

When many small boats lock through together, there may not be enough space along the wall to accommodate all of them. Break out your fenders and lines and raft up with the other boats if requested (Figure 7-25). The lockmaster will tell you where to go on the wall, and may tell you which boats are to raft with you.

Leaving the Lock

After the water in the lock has reached its desired level, wait for the lockmaster's signal before moving out. Again, move at a no-wake speed, paying close attention to the other boats that are getting underway at the same time.

Please note that the signals and procedures outlined here are general guidelines. Significant

variations exist in regulations from waterway to waterway and in lock design from one lock to the next, and it is important that you familiarize yourself with local conditions and procedures before using the installations (Figure 7-26).

Figure **7-26.** The northernmost of the two locks on the Dismal Swamp Canal, an alternative route to the Intracoastal Waterway for slow-moving sailboats heading south from Norfolk, Virginia, to Elizabeth City, North Carolina. The canal was partly surveyed by George Washington. In this sequence a sailboat is locked in and raised to the higher level. (PHOTOS BY DON LINDBERG)

River Charts

The Corps makes most of the charts used for river piloting, which differ in many respects from those used in coastal piloting. They are often published as spiral-bound books, with each page containing a chart of a section of the river. In this format, river charts can have large scales and still be handled conveniently aboard recreational boats.

Characteristics

Many river charts are little more than simple sketches that show the principal geographic features of the waterway, the channel and its sailing line, prominent structures, and fixed aids to navigation. Others, such as the chart of the Warrior River in Alabama, are aerial photographs on which symbols have been printed. Some charts, including those of the Mississippi, show the positions of navigation lights but do not show the lights' characteristics. An up-to-date copy of the *Light List* (see Chapter 5) will help you know which light you are viewing.

Depths of water seldom appear on river charts. Since river depths vary greatly from time to time, they would be meaningless. When a chart shows floating aids to navigation, consider their positions approximate and use them with caution. The Coast Guard moves them frequently and it also sets additional buoys during periods of low water to mark shoals that are not of concern when the water is higher.

Unlike coastal charts, landmarks such as smokestacks, water towers, and antennas do not usually appear on river charts. Often, only those structures close to the banks are shown, and then only by symbols and footnotes. Many of these symbols are unlike those on coastal charts, but there should be a key to the symbols on the front pages of the chartbook. It is best to spend some time studying your chart before you begin your voyage.

On most river charts, information about bridges—such as ownership, type of bridge, vertical and horizontal clearances, and location—can be found in the information block, or legend. The horizontal clearances of swing and drawbridges are given for both their open and closed states, vertical clearances are given for some bridges at pool stage and for others for normal high water, and locations are given by mile markers. Most bridge tenders can be reached on VHF-FM Channel 16 or 13.

Some river charts do not show geographical names for areas along their banks. Likewise, most do not include roads other than those that cross the river, so a good road map may be a useful supplement to your river chart.

A Chart of a Section of the Missouri River

At first glance, river charts may appear inadequate to boaters accustomed to coastal charts. Careful study will show you, however, that they have most of the features you need for safe boating on the river.

The chart in Figure 7-27 shows a section of the Missouri River. The river flows from left to right, which you can tell from the arrows on the river in the upper left and right corners. North is to the left and south is to the right, as indicated by the arrow with an N on it near the upper right side of the page.

As shown on the lower right of Figure 7-27, it is Chart No. 27. Revetments appear as cross-hatched areas at bends in the river, while dikes and wing dams jut out from the banks and appear as solid and dotted lines.

Mileage numbers are printed on the sailing line that marks the channel, and mileage markers appear at easily seen points such as the daybeacons at Sarpy, Bellevue Reach Upper, and Bellevue Reach. Since the Corps measures the Missouri from its mouth to its source, the mileage numbers decrease as you go downriver.

Daybeacons

As already discussed, daybeacons offer invaluable guidance to riverboaters, especially large commercial craft. They are printed on the chart in the order you see them as you move either up or down the river.

For example, when you pass Manawa at mile 604.6 going downstream (Figure 7-27, upper left), you see a red triangular passing daymark on the left descending bank. On the back of the triangle is a red diamond crossing daymark. If you look back upriver as you pass these daymarks, you see the red diamond, and know that the next daymark will be

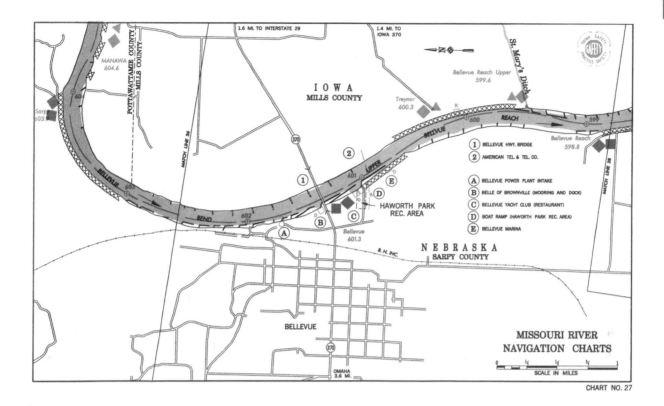

Figure **7-27.** A portion of a Missouri River chart.

a green diamond on the opposite bank. When you look downriver, you see the green diamond passing daymark at Sarpy and head for it.

Since the diamond at Sarpy has a green square on its back side, you know that the channel continues along the right descending bank. It continues there until Bellevue at mile 601.3, at which point you learn that the channel crosses over to the opposite bank and you head to the markers at Treynor. You can tell the course of the channel by observing the sailing line.

Navigation Lights

The locations of navigation lights are also shown on some river charts. A red disk between a red triangle and red diamond stands for a red navigation light. Some disks are green to correspond to the green lights they represent. As you would expect, red lights mark the left descending bank and green ones mark the right descending bank.

In some cases a disk has the letter P overprinted on it, indicating a privately maintained light. If it does not have the P, the U.S. Coast Guard maintains it. River charts do not show the characteristics of navigation lights, such as their colors and periods, but you can tell their characteristics by referring to the *Light List*.

Commercial Traffic

A variety of commercial traffic uses inland waterways. In some places you can see ships from foreign ports, cruise ships, and floating casinos, but most often, commercial traffic consists of tow boats with strings of barges. Usually, the barges are lashed alongside their tow boats or are pushed ahead of them, and are rigidly connected so that they can be maneuvered as a single unit. A string of barges such as this is a *composite unit*.

Oceangoing and River Tows

There is an important difference between oceangoing and river tows that recreational boaters should know about. Oceangoing tugs usually tow their loads well behind them, with long steel cables that connect the tugs with their tows and dip just below the water's surface. This presents a dangerous situation for boaters. **Never cut between an ocean-going tug and its tow.**

You and a River Tow

It takes a long distance for tows to get up speed or to stop. As a result, they stop only to break out a barge, to pass through a dam, or to tie up to the bank because the water is too low or too high. Tenders deliver provisions and fuel to them while they are underway.

An average commercial river tow is about 1,150 feet long with a beam of 105 feet. It draws 8.5 feet and weighs 60,000,000 pounds, and its engines develop as much as 5,600 horsepower.

In contrast, the average pleasure boat is less than 20 feet long with a beam of less than 8 feet. Its draft is 2 feet, and it weighs about 3,000 pounds.

Watch Out for the Tow

Obviously, commercial tows are big and you are small. It's like comparing a subcompact automobile with a train. The tug has 0.2 horsepower per ton, while you have 133 horsepower per ton and can stop quickly. It may take up to a mile to stop a down-bound tow when the river is running, and the tow also requires a lot of room in which to maneuver.

With your shallow draft, you can go bank to bank almost anywhere, but the tow is limited in where it can go, and cannot turn wherever it wishes due to its draft.

Some tugs have as many as three large propellers. Driven by a tug's large engines, they can produce a prop wash you can feel hundreds of feet behind them (Figure 7-28). The propellers also churn debris from the bottom that may be hazardous to small craft. It makes sense to give tows as wide a berth as possible.

The Tow's Blind Spot

The operator of a tug pushing a string of barges is in the pilothouse at the after end of the tow, as in Figure 7-29. Although most towboats have high pilothouses, there is always an area immediately in front of the tow that is blocked from view. This blind zone typically extends 600 feet or more ahead of the tow (Figure 7-30).

When boating near a tow, be sensitive to the

Figure **7-28.** **Top:** A towboat on the Lower Mississippi River near Baton Rouge, Louisiana. (PHOTO BY JAY J. BRANDINGER) **Bottom:** The backwash behind the towboat *Rachel* as it pushes its string through a lock on the Colorado River is eloquent testimony to the power of those props. (COURTESY U.S. ARMY CORPS OF ENGINEERS)

Figure **7-29.** A view from the bridge of the *Christopher M. Parsonage.* The *Parsonage* is pushing the equivalent of 665 railroad cars or 1,820 tractor trailers of grain and coke down the Mississippi River. Don't count on it stopping or turning quickly. (REPRINTED WITH PERMISSION FROM *SEAWORTHY: ESSENTIAL LESSONS FROM BOATU.S.'S 20-YEAR CASE FILE OF THINGS GONE WRONG* BY ROBERT A. ADRIANCE)

tugboat operator's field of view, and avoid running into the blind zone. It is tempting to move back to the center of a channel as soon as you pass a tow, but this usually means that you are moving into the blind zone or towing a skier into it. If you have an

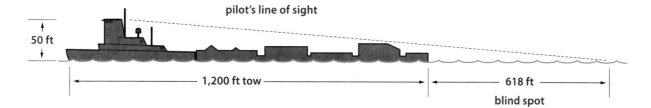

Figure 7-30. A towboat captain's blind spot extends far ahead of his tow. If you can't see him, he can't see you.

engine failure, strike a submerged object, lose someone overboard, or drop your skier, the towboat operator will never know, and could unwittingly run over you. Even if there is a lookout posted on the bow, the operator cannot stop the tow in time to avoid hitting a stalled boat or someone in the water.

Recently, in Philadelphia, a barge in tow ran over a small boat that was stranded in the Delaware River. The tugboat's pilot received an emergency cell-phone call from his wife and moved from the upper wheelhouse, which had better visibility, to the lower wheelhouse so he could hear better. He also turned down the ship's radio so he missed the Mayday calls from the stranded boat. Two people on the small boat were killed.

Communicating with Commercial Traffic

When you meet or pass a tow, remember that the sound signals for meeting head-on, crossing, and overtaking required by the Inland Navigation Rules are in effect, and you should use them to communicate with the tow and to respond to signals from the tow.

It is very possible that the towboat operator will not hear your sound signals, since there is a high noise level in the pilothouse from the tug's engines, and the pilothouse is often air-conditioned. The towboat operator will probably therefore expect your contact to be by VHF-FM radio.

Call the tow operator on Channel 16 and be ready to switch to Channel 13. Vessels working around docks or barge staging areas where the radio traffic is heavy may direct you to a different working channel. When you talk to a towboat, be certain that it is the towboat you are near and not one farther up or down the river.

If you find yourself in a narrow channel with a tow approaching, move to the edge of the channel. If there is still not room enough for the tow to pass, move out of the channel if the water is deep enough. If not, turn around and retreat to a safe position below the narrow channel. For practical purposes, the responsibility for avoiding a collision is yours.

Avoid meeting tows in a river bend. If you are monitoring your VHF-FM radio, you will know where the traffic is and should wait for the tow to pass through the bend if possible. If a tow catches you in a bend, move to the inside of the bend, since the towboat will follow the channel, which is most likely on the outside of the bend (Figure 7-31).

Obviously, a VHF-FM radio is essential equipment. Also, consider installing a radar reflector on your vessel, since towboats have radar and a radar reflector can help the towboat operator see you.

Before You Go

Before you venture out onto a river, study its chart to learn of hazards such as dams and low drawbridges and to gain a general orientation to the river. Being informed is better than being surprised.

If you are moving your boat from one body of fresh water to another, observe the precautions regarding zebra mussels.

Drawbridge signals and regulations are discussed in Chapter 6, which you should review before boating on a river. Although most highway and railroad bridges are high enough to permit the passage of most recreational craft beneath them, you may meet one that is not high enough. This is more likely to be the case if your vessel is a sailboat than if it is a motorboat.

Figure **7-31.** On the Black River in Louisiana below the Columbia Lock and Dam. (PHOTO BY JAY J. BRANDINGER)

Ways to Learn More

Chapman Piloting & Seamanship. 66th ed. Charles B. Husick. New York: Hearst Books, 2009. Chapter 22.

The One-Minute Guide to the Nautical Rules of the Road. Charlie Wing. Camden, Maine: International Marine, 2006.

Rules of the Road and Running Light Patterns: A Captain's Quick Guide. Charlie Wing. Camden, Maine: International Marine, 2004.

Practice Questions

IMPORTANT BOATING TERMS

In the following exercise, match the words in the column on the left with the definitions in the column on the right. In the blank space to the left of each term, write the letter of the item that best matches it. Do not use an item in the right-hand column more than once.

THE ITEMS

1. _____ navigable waterways
2. _____ left bank
3. _____ Western Rivers
4. _____ buoys
5. _____ revetment
6. _____ wing dams
7. _____ tailrace
8. _____ sailing line
9. _____ passing daymark
10. _____ crossing daymark

THE RESPONSES

a. left descending bank

b. triangle or square

c. marks channel

d. direct the current into the channel

e. includes navigable rivers, the Great Lakes, and the ICW

f. the Mississippi and its tributaries

g. facing of stone, concrete, etc.

h. diamond

i. not usually shown on river charts

j. whitewater below a dam

Multiple-Choice Items

In the following items, choose the best response:

7-1. Navigable waterways include

a. local lakes

b. the navigable rivers, Great Lakes, and ICW

c. all canals and rivers

d. all inland waterways

7-2. Which navigation rules are in force on navigable waterways?

a. U.S. ATON System

b. COLREGS

c. USWMS

d. Inland Navigation Rules

Multiple-Choice Items (continued)

7-3. What is the color of the ATONs on the right descending bank of a river?

a. red
b. green
c. yellow
d. white

7-4. River buoys are

a. easily located
b. lighted
c. black
d. usually not shown on river charts

7-5. The flow of a river's current is often directed by

a. revetments
b. dams
c. locks
d. wing dams

7-6. At night you know which side of a dredge the pipeline is on by

a. two red lights
b. two green lights
c. a white and a green light
d. a white and a red light

7-7. Regulatory marks are of two types:

a. signs and buoys
b. nuns and cans
c. dolphins and spherical buoys
d. spar buoys

7-8. River charts have

a. many details of landmarks
b. charted water depths
c. locations of buoys
d. information about bridges

7-9. Lakes include bodies of water that are

a. natural
b. impounded
c. made by damming rivers
d. all of the above

7-10. Which set of ATONs is used on the Western Rivers?

a. U.S. ATON System
b. USWMS
c. ICW
d. none of the above

7-11. Crossing daymarks are

a. diamond shaped

b. square
c. triangular
d. rectangular

7-12. When entering a lock, a red traffic signal means

a. do not approach
b. proceed with caution
c. enter lock
d. high-priority vessels can enter lock

7-13. Maintenance of the federal, navigable, inland waterways is the responsibility of

a. the U.S. Army Corps of Engineers
b. the U.S. Coast Guard
c. state authorities
d. local authorities

7-14. Dredge pipelines are marked by what color lights at night?

a. blue
b. green
c. yellow
d. white

7-15. In locking through, which vessels have the highest priority?

a. commercial
b. government
c. recreational
d. yachts

7-16. Most river charts are made by

a. the U.S. Coast Guard
b. the U.S. Army Corps of Engineers
c. National Oceanic and Atmospheric Administration
d. National Ocean Service

7-17. When communicating with commercial river traffic

a. call on Channel 16
b. change to a working channel when you have contact
c. be sure you know which vessel you are talking to
d. all of the above

7-18. Your speed should be reduced in canals because

a. they are small and dangerous
b. you need to watch out for other vessels
c. your wake will erode the banks
d. you will miss the scenery

Multiple-Choice Items (continued)

7-19. As you travel upstream, which bank is on your port side?

a. right
b. left
c. First National
d. left descending bank

7-20. Crossing daymarks mean

a. cross over at the next ATON
b. the river channel continues along the same bank
c. nothing to you since your vessel is very small
d. the river channel is on the side with the daymark

7-21. Danger areas in the Western Rivers and U.S. ATON systems are marked with

a. open diamonds
b. diamonds with cross marks
c. circles
d. rectangles

7-22. On the inside of a river bend

a. the current scours the channel
b. currents are in one direction at the surface and in the opposite direction below the surface
c. the current moves faster
d. silting and shoaling may occur

7-23. Wing dams and dikes

a. appear as solid or dotted lines on charts
b. are not usually shown on charts
c. cause silting
d. provide excellent anchorages

7-24. What structures have been described as "efficient, self-operating drowning machines?"

a. wing dams
b. high-rise dams
c. dikes
d. lowhead dams

7-25. Call the lockmaster on your VHF-FM radio using

a. Channel 13
b. Channel 6
c. Channel 22
d. Channel 16

7-26. River charts seldom show

a. the characteristics of navigation lights
b. locations of passing daymarks
c. locations of crossing daymarks
d. locations of navigation lights

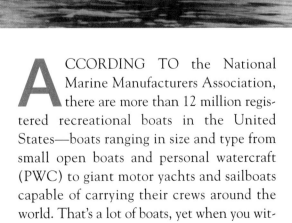

chapter 8

Boating Safety

The objectives of this chapter are to describe:

- ✔ The causes of small boat accidents and how to prevent them.
- ✔ The principles of safe personal watercraft operation.
- ✔ The dangers of immersion in cold water, the causes and symptoms of hypothermia, how to prevent hypothermia, and precautions to observe when assisting victims of hypothermia.
- ✔ How powerboats can best share the water with sailboats, how to help a sailboat in trouble, and how to aid a person overboard.
- ✔ The dangers and symptoms of carbon monoxide poisoning, its causes aboard ship, and its prevention.
- ✔ Sources of good weather information.
- ✔ Changes in surroundings that indicate a storm is approaching.

ACCORDING TO the National Marine Manufacturers Association, there are more than 12 million registered recreational boats in the United States—boats ranging in size and type from small open boats and personal watercraft (PWC) to giant motor yachts and sailboats capable of carrying their crews around the world. That's a lot of boats, yet when you wit-

Newer models of PWC can carry as many as four seated passengers and are highly maneuverable. (COURTESY BOMBARDIER RECREATION PRODUCTS)

197

ness the flotilla of boats swarming around a major coastal yachting center or a popular inland boating area on a summer weekend afternoon, you may find yourself wondering whether the real number isn't even larger than that.

With so many boats sharing the water, operating your boat safely and skillfully is the key to a pleasurable afternoon on the water. That message is woven throughout this book, but in this chapter we take a closer look at a few specific safety concerns that previous chapters have only mentioned.

Boating regulations and safety alerts are constantly changing at the federal and state levels, and it is the responsibility of the boat operator to keep current. The U.S. Coast Guard websites are a good source of information, and they also have links to state boating agencies.

Small Boat Safety

Passenger Briefing

Whether they are seasoned boaters or unaccustomed to being on a boat, all passengers should be briefed about the locations of life jackets, fire extinguishers, flares, and the first-aid kit, and should understand the procedures for using the boat's toilet, operating the radio in an emergency, handling lines, and recovering a person who has fallen overboard. They need to know the latter so that they can recover you should you fall overboard, or so that they can help themselves should they fall over. Before anchoring or docking, brief your passengers on the procedure. Should you be unlucky enough to face the possibility of a squall or gale that you can't beat back to the dock, brief your passengers on what will happen and what measures you may take. It helps to use a prepared checklist.

Boating Fatalities

Most boats in use today are less than 16 feet long, and more than 90% are less than 20 feet long. While most are stable and safe when used properly, small boats are more liable than larger ones to become unstable when used improperly. In part for this reason, and in part simply because there are so many

more small boats in use, nearly half of all boating fatalities occur in boats 12 to 16 feet long.

Contrary to popular opinion, about half of all boating fatalities occur on lakes, ponds, and reservoirs, and not on navigable waterways. Nearly half of all fatalities occur on weekend afternoons, and about half occur in calm weather and in full daylight.

Of boaters involved in fatal accidents, more than 80% of the accidents are due to operator error. Many probably do not even think of themselves as boaters, since about 25% fish and some hunt in boats. And they are not only young people; almost half are 26 to 50 years old. An example of this was a recent tragedy on Long Island Sound. A 34-foot power cruiser had 27 people on board to watch the Fourth of July fireworks. The boat suddenly rolled over and in the ensuing chaos, three children were trapped in the cabin and drowned. The Coast Guard is investigating how overcrowding, weather, and seamanship may have contributed to this sad event.

These victims have one thing in common with many motorists who do not buckle up: 78% are not wearing life jackets. In addition, a large percentage drink alcohol immediately before their accidents.

Most fatal boating accidents involve people who suddenly and unexpectedly find themselves in the water without life jackets. More often than not, this happens when they stand up to shoot waterfowl, land fish, start their engines, or raise their anchors, or for other reasons, and their boats capsize or swamp or they fall overboard. Sometimes the victims wind up in the water after a collision with another boat or object. Regardless of the cause, being able to swim is not sufficient protection if you find yourself in the water unexpectedly. Nearly 70% of people who lose their lives in boating accidents drown, even though most are "swimmers."

Sadly, most boating fatalities involve people who have life jackets on board but are not wearing them at the time of the accident. A life jacket aboard will not help you if you fall overboard without it and your boat floats away, or if you can't reboard the boat. If your boat capsizes and the life jackets are in the cabin, you and your passengers will probably not be able to get to them. Even small boats without cabins often trap life jackets under their thwarts, or seats, when they capsize.

The use of drugs and alcohol accounts for a very large number of boating fatalities, and is no more safe than operating an automobile under the influence. Furthermore, it's illegal to operate a boat under the influence of these substances.

The shock of a sudden plunge into cold water (less than 59°F) can have a severe effect on the body. Good swimmers in good physical condition can be immobilized within a few minutes, and death can occur even after a quick recovery from the water. This is independent of the risks of hypothermia, which involves the more gradual loss of body heat and subsequent loss of body functions even in relatively warm waters.

Small Boat Stability

Obviously, you want to avoid swamping or capsizing if at all possible. You can avoid swamping in two ways. First, don't go out in a small boat in rough water. Second, know how boats float and use this knowledge to your advantage.

When you go boating, regardless of the size of your boat, load it according to the weather. The rougher the weather, the more freeboard you need to avoid swamping. It is tempting to overload small vessels when you expect to be in calm, protected waters. Operating in shallow waters also causes boaters to not assess their risks properly. Seemingly safe movements such as standing to hand a drink to another passenger can sometimes cause a disaster by changing the boat's stability. Boat instability and overloading account for a very high fatality rate. This is part of the reason why boats less than 20 feet are required to display a capacity plate as described in Chapter 2. Never exceed your boat's capacity even in calm weather, and reduce its load if the weather deteriorates.

Things float because they displace a weight of water equal to their own weight. Thus, a boat will sink into the water only far enough to displace its own weight of water. The heavier the boat, the farther it must sink into the water before it can float, which means that the less weight you add to a boat, the higher it will float.

The stability of a boat—that is, its ability to resist capsizing—depends on its underwater shape and its centers of gravity and buoyancy. A boat's *center of gravity* (CG) is the center of its total mass. A sturdy object is stable when its center of gravity is over its base, and unstable when its weight is centered over a point outside the base.

Further, the higher the center of gravity, the less stable the boat. Piling things in a boat, or standing in a boat, raises its center of gravity and lessens its stability. The lower the center of gravity of a boat, the more stable it becomes. This is why many sailboats carry lead ballast on the bottoms of their keels to balance the heeling force of the sails, and it's also why a canoe feels so much more stable when you're sitting down than when you're standing up. The center of gravity of a boat varies with its load and where you place it, as shown in Figure 8-1.

Another consideration in the stability of a boat is its buoyancy. The buoyant force on a boat is equal to the weight of the water it displaces. The *center of buoyancy* (CB) is the center of the mass of the water the boat displaces. When a boat is at rest, or in equilibrium, the center of buoyancy is vertically aligned with the center of gravity, the

ATTENTION, PADDLERS!

Kayaks and canoes are small boats, and the information on small boat stability in these pages applies to you. Additional safety measures you should take include:

- Be prepared to enter the water. Wear a properly fitted PFD, and know how to swim.
- Never paddle alone.
- Know your skill level and limits, and avoid bad weather, great distances from shore, rough seas, and strong currents.
- Take a paddling course with hands-on instruction. It will teach you balance, use of stabilizing strokes, safe entry and exit on the water, and rescue and recovery skills.

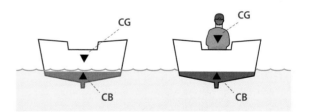

Figure **8-1.** The centers of gravity (CG) and buoyancy (CB) of a boat when empty and loaded. A boat is in perfect trim when its center of gravity is directly above its center of buoyancy, and the lower the center of gravity, the more stable the boat. When weight is added high in the boat, as by the addition of a passenger and gear in a small boat, the center of gravity rises and stability decreases. When weight shifts outboard or in the fore-and-aft direction, the center of gravity moves accordingly, and the center of buoyancy must likewise move (as in Figure 8-2) to achieve a new alignment with the CG.

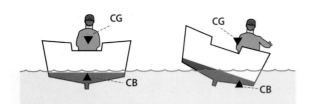

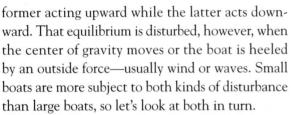

Figure **8-2.** The centers of gravity and buoyancy when a boater leans out in a small boat. The center of gravity shifts outboard, and the center of buoyancy must move outboard to achieve a new equilibrium. In this drawing the centers are back in alignment, but sometimes a careless boater will shift his weight too high and too far outboard to be countered by heeling, and the boat will swamp or capsize.

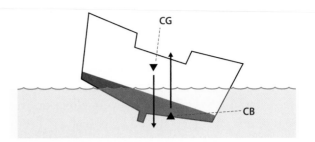

Figure **8-3.** The centers of gravity and buoyancy in a boat heeled by waves, wind, or a tight turn. This time the center of buoyancy moves, while the center of gravity does not. The resulting lever arm between the CG acting downward and the CB acting upward seeks to restore the boat to its upright position.

former acting upward while the latter acts downward. That equilibrium is disturbed, however, when the center of gravity moves or the boat is heeled by an outside force—usually wind or waves. Small boats are more subject to both kinds of disturbance than large boats, so let's look at both in turn.

Figure 8-1 shows two small boats from astern. The first is empty. In the second a person is seated on a raised seat. Notice that only the center of gravity has changed much from the first to the second. It has risen significantly and is farther from the center of buoyancy. If this elevated center of gravity moves off-center, which occurs, for example, if a person stands and leans to one side, it creates a long lever arm with the center of buoyancy, a force acting to heel the boat. In order to counter this, the center of buoyancy must move outboard to the same side as the leaning person, which is exactly what happens when the boat heels as in Figure 8-2. If the boat is small enough relative to the weight of the person, however, the center of buoyancy will not be able to move far enough outboard to get back in vertical alignment with the center of gravity. Put another way, the boat will not be

able to reach a new equilibrium when the person stands and leans to one side, and it will simply continue heeling until either the person falls overboard or the boat swamps or capsizes.

Now let's see what happens when the boat is heeled by a wave, by wind, or by the force of a tight turn at high speed. As Figure 8-3 shows, this time it is the center of buoyancy that moves, while the center of gravity does not change. This shift creates a force on the heeled side of the boat that acts to bring the boat back to a level position.

In either instance—whether the boat is heeled due to a shift in the center of gravity or the action of an outside force—its resistance to that heeling is often called *initial stability* by boat designers, and that resistance is greater in a flat-bottomed jonboat than in a round-bottomed canoe. The bottom line is that a canoe will roll and swamp or capsize with a smaller shift in the center of buoyancy than will a jonboat of similar length, and a smaller boat will roll more easily than a larger boat of similar hull shape. If you lean out over the side of a canoe, it may roll out from under you.

Boaters who are properly centered and seated low in a small boat do not seriously disrupt the boat's natural stability. If a boater stands up to shoot a gun, land a fish, reach for a pier, or for some other reason shifts his weight up and too far to the side, however, the boat's center of gravity may move outside the gunwale, and the boat will swamp or capsize (Figure 8-4).

Maintain Three-Point Contact

Once you take a seat in a small boat, stay seated, and be careful when leaning over the side. When

IF YOU CAPSIZE . . .

- Put on your PFD.
- Account for all your passengers.
- Stay with your boat if at all possible.
- Grab anything that floats.
- Try to attract the attention of other boaters nearby.
- Get people out of the water as soon as you can.

Figure **8-4.** Stepping on the gunwale of a canoe or small rowboat is a sure way to capsize it. (PHOTO BY JOE BRITVCH)

Figure **8-5.** Maintaining three-point contact for stability. (PHOTO BY DON LINDBERG)

you enter a small boat, or if you need to move about, maintain three points of contact as in Figure 8-5. Hold on to both sides of the boat and keep at least one foot on the deck. This keeps the center of gravity of the boat as low and as nearly centered as possible, helping to maintain the stability of the boat.

Stay with Your Boat

As discussed in Chapter 1, some boats have flotation built in at the factory. This means that if they capsize or swamp, they will stay afloat. Even a boat without such flotation may stay afloat if made of wood or if air is trapped within the hull. As long as your boat remains afloat, even awash, it is usually best to stay with it. Climb on it if possible. The

colder the water, the more urgent it is that you get out of it. You may be tempted to swim to shore, but be careful. It is difficult to judge distances in the water, and the shore may be farther away than you think. Also, if you stay with your boat, it is easier for would-be rescuers to see you.

Personal Watercraft

The past decade has seen a rapid increase in the number of PWC. Originally, the term "personal watercraft" included only those power-driven vessels designed to carry just one standing, kneeling, or sitting passenger, who steered by means of handlebars like those found on bicycles (Figure 8-6). The first sit-down model was introduced in 1987, and by 1993 fully 94% of PWC were sit-down models. The commonly accepted definition of a PWC today is "a vessel that uses an inboard motor powering a water pump as its primary source of power. In addition, it is designed to be operated by a person sitting, standing, or kneeling on the vessel, rather than sitting or standing inside the vessel."

The larger models of PWC now on the market can carry as many as four seated people, though they are still steered with handlebars (Figure 8-7). This discussion of PWC applies to them also.

Figure **8-6.** The first Jet Ski, introduced by Kawasaki in 1973. (COURTESY PERSONAL WATERCRAFT INDUSTRY ASSOCIATION)

Figure **8-7.** Newer models of PWC can carry as many as four seated passengers and are highly maneuverable. (COURTESY PERSONAL WATERCRAFT INDUSTRY ASSOCIATION)

Regardless of what these vessels are called, they are Class A motorboats (boats less than 16 feet long), not toys, and they are high-performance motorboats at that, and subject to all the laws that govern motorboats. When you operate a PWC, keep in mind that you are a boater, and must obey the laws governing our waterways just as any other boater must. It is also good to keep in mind that your PWC is one of the smallest boats on the water. Although it is highly maneuverable, it is also highly unstable and less visible than larger boats.

Operator Responsibility

With certain exceptions, PWC are subject to all the legal requirements outlined in Chapter 2 of this book. This means that their equipment must conform to U.S. Coast Guard standards and regulations when they are used on navigable waters, unless the manufacturer has applied for and received an exemption or exemptions from the Coast Guard. Exemptions may cover such things as capacity plates, safe loading requirements, flotation, fuel systems, and powered ventilation.

PWC must observe the Navigation Rules and all state and local laws and regulations. They should be properly registered and numbered, and their certificates of number must be aboard when they are underway. PWC are required to carry fire extinguishers.

Operators need both physical capability and maturity of judgment to operate these craft safely and responsibly.

Each person aboard must wear a life jacket (Figure 8-8). As discussed in Chapter 2, inflatables are not suitable for this purpose because of their inflating mechanisms. Furthermore, inflatable life jackets are incapable of providing resistance to impact. Printing on your life jacket should indicate its degree of impact resistance. Wear your life jacket and have your riders wear theirs when underway, since chances are good that all of you will spend some time in the water. You might also consider wearing a wet suit if the weather is cold, as hypothermia can occur more rapidly than you may think. Learn the procedures for righting and reboarding a PWC before you head out, and if you can't swim, don't drive or ride on a PWC.

Figure 8-8. PWC can provide family fun when operated responsibly. All passengers should wear inherently buoyant life jackets. Inflatable PFDs are inappropriate for PWC use because the constant soaking could trigger the inflating mechanism and because they provide no impact resistance. (COURTESY PERSONAL WATERCRAFT INDUSTRY ASSOCIATION)

It is advisable to wear some kind of shoes or protection for your feet when driving or riding on a PWC. This helps you keep your footing and avoid scrapes and bruises from underwater objects. You may also want to consider wearing gloves to protect your hands and to aid in moving your watercraft during docking and loading.

As with any vessel, the responsibility for what happens to or on a PWC rests with the skipper. The skipper has responsibility for any damage the PWC may cause, including damage from its wake, and must see that the PWC is operated legally. Among other things, this means not operating your PWC at night and observing all the Navigation Rules for overtaking, crossing, and meeting situations.

Operating any vessel can be stressful, but handling a PWC can be even more so. Be aware that wind, glare, sun, and water can be fatiguing. To boat safely, stay alert, and don't exceed your limitations.

Be Respectful of Others

Quite apart from your legal responsibilities, you should operate your PWC in a safe and courteous manner, with due regard for the rights of the swimmers, boaters, water-skiers, and anglers with whom you're sharing the water. Irresponsible operators have caused state and local agencies to enact restrictive laws controlling PWC. Don't add to the need for more laws, and be sure to obey the laws of the state in which you are boating.

Be mindful that noise carries farther over water than over land, particularly when there are no

- *Don't speed in a congested area.*
- *Don't speed in fog or stormy conditions.*
- *Don't operate in a swimming area.*
- *Don't operate close to dams.*
- *Don't cut through a regatta or marine parade.*
- *Don't cut across flats where people are fishing.*
- *Don't jump boat wakes.*
- *Don't race up to something and swerve at the last moment.*
- *Don't operate in very shallow water, and be aware of environmental issues.*
- *Don't go alone; cruise with at least one other PWC.*

other noises around. Since people place an especially high value on "peace and quiet" in the early morning and late afternoon, watch where you boat at those times. Stay away from homes, campgrounds, or other places where people retreat for peace and quiet.

Never operate a vessel while or immediately after drinking. A PWC is an agile and responsive craft, and operating conditions change with every wake or wave. Even small amounts of alcohol reduce your ability to respond effectively. You must be alert and in control.

Steering a PWC

PWC are fun boats—quick, exciting, fast, and highly maneuverable. Some can reach speeds of more than 60 miles per hour. Their power comes from a two-stroke inboard engine that may develop as much as 40 to 80 (or more) horsepower and that pumps in large amounts of water and ejects it at high speed through a special nozzle.

The nozzle turns to one side or the other to steer the boat, as described and pictured in Chapters 1 and 4. The operator and passengers also help steer by leaning and shifting their body weights much as they might do on a bicycle. Some PWC reverse direction by lowering a clamshell barrier behind the nozzle. This redirects the force of the jet forward, causing the vessel to reverse direction. Do not use reverse for braking. It is advisable to shift to neutral and to stop before reversing.

This arrangement of a relatively high-powered inboard engine, jet propulsion, and light weight means that PWC can accelerate rapidly and stop quickly. Since their pivot points are roughly 14 to 20 inches forward of their engines, they can also turn sharply.

Some Safety Considerations

The high speed and maneuverability of PWC create special safety issues. For example, if a PWC is moving at fast speed, its operator may not see an object in the water ahead in time to avoid hitting it.

Even at slow speeds, a PWC creates a lot of spray. This may blind its operator and cause an accident, so most PWC manufacturers recommend that operators wear goggles or wraparound eye protectors.

The ability of a fast-moving PWC to accelerate or to change direction rapidly can cause passengers or the operator to be thrown from the vessel and possibly injured. A sudden change in direction could place a PWC directly in the path of an oncoming vessel. Operators should always look carefully for other boats and objects before starting and before making quick maneuvers.

Do not operate a PWC at high speed unless you are thoroughly familiar with its operation. A beginning operator needs to learn that releasing the throttle or turning off the engine causes loss of directional control by stopping the flow of water through the nozzle. Thus, reducing power to avoid a collision—which may be your automatic reflex—can cause you to run into the very object you are trying to avoid. Consult your owner's manual or an experienced operator on how best to avoid obstacles.

If your PWC is not of the type that circles back when you fall off, it will have a lanyard and a kill switch. Be certain to fasten one end securely to your wrist or life jacket and the other to its appropriate place on the ignition switch. When (not if) you fall overboard, this will shut off the engine and stop the boat. If you don't connect the lanyard, your vessel may continue on without you, or it may circle back and run over you.

Learning to Operate a PWC

If you are learning how to operate a PWC, be cautious. Read the manual carefully and be sure you understand it fully. Pay particular attention to procedures for reboarding in deep water.

Before starting up, make certain the water is deep enough to avoid drawing sand into the jet-drive intake, since doing so can damage the impeller and possibly injure someone when the sand is ejected from the nozzle. Try not to operate your PWC in water less than 2 feet deep, and before starting up, check to see that there are no objects in the water that might enter the intake.

If the intake becomes clogged, stop the engine before you try to clear it. Do not reach into the nozzle when the engine is running and keep your hands, feet, hair, and clothing away from the intake.

Start slowly and get a feel for the vessel. A PWC responds differently to a lighter person than a heavier one, and differently with a full load than with a sole operator. When pulling a skier (which is illegal in some places) or another PWC, it may respond in a sluggish manner, and the resulting loss of control can create a hazardous condition (Figure 8-9).

A beginning operator has to concentrate on learning how to control the boat, and as a result is not fully aware of nearby swimmers, other vessels, and immovable objects close at hand. It makes sense to operate slowly until you master control of the vessel.

Some PWC are self-righting, while others require special techniques to right them after they turn over. Operators should be thoroughly familiar with the procedures outlined in their manuals before operating the vessels, and rental boat operators should see that renters know the procedures.

It makes good sense to stay within sight of land, whether you are alone or not, and to watch your gasoline use. Observe the One-Third Rule: use no more than a third of your fuel on the trip out, save a third for the trip back, and keep the other third in reserve.

Water Risks

Swimming Near Boats

Swimming near boats, or off docks, especially in a marina, presents a risk of electric shock drowning (ESD) since faulty wiring can mean low levels of alternating current are in the water. Since fresh water has lower conductivity than salt water, fatalities are more likely to occur in freshwater locations. To protect against ESD accidents, the American Boat and Yacht Council (ABYC) adopted standards in 2010 that require installation of an equipment leakage circuit interrupter (ELCI) on new boats. An ELCI responds to a potential fault by tripping the main circuit breaker and cutting power to the boat. However, ABYC standards are voluntary, and there is no requirement to retrofit older boats with ELCIs. There is also no standard that requires installation of ground fault circuit interrupters (GFCIs) at marinas and private docks. The best defense is to never swim near docks with energized 120-volt AC power.

Cold Water

Cold water presents two significant threats to the boater: *cold water immersion* (or cold shock) poses an immediate life threat, and *hypothermia* is the potentially lethal consequence of extended exposure to cold water. Research indicates that certain

Figure **8-9.** Pulling a skier with a PWC is illegal in some places. (COURTESY PERSONAL WATERCRAFT ASSOCIATION)

> **WARNING** *Hypothermia is a serious, life-threatening condition. It is difficult to treat and requires expert care. If you suspect hypothermia, seek prompt and competent medical attention.*

things happen to anyone who is immersed suddenly and perhaps unexpectedly in cold water:

- There is a gasp response on initial contact with the water, and if the person's face is in the water when the gasp takes place, it is possible that water will be aspirated (inhaled) and rapid drowning will ensue.
- There is an immediate and significant reduction in breath-holding capability.
- There is a very rapid loss of coordination and an early inability to move the hands and feet, followed by a loss of the ability to swim.
- Heart rate, breathing rate and effort, and blood pressure all increase dramatically, accelerating the loss of body heat.

Drowning

The common perception of a drowning person is either a lifeless floating body or someone flailing and shouting for help. There are actually many signs of distress and drowning, and it's not practical to ask boaters to memorize all the signs of drowning signs that emergency personnel are trained to recognize. The probability is very high that anyone who isn't behaving like an active normal swimmer is probably in some stage of drowning or distress. The Man Overboard section in Chapter 4 and this chapter cover how to react when encountering a distressed or drowning victim.

Even among people who are young, in good health, and wearing protective clothing, death from cold water immersion has been known to result within 3 to 5 minutes in water that is 59°F or colder. What can be done to minimize the risks of cold water? First and foremost, make sure that you and everyone on your boat wears a life jacket at all times. With a life jacket on, at least you will remain upright in the water and will be less likely to aspirate water when that first gasp occurs. Wear warm clothes, and select clothing made from fibers that retain warmth after becoming wet.

Hypothermia, a major killer in aquatic mishaps, is the gradual reduction of the body's core, or internal, temperature below the threshold of normal biological functions. Hypothermia is not freezing to death, nor is it frostbite. It can kill at temperatures

WARNING You have only a 50-50 chance of swimming 50 yards in 50°F water. This 50-50 "rule" emphasizes the rapidity with which hypothermia can occur. Another 50-50 rule says that a 50-year-old person has only a 50-50 chance of surviving 50 minutes in 50°F water.

TABLE 8-1	APPROXIMATE MEDIAN LETHAL EXPOSURE TIMES		
	Time (hours)		
Water Temperature (°F)	Floating with PFD	Treading Water	Swimming
35	1.75	1.25	0.75
45	2.50	1.75	1.00
55	3.50	3.00	2.00
65	7.75	5.75	4.50
70	18.00	13.00	10.00

well above freezing. In hypothermia, the body simply loses heat more rapidly than it can be replenished.

Anytime your body is unable to maintain its normal temperature, you are at least mildly hypothermic. Most people have experienced mild hypothermia from overexposure to winter weather, and it can occur at other times of the year in strong winds, especially if your clothing is wet.

Hypothermia occurs most rapidly when your body is immersed in cold water because water robs your body of heat at least twenty-five to thirty times faster than air of the same temperature. The shivering you may experience is one means your body employs to keep itself warm, but in cold water this stratagem can postpone only for a short time the onset of more serious symptoms. The colder the water, the more rapidly hypothermia occurs, but it can occur even in rather warm water if you are exposed to it for a long enough time. In water of 50°F, your predicted survival time is 1.5 to 3 hours.

Stages

Your body metabolizes food to get the energy it needs to operate and to maintain its temperature. Excess heat is eliminated by radiation and the evaporation of perspiration. When the body cools below its normal temperature, however, it responds defensively. Blood flow is redirected from nonvital surface tissues and large muscles to vital organs (brain, heart, lungs), and stored food is burned to generate more heat. One sign of the diversion of blood is the appearance of gooseflesh. Another sign is shivering.

As the core temperature falls and the body's resources decrease, shivering slows, then stops. The body begins a systematic shutdown, abandoning periphery circulation (arms and legs) while it seeks to maintain a constant temperature in its core. If you have been drinking alcohol, your capillaries will be dilated, and you will lose heat more rapidly, speeding the onset of hypothermia.

As cooling continues, speech becomes slurred and incoherent. You become increasingly lethargic and uncoordinated, and your respiration becomes shallow and erratic. You lose consciousness and eventually die.

Hypothermia occurs more rapidly in women than men because of their smaller average body sizes, and more rapidly still in children due to their small sizes and lack of body fat. Table 8-1 gives approximate survival times in water of various temperatures. Note how much survival time increases when you wear a life jacket.

Prevention

The precautions for prevention of hypothermia are well known. Most are "common sense" measures that you would normally take anyway.

CONSERVE YOUR HEAT. The simplest thing to do is to avoid situations that promote loss of body heat. This means keeping dry and out of the wind. If you fall overboard, get out of the water as soon as possible.

CLOTHING MAKES A DIFFERENCE. The clothing you wear makes a difference in the rate of heat loss. Synthetic fibers are effective in reducing heat loss when they are dry, but afford virtually no protection when wet. Wool retains a higher degree of its insulating properties when wet than most other fabrics.

INCREASE YOUR ENERGY RESERVE. Never go into a potentially hypothermic situation without having eaten a good meal. This is good practice for boating activities and anything that involves working or playing outside, especially in the cold.

Activity and Hypothermia

Your life jacket will help ward off hypothermia, and "jacket" styles offer better protection than "bib" styles. Besides trapping warmed water between it

WARNING *Swimming and treading water cause faster heat loss than remaining still.*

Treating a Hypothermic Victim
1. *Rescuers should do all the rescue work (not the victim).*
2. *Dry off the victim, if possible.*
3. *Keep the victim out of the wind.*
4. *Make the victim as comfortable as possible.*
5. *Ask for assistance on the radio.*
6. *Get medical assistance as soon as possible.*
7. *Cover the victim with warm clothing or other material.*

and your body, a life jacket helps you stay afloat with a minimal expenditure of energy. If you are not wearing a life jacket, you may need to tread water to stay afloat, and this uses energy and hastens hypothermia. Tests show that the average rate of heat loss of a person treading water is about 34% faster than for the same person remaining still in a life jacket.

FLOATING AND HEAT LOSS. If you aren't wearing a life jacket, try floating with your lungs full of air. Immerse your head in the water and raise it every 10 to 15 seconds to breathe. By this means, even nonswimmers can delay the possibility of drowning for many hours. But it presents problems in cold water, since so much heat is lost through your head. People who use this technique in 50°F water lose heat about 82% faster than if they were floating in a life jacket with their heads out of the water. Better wear a life jacket anytime you are underway!

SWIMMING AND HEAT LOSS. If your boat capsizes, your first impulse may be to swim to shore. This is dangerous at any time, and more so if the water is cold. The more you swim, the more heat your body generates, and this heat is lost rapidly in the cold water. In a short time your body may have exhausted its ability to generate heat.

GET OUT OF THE WATER. Studies show that the average person swimming in a life jacket cools 35% faster than when holding still. Instead of swimming to shore, climb onto your boat, if possible, which may enable you to balance your heat loss with the heat your body can generate.

HELP position

Figure 8-10. Conserving body heat. (REPRINTED WITH PERMISSION FROM "FEDERAL REQUIREMENTS & SAFETY TIPS FOR RECREATIONAL BOATS," U.S. COAST GUARD OFFICE OF BOATING SAFETY)

TABLE 8-2	STAGES OF HYPOTHERMIA
Body Temperature (°F)	**Visible Signs and Symptoms**
98–96	Intense, uncontrollable shivering; impaired ability to perform complex tasks
95–91	Violent shivering; difficulty speaking; sluggish movements; amnesia begins
90–86	Shivering replaced by muscular rigidity; muscle coordination impaired; erratic movements
85–81	Irrational; stupor; loss of contact with surroundings; pulse and respiration slow
80–78	Unresponsive; no reflexes; heartbeat erratic; loss of consciousness
Below 78	Failure of heart and lungs; internal bleeding; death

SOURCE: *U.S. COAST GUARD BOAT CREW SEAMANSHIP MANUAL*

If you find yourself in the water, do what you can to conserve your heat. Keep your clothes on, since they provide some insulation from heat loss, as does the air trapped in them.

Do not struggle or try to swim, either of which will cause you to lose the trapped air in your clothing and thus speed heat loss. Insulated clothing, minimal movement, clear thinking, and a life jacket provide the best possible defenses against cold water.

The HELP Position

If you are wearing a life jacket, draw your knees up into a **HELP** (heat escape lessening position) position (Figure 8-10). Make your body as compact as possible. If there are two or three people in the water, huddle together to conserve heat, and move about as little as possible.

If you are wearing a Type III life jacket, however, the HELP position may turn you facedown. Instead, bring your legs tightly together, keep your arms tight against your sides, and lean your head back to keep your face out of the water.

The greatest heat loss from your body is from your head, so keep it above water if possible. The next greatest loss is from your armpits and sides. Thus, in the HELP position, you press your arms against your sides, draw up your legs, and keep your head above water.

Helping Hypothermic People

If you try to rescue someone with hypothermia, be careful. The victim's energy resources are minimal, and he or she should do as little as possible to help in the rescue in order to avoid depleting what energy reserves he or she has left. Victims of hypothermia have died after being rescued because of their exertion during the process.

Visible signs of hypothermia are summarized in Table 8-2. If the survivor is rational and responsive, even if shivering dramatically, dry clothes or blankets, shelter from wind and water, and a period of inactivity may be all that is required. Critical hypothermia, however—especially if the victim is unconscious or only semiconscious—requires experienced medical assistance, and your best response is to secure that medical attention as soon as possible and keep the victim as sheltered, dry, and bundled as possible in the meantime. Remember how fragile a person is when in a hypothermic state. Death for a severely hypothermic individual can occur several hours after rescue.

If you have a VHF-FM radio aboard your vessel, contact the Coast Guard as soon as possible in any life-threatening emergency. Tell them your problem and request that they have an ambulance meet you at the nearest landing place, then ask them to advise you on first-aid methods. The Coast Guard has the specialized knowledge you need and will guide you in rewarming the victim.

Powerboats and Sailboats

We do not intend to teach you how to sail in this chapter; that would not be possible in the limited space available, since sailing involves complex skills and knowledge. We will try here only to increase your understanding of the unique characteristics of sailboats and suggest what you, as a powerboater, can do to share the waterways with sailboats safely and with mutual regard. To learn more about sailing, we recommend that you take the Auxiliary's sailing course.

Occasionally, you may find it necessary to help a sailboat or sailor in need. Giving help to a sailboat in distress requires a unique set of skills.

Sailing Skills

Sailboats under sail are at the mercy of the wind, and this restricts many of their options. It has only been in the last two centuries that boats could make much progress in the direction from which the wind was blowing. Square-rigged vessels, such as the *Mayflower*, the *Niña*, the *Pinta*, and the *Santa Maria*, sailed mainly downwind or nearly so. By complicated maneuvers, they could sail across the wind

Figure **8-11.** This double-ended sailboat is sailing *close-hauled* (sometimes also called *hard on the wind*) on starboard tack—i.e., sailing as close into the wind as it can go, with the wind coming over the starboard side and the sails pulled in close to the boat's centerline. Some of the crew is sitting high on the windward side to counter the heeling action of the wind, while the sails are trimmed to leeward. This boat can't turn to starboard without luffing sails and slowing down. (COURTESY MARSHALL MARINE)

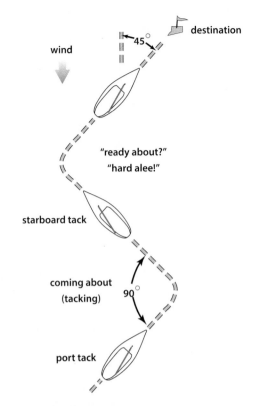

Figure **8-12.** Tacking to a windward objective. (REPRINTED WITH PERMISSION FROM *FAST TRACK TO CRUISING* BY STEVE AND DORIS COLGATE)

and at times even make progress against it, but for the most part they needed a wind from behind in order to get where they were going.

Tacking

The triangular sails of a modern sailboat are a relatively recent invention, enabling a boat to make progress into the wind. In sailing **downwind**, or "across," the wind (which sailors call *reaching*), a sailboat can maintain a fairly straight course if the wind is steady and the wake of passing vessels is not too disturbing. When sailing toward the wind, however, things change.

When a sailboat attempts to sail toward the wind—**upwind**, as sailors say—it must constantly change its direction. It first sails on a leg with the wind coming across one side of the boat, then turns in a new direction so the wind comes across the other side, ultimately sailing a zigzag course by a series of *tacks*. It keeps up these maneuvers, always coming closer to its destination until it finally arrives. This process of moving toward an upwind destination in a zigzag manner is called *tacking* (Figures 8-11 and 8-12).

When a sailboat is forced to tack upwind, the closest any one leg of its zigzag course can come to the direction from which the wind is blowing is usually 45° (Figure 8-13). Thus, for practical purposes, there is a 90° arc through which a boat cannot sail, and it can only proceed to a destination within that 90° sector in a zigzag fashion (Figure 8-12). Powerboaters need to know this and to be alert to sudden changes in direction of sailboats sailing upwind. Under all circumstances, powerboaters should give sailboats under sail (i.e., not using auxiliary power) the maximum room in which to operate. The narrower the passageway, for example an inlet or a channel, the more caution a powerboater needs to exercise.

Mooring and Anchoring

Sailboats must cope with other challenges as well. Chapter 4 covered the skills needed for mooring and anchoring a powerboat. These maneuvers are relatively easy for powerboaters but are more complicated for sailors. A boat under sail must (usually) approach a mooring or anchorage spot while heading into the wind (Figure 8-15), a maneuver that needs to be precisely timed for two reasons. First, as the boat loses headway, it becomes less and less easy to control with its rudder. Second, the boat should arrive at its mooring at the moment its forward progress stops. The wake of a passing motorboat can seriously interfere with a sailboat's mooring or anchoring approach.

When There Is Little Wind

Wakes from powerboats also affect sailboats adversely when there is little wind. Many sailors, particularly those on inland waters, find that it is a shortage of wind that most frequently taxes their patience and skills. When drifting slowly along, a sailboat responds only sluggishly to its helm, making it difficult to maneuver. The problem is compounded when the boat is confined to a narrow channel due to its draft.

Figure **8-14.** This sloop on San Francisco Bay is on a beam reach, with the wind coming directly over the starboard beam. The jib is rolled up, and instead the boat is flying a *reacher*, a sail with a fuller cut that is used only off the wind. Judging from the poised, attentive crew and the helmsman's intense focus, this boat is racing. (PHOTO BY MIKE BRODEY)

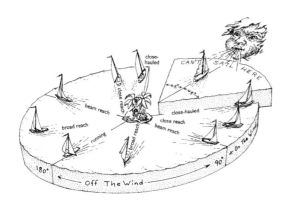

Figure **8-13.** The directions in which a modern sailboat can sail. (REPRINTED WITH PERMISSION FROM *THE COMPLETE SAILOR* BY DAVID SEIDMAN)

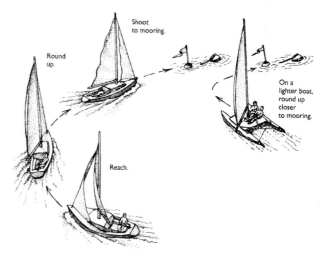

Figure **8-15.** Approaching a mooring. (REPRINTED WITH PERMISSION FROM *THE COMPLETE SAILOR* BY DAVID SEIDMAN)

Figure **8-16.** The Lido 14 is a reliable two-person sailing dinghy. When the wind is this light, even a small powerboat wake shakes the wind from the sails. This boat is on port tack, with the wind (what little there is) coming over the port side and the sails trimmed to starboard. (PHOTO BY NICK TARLSON)

Wind and Wake

Slowly drifting sailboats are particularly sensitive to disturbances created by the wakes of passing powerboats (Figure 8-16). Besides making a sailboat's passengers uncomfortable as the boat bobs helplessly on a powerboat's wake, a big wake can seriously reduce the boat's already slow progress and momentarily disrupt its directional control.

Bobbing in a wake can cause serious damage to a boat sailing downwind by precipitating an accidental *jibe*, which occurs when the boat inadvertently turns far enough off course to bring a wind from behind over the same stern quarter (port or starboard) on which the mainsail is set. When that happens, the wind may get behind the mainsail and swing it to the other side of the vessel in an uncontrolled manner. If the jibe is violent enough, it can cause damage to the vessel. Accidental jibes have even caused serious personal injury and have dismasted sailboats.

A rocking boat is dangerous to everyone on board. Accidental falls can occur, scalding water

might spill in the galley, or a swinging boom might hit an unwary passenger in the head. For all these reasons, passing powerboats should keep a safe distance from sailboats and keep their wakes to a minimum when passing. This may mean that the powerboat should slow enough that it comes down off plane and moves as a displacement vessel at idle speed while passing a sailboat.

Blocking the Wind

If you have watched sailboats race, you have seen some of the maneuvers they perform to gain advantages over their competitors. The outcome of a race usually depends on tactics and strategies. It's one-upmanship on the water.

One proven tactic is to block the wind from reaching a competitor's sails. The blocker moves into a position upwind of the boat he wants to pass, placing the target boat in his wind shadow. As a result, the blocked boat slows down, and by the time it regains its speed, the blocker may be well ahead of it.

The same thing may result when a motorboat moves upwind of a sailboat, and the larger the powerboat, the more pronounced the effect. If the wind is nearly calm, the sailboat may come to a stop or move in an uncontrolled manner. Thus, whenever possible, pass downwind of a vessel under sail.

Obscured Vision

The sails of a boat can obscure a skipper's vision, and the skipper may not see nearby vessels. This happens to sailboards as well. (A *sailboard* is essentially a surfboard with a sail, and the athletic endeavor of sailing it is called *windsurfing*.)

It is hazardous to approach a sailboat from any direction in which its skipper does not have you in full view. It is even more hazardous to approach a sailboard. Not only is the windsurfer's vision obscured, but frequently the windsurfer ends up in the water.

Special Navigation Rules for Sailboats

The unique characteristics of sailboats described above are the reason they are granted special consideration in the Navigation Rules.

Priority of Sailboats

One very important Navigation Rule creates an order of precedence for one vessel approaching another. As discussed in Chapter 6, and shown in the sidebar, this rule makes vessels not under command, vessels restricted in their ability to maneuver, fishing vessels, and sailing vessels under sail only stand-on to powerboats that are passing them.

In other words, power-driven vessels have the lowest priority and must keep out of the way of other vessels they are passing, including sailboats under sail only and other vessels that are unable to maneuver easily.

Since sailing vessels are more maneuverable, they must keep out of the way of vessels not under command, vessels restricted in their ability to maneuver, and vessels engaged in fishing. Sailing vessels lose their priority when they are overtaking other vessels. If the sailing vessel is operating its engine, it also loses its priority, since then it is considered a motor vessel, not a sailboat.

Sailing Races

During a sailing race, the competitors are governed by complex special rules. These have to do with things such as the overlap of two boats and the resulting right of way, the amount of room that one sailboat must give another one at a turning point, room to round marks on the race course, and stand-on status. Sailboat skippers use these rules to gain advantages over their opponents. It's all in the game!

Sailboat racing is such a finely tuned operation that it is easily interfered with by outside forces. This means that powerboats, including those that officiate races and stand by to assist competitors in time of need, should stay well behind the fleet to avoid making wakes that might change the outcome of the race. Powerboats should swing wide at the turning marks of the course to keep their wakes outside the fleet. Small centerboard sailboats often capsize during a race, and recovering themselves and resuming the race is part of the competition. You may stay nearby to offer assistance, but do not approach the boat unless requested. In sailboat races, it is the small things that determine the outcomes.

Carbon Monoxide Poisoning

Carbon monoxide is a colorless, odorless, highly poisonous gas that has about the same weight as air and mixes readily with it. It forms from the incomplete combustion of hydrocarbon fuels such as gasoline and diesel, and about 10% to 12% of the exhaust gas of an internal combustion engine is carbon monoxide. Carbon monoxide is poisonous because it reduces the ability of the blood to absorb oxygen.

Symptoms

Carbon monoxide is toxic in concentrations as small as one part per 100 parts of air. The symptoms of carbon monoxide poisoning include drowsiness, headache, dizziness, weakness, nausea, fainting, and coma, with prolonged exposure eventually resulting in death.

Most people know that they should not run their automobile engines in enclosed spaces such as a garage; what they may not know is that the engine in their boat produces the same gas. If you experience any of the symptoms associated with carbon monoxide poisoning, such as constant headaches when you boat, consider the possibility that you are being exposed to the gas. The early symptoms are not especially alarming and can easily be attributed to heat exhaustion or simply overtiredness. Survivors of near-fatal carbon monoxide poisoning

---

ORDER OF PRECEDENCE OF VESSELS

A vessel is stand-on to all vessels below it in the list:
- Overtaken vessel
- Vessel not under command
- Vessel restricted in ability to maneuver
- Vessel constrained by draft (International Rules only)*
- Fishing vessel
- Sailing vessel
- Powerboat
- Seaplane

*The Inland Rules do not recognize "vessels constrained by draft."

repeatedly describe simply falling asleep, unaware of the danger, before being fortuitously saved (Figure 8-17). Thus, you must be alert to the warning signs.

Carbon Monoxide and Ventilation

You may know that it is possible for a moving station wagon to pump exhaust gas in through its rear window. In some instances, people in the back seats of automobiles have died from carbon monoxide drawn into the vehicle from the exhaust.

The same condition can exist in the cockpit of a vessel that is enclosed on all sides except the stern. Alternatively, carbon monoxide may come from the exhaust of your generator (if your boat has one), from a hot-water heater, or from a galley stove. It may even come from a boat in an adjacent slip. If you experience any of the symptoms of carbon monoxide poisoning, search for the cause.

One owner of a new boat had it equipped with a carbon monoxide detector, which sounded continuously while the engine was operating and for several minutes after it was shut down. A representative of the boat manufacturer suggested that the alarm was faulty, but the headaches, nausea, and disorientation the owners and their children were experienc-

ing all suggested otherwise. The owners surmised that engine fumes might be entering the cabin through the head ventilation exhaust, which was located near the engine exhaust. When the installation was modified, the problem disappeared.

In another case, a boatowner's two young children were poisoned by carbon monoxide from a generator exhaust outlet located under the boat's swim platform. The boat was anchored in a Missouri lake on a hot day with the generator running to power the air conditioner, and the children were swimming when they were afflicted. One lost consciousness, and both were hospitalized with high levels of carbon monoxide in their systems. Both recovered fully. Only in retrospect did the owner and his wife piece together what had happened. According to Bob Adriance, author of *Seaworthy: Essential Lessons from BoatU.S.'s 20-Year Case File of Things Gone Wrong*, there have been several similar, well-documented cases (Figure 8-18).

Preventing Carbon Monoxide Poisoning

You can prevent carbon monoxide poisoning by making certain that your engine compartment is well ventilated and that the ventilation system is operating properly. In addition, be wary of completely enclosing your vessel if it was not designed for this purpose. Do not run your engine or generator while anyone is using the swim platform if the

Figure **8-17.** Carbon monoxide quickly overcame all four people without warning aboard this boat on Lake Powell, Arizona. One person was killed, and three were unconscious for 14 hours. The boat was moving slowly with the front end closed, and fumes entered the open stern via the station wagon effect. (REPRINTED WITH PERMISSION FROM *SEAWORTHY: ESSENTIAL LESSONS FROM BOATU.S.'S 20-YEAR CASE FILE OF THINGS GONE WRONG* BY ROBERT A. ADRIANCE)

Figure **8-18.** What's wrong with this picture? In this powerboat at cruising speed, the ensign in the stern is actually flapping forward rather than aft, due to a powerful station wagon effect—a sure indication that the engine exhaust is being sucked aboard over the transom. (REPRINTED WITH PERMISSION FROM *SEAWORTHY: ESSENTIAL LESSONS FROM BOATU.S.'S 20-YEAR CASE FILE OF THINGS GONE WRONG* BY ROBERT A. ADRIANCE)

exhaust outlets are located in the transom, and above all, be alert to the symptoms of carbon monoxide poisoning. Should they occur, immediately suspect the presence of carbon monoxide and search for its avenue of entrance to your boat.

It is a good idea to install a carbon monoxide detector in all closed spaces people occupy on your vessel. The U.S. Coast Guard recently stated that "Improvements in technology and reliability of carbon monoxide gas detectors have reached the point where their installation in accommodation spaces should be considered by all safety-conscious recreational boaters." Most boats with gasoline engines or generators and enclosed accommodations spaces built since August 1998 have a carbon monoxide detector. If your boat does not have one, you are well advised to install one.

It's important to install marine-rated carbon monoxide detectors because they have much more stringent performance requirements than home-rated detectors. This includes a greater operating temperature range, greater shock tolerance, greater resistance to outgassing, and better rejection of false RF alarms.

Weather

Boaters have a special need to know about weather. High winds, lightning, rough seas, and poor visibility are a few of the conditions that can make for uncomfortable boating.

There are two important principles of boating:

1. Know before you go.
2. Update while you are out.

These are particularly true where weather is concerned. Good weather information can be obtained in most locations from AM and FM radio, from television broadcasts after local news and, often, from a televised weather channel. Those with Internet access can obtain excellent weather information at www.weather.com, www.nws.noaa.gov/om/marine/home.htm or www.srh.noaa.gov (select a station near you). See www.navcen.uscg.gov for further details. You can also receive National Weather Service broadcasts on inexpensive shortwave receiving sets that use either household electrical current or batteries. The broadcasts are also available on the weather channels of your VHF-FM marine radio. In short, there is no reason for a boater to go out without knowing what kind of weather is in store for the day or even for several days.

CARBON MONOXIDE POISONING PREVENTION TECHNIQUES

1. Provide, maintain, and frequently check adequate engine, and generator compartment ventilation.
2. Install a carbon monoxide detector.
3. Be aware of the symptoms of carbon monoxide poisoning.
4. Be aware of any nearby boats that might be sending poisonous fumes your way.

WEATHER HAZARDS AND LOCAL KNOWLEDGE

Dangerous weather conditions come in several varieties. Among the conditions you should watch out for and avoid if possible are these:

- Heavy fog or otherwise reduced visibility can cause you to lose your bearings, increasing the risk of collisions or running aground.
- Thunderstorms bring high winds, reduced visibility, and the danger of lightning strikes.
- Lightning seeks the quickest and easiest path to ground, and when your boat is the tallest thing around, that makes you a target for a strike.
- High winds, no matter what their cause, can churn the water into heavy, breaking seas, increasing the risk of swamping, broaching, or yawing.

See Chapter 12 for more on predicting and avoiding bad weather.

"Local knowledge" means familiarity with the waters in which you routinely do your boating. Developing local knowledge is among the top things you can do to increase your safety—no matter what the weather. Keep yourself up to date on local boating conditions by:

- Reading the *Local Notices to Mariners* regularly (see Chapters 5 and 9).
- Checking with local sources, such as other boaters.
- Becoming familiar with such local hazards as shoals, lowhead dams (see Chapter 7), sandbars, and rocks.

In some circumstances, local conditions can change suddenly, and the wise boater is always on the lookout for signs of changing weather. Suppose you embark on a boating trip on a beautiful, sunny summer day, and are then surprised by a late afternoon thunderstorm. Evidence of such storms is readily visible from the following changes:

1. Clouds appear, looking more ominous over an hour or so.
2. Wind comes up or shifts noticeably.
3. Waves appear because of the wind.
4. The air takes on a cool bite.
5. If you are listening to AM radio, static is noticeable.
6. You suddenly realize that other boaters have disappeared.

While you can hope to return home before the storm hits, it may be wiser to find a cove where you can anchor and ride it out. In either case, as a safety precaution, have everyone put on a life jacket, stow all gear or secure it so that it cannot blow away, and head for safety. Turn on your navigation lights and review your sound signals for reduced visibility conditions. Controlling a small boat in large waves, with visibility badly reduced by rain, is no fun at all! We will explore the topic of weather more fully in Chapter 12.

Ways to Learn More

Chapman Piloting & Seamanship. 66th ed. Charles B. Husick. New York: Hearst Books, 2009. Chapters 7 and 11.

Confident Powerboating: Mastering Skills and Avoiding Trouble Afloat. Stu Reininger. Camden, Maine: International Marine, 2008.

Emergencies on Board: A Captain's Quick Guide. John Rousmaniere. Camden, Maine: International Marine, 2005.

Emergency First Aid On Board: A Captain's Quick Guide. Richard Clinchy. Camden, Maine: International Marine, 2007.

Heavy Weather Sailing: A Captain's Quick Guide. John Rousmaniere. Camden, Maine: International Marine, 2005.

Practice Questions

IMPORTANT BOATING TERMS
In the following exercise, match the words in the column on the left with the definitions in the column on the right. In the blank space to the left of each term, write the letter of the item that best matches it. Do not use an item in the right-hand column more than once.

THE ITEMS

1. _____ carbon monoxide
2. _____ PWC
3. _____ hypothermia
4. _____ safety lanyard
5. _____ wearing a life jacket
6. _____ riding aboard a PWC
7. _____ center of gravity
8. _____ a first sign of hypothermia
9. _____ human error
10. _____ center of buoyancy

THE RESPONSES

a. power-driven vessel
b. main cause of boating accidents
c. best defense against drowning
d. reduction of a body's core temperature below where normal biological functions can occur
e. formed by incomplete combustion of fuel
f. gooseflesh
g. center of the mass of water a boat displaces
h. shuts off engine if operator falls overboard
i. each person must have a life jacket
j. center of a mass

On-Board Medical Emergency Handbook: First Aid at Sea. Spike Briggs and Campbell Mackenzie. Camden, Maine: International Marine, 2008.

On-Board Weather Forecasting: A Captain's Quick Guide. Bob Sweet. Camden, Maine: International Marine, 2005.

On-Board Weather Handbook: Understanding and Predicting Conditions at Sea. Chris Tibbs. Camden, Maine: International Marine, 2008.

The Practical Encyclopedia of Boating: An A–Z Compendium of Navigation, Seamanship, Boat Maintenance, and Nautical Wisdom. John Vigor. Camden, Maine: International Marine, 2007.

The Practical Mariner's Book of Knowledge: 460 Sea-Tested Rules of Thumb for Almost Every Boating Situation. 2nd ed. John Vigor. Camden, Maine: International Marine, 2013.

Rough Weather Seamanship for Sail and Power: Design, Gear, and Tactics for Coastal and Offshore Waters. Roger Marshall. Camden, Maine: International Marine, 2006.

Seamanship Secrets: 185 Tips and Techniques for Better Navigation, Cruise Planning, and Boat Handling Under Power or Sail. John Jamieson. Camden, Maine: International Marine, 2009.

Seaworthy: Essential Lessons from BoatU.S.'s 20-Year Case File of Things Gone Wrong. Robert Adriance. Camden, Maine: International Marine, 2005.

Suddenly Overboard: True Stories of Sailors in Fatal Trouble. Tom Lochhaas. Camden, Maine: International Marine, 2013.

Weather Predicting Simplified: How to Read Weather Charts and Satellite Images. Michael William Carr. Camden, Maine: International Marine, 1999.

Title 46. Code of Federal Regulations. 2303-2306

www.mariovittone.com/2010/05/154

Multiple-Choice Items

In the following items, choose the best response:

8-1. A major cause of small boat fatalities is

a. being run over by large boats
b. being swamped by waves
c. loading too many people on board
d. falling overboard and drowning

8-2. A boat is less stable and more likely to capsize when it

a. is empty
b. is overloaded
c. has an evenly distributed load
d. is in deep water

8-3. PWC operators and riders should wear

a. life jackets
b. goggles or wraparound eye shields
c. wet suits in cold weather
d. all of the above

8-4. Which of the following fabrics will protect you most from hypothermia when they are wet?

a. synthetic fibers such as nylon
b. cotton
c. wool
d. rayon

8-5. The best thing you can do for a hypothermic person is

a. get immediate medical help
b. treat the person yourself
c. give a small drink of whiskey
d. help the person get up and move around to warm up

8-6. Motorboats are often disruptive of sailboats when

a. the sailboats are mooring
b. there is little wind
c. they block the wind
d. all of the above

8-7. Which of the following is correct?

a. about half of all boating fatalities occur on lakes, ponds, and reservoirs and not on navigable waterways
b. over half of boating fatalities occur on weekend afternoons
c. about half of all boating fatalities occur in calm weather and in full daylight
d. all of the above

Multiple-Choice Items (continued)

8-8. Standing in a boat raises its

a. center of gravity
b. center of buoyancy
c. blind spot
d. freeboard

8-9. Dangerous loss of steering ability on a PWC results from

a. releasing the throttle
b. standing on the PWC
c. overcorrecting after a turn
d. not using the safety lanyard

8-10. Which of the following is true?

a. hypothermia occurs more rapidly if you are wet than if you are dry
b. hypothermia occurs more rapidly in women than in men
c. hypothermia can occur in a strong wind even if you are dry
d. all of the above

8-11. The best thing you can do to ward off hypothermia if you find yourself in cold water is

a. start swimming to shore
b. keep moving
c. assume the HELP position
d. eat a good meal before you go

8-12. A hazard can be created in jet-drive boats by

a. hull vibration
b. debris caught in the intake
c. corrosion
d. slow reaction time caused by jet propulsion

8-13. The best way to prevent carbon monoxide poisoning is to

a. install a smoke alarm
b. burn clean fuel in your engine
c. keep air flowing through the vessel
d. stay in the stern area of the boat

8-14. What percentage of people who drown in boating accidents are able to swim?

a. 60
b. 70
c. 80
d. 90

8-15. Small motorboats (less than 20 feet long) have

a. oarlocks
b. capacity plates
c. loading instructions
d. all of the above

8-16. If your boat capsizes

a. have someone swim to shore for help
b. have someone stay with the boat
c. have everyone stay in the water and hold on to the boat
d. climb up on the boat and out of the water, if possible

8-17. Which of the following is correct?

a. the skipper is responsible for anything that happens to or on a PWC
b. the skipper is responsible for any damage caused by a PWC
c. the skipper is responsible for seeing that a PWC is operated legally
d. all of the above

8-18. In comparison to cold air, cold water robs the body of heat

a. much faster than air
b. slower than air
c. it depends on the humidity of the air
d. at the same rate as air

8-19. Under which of the following conditions will you lose heat most rapidly in cold water?

a. swimming
b. treading water
c. wearing a life jacket
d. using the HELP position

8-20. Sailboats can sail toward the wind by

a. tacking
b. running before the wind
c. jibing
d. maneuvering

8-21. Carbon monoxide is

a. colorless
b. odorless
c. poisonous
d. all of the above

part II MORE BOATING SKILLS

(COURTESY U.S. COAST GUARD)

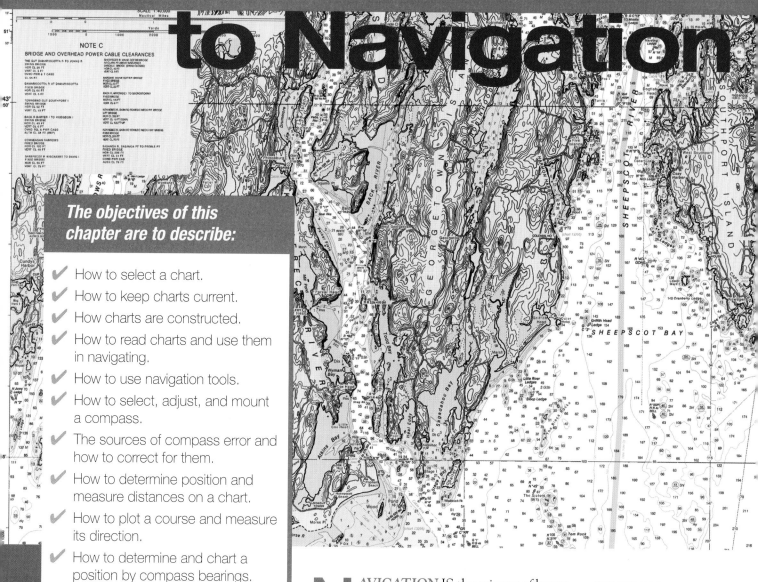

chapter 9

Introduction to Navigation

(COURTESY NOAA)

The objectives of this chapter are to describe:

✔ How to select a chart.

✔ How to keep charts current.

✔ How charts are constructed.

✔ How to read charts and use them in navigating.

✔ How to use navigation tools.

✔ How to select, adjust, and mount a compass.

✔ The sources of compass error and how to correct for them.

✔ How to determine position and measure distances on a chart.

✔ How to plot a course and measure its direction.

✔ How to determine and chart a position by compass bearings.

✔ How to compute speed, time, or distance when two of the three are known.

✔ How to make a dead-reckoning plot.

✔ The importance and use of *Tide Tables*.

✔ How to navigate with electronics.

NAVIGATION IS the science of knowing where you are and how to get to where you want to go. In this chapter we introduce you to navigation and give you some useful tools and techniques. If you would like to study navigation in greater depth, the U.S. Coast Guard Auxiliary teaches several classes that will enhance your skills and knowledge. Ask your instructor for more information. Navigational tools vary in complexity and cost. Limit yourself to the basic tools until you have an understanding of what you really need.

Your basic navigational tool kit should include (Figure 9-1):

- **Charts** of the area in which you boat
- A good **magnetic compass** for your boat
- A **course plotter** or **parallel rulers**
- **Dividers** or a **drafting compass**
- A fine-point (0.5 mm) pencil with medium-soft lead
- A good eraser

In addition, you may want to include a binocular, a handheld **bearing compass**, and some means of measuring water depth. You can measure water depth by a calibrated pole, a **lead line**, or an electronic depth sounder. And finally, with handheld global positioning system (GPS) receivers available for as little as $150, more and more boaters are making GPS central to their navigation. And little wonder: The accuracy and reliability of GPS are truly amazing. Remember, however, that use of GPS does not relieve you from chartwork. GPS coordinates mean nothing until you plot them on an up-to-date chart, nor will you know whether the course to your next GPS **waypoint** is a safe one until you find out from the chart whether it takes you across intervening ledges or shoals. And finally, any electronic device can fail at any time, no matter how reliable. It is for this reason that you should continue to maintain a dead-reckoning (DR) plot and keep track of your position by traditional means, despite using GPS.

We will return to the subject of electronic navigation later in this chapter. First, though, we'll explore the time-honored techniques of chart-and-compass navigation.

Nautical Charts

The word "map" usually applies to a land area, whereas a map of a water area is called a "chart." A *chart* is a representation of a portion of the earth's surface showing information useful to mariners. Quite simply, charts make navigation possible. Charts are printed on paper, though electronic charts are increasingly popular today. (We'll return to the subject of electronic charts later in this chapter.) Usually, charts are drawn *to scale*, which means that the sizes of objects on the chart are proportional to their actual sizes.

Your charts may show both water and land areas, and the land near the water may even show considerable detail. This is especially true if the details can help you pinpoint your location—that is, your *position*. Charts also include details such as the shape of a coastline, harbors, islands, ledges, shoals, water depths, navigation buoys and other aids to navigation, shipping lanes, underwater cables, shoreline topography, and landmarks such as radio towers, church steeples, stacks, large buildings, and other objects. And that's only a partial list.

Charts are technological marvels. If you were to write out all that information, it would take several large books to contain what is on a single nautical chart. Furthermore, the books would be hard to read and interpret.

Availability of Charts

The National Ocean Service (NOS) of the National Oceanic and Atmospheric Administration (NOAA) publishes charts of all U.S. waters other than navigable rivers. You can buy them directly from the NOS or from authorized chart sales outlets such as marinas and marine supply stores. These are the charts prepared by the Office of Coast Survey (OCS), the NOS's sister agency within NOAA.

Figure **9-1.** The basic piloting tools include a chart, a pair of dividers, a fine-point pencil, and parallel rulers (shown here) or a course plotter (not shown). (PHOTO BY RAY PAGES)

In addition, as mentioned in Chapters 5 and 7, charts of major river systems such as the Mississippi and Ohio are produced by the U.S. Army Corps of Engineers, and charts for the high seas and foreign waters are produced by the National Imagery and Mapping Agency, or NIMA (recently renamed National Geospatial-Intelligence Agency, or NGA).

Nautical chart catalogs list the available NOS charts. For example, *Nautical Chart Catalog 1* lists all NOS charts that cover the Atlantic and Gulf Coasts, including Puerto Rico and the Virgin Islands. Nautical chart catalogs should be available where charts are sold. In effect, a chart catalog is itself an overview chart of a large region on which the coverage areas of designated navigation charts are outlined.

Don't confuse the nautical chart catalogs with *Chart No. 1: Nautical Chart Symbols, Abbreviations, and Terms*. Although it has the word "chart" in its title, *Chart No. 1* is a book published jointly by NOAA and the Defense Mapping Agency that is useful for interpreting nautical charts. Though it is no longer available from the government for distribution through commercial chart agents, you can still obtain a print copy of *Chart No. 1* from the Government Printing Office, and you can view and download a digital version at www.nauticalcharts.noaa.gov. In addition, various commercial publishers offer *Chart No. 1* for sale (Figure 9-2).

Again as mentioned in Chapter 5, reproductions of government charts on waterproof paper or reformatted in bound volumes to cover defined regions are also available from commercial sources, and these will sometimes represent a significant savings or gain in convenience over the government charts. You can also obtain the latest edition of a chart from online print-on-demand services, and you can download free electronic charts in raster format (for use on a laptop computer or chartplotter) from the Office of Coast Survey website. (This web address, www.nauticalcharts.noaa.gov, will also direct you to print-on-demand charts, *Notices to Mariners*, and *Coast Pilots* in print or digital downloadable form.)

Finally, www.oceanservice.noaa.gov/dataexplorer offers interactive mapping tools and links to NOS websites (such as Marine Navigation and Tides and Currents) that provides more information and downloadable data. In some cases, users can view and interact with data. To get regular up-

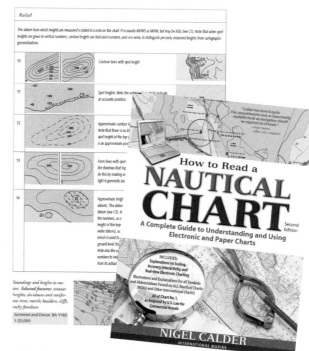

Figure 9-2. The government no longer prints *Chart No. 1*, which explains the symbols, abbreviations, and terms used on nautical charts, but various commercial editions are sold, including the one shown here.

WARNING *Always have up-to-date charts for your current area of operation. Study the Local Notices to Mariners and enter changes on your charts.*

dates via e-mail go to http:/cgls.uscg.mil/mailman/listinfo. Click on your local Coast Guard District, for example, Ninth-cg-dlnm. Once there, fill out and submit the form. The Coast Guard will then provide one-way updates you with the latest information on *Local Notices to Mariners* updates, *Light Lists*, and other marine-related information.

Dates of Charts

Information on charts changes from time to time. These changes appear in the *Local Notices to Mariners* published weekly by each Coast Guard District. As the information is outdated, your chart becomes less reliable, so be sure to use up-to-date charts. A new edition of a chart cancels previous editions and such "revisions" contain less significant changes.

You can access the *Local Notices to Mariners* on the Internet at www.navcen.uscg.gov. Click on Local Notice to Mariners, and select your district to get weekly updates.

Charts have dates to help you be certain that you have the most recent versions. The store where you buy your chart should have a copy of the NOS publication, *Dates of Latest Editions* (or view it online

Figure **9-3.** A Mercator projection shows lines of longitude as vertical, parallel lines, rather than converging at the poles. Compass courses plot as straight lines on a Mercator chart. There is some distortion of landmasses, which becomes progressively greater in the higher latitudes, but for charts of midlatitude local waters this is of no consequence. (REPRINTED WITH PERMISSION FROM *THE WEEKEND NAVIGATOR* BY BOB SWEET)

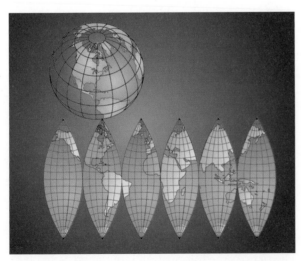

Figure **9-4.** Rendering the earth into a meaningful flat chart is a major challenge. If you simply unfold and flatten the earth's surface, you will get something like this figure, which is similar to a polyconic projection. (REPRINTED WITH PERMISSION FROM *THE WEEKEND NAVIGATOR* BY BOB SWEET)

at www.nauticalcharts.noaa.gov). Ask to see a copy before buying a chart. Get a current chart and keep it up to date by posting changes as they are reported. When you buy a chart from a print-on-demand source (see above), it will incorporate revisions referenced by *Local Notices to Mariners* through the date the chart is printed for you.

Chart Features

If the world were flat, chartmaking would be a much simpler process than it is. The central dilemma for all chartmakers is how to represent a curved surface on a flat chart.

Projections

One way to make a chart is to draw it on the surface of a globe. This accurately represents the earth's surface, but it would not be very useful on a small recreational vessel. It would take a huge globe to show the area where you are boating in any detail, and even if that were possible you'd have a hard time using it for navigation.

Another way to make a chart is by using a mathematical concept called *projection*, which enables a chartmaker to represent a curved surface on a flat sheet of paper. There are several distinct projection types, but only two need concern us here.

MERCATOR PROJECTIONS. Most nautical charts use the *Mercator projection*, in which points on the earth's surface are projected onto a cylinder wrapped around a globe as in Figure 9-3. After this, the cylinder is cut open and laid out to make a flat surface.

A chart made by Mercator's method is useful for navigation, although it has limitations. One important feature is that all angles are represented correctly, even in extreme northern and southern waters. This means that you can measure the angle of a course line from one point to another directly on the chart. With this knowledge, you can head your vessel where you want to go.

Unfortunately, Mercator projections introduce distortions both in north-south and east-west directions that become greater the farther north or south you go from the equator. Thus, on a Mercator projection, Greenland appears to cover a much larger portion of the earth's surface than it actually does. This distortion makes Mercator charts nearly unusable in polar or near-polar areas. If the area covered by a chart is small enough, however, the distortion does not present a serious problem where most recreational boating occurs.

POLYCONIC PROJECTIONS. Another common way to make a chart is by projecting the earth's surface onto a series of cones, which is called a *polyconic projection* (Figure 9-4). Great Lakes charts are most often conic projections, since this projection gives less distortion at high northern and southern latitudes. Mercator projections for the Great Lakes are available, however.

Chart Scales

A chart can show a small area at a large scale or a large area at a small scale, but showing a large area at a large scale would be impossible on a chart of usable dimensions. A harbor chart, for example, shows a comparatively small area at a comparatively large scale, frequently 1:20,000. At that scale, the drawing of a spit of land, a pier, or other object is 1/20,000th its actual size. Thus, a harbor entrance that is 1 inch wide on the chart would actually be 20,000 inches wide, or about 3/10 of a mile.

If the chart's scale is 1:40,000—as is true of some coastal charts—a 1-inch-wide island is actually about 3/5 of a mile wide. Conversely, the 3/10-mile-wide harbor entrance would be only 1/2 inch wide on this chart (Figure 9-5).

HARBOR AND COASTAL CHARTS. Harbor charts sometimes have a scale of 1:10,000, though 1:20,000 is more usual. Such a chart can show detail but cannot cover a large area. Coastal charts, on the other hand, usually have a scale of 1:80,000, which shows larger areas with less detail. Thus, small scales cover large areas, and large scales cover small areas in greater detail.

There are even smaller scales (for example, 1:100,000 or 1:1,000,000) for special purposes such as planning ocean passages. Some charts show an entire ocean on one sheet of paper. Select your charts to give the greatest amount of detail (largest scale) you need for each portion of your cruise. Use small-scale, large-area charts for overall voyage planning, and large-scale, small-area charts for maneuvering in harbors or other difficult areas. Sometimes it's handy to remember that "large scale means large detail, small scale means small detail."

Chesapeake Bay 12280 1:200,000

Chesapeake Bay 12263 1:80,000

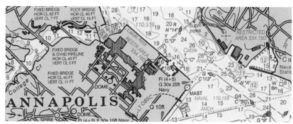
Chesapeake Bay 12282 1:25,000

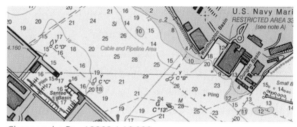
Chesapeake Bay 12283 1:10,000

Figure **9-5.** A series of chart extracts of the same area, varying in scale from 1:200,000 to 1:10,000. The smaller the second number in the ratio, the larger the scale and the more detailed the chart. (REPRINTED WITH PERMISSION FROM *HOW TO READ A NAUTICAL CHART* BY NIGEL CALDER)

WHICH CHART IS FOR YOU? You can get some charts in either of two forms, conventional or small craft. **Conventional charts** are ideal for use on large, flat navigation tables such as you would find on the bridge of a ship or at the nav station of a 40-foot boat, and for many waters, conventional charts are the only alternative the government offers. **Small-craft charts,** on the other hand, feature folded formats for use in the confined navigation spaces of a small boat (Figure 9-6). Several formats are used by NOAA, but they all feature sections of larger, conventional charts printed on smaller panels and

Figure **9-6.** A small-craft strip chart.

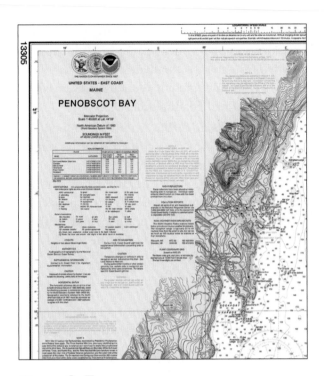

Figure **9-7.** The general information block of a nautical chart, showing chart number and title, projection, datums, and miscellaneous tide and other information. (REPRINTED WITH PERMISSION FROM *HOW TO READ A NAUTICAL CHART* BY NIGEL CALDER)

enclosed in a folder or booklet. Some are folded accordion style and stored in jackets, while others are printed on both sides of three or four sheets that are folded and bound in a protective cover. They are all designed to be easier to handle on small recreational craft, with each panel giving you access to a small portion of the area.

Small-craft charts usually have a scale of 1:40,000, but often have insets showing smaller areas at scales of 1:20,000, 1:10,000, or even larger. They also include ancillary information of interest to local boaters such as tide data, public marine facilities, weather information, and more.

NOAA uses water-resistant paper for its charts, but you may want to give your chart additional protection. Encase it in a plastic cover that will allow you to spread it out on a center console or a cockpit seat without worrying about rain, spray, or wind.

General Information Block

Before you use a chart, read its *general information block* (Figure 9-7). This is sometimes called the *chart block* and will tell you the chart's name. In the lower left corner of the chart you will find the edition number and date of publication.

The general information block will give you information such as the chart's projection, its scale, and its *vertical* and *horizontal datums*—a technical term for the benchmarks from which a chart's vertical and horizontal measurements are made.

HORIZONTAL DATUM. Formerly, most North American charts used the North American 1927 horizontal datum, referencing their latitude-longitude grids to a geophysical point in Meade's Ranch, Kansas, from which horizontal measurements were used to locate landmasses and other geophysical features. With the arrival of space satellites, more precise measurements than those based on the 1927 datum became possible, and many charts were redrawn to the North American 1983 datum. Most nautical charts today use the World Geodetic System 1984 (WGS-84) horizontal datum, which is fundamentally the same as the North American 1983 datum. The differences that result from these datums are very small and for most practical purposes inconsequential. You probably will never know what datum your chart uses unless you read its legend block.

If you are using GPS, however, the chart datum and GPS datum must be the same in order to avoid position error. Your GPS receiver's instruction manual will show you how to change your GPS datum, which is easy to do. This subject will be addressed later in this chapter in the Electronic Navigation section.

VERTICAL DATUM. The vertical datum of a chart also has important meaning for you. It helps you know how much water is under your vessel and how much vertical clearance there is under a bridge (Figure 9-8). NOS charts use **mean high water** (MHW) as the plane of reference for vertical clearances of bridges and high-tension power lines, and **mean lower low water** (MLLW) as the plane of reference for soundings, or depths. These terms are explained below; for the moment, it is enough to know that overhead clearances may be less than indicated on the chart during an extremely high tide, and depths beneath your boat may be less than indicated on the chart during an extremely low tide.

What Charts Show

Charts show heights and shapes of landforms; depths of water; locations of navigation buoys; locations and characteristics of lighted aids to navigation (ATONs); heights and ranges of fixed lights; and the locations of principal landmarks (including, but not limited to, church spires, water towers, smokestacks, cupolas, and radio towers), harbors, piers and other principal structures within harbors, ledges, sandbars, underwater cables, shipping channels, wrecks and other hazards, and a whole lot more (Figure 9-9). Charts also describe bottom types—such as sand, rock, or mud—using special abbreviations, information that is useful when you are trying to select a place to set an anchor (Figures 9-10 and 9-11). Each chart offers a rich trove of information in shorthand notation, and the key to interpreting the chart's symbology is really quite simple. We'll look at some of the basics here; the symbology used for ATONs (Figure 9-12) is described and illustrated in Chapter 5.

WATER DEPTHS. Water depths, or *soundings*, are among the most critical categories of information recorded on a chart. Shallow water is light blue on a chart, whereas deeper water appears as white. Shoal areas that uncover at low

tide are shown in green, and areas of land are a gold or tan color. This gives a ready visual reference without having to look at the numbers that show depth. Remember, though, that the areas of blue and white water vary in depth depending on the scale of the chart. As a rule of thumb, switch to a larger-scale chart when you move into the blue.

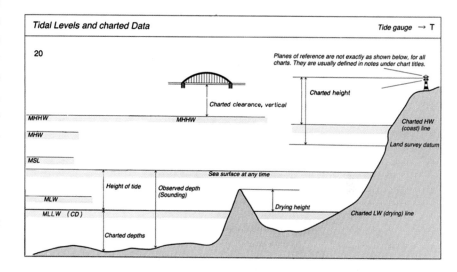

Figure 9-8. Vertical datums. NOS charts use mean lower low water (MLLW) as the reference datum for soundings, and mean high water (MHW) as the reference datum for vertical clearances beneath bridges. (REPRINTED WITH PERMISSION FROM *HOW TO READ A NAUTICAL CHART* BY NIGEL CALDER)

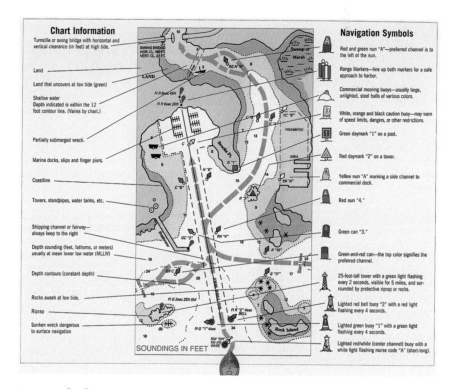

Figure 9-9. What charts show. In chart language, some symbols show visible features and others show hazards hidden beneath the water's surface. (COURTESY MAPTECH; REPRINTED WITH PERMISSION FROM *THE WEEKEND NAVIGATOR* BY BOB SWEET)

On most U.S. charts, water depths are in feet. Some charts, though, report depths in *fathoms* (a fathom is 6 feet, or about 2 meters), while some newer charts show depths in meters, and meters are used on charts published by Canada and many other countries. Read your chart's general information block to see what units it uses for reporting depths and heights.

To highlight local trends in water depth, cartographers connect points of equal selected depths with lines known as *contour lines*. These are, in effect, the mirror image of the contour lines that mark points of equal elevation on a topographic map of the land. Most U.S. charts use a 6-foot or 1-fathom interval for depth contours, and you'll see contour lines at depths of 6, 12, 18, 30, and 60 feet. **NOTES.** Charts also contain notes on their borders and in other clear spaces. These give you important safety information and information of a more general nature such as anchoring and precautionary areas. Read them.

For example, page G of Chart 11451 shows "Moser Channel (see note)." The note says, "Moser Channel—Overfalls that may swamp a small boat may occur at the bridge." This means that during certain tidal changes, tidal currents at this point oppose each other and create an overfall.

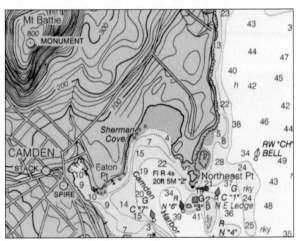

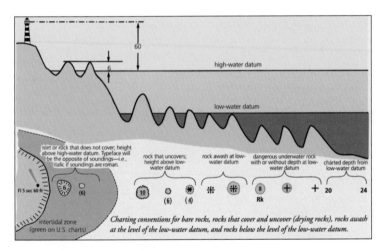

Figure **9-10.** It is essential to understand the chart symbols for rocks and ledges in order to avoid these hazards. (REPRINTED WITH PERMISSION FROM *THE WEEKEND NAVIGATOR* BY BOB SWEET)

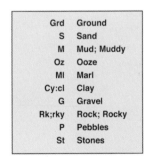

Grd	Ground
S	Sand
M	Mud; Muddy
Oz	Ooze
Ml	Marl
Cy:cl	Clay
G	Gravel
Rk;rky	Rock; Rocky
P	Pebbles
St	Stones

Figure **9-11.** Types of bottoms and their chart symbols.

Figure **9-12.** Selected features of nautical charts. **Top:** PA = position approximate, and TR = tower. Vertical, roman type is used for beacons and land features; slanted, italic type is used for hydrographic features. Soundings are in feet. Labels on depth contours are in italic—in a smaller font and lighter typeface—to distinguish them from spot soundings. Blue denotes shoal water—on this chart, less than 10 feet deep. Note the symbol for a dangerous wreck in the center of the chart. **Bottom:** Contour lines on land are every 20 feet, with every fifth one (100-foot intervals) bolder. The monument, spire, and stack are all accurately charted (positioning dot) and conspicuously visible as landmarks (capital letters). Buoy labels, unlike beacon labels, are italic. (REPRINTED WITH PERMISSION FROM *HOW TO READ A NAUTICAL CHART* BY NIGEL CALDER)

The note warns mariners that their boats may run head-on into an unexpected waterfall. It's much better to know this in advance than to learn it the hard way. **Read the notes on your chart.**

SHORE DETAILS. Charted details ashore include easily recognized structures, such as water towers, church steeples, and radio towers. Land contours are often charted, since bold headlands and coastal hills make useful landmarks, and bridges are described in detail.

The shoreline contour is another important feature and, as mentioned, is usually printed a golden color. If the shore is swampy or covers and uncovers with changes in water level, it is light green.

Keep in mind that structures that were once prominent enough to appear on your chart may no longer be there. Sometimes you can't see them because newer, larger buildings screen them from view. This is another reason to keep charts up to date. The U.S. Coast Guard Auxiliary and the U.S. Power Squadrons assist in gathering data to keep charts current.

AIDS TO NAVIGATION. These structures, both fixed and floating, serve as signposts, beacons, directional signals, and warnings of danger. They are your most important navigational aids. Refer to Chapter 5 for a discussion of ATONs.

LOCATION, DISTANCE, AND DIRECTION ON A CHART. Suppose your GPS receiver tells you that your present position coordinates are 41°31 north latitude, 70°39 west longitude (we'll talk more about latitude and longitude coordinates below). You can't use that information to orient yourself to the real world unless your local chart allows you to plot those coordinates; then you'll know right where you are in Vineyard Sound, Massachusetts. Charts therefore include latitude and longitude scales for plotting positions, and the latitude scale can also be used to measure distances on the chart. (The chart may also include a distance scale for the latter purpose, but it's nice to know you can use the nearest latitude scale when the distance scale is folded underneath and not conveniently accessible.)

Now suppose your destination is the channel marker bell off the mouth of Vineyard Haven, but you can't see the bell from your position. You need to know what compass course to steer. The chart gives you directions both in degrees true and de-grees magnetic. True directions come from lines of *longitude*, also called *meridians*—that run north to south—and from lines of *latitude*, also called *parallels*—that run east to west. Magnetic directions come from a **compass rose** overprinted in one or several places on the chart (Figure 9-13). We'll discuss all this in greater detail below, but first we'll look at the magnetic compass, which is every bit as important to navigation as the chart.

Ship's Compass

There are several types of *compasses*, and it's now common to have more than one type aboard. If you only have one compass aboard, it's best to have a liquid-filled magnetic one. Powerboats need steering compasses built to withstand the vibrations and pounding of boats moving at high speeds or through rough waters. The steering compass of a sailboat must be able to operate satisfactorily at large heel angles (Figure 9-14).

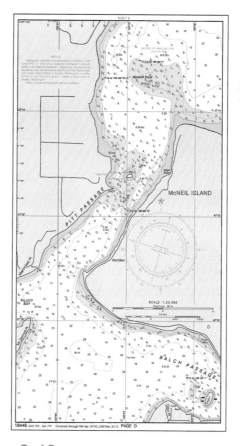

Figure **9-13.** A segment of Small-Craft Folio Chart 18455, from Puget Sound, showing lines of latitude (parallels), lines of longitude (meridians), and a compass rose. (COURTESY NOAA)

Types of Compasses

There are several kinds of compasses to choose from.

The *dry magnetic compass* uses a magnet to align its pointer to the magnetic poles. This type may be used as a handheld compass to obtain a bearing to an object. The compass pointer is inherently jittery. Handheld compasses may also utilize a pointer-damping technology.

The *liquid magnetic compass* uses the same technology as the dry compass, but the moving part is suspended in a liquid to dampen vibration and sudden swing movements. This has been the reliable standard for centuries.

The *gyrocompass* uses a spinning disk and the earth's rotation to automatically find geographic direction. They are the main compasses used on very large vessels since they find true north, not magnetic north, and are unaffected by ferromagnetic materials. They are expensive and need to be periodically recalibrated with a magnetic compass as they will drift over time, particularly as the instrument ages.

The *electromagnetic compass*, also known as the *fluxgate compass*, utilizes two or more small coils of wire around a core of highly permeable magnetic material to detect the direction of the horizontal component of the earth's magnetic field. The compass heading is easy to read directly from the compass or it can be digitized and connected to other devices, such as an autopilot. It also has the capability of canceling out any deviation caused by internal stray magnetic fields generated by other electronic equipment and/or metal close to the compass.

The *solid-state compass* utilizes a microelectrical mechanical system (MEMS) that employs a very small electronic sold-state device that can detect physical movements and magnetic fields. It can be used as a conventional compass as well as measuring the vessel's pitch and roll. It can be combined with the gyrocompass technology to become even more accurate. This technology can be employed in many other devices, including smart phones, GPS, and robots.

Marine Compass Features

The bowl of a marine compass is filled with a viscous oil or alcohol-based liquid that dampens vibrations and oscillations and keeps the compass card from swinging rapidly as your boat bounces. The card pivots on a needle point and thus remains more or less level as the boat pitches and rolls. The compass's construction allows for expansion and contraction of the fluid as temperatures change.

Protect your compass from excessive heat and direct sunlight. A compass may leak fluid from a ruptured seal if it overheats, and without its fluid, it is unusable.

You will find it useful to have a light to read the compass at night. A good compass comes with an internal red light, which illuminates the card in darkness yet does not impair night vision.

Large compasses usually are more stable and more finely calibrated than small compasses. Select one that is as large as practical for where it will be mounted.

Installing Your Compass

Install the compass where it will be easily visible from the helm, and so that its central pivot and **lubber's line** are parallel with your boat's keel. Any

Figure **9-14.** An array of small boat compasses. **Top left:** A front-reading powerboat compass. The yellow lubber's line is on the front surface of the glass bowl. Front-reading compasses are a bit counterintuitive and may take some getting used to. **Top right:** A top-reading powerboat compass. **Bottom left and right:** A binnacle-mount sailboat compass and a bulkhead-mount sailboat compass. (COURTESY RITCHIE NAVIGATION; REPRINTED WITH PERMISSION FROM *THE WEEKEND NAVIGATOR* BY BOB SWEET)

compass misalignment during installation will give a constant error in readings. Powerboat compasses are often mounted on a dash, a center console, or close by the helm in a pilothouse. Sailboat compasses are typically either binnacle mounted or installed in the cabin's aft bulkhead so as to be clearly visible from the helm. The choice of a front-reading, top-reading, or bulkhead-mount compass will depend on your installation location. Locate the magnetic compass as far as possible from radios, other electronic instruments, or masses of ferrous (iron) metal—especially audio speakers. This is not usually a problem on boats with outboard motors, but on inboards it may be a significant problem. Watch your compass card while at a pier. Does it move when you turn on an electric or electronic instrument? If so, move either the compass (or adjust it) or the instrument.

Adjusting Your Compass

Each type of compass has a unique alignment procedure you must perform after installing the compass. The alignment procedure for a liquid magnetic compass is standard. Take your boat to an area with several charted landmarks and one or more fixed ATONs (not buoys) that can be aligned with the landmarks to create ranges. Align and point your vessel toward each range and read your compass.

Compare these readings with the magnetic directions measured from your chart (see below). If the compass readings vary no more than 2° or 3° from what they should be, a boater traveling short distances may ignore these errors. Most people can't read such small differences on their compasses or steer a course that accurately anyway. If the differences are greater than 3°, however, make a note of them. You will want to either adjust your compass so as to remove these errors, which are called *deviations*, or compensate for the errors in the courses you steer.

A good compass has internal adjustable magnets that, when appropriately tuned, will counteract the magnetic influences aboard your boat that cause compass error. Don't try to adjust the compass unless you have time, patience, and special knowledge. Local professional compass adjusters can usually be found in the Yellow Pages. Note that

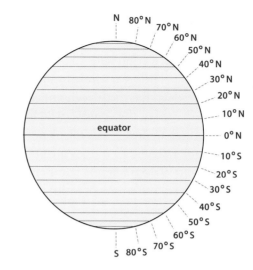

Figure **9-15.** Parallels of latitude.

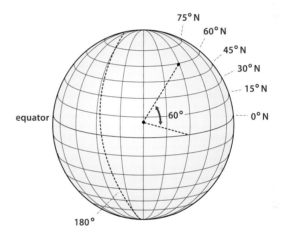

Figure **9-16.** Measuring latitude.

electronic compasses automatically compensate for most deviation.

Fixing Your Position

Navigation involves getting from where you are to where you want to be. To do this, you must be able to locate both your present position and the position to which you wish to move.

Great Circles

Lines of *latitude* (Lat) and *longitude* (Lo) provide a precise means of determining a position on the earth's surface. These lines are made by passing imaginary planes (flat surfaces) through the earth.

Parallels of Latitude

If an imaginary plane passes through the center of the earth, its intersection with the earth's surface is a *great circle*. The great circle formed by passing a plane through the earth's center perpendicular to the earth's axis is the *equator*, which is 0° latitude. Other lines formed by passing planes through the earth perpendicular to its axis are *parallels* of latitude (Figure 9-15). Each is parallel with the equator and every other line of latitude, but only the equator is a great circle.

Latitude lines encircle the earth in an east-west direction and measure angular distances north and south of the equator. These angles are measured in degrees, the symbol for which is °. Each degree can be divided into 60 minutes (60), and each minute can be divided into 60 seconds (60). In navigating, however, we most often use tenths of minutes rather than seconds, and you may be required to convert from seconds to "tenths" if the chart displays seconds. To illustrate how parallels of latitude are used, draw a line from the earth's center to the point where it intersects the equator as in Figure 9-16. Next, draw another line from the earth's center to a second point directly above the first and on another line of latitude. The angle between these lines (60°) describes the position of the sec-

ond point in relation to the equator. The second point can be either north or south of the equator. In Figure 9-16, the point is at 60°N latitude (abbreviated "Lat"). In Figure 9-17, the angle shows that Greenwich, England, is at 51°28 N latitude.

The angle between the two lines can vary from 0° to 90°, since the equator is 0° and the poles are Lat 90°N and Lat 90°S. A point halfway between the equator and either the north or south geographic pole is at an angle of 45°. It is either Lat 45°N or Lat 45°S, depending on whether it is north or south of the equator.

Longitude Lines

Planes that pass through both geographic poles form great circles on the earth's surface. These are called lines of longitude or *meridians*. On one side of the earth the lines are called the **upper branches**, and on the opposite side they are called the **lower branches**. Meridians run from north to south through the earth's poles and measure angular distances to the east or west of the *prime meridian*, which passes through Greenwich, England, and is designated as 0° longitude. You might ask why the prime meridian was chosen so as to pass through Greenwich. The answer has much to do with England's global dominance of the seas at the time this determination was made.

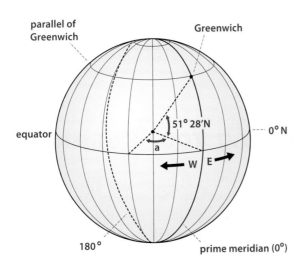

Figure **9-17.** Meridians of longitude are shown here. The Greenwich or prime meridian is 0° longitude, and longitude is measured east or west from there. The east and west longitudes converge on the opposite side of the globe from the prime meridian, at 180° longitude. Angle "a" in the drawing represents a west longitude.

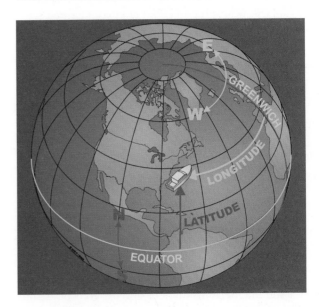

Figure **9-18.** Together, latitude and longitude measurements provide a coordinate grid system, giving each location on earth a unique "address." (REPRINTED WITH PERMISSION FROM *THE WEEKEND NAVIGATOR* BY BOB SWEET)

Note that all meridians are great circles. This is in contrast with lines of latitude, which, with the exception of the equator, are not great circles.

Now imagine a line drawn from the center of the earth to the intersection of the prime meridian with the equator, such as in Figure 9-17. Imagine, too, another line drawn from the center of the earth to a point where a different meridian intersects the equator to form angle "a." Angle "a" between these two meridians tells the position of the point relative to the prime meridian. The position may be east or west of the prime meridian.

If you go west from Greenwich one-quarter of the way around the earth, you are at Lo 90°W. If you go east one-quarter of the way around the earth, you are at Lo 90°E. If you go halfway around the earth, you are at Lo 180°. Lo 180°E and Lo 180°W are the same meridian.

Lo 180° is approximately the international date line (see the line of dashes on Figure 9-17). The date line follows Lo 180° except where it is contorted to exclude or include bodies of land. It is drawn west of Alaska, for example, so that all of Alaska will have the same calendar date.

As with degrees of latitude, degrees of longitude are divided into 60 minutes, and each minute is divided into 60 seconds.

Locating a Point on a Chart

You can describe any point on the earth's surface by its latitude and longitude (Figure 9-18). If a vessel's position is 44°00 N, 80°00 W, there is only one place on earth it can be. It is in Lake Huron. Similarly, Greenwich, England, is located at Lat 51°28 N, Lo 0°00 (Figure 9-17).

Since most charts are Mercator projections, true north is at the top. Parallels of latitude extend horizontally across the page, whereas meridians of longitude run vertically up and down the page. Indeed, one of the defining characteristics of a Mercator projection is its depiction of meridians as vertical lines that are parallel with one another. On a round globe, the meridians converge at both poles and thus are not parallel, and this explains why high-latitude landmasses are distorted on a Mercator chart. This feature is also one of the keys to the great utility of a Mercator projection, however, en-

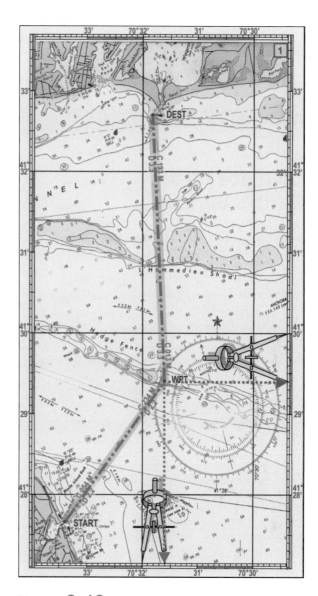

Figure **9-19.** Locating a position on a chart. Here a boater planning a trip plots a course on the chart that includes a turning point. To find the coordinates of that turning point, he uses dividers to measure its latitude and longitude as shown (and as described in this chapter). If he is using GPS, he can then enter those coordinates into his GPS receiver as a waypoint. (REPRINTED WITH PERMISSION *FROM THE WEEKEND NAVIGATOR* BY BOB SWEET)

abling the navigator to plot compass courses and bearings as straight lines on a chart.

Along the margins of a chart are black-and-white scales showing degrees, minutes, and tenths of minutes or seconds. The scales on the left and right margins are latitude scales, while those along the top and bottom are longitude scales.

You can describe any point on a chart using the latitude and longitude scales. Figure 9-19 illustrates their use in determining a position.

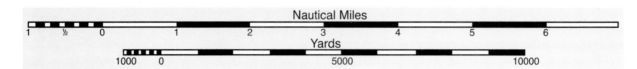

Figure 9-20. You will find a distance scale like this one on your nautical chart.

Distance on the Earth's Surface

You have probably heard the term *nautical mile* and wondered why it is used instead of the more common unit of distance, the statute or "land" mile. There is a good reason.

There are 360° in a circle. Each circle therefore has 360° x 60 or 21,600 minutes. The distance described on the earth's surface by 1 minute of arc along a great circle is 1 nautical mile. Thus, the circumference of the earth is 21,600 nautical miles. Since every minute of latitude is a minute of arc along a meridian, and since every meridian is a great circle, 1 minute of latitude is always equal to 1 nautical mile. This makes the nautical mile a convenient measure of distance.

Not all great circles are precisely the same length, however, since the earth is not quite a perfect sphere. In July 1, 1959, the length of 1 nautical mile was set officially at 1,852 meters (about 6,076 feet). This is ¹⁄₂₁,₆₀₀th of the distance around the earth at the equator. Since a statute mile is 5,280 feet (about 1,600 meters), 1 nautical mile equals 6,076 ÷ 5,280 or 1.15 statute miles. A *knot* is a speed of 1 nautical mile per hour. (Note that "knots per hour" is not a valid expression. Your speed might be 10 knots or 11.15 miles per hour, but it is *not* 10 knots per hour!)

There are two ways to measure the distance between two points on a chart.

Use the Chart's Scale

Most charts have distance scales, which show distances in nautical miles, statute miles or kilometers, and yards or meters (Figure 9-20). Mariners commonly use nautical miles to measure distance. The fastest and most convenient way to use these scales to measure the distance between two points is with dividers. Set one leg of the dividers on one point and

the other leg on the second point. Now move the dividers to a scale such as shown in Figure 9-20.

Put one leg of the dividers on one of the whole-number division points—for example, on 1, 2, or 3—such that the other leg of the dividers will fall somewhere within the subdivided portion at the left end of the scale. The whole-number division point is the number of nautical miles, statute miles, kilometers, yards, or meters, and the finer divisions to the left are tenths of a mile, kilometer, yard, or meter. On the "yard" scale, the finer divisions are each equal to 100 yards.

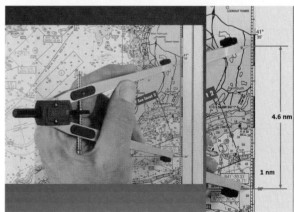

Figure 9-21. Using the latitude scale to measure distance. **Top:** Place one point of the dividers on the first location and the second point on the other location. **Bottom:** Without altering that setting, transfer the dividers to the latitude scale on the edge of the chart. One minute of latitude (but not longitude!) is exactly equal to 1 nautical mile. (REPRINTED WITH PERMISSION FROM *THE WEEKEND NAVIGATOR* BY BOB SWEET)

Use the Latitude Scale

The second way to measure distance on a chart is by use of its latitude scale, since 1 minute of latitude is always 1 nautical mile. Again, set the dividers to extend from one point on the chart to the other whose distance away you want to know (Figure 9-21).

Now, move the dividers to the latitude scale near the midpoint of the latitudes of your points, as in Figure 9-21. Place one leg of the dividers on a minute or a degree mark on the latitude scale. Place the other leg above it on the latitude scale as in Figure 9-21. Now count the minutes and tenths of minutes between the two points. Remember, 1 minute of latitude equals 1 nautical mile.

If the distance between the two points you are measuring is greater than the span of the dividers, set the span of the dividers equal to 1 nautical mile by using the latitude scale of the chart. Now "walk" the dividers from one end of the line joining the two points to the other, keeping count of the number of nautical miles measured. When you get near the end of the line, reduce the span of the dividers to equal the length of the last segment. Apply the dividers to the latitude scale to read the length of this segment in tenths of a mile, and add that to the number of whole nautical miles you counted.

The longitude scales on a chart cannot be used to measure distance. Figure 9-18 shows that, although latitude lines are spaced at equal intervals, longitude lines are closer together near the earth's poles than they are at the equator. Only at the equator does 1 minute of longitude equal 1 nautical mile.

On small-scale polyconic charts, such as those for the Great Lakes, you can measure large east-west distances most accurately by using the distance scale.

Use a Piece of Paper

If you don't have dividers, use a piece of paper to make your measurement. Make a mark on the edge of the paper, and place this on one of the points. Align the paper's edge with the two points and put another mark at the second point. Now move the paper to the latitude scale and read the distance.

WARNING *Use the latitude scales on the right and left of a chart to measure distance. Do not use the longitude scales at the top and bottom of the chart.*

Course Plotting

An important feature of Mercator and large-scale polyconic charts is that angles are represented correctly. Draw a line on a chart from where you are to where you want to go. This is a *course line*. The angle the course line makes with true north is the direction you should go to get where you want to be. In addition, the length of the line represents the distance you have to travel to get there.

Direction

Direction is measured clockwise from north and expressed in degrees. East is 90°, south is 180°, west is 270°, and north is 360° or 0°. The direction of a course line is its clockwise angle from north.

Measuring Direction

You can measure the direction of a course line drawn on a chart in several ways, but the two most common use a course plotter or parallel rulers. Whichever method you use, the first step is to *esti-*

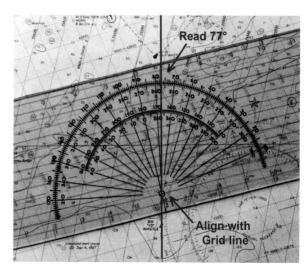

Figure **9-22.** Using a course plotter to measure direction on a chart. Slide one edge or one of the parallel lines of the plotter along the course line plotted on the chart until the plotter's bull's-eye aligns with a line of latitude or longitude. Then read the course direction in degrees true from the appropriate scale on the plotter. (PHOTO BY RAY PAGES)

mate the direction of the course line. The estimate will help avoid the common error of steering a course exactly opposite the intended one. When making your estimate, remember that a line has two ends, only one of which is in the direction you want to go. The other points in the opposite direction. These two directions are 180° apart, which means they are *reciprocals*.

A direction between north and east is between 0° and 90°. A direction between east and south is between 90° and 180°; between south and west, 180° to 270°; and between west and north, 270° to 360° (0°).

USING A COURSE PLOTTER

The **course plotter** is a protractor designed to measure courses and bearings on charts. It is particularly useful in small boats, since it needs little space. To use the plotter, first estimate the direction of the course line as outlined in the text on page 233.

Measuring Courses and Bearings

To measure a course (or a bearing), place a long edge or a line of the plotter along the course line. Now, slide the plotter along this line until the bull's-eye is over a meridian of longitude or a parallel of latitude. Read the course from the proper scale of the plotter. Note that the plotter has separate dedicated angular scales for measuring latitude and longitude. The scales are very similar, so it's easy to make an error and select the wrong one. Also, the reading may reflect the opposite intended direction, so the reciprocal course must be calculated.

Drawing a Course or Bearing from a Given Point

To draw a course or bearing from a given point, place the plotter in the general direction of the desired course or bearing. Next, place the point of your pencil on the point. Now, slide the plotter until one of its edges touches the point and the bull's-eye is on a meridian. Then, while keeping the plotter against your pencil and the bull's-eye over the meridian, slide the plotter up or down. When you have adjusted the plotter to the desired angle, draw the course or bearing line along its edge. Again, if your course or bearing is nearly north or south, use a parallel of latitude instead.

Extending a Course Line

You can easily extend a course line beyond the end of the plotter. First, spread your dividers and place them on the course line. Next, place one edge of the plotter against the dividers. You can now slide the plotter along the points of the divider and draw the extended course line.

USING A COURSE PLOTTER. A simple way to measure the direction of a course on a small vessel is with a *course plotter* (Figure 9-22). Align any of the lines or long edges of this see-through plastic tool with the course line. Slide it along the line until the bull's-eye is on a meridian or a parallel, and read the direction of the course line from the appropriate protractor scale on the plotter. Complete directions for using a course plotter are in the sidebar on page 234.

One of the great advantages of a course plotter is that you can read the course from any nearby line of latitude or longitude, at least one of which will always be handy on the portion of the chart you happen to be using. You must remember that the course measurement you obtain using this method will be in degrees true, not magnetic. This means that you will have to apply a correction before you can steer the course by your compass, as we'll discuss below.

USING PARALLEL RULERS. You may also measure the direction of a line by using the nearest *compass rose*. Each chart features at least one of these, and often two or three. A compass rose includes two concentric circles, each of which is graduated in degrees. The outer ring is oriented toward "true" or "geographic" north, just like the meridian lines, whereas the inner ring is oriented toward magnetic north—like a compass needle—as discussed below and illustrated in Figure 9-25. Thus, by using a compass rose, you can measure course directions in degrees true or degrees magnetic.

There are several ways to do this, but the easiest is with *parallel rulers*, which are a pair of hinged, articulated rulers designed so that they remain parallel with one another at all times while swinging apart or together (Figure 9-23). Align one edge of the rulers with the course line, then **walk** the rulers to the nearest compass rose by swinging the leading ruler toward the rose to the full extent of the hinged arms, then anchoring the lead ruler while you swing the trailing ruler so as to catch up. Then repeat. In this fashion you advance by increments across the chart, while retaining the original course direction, until the edge of the lead ruler passes through the center of the compass rose. Then read the direction from the *outer edge* of the compass rose for *degrees true*, or from the *inner edge* for *degrees magnetic*. For more about this choice, see below.

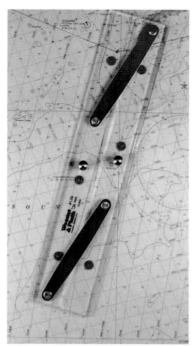

Figure **9-23.** Using parallel rulers to measure direction. From left to right, a course line is "walked" by increments over to the nearest compass rose, from which direction can be measured in degrees true or magnetic as desired. (REPRINTED WITH PERMISSION FROM *THE WEEKEND NAVIGATOR* BY BOB SWEET)

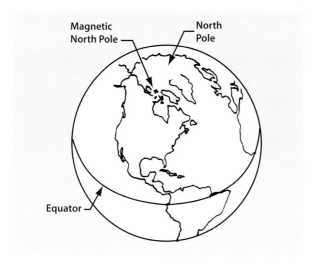

Figure **9-24.** The relative positions of the true and magnetic north poles.

The chief disadvantage of reading directions from a compass rose is that, when you're working in the cramped confines of a small boat, you rarely have room to spread out the entire chart flat. It's common to fold a chart so that the area of immediate interest is the part that shows, but it's also common to find that the nearest compass rose is *not* on the area of the chart that's showing. Therefore, major voyage planning is best done on a large table.

Sources of Compass Error

Even if you read your compass correctly, the reading may be in error. Two sources of compass error are variation and deviation.

Variation

The earth's core contains ferrous iron, and this creates a magnetic field around the earth, one end of which is the north magnetic pole. Unfortunately, the magnetic north pole is several hundred miles away from the geographic north pole (Figure 9-24), and it also changes gradually over time, wandering around the Canadian Arctic. (Fortunately, the change with time is predictable.) A compass needle points to the magnetic north pole, not the "true" north of the geographic north pole. The resultant error is called *variation*.

It should be noted that marine compasses do not really "point" in the way that hikers' compasses do. Beneath the card of a marine compass is a small bar magnet that aligns itself with the earth's magnetic field and remains aligned as the vessel turns.

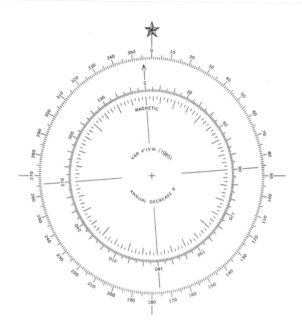

Figure 9-25. A compass rose. (REPRINTED WITH PERMISSION FROM *HOW TO READ A NAUTICAL CHART* BY NIGEL CALDER)

The card to which the magnet is attached *appears* to turn, but in fact it is the vessel that does so, while the card retains its orientation with respect to magnetic north. Thus, the compass is said to "point" toward magnetic north.

Variation is either easterly or westerly—i.e., magnetic north is either east or west of true north, depending on where you are. You can find your local variation by referring to the compass rose printed on your nautical chart. In Figure 9-25, the amount of the variation was 4°15 W in 1985, and at that time it had an annual decrease of 8 minutes. Thus, if you had been using this compass rose in 2005, the local variation would have been 1°35 W rather than 4°15 W. Since variation changes from place to place, a chart with two or more compass roses may show a slightly different variation on each rose. Use the variation noted on the compass rose closest to your position.

Notice that the compass rose has two protractor scales (Figure 9-25). As mentioned above, the outer ring represents directions with respect to true north, whereas the inner ring represents directions with respect to magnetic north after taking variation into account. Thus, another way to calculate the local variation as of the year the chart was issued is to compare magnetic north on the inner ring with true north on the outer ring.

The innermost gradations on a compass rose have more historical interest than practical value for recreational boaters. They are **compass points**. Since there are thirty-two points on the compass, each point represents 11.25°. At one time a practicing navigator was expected to be able to *box the compass*—name all thirty-two points: north; north by east; north northeast; northeast by north; northeast; northeast by east; etc.

Deviation

Variation is the same for all vessels in an area. *Deviation*, which is compass error caused by magnetic fields aboard the vessel, varies from one vessel to the next. The engine, steering wheel (including its spokes), dashboard instruments, electronic equipment, and bundles of wires may have magnetic fields. A radio speaker has an especially strong magnetic field. These local magnetic fields interact with the earth's magnetic field and the magnetic field of your compass and can cause the compass to deviate from magnetic north.

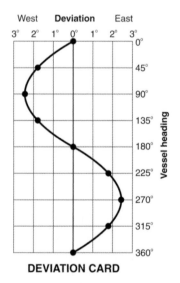

Figure 9-26. In theory, the deviation table you construct for your boat's steering compass could be plotted in a symmetrical curve like this one. In reality, your compass deviation may be highly skewed in one direction, east or west. (REPRINTED WITH PERMISSION FROM *BOATER'S BOWDITCH* BY RICHARD K. HUBBARD)

Some vessels do not cause deviation in their compasses. Outboard motors do not usually influence a compass because they are too far from it and contain less iron than inboards or stern drives. If your compass is far enough from the electronic equipment and other magnetic fields aboard your vessel, it should have little deviation.

Since your boat carries its local magnetic fields with it, deviation does not change from place to place, but it will change with the heading of the boat. As mentioned above, if the deviation of your compass is no more than $2°$ or $3°$ on any heading, and the distance to be traveled on this heading is short, you can safely ignore it. If, however, you find larger deviations after running ranges as described above, you may want to construct a **deviation table** and then use the data in the table to correct your compass courses (Figure 9-26).

Alternatively, again as mentioned above, you can have your compass adjusted by a professional adjuster. In most cases an adjuster can remove most of the deviation from your compass by tuning the compass's internal adjustable magnets. From that point forward you will not need to worry about deviation unless you rewire the boat, install new electronics, relocate your backup anchor to a nearby locker, install a new engine, or make some other change that may affect your boat's magnetic field. At that point you should recheck your compass.

Correcting a Compass Reading

We've seen how to measure the direction of a course line on a chart as an angle between the course and true north. This is the most convenient way to determine courses on a chart, but steering such a course by your compass without first adjusting it for variation and possibly for deviation can get you into trouble. If the local variation were 18°W and your boat's deviation on the chosen heading were 5°W, you'd be steering off at a 23° angle from the direction you really wanted to go. How can you tell in which compass direction to head your boat?

You can **correct** a compass reading to tell its direction with reference to true north. You can also **uncorrect** a true heading to derive the compass direction in which to head your boat.

A Helpful Memory Aid

Figure 9-27 shows a memory device that makes correcting or uncorrecting a simple procedure. The letters TVMDC stands for **T**rue, **V**ariation, **M**agnetic, **D**eviation, and **C**ompass. There are several ways to remember TVMDC; one is **T**ele-**V**isions **M**ake **D**ull **C**hildren.

Figure 9-27 has arrows on either side of the memory device. The ones on the left show that when uncorrecting a true heading, you add westerly variations and deviations and subtract easterly ones. The arrow on the right shows that when correcting a compass reading, you add easterly variations and deviations and subtract westerly ones.

To simplify, the memory device says, "Tele-Visions Make Dull Children, add **W**onder." So, when converting from true headings to compass headings, add westerly variations and deviations. It follows, then, that you would subtract easterly ones. If going from compass to true, do the opposite. Add easterly variations and deviations, and subtract westerly ones. This means that all you need to know is **TVMDC + W** and you can work out the rest.

Some Examples

Let's try an example. In an area in which the variation is 5°W, you measure a course heading on your chart and find it is 047° true. Since you are uncorrecting your heading and converting from true to compass, first add the westerly variation:

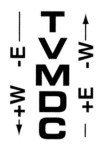

Figure 9-27. A memory device for correcting and uncorrecting compass readings.

$$047° + 5°W = 052°M$$

This is your magnetic heading; use an M to show it.

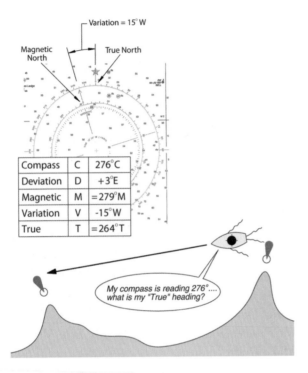

Figure 9-28. Deriving a true course from a compass reading. (REPRINTED WITH PERMISSION FROM *BOATER'S BOWDITCH* BY RICHARD K. HUBBARD)

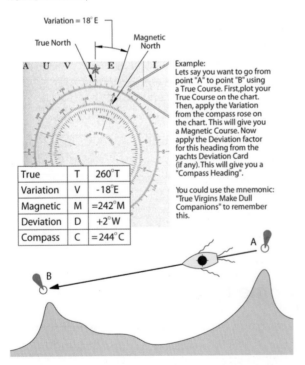

Figure 9-29. Deriving a compass heading to steer from a true course. (REPRINTED WITH PERMISSION FROM *BOATER'S BOWDITCH* BY RICHARD K. HUBBARD)

Then look at your deviation table and find that, for a course of 052°M, your deviation is 8°E. Now subtract the easterly deviation:

$$052°M - 8°E = 044°C$$

This is your compass heading; label it with a C (Figure 9-28).

Here's another example. Suppose the variation in the area where you are boating is 7°W and the compass reads 104°. According to your deviation table the deviation for a compass heading of 104° is 10°W. What is your true heading? This example asks you to correct a compass reading. This means that you will add easterly deviations and variations and subtract westerly ones:

$$104°C - 10°W = 094°M$$

Now subtract the westerly variation:

$$094°M - 7°W = 087°$$

Your true heading is 087°.

It is customary not to label a true course with a T; however, it is customary to label a magnetic course with an M. On some commercial charts, courses in channels are preprinted, and given in magnetic. On many commercially produced charts, directions are given in magnetic. Thus, the mariner can, after dealing with deviation, simply steer the compass course noted on the chart. This works well for short trips, but for longer voyages, convert magnetic to true.

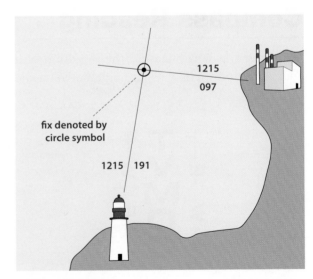

Figure 9-30. Position by crossed bearings on two landmarks.

Finding Your Position

The most common navigation problem is pinpointing your position. There are several compelling reasons for knowing where you are. For one, it's the first and most critical step in figuring out how to get where you want to go. Second, you can't be assured of avoiding ledges and other hazards unless you know your position relative to their charted locations. Otherwise, you would just be blundering around out there and trusting to luck. Third, knowing where you are is critical for managing your fuel supply and ensuring that you don't run out before you can refuel. And finally, in the event of an emergency, you need to be able to tell the Coast Guard or a towboat operator where you are.

A *line of position* (LOP) is a line that you draw on a chart such that it passes through your location. A single LOP does not tell you where you are. All you know is that you are somewhere along that line. **Crossing** two lines of position as in Figure 9-30, however, tells you where you are with some degree of certainty; you are at their intersection. You have made a *fix* and have determined your position. You can also get a fix by passing close aboard a charted object such as an aid to navigation. A buoy is not usually used to determine a fix, since it may be off-station, but a buoy works well enough when precision is not critical, or when the charted hazard it marks is clearly visible and confirms its

position, or when no fixed ATON or other landmark is available.

Since LOPs are the key to fixing your position, you need to know how to obtain an LOP. There are several ways.

Range LOPs

As mentioned in Chapter 5, a **range** offers one way to determine an LOP, and a very precise one at that. If you can line up two charted objects, you can draw a line through the objects toward your vessel (Figure 9-31). You are somewhere along this line, though just where, you can't know without a second LOP. In most coastal waters, opportunities for ranges abound. Line up a daybeacon in front of a church spire, or a prominent half-tide rock in front of the seaward end of a bold headland, or the end of an island in front of a radio tower on the distant mainland. As long as both objects are charted, they qualify as range markers.

Although you may not know where you are from a single LOP, you now know where you are not!

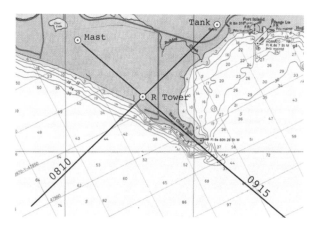

Figure **9-31.** A range line, obtained when any two charted objects are in line from your position, makes a perfect LOP. Neither compass bearings nor compass correction is necessary. (REPRINTED WITH PERMISSION FROM *BOATER'S BOWDITCH* BY RICHARD K. HUBBARD)

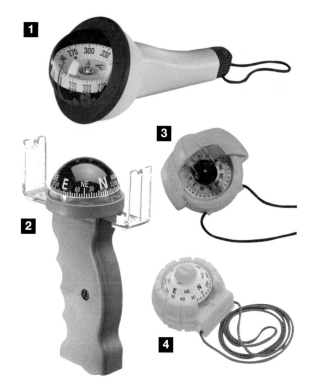

Figure **9-32.** A selection of hand bearing compasses. 1. A Plastimo hand bearing compass that can be fix-mounted as well. 2. A Davis model. 3. A Plastimo "hockey puck" model. 4. A Ritchie model for a small boat. (REPRINTED WITH PERMISSION FROM *THE WEEKEND NAVIGATOR* BY BOB SWEET)

Bearing LOPs

You will often get your LOPs with a magnetic compass. Using either a handheld bearing compass (Figure 9-32) or the boat's steering compass, select two or more identifiable landmarks or aids to navigation that appear on the chart. Three charted marks, and thus three LOPs, are preferable to two. If you must use only two marks, select them so that the angle between them, as seen from your position, is as close to 90° as possible.

Take the readings by pointing your handheld compass at each mark in turn. The direction to a mark is its *bearing*. If using your vessel's compass, head your vessel toward each mark and note your compass heading, which is also the bearing to the object.

After you have determined the bearings of two or more marks, the next step is to correct them. If using a handheld bearing compass, assume that its deviation is zero. If using your boat's compass, read the deviation from your deviation table. In either case, determine variation from the compass rose on your chart.

Suppose that at 1215 you took bearings on a tank and a monument by using your boat's compass (refer back to Figure 9-30). Suppose, also, that variation for the area is 12°E, the bearing to the tank is 088°C, and the bearing to the monument is 176°C. Let's also suppose that your deviation table shows that for a heading of 088°C the deviation is 3°W, and for a compass heading of 176°C it is 3°E.

The first step is to correct each compass bearing to a true bearing:

$$088°C - 3°W = 085°M$$

$$085°M + 12°E = 097°$$

The bearing of 176°C must also be corrected:

$$176°C + 3°E = 179°M$$

$$179°M + 12°E = 191°$$

After determining the true directions of the two charted marks, use your parallel rulers and a compass rose to determine where to draw the LOPs. To draw the first LOP, place one edge of the ruler so it passes through the center of the rose and

097° on the outermost scale. Now, walk the ruler to the tank and draw a line back toward your position.

Use the same method to draw the LOP from the monument. Your position is at the point where the two lines cross. This is your fix, and you should label it with a dot with a circle around it. Label the LOPs with the time above the bearing lines and the directions below the lines, as shown in Figure 9-30.

When drawing a line of position, do not run it through the charted mark. Instead, begin seaward of the mark and make the line long enough that it passes through your position. At some later time, you may wish to erase the line. If the LOP runs through the mark, you may destroy it when you erase the LOP.

CHECK YOUR WORK. Make an estimate to check your work. From your original sighting, you knew that the tank was in an easterly direction. It had a bearing of 088°C. That means that you are west of the tank and looking east, which is 090°. The true direction of the tank from your position is 097°, which is almost east.

In a similar manner, south is 180°. You observed the monument to be at 176°C, which means you are north of the monument and looking south toward it. The true direction of the monument from your position is 191°, which is a southerly direction.

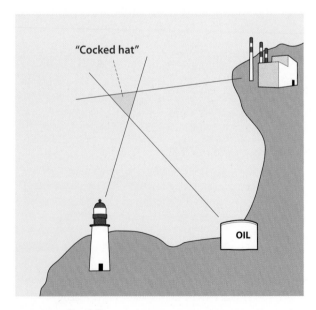

Figure **9-33.** A "cocked hat" formed by three lines of position.

If you had taken bearings on three marks, the three LOPs would, ideally, cross at a single point. In reality, this seldom happens. More often the intersections of the three lines form a small triangle, which navigators call a **cocked hat** (Figure 9-33). The smaller the triangle, the more exact your position is, since you assume that you are somewhere within the area of the triangle.

Remember, a fix obtained by this method is NOT where you are now if your vessel is moving. It is where you were when you took the sightings. In a fast boat, that could be "way back there."

Other LOPs

It should be apparent by this time that a range LOP is both simpler and more precise than a bearing LOP. Use range LOPs whenever possible.

There are, in addition, other possible ways of getting LOPs. One is to measure your distance from a charted object and use that to create a *circle of position* (COP). The object will be the center of the circle, and the measured distance will be the radius. It is possible, for example, to measure your distance off a lighthouse or bold headland of known height by measuring the vertical angle of the object with a sextant. You can also, sometimes, get a curve of position from a depth contour where the depth changes rapidly from place to place. Match the depth measured by your depth sounder with, say, the 30-foot depth contour on the chart (making due allowance for tide), and you can be reasonably confident of being somewhere over or near that local contour. Cross that curve of position with an LOP from another source, and you get an estimated position. Other techniques are possible too, and you can learn more about this in more advanced Coast Guard Auxiliary courses (see www.cgaux.org).

Common Conventions

When writing bearings on a line of position or a course line, write them using three digits, as in Figure 9-30. In this way, you will not confuse them with units of time or speed. Always write time with four digits using a 24-hour clock. For example, noon is 1200, 9:45 a.m. is 0945, and 3:20 p.m. is 1520.

Write speed with two digits. Thus, even if you do not identify the units of measure on an LOP or course line, you know what each is. A four-digit number is time, a three-digit number is direction, and a two-digit number is speed. Use leading zeros where necessary to bring the measures to their two-, three-, or four-digit forms.

Figure **9-34.** Some marine binoculars offer a built-in bearing compass that displays in the bottom of the magnified image (bottom). (COURTESY STEINER)

BINOCULAR

Most authorities recommend a 7 x 50 binocular, which magnifies objects seven times. In a pitching and rolling boat, it is difficult to steady a binocular stronger than 7 x 50 on an object, although there are binoculars with a stabilizing feature that will assist in steadying the image. The diameters of a 7 x 50 binocular's front (objective) lenses are 50 mm, which is important for nighttime use, since a diameter of less than 50 mm would not admit enough light for good vision in dim light.

Many boaters prefer a binocular with a built-in compass that shows in the bottom of the field of view (Figure 9-34, bottom). These offer a convenient and accurate way to take bearings on landmarks and ATONs, essentially replacing the hand bearing compass.

Figure 9-35. A powerboat instrument panel with speedometer display. (PHOTO BY NORMA LOCOCO)

	N - S		S - N		Average
RPM	**Time**	**Speed**	**Time**	**Speed**	**Speed**
800	6m 47s	8.85	8m 32s	7.03	7.94
1000	5m 46s	10.41	7m 31s	7.98	9.20
1200	5m 01s	11.96	6m 46s	8.87	10.42
1400	4m 28s	13.43	6m 13s	9.65	11.54
1600	4m 03s	14.82	5m 47s	10.38	12.60
1800	3m 42s	16.22	5m 01s	11.96	14.09
2000	3m 31s	17.06	4m 53s	12.29	14.68
2200	3m 24s	17.64	4m 41s	12.81	15.23

Speed Trial Tabulation Over Measured Mile

Figure 9-36. A table of engine speed versus boat speed.

Speed-Time-Distance

Suppose you plan to make a fishing trip to a distant point. How long will it take you to get there? You need a measure of your boat's speed and the distance to the fishing hole. When you know any two of these variables—speed, time, or distance—you can calculate the third.

Measuring Speed

Measuring a boat's speed is harder than it sounds. You can install a speedometer on a small boat, but this instrument is not especially accurate (Figure 9-35). Furthermore, it gives measures of speed through the water, and what you need is speed over the bottom, which may differ from speed through the water due to the effects of wind and current. This is one of the many navigation tasks that is performed far more simply and with greater accuracy and reliability by GPS, as we'll see below. But you should know how to work through these problems without GPS.

The Speed Table

Most small boats have *tachometers*, which measure the speed of your boat's engine in revolutions per minute (rpm). You can use this to construct a **speed curve** or **speed table** to tell your boat's speed through the water at various engine speeds (Figure 9-36).

To make a speed table, find two charted points about a mile apart in navigable waters (two navigation buoys would do, as it won't matter much for these purposes if one or both are slightly off-station),

and measure the charted distance between them. If you measure the distance in statute miles, the speed table you construct will be in miles per hour (mph). If you use nautical miles, it will be in knots.

Run the course between the two measured points, and then reverse course, timing your speed each way with a stopwatch. Run the course both ways at the same engine speed to cancel the effects of wind and current. Now, compute your speed in each direction and average the the two speeds. **Do not average times to compute the speed.**

Do this for a variety of engine speeds, averaging the two vessel speeds at each engine speed, and then use these averages to construct a speed table like the one shown in Figure 9-36. Remember, though, that this is your speed through the water, meaning that it is not corrected for wind and most especially not for current. If your speed through the water is 15 knots and you're heading downstream in a 5-knot current, your speed over ground is 20 knots, but if you turn around and head upstream, your speed over ground will fall to 10 knots. To derive speed over ground from speed through the water, you need to know what the current is doing. Later, in our discussion of GPS, you will see an easier method.

Computing Time, Speed, or Distance

If you know two of the time-speed-distance variables, you can compute the other one. For example, if you travel two hours at 60 statute miles per hour, how far have you gone? You have gone:

2 x 60 = 120 statute miles

In this formula, time is in hours, speed in statute miles per hour, and distance in statute miles. The formula used was:

Distance = Speed x Time
or D = S x T

Computing Distance

In navigating, we use the same formula, but measure time in minutes, speed in knots or nautical miles per hour, and distance in nautical miles.

Since time is expressed in minutes, it has been multiplied by 60. So we must do the same to the other side of the equation; thus, the formula becomes:

60D = S x T
or D = (S x T) ÷ 60   (1)

Computing Speed or Time

If you remember your algebra, you can use formula 1, above, to derive two others:

T = 60D ÷ S   (2)
S = 60D ÷ T   (3)

Formulas 1, 2, and 3 give you a means of computing distance, time, or speed. Use formula 3 to build your speed table. Again, if you remember your algebra, you need only memorize formula 1 to compute speed, time, or distance.

Some Examples

Suppose that you drive your boat at a speed of 20 knots for 12 minutes. How far have you gone?

D = (S x T) ÷ 60
or D = (20 x 12) ÷ 60
D = 240 ÷ 60
and D = 4 nautical miles

How long does it take to travel 4 nautical miles at a speed of 20 knots?

T = 60D ÷ S

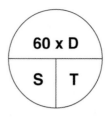

Figure **9-37.** Speed, time, and distance relationships.

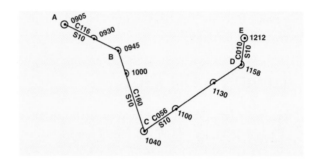

Figure **9-38.** A typical DR plot.

T = (60 x 4) ÷ 20
T = 240 ÷ 20
T = 12 minutes

How fast are you going if you travel 4 nautical miles in 12 minutes?

S = 60D ÷ T
S = (60 x 4) ÷ 12
S = 240 ÷ 12
S = 20 knots

An Alternate Method

A graphic representation of the information in the formulas is shown in Figure 9-37. To use this illustration, cover the answer you need. The formula for the answer remains uncovered. For example, if you want to compute speed, cover the S. The formula is 60 x D ÷ T. To find time, cover the T. The formula is 60 x D ÷ by S. To find the distance traveled, cover the 60 x D. You have S and T left. Distance equals S x T. Divide the result by 60.

Dead Reckoning

Navigators plan their voyages on paper charts using *dead reckoning* (DR). It is likely that the term was originally "deduced reckoning," which may have been abbreviated "ded reckoning" and later spelled "dead reckoning." Whatever the origin of the term, DR is used to plot cruises of 30 minutes or more.

A DR plot is a drawing on a chart of the courses you intend to follow (Figure 9-38), and includes notations of directions, intended speed, and DR positions at course changes and at 30-minute intervals. Intended speed is written below the line in two-digit form.

Drawing a DR Plot

Begin your DR plot at a known position or from your last known fix. The mouth of a harbor, an inlet, or a fixed aid to navigation is a good place to begin. Mark it on your course line with a dot and a full circle and the intended departure time.

If there are no obstructions between where you begin your plot and where you intend to go, you can draw a straight line between the two. More often, though, there will be obstructions or hazards that will cause you to travel an irregular course. Use the plotting tools to draw your intended course as a series of straight lines between your turning points. If possible, select turning points where there are suitable landmarks or aids to navigation.

After drawing the legs of your course line, measure their true directions using a course plotter or parallel rulers. Write these directions above the line for each leg using the three-digit form. If you wish, precede each direction with a C (to mean "course"). If you want to add compass directions to the course plot, follow them with a C for "compass."

Make your measurements and calculations carefully. In navigating, neatness and accuracy are essential, and small errors tend to be cumulative.

Now, use the dividers and the latitude scale to measure the lengths of the course legs. Using the part of the scale that is nearest to the midlatitude of each leg, measure carefully to the nearest tenth of a nautical mile.

As you travel over your planned course, you may be able to obtain intermediate fixes from ranges and bearings. Whenever you get the chance, you should do so. If you find this means that your DR course is different from your "real" course, you are most likely being set off course by wind or current. Make the

necessary adjustments to your DR plot to compensate for these influences. The farther you travel between fixes, the less accurate your DR plot will become, and the less confidence you can place in it.

A Sample Course

Let's see how this works in practice. In Figure 9-38, the course has four legs. The distance in nautical miles from point A to B is 6.6; from B to C, 9.2; from C to D, 13.0; and from D to E, 2.4.

Labeling a DR Plot

Since you know where you are at point A, you have a fix. Note this by a dot with a circle around it. A DR position is denoted by a dot with a half-circle around it, and each position is marked with the time.

Now estimate the speed that you intend to use on each leg of your cruise. Write the number below the course line using the two-digit form. You can precede the speeds with an S for "speed." A course line of 116° at a speed of 10 knots would look like:

C116

S10

If you desire to add compass direction to the plot, using a variation of 9°W and a deviation of 0°, it would look like this:

C116   C125C

S10

Making the Computations

Using the formula $T = 60D \div S$, compute the time needed to get from your departure to your first turning point at your intended speed. Remember, time is always in minutes, rounded off to the nearest whole minute, distance is usually in nautical miles and tenths of a mile, and speed is in knots.

If operating on the Great Lakes, rivers, or other bodies of water where charted distances are in statute miles, speed is in miles per hour. This is perfectly acceptable as long as you do not mix units. Use statute miles and miles per hour or nautical miles and knots. Also, if using statute miles, do not use latitude scales for measuring distances.

As shown in Figure 9-38, you expect your speed on each leg to be 10 knots. The computed times for the four legs are, therefore, 39.6, 55.2, 78.0, and 14.4 minutes. Rounded off, they are 40, 55, 78, and 14 minutes.

After calculating the time that should elapse between your departure and your arrival at the first turning point, add it to your departure time. If you start from point A at 0905, your estimated time of arrival (ETA) at point B will be 40 minutes later, or 0945. Since point B will be a DR position (unless you can fix your position with bearings, ranges, or other means when you arrive there), mark it with a dot and a half-circle. Label this point 0945.

Compute Each Half-Hour

Note: The choice of a 30-minute plotting interval in this illustration is arbitrary. For very slow-moving boats well away from hazards to navigation, 60 minutes might well be appropriate. Operators of fast boats might use a 15-minute interval. DR positions should also be plotted at the time of each course or speed change, and a new DR plot should be started whenever a position fix is obtained.

In our example, your trip to the first turn will include the start of a new half-hour, so calculate your predicted position for that time and plot it on your course line. Mark it with a dot and a half-circle. In this case, use the formula:

$$D = (S \times T) \div 60.$$

The question is, "Where will you be at 0930?" Applying the formula, you find that you will have traveled 4.2 miles. Using the dividers, place a dot and a half-circle at a point 4.2 miles from point A along your DR course line, and label this 0930.

Since you are going to show your predicted position each half-hour, you need to know where you will be at 1000. This is 15 minutes after you pass point B. In that 15 minutes you will travel 2.5 miles. Mark this point with a dot and a half-circle.

If all goes exactly according to predictions, you will arrive at point C at 1040, point D at 1158, and point E at 1212. In reality, of course, the vagaries of wind, tide, waves, and perhaps your own inconsistent steering and throttle control will cause your actual course line, speed, and distances covered to differ from those predicted. Compensating for these vagaries is a good part of the art of traditional piloting. In good visibility and safe waters, the differences won't matter much, but when visibility is poor or there are hazards on either side of your intended track, you'll want to steer as straight as possible, maintain as steady a speed as possible, keep your DR legs between charted landmarks and navigation buoys (preferably ones that are surrounded by safe water and that have easily recognized light or sound signals) as short as possible, and adjust your DR courses for current and leeway to the extent possible.

Most coastal currents are the result of tides, so we'll look at tides next. There are two ways to compensate for a tidal current: either predict what it will be ahead of time and adjust your DR course to cancel the expected influence, or note to what extent your predicted DR position varies from your next fix, and apply that difference to subsequent legs of the trip. Again, a GPS receiver takes all the guesswork out of this process, as we'll see below.

Tides

Tides are the regular rise and fall of coastal waters caused by the gravitational attractions of the moon and sun. The sun dwarfs the moon but is 370 times more distant, so its effect is subordinate to the moon's. Their effects are additive when both are in line with the earth—that is, at new moon, when the moon is between the sun and earth; and at full moon, when the moon is on the side of the earth

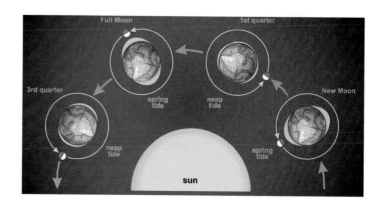

Figure 9-39. The spring tide–neap tide cycle. At new moon and again at full moon, the gravitational forces of the moon and sun are additive, and we experience the higher high tides and lower low tides known as spring tides. During the first and third quarters of the moon, the effects of the sun and moon partially cancel each other, and we experience the lesser tides known as neap tides. (REPRINTED WITH PERMISSION FROM *THE WEEKEND NAVIGATOR* BY BOB SWEET)

opposite the sun. At those times most coastal areas experience the run of higher high tides and lower low tides known as *spring tides*. When the moon is at right angles from the sun—i.e., in its first and third quarters—the sun partially cancels the gravitational attraction of the moon, and we experience the run of lower high tides and higher low tides known as *neap tides* (Figure 9-39).

Tides also vary greatly from place to place, due to complex interactions of local water depths, embayments, and other factors. In some places, such as Alaska and the Bay of Fundy, the mean range of the tides is greater than 30 feet. In others—for example, the Chesapeake Bay—it may be as little as 6 inches.

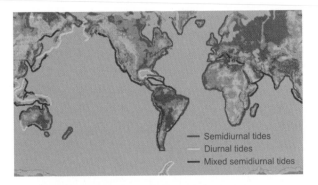

Figure **9-41.** Areas of the world with semidiurnal, mixed, and diurnal tides. (REPRINTED WITH PERMISSION FROM *THE WEEKEND NAVIGATOR* BY BOB SWEET)

On the Atlantic Coast there are two high tides and two low tides in each **tidal day** of about 24 hours and 50 minutes. (The tidal day is 50 minutes longer than the solar day because the moon completes about 12.5° of its orbit each solar day, which means that a given spot on the earth's surface must complete slightly more than a full revolution to "catch up" with the moon.) This is a *semidiurnal tide* (Figure 9-40). Both high waters are about equal in height, as are the low waters.

On the Pacific Coast, there are also two sets of tides each day, but one high tide is higher than the other, and one low tide is lower than the other. Such tides are called *mixed tides*. Along the Gulf Coast and in the Great Lakes, the tides are *diurnal*, with just one high and one low tide each day (Figure 9-41).

Obviously, mariners need some way of knowing how much water is under their keels at any particular time. To meet this demand, the NOS generates and updates tide tables for all of North America. The NOS no longer publishes these tide tables in book form, but they are available from commercial sources and are widely reprinted in smaller editions for local waters.

The datum used on U.S. charts for heights of objects on land and over water is *mean high water* (MHW). This is the average (mean) level of all high tides, and to get this average, all unusual

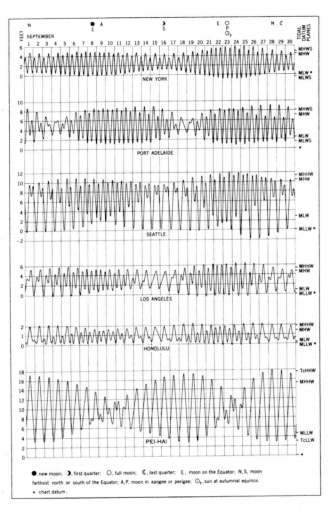

Figure **9-40.** Tidal variations over 3½ weeks for selected ports around the world. The spring tide–neap tide cycles are clearly visible. New York shows a semidiurnal tide. The other ports show mixed tides to various degrees; there are two highs and two lows in each lunar day, but one of the highs is substantially higher than the other, and one of the lows is lower. (REPRINTED WITH PERMISSION FROM *HOW TO READ A NAUTICAL CHART* BY NIGEL CALDER)

WARNING *Remember that datums are averages. At times there will be less vertical clearance under bridges and less water depth over shallows than shown on your chart.*

conditions such as storms are excluded. The clearances for bridges that appear on charts are the distances from the water's surface at mean high water to the lowest clearance under the bridge (worst case). Remember, this is the clearance at **mean high water**.

In the past, the datum for charted water depths differed according to the type of tides in an area. On the Gulf Coast and the Great Lakes, where there is only one low tide each day, and on the East Coast, where the two low waters each day are approximately equal, the datum was *mean low water* (MLW). On the Pacific Coast, where the heights of the two low waters each day are unequal, the datum was (and is) the average of the lower of the two. This datum is called *mean lower low water* (MLLW), and all U.S. charts are incorporating it in their new editions. Although the name of the chart datum has changed, indicated water depths will remain the same. On the East and Gulf coasts and the Great Lakes, MLLW will be the average of all low waters. On the Pacific Coast, only the lower of the two daily low waters will be averaged, as in the past. No matter where you are, you should bear in mind that actual water depths are likely to be less than charted depths on a spring low tide, and actual vertical clearances under bridges are likely to be less than charted clearances on a spring high tide.

Tide Tables

As mentioned, the NOS compiles data showing the times and heights of predicted tides for the Atlantic, Gulf, and Pacific coasts and for tidal rivers. Local tables made from these data are published in newspapers and are usually available from boating suppliers.

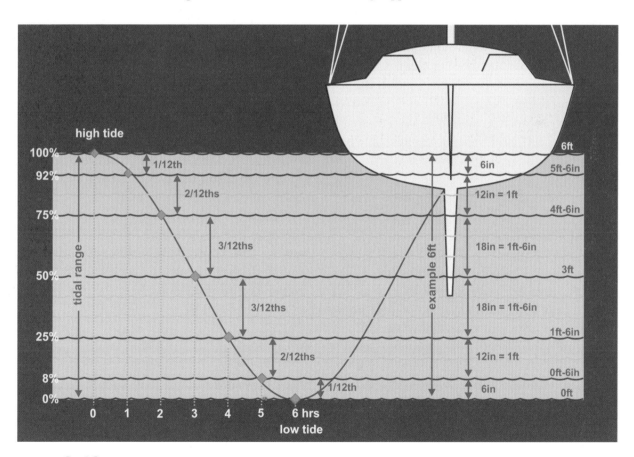

Figure **9-42.** You can use the Rule of Twelfths to estimate the height of tide at a given place and time. The rule assumes that, from the most recent low (or high) tide, the tide rises (or falls) one-twelfth of its range in the first one-sixth of its total time to rise (or fall), two-twelfths in the second sixth, three-twelfths in the third sixth, three-twelfths in the fourth sixth, two-twelfths in the fifth sixth, and one-twelfth in the final sixth. In areas of semidiurnal tide, each sixth of tidal rise or fall is roughly 1 hour. Once you obtain the local height of tide, apply it to the charted depth to obtain a working estimate of actual depth at the time of interest. (REPRINTED WITH PERMISSION FROM *THE WEEKEND NAVIGATOR* BY BOB SWEET)

You can also access these data from NOS on the Internet (www.oceanservice.noaa.gov). From the home page, select Tides and Currents, which will guide you through the tide prediction program. Alternatively, go to http://tidesandcurrents.noaa.gov, which will guide you to the NOS's tide predictions as well as Great Lakes water levels and other NOAA products.

Although the NOS data and the tables made from them are dependable, do not follow them unthinkingly. Local conditions such as storms, wind direction and strength, and barometric pressure affect tidal levels significantly.

The depths of water shown on your chart are averages, with some low tides being higher than the charted depths and some being lower. Tide tables tell you when to expect the next high or low tide, and also how much higher or lower than the mean the tide is *predicted* to be. Add or subtract this difference to the charted depth of the water to find out how much water *may* be under your keel at the next high or low tide. While doing so, don't forget to consider the amount of water your boat *draws*, or the distance your boat extends beneath the water's surface (Figure 9-42).

There are no tide tables for western rivers. NOS *Nautical Chart Catalog 4* lists available bulletins of lake and river pool levels by month, however, and some newspapers give pool levels daily. River pools are the lakes formed by dams.

Tidal Currents

In bays, estuaries, gulfs, and other coastal areas with substantial tides, it stands to reason that there must be substantial horizontal movements of water in and out with the tides, and indeed this is true. Where these tidal currents are weak relative to the speed of your boat, you can probably ignore them, but where they are substantial, they must be taken into account. Otherwise, your course over ground will diverge widely from your intended course, and you could navigate your boat into danger. We have already touched upon the two ways of compensating for tidal currents. The first is to observe how your course is being influenced, and counter that effect as you go along. The second is to obtain a prediction of the tidal current and apply a counteracting course adjust-

ment from the moment you begin the affected leg or legs of your journey. The latter approach requires *Tidal Current Tables*, which, like the *Tide Tables*, are prepared but no longer printed by the NOS. These are available from commercial publishers, and in smaller local editions from marine suppliers, or by visiting http://tidesandcurrents.noaa.gov.

Electronic Navigation

One of the most exciting developments to impact marine navigation is the advent of stand-alone electronic instruments to aid navigation. This movement started during World War II with the invention and implementation of loran (long range navigation). This system enabled vessels and aircraft to fix their positions without reference to surrounding landmarks or celestial bodies and with a precision and accuracy never before attained. After the war, loran became the primary electronic tool for marine coastal navigation. As receiver costs were lowered, the system became attractive to recreational boaters and soon found widespread usage.

The global positioning system (GPS) became the next evolution of electronic navigation. It became fully functional in 1994 and totally replaced loran in 2010. GPS receivers continue to improve, adding more and more exciting features and at costs well within the means of most boaters.

There are other electronic navigation tools that won't be covered here, including **radar** (for seeing objects in poor visibility) and **depth sounders** (for plotting assistance when used with charts showing water depths).

GPS

GPS is *everywhere!* This satellite-based system provides extremely accurate navigational information from any place on the globe that has an unobstructed view of the heavens. (But don't expect it to work in the deep valleys of West Virginia!)

There are 24 active satellites with about seven spares in the system, and they are arranged and programmed to provide continuous worldwide coverage at any time, day or night, no matter what the weather. Your receiver will tell you what satellites it is currently using (the satellites being used change as their usefulness increases and decreases), and where they are in your sky (Figure 9-43).

The system is managed by the U.S. Department of Defense. Prior to May 1, 2000, the system was randomly degraded (called Selected Availability, or SA) to keep enemies of the United States from using our own system to very accurately target their missiles. Since that date, SA is no longer in use. The end result is a public navigational system that is accurate to within 15 meters (49.2 feet) or less 95% of the time. (There is a military-only version that is even more accurate.)

During the period when SA was used, another system, *Differential GPS* (DGPS), was developed and deployed, mostly along the U.S. coasts and the shores of the Great Lakes. DGPS is a land-based supplement to GPS that effectively corrected the errors introduced by SA. This was necessary to provide continuously accurate information around harbors and inlets, where SA degraded the information enough to become dangerous.

DGPS requires a second receiver on the vessel, but it provides super-accurate (errors of less than 5 meters or 16.4 feet) information where it is needed the most—around the hard stuff. Thus, it remains useful even after the termination of SA.

GPS uses the time reception differences between several satellites and the receiver to establish multiple LOPs and, thus, an electronic fix. Usually, there are at least five and as many as twelve usable satellites available at any given time, and the receiver constantly chooses the most accurate satellites to use.

GPS receivers may be permanently installed or handheld. While permanently mounted receivers are likely to have more features and be somewhat easier to operate, the less expensive, lightweight receivers are usually just as accurate. Some of the handheld receivers are extremely feature-rich, and the principle of "more features equal more money" is very much the case. Just know that a unit with many features carries the downside of operational complexity, so the learning curve may be long and only constant practice will enable the operator to retain the skills.

The one operational necessity often overlooked by the user is that the datum used in your GPS receiver must match the datum on your chart. If there is a mismatch, the location you mark on your chart may be inaccurate.

Simple but very accurate GPS receivers are priced in the $100 to $150 range. These will satisfy the needs, though perhaps not all the wants, of most boaters.

GPS relies on the establishment of waypoints. Each *waypoint* is a pair of coordinates describing a unique location on the globe—usually either a place we want to go to or come from, or a place we want to be sure to avoid. Both systems enable the mariner to establish routes to follow by the use of one or more waypoints in sequence.

These waypoints are entered into the receiver (and also on the chart). The receiver will then tell the crew the bearing and distance to the waypoint, whether or not you are on course for the waypoint (and what to do to get back on course), your speed over the ground, your ETA, and when you have arrived without doing a calculation.

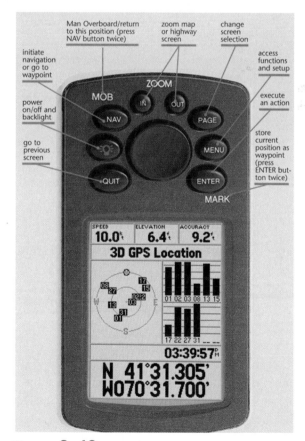

Figure 9-43. A handheld GPS receiver and its features.
(REPRINTED WITH PERMISSION FROM *USING GPS: A CAPTAIN'S QUICK GUIDE* BY BOB SWEET)

The one thing neither system will do is tell you what is between you and each waypoint, unless your receiver has a built-in moving map. There may be some very hard stuff in your path, such as rocks, and this is where a chart is needed. To keep good water under your keel at all times, lay out your course, with its waypoints, on the paper chart first, and then transfer the waypoint information into your receiver. Now you can have a pleasant voyage.

WAAS

There is another GPS enhancement called the *wide area augmentation system* (WAAS) that employs satellites that are stationary relative to the earth. They communicate with ground stations whose positions are accurately known, called geodetic markers. The ground stations determine the error in their basic GPS position. The resulting corrected information is transmitted to the WAAS satellites that in turn send the corrected data to GPS receivers. WAAS is standard in GPS receivers manufactured in the last few years. It is employed in the United States as well as neighboring countries. The same technology is employed throughout the world under different names. The stated horizontal accuracy of a GPS receiver with WAAS is 2.5 meters or 8.2 feet.

GPS Electronic Charting

The majority of recently manufactured nautical GPS receivers have built-in marine charts. You can display the current location of your vessel on these charts. Handheld units have the disadvantage of a small viewing screen. Fixed-mount GPS receivers have a larger display screen and often have more navigational features; they are often called *chartplotters* (Figure 9-44). Chartplotter features are gradually being incorporated into handhelds so the meaning of the term chartplotter is becoming blurred. The map screens in early GPS receivers displayed only in black and white and shades of gray but most GPS receivers manufactured today are in color. The quality of the color displays is excellent, even in direct sunlight.

GPS receivers can be integrated with other electronic navigation equipment through data communication lines. The National Marine Electronics Association (NMEA) has established standards that permit integrating most marine electronic devices. Older electronics conform to NMEA 0183 standard, which is slowly being phased out in favor of the newer NMEA 2000 standard. These standards are not electrically interchangeable, but can be connected with adapters. Some equipment manufacturers have unique interconnection systems. Equipment interconnection can be complicated, and should be investigated carefully when acquiring new equipment. Some GPS receivers allow split-screen display. For example, depth sounder information may be displayed on the GPS on one side of the screen while a marine chart is displayed on the other. The GPS receiver calculates all the navigation information that previously had to be done manually. GPS can calculate and display how much a vessel is off course, called *cross-track error*. Previously cross-track errors were difficult to compute and could only be estimated. Always remember that the GPS receiver with all its features doesn't know all the hazards that lie ahead. Also, when equipment power is lost you may have to rely on paper charts and a nonelectric compass. You still have the ultimate responsibility to navigate.

Electronic Chart Display Information System (ECDIS)

ECDIS is the most advanced electronic navigation technology. It can interface with existing chartplotters and other navigation equipment but it requires additional specialized equipment and software to use most of its features. It must be installed on new cargo ships of 3,000 tons or greater. There are no existing cruise ships large enough to require it. It obtains its raw navigational data from the existing sources such as GPS satellites and NOAA data, and the benefits are mainly in greater accuracy and sophisticated displays. For example, NOAA's latest wind vector displays are configured for ECDIS. It is currently very expensive, but with rapid advances in technology it may eventually become affordable for recreational boaters.

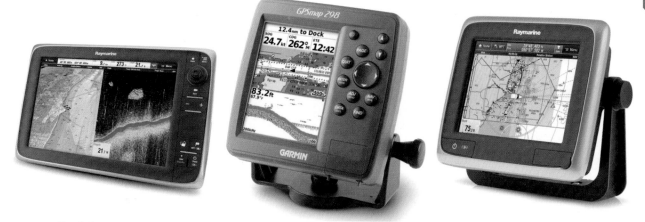

Figure **9-44.** A selection of chartplotters. Five- to 10-inch screens are typical, and many models can also display depth sounder and radar information if properly interfaced. (COURTESY GARMIN AND RAYMARINE)

GPS Operation

The following is a sequence of events for basic operation of a GPS receiver. The use of GPS is quite intuitive as long as you have a good understanding of basic navigation principles—which is why we've saved electronic navigation for the end of this chapter.

Imagine a simple trip in which you leave a marina or launch ramp, go to one or two buoys, then return to the starting point. With your unit's operating manual at hand, let's see what happens.

When the GPS receiver is turned on, it immediately searches the sky to locate the available satellites, displaying the serial number and relative signal strength of each satellite it locates. The unit selects the optimal satellites, and when it is satisfied that it knows its current location and is ready for use, the screen will change to display your current Lat/Lo coordinates (Figure 9-45). The receiver remembers the satellites it used last, so it may take awhile to find your current location the first time you use it. (It may be looking for the satellites over China, where it probably was built!) Subsequent initializations occur in seconds, however. If it fails to find four satisfactory satellites, it will either continue to search or announce that its accuracy is degraded or that it cannot be used. The GPS antenna requires relatively open access to the sky.

The receiver has a general menu, on which you will find all its main features listed. These include a *setup* feature. The setup menu allows you to adjust screen contrast and select things such as units of

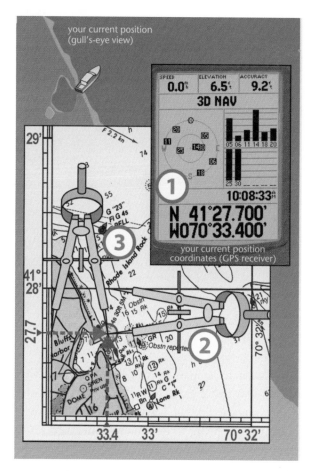

Figure **9-45.** Using GPS to figure out where you are. Read your latitude and longitude coordinates from your GPS receiver (1), then plot the latitude (2) and longitude (3) on your chart to locate your position. (REPRINTED WITH PERMISSION FROM *USING GPS: A CAPTAIN'S QUICK GUIDE* BY BOB SWEET)

measure, audible alarms, and datum. The default settings are usually good enough to become familiar with basic operations.

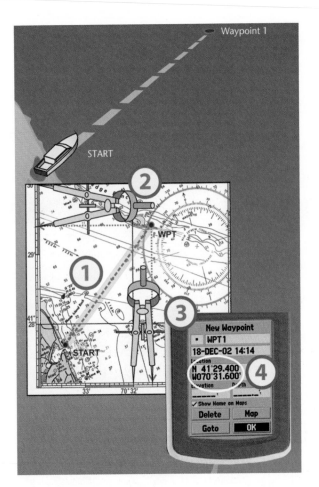

Figure **9-46.** Using GPS to figure out where you are going. Mark on the chart the position or waypoint you wish to go to, then plot the course from your current position to that destination (1), making sure there are no intervening ledges or other hazards. Next, use dividers to ascertain the latitude (2) and longitude (3) of the waypoint, and enter these coordinates into your GPS receiver (4). Your GPS will now give you the course and distance to the waypoint. (REPRINTED WITH PERMISSION FROM *USING GPS: A CAPTAIN'S QUICK GUIDE* BY BOB SWEET)

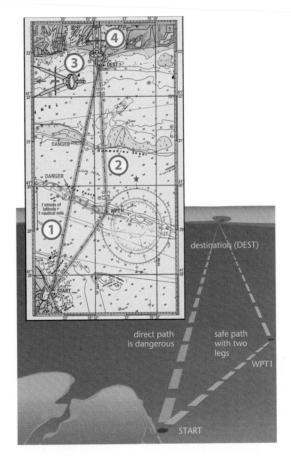

Figure **9-47.** Using GPS to navigate a route with more than one leg. In this example the direct route to your ultimate destination (1) would take you across a shoal, so you must add a dogleg (2) around the hazard. Once the coordinates of the destination are measured (3 and 4) and entered into your GPS receiver along with the coordinates of the intermediate waypoint (WPT1), you can store this sequence of two waypoints as a route. Selecting this route instructs the GPS receiver to direct you first to WPT1 and then to your destination waypoint. (REPRINTED WITH PERMISSION FROM *USING GPS: A CAPTAIN'S QUICK GUIDE* BY BOB SWEET)

The next step is to select the feature that allows you to program waypoints (Figure 9-46). There, you can add the waypoints of the trip you're planning. In order to do this, you need to know the Lat/Lo for each waypoint. If you have a GPS with electronic charts, the waypoints for your trip may be selected from a waypoint list or they may be derived by measuring them directly from a paper chart. The waypoint for your dock or launch ramp will not be there, but you can find it simply by moving the cursor over the relevant point. If you're using a simple GPS without electronic charts, you'll need to pick off the coordinates of your waypoints from the paper chart using dividers.

Once underway, select the first waypoint of the trip from the waypoint list (Figure 9-46). Press the **Go To** button, and the unit will display the course required to get to that waypoint. If your boat wanders off course, the unit provides instructions to get back on course. When you arrive at that waypoint, which might be a buoy or simply a safe water location in midchannel where you wish to change course, you should select the next waypoint from the list and press Go To again. Repeat this process until you reach your final destination.

Alternatively, you can add all these waypoints to a **Route** file, and when you select that route, the unit will automatically call up each waypoint in its proper sequence and provide the course to steer for the next waypoint. A feature called **Return**

Course will reverse the waypoints to provide directions to return home. Many other features augment the ones described here, including ones that provide the distance and time required to complete each leg of the trip. The only difference between this simple exercise and a longer, more complex trip is the number of waypoints to be entered (Figure 9-47). Also, you should review or **prequalify** the trip on an up-to-date chart to be sure the programmed route does not lead you into obstacles or across hazards. If it does, you'll have to program doglegs with additional waypoints to steer the boat around obstructions.

Some skippers with chartplotters bypass the entire process of using waypoints. They simply steer their boats visually, using the marker on the screen that shows their boat's real-time location superimposed on the chart. This technique can invite risks when operating in crowded areas, however, if the skipper spends too much time studying the chart and not enough time watching the helm.

Practice Your Art

It takes practice to become proficient at navigating. Practice it often, as it can slip away easily. No matter how proficient you become, though, practice the "buddy system." If you move into unfamiliar waters, it is advisable to travel with a companion vessel piloted by someone familiar with the area. Not only will you feel more comfortable, but you will probably have more fun in the process. And that is what it is all about.

A Further Invitation

See www.cgaux.org for the Auxiliary courses available to enhance your skills in this area.

Ways to Learn More

Boat Navigation for the Rest of Us: Finding Your Way by Eye and Electronics. Bill Brogdon. Camden, Maine: International Marine, 2001.

Chapman Piloting & Seamanship. 66th ed. Charles B. Husick. New York: Hearst Books, 2009. Chapters 13, 15, 16, 17, 18, and 21.

Emergency Navigation: Improvised and No-Instrument Methods for the Prudent Mariner. 2nd ed. David Burch. Camden, Maine: International Marine, 2008.

Fast Powerboat Seamanship: The Complete Guide to Boat Handling, Navigation, and Safety. Dag Pike. Camden, Maine: International Marine, 2004.

GPS for Mariners. 2nd ed. Bob Sweet. Camden, Maine: International Marine, 2011.

How to Read a Nautical Chart: A Captain's Quick Guide. Nigel Calder. Camden, Maine: International Marine, 2008.

How to Read a Nautical Chart: A Complete Guide to Using and Understanding Electronic and Paper Charts. 2nd ed. Nigel Calder. Camden, Maine: International Marine, 2012.

Outboard Boater's Handbook: Advanced Seamanship and Practical Skills. David Getchell. Camden, Maine: International Marine, 1994.

The Practical Encyclopedia of Boating: An A–Z Compendium of Navigation, Seamanship, Boat Maintenance, and Nautical Wisdom. John Vigor. Camden, Maine: International Marine, 2007.

The Practical Mariner's Book of Knowledge: 460 Sea-Tested Rules of Thumb for Almost Every Boating Situation. 2nd ed. John Vigor. Camden, Maine: International Marine, 2013.

Radar for Mariners. David Burch. Camden, Maine: International Marine, 2004.

Reed's Skipper's Handbook for Sail and Power. 4th ed. Malcolm Pearson. Camden, Maine: International Marine, 2005.

Seamanship Secrets: 185 Tips and Techniques for Better Navigation, Cruise Planning, and Boat Handling Under Power or Sail. John Jamieson. Camden, Maine: International Marine, 2009.

Using GPS: A Captain's Quick Guide. Bob Sweet. Camden, Maine: International Marine, 2004.

The Weekend Navigator: Simple Boat Navigation with GPS and Electronics. 2nd ed. Bob Sweet. Camden, Maine: International Marine, 2011.

MORE BOATING SKILLS

Practice Questions

IMPORTANT BOATING TERMS
In the following exercise, match the words in the column on the left with the definitions in the column on the right. In the blank space to the left of each term, write the letter of the item that best matches it. Do not use an item in the right-hand column more than once.

THE ITEMS

1. _____ datum
2. _____ longitude line
3. _____ 1 minute of latitude
4. _____ Mercator projection
5. _____ latitude line
6. _____ variation
7. _____ knot
8. _____ correct a compass reading
9. _____ direction a compass points
10. _____ nautical mile

THE RESPONSES

a. 1 nautical mile
b. compass error caused by earth's magnetic field
c. make adjustments for effects of variation and deviation
d. meridian
e. 1.15 statute miles
f. benchmark
g. parallel
h. magnetic north
i. 1 nautical mile per hour
j. used in most nautical charts

Multiple-Choice Items

In the following items, choose the best response:

9-1. The best binocular for use on a recreational vessel is

a. 50 x 7
b. 15 x 35
c. 7 x 50
d. 7 x 35

9-2. For overall planning on a long cruise, navigators should select a chart with

a. a small scale that shows a large area
b. a large amount of landmass shown
c. a large scale
d. an unknown date of revision

9-3. 1 minute of latitude equals

a. 1 statute mile
b. 1 nautical mile
c. 60 nautical miles
d. 60 statute miles

9-4. Charts are being revised to use only the following datum for soundings:

a. mean low water
b. low water
c. lower low water
d. mean lower low water

9-5. Which of the following measures distances north or south of the equator?

a. a great circle
b. latitude
c. longitude
d. the prime meridian

9-6. Which scale of a chart should never be used for measuring distances?

a. longitude scale
b. latitude scale
c. the chart's distance scale
d. none of the above

Multiple-Choice Items (continued)

9-7. The direction of a course is the angle it makes with a

a. line of position
b. the equator
c. line of latitude
d. meridian

9-8. You can find the amount of variation in your boating area by

a. finding the difference between the direction a magnetic compass points and the direction it should point
b. looking at a compass rose on the chart of the area
c. looking in the chart catalog
d. looking at *Chart No. 1*

9-9. If you measure the direction of a course line from a chart meridian, you have a

a. magnetic direction
b. compass direction
c. true direction
d. line of position

9-10. Variation is the difference between

a. your course heading and your intended heading
b. magnetic north and the direction your compass needle points
c. true north and magnetic north
d. a vessel's heading and its course direction

9-11. Deviation is a compass error caused by

a. the earth's magnetic field at your position
b. a cheap compass
c. proximity to the north geographic pole
d. magnetic influences aboard your vessel

9-12. The technical term for the benchmark from which a marine chart's vertical and horizontal measurements are made is

a. latitude
b. longitude
c. fathom
d. datum

9-13. Direction can be determined on a Mercator chart by using the

a. direction scale
b. variation
c. compass rose
d. chart block

9-14. A speed table is used to

a. determine speed from a tachometer reading
b. measure distances
c. calibrate your speedometer
d. tell you what the maximum legal speeds are

9-15. The vertical datum of a chart

a. helps you know how far apart two points are
b. is the North American 1983 datum
c. helps you know where you are
d. helps you know how much clearance there is under a bridge

9-16. To correct a compass reading

a. add easterly variations
b. add magnetic deviations
c. add westerly variations
d. add westerly deviations

9-17. Mercator projections are made by projecting the earth's surface onto a

a. cone
b. cylinder
c. chart
d. map

9-18. On a chart, shallow water is

a. white
b. light green
c. light blue
d. light yellow

9-19. If you travel at a speed of 12 knots for 10 minutes, you will have gone how far?

a. 2.0 miles
b. 2.0 nautical miles
c. 3.0 miles
d. 3.0 nautical miles

9-20. In an area with a variation of 12°E, your heading is 130° by your compass. The deviation for this heading is 3°W. What is your true heading?

a. 121°
b. 145°
c. 115°
d. 139°

Multiple-Choice Items (continued)

9-21. A position determined by the intersection of two LOPs is

a. an estimated position
b. a range line of position
c. a fix
d. an advanced line of position

9-22. A fix is labeled with

a. a dot and a circle
b. an X
c. a square
d. a half-circle

9-23. How long will it take you to go 3 miles at a speed of 20 knots?

a. 60 minutes
b. 6.67 minutes
c. 9 minutes
d. 12 minutes

9-24. How fast do you have to go to cover 6 nautical miles in 20 minutes?

a. 6.67 knots
b. 18 knots
c. 3 knots
d. 6 knots

chapter 10

Powering Your Boat

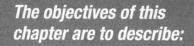

The objectives of this chapter are to describe:

✔ The types and characteristics of marine engines.

✔ The differences between two- and four-stroke engines.

✔ The fundamentals of marine engine operation and how to care for a boat's engine.

✔ The dangers of substituting automobile parts for marine engine parts.

✔ What to consider when selecting gasoline for your marine engine.

✔ The effects of alcohol on an engine's fuel system.

✔ The importance of the battery and how to maintain it properly.

✔ 110-volt electrical dangers.

✔ How to prevent galvanic action.

✔ Steps for winterization and spring commissioning of your boat.

✔ Basic troubleshooting for causes of engine failure.

RECREATIONAL POWERBOATS have come a long way since the internal combustion engine supplanted steam engines more than a century ago. After its invention, the internal combustion engine soon appeared in horseless carriages and in small boats, and recreational boating was off

(COURTESY BOMBARDIER RECREATIONAL PRODUCTS)

and running. We looked briefly at engines and drivetrains in Chapter 1; in this chapter we'll explore marine engines and their operation in greater depth.

Types of Marine Engines

Marine internal combustion engines can be classified according to their installation, their operating cycles, and the fuels they use.

Installation

One type of marine engine installation is entirely within a boat's hull, and the engine is linked to the boat's propeller by a propeller shaft. Since the engine and the gears that connect it to its propeller shaft are entirely inside the hull, the engine is called an *inboard* (Figures 10-1 and 10-2).

In a second type of installation, the engine itself is in the boat's hull, but it connects to the boat's propeller through a system of gears mounted on the outside of the transom. This is a *stern-drive engine*, sometimes called an *inboard/outboard* or I/O (Figure 10-3)

A third installation mounts the motor to the boat's transom or to a bracket attached to the transom. This is an *outboard* motor (Figure 10-4).

Operating Cycle

An internal combustion gasoline engine works by drawing in a mixture of fuel and air, compressing it into a smaller volume, igniting it to expand the gases and produce power, and exhausting the spent gases. *Two-cycle gas engines* combine the intake and compression steps and the expansion and exhaust steps and therefore require just one revolution of their internal parts to complete all four processes. *Four-cycle engines* require two revolutions because they complete each of the four steps

Figure **10-1.** Like most inboard-mounted engines, GM's Vortec marine engines are marinized adaptations of vehicle engines. The Vortec 8100 (left) is a big-block V-8 used in stern-drive and inboard boats, often in a twin-engine configuration. The engine delivers 392 hp at 4,600 rpm. Marine features include a high-torque marine camshaft and provision for marine ancillaries such as a seawater pump, external heat exchanger (to keep seawater out of the intake manifold), and marine oil cooler. The Vortec 5700 (right) is a small-block V-8 also used in stern-drive, inboard, and twin-engine applications. This engine delivers 292 hp at 4,800 rpm. Both engines burn regular unleaded gas, and both employ sophisticated electronic fuel injection and electronic ignition. The engines are shown as delivered to marine engine suppliers, who then add the ancillary components prior to reselling or installing the engines. (COURTESY GM POWERTRAIN)

Figure **10-2.** The Mercury 8-1S inboard engine was designed specifically for marine applications. (COURTESY MERCURY MARINE)

Figure **10-3.** The MerCruiser 5.0-liter Bravo stern-drive engine. (COURTESY MERCURY MARINE)

Figure **10-4.** Outboard motors are a popular form of power for small boats. (COURTESY YAMAHA)

Figure **10-5.** Yamaha's VZ 150 hp direct-injected outboard is representative of the new breed of direct-injected two-stroke outboards. (COURTESY YAMAHA)

Figure **10-6.** A cutaway view of Yamaha's 250 hp four-stroke outboard. (COURTESY YAMAHA)

separately. Two- and four-cycle engines are also called **two-stroke** and **four-stroke engines**, respectively (Figures 10-5 and 10-6).

Inboard and stern-drive engines are almost always four-stroke engines. Most outboards are two-stroke, although four-cycle outboards are becoming increasingly popular, for reasons outlined below.

Differences between Two- and Four-Stroke Engines

There are two major differences between engines with two- and four-stroke cycles (Figures 10-7 and 10-8). First, for a given power rating, two-stroke engines weigh less than four-stroke engines. On a

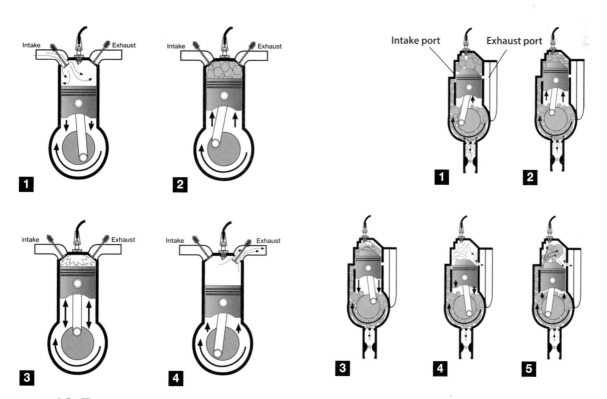

Figure **10-7.** **Left:** The four-stroke engine cycle illustrated. **Right:** The two-stroke engine cycle illustrated. (REPRINTED WITH PERMISSION FROM *OUTBOARD ENGINES* BY EDWIN R. SHERMAN)

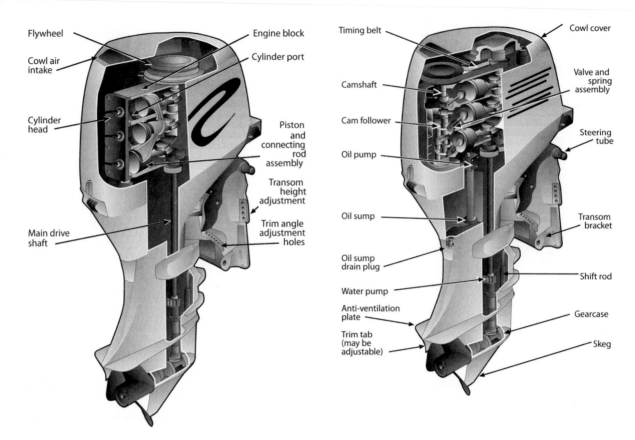

Figure 10-8. Cutaway comparisons of a two-stroke (left) and a four-stroke (right) outboard. (REPRINTED WITH PERMISSION FROM *OUTBOARD ENGINES* BY EDWIN R. SHERMAN)

small boat this is an important consideration, and this is the main reason why, formerly, almost all outboard engines were two-stroke.

The second difference is in the way the engines are lubricated. A four-stroke engine has a **crankcase** that holds oil to lubricate moving engine parts. The oil recirculates and is not burned with the fuel. The crankcase of a two-stroke gasoline outboard engine, on the other hand, does not contain oil. Instead, it is lubricated from oil mixed with the fuel.

Since two-stroke engines burn fuel less efficiently than four-stroke engines, and since their exhausts contain unburned oil along with unburned fuel, two-stroke engines are a greater source of water and air pollution than are four-stroke engines. This is why small engines such as lawnmower engines, all of which are two-stroke, contribute much more pollution than would be expected based on their proportionate use alone. The least polluting engines are four-stroke engines with fuel injection systems.

Beginning in 1998, the U.S Environmental Protection Agency (EPA) set emission standards

for marine engines that will, eventually, cut hydrocarbon emissions by as much as 75%, and this has forced two-stroke engines to become much more efficient. Two-stroke outboard engines with electronic fuel injection (EFI) are more efficient than carbureted engines, and direct-injected two-strokes are more efficient still.

Until recent years, it was necessary to add oil to the fuel in a two-stroke outboard engine's fuel tank or to buy premixed fuel, but most larger two-stroke engines now do this job for you. These engines have special reservoirs for storing oil, which is either metered into the fuel before it enters the engine or injected into the fuel as the fuel is injected into the engine. Motors with **variable-ratio oilers** (VROs) vary the amount of oil mixed with the fuel according to engine speed.

Be sure to use the proper oil in your two-stroke engine, one made especially for mixing with your fuel. There are separate types of oil for air- and water-cooled engines. Look at the label on the container. It should say "TC-W," for example, if it is for two-cycle, watercooled engines.

Four-stroke engines are heavier and more expensive than two-strokes, but their weights have decreased markedly in recent years, and they are much quieter. Four-strokes also are proving more reliable and durable than two-strokes, are more fuel-efficient (although direct-injected two-strokes are competitive), and, above all, cause less pollution because no oil is discharged with the exhaust. Their popularity is expanding rapidly as a result.

Type of Fuel

The third classification of marine engines is by the fuel they use—gasoline or diesel. Diesel engines operate more efficiently than gasoline engines, burning about 40% less fuel for a given power output. Diesel and gasoline fuel cost about the same, but diesel engines are less expensive to operate for most purposes (Figure 10-9).

Diesel engines have fewer moving parts than gasoline engines, which means greater reliability and fewer maintenance problems. Thus, diesel engines enjoy a reputation for long-term reliability.

Diesel engines have drawbacks, however. Because of the way they work, they are generally larger and heavier than gasoline engines (though precision engineering has reduced their size and weight substantially over the past two decades), and as a result, they are also more expensive. Over time, though, their higher initial cost is offset somewhat by savings in fuel and maintenance costs.

Also because of the way they operate, diesel engines vibrate more than gasoline engines and are noisier. The vibrations tend to loosen bolts, so crankcase and gearcase attachments must be checked and tightened periodically.

Figure **10-9.** Economy and reliability are reasons why most workboats, such as the fishing vessel pictured above, are diesel powered. (COURTESY NOAA)

Risks from Fuel

Gasoline is volatile; that is, it gives off fumes very easily. These fumes are highly flammable, and, being heavier than air, they can pool in a boat's bilge and other interior spaces, awaiting only a spark for ignition. In a confined area, they are explosive. (In an automobile, gasoline fumes escaping from the fuel tank, fuel line, or engine dissipate into the surroundings rather than pooling within the vehicle.) Many boat fires and explosions—sometimes fatal—have been caused by ignition of gasoline vapors. Coexisting safely with an inboard or stern-drive gasoline engine requires a level of diligence, but this diligence should become second nature after a short time. You shouldn't use gasoline mixed with ethanol. Ethanol is a solvent that can cause marine engines and fiberglass tanks to fail. Marine fuel dealers don't offer ethanol-enriched fuel.

Diesel fuel does not give off fumes as readily as gasoline, and the fumes it does give off have a higher flash point. This means that it takes a lot more heat to ignite diesel fuel than it does to ignite gasoline. Thus, diesel fuel has a deserved reputation for being safer than gasoline. This is the biggest reason why diesel engines have largely supplanted gas engines in auxiliary sailboats. In small powerboats, however, the larger power-to-weight ratio of a gas engine continues to favor it.

Diesel fuel is not entirely free from risk, however. Any fuel line can rupture and spew its contents onto a hot exhaust manifold, thereby igniting the fuel. If diesel fuel leaks into the bilge, any fire in the bilge will use it as a fuel.

Further, diesel fuel is subject to problems of its own. First, because it is injected into engines, it must be very clean and free of water. To ensure this, a diesel engine needs additional fuel filters, which should be changed frequently. A second disadvantage is that diesel fuel gels at very cold temperatures. To prevent this (should you ever find yourself boating on a frigid winter day!), add an inhibitor in cold weather. Third, a fuel-eating fungus can form in diesel fuel, and when present, it clogs fuel injectors. Special antimicrobial agents have been developed as fuel additives to retard fungus formation.

Diesel engines are the usual choice in boats longer than 35 feet for a number of reasons, including their greater fuel efficiency, reliability, durability, and safety. In addition, a diesel engine can run continously at 90% of its maximum rated engine speed without ill effects, whereas a gas engine burns excessive fuel and wears out prematurely when run continously at such high speeds. Further, a diesel develops more torque at cruising speeds than a gas engine. The net result is that a 200-horsepower (hp) diesel can cruise a 35-foot boat as fast as a 300 hp gas engine.

Diesel and gasoline engines are about equally popular in inboard boats between 28 and 35 feet long, each having distinct advantages and disadvantages. But gasoline remains the dominant fuel for the outboard, stern-drive, and smaller inboard boats that are the main focus of this book. Gasoline engines are quieter, less smelly, less expensive, and lighter than diesels, and in lightly used recreational boats the greater durability and operating economy of a diesel fail to outweigh its higher initial cost. For the balance of this chapter, therefore, although we will call attention to key distinctions between diesel and gasoline engines where appropriate, our discussion will center on gasoline engines.

Inboard Engines

An inboard engine is usually installed close to amidships and faces forward, as in an automobile with rear-wheel drive. It is connected to a propeller shaft by a clutch and a system of reduction and reverse gears housed in a marine transmission, or gearbox, at the back end of the engine. The clutch serves to disengage the crankshaft from the propeller shaft so that the engine can run without moving the boat. The clutch and associated gears also enable the boat to go forward or in reverse. This type of inboard drivetrain is termed an *in-line* or *direct-drive inboard*, with the engine, gearbox, and propeller shaft laid out in a straight line that often extends half the boat's length (Figure 10-10).

In some instances, the inboard engine faces aft, and its crankshaft is connected to a gearbox at the forward end of the engine. The gearbox redirects

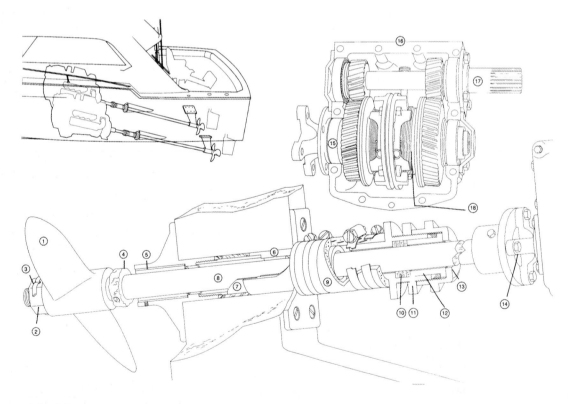

Figure **10-10.** Typical components of a direct-drive installation: (1) propeller; (2) retaining nut; (3) cotter pin; (4) zinc anode; (5) rubber sleeve (Cutless) bearing; (6) bearing; (7) stern tube; (8) propeller shaft; (9) flexible stuffing box; (10) packing rings; (11) locking nut; (12) compression spacer; (13) adjusting nut; (14) shaft coupling; (15) output shaft; (16) transmission, or gearbox; (17) input shaft; (18) clutch discs. (COURTESY JIM SOLLERS; REPRINTED WITH PERMISSION FROM *BOATOWNER'S MECHANICAL AND ELECTRICAL MANUAL*, THIRD EDITION, BY NIGEL CALDER)

the crankshaft torque sternward through a series of gears before mating with the propeller shaft. This form of installation is a *V-drive inboard*, and its chief advantage is that it permits the engine to be farther aft, leaving more room forward for accommodations or fuel tanks (Figures 10-11 and 10-12).

Regardless of the drivetrain type, most inboard engines require a **reduction gear**, the purpose of which is to allow the engine to turn at higher speeds than the propeller. This permits a larger, more efficient propeller to be mated with a compact, efficient, high-speed engine. If the prop were to turn at the same speed as the engine, it would have to be so small as to develop very little thrust. Gear ratios commonly range from 1.5:1 (1,500 revolutions per minute from the engine delivering 1,000 rpm to the propeller) to 3:1 (1,500 engine rpm delivering 500 propeller rpm).

Direct Drive vs. V-Drive

A direct-drive engine provides better fore-and-aft balance and economy than a V-drive. It is the simplest, least expensive, and most trouble free of all inboard engine installations. On the other hand, a V-drive engine is installed nearer the boat's stern, which moves the boat's center of gravity aft and can enhance desirable performance characteristics in appropriately designed hulls while making room forward for things such as accommodations, tankage, and storage.

Jet Drives

As we saw in Chapter 4, a jet drive consists of a power plant, usually a gasoline-powered inboard engine, turning an impeller (a small propeller) that is enclosed in a relatively narrow tube-like housing. The impeller sucks water into the housing and expels that water out the back of the boat through a steerable nozzle. This pumping and ejection action propels the boat through the water, and the boat is steered by directing the jet of water from the steerable nozzle on the stern of the boat. Personal watercraft (PWC) are powered by comparatively small jet-drive engines.

Since steering is accomplished by directing a jet of water, the boat *must* maintain a rather high throttle setting or the steering becomes sluggish. At very low throttle there is no steerage at all, and this accounts for many PWC accidents.

Most jet drives do not have a reverse gear, though some provide a reversing mechanism in the form of a metal shroud, or clamshell, that lowers over the jet-drive outlet and deflects the jet forward. This reverse mechanism should *not* be used for braking action.

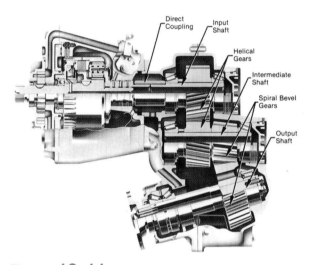

Figure **10-11.** Cutaway view of a BorgWarner V-drive. (COURTESY TRANS ATLANTIC DIESELS)

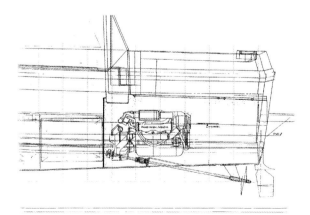

Figure **10-12.** A typical V-drive installation, this one in a planing catamaran designed by John Kiley. (COURTESY JOHN KILEY; REPRINTED WITH PERMISSION FROM *SORENSEN'S GUIDE TO POWERBOATS* BY ERIC SORENSEN)

Tunnel Drives

A *tunnel drive* is a variant of a direct drive in which the propeller shaft, after exiting the hull, is recessed into a trough, or tunnel, that extends aft to the stern. This enables the shaft's thrust angle to be more nearly parallel with the water's surface, thus converting the engine's power output more efficiently into forward thrust. The tunnel also acts as a protective shroud around the propeller, which is why tunnel drives are often chosen by boaters operating in shallow waters.

Instead of a tunnel drive, some hulls feature a shallower trough known as a *propeller pocket*, which is just a quarter to a third of the propeller diameter in depth. Though it does not completely house the propeller, a properly designed pocket will nevertheless reduce the propeller shaft angle, decrease the boat's draft, allow the engine to be moved farther aft, and accommodate a larger, more efficient propeller than a standard hull (Figure 10-13).

Stern-Drive Engines

In a stern-drive engine, the engine itself is coupled to an *outdrive*, which is a system of gears (analogous to the gearbox of an inboard engine) sometimes called the lower unit. The engine is mounted inside the boat near its stern, while the outdrive is mounted outside the hull, on the transom. The outdrive is articulated so that it can swing the propeller from side to side like an outboard propeller for steering. It can also be raised and lowered like an outboard lower unit, permitting easy removal of debris from the propeller and making it possible to operate in shallow waters. It cannot, however, be raised clear of the water—a disadvantage that is of more consequence in salt water than fresh.

Stern-drive units are considerably more expensive than direct drive, and their maintenance and

Figure **10-13.** Shamrock's PocketDrive shows how a recessed prop pocket can achieve reduced draft. (COURTESY SHAMROCK)

repair are also costly. Their gears are complex and easily damaged. Still, stern drives offer the speed and trim advantages of an outboard with an inboard's fuel efficiency and quietness, making them popular in boats less than 30 feet long. Stern drives, like outboards, are rarely found on boats longer than 35 feet (other than light racing boats), because their relatively small props simply don't develop enough thrust for bigger, heavier boats.

Outboard Motors

The third type of installation is an outboard motor, which fastens to a boat's transom or to a bracket that is in turn fastened to the transom. It consists of a power-generating mechanism (the powerhead), a clutch, a gearbox, and a propeller, all in one unit that can be raised out of the water. A few small outboards have built-in fuel tanks, but most draw their fuel either from a portable gas tank (the norm on boats smaller than 16 feet) or one that is permanently installed (the norm on boats longer than 20 feet).

Small outboards have pull starters, but larger ones have electrically operated starter motors and alternators that require batteries. Some small outboards lack clutches and reverse gears. With these, to reverse direction you must turn the motor around so the propeller faces forward.

Stern Drive or Outboard?

Which is better, an outboard or a stern drive? A definitive answer can't be given, but there are important differences in the two engines that should influence your choice.

Outboards weigh less than stern drives of comparable power. A 150 hp two-cycle outboard weighs about 300 to 400 pounds, whereas a stern drive of equivalent power weighs about twice as much. A four-stroke outboard is heavier than a two-stroke but lighter than a stern drive. These differences are important on a small, light boat, which is one reason why outboard power dominates in smaller boats.

On the other hand, a stern-drive engine will use 15% to 30% less fuel than a two-cycle outboard of comparable size, and the difference may be even greater at displacement and trolling speeds. Recent improvements in four-cycle outboards, however, have made them more fuel efficient and have narrowed the stern drive's efficiency advantage. A stern drive requires 6 or more square feet of deck space, whereas an outboard takes up no space within the boat. In addition, when the outboard is on a bracket, the boat can have a full transom.

Stern drives are usually quieter than outboards because the engines are in closed compartments. Four-cycle outboards are much quieter than two-cycle, however, and when the outboard is on a bracket and the boat has a solid transom, even a two-cycle outboard may be the quieter engine.

An important consideration for some owners is that outboard engines and their electrical parts are outside the boat, which somewhat reduces the danger of fire and explosion.

One other point is that boats usually outlast their motors, and outboard motors are easier to replace. If the outboard is small, it can be dismounted and taken to the repair facility. At the end of the day, the decision on the choice of drives is a complex one involving many trade-offs.

Engine Sizes

The International Congress of Marine Industry Associations (ICOMIA) has changed the method and units for measuring engine power, making it easier for boaters to compare engines. In the past, an engine's power was measured at its crankshaft, but this method failed to consider loss of power due to friction in the engine's gear train. As a result, the ratings were usually too high.

As of September 1, 1989, all measures of engine power are made at their propeller shafts except for inboard engines sold without transmissions. This results in lower ratings for marine engines. The reduction is about 5% to 10% for outboards, about 10% to 15% for stern drives because of their extra gears, and about 15% to 20% for inboard engines with hydraulic transmissions.

In addition, ICOMIA changed the units for rating engine power. Previously, the unit was hp, but the new standard is the kilowatt (kW). A kW is the equivalent of 1.34 hp, so if you want to know how many kW of power your 150 hp engine develops, divide 150 by 1.34, which tells you the engine offers about 112 kW of power. To change from kW to hp, multiply kW by 1.34.

A Special Warning!

All inboard and stern-drive engines look like automobile engines, and most use automobile engine blocks, but there are important differences between automobile and marine engines. Most marine engines use special devices for discharging exhaust fumes and cooling water. All marine fuel pumps, alternators, starters, distributors, and other electrical parts are designed specifically to prevent sparks or the release of fumes.

Much of this special "marinized" equipment is necessary since, unlike automobile engines, inboards and stern drives operate in enclosed spaces. Gasoline fumes can collect in these spaces, and equipment that can produce sparks may produce disastrous results. **Never repair a marine engine with automobile parts. The result may be a fire or an explosion.**

Selecting a Propeller

See Chapter 4 for an in-depth discussion of propellers. Matching your boat and engine with a propeller of the right size can make a big difference in performance. A propeller with too little diameter, pitch, or both cannot absorb the engine's full power output, and instead spins ineffectually, producing little thrust (Figure 10-14). It will lead to higher rpm than that recommended by the engine manufacturer, in extreme cases allowing the engine to race over its top rated rpm and destroy itself. A propeller that is too large for the engine, on the other hand—one with too much diameter or pitch—can lead to a laboring engine that will not be able to reach its full rated rpm and highest hp. The engine will smoke and foul its valves.

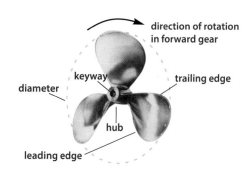

Figure **10-14.** A right-handed, three-bladed prop for an inboard engine. (COURTESY MICHIGAN WHEEL CORPORATION)

There are about fifteen variables that contribute to the proper selection of a propeller for a pleasure craft. Propeller analysis forms are available from propeller manufacturers and dealers, from boat dealers, and also on the Internet. The selection service is usually free, except for special cases that require naval architect services, and the actual selection process is usually accomplished using a computer program.

Induction Systems

The induction system of a gasoline-powered internal combustion engine brings fuel and air together, mixes them in the proper proportion, vaporizes the mixture, and delivers it to the engine. The most critical part of the system is the mixing and vaporizing, which is done by carburetors or fuel injection systems.

Carburetors

Carburetors are complex mechanisms. Modern carburetors operate in as many as four separate modes: idling, accelerating, normal cruise, and sustained high speed. They also operate smoothly through a wide range of engine and air temperatures.

Many outboard motors now have two or more carburetors, which increases their reliability and efficiency. It also increases their complexity. Because of this complexity and all the demands placed on carburetors, it is best to leave their adjustment or overhaul to specialists.

Fuel Injection

Fuel injection systems are replacing carburetors, and are a good response to the complex, critical, and expensive devices that carburetors have become.

Gasoline fuel injection systems use small computers ("little black boxes") to receive information from sensors that determine things such as fuel demand, throttle position, and engine temperature. Some computers also consider air temperature, barometric pressure, amount of carbon monoxide in the exhaust, and other factors.

The computers control the flow of fuel into units that mix it with air and vaporize the mixture before it is fed into the engine. The usefulness of fuel injection in marine gasoline engines has been well demonstrated.

Ignition Systems

After the fuel mixture enters an engine, there must be some means of igniting it. The burning fuel mixture provides the energy that powers the engine.

Diesel Engines

Diesel engines do not have ignition systems, though some do have igniters or glow plugs to help the starting process. Air and fuel are drawn into the engine and then highly compressed, which heats the mixture to a high enough temperature for self-ignition.

Gasoline Engines

The compression of the fuel-air mixture in a gasoline engine does not produce enough heat to ignite the fuel, so another means must be used. Instead, an electric current is generated and passed through a spark plug, producing a spark that ignites the gasoline-air mixture. The electrical current comes from one of three different sources.

Magneto Ignition

Small, two-stroke outboard motors have *magnetos* that are high-voltage generators built into the flywheels of the motors. When you pull the starter cord on this kind of motor, permanent magnets rotate and cause an electric current to be generated. This current is sent to the spark plugs at appropriate times, and the spark ignites the fuel and powers the motor.

A circuit breaker (usually called **points**) must be adjusted correctly to operate efficiently. A small electrical capacitor, called a **condenser**, is used to reduce arcing of the points. If the condenser fails, electricity is not delivered to the engine, and it will not run. If the condenser fails partially, the motor will start and run at fairly high speeds in neutral but will not run much above idle speed in gear. You should have the points and condenser inspected and replaced every 2 or 3 years, a job you probably can't do yourself, since special tools are required to remove the flywheel. Never replace breaker points without replacing the condenser.

Alternator-Battery Ignition

Some larger two-stroke gasoline engines and all four-stroke gasoline engines use a second method to create a spark to ignite the fuel. As in an automobile, the engine drives an alternator that creates an electrical current, which is stored in a battery. An ignition coil transforms the 12-volt current of the battery to the high voltage needed for igniting the fuel (Figure 10-15). Some outboards have an ignition coil on each cylinder, which increases the motor's reliability. If one or more coils should fail, it is still possible to operate the motor.

Older engines with battery-alternator ignitions often have breaker points, a condenser, a distributor, and an ignition coil (Figure 10-16), all of which deliver current to the spark plugs at the appropriate times. Inspect the points and condenser and replace them periodically, and check the distributor and its cap for cracks. Also, the ignition wire may deteriorate over time and can leak high voltage.

Electronic Ignition

There is a third, and newer, method of igniting the fuel in an engine called an **electronic ignition system** and it is used on all types of gasoline engines. It uses solid-state switching, sometimes called a **black box**, that replaces distributors, condensers, and

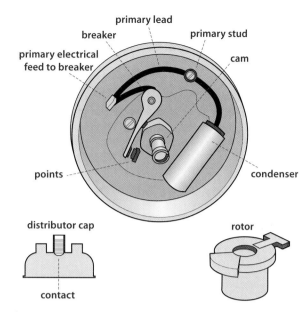

Figure **10-16.** A distributor shown with its cap and rotor both removed. In use the rotor would be installed on the camshaft in order to distribute electricity to the spark plugs in correct firing sequence as it spins. As the camshaft spins, it periodically lifts the breaker point away from the opposing stationary point, interrupting the low-tension electrical circuit (see Figure 10-15) and, through electromagnetic induction, building high voltage in the secondary windings of the coil, which is then fed via the rotor to the spark plugs. Elegant though it is, this electromagnetic arrangement is subject to wear and inefficiencies, and on newer gasoline engines the distributor, condenser, and points have been replaced by electronic ignitions with solid-state switching. Electronic ignition systems are more reliable and efficient but cannot be repaired by the amateur mechanic.

points, which are the least reliable parts of older ignition systems and the ones that require the most maintenance.

An electronic ignition system delivers a much hotter ignition spark for a shorter duration than either of the other systems. This makes starting easier, since it provides greater precision in timing the delivery of the electrical current to the engine.

Flame Arresters

Sometimes, when the fuel ignites, a backfire occurs. This is a small explosion through the air intake of the carburetor, and it can cause a fire or a major engine compartment explosion. Because of this, inboard and stern-drive gasoline engines must have flame arresters (Figure 10-17). Keep the flame arrester clean by using one of the special detergents available for this purpose.

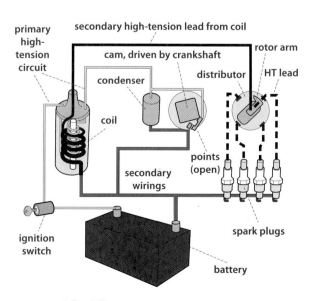

Figure **10-15.** Schematic layout of a traditional electromechanical ignition system, still found on older engines.

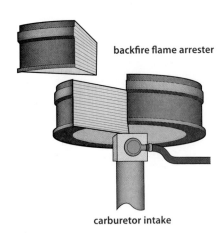

backfire flame arrester

carburetor intake

Figure **10-17.** A flame arrester can prevent an accidental explosion.

Outboard engines do not require flame arresters, since they do not operate in enclosed spaces.

Cooling Systems

The fuel that burns inside an internal combustion engine produces large amounts of heat, making it essential to have some way to cool the engine.

Air-Cooled Engines

Some very small outboard motors are air cooled by means of fans, but larger outboards, stern drives, and inboards produce too much heat to be cooled this way. Furthermore, stern drives and inboards are enclosed in compartments where there is insufficient air with which to cool them. Some other method of cooling them is necessary.

Water-Cooled Engines

Most marine engines are water cooled by one of two methods.

Open Cooling Systems

Internal combustion engines contain water channels through which water circulates. When that water is pumped into the engine from outside the boat, circulates through the channels, and is then dumped overboard, you have an *open circulation system*, also known as *raw-water cooling*.

Your engine's water intake may become clogged by weeds, trash, or other debris, which can cause the engine to overheat. If this happens, examine the intake and clear out any debris you find. Do not operate your engine if it is overheating, as this can severely damage it.

The engine's cooling system usually has a thermostat that blocks the flow of water through the engine until it warms up. Once the engine is warm, the thermostat opens and allows the cooling water to circulate. A faulty thermostat may stay open all the time and cause the engine to warm up slowly, or may fail to open and cause the engine to overheat. In either case, replace the thermostat.

Most marine engines have an impeller-type water pump. An *impeller* is a propeller-like device made of rubber or neoprene that is turned rapidly by the engine. This device has a relatively short life, one made even shorter if you run your engine without cooling water. If you have to run it when the boat is out of the water, supply water to it through a hose and an adapter.

Dual Cooling Systems

Some inboards and stern drives have *dual cooling systems*—also called *freshwater cooling*—in which a mixture of water and antifreeze circulates through the engine's water channels. This mixture is circulated by a pump like that on an automobile engine, and as the water circulates, it passes through a heat exchanger that cools it. This is a *closed circulation system*.

The **heat exchanger** serves the same purpose as an automobile radiator, but the exchanger is cooled by water and not by air as in an automobile. Seawater (or raw lake or river water) is pumped into the cooling system, circulated around the exchanger, and discharged out of the boat. In a dual cooling system, only the closed half of the system has a thermostat.

> **TIP** ***Keep fuel tanks full to mimimize condensation.*** *If you leave much head space in your fuel tanks, moisture in the air can condense when temperatures decrease, forming a layer of water. Because water is not miscible with and is heavier than fuel, the water falls to the bottom of the tank. After repeated cycles, this water accumulates and can create a problem. The solution is to keep the tanks full, refilling as necessary after each use.*

Cooling System Precautions

Modern marine engines can operate in either fresh or salt water without harm if cared for properly. Normally, you do not need to flush your engine with fresh water. Engines having iron or steel blocks, however, and open cooling systems should be flushed after each use in salt water. If you have operated your engine in polluted or brackish water, you may also wish to flush it.

Flushing is also helpful in reducing the spread of aquatic nuisance species (ANS), such as zebra mussels, from one body of fresh water to another, and can be done using a garden hose and a special adapter. If you are taking your boat from one fresh-water lake or river to another, flush your engine and take the other precautions recommended earlier.

Consult your owner's manual for instructions on engine operation and care in freezing weather. You will usually want to keep your outdrive or the lower unit of your outboard submerged in freezing weather, as this prevents possible damage, unless the water around the unit freezes. If you take your boat out of the water in freezing weather, keep its lower unit in its operating (down) position until all water has drained from it.

Gasoline Considerations

Changes in the lead content of gasoline in recent years have had serious implications for boaters. The removal of lead has resulted in lower octane ratings and, in some cases, the addition of alcohol to gasoline.

Leaded Gasoline

For many years, gasoline contained lead, which served two purposes: it lubricated and protected exhaust valve seats in four-cycle engines, and even a small amount of lead raised the octane rating of the gasoline.

The *octane rating* is a measure of a fuel's resistance to *premature detonation* (detonation before ignition). Premature detonation causes knocking or pinging in engines, which results in power loss and damage to engine parts, and it can destroy an engine in a few hours.

Most four-cycle engines manufactured since 1974 have induction-hardened valve seats that do not need lead for lubrication under normal conditions of operation. If your inboard or stern-drive engine is a 1973 or earlier model, you should probably add a lead substitute to the gasoline.

Octane Ratings

Prior to 1986, "regular leaded" gasoline had an octane rating (antiknock index, or AKI) of 89. In 1986, the EPA reduced the allowable lead content of gasoline, which meant that some regular-grade gasolines began having octane ratings of 87. Then in 1989, the EPA mandated the removal of all lead, and this resulted in regular-grade gasoline with an octane rating as low as 86. Premium unleaded gasoline continued to have octane ratings of 91 to 93.

To compensate for the lower octane ratings in lead-free gasoline, oil companies increased the amount of octane-boosting additives in their gasolines. Unfortunately, these additives cause carbon buildup in two-cycle outboards and other marine engines subject to hard use, which in turn leads to increased engine wear and decreased performance. In severe cases, engines freeze up completely.

Engine deposits can be reduced by using high-quality gasoline, which contains a detergent that combats carbon buildup. Each of the major oil companies uses a different trade name for its detergents, but all of their gasolines contain them. You can purchase detergent additives to add to your gasoline if it does not already contain them.

Consult your owner's manual or your dealer to see what octane rating your engine needs. If your outboard motor is a 1985 or earlier model, consult your dealer to see what adjustments to make for lower grades of gasoline. One tankful of 86 or 87 octane gasoline in a pre-1986 outboard motor can do irreparable damage if the motor has not been properly modified.

Premium Gasoline

One way to avoid the problem of premature detonation in pre-1986 outboards is to use premium unleaded gasoline. Such gasoline is expensive and possibly wasteful, however, and it may be cheaper to have the engine modified.

Any gasoline that eliminates premature detonation develops all the hp you can get from your motor. If you use more "powerful" gasoline than the engine needs, you do not get more power. So while the alternative to using 91 to 93 octane gasoline in a pre-1986 outboard could be costly engine repairs, using a lower octane gasoline for 1986 or later models of outboards should not cause any problems. Consult your owner's manual to see what grade of gasoline to use.

Reformulated Gasoline

The EPA has been working cooperatively with the petroleum and engine manufacturing industries to use a cleaner-burning fuel called **reformulated gasoline**. Some parts of the United States are required to use it, and about one-third of the nation's gasoline is reformulated. The fuel contains a chemical oxygen, which is either an alcohol or an ether. Because alcohol has an affinity for water, boaters should take the following precautions when using this fuel is inevitable:

- Ensure that the engine is in tune. Modern engines are designed to operate with these fuels when they are tuned properly.
- Keep fuel tanks and storage containers either full or empty so that they won't accumulate moisture.
- Use a water-separating fuel filter if you want maximum protection.
- Check fuel hoses for deteriation once a year. These lines may become brittle or soft on fuel systems produced before 1980, and in severe

cases may bleed enough to form droplets of gasoline on the hose. If you do not see gasoline on your fuel line, wipe it clean and check it in a few minutes by blotting the hose with a clean paper towel. Is the towel wet? If so, replace the hose. Fuel tank hoses and vent hoses should also be checked.

- Engines manufactured prior to 1986 may have internal parts containing rubber that deteriorate from reformulated fuel.
- Install a fuel shutoff valve on permanent fuel tanks (Figure 10-18).

Fuel Tanks

There is another consideration in the use of gasoline with an alcohol additive, in that alcohol may have an adverse effect on the fuel tank. Because alcohol has a strong affinity for water, alcohol dissolved in gasoline will sometimes come out of solution and combine with water. Also, boat fuel systems are open to the atmosphere, and moist air can therefore condense inside the fuel tank and leave water in the tank. One way to reduce condensation is to keep your fuel tank full at all times.

An alcohol-water mixture inside a fuel tank can corrode it, and the tank can then leak and become dangerous. Inspect your tank at least annually, and replace it if you see any sign of corrosion or leakage. If you replace it with a plastic one, be certain it is a "permanent" type with a label showing that it meets Coast Guard requirements. Such tanks have limited permeability—that is, they do not "sweat" gasoline excessively.

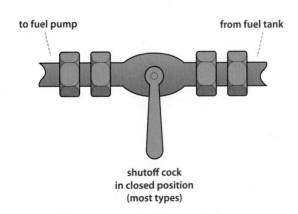

to fuel pump   from fuel tank

shutoff cock
in closed position
(most types)

Figure **10-18.** A fuel shutoff valve.

Batteries

Batteries are divided into cells with plates of two different metals surrounded by an electrolyte. In lead-acid batteries, the electrolyte is sulfuric acid and the metals are two types of lead, hence the name. Over the years, improvements have been made to the basic technology, and now boaters can choose from gel-cell batteries, absorbed-glass-mat batteries, and lithium-ion batteries. In *gel-cell batteries*, the electrolyte is a paste that the plates are suspended in. Gel-cells hold a charge much better but will sustain permanent damage if overcharged. Like gel-cells, *absorbed-glass-mat batteries* (AGM) are also sealed, but the electrolyte is retained in spongy fiberglass mats. They can stand up to overcharging better than gel-cells.

Unless your outboard engine starts with a pull starter, you need a battery (Figure 10-19). The battery is one of the most important items on your boat, and without it you can't start your engine, call for help, display lights, or pump the bilge if your only pump is electric. Since it is so important, many boaters have a second, backup battery. Such a backup is useless, though, if the batteries are not electrically isolated from each other. Should a fault develop in one battery, any other battery connected to it will also lose its charge.

Marine engines using lead-acid batteries should use *deep-cycle batteries*, which unlike automobile batteries, can be completely discharged and recharged through multiple cycles without being damaged. Deep-cycle batteries are especially useful for powering trolling motors.

Battery Switches

With a **battery isolation switch** you can use either of two batteries or both at the same time. While some of these switches should be operated only when the engine is stopped and the ignition switch is turned off, others can be used to switch from battery 1 to battery 2 or to Both while the engine is running. Determine which kind you have before you switch batteries, since failure to do so may damage the alternator. Do not use different kinds of batteries. Mixing battery types can lead to under- or overcharging.

Check Your Battery

If your batteries are not "maintenance free," check their fluid levels every month or two and add distilled water if the levels are low. When it is necessary to charge a dead battery, you will probably need to add water. During the charging, some water breaks down into hydrogen and oxygen, and these gases usually escape into the atmosphere. In a confined space, the hydrogen is highly explosive, so keep sparks away from it.

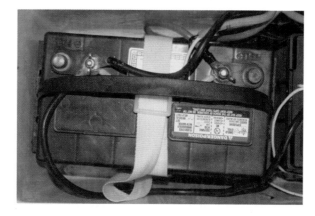

Figure **10-19.** A rugged battery strap is essential equipment. (PHOTO BY DON LINDBERG)

Checking Your Battery's Charge

You can check a lead-acid battery's charge with a **hydrometer**. Water has a specific gravity of 1.0. A fully charged battery has a specific gravity of 1.270 or more, while a discharged battery has a specific gravity of 1.150 or less.

If your boat has a **voltmeter**, you have a continuous check on the lead-acid battery's condition. When the ignition switch is turned on, a fully charged battery should register about 12.5 volts. If it registers 11 volts or less, it has lost its charge. If your battery is in good condition, the voltmeter will show a reading of about 13.5 to 14.0 volts when the engine is running.

An **ammeter** does not give the same information as a voltmeter, but instead shows the rate at which the alternator is delivering current to the battery when the engine is running. Its charging rate depends on the condition of the battery.

If the battery is low or fails to hold a charge, the ammeter will show a high delivery rate. As the battery charges up, the delivery rate will drop back and may be as little as zero.

You'll know something is wrong with the alternator if the ammeter shows "discharge" when the engine is running. If your alternator has a drive belt, it may be broken. Otherwise, the problem may be with the alternator itself.

Battery Failure

Sometimes, even with fully charged batteries, the starter will not engage and crank the engine. This usually results from loose or corroded battery terminals. If your starter will not operate, check the battery terminals. You may need only to tighten their clamps to correct the problem, or you may need to clean the terminals and clamps. A special brush is available for this purpose.

Crank the engine for a few seconds. Now feel the terminals. If they are more than slightly warm, you have poor or dirty connections.

If the battery cables are worn, or if they get hot when you are starting your engine, replace them. They are doing a poor job of delivering current from the battery, and may also be a fire hazard.

Corroded Terminals

The easiest way to approach the problem of corrosion on your battery terminals is to prevent it by coating the terminals and their clamps with petroleum jelly or grease.

If you haven't coated the terminals, they will corrode. To remove corrosion, make a solution of 2 tablespoons of baking soda in 1 pint of water. Turn the battery switch to Off and slowly pour the solution over the battery terminals. (Don't let any of it enter the battery.) It will fizz as carbon dioxide is released. Scrub the terminals with a brush if necessary, and then continue the treatment until the fizzing stops. Now, coat the terminals!

Some batteries have side-mounted terminals with wing-nut connectors. While side mounts are not subject to as much corrosion as top-mounted terminals, you may still need to clean them if you haven't coated them.

Secure Your Battery

Keep your batteries in secured and vented plastic containers with covers to prevent them from tipping over or tearing loose in rough water.

Covered containers will also help keep batteries from being accidentally short-circuited, which can happen if you drop a tool or some other metal object and it touches both terminals. A shorted-out battery makes a large spark, which can cause a fire or an explosion. Shorting is also hard on the battery and will reduce its life.

A short-circuited battery heats rapidly, and can become hot enough to boil its fluid and explode. This can also happen when you use the starter ex-

cessively. Protect yourself and your boat by putting the battery in a vented plastic container and securing the container.

When replacing a battery, remove the negative cable first and install it last. This prevents an accidental sparking if a tool should make contact between the battery's positive terminal and ground.

Use of Dual Batteries

Batteries last longer and perform better when you use them. If you have two batteries, don't use them both at the same time or use the same battery all the time. Instead switch from one to the other regularly.

If you're on a trip and will be anchored all night, use only one battery for the anchor light. This leaves the other battery for starting the engine the next morning.

Short Circuits

Batteries may be shorted out by anything metallic, such as tools or the jewelry you are wearing. Jewelry can also cause short circuits at electrical junction points, such as a fuse panel, the solenoid on the starter, or any bare wire. Don't wear necklaces, rings, bracelets, metal watch bands, or the like when working near the battery or any of the electrical connections aboard your boat, and be careful with all tools.

Although the electrical systems on most small recreational boats are 12 volts, short circuits can deliver dangerous amounts of energy for brief periods, and this energy can cause personal injury and pose a fire hazard. The metal causing the short circuit can be melted instantly. Having your wedding ring, for example, vaporized while it is still on your finger would be painful and could cause permanent injury.

The possibility of a short circuit is another strong argument for a battery isolation switch. The energy present in a short circuit can quickly melt the insulation on a wire and may ignite it or anything in contact with it, and electrical failures of this kind are the leading cause of fires aboard boats. It may be impossible to extinguish an electrically caused fire unless the batteries are disconnected, and even if the fire is extinguished, the fire may be rekindled if the batteries are not disconnected.

The easiest way to disconnect batteries is a battery isolation switch. If this switch is used to disconnect the batteries from the electrical system of your boat when it is not in use, an electrically caused fire is almost impossible. Just be certain to have the bilge pump wired directly to the battery so that when you leave your boat on the water and turn off the disconnect switch, the pump can operate independently.

Charging Your Batteries

Many pleasure boats are inactive for long periods, and their batteries lose their charge. This loss may be partial, and there may be sufficient reserve to start the engines. Nevertheless, that battery has experienced a penalty, and repeated loss of charge, small or large, shortens a battery's life. The ideal solution is to keep a low-level maintenance charge on the battery, called a *float charge*. Another, slightly larger charging level is called a *trickle charge*, but this is less ideal for long periods than a float charge. The constant use of carefully regulated charging equipment will most often provide a good payback by lengthening battery life.

The first step in charging your battery, if it doesn't have a built-in charging system, is to turn your battery isolation switch to the Off position. This reduces the possibility of an electrical spark being produced near the hydrogen and oxygen generated during the charging. Also, be careful to see that the area containing the battery is well ventilated so as to disperse the hydrogen and oxygen.

Unless your battery is a "no maintenance" one, before charging it, remove the caps that cover its cells to allow generated gases to escape. Check to see that the battery's plates are covered with fluid, and add distilled water if necessary—but do not overfill it. Carefully wipe up any spilled battery fluid; it is sulfuric acid, which is corrosive and can burn your skin or eat holes in your clothing. If you come in contact with battery acid, flush the area with water.

120-Volt Electrical Dangers

Whenever a boat is connected to a 120-volt alternating current (AC) from ashore or generated aboard, serious dangers may exist. The danger is

WARNING *Read owner's manuals for charging directions on low-maintenance, gel-cell, AGM, and lithium batteries.*

greatest in a boat with a metal hull, but it is also present in any boat with metal fittings, propellers, or outdrives below the waterline.

The most common source of AC problems is the connection between the boat and the power wiring ashore. If the fittings ashore will accommodate only two-prong connectors, the circuit is not grounded and is inherently dangerous. If the fittings accommodate three-prong connectors, a simple, plug-in, three-prong AC circuit tester, readily available at a variety of sources, can be used to test the correctness of the wiring. If the tester shows an incorrectly wired circuit, don't use it since such circuits are dangerous.

Even if the tester shows that the onshore 120-volt source is properly wired, the circuit should be protected with a ground fault circuit interrupter (GFCI or GFI). Portable, plug-in GFIs are available and you should carry one with you and use it whenever a circuit does not have a GFI. Plug it into the source, then plug the cable from your boat into it. Under some circumstances, if a short develops in the circuit, the GFI will immediately disconnect the power source.

All 120-volt appliances on board, such as stoves, refrigerators, and air conditioners, should be grounded to a common ground connection. If the "hot" wire of any of these appliances becomes grounded to its chassis or frame, all grounded metallic components of the boat are energized. A GFI will interrupt the flow of current immediately if this happens, but without one a hazard is present for anyone on the boat or in the water nearby. It is best to stay out of the water if nearby boats are connected to AC current ashore, but if you must go in the water to retrieve something, unplug your boat and nearby boats.

Direct-Current Problems

The direct current (DC) supplied by your battery can be a source of severe damage to metal parts of your boat. Unless the "hot" wire to your bilge pump is properly sealed from the bilge water, DC current can leak from the wire to metal fittings in the bilge, such as the propeller shaft, through-hull fittings, and other metallic parts of your vessel. It then seeks a ground and takes part of the metal with it, and this electrolytic action can rapidly destroy metal parts of a boat. Although potentially damaging to immersed metal parts, the 12-volt DC system by itself does not present a shock hazard to someone in the water.

Preventing Electrical Problems

You can take the following simple steps to reduce the hazards of damage from DC current:

- Keep electrical wiring out of the bilge.
- Use only watertight connections if there is any possibility of immersion in bilge water.
- Install a battery isolation switch.
- Make certain there is a fuse or a circuit breaker in the main distribution line from your batteries and as near to your batteries as possible.
- Use only fuses or circuit breakers of the recommended size in your accessories connection panel.
- If new wiring is added to your boat, be certain it is large enough to carry its intended load without overheating.
- Have any worn or frayed wires replaced by a competent marine electrician as soon as possible.
- Use multistranded, marine-rated wire with copper strands (not aluminum) that have been individually coated with tin.
- Inspect all metal fittings at frequent intervals for electrolytic or galvanic corrosion.

You can also reduce the potential damage and hazards of AC current by doing the following:

- Use a plug-in tester to screen for potential problems in the onshore service line.
- Don't use the onshore service line unless you know it is correctly wired.
- Install a GFI between your vessel and an onshore power source.
- Use a galvanic isolator that has been tested

and approved by Underwriters Laboratories to allow AC current to flow to ground while preventing stray DC current from following the same path.

- Properly fuse all AC circuits or install circuit breakers.
- Install new wire in your boat for any AC circuit and make certain that it is heavy enough to carry its intended load.

Maintenance

There are many things you can do to prevent problems. Most of these you do while tied up at a pier or ashore and before you are on the water and have engine failure.

This chapter describes several things you can do to keep your engine operating efficiently. Also read and carefully follow the manufacturer's recommendations in your owner's manual. It is important that you follow them exactly and don't take shortcuts.

For most boaters, maintenance procedures fall into three groups: routine maintenance, winterizing, and spring fitting out.

Routine Maintenance

Follow a periodic maintenance plan for your engine based on the manufacturer's recommendations. It helps to make a checklist of what you should do and when you should do it (Figures 10-20 and 10-21). You should also keep a log of the hours you run your engine; an engine hour meter helps in this respect but is not essential.

An important part of engine maintenance is keeping it clean. It is also imperative that you keep the compartment of an inboard or stern-drive engine clean. This is not just a matter of good taste, but is a safety consideration since oil in a bilge can be dangerous. Remember, it is against the law to pump out oily bilge water into the water around you, and doing it leads to environmental pollution, big fines, and embarrassment.

Lubrication

Systematic lubrication of your engine and its power transmission system is essential for optimal operation and long-time service (Figure 10-22).

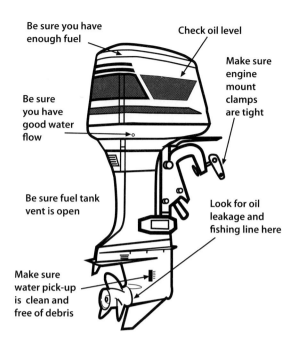

Be sure you have enough fuel

Check oil level

Make sure engine mount clamps are tight

Be sure you have good water flow

Be sure fuel tank vent is open

Look for oil leakage and fishing line here

Make sure water pick-up is clean and free of debris

Figure **10-20.** Typical points on an outboard engine that you should check daily. (REPRINTED WITH PERMISSION FROM *OUTBOARD ENGINES* BY EDWIN R. SHERMAN)

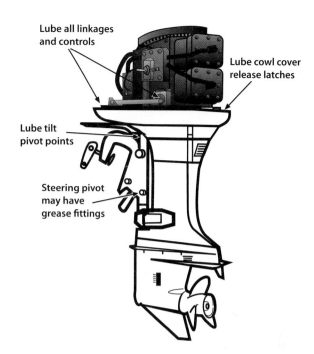

Lube all linkages and controls

Lube cowl cover release latches

Lube tilt pivot points

Steering pivot may have grease fittings

Figure **10-22.** Typical outboard engine lubrication points. (REPRINTED WITH PERMISSION FROM *OUTBOARD ENGINES* BY EDWIN R. SHERMAN)

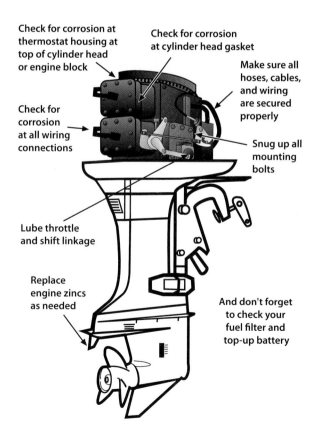

Check for corrosion at thermostat housing at top of cylinder head or engine block

Check for corrosion at cylinder head gasket

Make sure all hoses, cables, and wiring are secured properly

Check for corrosion at all wiring connections

Snug up all mounting bolts

Lube throttle and shift linkage

Replace engine zincs as needed

And don't forget to check your fuel filter and top-up battery

Figure **10-21.** Typical points on an outboard engine that you should check monthly. (REPRINTED WITH PERMISSION FROM *OUTBOARD ENGINES* BY EDWIN R. SHERMAN)

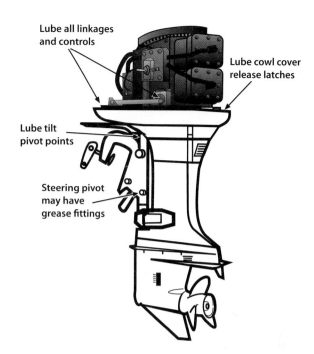

CRANKCASE OIL. Change the crankcase oil in your stern-drive or inboard engine at the intervals recommended by its manufacturer. Some manufacturers recommend changing the oil filter each time you change the oil, which may seem excessive, but why run clean oil through a dirty filter? While changing the oil in most marine engines is a dirty job, changing the filter adds little to it, so go ahead and change the filter when you change the oil.

Changing the oil in a stern-drive or inboard engine is not an easy task because of the inaccessibility of the drain plug.

PUMPING THE CRANKCASE. Pumps, either manual or electrically driven, are available to remove crankcase oil through the dipstick tube. Before you use a pump, warm your engine thoroughly (by running it for 10 to 15 minutes, preferably under gentle load) so that its oil is as thin as possible and will flow more easily. Be careful not to burn your hands with the hot oil.

WASH IT OUT. To clean hard-to-reach areas of the bilges, put a little water in them, then add about ½ cup of liquid detergent, preferably a nonfoaming one. After running your boat for a few hours, pump the bilge water into a container (not overboard) for easy and legal disposal. While the water and detergent are in the bilge, keep your electrically oper-

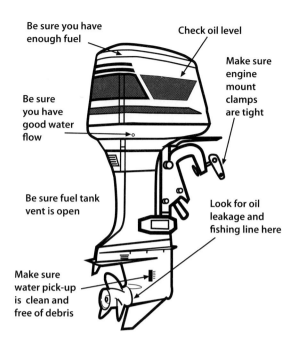

275

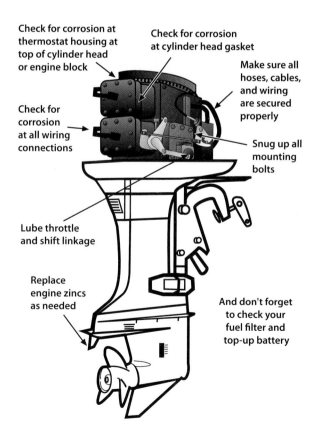

POWERING YOUR BOAT

ated bilge pump turned off to avoid an accidental overboard pumpout.

CHECK THE OIL LEVEL. In stern-drive and inboard engines, check the crankcase oil level each time you use your boat, before starting the engine. Also check the oil in the transmission at regular intervals, and change it according to the manufacturer's recommendation.

Lower Unit Care

Lower units on outboards and stern drives contain oil to lubricate their gears, and these units require special care (Figure 10-23). Each unit has two oil cap screws. The upper one is for checking the oil level, and the lower one is for draining old oil and adding new.

Change the gearcase oil at regular intervals. Some manufacturers recommend changing it at least once each season or each 100 hours of operation, whichever comes first, but you should also check it at other times to see if there is enough oil in the case and to be sure water has not intruded. The oil should be clear and without metal filings. If it is milky, it probably has water in it and needs immediate attention.

To check the oil, remove the upper cap. The oil should be at or just below this opening. To fill the case with oil, remove both plugs and drain the old oil. Then take the plastic squeeze bottle of new oil and cut the tip off the nozzle and insert the nozzle in the bottom hole of the lower unit. Fill it un-

til oil comes out of the upper hole, then replace both plugs. Some lower units use a thin oil and, in that case, the filling is done at the upper plug.

GREASE THE FITTINGS. Most outboards and outdrives have zerk fittings to lubricate moving parts and cover latches. Lubricate them with marine-type grease from a grease gun. In saltwater use, they should be lubricated every 30 days, but in fresh water you may do it every 60 days.

Many stern-drive engines have one or more zerk fittings or grease caps on the gears that connect the driveshaft to the lower unit. They are located in the engine compartment, and should be lubricated as recommended by the manufacturer.

CHECK HYDRAULIC FLUID. Some lower units and most larger outboards use hydraulic fluid in their lift mechanisms, and some also have hydraulic steering that uses hydraulic fluid. The hydraulic fluid for these purposes is stored in reservoirs, which you should check frequently to be sure they are full.

Checks While Lubricating

You can check several other things while you are changing the engine oil and filter.

CHECK YOUR BILGE PUMPS. This can be done by operating the pump switches manually. The pumps should operate with the main battery switch in the Off position; if they do not, first check the fuses or breakers, then check the battery and the wiring. Most pumps use a float to detect water level, and they can become sticky from debris.

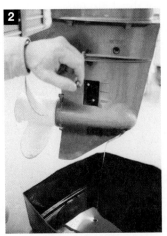

Figure **10-23.** Changing the gearcase oil in the lower unit of an outboard: 1. Loosening the gear oil drain screw in the gearcase. 2. The old gear oil is draining. 3. Inserting a tube of gear oil into the lower hole for refilling. 4. Once oil dribbles out of the upper hole, it's time to reinstall the upper screw. When that is tightened, you can withdraw the tube of gear oil. The vacuum in the gearcase will prevent the oil from dripping out while you reinstall the lower screw. (REPRINTED WITH PERMISSION FROM *POWERBOAT CARE AND REPAIR* BY ALLEN BERRIEN)

CHECK FOR OIL LEAKS. When there is oil in the bilge under the engine, look for its source. First, check to see if oil is leaking from the oil filter. If this is not the source, check the tightness of the crankcase bolts and transmission. Your oil filter should only be hand-tightened, but it should not leak. After you change the oil, start the engine and check to see if the filter is leaking. Oil in the bilge may be recovered with an oil absorber designed for that purpose (Figure 10-24). Baby diapers, although not as convenient, may also be used.

CHECK THE STUFFING BOX. If your engine is an inboard, check to see how much water is coming through the propeller's stuffing box. The amount of water in the bilge gives you some sign. A drip rate of a few drops per minute is normal. When the bilge water level or the drip rate is high, tighten the packing nut slightly, but do not overtighten it, since some water must come through for proper operation. If tightening the packing nut does not solve the problem, change the packing.

CHECK THE DRIVE BELTS. Check the condition and the tension of the drive belts on alternators and water pumps. They should be flexible and resilient, and should not have frayed edges. A belt-tension measuring tool is available, but few recreational boaters have them. Most simply press the belts at their midpoints. The belt driving the alternator should have about 3/4 inch of "give," while other belts should have about 1/2 inch.

Ignition System Maintenance

Check your spark plugs at least annually. If they are pitted, replace them with new ones. Always use the size and type recommended for your engine, and do not overtighten them. When reinstalling the ignition wires, put about 1 cc (0.06 cubic inch) of a silicone-based grease inside each rubber cover to help prevent poor connections due to corrosion. Type Z-5 is recommended and is available at most electronics stores.

Fuel System Maintenance

Many marine engines have fuel filters and these should be cleaned periodically for best motor performance (Figure 10-25). The filters usually have a fine-mesh wire screen, which can be cleaned by shaking it into a clean, dry cloth. You can also clean their containers with a clean, dry cloth.

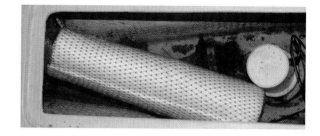

Figure **10-24.** Absorbing oil in a bilge. (PHOTO BY DON LINDBERG)

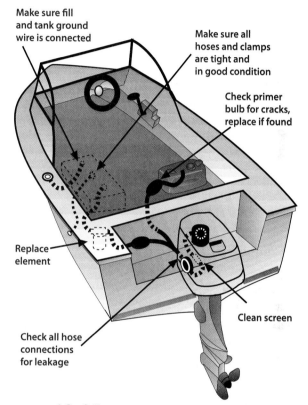

Make sure fill and tank ground wire is connected

Make sure all hoses and clamps are tight and in good condition

Check primer bulb for cracks, replace if found

Replace element

Check all hose connections for leakage

Clean screen

Figure **10-25.** Fuel system inspection points. (REPRINTED WITH PERMISSION FROM *OUTBOARD ENGINES* BY EDWIN R. SHERMAN)

WATER SEPARATION FILTER. If you have a water separation filter in your fuel line, change its element annually. A tankful of "wet" gas or water that collects in your fuel tank from condensation can cause your engine to run rough or ragged. You can sometimes correct this condition by slowing the engine speed and running it until the water is cleared out. If your engine is diesel and you get a tankful of wet fuel, open the fuel filter drain cock and drain the filter. It may be necessary to replace the fuel.

Cooling System

Both stern-drive and inboard engines have cooling system hoses, and these should be inspected whenever you open the engine hood or hatch. If one of them ruptures while underway and you do not have a spare, you have a serious problem. The hoses should be firm, so if they have soft spots or collapse easily, replace them.

Galvanic Action

Modern marine engines and lower units use a variety of metals. When you immerse two dissimilar metals in a solution such as salt water, an electrical current flows from the less noble to the more noble metal, and this galvanic current eats away the less noble metal. Although this occurs less rapidly in fresh water than in salt water, it does occur to some degree because of impurities in the fresh water.

SACRIFICIAL ZINCS. Zinc is one of the least noble of the metals, so zinc plates or bars are used to prevent destruction of metal parts by galvanic action. These zincs are attached to the lower units of outboards and stern drives, the rudders of inboards, and the heat exchangers of many engines with closed cooling systems. Instead of the galvanic action eating away parts of the engine or outdrive, it eats up the zinc, while the engine parts are protected. The zincs should be replaced when they are about half eaten away. If sacrificial metals are not effective, tests can be performed to measure the damaging galvanic currents and identify the corrective action.

Propeller Maintenance

Unless a propeller is damaged, it needs little attention. If it has been damaged, however, even if the damage is slight, you should repair or replace it, since damaged propellers can cause vibration and destroy propeller shaft bearings.

When installing your propeller, grease its shaft with a good-quality marine grease. This will make it easier to remove.

Propellers are expensive, so protect yours from theft by using one of the propeller locks available.

Winterizing Your Boat

There are several important guidelines for winterizing your boat if you do not plan to use it during the winter months. First, the more you do in the fall, the less there is to do in the spring. Second, the greater the danger of freezing, the more important it is to store your boat ashore. And third, list the things you have done to lay up your boat, and then check this list in the spring to see what you need to change back. For example, if you remove the bilge plug from the boat, include an item on the spring list to remind you to replace it. Fourth, consult your owner's manual for layup procedures not covered in the following general discussion. The manufacturer of your engine may recommend different procedures than those described here.

Crankcase Oil

Change the oil as described above. The old oil in your crankcase contains residual acids and may contain water, and these acids can damage an engine during the winter. Warm the engine, then drain the oil. Replace the filter and fill the crankcase with clean oil, then run the engine for several minutes to circulate the clean oil to all parts of the engine. (For a boat on land, connect a freshwater adapter to the engine to prevent overheating.) While the engine is running, check the filter for leaks. After shutting down the engine, check the oil level once more and top off as necessary, but do not overfill.

Dispose of the used oil in an environmentally responsible way. Ask your marina or your town's public works department how to do this.

Transmission Oil

It's a good idea to change the transmission oil of an inboard or stern-drive engine as part of your winterizing routine. Faithfully follow the manufacturer's recommendations for type and quantity of gear oil.

Fuel Tank

The long-standing recommendation for winterizing an installed fuel tank is to drain it, but this can cause more problems than it prevents. For one thing, an empty tank offers a large volume of unoccupied airspace in which condensation can occur over the winter. This water will accumulate in the bottom of the tank, to be ingested by your engine the first time you fire it up in the next season. For another thing, a tank full of gasoline vapors represents a greater risk of explosion than a tank full of liquid fuel.

For these reasons, the current trend is to leave the tank full for the winter, so that there is no airspace for condensation or explosive fumes to accumulate. To prevent the gasoline from degrading in long storage, add a fuel stabilizer, which will also prevent varnish and gum deposits from forming in the tank during layup. Stor-N-Start, made by Marine Development and Research Corporation (MDR), is one of the most widely distributed stabilizers. Do not fill the tank so completely that you have gasoline standing in the rubber fill and vent pipes, since this may soften the rubber. Following

WINTERIZE YOUR BOAT

Winterizing Checklist

i = inboard-powered boats
s = stern-drive-powered boats
o = outboard-powered boats
* = some engines—see your owner's manual for details
f = if your boat has this equipment
_ = all hoses that run below the waterline anywhere along their length must have double hose clamps at both ends

BEFORE HAULING OUT

TASK	APPLICATION
inspect fuel filter for water	i, s, o
change engine oil and filter and genset oil and filter	i, s, f
check coolant in freshwater-cooled engines	f
change transmission fluid and/or gear oil	i, s*
pump out holding tank	f
fill fuel tank and stabilize fuel	i, s, o
apply Teflon grease to fill caps and O-rings	i, s, o

AFTER HAULING OUT

TASK	APPLICATION
wash the boat's bottom	i, s, o
remove barnacles from running gear and through-hull fittings	i, s, o
check running gear and through-hulls for electrolysis, corrosion, and damage	i, s, o
change gear oil in lower unit	s, o
disassemble, clean, inspect, and overhaul raw-water strainer(s)	i*, s*
disassemble, grease, and reassemble seacocks	f
inspect hoses and hose clamps (especially below the waterline)	f, _
drain water tanks and winterize freshwater supply system	f

winterize water heater system	f
winterize shower drain system	f
winterize sink drains and icebox drain	f
check deck drains (scuppers) for water traps and winterize if necessary	f
winterize head and holding tank system	f
winterize engine	i, s
fog out engine with fogging oil	i, s, o
winterize genset	f
fog out generator with fogging oil	f
shut off fuel supply at tank	i, s, o
remove, wash, charge, check, and store batteries in warm place	i, s, o
seal engine inlet and exhaust with rags, plastic, and duct tape	i, s
clean engine with spray cleaner and rags or paper towels	i, s, o
spray light film of WD-40 over engine and machinery	i, s, o
establish a program for maintaining batteries over the layup season	i, s, o

INSPECTION CHECKLIST

TASK	APPLICATION
note engine water leaks	i, s, o
correct these by retorquing or replacing gaskets or hoses	i, s, o
grease all control linkages	i, s, o

TUCKING IN AND COVERING

- remove compass and electronics (store them at home)
- remove bilge drain plug and place in galley sink
- drain, pump, and sponge bilges dry
- add a little antifreeze to freeze-vulnerable nooks
- sprinkle rock salt in bottom of bilge near drain plug
- remove cushions to dry stowage place
- remove all food from cabinets and refrigerator
- open all lockers and compartments

(continued on next page)

WINTERIZE YOUR BOAT (continued)

REQUIRED TOOLS

- oil changing pump (hand or drill motor-powered)
- container for drained engine oil (empty milk or bleach jugs)
- plastic funnel for draining oil filter
- disposable aluminum meatloaf pan
- oil filter wrench
- oil filler spout (only needed for oil in old-fashioned cans)
- pocketknife
- antifreeze checker
- 5-gallon plastic jerry jug
- plastic dishpan
- lever-action pump-type oil can
- multimeter (analog or digital)
- battery terminal cleaner
- ruler
- needle-nose pliers
- combination wrenches
- screwdrivers
- bucket and sponge
- flush adapter and garden hose
- lever-action grease gun
- needle-tip adapter (for grease gun)

NECESSARY SUPPLIES

- motor oil
- oil filters (engine and genset)
- gear oil
- nylon washers for gearcase screws (stern drives and outboards only)
- fuel stabilizer
- factory-recommended marine grease
- white Teflon grease
- fogging oil
- WD-40 penetrating lubricant
- permanent antifreeze (ethylene glycol)
- nontoxic antifreeze (propylene glycol)
- rock salt
- Teflon thread paste
- wiping rags and spray cleaner (such as Fantastik or Formula 409)
- paper towels
- dish soap
- distilled water (for batteries)
- sheet plastic and duct tape
- fine-grade emery cloth

the engine manufacturer's recommendations for storage is a safe option. In the case of diesel fuel, add a deicer and an antimicrobial agent.

Gasoline Engine

A couple of simple steps will protect your engine if you are not going to use it for several months. After adding stabilizer to the fuel, run the engine for 10 to 15 minutes to make sure the stabilized fuel reaches the carburetor, where it will prevent varnish and gum from forming in the small passageways there.

Next, fog out the engine with a special-purpose fogging oil. This is essential for outboards and recommended for inboards and stern drives. To prepare for this, remove the nut that secures the flame arrester on top of the carburetor of an inboard or stern-drive engine, and remove the "rainhat" from the carburetor if so fitted. On an outboard engine, remove the plastic plugs near the air inlet for each carburetor. If you're doing this on dry land, you'll have to provide a source of cooling water. For an inboard or stern drive, take the raw-water intake hose off its seacock and immerse it in a bucket that

you will constantly recharge with a garden hose. For an outboard engine, connect a flush adapter and garden hose directly to the gearcase. (If your outboard controls will not allow you to advance the throttle in neutral, you will have to remove the propeller for the fogging operation.)

Now start the engine and let it run at fast idle, say 1,800 rpm. Spray the fogging oil into the carburetor throats of an inboard or stern drive or each carburetor air inlet on an outboard. Spray only enough to bog down the engine, then let it recover. Repeat. Finally, spray a heavy enough dose to stop the engine. The oil will coat internal surfaces and prevent rusting and freezing of moving parts. Be very careful while working around moving parts, and do not wear loose clothing.

Cover the carburetor vents with plastic and tie it tightly to prevent moisture-laden air from entering and corroding carburetor parts.

Cooling Systems

Fresh water left in a cooling system may freeze and damage the engine. If you have an outboard or stern drive on land or on davits, leave it in the normal operating position, at least until all water has drained from it.

If you don't have antifreeze in the closed portion of the cooling system, add it now. Fill it with a 50-50 mixture of water and permanent antifreeze (ethylene glycol), not pure antifreeze, as it will gel in very cold weather. You must run the engine to distribute the antifreeze internally, so this is a job done most conveniently before you haul the boat.

To winterize the raw-water side of your cooling system, wait until the boat is hauled. Remove the raw-water intake hose from its seacock as described above for fogging the engine, but this time immerse it in a bucket of nontoxic antifreeze (propylene glycol) rather than fresh water. Run the engine until the exhaust discharge on the ground shows that the antifreeze has worked its way through the system.

Care of Lower Units

Lower the outdrive or the outboard as far as possible to let the water drain out, making sure the drain holes are open. Check the owner's manual—some I/Os will not drain completely. Then check the level of the oil, and if you haven't replaced it during the operating season, replace it now, so it won't have to be done next spring.

Ignition System

Remove the spark plugs and inspect them, being careful not to drop them since this may crack their ceramic stems and make them useless. Replace any worn or pitted ones.

Store your batteries in a cool, dry place. If possible, connect them to a float charger to keep them fully charged, and make sure there is enough water to cover their plates. If you leave batteries in a boat that is stored outside, they will gradually discharge and then freeze.

You may want to leave a battery aboard to operate a burglar alarm or a bilge pump. If so, see that it has a full charge and enough water. Given enough time, an unused battery will discharge itself and be rendered useless, and a discharged battery will freeze.

Don't depend on a battery aboard to operate

your bilge pump. The pump, battery, or float switch can fail. If your boat has a chronic leaking problem, store it ashore.

Freshwater System

You must winterize your fresh (drinking) water system. Drain it and then add antifreeze, but do not use ethylene glycol, as it is poisonous and you don't want it anywhere near your freshwater system. Instead, use nontoxic antifreeze (propylene glycol), which is available at most marine supply stores. Some people who can't get nontoxic antifreeze use cheap vodka.

Heads

If your head has a holding tank, drain it and then add disinfectant and environmentally friendly antifreeze, which can be pumped through the bowl and into the tank.

For other heads, see the manufacturers' recommendations.

Spring Fitting Out

Look at your boat winterizing checklist to see which items you need to undo in the spring. For example, you will need to put in the hull drain plug and remove the plastic covers from the carburetor vents. If you did not do all of the things on the winterizing list, add them to your spring list.

Out of the Water

Before you put your boat in the water, reinstall the batteries. If you did not remove them, check the levels of their fluid and their charges, and add distilled water and charge them as necessary. Then clean and tighten the clamps.

In the Water

After your boat is in the water, check all seacocks. Before you start your inboard engine, loosen the stuffing box nut, then check to see that it is dripping several drops per minute. Inspect the rudder packing box for leaks.

You are now ready for your engine starting sequence.

Troubleshooting

The environment in which boats are kept and used is hard on everything on board, particularly electrical parts, so this is where problems most often occur. Failure of such equipment is usually the result of corrosion at electrical connections and switches.

For example, radios often fail because of faulty antenna connections, and the same problem may cause a light not to come on. Chances are you can get the terminals to work by brushing or shining them up with fine-grit sandpaper. Plug-in equipment may fail for the same reason, and cleaning the connectors can help.

Engine Will Not Turn Over

Say you get to your boat and prepare to start the engine. Of course you do all the right things, such as opening the hatch (if you have an inboard or stern drive) and leaning over and sniffing for fumes. If your boat has a through-hull fitting for cooling water intake, you turn it to the open position. Then you check the engine oil level and turn the blower on and let it run.

You also check the steering and the clutch and throttle control to see if they are operating. You lower the outboard or lower unit and pump the throttle full forward, full back, and then to its start position. Now, you insert the ignition key and turn it to start the engine. Nothing happens.

Check Your Clutch and Throttle Control

The first things to check if the starter doesn't work are the throttle and clutch controls, since a marine engine should not start unless it is in neutral. While some systems have separate throttle and clutch controls, in others they are combined in one control. If they are separate, put the clutch in the neutral position. If they are combined in one lever, you can usually pull the lever sideways to disengage it. Then keep it in neutral while you work the throttle forward and back.

Check Your Battery

When you turned the key, did you hear the starter solenoid click? If so, your problem is in the battery, the solenoid, or the starter. First, inspect the connections to the battery terminals. Are they clean and tight? If not, correct the problem.

If nothing happened when you turned the key, switch off the ignition, then turn on a lamp wired into the boat's 12-volt DC electrical system to see

✓ SPRING FITTING-OUT CHECKLIST

Inspect the following items, and service or replace them as needed:

- ☐ Lubricate all seacocks.
- ☐ Close all seacocks that you opened in the fall.
- ☐ Inspect hoses and hose clamps. Inspect the engine water intake strainer to see that it is free of corrosion and properly secured. Inspect the hull for cracks and blisters.
- ☐ Inspect zincs.
- ☐ Inspect the fuel tank for corrosion and leaks.
- ☐ Inspect the bilge blower hoses for leaks.
- ☐ If you have a stern drive, inspect the bellows for dried, cracked, or deteriorated spots.
- ☐ Inspect power steering and power trim oil levels.
- ☐ Inspect and lubricate steering and control cables.
- ☐ Inspect the fire extinguishers.
- ☐ Inspect the galley stove for loose fittings or leaking hoses.
- ☐ Inspect the bilge pump and float switch.
- ☐ Inspect your pyrotechnic distress signals. Replace outdated ones, but keep old ones aboard as spares.

if you have enough power to light it. If it lights, turn the ignition switch to the Start position. Does it still glow? If not, your battery is dead.

If you do not have a voltmeter or if the lamp fails to light, check the battery with a hydrometer. A battery that tests dead will need to be recharged. Check for some appliance that may have been left on and thus discharged the battery. If the battery will not take or hold a charge, replace it.

Check for Loose Connections

If the battery is charged and its terminals and connectors are clean and tight, check for loose wires or connections to the starter solenoid and tighten as required. Your engine should turn over. If it doesn't, the problem is probably with the solenoid and you should take the engine in for repairs unless you are a mechanic.

Engine Will Not Start

If the starter engages and the engine turns over but doesn't start, check to see if there is fuel in the tank and the fuel shutoff valve is open. If you have fuel, the problem is probably in the ignition system, contaminated fuel, or the air induction system.

Check to see if you have flooded the engine with gas. If so, you should smell fumes and waiting a few minutes should correct the problem. Check your bilge again for gasoline fumes and run your blower for at least 4 minutes. When you try again to start the engine, don't advance the throttle.

Check the fuel filter and the backfire flame arrester to see if they are clean. If they are dirty, gasoline or air will not enter the engine, since both are necessary for ignition.

Your engine will also not get fuel or start if it has a faulty fuel pump. Replacing it is a job for a mechanic.

After all of this, if your engine does not start, check the wires to the spark coil, from the spark coil to the distributor, and from the distributor to the spark plugs. A loose wire from the spark coil or to the distributor makes ignition impossible.

Engine Runs Rough

Sometimes an engine will start and idle smoothly but will run rough when accelerating or when at cruising speed. A wire could be loose at a plug, the coil, or the distributor. The same condition results if there is a damaged spark plug or one that is overdue for replacement, or if there is a crack in the distributor cap that may be too small to be easily seen.

If you replace the cap, be sure to use one designed for marine use that will not admit gasoline vapors.

Engine Idles but Does Not Develop Full Power

Sometimes an engine will idle but will not develop full power underway. There are several possible causes, including a faulty condenser, which has already been described.

The most common problem is too much oil in the fuel mixture of an outboard. You may have put too much oil in the tank, or your VRO may be malfunctioning.

The carburetor could be out of adjustment. It will lose power if the fuel-air mixture is too rich, and will also lose power and backfire if it is too lean. The same problem can result from a kinked fuel hose or a slight blockage in the fuel line.

Outboards that are primed with electrical primers have the same problem if the primer fails, since failure limits the amount of fuel reaching the engine. Have it repaired or replaced.

If you are underway and the engine overheats or loses power, turn it off. Weeds or other debris may have fouled the propeller. If you have an outboard or a stern drive, raise it or the outdrive and see if you have weeds or other debris on the propeller.

There are other problems and solutions beyond this general discussion. You can learn a lot by reading your owner's manual and by listening to mechanics. In this way, you can do many maintenance and repair jobs for yourself.

Ways to Learn More

Boat Maintenance: The Essential Guide to Cleaning, Painting, and Cosmetics. William Burr. Camden, Maine: International Marine, 2000.

Boatowner's Illustrated Electrical Handbook. 2nd ed. Charlie Wing. Camden, Maine: International Marine, 2006.

Chapman Piloting & Seamanship. 66th ed. Charles B. Husick. New York: Hearst Books, 2009. Chapter 6.

Diesel Engine Care and Repair: A Captain's Quick Guide. Nigel Calder. Camden, Maine: International Marine, 2007.

How Boat Things Work: An Illustrated Guide. Charlie Wing. Camden, Maine: International Marine, 2007.

Know Your Boat's Diesel Engine: An Essential Guide to Maintenance, Troubleshooting, and Repair. Andrew Simpson. Camden, Maine: International Marine, 2007.

Maintain and Improve Your Powerboat: More Than 100 Do-It-Yourself Ways to Make Your Boat Better. Paul Esterle. Camden, Maine: International Marine, 2009.

Marine Diesel Engines: Maintenance, Trouble-shooting, and Repair. Nigel Calder. Camden, Maine: International Marine, 2006.

Outboard Engines: Maintenance, Troubleshooting, and Repair. 2nd ed. Edwin Sherman. Camden, Maine: International Marine, 2008.

Powerboat Care and Repair: How to Keep Your Outboard, Sterndrive, or Gas-Inboard Boat Alive and Well. Allen Berrien. Camden, Maine: International Marine, 2003.

Powerboater's Guide to Electrical Systems: Maintenance, Troubleshooting, and Improvements. 2nd ed. Ed Sherman. Camden, Maine: International Marine, 2007.

Practical Boat Mechanics: Commonsense Ways to Prevent, Diagnose, and Repair Engine and Mechanical Problems. Ben Evridge. Camden, Maine: International Marine, 2009.

The Practical Encyclopedia of Boating: An A–Z Compendium of Navigation, Seamanship, Boat Maintenance, and Nautical Wisdom. John Vigor. Camden, Maine: International Marine, 2007.

The Practical Mariner's Book of Knowledge: 460 Sea-Tested Rules of Thumb for Almost Every Boating Situation. 2nd ed. John Vigor. Camden, Maine: International Marine, 2013.

The Propeller Handbook: The Complete Reference for Choosing, Installing, and Understanding Boat Propellers. Dave Gerr. Camden, Maine: International Marine, 2001.

Quick and Easy Boat Maintenance: 1,001+ Time-

Practice Questions

IMPORTANT BOATING TERMS

In the following exercise, match the words in the column on the left with the definitions in the column on the right. In the blank space to the left of each term, write the letter of the item that best matches it. Do not use an item in the right-hand column more than once.

THE ITEMS

1. _____ crankcase
2. _____ fuel injection
3. _____ diesel fuel
4. _____ induction system
5. _____ magneto
6. _____ gasohol
7. _____ removing battery
8. _____ zinc
9. _____ prevent gum formation
10. _____ impeller

THE RESPONSES

a. is built into flywheel
b. is replacing carburetors
c. stabilize your gasoline
d. most common water pump on marine engines
e. may destroy some fuel tanks
f. loosen negative terminal first
g. contains the lubricating oil
h. gels at low temperatures
i. brings fuel to the engine
j. sacrificial metal

Saving Tips. 2nd ed. Sandy Lindsey. Camden, Maine: International Marine, 2012.

Seamanship Secrets: 185 Tips and Techniques for Better Navigation, Cruise Planning, and Boat Handling Under Power or Sail. John Jamieson. Camden, Maine: International Marine, 2009.

Troubleshooting Marine Diesel Engines. 4th ed. Peter Compton. Camden, Maine: International Marine, 1997.

www.pureenergysystems.com/PESWiki/Directory/Bedini_SG/files/Vonwentzel-battery.pdf

www.batterystuff.com/kb/articles/battery-articles/lithium-battery-overview.html

Multiple-Choice Items

In the following items, choose the best response:

10-1. Diesel engines ignite their fuel

a. by a spark
b. by an ignition system
c. the same way as in a gasoline engine
d. by heat of compression

10-2. Diesel fuel has a safety advantage over gasoline because it is

a. less likely to explode
b. more efficient
c. cheaper to use
d. less odorous

10-3. One advantage of a stern-drive engine over an outboard motor is that it

a. weighs less, horsepower for horsepower
b. costs less
c. uses fuel more efficiently
d. is easier to replace

10-4. Marine engines can be classified by

a. how they are installed
b. the number of operating cycles
c. the type of fuel they use
d. all of the above

10-5. The easiest way to approach the problem of corrosion on battery terminals is to

a. tighten the terminals
b. spray them with a mixture of water and baking soda
c. turn off the switch when the battery is not in use
d. coat them with grease

10-6. Inboards, stern drives, and outboards get their names from

a. how they are installed
b. the fuel they use
c. the type of ignition they have
d. none of the above

10-7. Which of the following is a cooling system in current use?

a. air
b. open
c. dual
d. all of the above

10-8. If you have two batteries, you should have

a. no battery failure problems
b. a battery isolation switch
c. a hygrometer
d. a voltage regulator

10-9. If your engine has points and if you change them, always change your

a. distributor
b. carburetor
c. condenser
d. oil

10-10. An explosion through the air intake of a carburetor is a

a. power stroke
b. backfire
c. misfire
d. disaster

10-11. To protect your battery from accidental short circuits, the terminals should be

a. disconnected whenever the battery is not in use
b. smeared with marine grease
c. protected by a cover
d. allowed to build up a deposit of salts

10-12. One feature that you will find on a four-cycle engine that you never find on a two-cycle outboard motor is/are

a. a crankcase with oil
b. a condenser
c. points
d. a carburetor

Multiple-Choice Items (continued)

10-13. Modern outboard motors require

a. leaded gasoline
b. a lead substitute in the gasoline
c. less lead than a stern-drive engine
d. no lead in the gasoline

10-14. Proper lubrication in a two-stroke gasoline outboard engine is provided by

a. oil mixed in the gasoline or injected with the gasoline
b. marine grease packed in the bearings
c. oil pumped throughout the engine
d. oil in the crankcase

10-15. The first thing to check if your fully charged battery will not crank your engine is

a. your battery isolation switch
b. your battery terminals
c. the level of fluid in the battery
d. the voltage of the battery

10-16. Maintenance procedures include

a. routine
b. winterizing
c. springtime fitting out
d. all of the above

10-17. Sacrificial metals are used to keep other metals from eroding. They are made of

a. stainless steel
b. magnesium
c. zinc
d. copper

10-18. To prevent explosions from backfires, stern-drive and inboard engines are equipped with

a. marine-type parts
b. backfire flame arresters
c. sealed distributors
d. vapor locks

10-19. To protect against gasoline gum when your engine is not in use for a long period of time

a. flush it out with water
b. leave the tank full and add stabilizer to the fuel
c. fill your tank with diesel fuel
d. buy a high grade of gasoline that does not have gum in it

10-20. Most marine engines will start only in

a. forward
b. reverse
c. neutral
d. idle speed

10-21. The newest engines available use what kind of ignition system?

a. electronic
b. magneto
c. distributor
d. closed

10-22. Which of the following is an advantage of an outboard over a stern drive?

a. weighs more
b. uses fuel more efficiently
c. is easier to replace
d. is quieter

10-23. The principal reason for covering a battery is to

a. prevent dirt accumulation
b. create a thermal barrier
c. prevent accidental short circuits
d. retard evaporation of fluid

10-24. To check the oil level in the gears of an outboard or stern-drive lower unit

a. remove the upper screw cap
b. remove the lower screw cap
c. remove both screw caps
d. see if you can add additional oil

chapter 11

Lines and Knots for Your Boat

The objectives of this chapter are to describe:

✔ The art of handling and working rope known as marlinespike seamanship.

✔ Rope materials and construction.

✔ The selection, use, and care of rope.

✔ How to store rope.

✔ The rope-handling hardware your boat should have.

✔ Some useful knots.

✔ How to secure a boat's lines.

(PHOTO BY MOLLY MULHERN)

THIS CHAPTER discusses *marlinespike seamanship*, which is the art of handling and working rope on board. Its name comes from a tapered metal tool, called a *marlinespike*, which is used for working rope. We'll discuss the materials and constructions of rope that is optimized for specific purposes, and we'll look at the uses and care of rope as well as the onboard hardware that helps with line-handling tasks.

Line or Rope?

The last sentence of the paragraph above mentions line handling instead of rope handling. So when does a rope become a line? Simply put, when you buy it, you ask for **rope**, but when you bring it aboard your boat you call it **line**. Let's look at the few exceptions to this convention.

In traditional terminology, there are times when a rope is a rope. For example, the line used to move a bell's clapper to make the bell ring is a *bell rope*. *Bolt ropes* and *foot ropes* help control sails, while the tillers of sailing ships were once controlled with *tiller ropes*. Today, however, with the exception of the occasional bolt rope sewn into a sail, you won't find ropes in use on a boat.

There are times, though, when the word "line" is too generic for the task at hand. For example, the rope (usually a wire rope) that keeps a sailboat's mast from leaning forward or backward is a *stay*, and the

wire ropes that support a mast from side to side are called *shrouds*. Collectively, the stays and shrouds constitute a sailboat's *standing rigging*. The synthetic-fiber or wire ropes used to pull up a sailboat's sails are called *halyards*, and these are part of the boat's *running rigging*. An anchor line and its fittings constitute a *rode*, although you won't be misunderstood if you refer to it as an anchor line. The line that secures a dinghy to a larger boat is a *painter*. A *sheet* is a line that adjusts the trim of a sail.

While sailboats use lines extensively, powerboats use fewer lines and use them less often. Even aboard a powerboat, however, lines serve essential needs.

Rope Materials

With the exception of the wire rope used in a sailboat's rigging, virtually all modern ropes are made from synthetic fibers. The natural-fiber ropes of earlier generations—manila, sisal, hemp, jute, cotton, and flax—have disappeared from boats and from

TABLE 11-1 CHARACTERISTICS OF FIBERS

Material	Breaking Strength[1] (lbs.)	Stretch (%)	Abrasion Resistance	Specific Gravity[2]	UV Resistance	Relative Cost
Polypropylene	1,530	18–22	Fair	0.91	Fair	Low
Nylon	2,600	30–35	Excellent	1.14	Excellent	Medium
Polyester (Dacron)	3,470	15–20	Excellent	1.38	Excellent	Medium
High-tenacity polyethylene (Spectra)	8,160	2.3–3.9	Excellent	0.97	Fair	High
Aramid (Kevlar)	8,500	1.5–4.5	Fair	1.44	Fair	High
High-tenacity copolymer (Technora)	10,700	1.5–4.5	Fair	1.44	Fair	Very high
Liquid-crystal polymer (Vectran)	11,600	3.5–4.5	Very good	1.40	Fair	Very high
High-tenacity polyethylene (Dyneema)	12,000	2.0–4.0	Excellent	0.975	Very good	Very high

1. Breaking strength of single-braid 5/16 in. rope.
2. Floats in fresh water if < 1.00; salt water if < 1.025.

REPRINTED WITH PERMISSION FROM *KNOTS, SPLICES, AND LINE HANDLING: A CAPTAIN'S QUICK GUIDE* BY CHARLIE WING

the shelves of marine supply stores, and for good reason. Synthetic ropes have superior strength either wet or dry, and they can be engineered to optimize certain characteristics for specific jobs. Further, they resist mildew, rot, and damage by acids and alkalis. Heat and sunlight, however, *can* damage *some of* them, as we'll see. The characteristics of various synthetic fibers are shown in Table 11-1. We will mention such high-tech synthetics as Kevlar and Spectra as we proceed, but nylon and polyester predominate on boats and are perfectly satisfactory for every ordinary service.

Nylon Rope

The most commonly used synthetic fiber is nylon. It does not shrink when wet, and it also resists chafing. Nylon stretches more than any other synthetic or natural fiber rope. Even so, when you remove the stress, it springs back without damage to its fibers or construction.

Nylon's elasticity is both an asset and a liability. When used as an anchor or mooring line, it stretches and helps absorb the shock of a boat's surge. Your anchor is less likely to lose its hold, and the shock loads on your deck hardware are reduced.

On the other hand, since nylon stretches, you should not use it for lines that must stay tight. Thus, you would not use it in the running rigging of sailboats.

Nylon's ability to stretch can make it dangerous if it breaks under strain. In such a case, it may work like an elastic band. A serious accident can result, for example, when one boat is towing another and the hardware comes loose. The line may act as a slingshot and hurl the hardware like a missile.

Polyester Rope

Polyester rope is manufactured under a variety of trade names, but Dacron is the best known. The stretch rating of a polyester line will vary according to its construction (see below), but polyester in general has substantially lower stretch than nylon and is therefore used widely for sailboat halyards and sheets. Polyester can also be blended with other, even higher-tech synthetics to further increase strength and reduce stretch for specialized applications such as the halyards of racing sailboats. For example, a Spectra, Kevlar, Vectran, or Technora core can make a rope extremely strong and inelastic, while a polyester cover gives that rope better resistance to abrasion and sunlight and makes it easier to handle. Polyester can be formulated to give a rope excellent *hand* (feel)—flexible and soft. Resistance to chafing varies with the formulation but is always much higher than that of Spectra, Kevlar, and other higher-tech fibers.

Polypropylene Rope

Polypropylene rope is the least costly of the synthetic ropes, which explains its great popularity for lobster trap warps and other commercial fishing applications. Its other major advantage is that it floats, making it useful for ski towlines, painters, and for throwing PFDs to persons in the water. Its ability to float helps keep polyester rope out of a towing boat's propeller.

Polypropylene line deteriorates rapidly in sunlight, however, and it then *parts* (breaks) easily. Don't use it for anchor or mooring lines, or you will risk losing your anchor and, perhaps, your boat.

Polypropylene line also has the disadvantage of a hard, slippery texture. It may slip on a cleat, it can cut your hands, and knots tied in it often work themselves loose.

Special Ropes

Synthetic fibers are also used to make special types of ropes such as *shock cord*, a multistrand rubber

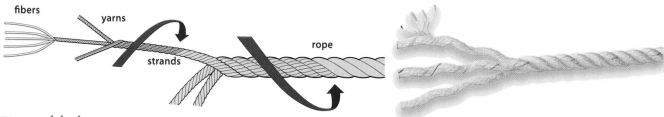

Figure **11-1.** **Left:** The composition of three-strand line. **Right:** Three-strand nylon line. (COURTESY NEW ENGLAND ROPES)

line with a synthetic cover and hooks or eyes on each end that make connecting it easy.

Shock cord can stretch up to twice its own length. Use it to hold things in place and to prevent halyards from slapping against the mast of a moored boat.

Wire Rope

The standing or permanent rigging on a sailboat is usually *wire rope*, and the running rigging with which sails are hoisted and trimmed is sometimes wire rope as well. Nearly all wire rope used on boats these days is stainless steel, which resists corrosion more successfully than galvanized steel (although, contrary to wide belief, stainless steel *will* corrode). Wire rope provides maximum strength and minimum stretch, which makes it useful also for the davits you see on big boats, by means of which they hoist their tenders clear of the water when making passages.

Rope Construction

Rope is made in one of three ways: laying, braiding, or weaving.

Laid Rope

Laid rope (also known as *cable-laid rope*) is made by twisting fibers together to form **yarns**, which are then twisted together in the opposite direction to form **strands**. The strands, in turn, are twisted together in the original direction to form the finished rope.

The direction in which the strands are twisted is called the *lay* of the rope. Thus, rope may be either *right-laid* or *left-laid*. To tell the lay of a line, hold up a length of the line. If the strands spiral upward to the right, the rope is right-laid. Most laid line used on boats has three strands twisted clockwise to form a right-hand lay, and is thus also called *three-strand line*. Three-strand nylon is the most popular choice for mooring pendants and anchor rodes, applications for which high stretch is an asset, not a liability (Figure 11-1).

Sometimes a larger line is desired. In this case, ropes are twisted together to form **cables** or **hawsers**.

Hawsers are used on tugboats and to moor large vessels.

Wire rope is also laid rope in that strands or bundles of wires are twisted together to make it. Figure 11-2 shows a selection of the wire rope constructions in use on boats—primarily sailboats. Wire rope for standing rigging is usually 1 x 19 (spoken as "one by nineteen"). This wire, consisting of nineteen equal elements wound around each other, is strong but not very flexible.

When wire rope is used for running rigging applications (most commonly halyards), 7 x 19 (seven elements, each composed of nineteen individual strands) is the most common choice, followed by 7 x 7 (seven elements with seven strands in each). Wire for running rigging is weaker but more flexible than standing rigging wire of the same diameter.

The 6 x 42 wire rope illustrated in Figure 11-2 has a fiber center, but is rarely seen in use anymore.

Braided Rope

A second way to make rope is by braiding, in which fibers are twisted into yarns, two to four yarns are bundled to make a strand, and the strands are then interwoven. *Braided rope* is smooth (like cotton clothesline), which makes it easier on the hands than laid rope. On the other hand, braided line can snag on pilings and other objects, in which case strands may break, weakening the rope.

Braided rope may be *single-* or *double-braid*. A double-braid rope has an outer braided cover over a separately braided inner core (Figure 11-3), whereas a single-braid line has a uniformly braided cross section (Figure 11-4). Double-braid rope is stronger, more durable, more resistant to stretching, and more expensive than single-braid rope of the same diameter and material. Single-braid rope is more supple and easier to handle, especially

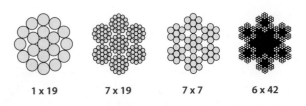

| 1 x 19 | 7 x 19 | 7 x 7 | 6 x 42 |

Figure **11-2.** Wire rope cross sections.

CORE

Figure 11-3. Two examples of double-braid rope, consisting of a braided core inside a braided cover. (TOP PHOTO BY JOE BRITVCH; BOTTOM PHOTO COURTESY NEW ENGLAND ROPES)

when constructed in whole or in part from spun fibers—i.e., from fibers that are a few inches long. Spun nylon or polyester rope is fuzzy, as opposed to continuous-filament rope, which is harder and has a shiny surface.

Small sizes of single-braid ropes, up to ⅜ inch, are used for sailbag ties, flag halyards, and similar special purposes. In larger sizes, single-braid polyester (often spun polyester) is popular for mainsheets, where ease of handling is prized and stretch matters less than it does for headsail sheets. Single-braid nylon is often used for docklines, where some stretch (though perhaps not as much as in an anchor rode) is an asset.

Figure 11-4. Two examples of single-braid rope, which is also called solid-braid because it has a uniform braid throughout when seen in cross section. (TOP PHOTO BY DON LINDBERG; BOTTOM PHOTO COURTESY NEW ENGLAND ROPES)

Most other braided rope used on boats is double-braid, which is stronger than laid rope of the same size and material. Single-braid rope is similar in strength but stretches less than laid rope of the same size and material. Braided rope costs more than comparable laid rope.

Various hybrids—both of synthetic materials and of construction methods—have been developed for specific applications. For example, *parallel-core braided polyester rope* consists of a core of parallel, unwoven polyester fibers encased in a braided cover (Figure 11-5). This construction is proving popular for sailboat halyards because it stretches even less than double-braid polyester. On highly competitve racing sailboats this trend is taken even further by substituting Spectra, Kevlar, or some other space-age fiber for the polyester in the parallel core.

Table 11-2 and Figure 11-6 summarize the characteristics of the most popular ropes, and Tables 11-3 and 11-4 show recommended diameters of three-strand or single-braid nylon ropes to use for docklines and anchor rodes on boats of various sizes.

Figure 11-5. Parallel-core rope has a core of parallel, unwoven fibers encased in a braided cover. (COURTESY NEW ENGLAND ROPES)

	Strength	Flexibility	Stretch	Cost
THREE-STRAND	Medium	Low	High	Low
SINGLE-BRAID	Medium	High	Medium	Low
DOUBLE-BRAID	High	Medium	Low	Medium
PARALLEL-CORE	Highest	High	Very Low	High

Figure 11-6. The characteristics of various rope constructions. (REPRINTED WITH PERMISSION FROM *KNOTS, SPLICES, AND LINE HANDLING: A CAPTAIN'S QUICK GUIDE* BY CHARLIE WING)

TABLE 11-2 APPROXIMATE BREAKING STRENGTHS OF ROPES

Diameter in inches	3/16	1/4	5/16	3/8	7/16	1/2	5/8	3/4
in millimeters	5	6	8	9.5	11	12	16	19
Polypropylene hollow-braid	550	980	1,530	2,200	2,990	3,910	6,110	8,800
Polypropylene three-strand	725	1,290	2,010	2,900	3,940	5,150	8,050	11,600
Nylon single-braid	940	1,670	2,600	3,750	5,100	6,660	10,400	15,000
Nylon double-braid	1,090	1,940	3,040	4,375	5,950	7,770	12,100	17,500
Nylon three-strand	940	1,670	2,600	3,750	5,100	6,660	10,400	15,000
Polyester single-braid	1,140	1,900	3,000	4,200	5,500	7,000	11,000	15,300
Polyester double-braid	1,200	2,000	3,000	4,400	6,600	8,500	14,400	20,000
with Spectra or Kevlar core	2,300	3,800	5,700	7,600	10,200	12,800	21,800	28,800
with Vectran or Technora core	2,720	4,500	8,000	10,000	15,000	18,000	31,000	42,300
Polyester braid with parallel core	1,600	2,700	4,400	5,500	7,400	9,600	15,000	21,600

REPRINTED WITH PERMISSION FROM *KNOTS, SPLICES, AND LINE HANDLING: A CAPTAIN'S QUICK GUIDE* BY CHARLIE WING

Webbing

Synthetic fibers are sometimes woven together to form a flat line called *webbing*. Webbing is used for a variety of purposes such as the retrieval line on a trailer, and you may have seen it used for the backs and seats of lawn chairs.

Webbing of woven nylon or polyester is very strong. Use it to tie down a dinghy on a larger boat or to hold a boat on a trailer. Webbing also makes good *sail stops* (ties used to hold a lowered sail to its boom) since it holds knots so well (Figure 11-7), and offshore sailors use webbing for their safety harnesses.

Measuring Rope

The older, traditional way to measure the size of fiber rope is by its circumference (the distance around the rope). Today, however, most marine suppliers and boaters describe it by its diameter. If you ask for 1/2-inch rope you will get one with a 1/2-inch diameter.

Small lines are suitable for securing small items, but most people have trouble holding onto them. The smallest line most people can conveniently hold has a 3/8-inch diameter. Thus, even

TABLE 11-3 DOCKLINES

Boat Length (ft.)	Bow/Stern Lines (ft.)	Spring Lines (ft.)	Rope Diameter (in.)
to 27	20	25	3/8
28–36	25	35	1/2
37–45	30	45	5/8
46–54	35	50	3/4
55–72	40	70	1

REPRINTED WITH PERMISSION FROM *KNOTS, SPLICES, AND LINE HANDLING: A CAPTAIN'S QUICK GUIDE* BY CHARLIE WING

TABLE 11-4 ANCHOR RODES

(recommended rode consists of 15 feet of chain plus 200 feet of three-strand nylon)

Boat Length (ft.)	Chain Rope Size (in.)	Diameter (in.)
to 25	3/16	1/4
26–35	1/4	1/2
46–54	3/8	3/4
55–72	1/2	1

REPRINTED WITH PERMISSION FROM *KNOTS, SPLICES, AND LINE HANDLING: A CAPTAIN'S QUICK GUIDE* BY CHARLIE WING

though a ¼-inch-diameter high-tech rope is as strong as ⅜-inch double-braid polyester, the latter is more likely to be chosen as a mainsheet because it's so much easier to handle (and also because it costs much less!). Choose larger line sizes for sheets, halyards, anchor lines, and mooring lines on anything but the smallest boats.

It is unwise to use small mooring and anchor lines. During a storm, these lines are under heavy stress. The surge of your boat can cause a line to part, and constant chafe can abrade and weaken it. For both these reasons, a thicker line will stand up better and longer than a thinner one, but there are limits. You need to select a line that's appropriate for the size of the cleat you will tie it to. In general, you will want to use the largest dock and anchor

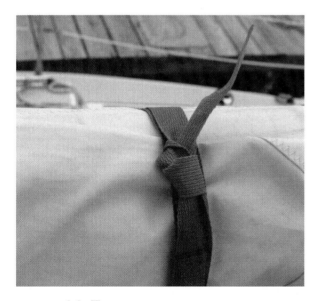

Figure **11-7.** Webbing used as a sail stop. (PHOTO BY DON LINDBERG)

lines that will lead fairly through your boat's chocks and tie properly to your boat's cleats and bitts.

Large lines have less stretch per pound of load than smaller lines of the same material and construction. Larger lines also take fewer turns around a winch to raise a sail, and offer more friction on the winch. Regardless of the size of the line, you may wish to wear gloves with palms but without fingers on a sailboat. They are designed to protect your hands from line burn while still keeping your fingers free.

The principal disadvantage of large lines is cost. Large lines cost more than smaller ones, and you will need larger cleats to which to tie them. On a sailboat, larger lines call for larger *blocks* (pulleys), which are also an added expense.

Care of Rope

All rope requires some care. Stainless steel wire rope needs the least. The time and trouble you take in caring for your lines will be repaid by greater safety and longer rope life.

Uncoiling Rope

Proper care begins as soon as you buy your rope. Open new coils carefully. The rope can easily tangle and kink, which makes handling it more difficult and can weaken its fibers.

Both braided and wire ropes usually come on reels or spools. If your rope came on a reel, roll it off. Do not try to uncoil it, as this introduces a kink in the rope with each turn taken off the reel. The same problem occurs if you take rope from a coil in an improper manner.

If you get a kink in the rope, remove it by working it out to the nearest end. You can make a kink disappear by putting a strain on the rope, but don't do it, because some of its fibers will break, weakening the rope at the point of the kink.

Overstressed Lines

Never overwork or overstress a line. You may not see it, but too big a load on a line breaks its fibers and weakens it. Check for deterioration by looking inside the rope. If you see a powdery material, re-place it. And if the line has decreased in diameter, it has been permanently stretched and weakened.

Dry Your Lines

Stow your lines in dry, well-ventilated places, such as on a shelf or grating, to prevent accumulation of moisture. Do not stow other materials on top of the lines.

You can stow synthetic lines wet, but doing so will introduce moisture into your hold or lockers. Although synthetic fiber will not rot, it will mildew, which makes it look and smell bad.

You should also keep your lines away from sources of heat such as exhaust pipes. Heat is harm-ful to synthetic fibers, as is battery acid.

Chafing

When lines rub against hard surfaces, even highly polished chocks, they will eventually chafe and weaken. Wrap your mooring and anchor lines with canvas or leather to prevent chafing where they pass through chocks or around cleats (Figure 11-8). Where mooring lines contact wooden or concrete piers, pass them through lengths of old garden hose to increase their useful life.

To get the most use out of a mooring or anchor line and to maintain its safety, turn it end for end pe-riodically to distribute chafing at different points. Docklines, too, can be end-for-ended in this manner.

Keep Your Lines Clean

Dirt, sand, salt, and oil are destructive to both nat-ural and synthetic fiber lines. Dirt, sand, and salt crystals cut the fibers, while oil weakens them. To wash a line, put it in a mesh bag or pillowcase and put it in a washing machine. In this way, it won't get tangled up, develop new kinks, or foul up the washing machine. Mild soap or detergent will help get the line clean and will not harm the fibers. If the line is stiff, use a fabric softener.

Fraying

The ends of all lines will fray and *unlay* (separate) unless you treat them to prevent it. If you don't

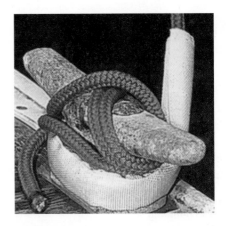

Figure **11-8.** A canvas sleeve protects this dockline from chafe where it passes around the cleat. (REPRINTED WITH PERMIS-SION FROM *ROUGH WEATHER SEAMANSHIP FOR SAIL AND POWER* BY ROGER MAR-SHALL)

care what the end of your line looks like, you can simply tie a knot in it, but this is unsightly and makes the line difficult to use, as the knot will not pass through chocks and blocks easily.

When a synthetic line is cut from a coil by an electric cutter, it does not need care immediately. When it is cut with a knife or otherwise, you can use a match to get the same result as an electric cutter. The heat will melt the end of almost any synthetic line, fusing the strands together and pre-venting them from unlaying. Eventually, though, the end will begin to unravel.

Another temporary means of treating the end of a line is to tape it with marine, electrical, or ad-hesive tape. Sooner or later the tape will come off, however, and the line will unravel.

A more permanent way to prevent fraying is by using an air-drying liquid plastic coating (such as Rope Dip) developed for this purpose and sold in marine supply stores. You can even color-code your lines by this means. This is useful on a sailboat, where several lines may end near each other.

Whipping the end of a line is another way to keep it from unraveling, one that will look better and last longer than heat-sealing or taping it.

Figure 11-9 shows a *plain whipping*, which is not permanent but will last a long time if done right. Start by forming a loop of whipping twine—which is also called *cord* or *small stuff*, and is most commonly sold in a waxed polyester construction, though nylon twine is also available. Place the apex of the loop about ½ inch from the end of the

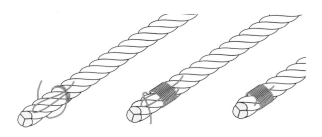

Figure **11-9.** A plain whipping. (REPRINTED WITH PERMISSION FROM *KNOTS, SPLICES, AND LINE HANDLING: A CAPTAIN'S QUICK GUIDE* BY CHARLIE WING)

rope. Using the long end of the twine, make eight or ten tight turns around the rope, working toward the rope end. Leave the anchored end of the twine exposed, because you will need it in a minute, and stop the turns before you cover the apex of the loop. Pass the working end of the cord through the loop, then pull the anchored end until the loop disappears under the turns. Clip the twine ends flush with the turns, and you're done.

To whip the end of a three-strand line permanently, use a *sailmaker's whipping* as in Figure 11-10. Start by unlaying the rope strands to about 1 inch from the end, then pass a loop of twine around one of the strands so that the apex of the loop points away from the rope end, rather than toward it as in the plain whipping. Then relay the strands back to their original position. Using the long end of the whipping twine, make eight or ten tight turns toward the rope end, leaving a generous bight of the loop exposed under the first turn. Then place the exposed portion of the loop back over its original strand, and pull tight using the anchored end of the twine. Finally, tie the twine ends tightly with a square knot, and trim the ends.

For a more or less permanent whipping that will work on braided as well as laid line, try a *sewn whipping*, as in Figure 11-11. Thread waxed whipping twine through the eye of a heavy needle, then make two stitches through the rope about $\frac{1}{2}$ to $\frac{3}{4}$ inch from the end. Follow with eight to ten tight turns toward the end, then make a stitch through a third of the rope's circumference so that the needle emerges about 120° from its entry point. Pull taut. Now pass the needle and twine back over the turns and make a mirror-image stitch at the beginning end of the whipping. Again pass needle and twine over the turns for a second 120° stitch that begins where the initial stitch emerged. Repeat until you have three double stitches spaced at 120° intervals around the rope end, then take a final stitch and trim the twine ends. Besides being decorative, a whipping like this is very functional.

Care of Wire Rope

Wire rope will serve you well if you take care of it. One of the worst things that can happen to it is to get a kink in it, as this weakens it.

Be careful when you run your hand along a wire rope. Under stress, some of the small wires break and then stick out from the rope. Examine wire rope from time to time by running your hand up and down the wire while wearing cotton gloves. If a glove catches on anything, you've most likely found a broken strand, which is often called a *fishhook* or *meathook*.

Any such break indicates that the wire is damaged, and its load-carrying ability has been compromised. If you find more than a few fishhooks, consider replacing the wire. Wire rope ends are usually covered by *swaged terminals*, which are metal

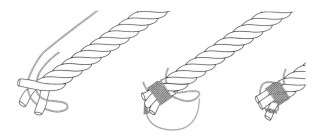

Figure **11-10.** A sailmaker's whipping. (REPRINTED WITH PERMISSION FROM *KNOTS, SPLICES, AND LINE HANDLING: A CAPTAIN'S QUICK GUIDE* BY CHARLIE WING)

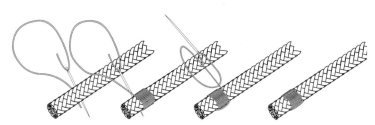

Figure **11-11.** A sewn whipping. (REPRINTED WITH PERMISSION FROM *KNOTS, SPLICES, AND LINE HANDLING: A CAPTAIN'S QUICK GUIDE* BY CHARLIE WING)

sleeves that are machine-crimped around the wire. The terminal is usually forged with an end fitting by means of which the wire can be connected to a mast tang, a turnbuckle, or other hardware (Figure 11-12). When swaged fittings deteriorate, they usually don't show signs of weakness during inspection. A failure in a sailboat's standing rigging will usually occur during periods of great stress, such as a storm, which is the last time you want this problem to happen. To avoid this, regular, highly critical inspections of your boat's rigging, especially the wire rope, are recommended. Boats exposed only to mild weather and waves should be inspected at least every 10 years, while boats exposed to heavy weather and waves should be inspected at least

every 5 years. All rigging should be inspected thoroughly before any extended offshore passage.

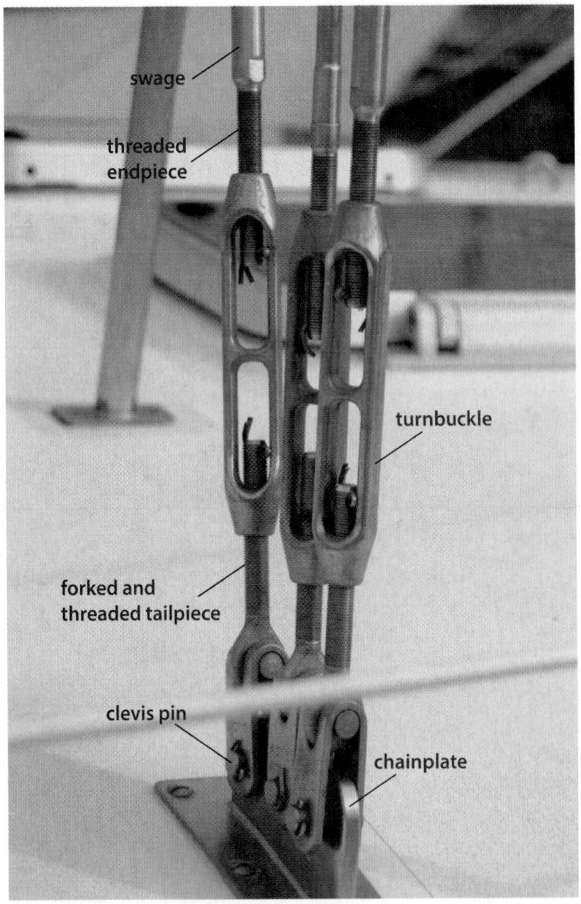

Making Up a Line

Stow your lines neatly when they are not in use. How you stow lines depends on their intended uses. There are three methods of making up line—coiling, faking, and flemishing.

Coiling a Line

If you plan to stow a line in a compartment or locker or hang it from a peg, coil it. Coil right-laid rope clockwise, and coil left-laid rope (if you ever encounter any) counterclockwise. Assuming the line is right-laid, start by holding it in your left hand. Run your right hand down the line and sweep the line back to your left hand to form a single loop, then repeat. Continue adding loops until you have coiled all the line.

When you coil the end of a cleated halyard in this fashion, the most convenient place to store the coil is on the halyard cleat. To do so, simply reach through the coil to grasp the line between the cleat hitch and the first bight of the coil. Pull that part of the line through the coil to form a loop, twist the loop once or twice, and hook it over the horn of the cleat (Figure 11-13). There you have it—a neat coil, hung off the deck and out of the way, yet easily loosened when the time comes to lower the sail.

If you are simply coiling an unused line for

Figure **11-12.** Sailboat forestays, backstays, and shrouds terminate on deck in swaged end fittings with threads that screw into turnbuckles like these three, which are for a sailboat's starboard shrouds. The turnbuckles are attached to well-anchored chainplates and are used to adjust the tension of the stay or shroud. The wire rope shrouds are not visible in this photo; they're crimped into the swages just above the field of view. (PHOTO BY DON LINDBERG)

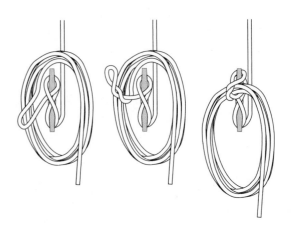

Figure **11-13.** An easy way to hang a coiled halyard from a mast cleat. This coil will also be quick to undo when it's time to lower the sail. (REPRINTED WITH PERMISSION FROM *KNOTS, SPLICES, AND LINE HANDLING: A CAPTAIN'S QUICK GUIDE* BY CHARLIE WING)

stowage and wish to hang the coil, release the last loop of the coil and wind the longer end thus created several times around the coil. Then reach through the coil and pull a loop from the last winding you just completed through the coil, then up and over the top of the coil. Pull on the running end to cinch the loop, and you have created a **gasket coil**, which can be hung in a locker or cabin for stowage (Figure 11-14).

Faking Down a Line

On a small boat you can usually stow your anchor line by letting it fall into its well. If this is not feasible, try faking it down or flemishing it. **Faked lines** run with less resistance than coiled lines in fast runoffs, and with less chance of tangling or snagging. Mooring lines, anchor lines, heaving lines, lead lines, running rigging, and other lines can all be faked to good advantage. Faking is sometimes known as **flaking**.

Faking down a line consists of laying it onto the deck or into the anchor locker in figure eights called *fakes*, as in Figure 11-15. The fakes may overlap or lie clear of each other. Faking down prepares the line to run out rapidly without fouling or kinking. Keep clear of a line when it is running out, or you could become snarled in it.

Flemishing a Line

To give a line a neat, ornamental look, **flemish** it. To do so, coil the line flat on a deck or pier like a spring, with each coil encircling the preceding one. Coil right-laid line clockwise. When you have finished, you can tighten the coil by laying both hands flat on the line at the center of the coil. Now, turn your hands in the direction that tightens the coil. The result is a tight, attractive mat (Figure 11-16).

A flemished line looks great. Flemish the ends of your mooring lines, and you will be less likely to trip over them. But don't leave a flemished line on a varnished surface very long, especially overnight. The trapped moisture will spoil a varnished finish, and if left for several days on a fiberglass surface, the line may leave a nasty dirt stain.

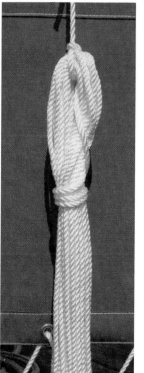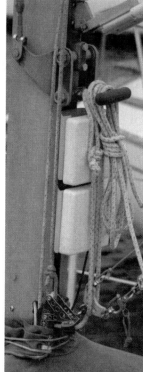

Figure **11-14.** A gasket coil is used to coil a line for stowing (left), and is also used for lines on deck that do not need to be adjusted fequently or quickly, such as this boom vang (right). (PHOTOS BY DON LINDBERG)

Figure **11-15.** Faking down a line. (PHOTO BY JOE BRITVCH)

Figure **11-16.** Flemishing a line. (PHOTO BY DON LINDBERG)

Knots, Bends, and Hitches

Lines are used for pulling, holding, lifting, and lowering. Before they can do these things, however, you must fasten them to something.

How you fasten a line depends on what you intend to do with it. In its more general sense, a *knot* is any series of loops, turns, and tucks in a line that modifies the rope itself or that connects it to another line or to some other object. In its narrower sense, however, a *knot* is formed in the line itself, whereas a *bend* ties one line to another, and a *hitch* joins a line to a spar, ring, or other object. There are exceptions to these conventions, as you will see. In any event, knots, bends, and hitches are all known collectively as **knots**.

You can learn something about tying knots by reading about them. If you are to become proficient, though, you must practice. Fortunately, just a few knots will serve all your ordinary needs.

Knots and Line Strength

All knots depend on friction created by turns in the line for their holding power. Under strain, friction weakens a line by breaking some of its fibers. Lines also weaken at splices, because these too depend on friction, but splices weaken a line much less than

other knots do. You can see how knots and splices weaken lines in Table 11-5.

Characteristics of Good Knots

A good knot, bend, or hitch will hold well without slipping. It serves a practical purpose and does what you want it to do. It is easy to tie, and it is also easy to untie. If you can't untie a knot after you have used it, you will lose at least a portion of the line.

Parts of a Line

The parts of a line have names. These make it easier to describe how to tie knots and to talk about them.

The end of a line in which you're tying a knot is its *working end*. The other end of the line, which is usually tied to the vessel or to a load of some kind, is the *bitter end*. On some boats, you tie the bitter end of an anchor line to a *bitt*—a heavy and firmly mounted piece of wood or metal on the foredeck used for securing lines. On other boats, the bitter end of the anchor rode is tied to a ringbolt in an underdeck anchor locker.

A line has a *standing part*, which is the main part of the line leading away from the knot you are tying and toward the load. Any bend or loop in the line is a *bight*, which becomes a loop if the line crosses itself (Figure 11-17). When the bight is around an object or the rope itself, it's a *turn*. When it is wrapped one and a half times around the object to form a complete circle, as in Figure 11-17, it is a *round turn*. An *overhand loop* is a small circle in the standing part of the line made by crossing the working end over the standing part. In an *underhand loop*, the working end crosses under the standing part.

A word of caution in tying knots. Synthetic line is slick, and some knots will pull out of it unless you leave an extra amount of line projecting beyond the knot. Pull the knot tight.

Some Useful Knots

The array of available knots can be confusing, but you don't need to know them all. A working fa-

TABLE 11-5	CHARACTERISTICS OF FIBERS	
How Knots and Splices Reduce Strength of Rope		**Percentage of Breaking Strength Remaining**
Knots	No knots or splices	100
	Anchor or Fisherman's Bend	76
	Timber Hitch	70–65
	Round turn	70–65
	Two half hitches	70–65
	Bowline	60
	Clove Hitch	60
	Sheet Bend or Weaver's Knot	55
	Square or Reef Knot	45
Splices	Eye Splice (over thimble)	95–90
	Long Splice	87
	Short Splice	85

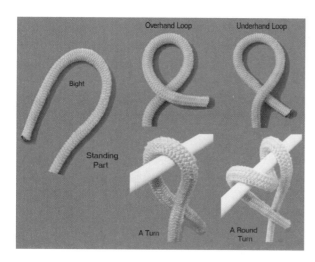

Figure **11-17.** Some knotwork terminology. (PHOTO BY JOE BRITVCH)

miliarity with a few good knots is better than a superficial knowledge of many seldom-used knots.

The knots, bends, and hitches described in this chapter are all functional. They serve many purposes, and, except as noted, are as easy to untie as they are to tie.

Stoppers

A *stopper knot* is a knot tied in a line to prevent it from running all the way through a block. There are two commonly used stoppers.

OVERHAND KNOT. An *overhand knot* can be used not only as a stopper (Figure 11-18), but also to temporarily prevent a freshly cut rope from unlaying or unraveling. It is not a good knot, however, since it jams under tension and is then difficult to untie. Tie it by making an overhand loop in the standing part of the line, then passing the working end up through the loop and pulling it tight.

FIGURE-EIGHT KNOT. A *figure-eight knot* (Figure 11-19) makes a better stopper than an overhand knot when heavy loads may occur. It can be untied easily after it has been jammed. Use it on all lines that you want to prevent from running through blocks, but do not use it on spinnaker sheets, which should always be free to run in an emergency. To tie a figure-eight knot, first form an underhand loop, then pass the working end over the standing part, then under and finally up through the loop. Untie the knot by pushing the working end back through the loop.

Figure **11-18.** The overhand knot, shown cinched up and loose. (PHOTO BY DON LINDBERG)

Figure **11-19.** The figure-eight knot. (PHOTOS BY DON LINDBERG)

Note: You can make this knot bulkier by adding one or more round turns of the working end around the standing part before finally passing the working end up through the loop. The knot is then called a *stevedore knot* (Figure 11-20).

Reef Knot

A *square knot* is sometimes called a *reef knot* because it can be used to secure a reefed sail to a boom. More generally, you can use it whenever you need to tie together two lines of equal diameter or the two ends of a single line, as when tying packages. If you try to use it with lines of unequal size, however, it will probably slip and untie.

A reef knot is useful only when not subject to a heavy or critical load. Under a heavy load it jams and becomes difficult to untie. Further, if you apply unequal tension, such jerking on one side, it is apt to capsize into two half hitches, and when it does it may slip. And if the knot fetches up against an obstacle or restriction, as when running through a pulley, it may come completely undone. For all these reasons, the reef knot should be avoided on a boat except for noncritical applications.

To tie a reef knot, hold one line in your left hand and the other in your right. Now pass the end in your left hand over and under the line in your right hand. Following this, pass the same end back over and under, this time working right to left. When you finish, it should look like Figure 11-21. The end of each line should emerge from the side it

entered and lie parallel to its own standing part. If it doesn't, you have tied a *granny knot*, which will slip under tension.

Sheet or Becket Bend

The *sheet* or *becket bend* is also called a *weaver's knot*. Use it to join lines of equal or different diameters. There are three forms of the knot: the sheet bend, the double sheet bend, and the slippery sheet bend.

SHEET BEND. Tie a *sheet bend* by forming a bight in the larger line. Pass the working end of the smaller line up through the bight, around both parts of the larger line, and back under itself. If you are going to stress this knot, tie the ends of both lines to their standing parts with small stuff. If not tied down, alternate loading and unloading of the knot can untie it (Figure 11-22A).

DOUBLE SHEET BEND. A *double sheet bend* offers more security than a sheet bend, and is especially needed when one line is considerably larger than

Figure **11-20.** Take an added turn or two with the working end before you make the final tuck in a figure-eight knot, and you get a stevedore knot, which is bulkier than a figure-eight knot. (REPRINTED WITH PERMISSION FROM *NAUTICAL KNOTS ILLUSTRATED,* REVISED EDITION, BY PAUL SNYDER AND ARTHUR SNYDER)

Figure **11-21.** The square or reef knot. (PHOTOS BY DON LINDBERG)

the other. Tie a double sheet bend by forming a bight in the larger line. Next, pass the working end of the smaller line up through the bight and around the standing part of the larger line. Now take another turn around the standing part of the larger line with the smaller line and pass it back under itself (Figure 11-22B).

SLIPPERY SHEET BEND. A *slippery sheet bend* is a variation of a sheet bend and is tied the same way, except that you don't tuck the line under itself. Instead, form a bight in the end of the smaller line and tuck this bight under the standing part of the smaller line (Figure 11-22C).

A slippery sheet bend is easier to untie than a sheet bend, but it is also less secure. Any knot is "slippery" if it ends in a bight, which makes it easy to untie under tension.

Clove Hitch

Use a *clove hitch* to tie a line to a piling or bollard or a fender to a rail (Figures 11-23 and 11-24). This knot is wonderfully quick and convenient to tie, but be careful as it will slip if not under constant tension. For example, the loading and unloading of a line caused by a boat surging on its moorings can undo the knot. Thus, a clove hitch is a temporary means of securing a boat. It will also jam under load, and if you can't ease the tension on the line, you will find it difficult to untie.

Tie a clove hitch by passing the working end of the line twice around the object to which it is to be tied. The first pass is below the standing part of the line (Figure 11-23). The second is above the standing part. Finish by passing the working end under the second loop.

Figure **11-23.** A clove hitch over a post. (PHOTO BY JOE BRITVCH)

Figure **11-24.** A clove hitch used to store a gasket coil temporarily on a lifeline. (REPRINTED WITH PERMISSION FROM *NAUTICAL KNOTS ILLUSTRATED*, REVISED EDITION, BY PAUL SNYDER AND ARTHUR SNYDER)

Figure **11-22.** **Left to right:** The sheet bend (A), the double sheet bend (B), and the slippery sheet bend (C). (PHOTOS BY DON LINDBERG)

You can also tie a clove hitch by forming two underhand loops in the standing part of the line, with the second loop on top of the first (Figure 11-25). You can now pass both loops over a bollard or piling.

To make a clove hitch more secure, run the working end over the standing part of the line and then through the loop thus formed (see below). You have now tied a half hitch, which will prevent the working end from slipping out of the clove hitch.

Two Half Hitches

Two *half hitches* are the same as a clove hitch tied around the standing part of a line (Figure 11-26). To make them, pass the working end of the line around the object to which the line is to be tied. Now, pass the working end of the line over the standing part and through the loop thus formed. This forms the first half hitch.

Form the second half hitch in the same way: pass the working end over the standing part and back through the resultant loop.

You can tie lines to rings, spars, piles, and posts

Figure **11-25.** An alternate way to tie a clove hitch. Make both loops as shown prior to passing them over a bollard or piling. (PHOTO BY DON LINDBERG)

Figure **11-26.** Two half hitches. (PHOTO BY JOE BRITVCH)

with two half hitches. Under tension, two half hitches are easier to untie than a clove hitch, and they make a more permanent knot than a clove hitch. Under tension, the knot tightens, but even so, it is easy to untie.

To further improve this knot, precede it with a round turn, which distributes the load over a longer length of line, reduces chafe, and makes the knot both secure and easier to untie (Figure 11-27). You'll find numerous uses on board for a *round turn and two half hitches*.

Anchor or Fisherman's Bend

Use an *anchor* or *fisherman's bend* to tie an anchor line to an anchor fitting such as a ring (Figure 11-28). You can also use it to tie a fishing line or leader to the eye of a fishhook, or more generally for bending a line to any object. It's a wonderfully secure knot, since it develops considerable friction. At the same time, there is less line chafe where it goes around the fitting.

Begin the knot by passing the working end around the object twice, forming a loop and a turn. Then pass the working end over the standing part and through the loop and the turn. Following this, you again pass the end over the standing part and between the standing part and itself.

Actually, the anchor bend is much like two half hitches. Instead of passing around the object once, though, it passes twice. Additionally, you tie the first half hitch through the two loops instead of between the standing part and itself.

To make the knot more secure, seize the working end to the standing part with twine.

Figure **11-27.** A round turn and two half hitches. (REPRINTED WITH PERMISSION FROM *NAUTICAL KNOTS ILLUSTRATED*, REVISED EDITION, BY PAUL SNYDER AND ARTHUR SNYDER)

Figure **11-28.** The anchor bend. For greater security, seize the working end to the standing part with twine. (PHOTO BY DON LINDBERG)

Figure **11-30.** A rolling hitch can be tied around another line to take the strain off it. Pulling on the braided line will tighten the grip of the rolling hitch around the three-strand line. Sailors sometimes use this technique to take the strain off a jibsheet long enough to clear overrides from a winch drum. (PHOTOS BY JOE BRITVCH)

Rolling Hitch

When you tie a *rolling hitch*, you tie one line to the standing part of another (Figure 11-29). Use it to tie a line to the working end of a second line. When tension is put on the first line, it releases the tension on the second. This allows you to adjust the second line. It can be used, for example, to take the strain off a jibsheet while you clear an override from the sheet wraps on a winch or relocate a block (Figure 11-30). You can also use it to adjust fender lines and awning tie-downs, or to adjust the tie-down lines on a dinghy lashing or a rooftop load on your car.

Tie the knot by passing the working end twice around the line to be held, as in Figure 11-29. In each of these turns, the working end passes over its own standing part. Then take a third turn around the line you want to hold, this time passing the working end under itself to form a half hitch. You must tie the first two turns on the side from which you will apply tension on the standing part.

Bowline

The *bowline* is a means of forming a temporary loop of fixed size at the end of a line (Figure 11-31). It is the **king of knots** because of its many everyday uses on boats and elsewhere. A bowline is easy to untie even after being placed under a heavy load. Just push the working end back through the loop around the standing part.

On board, bowlines tie lines to fittings, jibsheets to the clews of sails, and lines to anchors, among many other tasks (Figure 11-32). You can also use them to join lines of unequal sizes, loop to loop. You can even use a bowline as a temporary boarding lad-

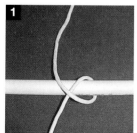 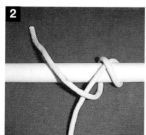  

Figure **11-29.** A rolling hitch tied around a rail, as you might do to hang fenders, for example. (PHOTOS BY JOE BRITVCH)

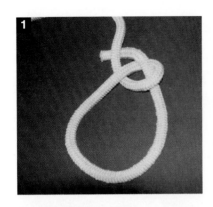
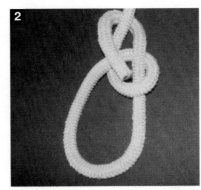
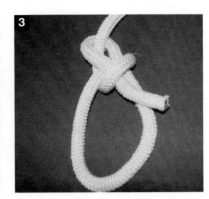

Figure **11-31.** Tying a bowline. (PHOTOS BY JOE BRITVCH)

Figure **11-32.** Bowlines in jibsheets. (REPRINTED WITH PERMISSION FROM *NAUTICAL KNOTS ILLUSTRATED,* REVISED EDITION, BY PAUL SNYDER AND ARTHUR SNYDER)

der by lowering it over the side and tying the standing part to a cleat on the opposite side of the boat. If you use a bowline to tie a line to an anchor, consider using a thimble to prevent chafing.

To tie a bowline, first make a small overhand loop in the standing part of the line as in Figure 11-31, leaving enough line at the working end to form a loop of the size you desire. Next, pass the working end up through the small loop, around the standing part, and back down through the small loop. Pull the knot tight. The knot is usually tied with the working end inside the loop.

Splices

When you want a more permanent way to join two lines or to form a loop (called an *eye*) in the end of a line, tie a *splice* rather than a knot. Splices are more time-consuming than the knots discussed above, but they cause less reduction in rope strength (see Table 11-5) and hold up remarkably well in long-term use.

You can buy mooring and docklines with eye splices already in place at one or both ends, and sailmakers and marine equipment suppliers sell sheets and halyards with custom splices. Many boating enthusiasts find pleasure in splicing their own lines, however, and the ability to do so is still seen as a sign of competent seamanship.

You can splice any fiber line, though a splice in laid line is simpler. Splicing double-braid line is more difficult, but it can be done.

Short Splice

You can join two pieces of laid line of the same size with a short splice (Figure 11-33) or a long splice. A *short splice* increases line diameter by about 40% and is thus inappropriate for any line that will pass through a block. A *long splice,* on the other hand, while it does not increase line diameter, does decrease line strength more than the short splice and is therefore not shown here. When you need a long length of line that will pass through blocks, you would do better to buy new rope than to splice two lengths of line together. For other applications, however, a short splice is a good solution.

To practice making a short splice, equip yourself with some laid line about $3/8$ to $1/2$ inch in diameter. You will need some tape or small stuff—any kind will do, since it is used only until you complete the splice. You will also need a fid or a marlinespike.

Lash or tape both lines about 16 diameters from their ends; if the lines are $1/2$ inch in diameter, this means you will tape or lash them about 8 inches from their ends. Unlay the lines to the tapes, then tape or lash the ends of the strands to keep them from untwisting as you make the splice.

1 Unlay all 6 strands 1" for each 1/16" of rope diameter and tape ends. Tape ropes to prevent further unlaying, and marry the ropes.

2 Remove one of the rope tapes. Cross a strand end over its adjacent and under the next.

3 Continue tucking strand over and under for a total of 4 tucks (6 for nylon).

4 Repeat Steps 2 and 3 for second strand.

5 Repeat for third strand against the lay.

6 Remove remaining tape and pull on loose strands to snug splice. Repeat Steps 2–5 going in opposite direction.

Figure **11-33.** Making a short splice. (REPRINTED WITH PERMISSION FROM *KNOTS, SPLICES, AND LINE HANDLING: A CAPTAIN'S QUICK GUIDE* BY CHARLIE WING)

Next, *marry* the two unlaid ends by alternating the strands of one rope with the strands of the other as shown in Figure 11-33. Then remove the tape or lashing from one of the lines; this is the one you will tuck into first.

Take one of the strands from the line you will

be tucking, and cross it over the adjacent strand on the other line, then under the next strand after that, opening a space for the tuck with a fid or marlinespike if necessary. Continue tucking this strand—over one, then under one—for a total of four tucks, or six for nylon. Then repeat this process with each of the other two strands in the line you are tucking.

Remove the tape or lashing from the line you have been tucking, and repeat the process with the three remaining untucked strands, this time working in the opposite direction. When you are done, cut off the ends of the strands to within about 1/4 inch of the standing part, and roll the completed splice between your hands or under your foot to finish it. With practice, you can do the splice quickly and neatly. One way to make a synthetic rope splice tight is by placing it in boiling water, which shrinks the rope.

Eye Splice

Tucking an *eye splice* is much like tucking the first half of a short splice (Figure 11-34). The tucks, though, are made back into the standing part of the same rope on which you are making the eye. To begin, unlay and tape the end of the line much as before, but this time you might unlay a slightly longer length—say, 20 diameters, or 10 inches for a 1/2-inch line. Form the eye to the size desired and lay the unlaid end along the standing part. Make the size of the eye just large enough to pull it over a cleat one horn at a time. *Seize* (lash) or tape the standing part to mark the entry point.

Using a fid or marlinespike if necessary, raise the strand of the standing part closest to the seizing and tuck the closest unlaid strand under it. Next, pass the adjacent unlaid strand over the strand you just tucked the first strand under, and tuck it under the next strand of the standing part. Finally, turn the whole splice over and tuck the last strand under the remaining strand on the standing part. Remove the seizing from the standing part and pull the tucks tight. Continue with the next sets of tucks in the same order and the same manner. Use four sets of tucks in polyester and six in nylon line. To taper the splice for a neater finish, remove half the fibers in each unlaid strand before you make the last tuck. When the tucks are completed, cut

① Unlay rope 5" for each 1/4" of diameter. Tape both rope and strand ends to prevent further unlaying. Form the eye and seize rope to mark entry point.

② Raise the strand closest to the seizing (use a fid if necessary) and tuck the closest unlaid strand through. Proceeding in the direction of twist, raise the next strand and tuck the corresponding strand through.

③ Raise the third strand and finish the first series of tucks with the remaining unlaid strand. Remove the seizing and tug on the strand ends to tighten throat.

④ Following the same order, tuck each strand over and under for a total of 4 tucks (6 for nylon). For a neater appearance, taper the last tuck by removing half of the fibers in each strand.

Figure **11-34.** Making an eye splice in laid line. (REPRINTED WITH PERMISSION FROM *KNOTS, SPLICES, AND LINE HANDLING: A CAPTAIN'S QUICK GUIDE* BY CHARLIE WING)

SPLICING DOUBLE-BRAID ROPE

Eye splices can also be made in double-braid line (Figure 11-36). The technique involves substituting core for core and cover for cover. This splice is difficult and time-consuming, but it is also extremely useful, and the result is strong and permanent.

To make this splice you need a tubular, hollow fid as shown at the top of page 307, the size of which must be proportional to the line being spliced.

Figure **11-35.** An eye splice around a thimble, here used in the connection between a nylon anchor rode and a length of chain. The thimble prevents the shackle from chafing through the nylon. (PHOTO BY DON LINDBERG)

the strands about ¼ inch from the standing part, then pound and roll the splice to even it out.

For a chafe-resistant eye, you can tie an eye splice around a *thimble* (Figure 11-35), which is a metal (usually galvanized steel), teardrop-shaped fitting with arms that are concave in cross section to accept a tightly fitted eye splice. The thimble then provides a protective rubbing surface to prevent the line from chafing. A classic application for a thimbled eye is in the end of a mooring pendant that connects to the mooring buoy or chain, or in the end of an anchor rode that connects to the anchor or to a length of chain.

Securing Lines

There are many special fittings for securing lines, used both on boats and piers. Fewer such fittings are necessary on powerboats than on sailboats.

Through-Bolt Your Fittings

Hardware for securing lines on a boat is attached to the hull or the spars (mast, boom, spinnaker pole, etc.). From time to time, these fittings are subject to considerable stress. For this reason, all deck fittings should be bolted through the deck or gunwales rather than just screwed to them (Figure 11-37).

On all but the smallest boats, the bolts should also go through a backing plate beneath the deck

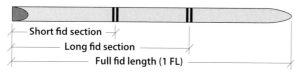

- Short fid section
- Long fid section
- Full fid length (1 FL)

Lengths of Tubular Fid Sections			
Rope Diameter in. (mm)	Short Section in. (mm)	Long Section in. (mm)	Full Length in. (mm)
1/4 (6)	2 (51)	3 1/2 (89)	5 1/2 (140)
5/16 (8)	2 1/2 (64)	4 1/4 (108)	6 3/4 (171)
3/8 (9)	3 (76)	4 3/4 (120)	7 3/4 (197)
7/16 (11)	3 1/2 (89)	6 (152)	9 1/2 (241)
1/2 (12)	4 (101)	7 (178)	11 (279)
9/16 (14)	4 1/2 (114)	8 (203)	12 1/4 (311)
5/8 (16)	5 (127)	9 1/2 (241)	14 (356)
3/4 (19)	5 3/4 (146)	11 (279)	16 (406)

Figure **11-36.** Making a double-braid eye splice. (TABLE AND ILLUSTRATIONS REPRINTED WITH PERMISSION FROM *KNOTS, SPLICES, AND LINE HANDLING: A CAPTAIN'S QUICK GUIDE* BY CHARLIE WING)

1 Tie a slip knot 8 fid lengths (FL) from end. Mark Point "A" 1 FL from end. Form an eye of the desired size (around a thimble if one is used), and mark Point "B" next to Point "A."

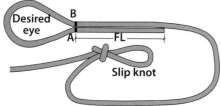

2 Pry open the cover at "B" and extract a small loop of the core. Mark the core "C." Extract the free end of the core and tape its end. Pinch and tape the end of the cover, as well.

3 Pull cover back toward slip knot and mark Point "D" 1 short fid length (see table above) from "C." Mark Point "E" 1 short + 1 full fid length beyond "D."

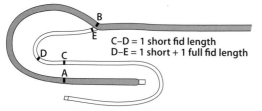

C–D = 1 short fid length
D–E = 1 short + 1 full fid length

4 Insert the end of the cover into the fid. Insert the fid at "D" and exit at "E." Continue pulling the cover through until "A" just appears. Remove the fid and the tape.

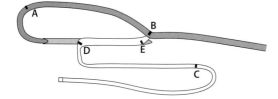

5 Now taper the exposed cover. Starting at "A" mark every 7th pic (pair of parallel ribs) running at one angle. Then count off 4 pics from "A," and mark every 7th pic running at the opposing angle. Cut one strand at each mark and remove the cut strand ends. Pull the tapered cover back until the end just disappears.

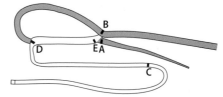

6 Insert the free end of the core into the fid. Insert the fid at "A" and exit at "B."

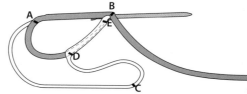

7 Pull on the core's free end until cover and core eyes match in size.

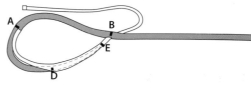

8 Insert the core end into the fid again, reinsert the fid at "B," and push it as far as you can into the rope's standing part. Pull the fid and core through the cover and cut off the excess core.

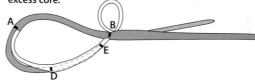

9 Grip the slip knot and work the cover toward the eye so that "E" and "D" disappear. Continue up to Point "A."

D (inside)   E (inside)

10 Secure the splice with waxed twine. Take 5 stitches through the throat of the splice, leaving a long tail. Switching the needle to the tail, take another 5 stitches at 90° to the first row of stitches.

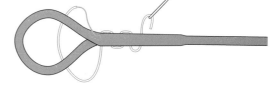

11 Tie the ends of the twine in a reef knot, and trim the ends.

to make the fitting more secure and to distribute the load. If you have a cleat on a gunwale, glue or otherwise attach a metal plate or a piece of ¾-inch marine plywood under the gunwale. Now, drill holes through the gunwale and the plate and fill them with marine caulking before bolts are inserted in them. (The caulking prevents water from entering and damaging the inner layers of the gunwale.) Secure the bolts of the fitting with appropriate nuts and washers. It's worth the effort, since a fitting that comes loose under severe stress can be dangerous. It is also easier to through-bolt a fitting than to patch a deck after a fitting has pulled loose.

Cleats

There are several types of cleats, and each serves a specific purpose.

Horn Cleats

Horn cleats are anvil-shaped fittings, with either open or closed bases. You tie anchor rodes, mooring and docking lines, sheets, and halyards to them, and they are the most common fittings for lines on small boats. Horn cleats are also called *mooring cleats*.

One way to secure a line to a horn cleat is by *belaying* it (Figure 11-38). To do so, take one complete turn around the cleat. Do not make more than one complete turn, as the line may jam on itself under tension or take up too much space on the horns. A lead-in angle of 10° to 20° also helps prevent jamming, and a good cleat installation provides such an angle from a block or chock to the cleat.

After you take a full turn around the cleat, lead the line over the cleat and around its horns to form a figure eight. Make two or more figure eights and pull the line tight. This way of belaying permits you to take the line off the cleat rapidly.

When you belay to a horn cleat and leave your boat unattended, the connection needs to be more secure. To do this, make only one figure eight and finish off with an underhand loop over one of the horns. This hitch is called a *weather hitch* (Figure 11-38). When making a weather hitch, be sure to have the line continue in a fair figure eight as shown to develop maximum friction.

Jam Cleats

A *jam cleat* is similar to a horn cleat, but with one important difference. One of the horns forms a tapered slot into which the line is "jammed" (Figure 11-40). This allows you to secure and release a line quickly, since you need less than a full turn to hold it.

Jam cleats usually secure sheets on sailboats, but they can also be used to secure a centerboard pendant to control its position or depth.

Install a jam cleat so the tapered slot faces the direction from which the line approaches. Thus, the first turn around the base of the cleat will not bind line, but the next turn binds and holds it. A jam cleat accommodates only one line size. If you

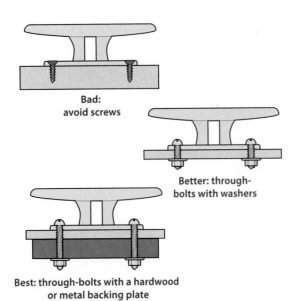

Bad:
avoid screws

Better: through-bolts with washers

Best: through-bolts with a hardwood or metal backing plate

Figure **11-37.** Bad, better, and best ways to install a cleat on deck.

Figure **11-38.** Belaying a line on a cleat. Note the lead-in angle to prevent the belay from jamming, the full turn around the base of the cleat, and the weather hitch that finishes the belay. (PHOTO BY DON LINDBERG)

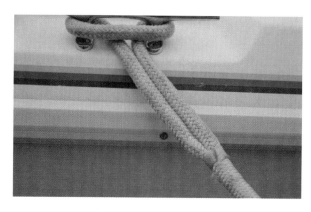

Figure **11-39.** Another way of securing a dockline to a horned deck cleat. The eye of the line is fed through the base of the cleat, then looped over the horns for a secure and quick belay. Notice the seizing on the throat of the eye splice to make it more secure. (PHOTO BY JOE BRITVCH)

use either a larger or smaller line than that for which it is specified, it will not function properly.

Cam Cleats

A *cam cleat* has two moving, serrated, cam-shaped jaws for holding a line (Figure 11-41). The jaws are spring-loaded and rotate open to release the line when you pull it. When the standing part of the line pulls against the cleat, it tightens.

In use, place the line over the teeth and pull it through and down to open the cams. Tighten the line simply by pulling it in. To ease or release it, first pull the line and lift it out of the cam jaws.

Cam cleats are suited only for small sailboats. They must be installed in the correct direction, since they work only one way, and they can be hard

Figure **11-40.** A jam cleat (top), showing the tapered slot that "captures" a line of matching diameter (bottom). (PHOTOS BY DON LINDBERG)

to release when there is a heavy load on the line such as during a high wind. Unfortunately, this may be the time you most want to let the line go quickly.

Turnbuckles

A *turnbuckle* is a threaded fitting that pulls two eyes together (Figure 11-42). On sailboats, turnbuckles are used as terminals on the wire rigging that supports the mast. The threaded bolts enable you to tension the shroud or stay. The bolts need to be locked in place to keep them from working loose after they have been adjusted, and there are several ways to do this. Perhaps the most common is to insert cotter pins or split rings through holes in the ends of the bolts.

Samson Posts

Larger boats have samson posts instead of cleats for anchoring or mooring (Figure 11-43). A *samson post* is a column of wood or metal with a pin or bar inserted through it near the top. To secure a line to the post, first take several turns around its

Figure **11-41.** A cam cleat in use. The direction of the load is toward the camera, and pulling the line in this direction only causes the jaws to tighten further. To release the line, a crewmember on the far side of the cleat will have to jerk the line straight upward, out of the jaws, while pulling it toward him or her. (PHOTO BY DON LINDBERG)

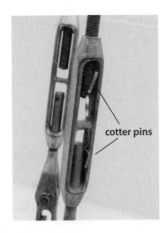

Figure **11-42.** Cotter pins have been inserted in the turnbuckle in the foreground to prevent the threaded fittings from turning. The pins have yet to be inserted in the turnbuckle in the background. (PHOTO BY DON LINDBERG)

Figure **11-43.** A line secured to a samson post on the foredeck of a boat. (PHOTO BY JOE BRITVCH)

WARNING *When attaching or detaching any line, be sure the line doesn't come under tension WITH YOUR FINGERS IN THE WAY.*

base, then finish with an underhand loop on each pin as if securing to a cleat.

Bow Bitts

Large boats may have bow bitts instead of samson posts or cleats (Figure 11-44). *Bow bitts* are a pair of circular metal columns on a common base, and each column has a lip around its top. To secure a line, take a complete turn around the bitt or post nearest the standing part of the line, then make a series of figure eights around the bitts.

Chocks

Lines from cleats, samson posts, and bitts are usually led through U-shaped fittings called *chocks* (Figure 11-45), which limit the direction of the pull on a cleat, help prevent chafing of the line, and prevent the line from damaging the boat. Lines are often equipped with chafing gear where they pass through chocks to further reduce chafing.

Other Hardware Items

A *winch* helps pull in a loaded line such as an anchor rode, a jibsheet, or a halyard. It consists of a metal drum with a series of gears inside, fastened to a secure base. An anchor winch, called a *windlass*, may have an electric motor, as might a winch used to help load a boat onto a trailer. Sailboat winches for sheets and halyards are turned manually with a handle.

Drums of winches on sailboats rotate clockwise, as viewed from the top end of the drum. Thus, you must wrap the line clockwise around the drum for the winch to work. The number of wraps depends on the load on the line, since the winch does its work through friction. While four turns are usu-

Figure **11-44.** A line secured to bow bitts. (PHOTOS BY JOE BRITVCH)

ally the most required for synthetic line, wire rope (as for a halyard) may require six turns.

Some sailboat winches provide two gear ranges to afford more pulling power. Turning the handle clockwise on these winches provides normal power, and turning it counterclockwise changes gears and increases the pulling capability. The drum turns in a clockwise direction in either mode.

On a large sailboat, two people may be needed to operate a winch. One person cranks the winch, while the second keeps a strain on the tail (working) end of the line as it comes off the drum. The second person also secures the line to a cleat after the sail is properly trimmed.

Self-tailing winches eliminate the need for the second person to serve as a tailer, which is a great advantage on a shorthanded boat or when working in a confined space (Figure 11-46). The top of the drum contains a notched channel that holds the line as it feeds off the drum. On a self-tailing winch, the notched channel also acts as a cleat to hold the line.

Lead Lines

A *lead line* is a line weighted with lead on one end that is sometimes used to measure water depths up to 100 feet (Figure 11-47). At least 5 pounds of lead is recommended on a line of braided cotton, which lays better on the deck than a synthetic line, making it easier to throw. The line should be 150

to 200 feet long so you can throw it out ahead of the boat.

Mark the line at standard depth intervals with strips of tape or leather or with knots. Plastic strips with large numbers are available for this purpose and attach easily to the line. They are difficult to read in the dark, however, and many mariners prefer markings that can be "read" by feel.

In use, you cast the lead forward with an underhand swing while the boat is moving forward slowly. The speed must be slow enough that the lead reaches the bottom by the time the line stands vertically. Subtract the vertical distance from the

Figure 11-46. A self-tailing winch. Note that the turns on a winch drum are always clockwise. (PHOTO BY DAVID J. SHULER)

Figure 11-45. Chocks like these, on the foredeck of a sailboat, protect lines and the boat from chafe and damage. (PHOTO BY DON LINDBERG)

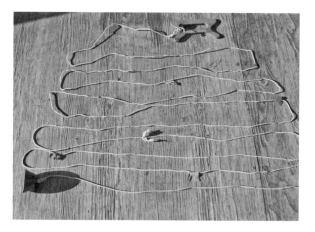

Figure 11-47. A lead line, showing the lead itself and the depth-interval markers. (PHOTO BY ED SWEENEY)

hand of the person casting the lead to the water from the length of the line paid out to get the water's depth.

Samuel Clemens got his pen name of Mark Twain from a lead line. The name comes from a Mississippi riverboat sounding "by the mark, twain" or 2 fathoms (12 feet).

Some leads have hollowed-out portions in their bottoms, which can be filled with a sticky material such as tallow or bedding compound. This material will collect a small sample of the bottom sediment on contact. Since nautical charts usually note the character of the bottom, the sample may help you confirm your position, and it can also tell you whether the bottom will provide good holding for an anchor.

Dipping the Eye

At times you must put the eye of your mooring line over a piling on which there is already a line. It is poor etiquette to place your line on top of one that is already there, and it may also be dangerous. If the other boat leaves before you do, the owner is likely to remove your line so that he can cast off, and he may or may not return your line to the piling.

To avoid the problem and to be courteous, *dip the eye* of your line by passing it up through the eye of the first line before dropping it over the piling (Figure 11-48). The other line can then be removed first. If you leave first, simply reverse the process. In this way you can free your line without removing the other line.

Ways to Learn More

Chapman Piloting & Seamanship. 66th ed. Charles B. Husick. New York: Hearst Books, 2009. Chapter 23.

The Essential Knot Book: Knots, Bends, Hitches, Whippings, and Splices. 3rd ed. Colin Jarman. Camden, Maine: International Marine, 2003.

Knots, Bends, and Hitches for Mariners. The U.S. Power Squadrons. Camden, Maine: International Marine, 2005.

Knots and Splices. Colin Jarman. Camden, Maine: International Marine, 2006.

Knots, Splices, and Line Handling: A Captain's Quick Guide. Charlie Wing. Camden, Maine: International Marine, 2004.

The Marlinspike Sailor. Hervey Smith. Camden, Maine: International Marine, 1993.

Nautical Knots Illustrated. Paul Snyder and Arthur Snyder. Camden, Maine: International Marine, 2002.

Pocket Guide to Knots. Lindsey Philpott. Camden, Maine: International Marine, 2007.

The Splicing Handbook: Techniques for Modern and Traditional Ropes. 3rd ed. Barbara Merry. Camden, Maine: International Marine, 2010.

Figure **11-48.** To *dip the eye*, pass your dockline through the eye of your neighbor's line before dropping the loop over the post. That way, if your neighbor leaves first, he can cast off without untying your line. (PHOTO BY DON LINDBERG)

Practice Questions

IMPORTANT BOATING TERMS

In the following exercise, match the words in the column on the left with the definitions in the column on the right. In the blank space to the left of each term, write the letter of the item that best matches it. Do not use an item in the right-hand column more than once.

THE ITEMS

1. _____ nylon
2. _____ ski rope
3. _____ standing part
4. _____ Dacron
5. _____ turn
6. _____ hitch
7. _____ bend
8. _____ anchor bend
9. _____ bowline
10. _____ clove hitch

THE RESPONSES

a. polypropylene
b. fisherman's bend
c. polyester
d. main part of a line
e. forms a temporary loop
f. will slip if not under tension
g. ties one line to another
h. elastic
i. line attached to an object
j. bight around an object

Multiple-Choice Items

In the following items, choose the best response:

11-1. Which of the following types of line will float?

a. polypropylene
b. polyester (Dacron)
c. nylon
d. all of the above

11-2. Most boatowners prefer ropes made from

a. natural fiber
b. wire
c. synthetic fiber
d. a mixture of synthetic and natural fibers

11-3. Which of the following types of line stretches the most?

a. manila
b. polypropylene
c. nylon
d. polyester

11-4. Whipping a line is done to

a. make it easier to manage
b. reduce stretching
c. cover a damaged spot
d. keep it from unraveling

11-5. Wrap your mooring and anchor lines with canvas or leather to prevent

a chafing
b. soiling
c. bleaching from the sun
d. whipping

11-6. A square knot is useful

a. for most purposes
b. when you are in a hurry
c. if it is not subject to a heavy load or critical load
d. for mooring a boat

Multiple-Choice Items (continued)

11-7. A bowline is useful when you want

a. a temporary, fixed-size loop in the end of a line
b. to tie two lines together
c. to tie a line to a cleat
d. to tie up to a mooring

11-8. The "king of knots" is the

a. square knot
b. half hitch
c. clove hitch
d. bowline

11-9. Protect synthetic and natural fiber lines from

a. kinks
b. mildew
c. dirt
d. all of the above

11-10. The best knot for tying different-size lines together is the

a. sheet bend or becket bend
b. square knot
c. bowline
d. clove hitch

11-11. Make an eye splice in a manner similar to a

a. short splice
b. back splice
c. long splice
d. dual splice

11-12. One of the most secure knots for attaching a line to an object is the

a. weaver's knot
b. sheet bend
c. clove hitch
d. anchor bend

11-13. Pulleys on a boat are called

a. blocks
b. sheets
c. winches
d. hitches

11-14. A horn cleat is

a. used to hold up a boat's rail
b. a device through which a line is passed
c. a means of warning nearby vessels
d. an anvil-shaped fitting

11-15. Which of the following is used to moor a vessel?

a. a cleat
b. a bitt
c. a samson post
d. all of the above

11-16. Lead lines are used

a. to pass a line from one boat to another
b. where strength is important
c. to measure the depth of the water
d. all of the above

11-17. The half hitch you use as the last step in securing a line to a cleat is called a

a. clove hitch
b. weather hitch
c. anchor bend
d. wedding hitch

11-18. If you tie a line to itself, it is called a

a. bend
b. hitch
c. knot
d. reef

11-19. The tool used in working rope is called a

a. splicer
b. awl
c. pick
d. fid

11-20. The best type of line for anchoring and mooring is

a. nylon
b. Orlon
c. Dacron
d. polypropylene

11-21. The end of a line tied to a vessel is the

a. working end
b. standing end
c. bitter end
d. whipped end

11-22. To make a clove hitch secure, finish tying it by adding a

a. half hitch
b. square knot
c. reef knot
d. bowline

chapter 12

Weather and Boating

The objectives of this chapter are to describe:

✔ Weather information sources.

✔ Basic weather patterns.

✔ Storm forecasting and precautions.

✔ Go, no-go decision making.

✔ A personal weather equipment and experience checklist.

BOATERS HAVE a special need to know about weather. The effects of storms can be devastating on land, but at sea they can be even worse. High winds, lightning, rough seas, and poor visibility may accompany storms on the water. If you are caught unprepared by a severe storm, your

(PHOTO BY DEREK KEY)

recreational outing can end in disaster, but it doesn't have to.

The first rule for avoiding weather problems is to "know before you go." There are many readily available sources for good weather information. If bad weather is in the offing, don't go out.

The second rule is to recognize that weather is always changing, and that forecasts are not always accurate. This chapter will cover the chief indicators of impending adverse weather that you can observe on board.

The third rule is to implement defensive measures in a timely fashion when caught in unexpected weather conditions. There are well-tested tactics that can see you and your boat through severe weather and sea conditions.

Weather Information

The science of weather observation and forecasting has made incredible advances in the past decades. With satellite imagery, radar, and other methods of information gathering, accurate weather data are produced for almost every place in the world—certainly everywhere in the United States.

The distribution of these weather data has also undergone immense improvement. Television, from both national and local stations, offers weather reporting and forecasting programs throughout the day and night. Of course, The Weather Channel gives incredibly accurate weather summaries for the entire country, and the national forecast is usually followed by local weather reports and forecasts (Figure 12-1).

Likewise, both FM and AM radio stations broadcast almost continuous local weather information, which is highly useful though not specifically targeted to mariners. Near the coasts and large inland waterways, TV and radio stations often provide regional marine weather broadcasts.

Thus, there is little excuse for not knowing what the weather is doing and will do. Boaters need not be surprised unless they are boating in remote areas. Even there, timely weather information is available using shortwave (see below), marine single-sideband, or ham radio.

Having said that, a forecast *can* be inaccurate. Therefore, boaters should get their information

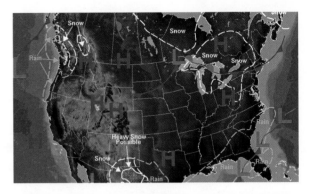

Figure **12-1.** A weather map showing low- and high-pressure areas along with fronts and areas of precipitation associated with the lows. (COURTESY NOAA)

from more than one source—the more the better. Experienced boaters also depend on their own weather knowledge to make "go, no-go" decisions, but the proper context for your own observations is provided by the regional weather forecasts you obtain before you head out and perhaps update while you're on the water. Note that "skipper error" in failing to seek out available weather information is what dooms most boats and crews to the ravages of bad weather.

Telephone Information

In some locales, principally large metropolitan areas, recorded telephone marine weather forecasts are available. If you use them, call while you are planning your cruise, then call again just before you leave to get the latest update. Check with the service to see how often it updates its forecasts.

National Weather Service

The National Weather Service (NWS) continuously broadcasts weather information over its network of FM weather stations. Its forecasts focus on specific locales and give marine weather conditions where applicable. The NWS updates its forecasts as soon as new information is available. If severe weather develops, the NWS immediately broadcasts the information. (Note, however, that sometimes the development is so fast that the NWS can't keep up with it.)

You can receive NWS broadcasts on inexpensive, narrow-band FM receiving sets that use either household electrical current or batteries. The broadcasts are also available on the weather channels of your VHF-FM marine radio. You should be able to receive NWS broadcasts on one or more of their broadcasting frequencies. If you have a VHF-FM radio or a narrow-band receiving set aboard your vessel, you can receive the latest information while you cruise. See Chapter 13 for more on NOAA's VHF-FM frequencies.

Internet

The Internet now provides a wide array of weather information, ranging from historical weather recitals to the current conditions any place on the globe. Boaters may obtain long- and short-range forecasts and detailed weather maps depicting reported conditions. There are also websites that provide both basic and advanced weather education. With the recent advent of wireless technology, it is often possible to access the Internet from a boat, while underway, using a PC, tablet, or other Internet access devices such as mobile phones. You can use weather facsimile receivers (WEFAX) areas where you can't access the Internet or use mobile phones.

A good place to start for weather information is the Coast Guard site www.uscg.mil/news/stormcenter which will identify the major links to federal weather related websites. This site provides essential storm information, as well as providing links to:

- Tides and storm surge information
- Boating safety issues
- Tropical storms worldwide
- National Weather Service
- NOAA marine weather information web page
- And many others

NOAA's National Weather Service (NWS) website is www.nws.noaa.gov or simply www.weather.gov. It provides local weather by ZIP code, and a searchable map that shows the current weather alerts. You can also link to offshore and high-seas weather forecasts, or go directly to www.opc.ncep.noaa.gov/marine_areas.php. There are other websites that display weather information differently than the NWS, but the essential weather source information comes from the NWS.

Other Information Sources

For those who cruise long distances and for commercial shipping interests, coded weather data are broadcast by shortwave radio, and facsimile weather maps are also available from shortwave broadcasts. You can detect an electrical storm by the static on an AM radio tuned to a broadcast station. You can detect a storm even if it is so far away that you can't see or hear it. Static is an irritation for landlubbers but a timely warning for mariners.

Wind and Boating

Fog, heavy rain, sleet, and snow create problems for boaters by reducing visibility. In severely reduced visibility you become more vulnerable to collisions and groundings. You may be unable to navigate back to port. Serious though these problems are, however, they are often mild in comparison with those created by wind.

We all know that vicious winds accompany gales, thunderstorms, tornadoes, waterspouts, tropical storms, hurricanes, and other extreme weather conditions. But the wind does not have to be gale force or stronger to create dangerous boating conditions. Even fairly mild winds can create rough seas.

Storm winds cause indirect as well as direct

SOME SOURCES OF WEATHER INFORMATION

AM and FM radio stations
Local TV
National TV, including the Weather Channel
The Internet, including www.weather.com (The Weather Channel), www.uscg.mil/news/stormcenter (Coast Guard Storm Center), and www.nws.noaa.gov (the National Weather Service)
Marine VHF radios, Channels 1 through 10 (see Chapter 13)
Shortwave and marine SSB radio, as well as ham radio (for those who are qualified)
Newspapers
Telephone (recorded messages)
CB radio (you can ask others, nearer the bad weather, about conditions)

problems. Strong winds blowing onshore will pile up water ahead of a storm system or hurricane, and this effect is amplified by the water's rise in response to falling atmospheric pressures. This so-called *storm surge* may raise local sea levels as much as 18 to 20 feet ahead of a hurricane, and the results can be particularly destructive when the peak surge coincides with local high tide. Hurricane surges may extend inland for hundreds of miles.

Winds do not have to be of hurricane force to create a surge that will inflict significant damage. In strong winds such as the northeasterly gales that sometimes strike the Northeast coast, the water levels of bays and sounds rise beyond those of normal tides. Moored boats may rise as far as their mooring lines will permit and will sink if the water rises farther. Docked boats may rise above the pil-ings to which they are tied and be impaled on them as the water level falls (Figure 12-2). Boats in covered slips may be crushed against the roofs.

Wind and Waves

The most common wind-related problem faced by boaters, however, is rough water. Large breaking waves can overturn or swamp small boats, and as we have already seen, breaking waves can make small boats yaw, broach, or pitchpole.

Most waves are caused by wind and continue to grow from it. Up to a point, the longer the wind blows from a constant direction and the greater the uninterrupted expanse, or *fetch*, over which it blows, the higher the waves will build. Eventually, the waves reach a maximum height for the given

TABLE 12-1 BEAUFORT WIND SCALE

Beaufort Number	Wind Description	Mean Wind Speed Equivalent (knots)	Sea Conditions	Mean Wave Height (meters)	Mean Wave Height (feet)
0	Calm	< 1	The sea is like a mirror.	—	—
1	Light air	1–3	Ripples without foam crests.	0–0.1	0–0.3
2	Light breeze	4–6	Small wavelets. Crests look glassy but do not break.	0–0.2	0–0.6
3	Gentle breeze	7–10	Large wavelets; crests begin to break; a few whitecaps.	0–0.6	0–2
4	Moderate breeze	11–16	Small waves becoming longer; frequent whitecaps.	1	3.3
5	Fresh breeze	17–21	Moderate waves with a more pronounced long form; many whitecaps. A little spray.	2	6.6
6	Strong breeze	22–27	Large waves begin to form; extensive whitecaps. Some spray.	3	9.8
7	Near gale	28–33	Sea heaps up, and white foam blows in streaks in the direction of the wind.	4	13
8	Gale	34–40	Moderately high waves of greater length; edges of the crests begin to break into spindrift; streaks of foam.	5.5	18
9	Strong gale	41–47	High waves; crests begin to tumble; dense streaks of foam. Spray may affect visibility.	7	23
10	Storm	48–55	Very high waves with long toppling crests. The sea appears white as foam is blown off in dense bands. Spray affects visibility.	9	29.5
11	Violent storm	56–63	Exceptionally high waves limit visibility. The edges of the wave crests are blown into froth. The sea is covered with blowing spray.	11.5	38
12	Hurricane	64+	Seas tumultuous. The air is filled with foam. The ocean is totally white with driving spray. Visibility seriously reduced.	14	46

fetch and wind speed, at which point the seas are said to be *fully developed* (Table 12-1).

Swells

Swells are waves that have traveled a long way from the storm that created them. As they travel, their heights decrease, the distance between them increases, and they assume the rounded shape of a sine curve. Even large swells are not dangerous to boats, though they may be uncomfortable for boaters.

Breaking Waves

As waves approach shore, they begin to "feel" the rising seabed, and this friction slows the speed of each wave's bottom. At the same time, the crests, which are not slowed by friction, begin to overrun their bases. As the water continues to shoal, the crests eventually become unstable and spill or plunge forward as *breakers*. A series of breakers approaching a shore constitutes surf, but breakers can also occur in navigable waters in the right circumstances. For example, when incoming waves encounter an ebb current—such as in the entrance to an inlet—the seas will rise and steepen and may begin to break. In a breaker, the energy that has been locked inside a deep-water wave is translated into the violent momentum of white, breaking water. In a big breaking sea, tons of seawater may be hurled forward at speeds approaching 40 miles per hour. Breaking seas are a real danger to small boats.

Wave Height

A prediction of "seas 3 to 5 feet" means that 70% of the waves are expected to be between 3 and 5 feet high. This is what is known as the *significant wave height*. Of those, 15% will be less than 3 feet high, and 15% will be more than 5 feet. Be prepared for the occasional wave that may be 7 or more feet high. Never anchor from the stern of your boat. Your boat may be swamped by an "occasional" wave or severe wake. It can happen in fairly calm seas.

Figure 12-2. The storm surge from Superstorm Sandy late in October 2012 left over 65,000 boats damaged, lifting many off floats and dropping them ashore, like these in Oceanville, NJ. Many boats that were already hauled out and in winter storage were damaged by high water that floated them off their jackstands. (COURTESY U.S. FISH AND WILDLIFE)

TABLE 12-2 WAVE HEIGHT

Significant wave heights as a function of wind speed, duration, and fetch

Fetch in n. miles	Force 4 (11-16 knots)			Force 5 (17-21)			Force 6 (22-27)			Force 7 (28-33)		
	time in hours	height in feet	period in seconds	time	height	period	time	height	period	time	height	period
10	3.7	2.6	2.4	2.2	3.5	2.8	2.7	5.0	3.1	2.5	6.0	3.4
20	6.2	3.2	2.9	5.4	4.9	3.3	4.7	7.0	3.8	4.2	8.6	4.3
30	8.3	3.8	3.3	7.2	5.8	3.7	6.2	8.0	4.2	5.8	10.0	4.6
40	10.3	3.9	3.6	8.9	6.2	4.1	7.8	9.0	4.6	7.1	11.2	4.9
50	12.4	4.0	3.8	11.0	6.5	4.4	9.1	9.8	4.8	8.4	12.2	5.2
60	14.0	4.0	4.0	12.0	6.8	4.6	10.2	10.3	5.1	9.6	13.2	5.5
70	15.8	4.0	4.1	13.5	7.0	4.8	11.9	10.8	5.4	10.5	13.9	5.7
80	17.0	4.0	4.2	15.0	7.2	4.9	13.0	11.0	5.6	12.0	14.5	6.0
90	18.8	4.0	4.3	16.5	7.3	5.1	14.1	11.2	5.8	13.0	15.0	6.3
100	20.0	4.0	4.4	17.5	7.3	5.3	15.1	11.4	6.0	14.0	15.5	6.5
120	22.4	4.1	4.7	20.0	7.8	5.4	17.0	11.7	6.2	15.9	16.0	6.7
140	25.8	4.2	4.9	22.5	7.9	5.8	19.1	11.9	6.4	17.6	16.2	7.0
160	28.4	4.2	5.2	24.3	7.9	6.0	21.1	12.0	6.6	19.5	16.5	7.3
180	30.9	4.3	5.4	27.0	8.0	6.2	23.1	12.1	6.8	21.3	17.0	7.5
200	33.5	4.3	5.6	29.0	8.0	6.4	25.4	12.2	7.1	23.1	17.5	7.7
220	36.5	4.4	5.8	31.1	8.0	6.6	27.2	12.3	7.2	25.0	17.9	8.0
240	39.2	4.4	5.9	33.1	8.0	6.8	29.0	12.4	7.3	26.8	17.9	8.2
260	41.9	4.4	6.0	34.9	8.0	6.9	30.5	12.6	7.5	28.0	18.0	8.4
280	44.5	4.4	6.2	36.8	8.0	7.0	32.4	12.9	7.8	29.5	18.0	8.5
300	47.0	4.4	6.3	38.5	8.0	7.1	34.1	13.1	8.0	31.5	18.0	8.7
320				40.5	8.0	7.2	36.0	13.3	8.2	33.0	18.0	8.9
340				42.4	8.0	7.3	37.6	13.4	8.3	34.2	18.0	9.0
360				44.2	8.0	7.4	38.8	13.4	8.4	35.7	18.1	9.1
380				46.1	8.0	7.5	40.2	13.5	8.5	37.1	18.2	9.3
400				48.0	8.0	7.7	42.2	13.5	8.6	38.8	18.4	9.5
420				50.0	8.0	7.8	43.5	13.6	8.7	40.0	18.7	9.6
440				52.0	8.0	7.9	44.7	13.7	8.8	41.3	18.8	9.7
460				54.0	8.0	8.0	46.2	13.7	8.9	42.8	19.0	9.8
480				56.0	8.0	8.1	47.8	13.7	9.0	44.0	19.0	9.9
500				58.0	8.0	8.2	49.2	13.8	9.1	45.5	19.1	10.1
550							53.0	13.8	9.3	48.5	19.5	10.3
600							56.3	13.8	9.5	51.8	19.7	10.5
650										55.0	19.8	10.7
700										58.5	19.8	11.0
750												
800												
850												
900												

Note that fully developed seas exceed the wave heights shown in Table 12-1, from which you can extrapolate estimated wave heights for winds stronger than Force 7.

In large bays, lakes, sounds, and at times in coastal areas, wave heights can change abruptly with a change in weather (see Table 12-2). Waves can go from 2 to 4 feet to 6 to 10 feet in just a few minutes.

Waves in Shallow Water

Waves are influenced not only by wind speed, wind duration, and fetch, but by water depth as well. Wind over shallow water generates steep waves that are close together. Two- to 4-foot waves in shallow water can present a serious hazard for small boats, while in deep water, waves of the same height have more gradual slopes and are farther apart.

Understanding Weather

The knowledge that wind causes waves begs the question, "What causes wind?" To answer this question, you need to understand a few things about weather.

There is also another reason you need to know

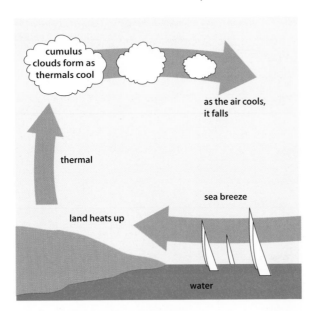

Figure **12-3.** Sea breeze dynamics. Heated air rises over land as the day advances, to be replaced by cooler air flowing in from seaward, as shown here. When a land breeze forms at night, this process is reversed. The air over land cools more rapidly than the air over the sea, and the resultant wind blows from the land toward the sea. A nighttime land breeze is rarely as strong or steady as a daytime sea breeze. (REPRINTED WITH PERMISSION FROM *GARY JOBSON'S CHAMPIONSHIP SAILING* BY GARY JOBSON)

something about weather. You have learned how to get good weather information. Now you need to be able to answer the question, "Does what I see mean the weather is changing?" If it is, you may want to change your plans. If you are on the water, you may wish to seek shelter.

Knowing something about weather can help you avoid some of its perils such as high winds, thunderstorms, lightning, heavy rain, fog, and other hazards to boating. It can also help you anticipate and know how to react to conditions such as squall lines, microbursts, and wind shear.

Weather and Heat

Heat from the sun warms the air, and this in turn causes wind and weather. There are two basic facts at the heart of this dynamic: warm air is lighter than cold air, and warm air can hold more moisture than cold air. Because it is lighter, warm air rises. As it rises, warm, moist air expands and cools and must therefore lose some of its moisture in the form of clouds, rain, hail, or snow.

Heat and Air Pressure

When land or water is heated, some of that heat radiates into the air above, which expands and becomes less dense when warmed. The heated air rises, which reduces the air pressure locally.

Cooler air from surrounding areas then flows into the low-pressure area caused by the rising air. Like water, air always flows from areas of high pressure toward areas of low pressure. This moving air is *wind*. The greater the difference in pressure between areas overlaid by warm and cool air, the stronger is the wind.

Land and Sea Breezes

Unequal heating of land and water causes land or sea breezes. During the daytime, land heats more rapidly than water. Thus, air rises over the land, and the air over the water flows in to take its place. This is a *sea breeze* (Figure 12-3). At night, the land loses heat more rapidly than the water. The cooler air over land then moves under the warmer ocean air in what is called a *land breeze*. This diurnal movement of air is often conducive to the formation of fog.

Heat and Temperature Changes

Other factors affect the temperature changes in an air mass. Thick vegetation or swampy land is slower to warm and slower to cool than arid, barren land. Thus, the dry air above a desert gets hotter by day and cooler overnight than the air over a rainforest. These and other factors cause differences in air pressure, amounts of moisture in the air, and the strength of the resulting wind.

Global Air Circulation

The ultimate engine for earth's weather is the unequal distribution of heat over the planet's surface. Simply put, the tropics receive more heat energy from the sun than the poles, and the result is a continual poleward transport of heated air (and heated water in the form of ocean currents) from the equatorial regions. Heated air rises in a broad band called the *doldrums* between roughly 15°N and 15°S—an area of light and baffling winds punctuated by violent thunderstorms—and when it reaches the upper troposphere it flows poleward both north and south. At roughly 30° north and south of the equator—the latitude of St. Augustine, Florida, in the northern hemisphere—some of the air has been cooled enough to subside, forming a band of high pressure and light and variable winds called the *horse latitudes*. The rest of the upper-atmosphere air from the tropics continues poleward, subsiding over arctic and Antarctic areas.

This poleward movement of air aloft must be balanced by an equatorward movement of air at the surface, and so it is. Part of the air that sinks at around 30° north and south flows back toward the low-pressure doldrums region to replace what has risen aloft there. In the northern hemisphere this north-to-south surface flow is deflected to its right by the spinning of the earth, and in the southern hemisphere the south-to-north movement is deflected to its left. The result is the northeast and southeast *trade winds*, respectively (Figure 12-4).

The rest of the air that sinks at 30° north and south flows poleward at the surface, and is deflected to the right in the northern hemisphere and to the left in the southern hemisphere to form the **prevailing westerlies** that characterize the circulation patterns of the middle latitudes, including most of the United States.

Along the polar front, at about 60° north and south, the prevailing westerlies run into high-latitude **easterlies** flowing from the poles toward lower latitudes, which forces the comparatively warm, moist air of the westerlies aloft. Rising air always causes instability—this is why bad weather is associated with low pressure—so it comes as no surprise that the polar front is a zone marked by frequent severe storms.

The Coriolis Force

The *Coriolis force* affects anything that moves over the earth's surface, through the air, or through water, including birds, missiles, aircraft, ocean and air currents, and submarines. Though called a "force," it is in fact a complex response to the earth's rotation, and so is more properly called the **Coriolis effect**. For the purposes of understanding weather, it is sufficient to recognize that the Coriolis force/effect does exist, and

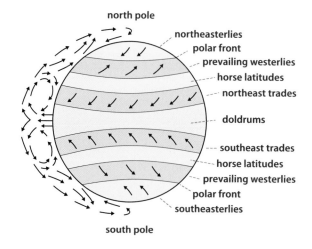

Figure **12-4.** Global atmospheric circulation patterns.

that it causes both winds and ocean currents to be deflected to the right in the northern hemisphere and to the left in the southern hemisphere. This is why surface air flowing toward the equator from the horse latitudes becomes the northeast and southeast trade winds, and it's why surface air flowing poleward from the horse latitudes becomes the prevailing westerlies of the middle latitudes.

Columbus and Wind Patterns

Columbus took advantage of the northeast trade winds and the prevailing westerlies when he came to the "new world." His square-rigged sailboats were best at sailing before the wind. He sailed down the coast of Africa to the belt of the northeast trade winds, then turned west. No wonder his crews were upset. Day after day the wind blew from astern. How were they going to get home?

But Columbus understood the trade winds. When he left the West Indies, he sailed north until he came to the prevailing westerlies. He then sailed east. Is it any wonder that St. Augustine became a replenishing port for food and water for Spanish ships returning from the New World? It is on the Florida coast at 29°53 N latitude, 7 nautical miles south of 30°N latitude.

Temperature and Humidity

One more factor is necessary to explain weather. As has already been stated, warm air can hold more moisture than cool air. You see the result of this on a summer day when you mix a cool drink: the glass cools the warm, moist air that contacts it, the air can't hold as much moisture as when it was warmer, and some of it condenses on the glass.

The temperature at which moisture begins to condense on the glass is the *dew point*. The more moisture the air contains, the more *humid* it is. If there is no change in temperature, the more humid the air, the higher its dew point. In other words, moisture condenses out of saturated air when the temperature is lowered only slightly.

Contrary to popular belief, moist air is lighter than dry air. When it's warm, moist air is even lighter, and it therefore rises rapidly. Cold, dry air descends. Warm air over cold ground or water is stable; cold air over warm ground or water is unstable.

Moisture and Energy

It takes enormous amounts of energy to change water from a liquid to a vapor. When water vapor condenses back to a liquid, this energy is released. When you heat water, it takes relatively little heat to raise its temperature to the boiling point, but it takes many more times that amount of heat to change it into steam. When the steam changes back into a liquid, that same amount of heat is released. This is why steam burns flesh so badly, and it also accounts for the violence of some storms. In a storm, the moisture in the air changes back to a liquid and releases its pent-up energy.

Air Masses

In the temperate regions between roughly 30° and 60° north and south—that is, between the horse latitudes and the arctic regions—weather systems move generally west to east, steered by the prevailing westerlies at the surface and by east-flowing jet streams aloft.

These upper-atmosphere jet streams, which average more than 50 knots and can reach 200 knots or more, are concentrated around 30° north and south (the **subtropical jet stream**), where air is subsiding, and over the polar fronts around 60° north and south (the **polar jet stream**), where air is rising. These boundary zones in the planetary atmospheric circulation are regions of rapid horizontal temperature change, and horizontal temperature gradients are what cause wind both aloft and on the surface. The jet streams migrate poleward and equatorward with the seasons. In the northern hemisphere winter, for example, the subtropical jet stream may disappear entirely from North American weather maps, while the polar jet stream dips far south, sometimes steering arctic air all the way to Florida.

Middle-latitude weather is dynamic and constantly changing, dominated by an endless, generally west-to-east parade of distinctive air masses. For purposes of this book we'll put aside the complex atmospheric mechanics that form these systems and just accept their existence, so familiar to mariners.

These air masses move over the earth's surface and determine much of our weather. As they move they tend to retain the moisture, pressure, and temperature characteristics they acquired upon formation. As we might expect, air masses with high pressure, called *highs*, contain cool, dry air. Low-pressure areas, or *lows*, are characterized by warm, moist air.

Air pressure is a function of the weight or mass of the atmosphere above us. At sea level the air pressure is approximately 14.7 pounds per square inch (psi). We call 14.7 psi *one atmosphere* of pressure. On weather maps or synoptic charts, areas of low and high pressure are delineated by *isobars*, generally concentric circles that connect points of equal atmospheric pressure and show how air masses are moving. Air masses move as the atmosphere tries to erase its horizontal pressure gradients, with the air in high-pressure areas flowing toward low-pressure areas and creating wind in the process.

A high-pressure area contains cooler air, and the higher the altitude, the cooler the air. This cooler air above weighs more than warmer air below. Gravity causes the cooler air to sink, causing higher barometric pressures. High-pressure cells generally are areas of clear and stable weather.

The lows denote areas where air is rising, which is why barometric pressures are lower there. Since rising air will cool and will eventually become supersaturated, low-pressure cells are areas of instability marked by precipitation and often by strong winds.

Isobars are usually more closely spaced around lows than highs, denoting stronger winds in the lows. A high might be 1,000 or more miles across, while a low tends to be more tightly coiled—typically 400 or fewer miles across. Simply put, good weather is associated with highs, bad weather with lows.

Surface winds spiral inward toward the center of a low, counterclockwise in the northern hemisphere and clockwise in the southern hemisphere. The winds spiral outward from a high, clockwise in the northern hemisphere and counterclockwise in the southern hemisphere (Figure 12-5). The characteristics of highs and lows can be summarized as in Table 12-3.

It is useful to know where the high and low pressure areas are in relation to you. Lows are a source of bad boating weather, and the highs that are moving toward them may be preceded by strong winds that create waves and bad boating conditions. The area between a high and a nearby low may have stormy weather.

To locate highs and lows in the northern hemisphere, stand with your back to the surface wind

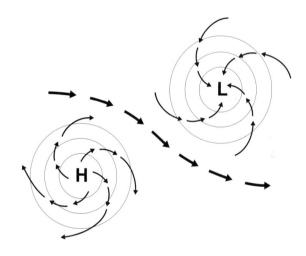

Figure **12-5.** Air circulates clockwise around highs and counterclockwise around lows in the northern hemisphere. Where a high is close to a neighboring low, you may see strong winds between the two systems.

TABLE 12-3	CHARACTERISTICS OF MIDLATITUDE HIGH- AND LOW-PRESSURE SYSTEMS	
	High	**Low**
Weather	Generally fair	Stormy, precipitation
Temperature	Stable—long periods	Cool to warm changing to colder
Average motion (west to east)	Winter: 565 nm/day	Winter: 660 nm/day
	Summer: 390 nm/day	Summer: 430 nm/day
Winds	Moderate, rising near edge	Strong and changing with possible high seas
Pressure (typical)	Rapid rise on approach, slow decline on retreat	Rapid fall on approach, slow rise on retreat
Clouds	Sparse, near periphery	Wide variety, all altitudes

(Figure 12-6). Now turn 45° to your right. This aligns you with the wind aloft. The high-altitude wind is always rotated from the surface wind in this fashion unless the surface wind is affected by local conditions such as buildings. After you have turned 45° to your right, the closest low is normally to your left, and the high is to your right. The low- or high-pressure area to the west is usually the one that will reach you. The one to the east has already

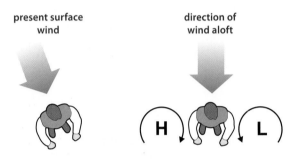

Figure 12-6. Using Buys Ballot's Law to determine the direction of a low-pressure system.

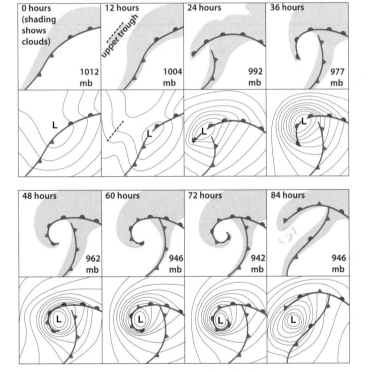

Figure 12-7. Typical life cycle of a northern hemisphere low. It begins as a kink in the isobars, with cold air advancing on warm air. As more isobars close around the low, winds increase. After 84 hours and perhaps thousands of miles from the point of its formation, this low is dissipating. (ADAPTED FROM BOATER'S BOWDITCH BY RICHARD K. HUBBARD)

passed. If low pressure is to the west, your local weather conditions may deteriorate.

In practice, you listen to what the weatherperson tells you, but you also weigh this with local circumstances, since local conditions can often vary dramatically from those indicated by the "big picture." Learning your local conditions can make your sailing or boating much easier and safer.

Fronts

The lows that drive our middle-latitude weather form along the boundaries between adjacent air masses—for example, between the cold, dry air mass that persists over Canada and the warm, moist air mass that recurs over the southern United States (Figure 12-7). A low is born when a kink forms along this boundary and begins a counterclockwise rotation (northern hemisphere). East of the kink, southerly warm air starts to override colder air to the north and east, while to the west, northerly cold air pushes south and east, displacing the warmer air ahead of it. The resultant frontal zones (called *fronts*) separating regions of cool or colder air from warm assume the shape of an inverted V, with the low at the apex. Across a frontal zone, temperature, humidity, air pressure, and wind often change abruptly over a short distance. Fronts are the sites of most large-scale weather conditions such as winter rainstorms, sleet, and snow. They are also the source of many boating problems.

The newly formed system migrates eastward, steered by the overhead jet stream that follows and defines the air mass boundary, until the low dissipates several days later. The isobars surrounding the low show distinct bends along fronts, marking abrupt shifts in wind direction there.

Types of Fronts

Fronts are named for the type of air that is arriving. When a mass of cold air catches up with a mass of warmer air, a *cold front* forms. If the overtaking air mass is warmer than the overtaken mass, the front is a *warm front*. When neither air mass is overtaking the other, the front is *stationary*.

A cold air mass may approach a warm air mass and form a cold front. If the cold air mass then slows to a stop, a stationary front forms. If the cold air mass then moves back toward where it came from, a warm front forms. The air behind a warm front is warmer than the air ahead of it.

On a weather map, commonly recognized symbols designate each of these three fronts (Figure 12-8). A heavy line with pointed barbs on the advancing side represents a cold front. (As a memory aid, think of the pointed barbs as icicles.) A warm front is denoted by a heavy line with rounded barbs on its advancing edge. (Think of the rounded barb as suns.) A stationary front is indicated with alternating rounded and pointed barbs. The pointed barbs point toward the warm air, while the rounded barbs point toward the cold air.

If the map is in color, such as on TV, cold fronts are blue, warm fronts are red, and stationary fronts have blue and red segments.

Changes as Fronts Pass

When a front passes, there are noticeable changes in air properties. If the overtaking air mass is moving rapidly, the zone between the air masses is narrow and the changes are abrupt. If the zone is wide and diffuse, the changes are more gradual. When the change is abrupt, the weather is more violent.

TEMPERATURE DIFFERENCES. As a front passes, the changes in temperature are usually pronounced. The air behind a cold front is always colder than the air in front of it. In a warm front, the overtaking air is warmer than the air it is overtaking.

MOISTURE. The moisture content of air in the two masses is usually significantly different. Behind a cold front the air is drier than the air in the overtaken mass. The air behind a warm front has more moisture than the air in front of it. When a cold

front passes in the winter, you expect clear, cold, dry air to follow. Ahead of it, you expect rain or sleet. You expect moist air and probably fog when a warm front passes. Ahead of it may be snow, rain, or fog.

WIND. Wind always changes across a front. The change may be in direction or in speed or both. The wind shift as a front passes in the northern hemisphere is almost always clockwise. For example, if it is blowing from the southwest before the front passes, it will change to northwest after it has passed. The shift is usually abrupt, and higher winds occur. These may pose a danger for small craft. If you are on the water when such a shift occurs, head your vessel into the wind.

PRESSURE. Pressure is higher in the cold air. Thus, when a frontal passage ushers in colder air, the air pressure usually rises abruptly. When a front brings warmer air, the pressure usually falls until the front passes. It then remains steady or may decrease slightly. The important thing to remember is that when a front passes, a change in pressure occurs. If you have a *barometer*, you can measure the change in air pressure.

A barometer is most useful for predicting changes in weather. A falling barometer means that a low-pressure system is approaching; a rising barometer means that the low is passing and a high is approaching. Not all changes in barometric pressure are significant, but a rise or fall of 0.02 inch or more per hour usually indicates changing weather. The more rapid the rise or fall, the greater the expected change.

Cold Fronts

Cold fronts move at speeds of 10 to 30 knots, depending on the time of year (Figure 12-9). They are two to three times as fast in winter as in summer. If a cold front is moving fast, the zone between it and the warm air mass in front of it will be narrow, and the changes in weather will be abrupt. Thus, if a cold front is moving fast, there will probably

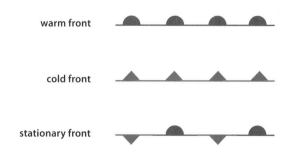

Figure **12-8.** Representations of fronts on weather maps.

WARNING *If a cold front is approaching, or has arrived, use extreme caution. This includes not boating or returning to port.*

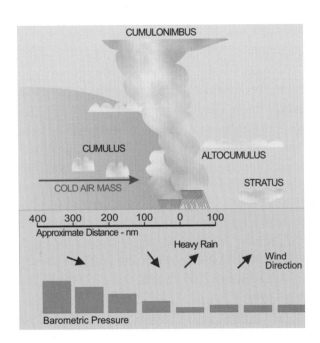

Figure **12-9.** An idealized cross section through an advancing cold front shows the characteristic northern hemisphere sequence of cloud types, wind changes, and barometric pressure changes. (REPRINTED WITH PERMISSION FROM *ONBOARD WEATHER FORECASTING: A CAPTAIN'S QUICK GUIDE* BY BOB SWEET)

be a line of strong winds in front of it called a *squall line*. Wind speeds in squall lines are often as high as 30 to 60 miles per hour, with gusts as high as 80 to 100 miles per hour. Squall lines present dangerous boating conditions. In and behind them, typically, there is heavy rain, followed by clearing.

The air behind a cold front is denser than the air in the warm mass it is overtaking. This is so because dry air is heavier than wet air, and cold air is heavier than warm. As a result, the cold air wedges in under the warm, moist air it is overtaking, and this forces the warm air to rise.

If the air temperature difference on the two sides of the front is small, the slope of the warm air rise is gradual. The frontal area is broad and its stormy weather is not severe. If the temperature difference is large, however, the warm air rises rapidly. The frontal zone is narrow and the resulting weather is severe.

When the warm, moist air in the mass preceding a cold front rises, it cools, and can no longer hold all its moisture. Some of it condenses to form clouds. If it condenses still further, precipitation occurs. As the moisture condenses, it releases the en-

ergy it absorbed in changing from a liquid to water vapor. This gives the storm its energy.

When a cold front passes, the abrupt shift in wind direction may create *wind shear*, in which strong circular wind currents (eddies) occur along the mixing zone. If the zone is very narrow, the eddies may be strong.

A vessel passing across the mixing zone is subject first to strong winds from one direction, and a short time later to equally strong winds from the opposite direction. Wind shear has caused airplane crashes, and sailboats have been dismasted by it. Powerboats may be subjected to severe yaw and may capsize.

If the difference in temperature between the two air masses is small, the precipitation is usually light. If the difference is larger, more violent storms occur. Frequently, the storms that occur are thunderstorms that may include strong winds, wind shear, lightning, heavy rain, hail, and sometimes tornadoes. Needless to say, this is not good boating weather.

Warm Fronts

Warm fronts travel much more slowly than cold fronts (Figure 12-10). The zones between warm fronts and the cold air that precedes them are wider and more diffuse than those that precede cold fronts. Thus, the changes as warm fronts approach are more gradual and less violent.

As a warm front approaches, air pressure starts to fall steadily and winds increase. A steady rain begins to fall. The temperature begins to rise. Air pressure falls slightly but steadily.

The air in a warm air mass is warmer and holds more moisture than the air in a cold air mass. Warm, moist air is lighter than cold, dry air. As a result, the warm, moist air rides up and over the cold air in front of it. The slope of the rise is very gradual, however, and the frontal area may be hundreds of miles wide. Some fog will probably form.

The rising warm, moist air cools and its moisture condenses. Since the slope of the rise is gradual, clouds are formed well in advance of any precipitation, which is gentle. Rain or snow may occur, but you would not expect violent weather such as in a thunderstorm. Warm front weather seldom presents violent boating conditions, but the

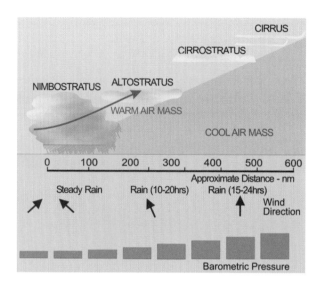

Figure **12-10.** The characteristic cloud, wind, and barometric pressure changes that accompany an advancing warm front. (REPRINTED WITH PERMISSION FROM *ONBOARD WEATHER FORECASTING: A CAPTAIN'S QUICK GUIDE* BY BOB SWEET)

fog that may accompany it can be a problem. Be alert for fog near a warm front.

Clouds and Fronts

Three types of clouds accompany fronts—cirrus, stratus, and cumulus (Figure 12-11). All are the result of moisture-laden air carried aloft. As air rises, it cools, and some of its moisture condenses to form a cloud. The rapidity with which warm, moist air ascends determines the structure of the cloud. In general, clouds get their names from their shapes and their altitudes.

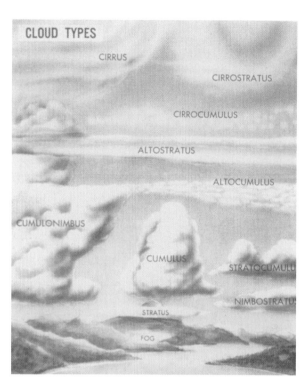

Figure **12-11.** Principal cloud types and their relative altitudes.

High-level clouds have a prefix of *cirro-*. In Latin, *cirro* means "curl," which often describes their appearance. These clouds have altitudes of 20,000 feet or higher. *Cirrus clouds* are thin, high-level clouds made of ice crystals (Figure 12-12). They are often called **mares' tails** and may be as high as 50,000 feet. *Cirrostratus clouds*, the lowest of the high-level clouds, are flat. Their altitudes

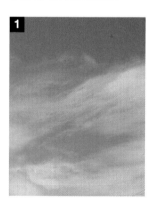
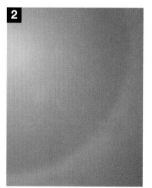
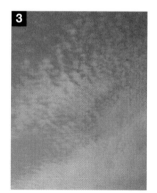

Figure **12-12.** High-altitude clouds are either cirrus or begin with the prefix *cirro*. Composed mainly of ice crystals, these clouds have a bright, wispy appearance. 1. The highest of the group, cirrus, may be isolated tufts, streaks, feather-like plumes, or curved lines called *mares' tails*. Cirrus can be the first indicator of an approaching warm front, sometimes thickening at such times. 2. Cirrostratus clouds form a thin veil that can produce a halo effect around the sun or moon. When these replace cirrus, they may indicate that the precipitation of an approaching warm front is about 24 hours away. 3, 4. Cirrocumulus clouds are thin and patchy, and are sometimes called *mackerel sky*. When more fully developed, as in (4), their wavy appearance indicates turbulent air but not necessarily the approach of bad weather. (PHOTO #4 BY JAY BRANDINGER)

vary from 20,000 to 30,000 feet. They cause halos around the sun, and hint at lower clouds to come.

Middle-level clouds have the prefix *alto-*. Their average altitude is about 10,000 feet (Figure 12-13). They may be *altocumulus* or *altostratus*, depending on whether they are puffy or flat.

Stratus clouds are flat and frequently layered (Figure 12-14).

Cumulus clouds are the fluffy, piled-up clouds often seen in summer skies (Figures 12-15 and 12-16). They are usually "fair weather" clouds but they

Figure **12-13.** Midlevel clouds begin with the prefix *alto* and have altitudes between 6,000 and 20,000 feet. 1. Altostratus clouds form a sheetlike layer. They may result from thickening and lowering of cirrostratus clouds, and when they do, they may indicate the closer approach of a warm front. 2, 3. Altocumulus clouds are common late in the day and can give us beautiful sunsets—the "red sky at night" that suggests a fine day tomorrow. (PHOTO #2 BY MIKE BRODEY; PHOTO #3 BY BOB DENNIS)

Figure **12-14.** Low-level clouds (under 6,500 feet) acquire a thick, ominous look. 1, 2. Sheetlike, stratified clouds known as stratus often result from a lowering and thickening of altostratus. They look more threatening the lower and darker they get. 3. Stratocumulus clouds are lumpier than stratus and hold a lot of moisture. 4. Nimbostratus clouds are low and dark and almost always accompanied by precipitation, often in association with a warm front.

can develop into towering *cumulonimbus* clouds (Figure 12-17) in the right circumstances. Thunderstorms are produced from cumulonimbus clouds.

The importance of clouds lies in what they can tell you about weather. Cumulonimbus clouds tell you that thunderstorms are forming. Altostratus clouds tell you that a warm front is approaching. Small cumulus clouds are a harbinger of fair weather. In general, as a front approaches, clouds become progressively lower and thicker.

WEATHER CLUES FROM CLOUDS. Clouds carry other weather clues as well (Table 12-4). When you see clouds moving in a leisurely fashion across the sky, you can expect continued fair weather. You can look for wind and rain when they scud rapidly overhead. When small clouds decrease or melt away toward sunset, expect fair weather. Increasing and lowering clouds mean unsettled weather ahead.

COLD FRONT CLOUDS. About 150 miles ahead of the usual cold front are high sheets of altocumulus clouds. In the summer, the front is probably about

12 hours away, but in the winter, the front may be only a few hours away.

As the front nears, *nimbus* and, perhaps, cumulonimbus clouds appear (Figure 12-17). Nimbus clouds are those from which rain is falling. They are the lowest of the clouds.

Figure **12-17.** Cumulonimbus clouds result when cumulus clouds build up to great heights (2 to 5 miles) as a result of extreme instability and violent thermal activity. These are thunderclouds, and when fully formed show the characteristic anvil top (bottom). Expect heavy showers, strong wind gusts, and lightning when these approach. (TOP PHOTO BY BOB DENNIS)

Figure **12-15.** When not vertically developed, cumulus clouds are the innocent puffballs that mark fair weather in the summer sky.

Figure **12-16.** Cumulus clouds often form over islands at sea.

TABLE 12-4 **WEATHER CLUES FROM CLOUDS**	
Clouds	**Precipitation**
Cumulonimbus—*vertical, developed cumulus*	Rain, possible thundershowers, possible hail, tornadoes
Cirrus—*thin, high level*	None
Stratus—*flat, often layered*	Possible light drizzle
Cumulus—*white, puffy*	None (but may be windy)
Altocumulus—*puffy, middle level*	None
Altostratus—*flat, middle level*	Light rain or snow possible
Nimbostratus—*flat, low level*	Heavy, steady rain
Nimbus—*lowest of clouds*	Rain is falling

As the cold front passes, the clouds rise and become stratocumulus or altocumulus and possibly cumulus. The storm is over. You can probably expect at least two to three days of cool or cold or less cloudy dry weather.

WARM FRONT CLOUDS. High, thin cirrus clouds extend as much as 1,000 miles ahead of a warm front. These are clouds formed from warm, moist air that has risen up and over the retreating cold air mass. As the front slowly advances, the clouds thicken and lower. High-level cirrostratus clouds become midlevel altostratus clouds, and rain or snow begins to fall.

After the warm front passes, rain or snow may continue to fall while the clouds gradually rise. The wind direction veers, or shifts clockwise—for example, from southeast to southwest. Rain, mist, or fog may linger. Some clearing begins.

Deck-Level Forecasting

You can synthesize what we've covered so far to create your own deck-level forecasts, either to confirm or interpret what region-wide forecasts are telling you. You should log your observations at regular intervals. Record wind direction and speed, cloud type and direction, and how much of the sky is cloud-covered. The directions and relative speeds of the mid- and high-level clouds will give a hint of the direction of the approaching low. See the sidebar opposite for how to refine a regional forecast with your own observations.

DECK-LEVEL FORECASTING

Approaching Low

Clouds: high cirrus, gradually lowering and thickening to altostratus
Wind: backing to southeast and possibly increasing
Barometer: begins to fall (2 to 10 mb in 3 hours)
Offshore: swell increases, with decreasing period

What to Expect:

Rain: Within 15 to 24 hours
If low is west to northwest and passing to your north, you will see fronts.
If low is west to southwest and passing to your south, you will not see distinct fronts, but wind will shift from southeast to east, northeast, then north to northwest.

Approaching Warm Front

Cirrus or cirrocumulus clouds: front is more than 24 hours away
Lowering, thickening clouds (cirrostratus to nimbostratus): front is less than 24 hours away
Rain: begins lightly, then becomes steady and persistent
Barometer: falls steadily; a faster fall indicates stronger winds
Wind: increases steadily, stays in the southeast
Visibility: deteriorates, especially in rain

Passing Warm Front

Sky: lightens toward western horizon
Rain: breaks

Wind: veers from south to southwest and may increase
Barometer: stops falling
Temperature: rises

Within Warm Sector

Wind: steady, typically from the southwest, will strengthen ahead of cold front
Barometer: steady—may drop shortly ahead of cold front
Precipitation: mist, possible drizzle
Clouds: variety of cumulus clouds

Approaching Cold Front

Wind: southwesterly, increasing; line squalls possible up to 100 miles ahead of front
Barometer: begins brief fall, could be rapid
Clouds: cumulonimbus build to the west
Temperature: steady
Rain: begins and intensifies, but duration is short (1 to 2 hours typical)

Passing Cold Front

Wind: veers rapidly to west or northwest, gusty behind front
Barometer: begins to rise, often quickly
Clouds: cumulonimbus, then nimbostratus, then clearing
Temperature: drops suddenly, then slow decline
Rain: ends, gives way to rapidly clearing skies, possibly with leftover altocumulus or stratocumulus

Fog

Fog is a cloud in contact with the earth's surface. It consists of water droplets or ice crystals, which form when air is cooled below its dew point. Fog is the most frequent cause of limited visibility and also the most common weather hazard (Figure 12-18). The speed with which fog can form makes it especially hazardous; it is not unusual for visibility to drop to less than 1 mile in a few minutes.

Conditions Favoring Fog Formation

Moisture-laden air is essential for fog formation, which means that the conditions are especially conducive to fog in coastal areas. Fog can and does occur anywhere, however. It usually forms around microscopic particles such as dust, soot, and chemicals, and thus occurs frequently in industrial areas.

Advection Fog

Of the several types of fog, the one of greatest concern to boaters is *advection fog*, which occurs in coastal waters and is caused by warm, moist air blowing over cold water. It is a concern for boating since it moves rapidly in dense fogbanks that can overtake and surprise unwary boaters.

Predicting Fog

Fog can be forecast with a moderate degree of accuracy. Factors that aid predictions are historical, wind strength, air temperature, air moisture, the air temperature–dew point difference, and other information such as sky appearance (Figure 12-19).

Historical predictions are based on questions such as "Did fog form last night?," and "Are the conditions the same tonight?" If the answers are yes, then it is likely that fog will form again tonight.

Wind strength is important in fog formation. A warm, damp, gentle, steady wind without gusts favors the formation of fog. This is especially true if the wind is warmer than the water.

WARNING *Advection fog can reduce visibility to a few feet in a matter of minutes.*

Figure **12-18.** The thicker the fog, the more slowly and carefully you should progress. (PHOTO BY JOE BRITVCH)

Figure **12-19.** A morning fog, like this one on the Strawberry Reservoir in Utah, will often dissipate as the day progresses. (PHOTO BY MART GARDNER)

FOG PRECAUTIONS

1. Mark your position prior to entering the fog area.
2. Reduce speed.
3. Assign lookouts to both look AND listen.
4. Consider anchoring if out of shipping channels.
5. Give appropriate (bell and/or whistle) sound signals.

If the air temperature and the dew point in early evening are within 10° of each other, you can expect fog. The air is carrying almost all the moisture it can hold. Any lowering of its temperature will cause the formation of water droplets.

A variety of other factors aid in predicting fog. A hazy sky that is not very blue is a forerunner of fog. When the sky is like this, the horizon is poorly defined. At night, halos around lights mean high air moisture content. Finally, is the time of the year right for fog?

Fog Precautions

As with other bad weather, it is advisable not to boat in fog; if it's foggy, don't go!

If you are on the water and fog settles in, take note of your position. Record it and the time. If you do not know where you are before the fog settles in, you will not know later on.

The next important thing is to reduce your speed. Assign lookouts at the bow and stern to watch and to listen. Listening in a fog is even more important than watching. The direction of sound is difficult to determine since the water droplets distort it. If you need to hear better, stop your engine and **listen**. If you are out of shipping lanes and other frequently traveled waterways, consider stopping and anchoring. You can hear better under these conditions.

Above all else, remember the sound signals you must give when underway or anchored in fog. If you have forgotten them, refer to Chapter 6 to refresh your memory.

Nonfrontal Weather

Stormy weather can also occur in the absence of lows or fronts. Nonfrontal weather includes thunderstorms, tornadoes and waterspouts, and tropical storms.

Thunderstorms

As already discussed, thunderstorms may accompany cold fronts, but they can also occur in nonfrontal weather. Summer thunderstorms are usually of this type. Regardless of its cause, a thunderstorm is probably the storm most feared by boaters. A thunderstorm may arise in a short time and produce powerful winds. Cumulus clouds in the morning may mean thunderstorms later in the day. Boaters should listen to National Weather Service radio broadcasts or other forecasting media.

The winds, heavy rains, and lightning in thunderstorms are dangerous. The National Weather Service calls a thunderstorm **severe** if its winds are 50 knots or greater and/or if it contains hail that is ½ inch or larger. And when a tornado is embedded in a thunderstorm, it is especially severe.

Thunderstorms form in rising, moist air. The advancing edge of a cold front or surface heat can provide the lift. There are usually three stages in the formation of any thunderstorm (Figure 12-20).

Stage One

In the first stage, the land or water surface heats, and the air above it heats and rises. If the air is moist, some of its moisture condenses and light, fluffy cumulus clouds form. Cloud development may not stop with small cumulus cloud formation, however. If there is enough heat, the air will continue to rise, and towering cumulus clouds will develop vertically. They may rise in a column 15,000 to 25,000 feet high at this stage. In rising to these heights, the air temperature may cool as much as 80°F to well below freezing at the top of the cloud. Even so, the air is still warmer than the surrounding air. As the air cools, its moisture condenses, releasing large amounts of heat. This heat energy is the power behind the developing storm.

Stage Two

In the second stage, the storm matures. At this point, clouds often reach a height of 40,000 feet, but heights of up to 80,000 feet have been recorded. The higher the cloud, the greater the release of energy and the more severe the storm.

As the air rises, its water vapor condenses and precipitation occurs at the outer edges of the column. The falling rain or hail further cools the air in the column, creating downdrafts and heavier rains. Air is still rising in the center of the column, bringing in more moisture. This air may reach a speed of as much as 6,000 feet per minute.

The rising air may catch descending hailstones, if there are any, and carry them back up the column. During the trip up the column, more moisture forms on the hailstones and freezes. Thus, the hailstones grow in size. If the updrafts are strong enough, a hailstone may make several trips up and down the column, growing in size with each trip.

The cold, descending air accelerates and may reach speeds of as much as 2,500 feet per minute. When it reaches the surface it spreads outward. This produces strong, gusty winds, a sharp temperature drop, and a rapid rise in pressure. The surface wind is a called a *plow wind*, and its leading edge is the *first gust*.

Wind shear occurs frequently in squall lines that appear before thunderstorms. A squall line is a row of black, towering clouds that may reach heights of 40,000 or more feet, and they often de-

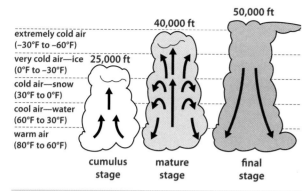

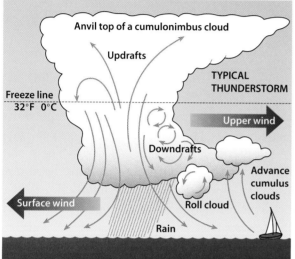

Figure **12-20.** **Top:** The three stages of thunderstorm development. **Bottom:** A maturing storm. The anvil top points in the storm's direction of travel. (BOTTOM ILLUSTRATION REPRINTED WITH PERMISSION FROM *BOATER'S BOWDITCH* BY RICHARD K. HUBBARD)

Figure **12-21.** Clouds like these indicate the approach of a squall line and are often associated with a thunderstorm embedded in or preceding a cold front. Expect rapid wind shifts and strong gusts. (COURTESY NOAA)

velop ahead of cold fronts in moist, unstable air (Figure 12-21). They may also develop in unstable air far from any front. As the squall line passes, there is an abrupt change in wind direction—a wind shear. Squall lines present a serious weather hazard for boaters.

Stage Three

In stage three the storm continues to move. You may be able to tell the direction of its movement from the anvil-shaped top of the cloud. The anvil points in the direction toward which the cloud is moving.

At this point, the falling air cools the earth's surface and the storm loses part of its energy source—hot air. The entire cloud becomes sinking air. With no ascending air to cool, rain stops. The storm dies.

When Thunderstorms Form

On some summer days, afternoon cumulus clouds are capable of turning into thunderstorms if there is enough moisture in the air. Keep an eye on growing cumulus. You may be able to run for safety before there's any danger.

In hazy weather, however, you may not see the thunderstorms forming. Haze limits visibility and is ideal weather for thunderstorms. On such hot, muggy, hazy afternoons, you should be alert for static on your AM radio, the sound of distant thunder, and/or the flicker of lightning. Stay close to port so you can run in if necessary. If you are sailing and do not have auxiliary power, be especially alert, and perhaps shorten sail. The winds may die shortly before the storm begins. This is no time to be becalmed. If there is a threat of bad weather, have all hands don their life jackets, batten your hatches, and tie down all loose equipment. Considerer anchoring.

Lightning

Lightning is a serious boating hazard. It is a giant electrical spark arcing between clouds, within clouds, and between clouds and the ground. Never take shelter under a tree when you are on land, because lightning usually strikes the tallest object around. When you are out on the water, *you* may be the tallest thing for miles around (Figure 12-22).

The best way to escape the dangers of lightning is to avoid it. This is a strong argument in favor of understanding weather. The more "weather-wise" you become, the less likely you are to be caught out on the water in a thunderstorm.

HOW FAR AWAY IS THE STORM? Lightning heats air. This makes it expand rapidly and creates a partial vacuum. It then cools rapidly and rushes back in to fill the vacuum. The sound of the air rushing into the vacuum is thunder. For practical purposes, you can consider that lightning and thunder occur at the same time.

You will see the lightning before you hear the thunder. Sound travels much more slowly than light, about 1,100 feet per second. It takes sound about 5 seconds to travel 1 statute mile or 1.7 kilometers, whereas light travels 186,000 miles per second.

> **WARNING** When you see a flash of lightning, count slowly, "one thousand and one, one thousand and two, one thousand and three..." Each five counts tells you the lightning is about 1 mile away. Be careful that you relate the sound to its appropriate flash. This may be difficult if the lightning is nearly continuous.
>
> Any heavy weather, tornadoes, or waterspouts that appear not to change their position relative to you may be moving toward you.

Figure **12-22.** Lightning over the shore. (COURTESY NOAA)

GROUND YOUR BOAT? You can lessen the danger of a lightning strike by staying off the water during thunderstorms. You can also lessen it by having a **grounding system** installed, similar to those found on buildings and other land structures. A grounding system may prevent a lightning strike or it may provide lightning a path to reach ground (water) without causing damage or injury to you or your boat.

Most physicists believe that a good grounding system serves to lead lightning into the water by the most direct means. They also believe that a good grounding system can prevent or lessen lightning strikes.

According to physicists, a good grounding system neutralizes the difference in electrical potential between the water and the air and prevents static buildup. This is the reason farmers put lightning rods on buildings such as barns. There are, though, no guaranteed safeguards against lightning. It is very unpredictable and powerful.

The installation of a grounding system is a job for a professional. Don't try it yourself, and don't assume that the builder of your boat provided any lightning protection for it.

Microbursts

In 1976 the U.S. government identified microbursts as possible hazards to landing aircraft and to pleasure boats. The downdrafts from thunderstorms act in the same manner as the downdrafts in front of squall lines. Cold downdrafts meet warm air and cause wind directions to change suddenly. These downdrafts radiate out from the thunderheads where they hit the surface in what is called a *microburst*. A microburst is strongest in the direction in which the thundercloud is moving, and its winds may exceed 100 knots (Figure 12-23). Microbursts may occur even when there is no rain below a thunderhead. A *dry microburst* occurs when falling rain in a thunderhead evaporates before it reaches the earth's surface. Because there is no visible sign of wind shear, it is difficult to predict.

Microbursts can occur several miles away from an associated squall line. Even if it is not raining, be alert for a possible squall. Near a thunderstorm, these may be from a direction different from the prevailing wind.

If You Are Caught

If you are boating and find yourself in a thunderstorm, have each person aboard don a life jacket. Next, pinpoint your exact location before the storm arrives. Heavy rain will reduce your visibility.

Reduce your boat's speed or reduce sail, and keep a sharp lookout for other boats and obstructions. Secure all hatches and ports. Strap down or stow in lockers all loose gear on or belowdeck.

Once the storm hits, try to take the first (and heaviest) gusts of wind on your bow, not abeam. Heading into the wind is the most seaworthy position for most small boats. Approach waves at a 45° angle. This will keep your propeller under water, and it also reduces pounding and provides a safer and more comfortable ride.

Stay low in the boat. Don't make yourself the tallest target. Keep away from all metal objects. Lightning does not have to strike a boat directly for strong electrical charges to be aboard. If it strikes the water near your boat, it may affect the metal parts on the boat.

Tornadoes

A *tornado* is a whirlpool of air with a relatively small diameter that extends downward from a cumulonimbus cloud. It has a funnel-like appearance. The average diameter of the funnel is about 750 feet, and the wind speed at its center may exceed 250 knots.

Tornadoes are usually spawned in the squall lines ahead of cold fronts (Figure 12-24). They also occur frequently in hurricanes, however, and can even occur in calm, sunny weather.

Tornadoes usually form over land and then sometimes move out over water. A tornado over

water is different from a similar-appearing phenomenon called a waterspout (see below).

Tornadoes always have a counterclockwise circulation and almost always move from southwest to northeast, although they sometimes move in the opposite direction. If a tornado appears to be standing still or growing larger, watch out! It is moving toward you. Move at right angles to its path as fast as you can, and you may avoid it.

Waterspouts

Waterspouts come from two different sources. The first is a tornado that has gone out to sea, which is not a true waterspout. Since it is over water, though, it may contain large quantities of water. Both the water and the tornado's wind make it dangerous for boaters (Figure 12-25).

✓ STORM-AT-SEA SAFETY CHECKLIST

- ☐ Have ALL aboard don life jackets.
- ☐ Close ports and hatches, and stow gear.
- ☐ Pinpoint and write down your exact location.
- ☐ Reduce speed.
- ☐ Keep a sharp lookout for boats, floating objects, shallow water, and the shore.
- ☐ Head into the wind.
- ☐ Approach waves at a 45° angle.
- ☐ Stay low in the boat.
- ☐ Keep away from all metal objects.

A FEW POINTERS ON LIGHTNING

- The more frequent the lightning, the more severe the storm.
- Lightning strikes increase in number as the storm grows.
- Decreasing lightning means the storm is dying.
- At night, frequent distant flashes along a large sector of the horizon suggest a probable squall line.

Figure **12-23.** A microburst. (COURTESY NOAA)

Figure **12-24.** A tornado. (COURTESY NOAA)

True waterspouts, unlike tornadoes, do not develop in weather fronts. They usually occur in fair weather and always over water. Their winds may circle either clockwise or counterclockwise, almost more like dust devils over land than tornadoes. Waterspouts may have diameters of 20 to 200 feet and are more common in the tropics than in the middle latitudes.

Unlike tornadoes, which form in clouds and grow downward toward the earth (and may or may not reach the earth), waterspouts form close to the water's surface and grow upward. They are usually small, of short duration, and less dangerous than tornadic waterspouts.

Although waterspouts are less violent than tornadoes, they are a danger to boats. They may last from 10 minutes to half an hour, and as they subside, they dump large quantities of water that can swamp a small boat.

Tropical Storms

Tropical storms are nonfrontal storms that form in the tropics. They have counterclockwise circulation in the northern hemisphere.

Figure **12-25.** Twin waterspouts. (COURTESY NOAA)

Tropical Waves

Tropical storms usually begin as tropical waves of low pressure and move from east to west in the trade wind belt. Good weather precedes tropical waves and extensive cloudiness follows them, often accompanied by rain and thunderstorms. Tropical waves occur in all seasons, but they are more frequent and stronger in summer and early fall. Tropical waves can develop into tropical cyclones.

Tropical Cyclones

A *tropical cyclone* is a general term for any low-pressure area that forms over warm, moist, tropical waters. The strength of tropical cyclones comes from the heat of the water over which they form. Over cold water, they lose strength.

Tropical cyclones are classed according to their intensities based on average 1-minute wind speeds. Wind gusts may be as much as 50% higher than the average wind speed.

There are three classes of tropical cyclones: **tropical depressions**, **tropical storms**, and **hurricanes** or **typhoons**. Additionally, hurricanes are called different names, depending on where they occur. An intense tropical cyclone in the Atlantic and eastern Pacific is a hurricane; in the western Pacific Ocean, it is a typhoon; and in the Indian Ocean, it is a cyclone. No matter what their names, they are serious storms. Among other factors, hurricanes require water temperatures of at least 79°F for their formation as they absorb tremendous amounts of energy from the water over which they form.

WINDS IN TROPICAL CYCLONES. The sustained winds in tropical cyclones are:

- Tropical depressions: up to 34 knots
- Tropical storms: 35 to 63 knots
- Hurricanes or typhoons: 64 knots or more

Hurricanes

On land, the greatest property destruction and loss of life in a hurricane usually results from the storm surge. Hurricane-force winds pile up the sea before them—in effect, the entire sea rises up—and this surge may extend for up to 100 miles along the coast to the right side of the storm's path of advance. Storm waves then roll ashore on top of this surge, resulting in storm surge heights from about 4 feet to over 18 feet.

Your boat will probably need more protection from the storm surge than from the wind. Even so, protection from the wind is not unimportant because windblown objects may damage it. There are many suggested ways to protect your boat in a hurricane, but none of them is completely satisfactory. If you live in a hurricane-prone area, get advice from seasoned boaters. Weigh the advice, then make up your own mind.

Well-developed hurricanes average 300 miles in diameter. At the center or *eye* of a hurricane is a low-pressure area that may be 15 to 25 miles in diameter. Since the winds of a hurricane rotate strongly, the center is a very low-pressure area of light winds. Although the sea below the eye is heavy and confused, the wind in the eye seldom reaches 15 knots.

The Atlantic Ocean hurricane season is June through November, although hurricanes also occur in other months (Figure 12-26). Early- and late-season hurricanes usually form in the Gulf of Mexico and the Caribbean Sea and develop rapidly. The mid-season storms of August and September may begin as tropical waves coming off the coast of Africa, and they develop slowly.

Hurricanes also begin off the west coast of Mexico. These usually do not present threats to the continental United States, but may reach the Hawaiian Islands and beyond.

The National Weather Service is a continuous source of information for tropical storms and hurricanes. Keep abreast of its warnings and heed them.

Don't wait until the last minute, though, to take measures to protect your boat. You may find safe harbors filled and storm equipment no longer available. Besides, you may find your time occupied in taking care of your family and home.

The Weather Channel on cable and satellite TV offers excellent coverage of hurricanes and other serious storms.

Water and Air Temperature

Water and air temperatures are also important to the comfort and safety of recreational boaters. Cold air temperatures require boaters to wear additional clothing. Cold air temperatures also mean that it

Figure **12-26.** Superstorm Sandy bearing down on the U.S. East Coast, October 29, 2012. (COURTESY NOAA)

WARNING *Above all, do not stay on your boat during a hurricane, even a minimal one!*

is more difficult to start engines—or to restart them after a day of fishing. Cold water temperatures increase the risk of cold shock and hypothermia in the event of falls overboard. U.S. Coast Guard recreational boating accident statistics indicate that the risk of fatalities associated with accidents increases dramatically as a function of water temperature.

The Jet Stream

The winds that are experienced at the earth's surface throughout the middle latitudes are caused by the interactions of low-pressure and high-pressure air masses. These surface air masses are steered by strong, high-altitude winds (18,000 feet or higher) that move west to east around the earth in sinusoidal paths. What we call a *jet stream* is a narrow, especially strong concentration of this upper-altitude flow. A complete explanation of the effects of jet streams on surface weather is beyond the scope of this chapter and is unnecessary for the deck-level forecasting presented above.

The Go, No-Go Decision

Where you boat is of great importance to your boating safety and enjoyment as it relates to weather. Your boat type and size, its equipment, and your ability to operate it also weigh heavily on your personal go, no-go decision making.

If you have a small boat and are boating on a small lake, with the shore nearby, your need for navigational equipment is minimal. You won't need much beyond a handheld compass and a VHF radio. After all, if fog develops, you can simply steer a steady compass course and land will appear sooner or later; maybe not exactly where you want it to be, but dry land will happen! On the other hand, if a squall line develops with attendant high winds and waves, you and your passengers should be wearing life vests, have a communication device to ask for assistance, and have a plan B for escape, at the very least.

✓ GO, NO-GO CHECKLIST

☐ Is the forecast and current weather suitable for the planned cruise?

☐ Does my boat have the equipment necessary for safe operation under any situation that might arise?

☐ Do my crew and I have confidence that we can successfully operate such equipment in the expected conditions?

☐ Do my crew and I have the necessary clothing, food, water, first-aid equipment, and training appropriate to the voyage?

☐ Do I understand how to ask for weather information while underway?

☐ Is my boating knowledge of all safety aspects, such as the Rules of the Road, up to date?

☐ Can I successfully navigate to safety if my electronic equipment fails?

☐ Do I have a plan B in case the original plan won't work?

☐ Have I filed an appropriate float plan with a responsible person?

☐ What is my comfort level in this situation?

A trip south along the California coast in a 42-foot cabin cruiser, however, presents the skipper and crew with a wholly different set of concerns and requirements. The chances of encountering fog are excellent! Is your vessel equipped with radar and loran or GPS? If not, and if you encounter fog, drop the hook or, perhaps, just don't go in the first place.

Regardless of the size of your boat or where you intend to take it, before you make the go, no-go decision, ask the following questions: Do you and your crew know how to use the equipment you have? Do you regularly practice using foul weather equipment in good conditions, so that when the bad stuff arrives it is a natural process to transition from visual cruising to marginal visual cruising? If you and your crew cannot answer such questions positively, then leave your ego at the dock—and probably your boat, also.

Creating Your Personal Go, No-Go Checklist

It is next to impossible to provide an all-encompassing go, no-go decision-making framework that will serve for all situations. There are too many variables of environment, weather, equipment, and skipper experience and comfort level.

The following checklist may be helpful, however. Personalize and expand it to suit your boat and the type of boating you do, and have a safe, pleasant day (or month!) on the water.

Ways to Learn More

Chapman Piloting & Seamanship. 66th ed. Charles B. Husick. New York: Hearst Books, 2009. Chapter 24.

Heavy Weather Sailing: A Captain's Quick Guide. John Rousmaniere. Camden, Maine: International Marine, 2005.

On-Board Weather Forecasting: A Captain's Quick Guide. Bob Sweet. Camden, Maine: International Marine, 2005.

On-Board Weather Handbook: Understanding and Predicting Conditions at Sea. Chris Tibbs. Camden, Maine: International Marine, 2008.

Rough Weather Seamanship for Sail and Power: Design, Gear, and Tactics for Coastal and Offshore Waters. Roger Marshall. Camden, Maine: International Marine, 2006.

Weather Predicting Simplified: How to Read Weather Charts and Satellite Images. Michael William Carr. Camden, Maine: International Marine, 1999.

Practice Questions

IMPORTANT BOATING TERMS

In the following exercise, match the words in the column on the left with the definitions in the column on the right. In the blank space to the left of each term, write the letter of the item that best matches it. Do not use an item in the right-hand column more than once.

THE ITEMS

1. _____ high
2. _____ front
3. _____ dew point
4. _____ fair weather clouds
5. _____ cirrus clouds
6. _____ nimbus clouds
7. _____ swells
8. _____ thunderstorm
9. _____ middle-level clouds

THE RESPONSES

a. small cumulus clouds
b. rain clouds
c. alto-
d. zone between two air masses
e. cool or cold, dry air
f. waves that have traveled a long way
g. cumulonimbus
h. water vapor condenses
i. ice crystals

Multiple-Choice Items

In the following items, choose the best response:

12-1. A condition favoring fog formation is
a. a cold front
b. moisture-laden air
c. nonfrontal weather
d. air moving over warm water

12-2. The temperature behind a cold front is
a. higher than that in front of it
b. lower than that in front of it
c. about the same as that in front of it
d. none of the above

12-3. The air pressure behind a cold front is
a. higher than that in front of it
b. lower than that in front of it
c. about the same as that in front of it
d. none of the above

12-4. The majority of weather systems in the United States come from a(n)
a. easterly direction
b. southerly direction
c. westerly direction
d. northerly direction

12-5. Which one of the following is the best source of marine boating weather information?
a. National Weather Service
b. TV broadcasts
c. newspapers
d. telephone

Multiple-Choice Items (continued)

12-6. In the northern hemisphere, winds flow around and into a low in what direction?

a. westerly
b. easterly
c. clockwise
d. counterclockwise

12-7. Warm air

a. rises
b. falls
c. is very dry
d. is present in high-pressure areas

12-8. Warm moist air, in comparison with dry, cool air is

a. heavier
b. lighter
c. higher pressure
d. about the same weight

12-9. Stand with your back to the surface wind and then turn 45° to your right. A low-pressure area will be

a. in front of you
b. behind you
c. to your right
d. to your left

12-10. A high-pressure air mass is characterized by

a. warm, moist air
b. counterclockwise rotation
c. calm winds
d. cool, dry air

12-11. The fastest-moving fronts are usually

a. warm fronts
b. stationary fronts
c. cold fronts
d. occluded fronts

12-12. A hurricane is a tropical storm with sustained winds

a. greater than 50 knots
b. less than 64 knots
c. 64 knots or greater
d. blowing from the south

12-13. A tropical cyclone is

a. a whirling, funnel-shaped wind
b. a low-pressure area over warm, tropical waters
c. a local storm
d. a thunderstorm over the Caribbean

12-14. Clouds from which rain is falling are called

a. stratus
b. cirrus
c. nimbus
d. cumulus

12-15. The main problem in thunderstorms, tornadoes, tropical storms, etc., is

a. heavy rain
b. wind
c. lightning
d. reduced visibility

12-16. Which of the following poses the most serious problem for boaters?

a. fog
b. wind
c. rain
d. sleet

12-17. The height of wind-created waves depends on

a. how long the wind has been blowing
b. the extent of the fetch
c. the strength of the wind
d. all of the above

12-18. Fog occurs most often near a

a. warm, dry surface
b. cold front
c. large body of cold water
d. warm front

12-19. A particularly dangerous phenomenon that can occur several miles away from a thunderstorm and a squall line is a

a. willy-willy
b. microburst
c. cyclone
d. fetch

12-20. Fronts are named for the kind of air that is

a. in front of them
b. behind them
c. being displaced
d. being cooled

12-21. Thunderstorms form ahead of

a. cold fronts
b. warm fronts
c. stationary fronts
d. occluded fronts

Multiple-Choice Items (continued)

12-22. On a colored weather map warm fronts are

    a. blue
    b. red and blue
    c. red
    d. orange

12-23. Weather is caused by

    a. wind
    b. rain
    c. heat
    d. all of the above

12-24. Thunderstorms are produced by

    a. cumulus clouds
    b. stratus clouds
    c. cirrus clouds
    d. cumulonimbus clouds

12-25. The clouds in front of a warm front are

    a. cumulus
    b. stratus and cirrus
    c. nimbus
    d. cumulonimbus

Your Boat's Radio

The objectives of this chapter are to describe:

✔ The types of radios in use on recreational boats.

✔ The functions of marine radios and their proper use.

✔ The necessity for, and how to obtain, a station license.

✔ When a radio operator's license is needed and how to get one.

✔ What to look for when buying a radio.

✔ The limits of VHF-FM radios.

✔ How to select an antenna.

✔ How to make a radio check.

✔ How to make distress, urgency, and safety calls.

YOUR BOAT'S radio is your link to the outside world. It enables you to get weather information, learn of hazards to navigation, communicate with other boats and shoreside facilities, and get help if you need it. Boats carrying six or more passengers for hire, as well as many other commercial vessels, must

A Coast Guard Auxiliarist use a fixed-mount VHF radio or his boat on the Washington North Carolina, waterfront (PHOTO BY DON LINDBERG)

have radio equipment. Although most privately operated boats are not required to have radios, it is nevertheless advisable to carry one or two.

Communications on the Water

When you're on your boat, you can communicate with other boats or with people onshore in several ways. These include VHF-FM radio, single-side-band (SSB) radio, amateur (ham) radio, citizens band (CB) radio, and cellular telephone. SSB and ham radio are not often used by coastal and inland boaters but come into their own beyond VHF and cell phone range. Offshore boaters are well advised to carry, in addition, an emergency position-indicating radio beacon, or EPIRB.

Coastal and Inland

VHF-FM Radios

VHF-FM radios are the most commonly used marine radios and also the most useful. Two types are available: full-sized, fixed-mount radios (Figure 13-1), which typically offer the legal maximum transmitting power of 25 watts, and handheld portables (Figure 13-2), which offer 5 or 6 watts of peak power and are limited to close-range communications. You can use VHF-FM radios to call for help, to arrange for a marina berth, to get weather information, to call home, or to talk with other boaters. A handheld set is a good standby if your fixed-mount radio fails. Note that it is against Federal Communications Commission (FCC) rules to transmit from a handheld VHF-FM radio onshore.

VHF communications are essentially limited to

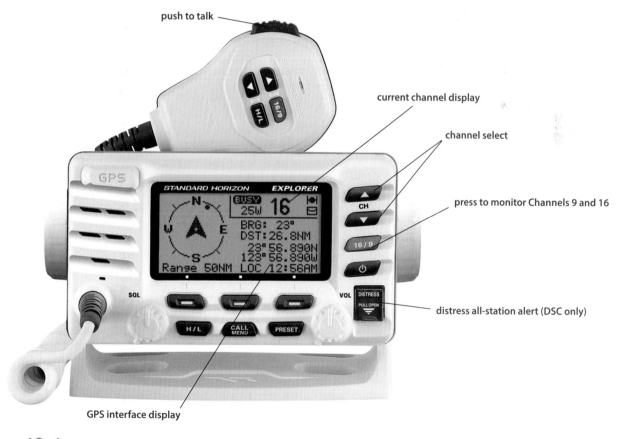

Figure **13-1.** A fixed-mount VHF-FM radiotelephone with digital selective calling (DSC) capability. The advantages of a DSC-equipped radio are discussed in this chapter. This radio is interfaced with a GPS receiver and thus displays the boat's latitude and longitude coordinates. In the event of an automated distress call (see DISTRESS button at lower right), these coordinates will be transmitted with the call. (COURTESY STANDARD HORIZON)

Figure 13-2. A handheld VHF-FM radio offers a maximum communications range of 3 to 5 miles. (COURTESY STANDARD HORIZON)

line-of-sight between the transmitting and receiving antennas, which means that the average maximum ship-to-ship range of a fixed-mount VHF-FM radio is about 10 to 15 miles, depending on the height of its antenna. A masthead antenna, or one installed high on a powerboat's flybridge, might reach up to 20 miles at 25 watts in ideal conditions. The ship-to-shore range may be 20 to 30 miles, depending on the height of the onshore antenna as well as the ship-board antenna. A handheld VHF-FM radio has not only less power but less antenna height (with its stubby, integral antenna) than a fixed-mount unit, and thus offers a maximum range of 3 to 5 miles.

Citizens Band Radios

CB radios are inexpensive and popular. In many inland areas CBs are common on boats, and often are the only radios on board. They serve useful functions on lakes and rivers where the Coast Guard does not maintain a presence, and are the only radios many river marinas have. A CB can serve as an emergency backup for your VHF-FM.

CBs have several limitations, however, such as their short range. Also, there are so many sets in use that the channels are often overcrowded, and many CB owners fail to exercise discipline and proper radio etiquette and overpower other stations. In addition, there is no common distress channel. Furthermore, CBs are AM radios and, therefore, susceptible to static caused by lightning, which means that in a storm, when you might need them most, they are least reliable.

Channel 9 is the channel most often used for emergency calling, but the Coast Guard does not monitor it. For all these reasons, the Coast Guard does not encourage the use of CBs as the first or only means of radio communication for boaters.

Cellular Telephones

In recent years, the use of cell phones has gained popularity, and receiving stations are widespread. Although cell phones are not marine radios, they may serve in an emergency. You may be able to use your cell phone to call for help on rivers and lakes where the Coast Guard does not maintain a presence, and some Coast Guard stations will answer when "*CG" is pressed.

There are drawbacks to the use of cell phones in an emergency, however. First, you may be too far from the nearest relay tower for your signal to be received, although the proliferation of cell towers has reduced this problem enormously in recent years. Second, the time required to relay your call from a 911 operator to the Coast Guard might be critical, and if the call is dropped, the Coast Guard might not be able to call you back. Further, although the locations of SSB and VHF-FM radios can be pinpointed by means of radio direction finders, this is not true of cell phones. Newer cell phones incorporate a GPS chip so their location can be tracked, but that feature is limited over water, so if you don't know where you are, your telephone signal may not help rescuers locate you. Additionally, an emergency call by cell phone does not alert nearby boaters to your distress and may thereby deny you the most immediate assistance available.

Offshore
Single-Sideband Radios

For boats operating beyond VHF range, an SSB radio provides a valuable link to shoreside communications and emergency help. The range of an SSB radio varies with time of day, season, and the frequency used, from as little as 25 miles to worldwide. Specific information on frequency selection can be found in the operator's manual that comes with the radio.

SSB radios cover the marine portion of the medium-frequency (MF) band (2.0 to 3.0 MHz) and the international marine channels in the high-frequency (HF) band (3.0 to 23.0 MHz). These radios include distress, safety, and calling channels; ship-to-ship channels; and public correspondence channels that can connect you through a High Seas marine operator to the land-based public telephone system. With an SSB radio you can also access worldwide weather forecasts and limited e-mail messaging far at sea.

Four Coast Guard stations within the continental United States, and one in Hawaii, monitor the SSB distress and calling frequency of 2,182 kilohertz (kHz).

Since few recreational boaters have SSB radios, we will not discuss them at length in this chapter. You probably do not need one unless you are planning an offshore passage or a voyage to a foreign port.

Amateur (Ham) Radios

If you are a shortwave amateur operator, called a **ham**, you might use a shortwave radio aboard your boat. Many ham operators have found their sets useful in marine and other emergencies, such as severe storms and other disasters. These radios operate in eight medium- and high-frequency bands that are interweaved with SSB frequencies and can reach around the globe. There are 420,000 licensed ham operators in the United States, more than 100,000 of whom may be on the air at any time and willing to assist you.

Before using the amateur radio service, you must pass an FCC examination and obtain a license and an assigned call sign. There are eighteen amateur maritime networks throughout the world, and they cover international as well as coastal waters. These networks operate 24 hours a day, with operators trained to handle emergency traffic and to provide the licensed amateur with an excellent communications network. A shore-based ham can patch you through the telephone lines to your home without the fees charged by SSB High Seas marine operators. Many amateur radio operators are listed in telephone directories. For all these reasons, ham radio remains popular among long-distance cruisers as a way to maintain contact with their homes.

You should be aware, however, that the Coast Guard does not monitor ham frequencies as it does VHF and SSB emergency frequencies. Because ham radio is of limited use for near-shore boating, this chapter will not discuss it in depth.

Distress-Signaling Devices

EMERGENCY POSITION-INDICATING RADIO BEACONS. An EPIRB is a portable transmitter that can be activated manually or automatically (by immersion) to summon help offshore. Several types are available, but the best transmit a coded signal at 406 MHz that is received by orbiting satellites and relayed to search-and-rescue personnel in the nearest ground station (Figure 13-3). Since the EPIRB is registered, rescue personnel will know the identity of the vessel in distress, and the receiving satellites will pinpoint its location—especially if the EPIRB incorporates a GPS unit.

An EPIRB is only a transmitter; it does not receive, and it does not permit voice communications. In contrast with a VHF or SSB emergency call, search-and-rescue personnel cannot tell the nature of the distress. Nevertheless, an EPIRB transmission is effective for quick response, and every boat venturing offshore should carry an EPIRB for use as a last resort.

PERSONAL LOCATOR BEACONS. Personal locator beacons (PLBs) are personal versions of EPIRBs. EPIRBs are registered to a vessel while PLBs are registered to individuals. PLBs are used to locate people in distress on land and water. Like EPIRBs, they transmit at 406 MHz. They communicate with the

Figure **13-3.** A 406 MHz EPIRB. (REPRINTED WITH PERMISSION FROM *ROUGH WEATHER SEAMANSHIP FOR SAIL AND POWER* BY ROGER MARSHALL)

Cospas-Sarsat satellite tracking system, which, when necessary, transmits distress signals to the appropriate search-and-rescue organization(s).

SATELLITE PERSONAL MESSENGER. The SPOT Satellite GPS Messenger (www.findmespot.com) uses the Globalstar network (SPOT LLC is a subsidiary of Globalstar). It processes emergency and non-emergency messages. All transmissions go through the private GEOS International Emergency Response Coordination Center (IERCC). Emergency transmissions are forwarded to the appropriate agencies. SPOT devices can also automatically transmit signals to report the holder's changing locations. The signal is not as strong as devices using 406 MHz when transmitting from remote areas.

INREACH. The DeLorme inReach (www.inreach. delorme.com) is a two-way communications system for processing any type of emergency. It utilizes the Iridium satellite network. You can use a dedicated inReach transmitter/receiver or load the inReach feature to Apple iOS and Android OS devices. Emergency transmissions are forwarded to GEOS IERCC for further action. InReach can process text messages and e-mail as well as track the movements of the caller.

AUTOMATIC PACKET REPORTING SYSTEM. The Automatic Packet Reporting System (APRS; www.aprs.org) is a VHF digital protocol system used by amateur radio operators for a wide variety of applications that may include emergencies. The messages are repeated for a specific time period awaiting a voluntary response. However, there is no guarantee that APRS signals will be forwarded to emergency responders.

Functions of Radiotelephones

VHF-FM and SSB marine radios serve three important communications functions—sending and receiving safety, operations, and commercial messages. No other type of message is permissible.

Safety Messages

There are three types of safety messages: distress, urgency, and safety. Use distress messages when you face or are witness to grave or imminent danger to life or property and you need immediate help. Use urgency messages when there is a chance that a dangerous situation may become life threatening. Safety messages relay important information about weather or safety of navigation. We'll look at the protocols for each type of message later in the chapter.

Operations Messages

Operations messages deal with exchange of information about navigation or the movement or management of vessels. For example, you can call a lockmaster for instructions, or you may call a bridge tender to open a drawbridge (Figure 13-4). You may also call a marina to secure a berth or arrange for boat repairs, and you can exchange information about fishing or scheduling a rendezvous with other vessels.

Don't chitchat on your marine radio, however. Idle chatter is against the rules because it clutters up important channels and interferes with essential communications.

Commercial Messages

These messages concern the business in which a commercial vessel is engaged. Recreational boaters should not use the radio channels designated for commercial communications.

Licenses

VHF-FM radios, EPIRBs, and radar units do not require station licenses when used on most recreational vessels. Power-driven recreational vessels that are 20 meters (65 feet) or more long do require station licenses, however, and you'll need a station license for your VHF-FM station if you travel to a foreign port or communicate internationally. Under some circumstances, you may also need an operator's permit.

Additionally, a VHF-FM radio equipped with digital selective calling (DSC) should be registered with an entity that will assign a Maritime Mobile Service Identity (MMSI) number, which will automatically identify your boat when you transmit over the radio (see below). There is a charge for this registration when you apply through the FCC, but there is no charge when you apply through BoatU.S. or Sea Tow Services International. Note also that although EPIRBs operating at 406 MHz don't require a license, they do require registration.

Station License

You must have a ship station license for an SSB radio. Furthermore, if you have an SSB radio, you also need a VHF-FM radio. To get a license for an SSB from the FCC, you must show a need for the radio.

Apply to the FCC using FCC Form 605. You may be able to get a copy of this form from a marine radio dealer or you can get it on the Internet at www.fcc.gov/formpage.html. If you buy an SSB radio, the form may be packaged with it. You can also get forms from the FCC or by calling 1-800-418-3676. Be certain the form is current.

Submit your application with the required fee to the Federal Communications Commission, Wireless Bureau Applications, P.O. Box 358130, Pittsburgh, PA 15251.

Use Schedule F of FCC Form 605 for temporary authority to operate your ship's SSB and VHF-FM radio stations after you have mailed in your application. Until you get your station license, use your boat's registration number for your call sign. You must post the temporary permit near the ship's radio, and it is good for 90 days, by the end of which time you should have received your permanent license.

If you change your mailing address, your legal name, or the name of your boat, and if you are re-quired to have a station license, let the FCC know in writing. Also tell the commission in writing if you sell your boat, and return your license. If you replace your SSB radio or its companion VHF-FM radio with another set that operates on the same frequencies, you do not need to do anything.

Even though you may not be required to have a station license, you are responsible for complying with all FCC regulations on the proper use of marine VHF-FM radios. Those regulations of importance to recreational boaters are described in the sections that follow.

Operator's Permit

An operator's permit is not needed to use your VHF-FM radio in domestic or international waters if your vessel is less than 20 meters. If you plan to dock in a foreign port, however, you must have a restricted radiotelephone operator's permit (RP). Also, if you leave a foreign port to enter and dock at a U.S. port, you must have an RP. Use FCC Form 605 (which is a multipart form) to apply for your RP. The fee is subject to change. The RP is good for your lifetime.

Selecting Your VHF-FM Radio

All marine radios must be acceptable to the FCC, which means they meet required minimum technical standards. Such radios carry labels certifying compliance.

VHF-FM radios differ widely in price and basic characteristics, so shop around to see what is available before you buy. When looking at sets, ask about their sensitivity, selectivity, audio output, signal strength, available channels, type of channel selector and readout, and the amount of current they use.

Global Maritime Distress and Safety System

GMDSS is an emergency communications system that will, when fully implemented, allow recreational boaters to send automated digital distress messages that include the boat's identity and location, leaving the boater free for emergency actions

Figure **13-4.** One example of a VHF-FM operations message is calling a bridge tender. The Figure Eight Island bridge on the Intracoastal Waterway in North Carolina, at Mile 278, is a single-pivot swing bridge with a vertical clearance of 20 feet. It opens on the hour and half-hour, but you can follow commercial traffic through at other times. Bridge tenders in Virginia, North Carolina, and Georgia monitor VHF Channel 13, whereas in South Carolina and Florida they use Channel 9. (PHOTO BY GENE HAMILTON)

while the message transmits. To use GMDSS, your radio must be equipped with DSC capability. All fixed-mount VHF radios (Figure 13-5) manufactured since 1999 are DSC-capable, but most handheld VHFs (Figure 13-6) are not.

While all marine transceiver radios, including HF and SSB, can be equipped with DSC, the VHF-DSC radio will be the combination used by the great majority of recreational boaters. Don't forget that VHF radios have a limited range, no more than 30 to 50 miles and quite possibly less. If your cruising takes you farther than that from land stations or possible ship stations, you may want to consider an SSB.

Channel 70 is the frequency reserved for digital distress calls on a VHF radio. Each DSC radio must be programmed with its own data relating to the boat and owner, and these data are encoded in a unique nine-digit number, your MMSI number. When the DSC distress button or switch is activated, an automated signal is sent out with the identity of the boat, its position (assuming the radio is interfaced with a GPS receiver), the current time, and (if selected by the user) the nature of the distress. Any ship or land station that is within range and monitoring Channel 70 will receive the signal. Both transmitter and receiver may then switch to Channel 16 or another VHF working channel for voice communications.

As of early 2006, the Coast Guard is monitoring Channel 70 DSC calls out to 50 miles offshore between Maine and Maryland, and expects to institute similar coverage throughout the East Coast and Gulf of Mexico by the end of 2007. West Coast coverage may not be operational until 2009. In the interim, Sea Tow Services International monitors Channel 70 near shore, though its towers do not give it the range of Coast Guard towers. (This is the same company that now handles maritime phone calls, a service formerly provided by MariTEL.) Because its Channel 70 monitoring program is taking longer than expected to roll out, the Coast Guard will continue to monitor Channel 16, the voice-only distress channel, through at least 2010.

To begin using GMDSS, first make sure your VHF radio is DSC-equipped. You will then need to obtain an MMSI number. This can be done for a fee by contacting the FCC directly as described above, or without a fee by contacting BoatU.S. at BoatU.S.

MMSI Program, 880 South Pickett Street, Alexandria, VA 22304; 1-800-563-1536; MMSI@BoatUS.com; or online at www.boatus.com/mmsi. The same service is provided by Sea Tow online at www.seatow.com/boating-safety/mmsi. As of 2006, MMSI numbers obtained from BoatU.S. or Sea Tow are not included in the FCC database, which feeds the international database. What this means is that unless your MMSI is obtained directly from the FCC, it will not properly identify your boat in international waters. Hopefully this will be rectified, but the deficiency makes little difference to boaters operating in U.S. coastal and inland waters.

After obtaining the MMSI number, program your radio with the number and other information, following the radio manufacturer's instructions. Then familiarize yourself with DSC radio procedures, which include the requirement to monitor Channel 70 (along with Channel 16) when at sea with the radio on.

For more information on DSC and GMDSS, consult the U.S. Coast Guard website at www.navcen.uscg.gov/.

Automatic Identification System

In the Automatic Identification System (AIS), your GPS position, course, and speed are automatically broadcast to all vessels around you. Other transmitted information includes the vessel's identification, the vessel's description, and the local sea state. The full complement of transmitted data may

Figure **13-5.** A Coast Guard Auxiliarist uses a fixed-mount VHF radio on his boat on the Washington, North Carolina, waterfront. (PHOTO BY DON LINDBERG)

include as many as 84 different types of messages. The installation is mandatory on very large vessels and smaller vessels will be phased in over time. Vessels that are not required to have AIS may install systems to receive the safety benefits. Other vessels may install a receiver only, although they may incur a small time delay in receiving their message due to the massive amount of data being processed. AIS data is communicated via VHF-FM marine radios equipped with DSC and configured to receive channels 87B and 88B. Some AIS information is translated and made available on the Internet at www.marinetraffic.com/ais.

There are AIS text-only receiver display systems. The more comprehensive information may be displayed on an AIS-enabled GPS or computer systems. AIS transmission data may be disabled by the vessel for security purposes.

Sensitivity

The *sensitivity* of a radio helps determine its ability to pick up distant signals. The less microvoltage a set needs to reach the 20-decibel (dB) sound level, the more sensitive it is. Thus, a radio using 0.5 microvolt is more sensitive than one using 2.5 microvolts. If a set is too sensitive, however, it may "talk" continuously when close to shore. If possible, sample several radios on friends' boats and select the model that performs best.

Selectivity

Selectivity is a measure of how well a receiver rejects signals from other channels close to the channel you are using. The units for selectivity are also decibels, but selectivity is expressed in negative decibels. A set with a –0.75 dB selectivity will do a much better job than one rated at –0.55 dB.

Audio Output

Audio output measures the loudness of the radio. Your radio needs to be loud enough to be heard over the sound of your engine.

Small radios usually have small speakers and do not produce loud sounds. Thus, handheld VHF-FM radios usually do not produce sounds as loud as fixed-mount ones. If the radio has an outlet for an

Figure 13-6. A Coast Guard Auxiliarist using a handheld VHF. (PHOTO BY JOE BRITVCH)

external speaker, you can use one to improve the sound level and audio quality.

Signal Strength

Your VHF-FM set must be able to transmit on a power of 1 watt. Most fixed-mount VHF-FM radios provide, in addition, a maximum power setting of 25 watts, while most handheld sets transmit on a "low" power of 1 watt and a "high" power of 5 watts. One watt is more than enough power for short distances, and it is mandatory to use the 1-watt setting when transmitting in a harbor. Make it a point to evaluate the signal strength of a VHF-FM radio before buying it.

Signal Suppression

When two VHF-FM radios are transmitting on the same channel in the same area, the stronger one "steps on" or suppresses the weaker. Unlike AM radios, which can receive two stations at the same time, an FM radio receives only the stronger station. Limit your signal distance by using the lowest power needed for your communication, and don't reach out of your area and, perhaps, inadvertently suppress an important communication from another vessel.

Line-of-Sight Transmission

VHF-FM is essentially a line-of-sight system (Figure 13-7 and Table 13-1), reaching only slightly

TABLE 13-1	**VHF COMMUNICATIONS RANGE**				
Range (in nautical miles) as a function of transmitting and receiving antenna heights					
Transmitting Antenna Height	Receiving Antenna Height				
	5 ft.	10 ft.	25 ft.	100 ft.	250 ft.
5 ft.	5	7	9	15	23
10 ft.	9	10	11	18	25
30 ft.	10	12	13	20	28
60 ft.	12	14	15	21	30

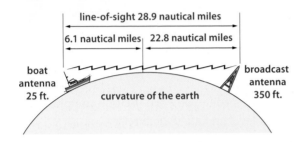

Figure **13-7.** Since VHF range is limited to a line-of-sight between the transmitting and receiving antennas, antenna height makes a big difference in effective range. In this example, a boat 29 miles at sea with an antenna height of 25 feet can receive transmissions from a U.S. Coast Guard 350-foot broadcast tower onshore. Communications between two boats with 25-foot antenna heights, however, would be limited to about 12 miles.

beyond the antenna's horizon. This is sufficient for most marine communications. Important land stations, such as a Coast Guard station, are equipped with high antennas, and these increase the Coast Guard's range of reception and transmission. Whenever one antenna can "see" another, communication is possible.

With 25 watts of power, an installed VHF-FM radio is limited by antenna height rather than power, and it will reach as many stations as it could reach with more power. A more powerful radio would only send its signal farther out into space.

Available Channels

The VHF-FM frequency band includes 73 channels, of which 55 are in use in the United States. Modern marine radios have all the channels required and needed. Even low-priced radios are full-channel capable. There are, however, eight channels that are blocked and reserved for government

use: 3, 21, 23, 61, 64, 81, 82, and 83. Any of these can be unblocked with proper justification.

U.S. and International Channels

Your VHF-FM radio may have a two-position switch labeled "USA" and "International." This is because the channel frequencies used in the United States differ, in some instances, from those used in foreign countries. Where there is a difference, the USA channel number includes the letter A.

For example, one of the channels used by the Coast Guard is Channel 22. Since the U.S. Channel 22 has a different frequency than a foreign Channel 22, the Coast Guard channel is 22A, which you say as "22 alpha." If the Coast Guard tells you to shift to 22 alpha, be certain that your switch is in the USA position. AIS is used worldwide so the assigned channels are AIS1 and AIS2.

Channel Selector

During a transmission to another vessel or a coastal station, it is necessary to switch from the calling channel to a working channel. On many older sets this is done with a rotary dial, which may have small numbers that are difficult to read, especially in poor light.

Newer sets have number pads for channel selection and digital readouts, making them easier to use. The digital readout is even easier to read in dim light than in good light, and a good set includes a dimmer switch for nighttime operation.

You can buy a scanning set that will scan as few as two channels or as many as the total available, though it will not scan the weather channels. Just be certain that the scanner you purchase includes

Channel 9 as well as Channel 16. If a message comes in on a preset channel, the set automatically switches to that channel.

Power Usage

The amount of electrical current a radio uses is important. The *amp draw* is a measure of the power a radio uses when sending or receiving that also shows how much drain is imposed on your battery. For handheld radios, it gives some idea of how long you can operate the radio before recharging the battery. The batteries of most handheld sets need charging after about 3 hours of use.

While efficient handheld radios draw as little as 0.02 amp on standby and 0.8 amp when sending, efficient fixed-mount radios require as little as 0.2 amp on standby and about 5.0 amps when transmitting.

Installation

You can install a fixed-mount VHF-FM radio yourself, but you cannot repair or adjust it, since this might change its transmitting characteristics. Only FCC-licensed General Class commercial operators can make repairs or adjustments.

Improper power and antenna connections can impair performance or cause equipment damage. When you install your radio, keep it and its speaker as far away from your compass as practicable, and be sure that the power connections are secure and correct. The positive lead from the radio should go to the positive power terminal on the vessel, or the positive terminal on the battery, and should have an in-line fuse. DSC-capable radios also need a cable connection to the GPS in order for DSC to function. On a 12-volt system, the positive lead is usually red and the negative lead, which goes to the negative terminal, is usually black. There should also be a fuse somewhere in the positive (red) lead. Installation is not difficult.

Your Radio Antenna

Select a good-quality antenna in the right frequency band for your radio (e.g., a CB antenna should be used only for a CB transmitter, and SSB antennas are designed only for SSB transmitters). If you use the wrong antenna, you will greatly reduce your ability to transmit and receive. You may also damage your transmitter if you attempt to transmit without an antenna.

Place the antenna as high in your boat as you can. Sailors often place their antennas at the masthead, thus increasing their range, and most powerboats use 8-foot-long antennas. When you install one, allow enough room to lay it down for trailering and passing under low bridges.

The *ferrule* is the nylon or metal fitting at the bottom of the antenna. Nylon is good and will serve you well on lakes and in calm to moderate seas. If you plan to fish or cruise in rougher weather, however, a metal ferrule is advisable.

Nylon or metal (usually stainless steel) mounts connect antennas to boats. You should match the mount to the ferrule—if the ferrule is nylon, use a nylon mount, and use a metal mount with a metal ferrule.

Gain is a measure of an antenna's effectiveness. The higher the gain, in theory, the farther you can communicate within the line-of-sight envelope for VHF transmissions. It is tempting to select a higher-gain antenna than needed, but don't do it.

RADIO USAGE CAVEATS

- Do not send false distress and emergency messages.
- Do not use obscene, indecent, or profane language.
- Observe the confidentiality of others' messages (except in emergency situations or broadcasts of general use).
- Do not use your radio when the boat is on land.
- Listen on your selected channel before transmitting your message, so as not to "step on" a communication in progress.
- Shift to a working channel immediately after contact has been made on the calling channel (except in an emergency situation).
- Learn and practice the correct radio usage techniques and language. Rehearse your message (to yourself) **before** making the transmission.
- Think through your responses **before** responding. (Responses don't have to be given immediately. You can simply say "Wait." Think through your response, then respond.)
- Speak slowly and distinctly.

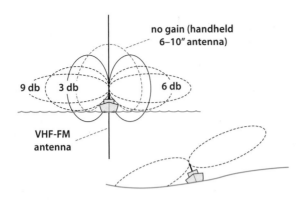

Figure 13-8. Typical radiation patterns of VHF-FM radio antennas. A 9 db gain antenna, which might be 24 feet long, offers greater potential range but also a vertically compressed signal. When the boat rolls, you might be transmitting down into the sea on one side of the boat and up into space on the other side. Many powerboaters choose a 6 db, 8-foot antenna as a good compromise.

> **WARNING** *Be careful about giving credit-card information over a radio channel. It is NOT secure.*

Theory aside, with a high-gain antenna, you may not be able to communicate at all.

Figure 13-8 shows why, illustrating the radiation patterns of 3 dB, 6 dB, and 9 dB gain antennas. On land or in a very stable boat you might select a 9 dB antenna. In a pitching and rolling vessel, though, the flat, vertically compressed signal of a 9 dB antenna sometimes will point at the sea and sometimes will point up in the air, so much of its signal is wasted. Most small boats should avoid antennas with gain ratings above 6 dB.

When installing your antenna, keep it away from masts, shrouds, stays, or other metal that might shield it. If the antenna cable is 25 feet long or less, you can use the cable that came with the antenna, but if a longer cable is needed, use a low-loss cable. Keep the cable as short as possible.

Operating Your VHF-FM

Before you turn your radio on, check that the **high power–low power switch** is in the 1-watt position. This is where you will operate most of the time. Use this position when communicating with vessels or marinas nearby. The high position, 25 watts, is normally used for cruising and especially for distress calls. Check, also, to see that the **USA/International switch** is in the USA position, often labeled "A or B."

Your VHF-FM radio is a *transceiver*, which means that it is both a transmitter and a receiver, but it can only perform one of these functions at a time. When you turn on the radio, it is ready to receive. To send, press a button or a switch. You will usually find a **push-to-talk button** on the microphone.

The volume control usually doubles as the **On/Off switch**. When you turn it, it first turns the radio on, then increases the receiving volume. It has no impact on your transmission strength, however; the high power–low power switch controls that.

Another important switch, the **squelch control**, stops the constant noise you hear when not receiving a signal from another radio. Turn it up until the static just disappears, but no farther. Too much squelch lowers the ability of your radio to receive signals, so set it just high enough to make the static disappear and to screen out signals that are so far away that you can't understand them.

Maintain a Radio Watch

You do not have to keep your radio turned on whenever you're boating. When it *is* on, however, and when it's not being used for messages, you should keep it tuned to Channel 16 (unless it's a scanner model, in which case you should include Channel 16 in the scan pattern).

You will do far more listening than talking. Your radiotelephone is a busy party line with many users, and it is also vital for emergency communications. Always listen carefully before transmitting to see if someone else is using the channel or if there is an emergency condition in effect. When you listen, adjust the squelch so you can understand distant signals.

Radiotelephone Station Log

A radio log is a record of calls made and received by a station, as in the accompanying sample. Each page of the log should be numbered, should include the name of the vessel and its call sign, and should be signed by the operator. Entries should show the

RADIOTELEPHONE STATION LOG

Vessel Name:_____   Vessel Call Sign:_____   Page #_____

| Date | Local Time Symbol | | Channel or Frequency Used | Station Called or Calling | Message | Operator's Signature |
	Time Begun	Time Ended				

time each watch began and ended using 24-hour military time.

If your boat is less than 65 feet long, you do not need to keep a radio log, but you must record as completely as possible all emergency signals and communications you hear and keep this log for at least 3 years. Keep it for a longer time if it concerns communications under investigation by the FCC or against which claims or complaints have been filed.

Channels Have Special Purposes

Each VHF-FM channel has an assigned frequency. For example, Channel 16 has a frequency of 156.800 MHz for receiving and sending. We will not discuss VHF-FM frequencies, though, since you do not need them. Use channel numbers, which are keyed to frequencies by the radio, to tune your set. (SSB radios use frequency settings, not channels. The SSB distress and calling frequency is 2182 kHz.)

TABLE 13-2	VHF-FM CHANNELS USED FOR VARIOUS NONCOMMERCIAL MESSAGES
Type of Message	**Suitable Channels**
Distress, Urgency, Safety, and Calling	16
Boater Calling Channel	9
Intership Safety	6
Coast Guard Liaison	21A, 22A
Noncommercial[1]	68, 69, 71, 72, 78A
Public Correspondence (Marine Operator)	24, 25, 26, 27, 28, 84, 85, 86, 87, 88[2]
Port Operations	1, 5[3], 11, 12, 14, 20[4], 63, 65, 66, 73, 74, 77[5]
Navigational	13
Maritime Control	17
Digital Selective Distress and Calling	70
Automatic Identification System	AIS1, AIS2
Weather[6]	WX1 (162.550 MHz) WX2 (162.400 MHz) WX3 (162.475 MHz)

1. Working channels for recreational boats only. Other channels are reserved for working vessels.
2. Only for use in the Great Lakes, the St. Lawrence Seaway, and Puget Sound and its approaches.
3. Available only in the Houston and New Orleans areas.
4. Channel 20 used only for ship-to-coast messages.
5. Channel 77 is limited to intership communications to and from pilot boats.
6. Weather channels are "receive only."

Table 13-2 summarizes the VHF-FM channels and their uses. Begin most calls on Channel 16, and begin all distress, urgency, and safety messages on Channel 16 unless you're using Channel 70 with a DSC radio.

Channel 9 is both an intership and ship-to-shore channel, and is often used by marinas and yacht clubs. Boaters often switch to Channel 9 after contacting another boat on Channel 16, and Channel 9 is an alternate calling channel as well.

Shift to Channel 6, the intership safety channel, for ship-to-ship safety messages. If you have an emergency and the Coast Guard or the Auxiliary comes to your aid, it may communicate with you on Channel 6.

If you call the Coast Guard, it may request that you switch to one of its working channels, such as Channel 22A (USA setting), the Coast Guard Liaison channel. You should initiate your call on Channel 16, however.

A message on any noncommercial channel must be about the needs of your vessel. Typical uses include fishing reports, rendezvous, repair scheduling, and berthing. Channel 72 is only for ship-to-ship messages.

Public correspondence channels connect your ship's radio with a telephone operator ashore. Through these channels, you can call any telephone. This service was formerly provided by Mari-TEL on a charge-per-call basis, and is now (after a 2-year service lapse) provided by Sea Tow on a subscription basis. The primary channels for this service are 26, 27, and 28, and Sea Tow expects to be operational nationwide by the end of 2006. If you plan to use ship-to-shore telephone service, find out which channel to use in your area, and arrange your subscription in advance. Since marine telephone conversations can be heard by anyone with a VHF-FM marine radio, you would not want to broadcast your credit-card number. Consult your telephone directory for information on how to call a marine operator using a public correspondence channel. There are no restrictions on the content of public correspondence calls. Remember, though, that your call is over public airways and is not secure.

In some ports, vessel traffic service systems use Channels 11, 12, and 14. The port operations channels are for directing the movement of ships in or near ports, locks, or waterways, and messages must be about the handling, movement, and safety of ships.

Channel 13 is the working channel at most locks and drawbridges. The navigational channels are bridge-to-bridge channels. These "bridges" are ships' bridges, the places from which they are controlled. Navigational channels are available to all ships, but the messages must be about vessel navigation—for example, passing or meeting other vessels. Keep your message short. No communication between two ships should exceed 3 minutes after the ships have made contact, and your transmission power should not be more than 1 watt.

You can talk to ships and coast stations operated by state or local governments on the maritime control channel, Channel 17. Your message must be about regulation and control, boating activities, or assistance to ships.

Channel 70, the digital selective calling channel, is an alternative channel for distress, safety, and general-purpose calling with a DSC-capable VHF radio. **Do not use this channel for voice transmissions.** Assuming both boats have digital radios, you can call a fellow boater's MMSI number on Channel 70 much as you dial a cell phone number. His radio will sound an alarm to alert him to the incoming call, and when he presses a button to acknowledge, both radios will switch automatically to a working channel for a voice conversation. This is the chief advantage of a digital radio for routine communications.

In addition to the primary three weather frequencies given in Table 13-2, there are as many as seven other VHF receive-only weather frequencies. Some have special applications, however, and some carry regional weather only in certain locations. Scanning the frequencies will show you which weather channels are available in your waters.

Some No-Nos

Do not send false distress or emergency messages. Hoaxes can lead to loss of life. The Coast Guard answers every distress call regardless of the weather or other conditions. These calls often are sent by children who do not realize the seriousness of their hoaxes.

The Coast Guard works closely with the FCC to identify offenders. Both the Coast Guard and the FCC have direction-finding equipment available, which means that when you are in waters where the Coast Guard has a presence, it is very likely that the location of your broadcast can be pinpointed. The misuse of Channel 16 is serious enough that it is a Class D felony; offenders are liable for a $5,000 fine plus all costs the Coast Guard incurs as a result of the hoax. So guard your radio against unauthorized use, because you are responsible for it.

Obscenity, Indecency, and Profanity

When using your radio, you are using an extensive party line and can assume that other people are listening. You therefore have a compelling moral obligation as well as a strict legal responsibility to watch your language. It is a criminal offense to use obscene, indecent, or profane language, and the penalty is a fine of up to $10,000, imprisonment for up to 2 years, or both.

Secrecy of Communication

The Federal Communications Act protects the secrecy of radio communications. You must not communicate the contents of any radio message to anyone other than the addressee or the addressee's agent or attorney unless you are authorized to do so. If you intercept a message, you must not use its contents for your own benefit or the benefit of other people.

This secrecy requirement does not apply to distress messages, however, nor does it apply to radio broadcasts meant for general use.

Using Your VHF-FM Radio on Land

Do not use your radio to transmit when your boat is on land—while it is on a trailer, for example. Also, do not make general calls except in an emergency or when your radio is being tested. Instead, direct your calls to a particular station.

Copies of the Rules

Recreational boaters do not need to keep copies of the FCC rules aboard their vessels. You can view the rules by going to www.fcc.gov/oet/info/rules.

Rules Violations

If the FCC believes that you have violated the rules, it may send you a written notice of the violation. A violation notice that covers a technical radio standard will require you to stop using your radio until the problem is fixed. You may be required to have your radio tested and the results sent to the FCC, and the commercial operator who conducted the test must sign the results.

If the FCC finds that you have willfully or repeatedly violated the Federal Communications Act or the rules, it may revoke your license if you have one. You can also be fined or even sent to prison, as mentioned above.

Calling Another Station

To call another station, first turn the radio on and make sure it is on low power. Tune it to your chosen calling channel—often Channel 16—and listen for a few moments to make sure no one else is using it. Next, press the microphone button and speak directly into the microphone. Hold the microphone 2 to 4 inches from your mouth, use a normal tone of voice, and speak clearly. Switch to high power if you suspect that the other station is too far away to hear you.

Call the other station by saying the name of the vessel or station you are calling three times, followed by your vessel's name one time. The reason for this is that the receiving vessel may not be sure of your first call, or the radio may be on scan mode and not be set to your channel for a moment. An example is, "*Sundance, Sundance, Sundance,* this is *Rusty Nail,* over."

Do not add unnecessary words such as "Come in, Bob," or "Do you read me?" These only add to the traffic on the channel. Also, calling in reverse, with your vessel's name first, is improper and confusing.

After you have called the other station, release the microphone button. If you continue to press the button, you won't be able to hear the other station's response. When you send, press the button, but when you want to listen, release it.

Do not call the same station for more than 30 seconds at a time. If you do not get a reply, wait at least 2 minutes before calling again. After three attempts, wait at least 15 minutes before calling again.

When the other station answers, immediately request that it switch to a working channel. Table 13-2 lists the channels to use for the kind of message you wish to send. Know which channel you want to switch to before you call.

After reaching the other station, switch to a working channel and send your message. If you expect an answer, end your transmission with the word "Over." If you do not expect an answer, say "Out." Do not say "Over and out."

Be sure to identify your station by giving your FCC call sign (if one has been issued) at the beginning and end of each message. You must do this in English.

Keep your communication brief, and when you are through, give your vessel's name and call sign. The other station should also give its name and call sign. After this, switch back to the calling channel.

Public Correspondence Calls

If you want to place a telephone call, first turn the radio on. Next, switch to a public correspondence channel and listen to be sure it is not currently in use. Then press the microphone button and say, "[Name of coast station] this is [your call sign or vessel's name]."

When the marine operator answers, say, "This is [name of boat, call sign, and billing number assigned], placing a call to [city and telephone number]." Except for distress calls, you need to be a subscriber to the service from the company that owns the coast station.

Ship-to-Ship Calls Through a Coast Station

Although you usually make a call to another ship by calling it directly, you can do it through a coast station as well. Use the same procedure as you do for ship-to-shore calls. You might make such a call if the vessel you are calling is too far away for you to reach directly. Remember, the coast station has a high antenna.

TABLE 13-3 PROCEDURE WORDS (PROWORDS)

Procedure Word	Meaning
OUT	This is the end of my transmission to you. No answer is required or expected.
OVER	This is the end of my transmission and a response is expected. Go ahead, transmit. (Omit when it is clearly not needed.)
ROGER	I received your last transmission okay.
WILCO	Your last message has been received and understood, and will be complied with.
THIS IS	This transmission is from the station whose name and call sign follows immediately.
FIGURES	Figures or numbers follow; for example, "Vessel length is FIGURES 2 3 feet."
SPEAK SLOWER	Your transmission is difficult to understand. Speak slower.
SAY AGAIN	Repeat.
WORDS TWICE	It is difficult to understand you. Give each phrase twice.
I SPELL	I shall spell the next word phonetically. (Used when a proper name is important in the message; for example, "Boat name is *Martha*. I spell—Mike, Alfa, Romeo, Tango, Hotel, Alfa.")
WAIT	I must pause for a few seconds; stand by for further transmission.
WAIT OUT	I must pause for longer than a few seconds. I will call you back.
AFFIRMATIVE	You are correct, or what you have transmitted is correct.
NEGATIVE	No.

Shore-to-Ship Calls

To call a vessel from a shore telephone, you need to know where the vessel is. Then dial 0 (zero) and ask the operator to connect you to or give you the phone number of the marine operator nearest the vessel. Tell the marine operator the name of the vessel you are calling, and also the call sign of the vessel's radio station, if you know it.

Once connected with the vessel, remember that the ship station operates using a push-to-talk radio. Don't try to break in while the ship station is transmitting, but wait until you hear, "Over." When you are through, hang up.

Limited Coast Stations

Limited coast stations serve the operational and business needs of vessels. Some, such as those operated by a harbormaster or at a drawbridge, also serve a safety function. Limited coast stations are not open to public correspondence.

Yacht clubs with docking facilities, marina operators, boaters, dockside restaurants, marine police, towing services, and others operate limited coast stations. There is no charge for communications services incidental to their business.

Call a limited coast station on its working channel. If that doesn't work, try the local calling channel, but be ready to switch to a working channel. A limited coast station calls vessels on the local calling channel, so you do not need to monitor its working channel if you are expecting a call.

Procedure Words

A key to efficient use of radiotelephone time is the use of *procedure words*, or *prowords* for short. These words are a form of shorthand, and you can see from Table 13-3 how much they reduce transmission time.

Don't be sensitive about using prowords. No one will think you are showing off by using terms such as "wilco" if you use them correctly.

Beware of other words in common use that sound like prowords, but accomplish nothing. For example, following several unanswered calls to a boat on Channel 9, you may hear something such as, "Negative contact. This is [boat name], out." This is meaningless. Anyone listening knows there was no contact, and, worse still, the unnecessary announcement could have masked another call.

Phonetic Alphabet

When radio signals are weak and reception is poor, you may need to spell words or to express numbers in clear ways. The phonetic alphabet and its pronunciation appear in Table 13-4. In use, the person sending the message says, "I spell," and then gives the phonetic spelling of the word or words. The proper use of the phonetic alphabet reduces misunderstandings.

TABLE 13-4	PHONETIC ALPHABET	
Letter	**Phonetic Equivalent**	**Pronunciation**
A	Alfa	*Al*[1] fah
B	Bravo	*Brah* voh
C	Charlie	*Char* lee
D	Delta	*Dell* tah
E	Echo	*Eck* oh
F	Foxtrot	*Foks* trot
G	Golf	Golf
H	Hotel	Ho *tell*
I	India	*In* dee ah
J	Juliet	Jew lee *et*
K	Kilo	*Key* loh
L	Lima	*Lee* mah
M	Mike	Mike
N	November	No *vem* ber
O	Oscar	*Oss* cah
P	Papa	Pah *pah*
Q	Quebec	Keh *beck*
R	Romeo	*Row* me oh
S	Sierra	See *air* rah
T	Tango	*Tan* go
U	Uniform	*You* nee form
V	Victor	*Vik* tah
W	Whiskey	*Wiss* key
X	X-ray	*Ecks* ray
Y	Yankee	*Yang* key
Z	Zulu	*Zoo* loo

1. Emphasis is on the **bold**, *italic* part of the word.

TABLE 13-5	PRONUNCIATION OF NUMBERS
Number	**Pronunciation**
0 (Zero)	Zero
1 (One)	Wun
2 (Two)	Too
3 (Three)	Thuh ree
4 (Four)	Fo wer
5 (Five)	Fi yiv
6 (Six)	Six
7 (Seven)	Seven
8 (Eight)	Ate
9 (Nine)	Niner

Numbers

Closely allied to the phonetic alphabet is the manner of pronouncing numbers. In a message, if you spell out a number, you precede it by saying, "Figures . . ." The correct pronunciations of the numbers are given in Table 13-5.

If your vessel is in distress and you can't give its exact location, the Coast Guard may request that you make a "long count" during which it will home in on your signal with a radio direction finder to determine where you are. If the Coast Guard asks you to give a long count, say slowly, "Wun, Too, Thuh ree, Fo wer, Fi yiv, Six, Seven, Ate, Niner, Zero, Zero, Niner, Ate, Seven, Six, Fi yiv, Fo wer, Thuh ree, Too, Wun." A short count goes from Wun to Fi-yiv, repeats Fi-yiv, and goes back down to Wun.

Routine Radio Test

It's reasonable to question whether your radio is working as it's possible for a radio to receive properly but not transmit. To test your radio, use Channel 9 or a working channel. Do not use Channel 16 for routine radio tests. An example of a radio test call is, "This is *Rusty Nail*, radio check, over." Wait for 1 minute, and do not repeat more than three times. If you don't get a response, your radio may not be working. However, if you are in a remote area, or an area where there is little vessel traffic, you may want to repeat the test.

DSC-equipped radios purchased after March 2011 must have a testing capability. Transmitting a test call (not a routine DSC call) to 003669999 will trigger a reply from any U.S. Coast Guard Rescue 21 station within range. If your radio does not have a testing capability, you can test it by sending a DSC message to another DSC-equipped radio.

Distress, Urgency, and Safety Calls

If your vessel is in distress, you may use any means, in addition to your radio, to attract attention and get help. Often visual signals such as flags, flares, lights, and smoke or audible signals such as your horn or a whistle will get the attention and help you need.

If you can't use visual or audible signals, use your VHF-FM radio. Initiate your call on Channel 16, but remember, you can use it or any other channel, including the public correspondence channels, to request emergency help.

Spoken Emergency Signals

There are three spoken emergency signals that show the degree of severity of the emergency. All three signals are initiated on Channel 16. Distress and urgency messages are then given on Channel 16, while safety messages are given on a working channel.

Distress Signal: Mayday

The distress signal, Mayday, precedes a distress message about a grave and imminent danger and a request for immediate help, and this signal has pri-

ority over all other calls. The word "mayday" comes from the French expression, *m'aidez,* which means "Help me." If you use it, speak the word three times, "Mayday, Mayday, Mayday."

SENDING A DISTRESS CALL. You send a voice distress signal and message on Channel 16. During the emergency, remain on that channel. Provided you are being received on Channel 16, you do not want to risk losing contact by switching to another channel.

After the initial contact, the following message sequence should be broadcast slowly and distinctly:

1. The distress signal **Mayday**, spoken three times.
2. The words **This is**, spoken once.
3. The **name of your vessel**, spoken three times, and **your call sign**, spoken once.
4. The distress signal **Mayday**, spoken once.

DISTRESS COMMUNICATION FORM

Instructions: Complete this form now (except for items 6 through 9) and post near your radiotelephone for use if you are in distress.

SPEAK: SLOWLY—CLEARLY—CALMLY

1. Make certain your radio is turned on.
2. Select **VHF-FM Channel 16** or **2182 kHz for your SSB.**
3. Press microphone button and say: **MAYDAY—MAYDAY—MAYDAY.**
4. Say: **THIS IS**_____
   (Your boat name, repeated three times, and your call sign.)
5. Say: **MAYDAY**_____
   (Your boat name)
6. **TELL WHERE YOU ARE.** (What navigational aids or landmarks are you near? What direction and distance are you from a landmark? What is your latitude and longitude? What are your loran coordinates?)
7. **STATE THE NATURE OF YOUR DISTRESS.**
8. **GIVE NUMBER OF PEOPLE ABOARD AND CONDITIONS OF ANY INJURED.**
9. **ESTIMATE CURRENT SEAWORTHINESS OF YOUR BOAT.**
10. **BRIEFLY DESCRIBE YOUR BOAT:** _____ FEET; _____
    (Length)   (Type)
    _____ HULL; _____ TRIM; _____ MASTS;
    (Color)   (Color)   (Number)
    _____
    (Anything else you think will help rescuers find you.)
11. Say: **I WILL BE LISTENING ON CHANNEL** _____ 16/2182 _____
    (Cross out one that does not apply).
12. End message by saying: **THIS IS**_____**OVER.**
    (Your boat name and call sign)
13. Release microphone button and listen. Someone should answer. **IF THEY DO NOT, REPEAT CALL, BEGINNING AT ITEM #1 ABOVE. IF THERE IS STILL NO ANSWER, CHECK TO SEE IF YOUR SET IS TURNED ON, IS ON HIGH POWER, AND IS ON CHANNEL 16 IF IT IS VHF-FM OR 2182 kHz IF IT IS SSB.**

5. The **name of your vessel**, spoken once.

6. The **position of your vessel** either by latitude and longitude or by a bearing (either true or compass) and distance from a well-known landmark. You can give it any way that will assist in locating you.

7. The **nature of your distress**: for example, taking on water, sinking, or fire.

8. The **kind of help needed**.

9. Any **other information** that might help. This might include the length or tonnage of your vessel, the number of people on board, and the number of people needing medical attention. It helps to give a description of your vessel, including the color of its hull, deck, cabin, and masts.

10. When you are through, say, "**I will be listening on Channel 16**."

11. End your message by saying, "**This is [your boat name and call sign], over**."

Release the microphone button and listen. Someone should answer. If you do not receive an answer, repeat your call beginning at #1 above.

DISTRESS CALLS ON A DSC-CAPABLE VHF-FM RADIO

If your radio is DSC-capable—as all fixed-mount VHF radios manufactured since 1999 are—and if the radio is properly registered, properly interfaced with your boat's GPS receiver, and programmed with the proper MMSI for emergency calling, a distress call is largely automated. The procedure is as follows:

1A. Lift the cover and press the Distress button. If the display reads "Undesignated," press the button for 3 to 5 seconds. The radio transmits a single "Mayday" alert in a digital signal containing your identity and location over Channel 70 to the Coast Guard, Sea Tow, and/or nearby ships.

1B. If the display provides a choice between "Undesignated" and "Designated," selecting "Designated" calls up a menu that allows you to specify the trouble you are in. Then press the button for 3 to 5 seconds to send the signal.

2. When the call is acknowledged digitally by another DSC-equipped radio, you will hear a tone.

3. If your radio does not switch automatically to Channel 16 for voice transmission, press the Cancel/Clear button.

4. On Channel 16, send a voice message concerning your situation (see above), and talk to rescuers and other vessels.

To help you recall the above steps in an emergency, refer to the accompanying Distress Communication form. Copy it, fill it in except for items 6 through 9, and post it near your radio.

ACKNOWLEDGING A DISTRESS MESSAGE. If you hear an unanswered distress message, you must answer on Channel 16. You can wait a short time for others to acknowledge if you are reasonably certain that the distressed vessel is not in your vicinity. Wait, also, in waters where there are reliable communications with the Coast Guard.

After you acknowledge receipt of the distress message, wait a short time. There may be others in a better position to help than you are, and they should also acknowledge receipt.

When you are sure you are not interfering with other distress-related communications, contact the vessel in distress and tell them what assistance you can give. If the vessel is in your area, you are obligated to render any possible assistance. Make sure the Coast Guard knows about the distress and relay the distress message if necessary.

If you can't reach the Coast Guard directly, call the nearest marine operator. This is especially important if the distressed vessel is beyond reach of the Coast Guard and you are between the Coast Guard station and the distressed vessel.

You acknowledge receipt of a distress message by saying the name and call sign of the distressed vessel three times. Follow this by saying, "This is" and your vessel's name and call sign. Do this three times, then add, "Received Mayday."

After a momentary pause to ensure that you are not interfering with a vessel better situated to help, send the following: Start with the "Mayday," then give the name and call sign of the distressed vessel. Continue with "This is," and give your vessel's name and call sign. Tell where you are, your speed, and how much time it will take you to reach the other vessel.

A vessel or shore station that learns a vessel is in distress should send a distress message when the vessel in distress can't send the message itself. It may also do so if more help is needed. If it hears an unacknowledged distress message and is not able to assist, it should send a distress message.

In such a case, the transmission consists of the radiotelephone alarm signal (if available) followed by "Mayday relay, Mayday relay, Mayday relay."

You then say, "This is," and give the name and call sign of your vessel or shore station three times. If you send a distress message under these conditions, contact the Coast Guard.

IMPOSING SILENCE. The vessel in distress or the station in control of distress communications may impose silence on any station that interferes by sending "Seelonce Mayday." ("Seelonce" is the French pronunciation of the word "silence.") Any other station that believes it is essential to impose silence may do so by sending "Seelonce Distress," followed by the name and call sign of the station imposing the silence.

After distress communications have ceased, or when silence is no longer necessary, the station in control ends the silence. It does so on Channel 16 by sending the following: "Mayday, to all stations, to all stations, to all stations, this is [name and call sign of station ending the distress], [the time], [name and call sign of vessel in distress], Seelonce Feenee." ("Seelonce feenee" is the French pronunciation of *silence fini*, meaning "silence finished.")

Urgency Signal: Pan-Pan

The urgency signal, **Pan-Pan**, announces that an urgent message follows. "Pan" (pronounced PAHN) comes from the French word *panne*, which means urgency, and should be used when the safety of a vessel or person is in jeopardy. Only a distress signal has a higher priority.

Urgency signals and messages are sent on Channel 16 in situations such as the following:

- Loss of a person overboard, but only when help is needed.
- Repeating an urgent storm warning from an authorized shore station.
- Loss of steering or power in a shipping lane.

SENDING AN URGENCY CALL. The urgency signal and message usually include the following:

1. The urgency signal **Pan-Pan**, spoken three times.
2. **To all stations** (or a particular station).
3. The words **This is**.
4. The **name of your vessel**, spoken three times, and your call sign, spoken once.
5. The **urgency message** (describe the problem).
6. The **position and description of your vessel**

and any information that will help responding vessels.

7. The words **This is**.
8. The **name of your vessel** and its **radio call sign**, spoken once.
9. The proword **Over**.

Safety Signal: Sécurité

The safety signal announces a message about safety of navigation or an important weather warning. It is the French word *sécurité*, pronounced "say-cur-ee-tay," and is said three times. Safety signals have higher priorities than any other messages except distress and urgency messages.

Most safety messages are initiated by the Coast Guard, and are announced on Channels 9 and 16 and given on a Coast Guard working channel, usually Channel 22A. If you have a safety message to send, announce it on Channel 16 and give it on a working channel.

Any message headed by one of the emergency signals has priority over other messages. Continue to listen but don't transmit, and be prepared to help if you can.

The decision about which emergency signal to use is the responsibility of the person in charge of the vessel, and sometimes there is no clear line to separate one signal from the other. Also, what starts as a routine problem might develop into a serious one. Running out of gasoline is not an emergency; running out of gasoline in a shipping lane might be an urgency situation, however, and running out of gas in a shipping lane with large ships headed toward you is more serious still.

SENDING A SAFETY MESSAGE. Initiate the safety call on Channel 16. The following is an example of a safety message from the vessel *Barbara Ann*, which has radio call sign WX 3456: "Sécurité, sécurité, sécurité. This is *Barbara Ann*, Whiskey X-Ray 3456. Shift to Channel [local working channel] for safety message. This is *Barbara Ann*, Whiskey X-Ray 3456. Out."

On the working channel the message might be as follows: "Sécurité, Sécurité, Sécurité. This is *Barbara Ann*, Whiskey X-Ray 3456. A log approximately 20 feet long, 2 feet diameter is adrift off Haines Point in the Potomac River. This is *Barbara Ann*, Whiskey X-Ray 3456. Out."

Many skippers prefer to contact the Coast Guard and let them give the Sécurité call.

Note: If you have not been assigned a call sign by the FCC, use only your boat name.

Crew Training

More than one person on board should know how to operate your vessel and your radio. Give your guests a brief introduction to your radio when you describe your vessel's operation and safety features, and fill out a Distress Communication Form and post it so that anyone on board can summon help in an emergency.

This may seem too cautious, but many emergencies could have had better outcomes if someone aboard other than a stricken skipper knew how to operate the radio or start the boat's engine. Many emergency broadcasts fail to summon help because the rattled operator does not turn on the power, or calls on the wrong channel, or forgets to depress the press-to-talk button. Others fail because the squelch is too high or the press-to-talk button isn't released and the return message isn't received.

Ways to Learn More

A Boater's Guide to VHF and GMDSS. Sue Fletcher. Camden, Maine: International Marine, 2002.

The Boatowner's Guide to GMDSS and Marine Radio: Marine Distress and Safety Communications in the Digital Age. U.S. Power Squadrons. Camden, Maine: International Marine, 2005.

Chapman Piloting & Seamanship. 66th ed. Charles B. Husick. New York: Hearst Books, 2009. Chapter 20.

Marine Amateur Radio: Selection, Installation, Licensing, and Use. U.S. Power Squadrons. Camden, Maine: International Marine, 2005.

Using VHF and SSB Radio: A Captain's Quick Guide. Bob Sweet. Camden, Maine: International Marine, 2004.

http://en.wikipedia.org/wiki/Distress_radiobeacon

Practice Questions

IMPORTANT BOATING TERMS

In the following exercise, match the words in the column on the left with the definitions in the column on the right. In the blank space to the left of each term, write the letter of the item that best matches it. Do not use an item in the right-hand column more than once.

THE ITEMS

1. _____ distress signal
2. _____ VHF-FM
3. _____ urgency signal
4. _____ safety signal
5. _____ Public correspondence channels
6. _____ Out
7. _____ I spell
8. _____ Channel 16
9. _____ Wilco
10. _____ Over

THE RESPONSES

a. Sécurité

b. I am through but I expect a response

c. I am through and I do not expect a response

d. Pan-Pan

e. message received, will comply

f. distress, urgency, and safety

g. Mayday

h. most commonly used marine radio

i. use phonetic alphabet

j. public telephone system

Multiple-Choice Items

In the following items, choose the best response:

13-1. VHF-FM licenses are issued by the

a. Coast Guard
b. state in which you live
c. FCC
d. marine patrol

13-2. You will need an operator's license for your VHF-FM if you

a. broadcast on your station
b. plan to dock in a foreign port
c. want to communicate with the Coast Guard
d. all of the above

13-3. If a VHF-FM channel number has the letter A attached to it, this means the channel is

a. an alternate one
b. already in use
c. available
d. USA only

13-4. Before you transmit

a. listen to see if someone else is using the channel
b. write out what you want to say
c. review the correct procedure
d. give your station call letters

13-5. At the beginning and end of each message, you must

a. state your name
b. give your call sign
c. turn your radio on and off
d. tell who you are calling

13-6. The most important purpose of a marine radiotelephone is

a. to arrange for boat repairs
b. to contact other skippers to find out where the fish are biting
c. to keep in touch with your home so they will know everything is okay
d. safety

13-7. Radios equipped with digital selective calling (DSC)

a. use Channel 70 to transmit its digital information
b. have a seven-digit MMSI number assigned

c. can transmit location data without using any external equipment
d. are designed to have voice communication on the same channel as digital data

13-8. If you set your squelch control too low you will

a. reduce your ability to receive signals
b. lower your transmission power
c. interfere with weaker stations
d. receive too many stations

13-9. The distress signal that is used to indicate grave and imminent danger and to request immediate assistance is

a. Pan-Pan (said three times)
b. Sécurité (said three times)
c. Mayday (said three times)
d. radio check (said three times)

13-10. Which channel is the Coast Guard liaison channel?

a. 6
b. 16
c. 22A
d. 83

13-11. When you have completed your radiotelephone communication and do not require a reply, use the proword(s)

a. over and out
b. over
c. wilco
d. out

13-12. If you hear "Seelonce Mayday" on your marine radio, you know that

a. a Mayday is in progress
b. you are not supposed to use your radio
c. radio silence is requested
d. all of the above

13-13. The range of your VHF-FM radio depends on

a. the height of your antenna
b. the height of the receiving antenna
c. the gain of your antenna
d. all of the above

Multiple-Choice Items (continued)

13-14. Keep a watch on the calling channel at all times except when

a. you are communicating on another channel or when your radiotelephone is not turned on
b. you are underway
c. no one is using the calling channel
d. you are maintaining a watch on another channel

13-15. A radio message concerning weather or safety of navigation is preceded by the word(s)

a. Mayday
b. Pan-Pan
c. Now hear this
c. Sécurité

13-16. Do not call a Coast Guard Station on Channel 16 to request

a. a radio check
b. assistance
c. a tow
d. a message be relayed

13-17. Although you may install your VHF-FM radio, any repairs or internal adjustments must be made by

a. a Coast Guard Auxiliarist communication specialist
b. a qualified electrician
c. a shortwave ham
d. an FCC-licensed general class commercial operator

13-18. Although a CB radio may be useful, it should not be seen as a means of

a. getting fishing information
b. contacting the Coast Guard
c. chitchat with other operators
d. calling home

13-19. When calling another vessel, the preliminary call must not exceed

a. 10 seconds
b. 30 seconds
c. 1 minute
d. 2 minutes

13-20. If you can't reach a limited coast station on its working channel, call it on

a. Channel 6
b. the local calling channel
c. Channel 16
d. Channel 22A

13-21. If another station answers your call, and you identify yourself, then

a. wait 10 seconds before talking
b. ask the other station to identify itself
c. request that it switch to a working channel
d. give your message

13-22. If you do not get a reply to your call to another station wait

a. at least 1 minute before trying again
b. at least 2 minutes before trying again
c. at least 3 minutes before trying again
d. at least 5 minutes before trying again

13-23. After you have tried three times to call another station, wait at least

a. 10 minutes before calling again
b. 15 minutes before calling again
c. 20 minutes before calling again
d. 30 minutes before calling again

13-24. An urgency message is preceded by the urgency signal

a. Sécurité
b. Mayday
c. Pan-Pan
d. all of the above

13-25. If you willfully or repeatedly violate the communications act or the FCC rules, you may

a. have your license revoked, if you have one
b. be fined
c. be sent to prison
d. any of the above

Your Responsibilities as a Boat Operator

CHAPTER 2 FEATURED the items required by federal law for safe and enjoyable boating. Those are just part of the responsibilities you have as a boat operator. This section will discuss responsibilitites to your passengers, to other boaters, to Homeland Security, and your environmental obligations.

Responsibilities to Your Passengers and Others

In most states you are responsible for any damage your boat may cause other boats or for injuries suffered by your passengers or others. Under federal law, reckless and negligent operation of a boat is a crime and punishable by law. For grossly negligent operation, you may be fined up to $5,000 or imprisoned for 1 year, or both. You are responsible for anything your boat does or anything that happens to or on your boat—if you are present or if it is used with your express or implied consent. For example, if your wake rocks another vessel and breaks dishes in its galley, you are responsible. If this happens when hot food is being prepared or served, you are liable for any personal injury. The courteous thing to do when passing another vessel is to slow down enough that you do not create a large wake.

Federal law requires you to provide whatever assistance you can to anyone at sea in need of help. However, it does not require you to endanger your passengers, your vessel, or yourself while doing so.

If you render assistance, you are protected by the "Good Samaritan" clause of the Federal Boat Safety Act of 1971. This act says that if you "gratuitously and in good faith" render assistance and there is no objection, you cannot be held liable for anything you do or don't do, provided you act as an ordinary, reasonable person would have acted under the same or similar circumstances.

Substance Abuse

Recreational boating is an activity that people engage in for fun. Many people focus their entire social lives around boats. Some of these social activities include consumption of alcohol and other mood-altering substances.

Unfortunately, as with automobiles, alcohol is a contributing factor in many boating accidents and deaths. Legal issues aside, drugs and alcohol have no place on a boat. Operating a boat is usually a simple, relaxed affair. But a single wrong choice, a single moment of inattention, can turn an afternoon outing into a disaster. The sea can be very unforgiving.

Over 700 people a year die in boating accidents. A large number of these deaths involve alcohol, used either by the victim or by another person involved in the incident. Add to this number the thousands who are injured each year, and a frightening picture emerges of needless suffering and expense directly related to the use of alcohol and other drugs. The federal minimum blood alcohol concentration (BAC) at which a person is considered "under the influence" has been lowered recently from 0.10% to 0.08%, which reinforces the concerns regarding alcohol abuse.

Boating, pleasant as it is, can be a stressful activity. After only a few hours on the water, a normal, healthy boat operator's perceptions and judgment are impaired even without alcohol or drugs. Unaccustomed exposure to fresh air, glare, ultraviolet light, motion, and noise can impair you as much as if you were legally intoxicated.

If you doubt that these factors can alter behavior, spend a couple of hours at a launching ramp. See how otherwise rational people try to load their boats on trailers. Add a few drinks or substance use and you have an explosive situation.

If you have been drinking or using drugs, your chances of surviving an accident are greatly reduced. Alcohol and depressant drugs lower your resistance to hypothermia, a serious medical problem. Intoxicated people who fall into the water are much more likely than sober ones to become disoriented. They may swim downward rather than toward the surface. Just when good judgment and mental sharpness are needed most, they are muddled by the intoxicants.

Illegal drugs are just that—illegal. If you or guests on your boat are found in possession of or using illegal drugs, the results may be devastating for all involved. At the least, under the zero tolerance rule, you stand to lose your boat and other personal assets. You may also lose your freedom.

Even legal drugs may impair physical ability and judgment. Antihistamines, "seasickness" pills, sedatives, tranquilizers, etc., can all affect you adversely.

Speed Regulations

Most speed regulations are local ordinances or state laws or regulations. Federal regulations require that you proceed at a safe speed so you can take proper and effective action to avoid collision. You must be able to stop in a distance appropriate to the circumstances and conditions. To determine safe speed, things such as visibility, traffic density, maneuverability of your vessel, and wind and sea state are considered.

A speed limit and no-wake sign at a marina entrance. (PHOTO BY BOB DENNIS)

State and Local Regulations

You are responsible for obeying all state and local regulations. Their purpose is to protect you and other people. They vary from location to location but include things such as: (1) using a kill switch on a PWC, which shuts off the engine if the operator falls away from the helm or overboard, (2) speed and wake regulations, (3) operator's license, (4) a requirement for a rearview mirror and observer if towing skiers, (5) age restrictions for operating or renting boats, and (6) laws regulating the operation of personal watercraft. You can consult your local police department or marine patrol for further information.

In most states, a PWC must have a kill switch unless the PWC is designed to circle back to its operator when the operator falls overboard. The kill switch is to be fastened to the operator by means of a lanyard whenever the vessel is in operation.

Boating Accident Reports

The operator of a vessel involved in an on-the-water accident must stop, render assistance, and offer identification. Notify local authorities immediately if a person disappears from a vessel or a death occurs.

A written accident report is required within 48 hours if a person dies, disappears from a vessel, or requires treatment beyond first aid. A written report is to be filed within 10 days if a vessel is lost or damage to it or other property exceeds $2,000.

File the report forms with the state authorities that have jurisdiction over the waters on which the accident happened. Accident reports are used to compile safety data. Information contained in them is not made public.

A generic Boating Accident Report form, which includes most state requirements, can be found in Appendix C.

Law Enforcement and Homeland Security

Boardings

Federal regulations require that vessels underway, when hailed by the Coast Guard, heave-to or maneuver in such a way that an officer can come aboard. Other federal, state, and local law enforcement officials may also come aboard and examine your boat. With the exception of customs, you can recognize such boats by their markings, their blue lights, and the uniforms the personnel wear.

Homeland Security

As a recreational boater, you share in keeping our waterways, marinas, and harbors safe and secure. It is important to know and observe security zones or restricted areas. Be aware that naval vessels (including Coast Guard vessels) maintain security zones. Within 500 yards of a naval vessel you must slow your boat to a minimum speed, and you must maintain a 100-yard distance from the naval vessel. If you must pass within 100 yards, hail the naval vessel on VHF-FM Channel 16 to get permission to pass.

Do not tie up to or obstruct any aid to navigation, and never anchor under bridges.

The Coast Guard's America's Waterway Watch program is a way for you as a recreational boater to assist in Homeland Security. Because you know your own harbors and marinas, you know what is ordinary and what is not. If there is immediate danger to someone's life or property, call 911. Report any suspicious activity to the National Response Center's Hotline, 1-877-24-WATCH.

America's WATERWAY WATCH

REPORT SUSPICIOUS ACTIVITY TO

877-24-WATCH

Environmental Concerns

Cleansers, Chemicals, and Paints

Purchase the least toxic product able to do the job and use lots of elbow grease. Clean spills with a rag, not a hose. Share leftover boat cleaning and painting supplies with other boaters or dispose of them safely onshore. Conduct all sanding, scraping, and painting away from the water and use a vacuum sander and tarps to collect particles.

Discharge of Fuel and Oil

All vessels under 100 gross tons are to have a fixed or portable means of discharging oily bilge slops into a container. A bucket or bailer is acceptable. Any discharge that causes a sheen on the water is a violation of the Federal Water Pollution Control Act.

When spilled, a single quart of motor oil can

create a 2-acre slick (three football fields), fouling the water's surface and impacting marine life. Every year Americans spill or throw away more than thirty times the oil that was spilled from the *Exxon Valdez*. Use absorbent wipe "bilge pillows" to remove oily water from your bilge. Recycle used oil at a local recycling facility. Learn how to gauge when your tank is almost full and don't "top it off." Keep your engine or engines well tuned and check frequently for possible oil or grease leaks.

If your vessel is 26 feet or more in length, you must post a placard stating the federal oil discharge requirements. The placard shall be at least 5 by 8 inches and made of durable material. Post it in the machinery spaces or at the bilge and ballast pump

DISCHARGE OF OIL PROHIBITED

The Federal Water Pollution Control Act prohibits the discharge of oil or oily waste into or upon the navigable waters and contiguous zone of the United States, if such discharge causes a film or sheen upon, or discoloration of, the surface of the water, or causes a sludge or emulsion beneath the surface of the water. Violators are subject to a penalty of $5,000.

DISCHARGE OF OIL PROHIBITED
The Federal Water Pollution Control Act

prohibits the discharge of oil or oily waste into or upon the navigable waters of the United States, or the waters of the contiguous zone, or which may affect natural resources belonging to, appertaining to, or under the exclusive management authority of the United States, if such discharge causes a film or discoloration of the surface of the water or causes a sludge or emulsion beneath the surface of the water. Violators are subject to substantial civil penalties and/or criminal sanctions, including fines and imprisonment.

Report all discharges to the
National Response Center at 1-800-424-8802
or to your local U.S. Coast Guard office
by phone or VHF radio, Channel 16.

OIL POLLUTION ACT

As a recreational boater, be aware of your potential liability under the Federal Oil Pollution Act of 1990. You may be assessed the cost of actions taken to prevent a spill, to remove oil, or to pay for damages resulting from an oil spill for which you are responsible. If your boat runs aground, sinks, or spills oil in some manner, you could be liable for prevention or cleanup costs of up to $500,000.

through liability insurance. Most recreational boat insurance policies will not protect you from liability under the Oil Pollution Act. If your policy does not have an oil pollution clause or if the clause is vague, consider purchasing pollution insurance.

Also help ensure that others obey the law. You are encouraged to report any polluting discharge you see to the nearest U.S. Coast Guard office. Report its location, source, size, color, substance, and the time you saw it. Do not take samples of any chemical discharge. If you are uncertain of what the discharge is, keep flames away. Avoid physical contact and inhalation of vapors. The Coast Guard oil spill and pollution telephone number is 1-800-424-8802.

Plastics and Garbage

There is an international agreement that regulates and controls the discharge of ship's garbage named the International Convention for the Prevention of Pollution from Ships (MARPOL). Each country working with MARPOL issues their own instructions to comply with these regulations. As of this printing, the United States is creating new instructions to incorporate MARPOL regulations dated January 1, 2013. These regulations are published as Code of Federal Regulations (CFR Title 33, 151). http://www.ecfr.gov/cgi-bin/text-idx?c= ecfr&tpl=/ecfrbrowse/Title33/33tab_02.tpl

Smaller recreational vessels are prohibited from discharging any garbage in any waters. Large vessels employing garbage maceration devices and incineration devices have very limited discharge authority. The discharge of waste is prohibited on the Great Lakes and their contributory waters.

Vessels 26 feet and over in length must post one or more placards listing at-sea garbage restrictions. Vessels 40 feet and over having a galley and berths must have a written trash disposal plan, and name the person in charge of the plan.

Plastic trash may not be dumped in any navigable waters.

Food garbage includes maintenance waste such as cooking oil, and grease; it includes domestic waste, which we usually call "trash." It doesn't include fresh fish or fish parts.

"Dishwater" is the liquid residue from manual or automatic dishwashers. Its definition assumes

**DUMPING OF GARBAGE *PROHIBITED*
IN THE GREAT LAKES
and connecting or tributary waters**

Violators are subject to a civil penalty of up to $25,000, a criminal fine of up
to $500,000 and imprisonment for up to 6 years for each violation.

Report marine pollution incidents to the National Response Center at
1-800-424-8802 or to your local Coast Guard office by phone
or VHF radio, channel 16.

 Help keep the Great Lakes great!

This placard meets the requirements of 33 CFR 151.59 for vessels operating solely on the Great Lakes and their
connecting or tributary waters.

that the dishes and cooking utensils have been pre-cleaned to remove food particles that would interfere with the operation of automatic dishwashers. If they haven't been pre-cleaned, the water they are washed in is considered garbage.

"Gray water" is water from a dishwasher, shower, laundry, bath, or washbasin. It does not include waste from toilets or urinals. It is not classed as garbage.

"Dunnage" is cargo-associated waste. It includes lining and packing materials that float. It also includes the containers and boxes your fish bait came in.

If a recreational boating facility can provide wharfage or other services for ten or more vessels, it has to have a means of garbage disposal. Facilities include marinas, yacht clubs, and attended launching ramps. Vessels that are conducting business with the facility or marina qualify for the service. The terminal or marina can charge reasonable fees for its service.

Violators of these federal regulations may be faced with Federal Class D felony charges which may incur imprisonment up to 10 years, in addition to a maximum fine of $250,000.

FLOAT PLAN

INSTRUCTIONS: Complete this plan before you go boating and leave it with a reliable person who can be depended upon to notify the Coast Guard, or other rescue organization, should you not return or check-in as planned. If you have a change of plans after leaving, be sure to notify the person holding your Float Plan. For additional copies of this plan, go to: **www.floatplancentral.org**

nws.cgaux.org

Do NOT file this plan with the U.S. Coast Guard

www.uscgboating.org

VESSEL

IDENTIFICATION:

Name & Home Port_____

Doc/Registration No._____

Year & Make_____

Length _____(ft/M) Type _____ Draft _____(In/CM) Hull Mat._____

Hull Color(s)_____

Prominent Features_____

_____

PROPULSION:

Primary - Type _____ No. Eng.____ Fuel Capacity_____(gal/L)

Auxiliary -Type _____ No. Eng.____ Fuel Capacity_____(gal/L)

TELECOMMUNICATIONS:

Radio Call Sign _____

DSC MMSI No. _____

Radio-1: Type _____ Ch./Freq. Monitored _____

Radio-2: Type _____ Ch./Freq. Monitored _____

Cell Phone No. _____

Pager No. _____

NAVIGATION: (Check all on board)

☐ Maps   ☐ Charts   ☐ Compass   ☐ GPS / DGPS

☐ Radar   ☐ Loran C   ☐ Sounder   ☐ _____

SAFETY & SURVIVAL

VISUAL DISTRESS SIGNALS:

☐ Day Only type

☐ Night Only type

☐ Day & Night type

PFDs: (Do not count Type IV devices)

_____ Quantity On Board

AUDIBLE DISTRESS SIGNALS:

☐ Horn / Whistle

☐ Bell

☐ _____

GROUND TACKLE:

☐ Anchor: Line Length_____(ft/M)

OTHER GEAR:

☐ Life boat / Life raft

☐ Dinghy / Skiff

☐ Food & Water

☐ EPIRB _____

☐ Foul Weather Gear

☐ Flashlight / Searchlight

☐ Signal Mirror

☐ Drogue / Sea Anchor

☐ _____

☐ _____

PERSONS ON BOARD

OPERATOR:

Name _____

Address _____

City _____ State _____ Zip Code _____

Vehicle (Year, Make & Model):_____

Trailer will be parked at:_____

PASSENGERS/CREW: Name & Address

1. _____
2. _____
3. _____
4. _____
5. _____

Attach "Supplemental Passenger List" if additional passengers or crew on board.

	Age	M/F	Notes (Special medical condition, Can't swim, etc.)
Operator	___	___	

Has experience: w/Boat ☐   w/Area ☐

Home phone: _____

Vehicle License No.: _____

Trailer License No.: _____

Passengers/Crew	Age	M/F	Notes (Special medical condition, Can't swim, etc.)
1.	___	___	_____
2.	___	___	_____
3.	___	___	_____
4.	___	___	_____
5.	___	___	_____

ITINERARY

	DATE	TIME	LOCATION	MODE OF TRAVEL	REASON FOR STOP	CHECK-IN TIME
Depart						
Arrive						
Depart						
Arrive						
Depart						
Arrive						
Depart						
Arrive						
Depart						
Arrive						
Depart						
Arrive						
Depart						
Arrive						

Attach "Supplemental Itinerary" if space for additional destinations is needed.

Contact 1: _____ Phone Number _____

Contact 2: _____ Phone Number _____

If you have a genuine concern for the safety or welfare of any persons on board the Vessel described above, who have not returned or checked-in in a reasonable amount of time, then follow step-by-step instructions on the **Boating Emergency Guide™** included with this plan, or on the World Wide Web at:

www.floatplancentral.org/help/BoatingEmergencyGuide.htm

Rev 2007.05.11

1 of 2

BOATING EMERGENCY GUIDE™

You will need the following items before you begin: 1) the **Float Plan** if one was given to you, 2) **Pen** or **Pencil**, 3) Clean sheet of **paper** or **Writing Tablet**, and 4) your local **Telephone Directory**.

Step 1

Do you have a genuine concern for the safety or welfare of any persons on board the Vessel described above, who have not returned or checked-in in a reasonable amount of time?

If YES, then continue with **Step 2**, otherwise STOP, no further action is required.

Step 2

Were you given a prepared Float Plan by anyone on board the vessel?

If YES, then continue with **Step 3**, otherwise got to **Step 5**.

Step 3

On the Float Plan, locate the two Contact lines below the Itinerary at the bottom of the Float Plan. Call Contact number 1…

IF	THEN
A person answered the phone…	Take notes during your conversation. 1. Let the person know you are responding to a late return or check-in by the individuals designated on the Float Plan. 2. Determine if the person you are talking to or anyone else at that location, has recently had contact with anyone on the vessel, and when and where that contact occurred. 3. Are you still concerned about the safety or welfare of any persons on board the vessel?

IF	THEN
Yes	Continue with **Step 4**.
No	STOP. No further action is required.

IF	THEN
Otherwise…	Continue with **Step 4**.

Step 4

Call telephone number for Contact number 2…

IF	THEN
A person answered the phone…	Take notes during your conversation. 1. Let the person know you are responding to a late return or check-in by the individuals designated on the Float Plan. 2. Determine if the person you are talking to or anyone else at that location, has recently had contact with anyone on the vessel, and when and where that contact occurred. 3. Are you still concerned about the safety or welfare of any persons on board the vessel?

IF	THEN
Yes	Continue with **Step 6**.
No	STOP. No further action is required.

IF	THEN
Otherwise…	Continue with **Step 6**.

Step 5

Take a moment to jot down the facts you know about each item in the checklist below.

> Do NOT speculate. Speculation about a detail may mislead Search And Rescue (SAR) personnel, and add to the overall search and rescue time, adversely affecting the outcome.

❑ Period of time the vessel has been overdue.

❑ Purpose of the trip or voyage.

❑ Description of the Vessel (type, size, color, features, etc.)

❑ Vessels departure point and destination.

❑ Places the Vessel planned to stop during transit.

❑ Navigation equipment on board (such as GPS, Loran C, Radar, Compass, Sounder, etc.)

❑ Number of people on board the Vessel, as well as personal habits e.g. dependability, reliability, etc.

❑ Was the Vessel already moored, or did a vehicle tow it to the launch point?

❑ License plate number and description of the tow vehicle, and/or passenger transport vehicle.

❑ Communications equipment on board, including type of radio and frequencies monitored, cellular telephone numbers of any persons on board.

❑ Additional points of contact along the vessels planned route.

❑ Where there any pending commitments e.g. work, appointments, etc.

Continue with **Step 6**.

Step 6

1. Contact your local Law Enforcement agency (Police or Sheriff).

2. Let the dispatcher know that you are responding to a late return or check-in by the persons on board the vessel.

3. The dispatcher will instruct you from here.

> **Note:** The dispatcher will provide you with the necessary contact or agency connection *(if one was not provided for you on the Float Plan)* to get a Search And Rescue mission started. This is usually handled this way because it puts you closest to the agency conducting the actual search and rescue, eliminating an unnecessary middleman.
>
> If the dispatcher would like a follow-up call from you on the outcome of the rescue, they will let you know.

4. Continue with **Step 7**.

Step 7

Be patient… you've done everything you can possibly do for now. It is important to stay off the telephone, so emergency personnel can contact you with additional information and/or questions concerning the search and rescue effort.

STOP--End of Guide

Float Plan Central™ is a service of the U.S. Coast Guard Auxiliary
www.floatplancentral.org

Boating Accident Report Form

BOATING ACCIDENT REPORT

States have different requirements for accident reporting. Each state specifies what conditions require you to report an accident (for example: death, injury or property damage exceeding $500), how soon the report must be filed after an accident occurs, and to whom the accident must be reported. Most states have their own Accident Report form, but the information collected will be very similar to that shown below. All reports are confidential. Indicate those not applicable by "NA" **Complete all blocks and both sides.**

INFORMATION ABOUT BOAT OPERATOR

Name and address of operator

Operator's phone #

Name and address of owner

Age of operator
Date of birth

Owner's phone #

Is this boat rented? ☐ Yes ☐ No

Number of persons on board

Operator's experience

This type of boat
☐ Under 20 hours
☐ 20 to 100 hours
☐ 100 to 500 hours
☐ Over 500 hours

Other type of boat
☐ Under 20 hours
☐ 20 to 100 hours
☐ 100 to 500 hours
☐ Over 500 hours

Formal instruction in boating safety
☐ None ☐ State ☐ USCG Auxiliary
☐ U.S. Power Squadrons ☐ American Red Cross
☐ Other *(specify)* _____

INFORMATION ABOUT OPERATOR'S BOAT

Boat registration # | Boat name | Boat make | Boat model | Hull I.D. #

Type of boat
☐ Open motorboat
☐ Cabin motorboat
☐ Auxiliary sailboat
☐ Sailboat
☐ Row boat
☐ Canoe
☐ Other *(specify)*

Hull material
☐ Wood
☐ Aluminum
☐ Steel
☐ Fiberglass
☐ Rubber/Vinyl
☐ Other *(specify)*

Engine
☐ Outboard
☐ Inboard gasoline
☐ Inboard diesel
☐ Inboard-outboard
☐ Jet
☐ Other *(specify)*

Propulsion
☐ Number of engines
☐ Total horsepower
☐ Type of fuel

Construction
Length _____

Year built _____

Has boat had a safety examination? *(specify)*
☐ None ☐ State/local examination ☐ Other
☐ USCGAux/USPS Vessel Safety Check
For current year? ☐ Yes ☐ No

ACCIDENT DATA

Date of accident | Time _____ ☐ am ☐ pm | Body of water | Precise location

State | Nearest city or town | County

Weather
☐ Clear ☐ Rain
☐ Cloudy ☐ Snow
☐ Fog ☐ Hazy

Water conditions
☐ Calm (waves less than 6")
☐ Choppy (waves 6" to 2')
☐ Rough (waves 2' to 6')
☐ Very rough (greater than6')
☐ Strong current

Wind
☐ None
☐ Light (0-6 mph)
☐ Moderate (7-14 mph)
☐ Strong (15-25 mph)
☐ Storm (over 25 mph)

Visibility
Day | Night
☐ Good ☐ Good
☐ Fair ☐ Fair
☐ Poor ☐ Poor

Estimated temperature
Air _____ ° F
Water ____ ° F

Operation at time of accident
(check all applicable)

☐ Commercial activity ☐ At anchor
☐ Cruising ☐ Tied to dock
☐ Maneuvering ☐ Fueling
☐ Approaching dock ☐ Fishing
☐ Leaving dock ☐ Hunting
☐ Water skiing ☐ Skin diving/
☐ Racing   swimming
☐ Towing ☐ Being towed
☐ Paddling ☐ Other *(specify)*
☐ Drifting _____

Type of accident
☐ Collision with boat
☐ Collision with fixed object
☐ Collision with floating object
☐ Grounding
☐ Capsizing
☐ Flooding/ swamping
☐ Sinking
☐ Hit by boat or propeller

☐ Fire or explosion (fuel)
☐ Fire or explosion (other than fuel)
☐ Fallen skier
☐ Falls overboard
☐ Falls in boat
☐ Other *(specify)*
_____

What, in your opinion, contributed to the accident? *(check all applicable)*

☐ Weather ☐ Drug use
☐ Excessive speed ☐ Fault of hull
☐ No proper lookout ☐ Fault of machinery
☐ Restricted vision ☐ Fault of equipment
☐ Overloading ☐ Operator inexperience
☐ Improper loading ☐ Operator inattention
☐ Hazardous waters ☐ Other *(specify)*
☐ Alcohol use _____

FIRE EXTINGUISHERS

Were fire extinquishers used? ☐ No ☐ Yes
Type(s) _____ Quantity: _____

PROPERTY DAMAGE

Describe property damage

Name/address of owner of damaged property

Estimated amount of property damage
This boat $ _____ Other boat $ _____
Other property $ _____

PERSONAL FLOTATION DEVICES (PFDs)

Was the boat adequately equipped with U. S. Coast Guard-approved personal flotation devices? ☐ Yes ☐ No
Were they accessible? ☐ Yes ☐ No Were they serviceable? ☐ Yes ☐ No
Were they used by survivors? ☐ Yes ☐ No Were they adjusted? ☐ Yes ☐ No
Were PFDs properly used? ☐ Yes ☐ No What type? ☐ I ☐ II ☐ III ☐ IV ☐ V

Were they sized? ☐ Yes ☐ No
Was the boat carrying non-approved PFDs? ☐ Yes ☐ No
Were they accessible? ☐ Yes ☐ No
Were they used? ☐ Yes ☐ No If yes, indicate kind: _____
(include any comments on PFDs under Accident Description on other side)

		DECEASED				
Name	Address	Date of birth	Was the victim... ☐ Swimmer ☐ Non-swimmer	Death caused by ☐ Drowning ☐ Other ☐ Disappearance	Was a PFD worn? ☐ Yes ☐ No What type?	
Name	Address	Date of birth	Was the victim... ☐ Swimmer ☐ Non-swimmer	Death caused by ☐ Drowning ☐ Other ☐ Disappearance	Was a PFD worn? ☐ Yes ☐ No What type?	
Name	Address	Date of birth	Was the victim... ☐ Swimmer ☐ Non-swimmer	Death caused by ☐ Drowning ☐ Other ☐ Disappearance	Was a PFD worn? ☐ Yes ☐ No What type?	

	INJURED			
Name	Address	Date of birth	Nature of injury	Was medical treatment required? ☐ Yes ☐ No
Name	Address	Date of birth	Nature of injury	Was medical treatment required? ☐ Yes ☐ No
Name	Address	Date of birth	Nature of injury	Was medical treatment required? ☐ Yes ☐ No

ACCIDENT DESCRIPTION

Describe sequence of events. If it applies, include any information about failure of equipment, use or non-use of PFDs, influence of drugs or alcohol, etc. If diagram is needed attach it separately. Continue this description on additional sheets if necessary.

VESSEL # 2		
Name of operator	Address	Boat #
Phone #		Boat name
Name of owner	Address	

WITNESSES		
Name	Address	Phone #
Name	Address	Phone #
Name	Address	Phone #

INFORMATION ABOUT PERSON COMPLETING THIS REPORT		
Name	Address	Phone #
Signature		Date submitted

Qualification (check one) ☐ Boat operator ☐ Boat owner ☐ Investigator ☐ Other (specify)

TO BE FILLED OUT BY REPORTING AUTHORITY ONLY — USE AGENCY DATE STAMP			
Causes based on (check one) ☐ This report ☐ Investigation ☐ Could not be determined ☐ Investigation and this report	Name of reviewing office		Date received
	Primary cause of accident	Secondary of accident	Reviewed by

Fact Sheet

United States Coast Guard Auxiliary
**America's
Volunteer
Lifesavers**ᔆᴹ

Digital Selective Calling Radios

Digital Selective Calling (DSC) is a VHF radio technology that provides recreational boaters with two unique features that will be discussed below. To be fully functional three items must be available:

- A DSC radio
- A Maritime Mobile Service Identity (MMSI) number
- A compatible GPS or Loran unit

The MMSI is a unique nine (9) digit number that is assigned to a DSC radio station. If the boater has a valid Federal Communications Commission (FCC) station license or plans to operate in international waters they need to contact the FCC to get an MMSI. Otherwise, they can register with BoatU.S. or SEA TOW Services by obtaining an MMSI Assignment form. Forms are available on the BoatU.S. website **www.BoatUS.com/mmsi** or by calling 1-800-563-1536 and the SEA TOW Services website **--**.

Some important points to consider are:
- Each vessel you own needs to have a discrete MMSI to be properly identified.
- The boater needs to keep their MMSI Assignment data current.
- Depending on the make and model of the DSC radio, it may limit the number of times you can try to program your MMSI number into the radio. Typically the radios offer you two (2) chances before locking out future attempts, forcing you to send the radio back to the manufacturer.

DSC technology makes a VHF radio function more like a telephone. It allows boaters to send a digital call directly to another DSC-equipped vessel or shore station.

- In an emergency, one push of a button and the DSC radio will send an automated digital distress alert consisting of your identification (MMSI), and position (if the radio is connected to a GPS or loran unit) to other DSC-equipped vessels and rescue facilities.
- You can privately hail another DSC-equipped vessel, or shore station, if you know their MMSI. It is similar to having a VHF phone number that "rings" the radio called and then automatically switches you to a predetermined working channel.

Rescue 21 is the Coast Guard system that will provide the Mayday response capability described above. For more details on the Rescue 21 System and its availability in your area visit **www.uscg.mil/rescue21**.

The Global Maritime Distress and Safety System (GMDSS) is the international system governing safety radio equipment on commercial ships. For more information on GMDSS visit **www.NAVCEN.USCG. gov/**.

Rev 1

MMSI Registration Form

*Denotes a required field. These fields must be completed in order to receive an MMSI #.

*OWNER'S FIRST NAME:_____ *OWNER'S LAST NAME:_____
OR COMPANY NAME:_____

* STREET ADDRESS:_____ * CITY:_____ * STATE:_____
* ZIP CODE:_____ PROVINCE, MAIL CODE, COUNTRY:_____ *OWNER'S HOME PHONE:_____
OWNER'S WORK PHONE:_____ EMAIL ADDRESS:_____ (Confirmation will be sent to email
address, if provided)

*NAME OF PRIMARY EMERGENCY CONTACT ASHORE:_____ *PRIMARY CONTACT HOME
PHONE:_____ PRIMARY CONTACT WORK PHONE:_____
NAME OF ALTERNATE CONTACT ASHORE:_____ ALTERNATE CONTACT HOME PHONE:_____
ALTERNATE CONTACT WORK PHONE: _____

VESSEL NAME: _____ RADIO CALL SIGN: _____
VESSEL WIRELESS PHONE 1: _____ WIRELESS 2: _____
VESSEL WIRELESS PHONE 3: _____ WIRELESS 4: _____
INMARSAT TELEPHONE #: _____
VESSEL FLAG STATE (Usually USA): _____

*SHIP CLASSIFICATION (SEE TABLE BELOW):_____
EX-SHIP NAME (IF KNOWN): _____
EX-CALL SIGN (IF KNOWN) :_____ EPIRB ID CODE: _____
*VESSEL REGISTRATION NUMBER:_____ OR *DOCUMENTATION NUMBER:_____

*VESSEL HOME PORT: (Marina Name or Residence)_____
PORT CITY: _____ PORT STATE: _____
ALTERNATE VESSEL HOME PORT:_____

*CAPACITY (# OF PERSONS EXPECTED TO BE ON BOARD): _____
SHIP'S RADIO INSTALLATION (VHF, DSC, MF/HF WITH DSC, MF/HF W/O DSC,
AIS TRANSPONDER, CELL PHONE, ETC.):_____

REMARKS (BOAT LENGTH, COLOR, TYPE, ETC.):_____

*SHIP CLASSIFICATION TABLE

DUN–KETCH   MTB–MOTOR BOAT
SLO–SLOOP   YAT–YACHT
GOL–SCHOONER   VLR–SAILING SHIP
SAE–RESCUE VESSEL XXX–UNSPECIFIED

*Note: If XXX-Unspecified, please be sure to describe the vessel in the remarks section

WHEN COMPLETE, FAX THIS FORM TO:
703-461-2840

OR SUBMIT BY MAIL TO:

BoatU.S. MMSI Program
880 S. Pickett St.
Alexandria, VA 22304

appendix E

Metric Conversion Tables

ENGLISH TO METRIC*			METRIC TO ENGLISH		
When you know	Multiply by	To find	When you know	Multiply by	To find
1 inch (in)	2.54	centimeters (cm)	1 centimeter (cm)	.39	inch (in)
3 feet (ft)	91.44	centimeters (cm)	1 centimeter (cm)	.03	feet (ft)
1 yard (yd)	.91	meters (m)	1 meter (m)	39.37	inches (in)
1 mile (mi)	1.61	kilometers (km)	1 meter (m)	1.10	yards (yd)
			1 kilometer (km)	.62	mile (mi)

SOME COMMON EQUIVALENTS			
English	Metric	Metric (approximate)	English (approximate)
		1 kilometer (km)	3280 ft 9.6 in
1 statute mile (mi)	1.61 km	1000 meters (m)	3280 ft 9.6 in
		500 m	1640 ft 5 in
.62 statute mile	1 km	200 m	656 ft 2 in
1000 ft	.2 km	150 m	492 ft 1 in
5 ft	1.5 m	100 m	328 ft 1 in
8 ft	2.4 m	75 m	246 ft 1 in
10 ft	3.0 m	60 m	196 ft 10 in
12 ft	3.6 m	50 m	164 ft 0 in
16 ft	4.8 m	25 m	82 ft 0 in
20 ft	6.0 m	20 m	65 ft 7 in
24 ft	7.2 m	12 m	39 ft 5 in
30 ft	9.0 m	10 m	32 ft 10 in
40 ft	12.0 m	8 m	26 ft 2 in
50 ft	15.0 m	7 m	23 ft 0 in
60 ft	18.0 m	6 m	19 ft 8 in
		5 m	16 ft 5 in
		4.5 m	14 ft 10 in
		4.0 m	13 ft 1 in
		3.5 m	11 ft 6 in
		2.5 m	8 ft 2 in
		2.0 m	6 ft 7 in
		1.5 m	4 ft 11 in
		1.0 m	3 ft 4 in
		.9 m	35.4 in
		.6 m	23.6 in
		.5 m	19.7 in
		1 centimeter (cm)	.39 in
		300 millimeters (mm)	11.8 in
		200 mm	7.9 in

*Approximate conversions from English to Metric measures and Metric to English measures.

Vessel Safety Check

U.S. COAST GUARD AUXILIARY

Be a Safer Boater, Learn from the Best.

Benefits of a Vessel Safety Check

For over 50 years, members of the Coast Guard Auxiliary have been especially trained to provide free safety checks of recreational boats. The safety checks are conducted with the boater's consent to verify equipment compliance with all federal, state, and local boating regulations.

During the safety check, the Auxiliary's vessel examiner will explain both the value and function of your boat's safety equipment, plus discuss "Best Boating Practices" to ensure a safe, fun day on the water for you and your family and friends.

For more information, call the Coast Guard Auxiliary Public Information Hotline at 1-877-875-6296.

Take a Virtual Vessel Safety Check or Sign up for a VSC online! Visit our website: www.safetyseal.net

A Vessel Safety Check can reduce the potential for accidents and injury by educating you as to the value and use of marine safety equipment, and other best on-the-water safety practices.

A Vessel Safety Check may save you money by preventing citations due to noncompliance with federal, state, and local regulations, by identifying safety equipment–related insurance discounts, and by increasing awareness of "best practices" to avoid costly breakdowns or accidents.

- Personalized One-on-One Education
- An Informed Boater Is a Safer Boater
- It's FREE
- It's Fast
- It's NOT a Law Enforcement Activity
- Up-to-Date Federal, State, and Local Boating Regulations
- Other Safety Suggestions

DO YOU WANT TO
Be a Better Boater,
Learn from the Best,
Be Part of the Action . . .

THEN, VOLUNTEER TO MAKE A DIFFERENCE!

Consider furthering your boating knowledge and safety on the water by joining the U.S. Coast Guard Auxiliary.

WHO WE ARE

The U.S. Coast Guard Auxiliary is the uniformed, volunteer civilian component of the Coast Guard team. Created by an Act of Congress in 1939, the Auxiliary directly supports the Coast Guard in all their missions, except military and law enforcement actions. Auxiliary membership is open to U.S. citizens 17 years of age and older.

How You Can Help Make A Difference

As a member of the Coast Guard Auxiliary, you will be able to choose from many exciting opportunities for service:

- Help Save Lives—Through boating safety instruction in the classroom, through Vessel Safety Checks, or in on-the-water operations.
- Increase Your Skills—Take advantage of advanced training on the water, in leadership, or through many courses available through the Auxiliary and Coast Guard. As a member of the Auxiliary, there are no fees for any of these courses.
- Support the Coast Guard—Become qualified to serve at Coast Guard units in radio watchstanding,

Saving lives through education is a satisfying mission! (PHOTO BY JOSEPH CIRONE)

Vessel Safety Checks provide the opportunity to engage in individual safety education. (PHOTO BY BOB DENNIS)

One benefit of on-the-water training is assisting the Coast Guard in search-and-rescue missions. (PHOTO BY KEN SOMMERS)

marine environmental protection, Homeland Security, and other operational and administrative support.

- Fun and Fellowship—Enjoy the company of fellow Auxiliarists, whether during training missions, at meetings, or social events. We enjoy our work and we enjoy each other's company!

Join the over 30,000 men and women who have volunteered to make a difference!

Call the Coast Guard Auxiliary Public Information Infoline at 1-877-875-6296 or visit our website at www.cgaux.org and select "Join the Auxiliary."

Harbor patrol is another important function of the Auxiliary. (PHOTO BY MICHAEL BRODY)

Auxiliarists gather together for dinner after a day of Vessel Safety Checks. (PHOTO BY NOREEN FOLKERTS)

Become an
Associate Member

Interested in Supporting the
U.S. Coast Guard Auxiliary?

You can help by . . .

Your tax-deductible financial contribution to and/or Associate Membership in the Coast Guard Auxiliary Association, Inc., the financial support organization of the Auxiliary, can help in tremendous ways.

One-hundred percent (100%) of your contribution supports the activities, programs and missions of the United States Coast Guard Auxiliary—*America's Volunteer Lifesavers ®!*

Go to www.cgauxa.org for information on donating or becoming an Associate Member of the

**Coast Guard Auxiliary
Association, Inc.** CG AuxA

The Coast Guard Auxiliary Association, Inc. is a 501(c)(3) Non-profit Corporation under the laws of the District of Columbia for the purpose of supporting the U.S. Coast Guard Auxiliary and its missions with funds, support functions, and business management.

Coast Guard Auxiliary Association
9449 Watson Industrial Park
Saint Louis, MO 63126
314-962-8828
www.cgauxa.org

Preventative Boat Maintenance Checklist

These are suggested items for a typical small boat and trailer checklist. It is not all inclusive, and it may contain items that are not applicable to your boat. It is designed to assist in the preparation of your personalized checklist. (It does not include items to be checked before every departure, such as fuel.)

BOAT

- ☐ Alternator
- ☐ Anchor/rode
- ☐ Battery charger
- ☐ Battery connections
- ☐ Battery tie-downs
- ☐ Belts
- ☐ Bilge cleanliness
- ☐ Bilge pump
- ☐ Boathook
- ☐ Canopy
- ☐ Compass
- ☐ Deck railing
- ☐ Emergency flares/light
- ☐ Engine controls
- ☐ Engine exhaust
- ☐ Engine tune-up
- ☐ Fire extinguishers
- ☐ First-aid kit
- ☐ Fuel filter
- ☐ Fuel vents
- ☐ Gauges
- ☐ GPS/loran
- ☐ Horn

- ☐ Hoses
- ☐ Hull condition
- ☐ Hull lettering
- ☐ Life ring
- ☐ Lower unit condition
- ☐ Lower unit oil
- ☐ Navigation lights
- ☐ Power trim control
- ☐ Propeller
- ☐ Radar
- ☐ Radio
- ☐ Registration
- ☐ Rub rails
- ☐ Searchlights
- ☐ Seats
- ☐ Spare parts/storage
- ☐ Steering
- ☐ Throttle operation
- ☐ Tools
- ☐ Transducer
- ☐ VHF-FM radio/antenna
- ☐ Windshield wipers
- ☐ Wiring/terminals

TRAILER

- ☐ Brakes/fluid
- ☐ Hitch
- ☐ Jack
- ☐ Lights
- ☐ Rollers
- ☐ Safety chains
- ☐ Springs

- ☐ Tie-downs
- ☐ Trailer tires
- ☐ Wheel bearings
- ☐ Winch
- ☐ Winch cable
- ☐ Wiring

answer KEY

	Chapter 1		Chapter 2		Chapter 3		Chapter 4		Chapter 5		Chapter 6		Chapter 7
1.	j	1.	h	1.	f	1.	g	1.	i	1.	g	1.	e
2.	i	2.	f	2.	e	2.	e	2.	e	2.	c	2.	a
3.	a	3.	c	3.	c	3.	a	3.	b	3.	f	3.	f
4.	g	4.	j	4.	b	4.	d	4.	a	4.	e	4.	i
5.	b	5.	a	5.	j	5.	b	5.	c	5.	a	5.	g
6.	e	6.	b	6.	a	6.	i	6.	d	6.	h	6.	d
7.	h	7.	d	7.	d	7.	c	7.	f	7.	i	7.	j
8.	d	8.	e	8.	g	8.	j	8.	j	8.	d	8.	c
9.	c	9.	i	9.	i	9.	h	9.	g	9.	b	9.	b
10.	f	10.	g	10.	h	10.	f	10.	h	10.	j	10.	h

1-1	a	2-1	d	3-1	c	4-1	c	5-1	a	6-1	c	7-1	b
1-2	c	2-2	b	3-2	a	4-2	b	5-2	b	6-2	c	7-2	d
1-3	b	2-3	c	3-3	d	4-3	b	5-3	d	6-3	d	7-3	b
1-4	d	2-4	b	3-4	b	4-4	a	5-4	c	6-4	a	7-4	d
1-5	a	2-5	d	3-5	a	4-5	a	5-5	a	6-5	d	7-5	d
1-6	a	2-6	c	3-6	d	4-6	b	5-6	a	6-6	d	7-6	a
1-7	c	2-7	b	3-7	d	4-7	d	5-7	b	6-7	b	7-7	a
1-8	d	2-8	c	3-8	b	4-8	d	5-8	d	6-8	b	7-8	d
1-9	a	2-9	b	3-9	d	4-9	a	5-9	b	6-9	d	7-9	d
1-10	d	2-10	d	3-10	c	4-10	d	5-10	a	6-10	b	7-10	a
1-11	a	2-11	c	3-11	b	4-11	b	5-11	d	6-11	c	7-11	a
1-12	d	2-12	a	3-12	d	4-12	c	5-12	c	6-12	d	7-12	a
1-13	a	2-13	a	3-13	b	4-13	b	5-13	a	6-13	a	7-13	a
1-14	b	2-14	d	3-14	a	4-14	a	5-14	b	6-14	c	7-14	c
1-15	d	2-15	c	3-15	d	4-15	b	5-15	c	6-15	a	7-15	b
1-16	a	2-16	b	3-16	b	4-16	d	5-16	a	6-16	a	7-16	b
1-17	c	2-17	b	3-17	b	4-17	c	5-17	c	6-17	c	7-17	d
1-18	c	2-18	d	3-18	d	4-18	c	5-18	d	6-18	d	7-18	c
1-19	b	2-19	c	3-19	c	4-19	a	5-19	b	6-19	c	7-19	a
1-20	a	2-20	a	3-20	b	4-20	c	5-20	a	6-20	b	7-20	d
		2-21	b	3-21	c	4-21	d	5-21	c	6-21	c	7-21	a
		2-22	a	3-22	c	4-22	c			6-22	d	7-22	d
		2-23	d	3-23	d	4-23	d			6-23	d	7-23	a
		2-24	c	3-24	b					6-24	a	7-24	d
		2-25	d									7-25	d
												7-26	a

Chapter 8		Chapter 9		Chapter 10		Chapter 11		Chapter 12		Chapter 13	
1.	e	1.	f	1.	g	1.	h	1.	e	1.	g
2.	a	2.	d	2.	b	2.	a	2.	d	2.	h
3.	d	3.	a	3.	h	3.	d	3.	h	3.	d
4.	h	4.	j	4.	i	4.	c	4.	a	4.	a
5.	c	5.	g	5.	a	5.	j	5.	i	5.	j
6.	i	6.	b	6.	e	6.	i	6.	b	6.	c
7.	j	7.	i	7.	f	7.	g	7.	f	7.	i
8.	f	8.	c	8.	j	8.	b	8.	g	8.	f
9.	b	9.	h	9.	c	9.	e	9.	c	9.	e
10.	g	10.	e	10.	d	10.	f			10.	b
8-1	d	9-1	c	10-1	d	11-1	a	12-1	b	13-1	c
8-2	b	9-2	a	10-2	a	11-2	c	12-2	b	13-2	b
8-3	d	9-3	b	10-3	c	11-3	c	12-3	a	13-3	d
8-4	c	9-4	d	10-4	d	11-4	d	12-4	c	13-4	a
8-5	a	9-5	b	10-5	d	11-5	a	12-5	a	13-5	a
8-6	d	9-6	a	10-6	a	11-6	c	12-6	d	13-6	d
8-7	d	9-7	d	10-7	d	11-7	a	12-7	a	13-7	a
8-8	a	9-8	b	10-8	b	11-8	d	12-8	b	13-8	d
8-9	a	9-9	c	10-9	c	11-9	d	12-9	d	13-9	c
8-10	d	9-10	c	10-10	b	11-10	a	12-10	d	13-10	c
8-11	c	9-11	d	10-11	c	11-11	a	12-11	c	13-11	d
8-12	b	9-12	d	10-12	a	11-12	d	12-12	c	13-12	d
8-13	c	9-13	c	10-13	d	11-13	a	12-13	b	13-13	d
8-14	d	9-14	a	10-14	a	11-14	d	12-14	c	13-14	a
8-15	b	9-15	d	10-15	b	11-15	d	12-15	b	13-15	d
8-16	d	9-16	a	10-16	d	11-16	c	12-16	b	13-16	a
8-17	d	9-17	b	10-17	c	11-17	b	12-17	d	13-17	d
8-18	a	9-18	c	10-18	b	11-18	c	12-18	d	13-18	b
8-19	a	9-19	b	10-19	b	11-19	d	12-19	b	13-19	b
8-20	a	9-20	d	10-20	c	11-20	a	12-20	b	13-20	c
8-21	d	9-21	c	10-21	a	11-21	c	12-21	a	13-21	c
		9-22	a	10-22	c	11-22	a	12-22	c	13-22	b
		9-23	c	10-23	c			12-23	c	13-23	b
		9-24	b	10-24	a			12-24	d	13-24	c
								12-25	b	13-25	d

abaft: Toward the rear (stern) of the boat. Behind.

abeam: At right angles to the keel of the boat, but not on the boat.

adjusting a compass: A good compass has internal magnets to adjust it for magnetic influences aboard a boat that cause compass error. Otherwise adjusting should be done by a professional.

adrift: Floating loose, not on moorings or towline.

advection fog: A type of fog that occurs when warm air moves over colder land or water surfaces; the greater the difference between the air temperature and the underlying surface temperature, the denser the fog.

aft: At the stern or back of a vessel.

aground: A vessel touching or fast to the bottom.

aid to navigation (ATON): Lighthouses, lights, buoys, sound signals, racon, radiobeacons, electronic aids, and other markers on land or sea specifically intended to help navigators determine position or safe course, or to warn them of dangers or obstructions to navigation.

air-cooled engine: A motor such as a small outboard that is cooled by having air blown over it.

alternating current (AC): An electric current, usually 120 volts, that reverses its direction at regularly recurring intervals.

alternator: An electric generator for producing alternating current.

altocumulus clouds: "Piled up" clouds at middle altitudes.

altostratus: A cloud formation similar to cirrostratus but darker and at a lower level.

amateur radio: Shortwave radio useful in marine and other emergencies. Operates in eight frequency bands and can often reach around the globe.

amidships: In or toward the center portion of the vessel.

ammeter: An instrument for measuring electric current in amps.

amp draw: The amount of electrical current a radio set uses when sending or receiving a message.

anchor: Device used to secure a boat to the bottom of a body of water.

anchor bend: The most secure knot for bending a line to an object.

antifreeze: A substance added to a liquid, such as the water in an engine, to lower its freezing point.

aquatic nuisance species (ANS): Foreign plants and animals that are invading U.S. waters.

articulated beacon: A beacon-like buoyant structure, tethered directly to the seabed and having no watch circle. Called "articulated light" or "articulated daybeacon," as appropriate.

astern: Behind the vessel. Direction of movement, opposite of ahead.

athwartships: Across or at right angles to the centerline of a boat; rowboat seats are generally placed athwartships (thwarts).

audio output: Tells the loudness of a radio.

available channels: The VHF-FM frequency band includes 73 channels of which 55 are in use in the United States.

backfire flame arrester: A part of an engine that prevents a fire or explosion when the fuel ignites and a backfire occurs.

back splice: A method of splicing rope that is an alternative to whipping the rope end; it increases rope diameter by 40% and provides a handle.

band: A range of radio frequencies, such as the medium-frequency band or the high-frequency band.

barometer: An instrument for measuring the air pressure.

barometric pressure: The pressure of the atmosphere; usually expressed in terms of the height of a column of mercury.

beam: The greatest width of the boat.

bearing: The direction to an object, given as a horizontal angle from a line of reference.

bearing compass: A handheld compass used to take bearings and determine your position.

becket: A looped rope, hook and eye, strap, or grommet used for holding ropes, wires or spars in position.

belay: To make a line fast. Also a command to stop.

bend: To attach a line to another line. Also, to attach a line to a spar or stay.

bight: A long and gradual bend or recess in the coastline that forms a large, open receding bay. Also, a bend in a river or mountain range. Also, a curve made in a rope by doubling it back on itself.

bilge: The lowest spaces in a vessel's hull.

bilge pump: Pump used to clear water or liquid from the bilge.

binocular: A tool used to magnify objects that is particularly useful in piloting.

bitt: A heavy and firmly mounted piece of wood or metal used for securing lines.

bitter end: The inboard end of a rope or cable.

black box: A small computer used in a gasoline fuel injection system.

block: A device consisting of a case enclosing one or more sheaves through which a line may be led to increase mechanical advantage or to change direction.

boathook: A pole with a hook or spike at the end, commonly used to facilitate line handling.

bollard: A heavy post set into the edge of a wharf or pier to which the lines of a ship may be made fast.

bolt rope: Line attached to the foot and luff of a sail to give it strength or to enable it to be attached to the spars.

boom: A spar attached horizontally to the mast for extending the foot of the sail.

boomkin: A short spar or structure projecting from the stern of a vessel to which the mizzen sail is sheeted.

bottoms, types of: The types of ocean bottom materials such as sand, clay, and mud that are described on nautical charts.

bow: Forward end of a vessel.

bow bitt: A post fixed on the deck of a ship near the bow for securing lines.

bow line: A docking line leading from the bow.

bowline: A knot used to form a temporary eye in the end of a line.

bowsprit: A spar extending forward from the bow.

braided rope: A rope made by interweaving individual fibers or by weaving three or four strands of fiber.

branch: The upper or lower half of a line of longitude or meridian that passes through both geographic poles.

breaking wave: A wave cresting with the top breaking down over its face.

bridge clearance: Vertical datum of a chart tells how much vertical clearance there is under a bridge.

broach: The uncontrolled turning of a boat parallel to the waves, subjecting it to possible capsizing.

broad on the bow: A direction midway between abeam and dead ahead.

buoy: A floating aid to navigation of defined shape and color, which is anchored at a given position and serves as an aid to navigation.

cable: A large line made by twisting ropes together. Cables are used on tugboats and to moor large vessels.

call sign: Unique letter-and-number vessel identifier issued to vessels that are required to carry radio equipment and also to voluntary vessels calling at foreign ports.

calling channel: The designated channel for station-to-station contact and distress calling.

cam cleat: A cleat with two moving, serrated cam-shaped jaws for holding a line. The spring-loaded jaws rotate open to release the line when you pull on it, and the cleat tightens when the standing part of the line pulls against it.

capsize: To turn a vessel bottom side up.

carbon dioxide: A heavy colorless gas that does not support combustion and is formed in animal and human respiration.

carbon monoxide: A colorless, odorless, and highly poisonous gas that has about the same weight as air and mixes readily with it.

carburetor: An apparatus for supplying an internal combustion engine with an explosive mixture of vaporized fuel and air.

caulk: To stop up and make watertight by filling with a waterproof compound or material.

cavitation: The rapid building and subsequent explosion of bubbles caused by, and interfering with, the action of the propeller. Destroys lift, and can actually damage the metal, the propeller, and supports.

centerboard: A plate, in a vertical fore-and-aft plane, that is pivoted at the lower forward end, and can be lowered or raised through a slot in the bottom of the boat to reduce leeway; movable keel used by sailboats.

centerline: An imaginary line down the middle of a vessel from bow to stern.

center of gravity: Point in a vessel where the sum of all moments is zero. With the vessel at rest, the center of gravity and the center of buoyancy are always in a direct vertical line.

chafing: The wearing away of lines as they rub against hard surfaces, which weakens them. Chafing can be prevented by wrapping lines with canvas or leather where they pass through chocks.

chain: A cluster of land antennas located usually along a shoreline that are part of loran. A chain consists of one master and one or more slave antennas.

channel selector: The dial or button used on any of several possible pieces of equipment to switch from the calling channel to a working channel during a transmission to another vessel or a coastal station.

chart: A printed or electronic geographic representation generally showing such things as depths of water, aids to navigation, dangers, and adjacent land features useful to mariners.

chock: A metal fitting through which anchor or mooring lines are led. May be open or closed.

circuit breaker: A switch that automatically interrupts an electric circuit under an infrequent abnormal condition.

cirrostratus: A fairly uniform layer of high stratus clouds darker than cirrus.

cirrus: A wispy cloud usually of minute ice crystals formed at altitudes of 20,000 to 40,000 feet.

citizens band radio: A range of radio wave frequencies that in the United States is allocated for private radio communications.

cleat: A fitting to which lines are made fast. The classic cleat to which lines are belayed, approximately anvil-shaped.

clew: The after, lower corner of a sail.

clove hitch: A hitch for temporarily fastening a line to a spar, ring, post, or piling.

coast station: The radio station at a land-based post; for example, a U.S. Coast Guard unit, a tugboat company, or a fishing company.

coil: To lay a line down in circular turns.

cold front: An advancing edge of a cold air mass.

color-code lines: Using a material such as an air-drying plastic to make the end of each line a different color. This is particularly useful on a sailboat where several lines end near each other.

COLREGS 72: The 1972 International Regulations for Prevention of Collisions at Sea, commonly called the International Rules.

commercial messages: Messages that concern economic and commercial matters directly related to the use of a boat.

compass: Instrument for determining direction.

compass rose: A circle graduated in degrees, clockwise from 000 at true north to 360. It may also be graduated in points. It is printed on nautical charts for determining directions.

condenser: An apparatus in which gas or vapor is condensed.

cooling system: Any of several systems used to cool an internal combustion engine by using things such as air or water.

Coriolis force: The deflective effect of the earth's rotation on an object in motion that causes it to divert to the right in the northern hemisphere and the left in the southern hemisphere.

correcting a compass: You can correct a compass reading to tell its direction with reference to true north.

corrosion: To wear metals away gradually, usually by chemical action.

course line: The horizontal direction in which a vessel is steered or intended to be steered, expressed as angular distance from north.

course plotting: Drawing a line on a chart from where you are to where you want to go.

crankcase: A case in an engine that holds oil to lubricate moving engine parts.

cruiser: A somewhat more seaworthy craft that usually affords some sort of living quarters.

cuddy: A small shelter cabin in a boat.

cumulonimbus: A cumulus cloud often spread out in the shape of an anvil extending to great heights.

cumulus clouds: Clouds with vertical development.

current usage: The amount of electrical current a radio set uses, or the amp draw.

cyclone: A storm that rotates about a system of low atmospheric pressure, advances at a speed of 20 to 30 mph, and often brings heavy rain.

daggerboard: A plate, in a vertical fore-and-aft plane, that can be lowered through a slot in the bottom of a sailboat to reduce leeway.

Danforth anchor: A patented lightweight anchor characterized by long narrow twin flukes pivoted at one end of the relatively long shank.

datum: The technical term for the baseline from which a chart's vertical measurements are made (i.e., heights of land or landmarks, or depths of water).

davits: Mechanical arms extending over the side or stern of a vessel, or over a seawall, to raise or lower a smaller boat.

daybeacon: A fixed structure having one or more daymarks, which is used in shallow water.

daymark: A signboard attached to a fixed structure to convey navigational information presenting one of several standard shapes (square, triangle, rectangle, diamond, octagon) and colors (red, green, orange, yellow, or black). Daymarks usually have reflective material indicating their shapes.

dead ahead: A relative bearing of 000°.

dead reckoning (DR): The practice of estimating position by advancing a known position for course and distance run. The effects of wind and current are not considered in determining a position by dead reckoning.

decibel (dB): A unit of measure for expressing the relative intensity of sounds.

deep-cycle battery: A kind of battery used in a marine engine that can be discharged and then recharged.

depth sounder: An electrical device used with charts showing water depths to plot courses.

deviation: The effect of the vessel's magnetic fields upon a compass. Deviation is the difference between the direction that the compass actually points and the direction that the compass would point if there were no magnetic fields aboard the vessel.

dew point: The temperature at which a vapor begins to condense.

Differential GPS (DGPS): A land-based supplement to GPS, which corrected the error introduced by Selected Availability (SA). This was necessary to provide continuously accurate information around harbors and inlets, where SA degraded the information enough to become dangerous.

digital selective calling (DSC): A technique using digital codes that enables a radio station to establish contact with, and transfer information to, another station.

dike: A man-made structure projecting from the shore into a waterway to control shoaling and to maintain a navigable channel.

dinghy: A small open boat. A dinghy is often used as a tender for a larger craft.

dip the eye: To bring the eye of a line up through the eye of a line that is already on a piling and then drop it over the piling. This way the line already there can be removed first.

direct current (DC): A constant electric current that flows in only one direction.

direct drive: The simplest, least expensive, and most trouble free of all inboard engine installations.

directional light: A light illuminating a sector or very narrow angle and intended to mark a direction to be followed.

direction finder: Equipment used by search-and-rescue services and salvage operators to locate the approximate source of radio emissions.

displacement hull: A type of hull that plows through the water displacing a weight of water equal to its own weight, even when more power is added.

distress communication form: A form for boaters to complete and post near the radiotelephone to help them remember the steps to take in an emergency.

distress signal. See *Mayday*.

distress system: The system of emergency visual, audible, and radio signals used to attract attention and get help.

distributor: An apparatus for directing the secondary current from the induction coil to the various spark plugs in an engine in the proper firing order.

diurnal: Having a period or cycle of approximately one tidal day. Thus the tide is said to be diurnal when only one high water and one low water occur during a tidal day, and the tidal current is said to be diurnal when there is a single flood and single ebb period in the tidal day. A rotary current is diurnal if it changes its direction through all points of the compass once each tidal day.

dividers: An instrument consisting of two pointed legs joined by a pivot, and used principally for measuring distances or coordinates. An instrument having one pointed leg and the other carrying a pen or pencil is called a "drafting compass."

documentation: A special federal license or registration for a vessel. A vessel of 5 or more net tons, owned by a U.S. citizen, may be documented as a yacht. The process is administered by the U.S. Coast Guard.

dolphin: A structure consisting of a number of piles driven into the seabed or riverbed in a circular pattern and drawn together with wire rope. Used for mooring and to protect other structures.

double-braid rope: Braided rope that has an outer braided cover over a separate inner braided core.

double sheet bend: A secure knot used to tie together two lines of unequal diameter.

draft: The vertical depth from the bottom of the keel to the top of the water.

drag: The forces opposing the direction of motion due to components such as friction and profile.

electronic charting: Charting a course using tools such as GPS (global positioning system).

emergency call: A call made using a radiotelephone to get help during an emergency.

emergency position-indicating radio beacon (EPIRB): A device that emits a continuous radio signal alerting authorities to the existence of a distress situation and leading rescuers to the scene.

engine, diesel: An engine that burns diesel fuel and operates more efficiently than a gasoline engine.

engine, four-cycle: An engine that requires two revolutions of its internal parts to complete the internal combustion process.

engine, gasoline: An engine that burns gasoline.

engine, two-cycle: An engine that requires one revolution of its internal parts to complete the internal combustion process.

engine power: As of September 1, 1989, all measures of engine power are made at their propeller shafts except for inboard engines sold without transmissions.

equator: Great circle formed by passing a plane perpendicular to the axis of rotation of the earth at a point 90° from the north and south poles.

eye splice: A permanent loop spliced in the end of a line.

fairway: The main thoroughfare of shipping in a harbor or channel.

faking: Laying out a line in long flat bights, that will pay out freely without bights or kinks.

fathom: A nautical measure of length, 6 feet, used for measuring water depth and length of anchor rode.

Federal Communications Commission (FCC): The federal government organization that manages the radio spectrum within the United States.

fender: A cushion, placed between boats, or between a boat and a pier, to prevent damage.

ferrule: A nylon or metal fitting at the bottom of an antenna.

fetch: The unobstructed distance over which the wind blows across the surface of the water.

fiberglass: Resin reinforced with fibrous glass (or glass-reinforced plastic) used in boat construction. Its forms are mat, cloth, woven roving, and chopped strands.

fid: A tapered, pointed tool used to separate strands of rope when splicing.

figure-eight knot: A knot in the form of a figure eight usually tied at the end of a line as a stopper to keep the end of the line from passing through a block or fairlead.

fisherman's bend: A hitch for making fast to a mooring buoy or spar or to the ring of an anchor.

fitting: Generic term for any part or piece of machinery or installed equipment.

fix: A geographical position determined by passing close aboard an object of known position determined by the intersection of two more lines of position (LOPs) adjusted to a common time, determined from terrestrial, electronic, and/or celestial data. The accuracy, or quality, of a fix is of great importance, especially in coastal waters, and dependent on a number of factors.

fixed light: A light showing continuously and steadily, as opposed to a rhythmic light. (Do not confuse with "fixed" as used to differentiate from "floating.")

flashing light: A light in which the total duration of light in each period is clearly shorter than the total duration of darkness, and the flashes of light are all of equal duration. This term is commonly used for a light that exhibits only single flashes that are repeated at regular intervals.

flemish: A decorative method of coiling a line flat on the deck or dock.

floating aid to navigation: A buoy that is secured in its assigned position by a mooring.

float plan: A document that describes the route(s) and estimated time of arrival for a particular voyage. The float plan generally includes description of the vessel, radio and safety equipment carried, planned stops, names of passengers, and other pertinent information.

flood current: The horizontal movement of a tidal current toward shore or upstream in a tidal river or estuary. In the mixed type of reversing tidal current, the terms "greater flood" and "lesser flood" are applied respectively to the flood currents of greater and lesser speed of each day. The terms "maximum flood" and "minimum flood" are applied to the maximum and minimum speeds of a flood current having a speed that alternately increases and decreases without coming to a slack or reversing.

fluke: The flat palm-shaped or shovel-shaped part of an anchor that digs in to prevent dragging.

foot rope: A rope used to help control sails on a sailboat.

forward: Toward the bow of the boat.

fraying lines: When the ends of lines begin to come apart, which can be prevented through treatments such as tying, heating, or taping the ends.

frequency setting: A frequency is the number of vibrations or radio waves per unit of time. It determines the pitch of a sound and is reckoned in cycles per second with one up-and-down vibration or oscillation equaling one cycle, called a Hertz.

front: The juncture or boundary between two air masses of different temperatures.

gain: Antennas differ in gain; the higher the gain, the farther you can communicate.

galley: The kitchen area of a boat.

galvanic action: An electrical current that passes between two dissimilar metals when they are immersed in a solution such as salt water and that will eat away one of the metals.

gasoline, leaded: Gasoline to which lead has been added to lubricate and protect exhaust valve seats in engines and to raise the octane rating.

gasoline octane rating: A measure of a fuel's resistance to premature detonation, or detonation before ignition.

general information block: A block of information on a nautical chart that gives information such as the chart's projection, its scale, and its vertical and horizontal datums, or benchmarks from which a chart's vertical and horizontal measurements are made.

give-way vessel: A term from the Navigation Rules used to describe the vessel that must yield to another in a situation where risk of collision exists. (Formerly called "the burdened vessel.")

Global Maritime Distress and Safety System (GMDSS): A worldwide system for dealing with distress situations at sea.

global positioning system (GPS): A satellite-based radio navigation system that provides precise, continuous, worldwide, all-weather, three-dimensional navigation for land, sea, and air appplications.

government channels: Eight radio channels that are blocked and reserved for government use: 3, 21, 23, 61, 64, 81, 82, and 83.

grapnel: A straight-shank anchor with four or five curved claw-like arms and no stock; used mostly for recovering lost articles or objects.

ground fault circuit interrupter (GFCI): A device used to protect a wired circuit from becoming dangerous.

ground tackle: A collective term for the anchor and its associated gear.

gunwale: The upper edge of a boat's sides.

half hitch: The simplest kind of hitch; a knot made by passing the end of the rope around the rope and then through the loop just made.

halyard: A line or wire used to hoist a spar, sail, or flag.

"ham." See *amateur radio.*

handheld radio: A portable type of VHF-FM radio commonly used on boats.

harbor chart: A chart that shows the features of the harbor, anchorages, and protection for ships.

hatch: An opening in a boat's deck fitted with a watertight cover.

hawser: A heavy rope or cable used for mooring or towing.

head: A marine toilet. Also the upper corner of triangular sail.

heading: The instantaneous direction of a vessel's bow. It is expressed as the angular distance relative to north, usually 000°, clockwise through 359°. "Heading" should not be confused with "course." A heading is constantly changing as a vessel yaws back and forth across the course due to the effects of sea, wind, and steering error. It is expressed in degrees of either true, magnetic, or compass direction.

headway: The forward motion of a boat through the water. Opposite of "sternway."

heat exchanger: A part on an engine that cools water as it passes through.

heave-to: To bring a vessel up in a position where it will maintain little or no headway, usually with the bow into the wind or nearly so. To stop.

helm: The wheel or tiller controlling the rudder.

helmsperson: The person who steers the boat. ("Helmsman" is the traditional name.)

hitch: A knot used to secure a rope to an object or to another rope.

hold: A compartment belowdeck in a large vessel, used solely for carrying cargo.

horn cleat: An anvil-shaped fitting used for tying up anchor rodes, mooring and docking lines, sheets, and halyards.

horse latitudes: Either of two belts or regions near 30°N and 30°S latitude characterized by high pressure, calms, and light baffling winds.

horsepower: A unit of power equal, in the United States, to 746 watts.

houseboat: A popular modification of the cruiser, which can offer all the conveniences of home.

hull identification number (HIN): A number that includes the manufacturer's identification code, hull serial number, date of certification, and model year, displayed on the boat's hull.

humidity: Moisture in the air.

hurricane: A large, tropical storm, measuring hundreds of miles in diameter, having steady winds in excess of 64 knots. It is called a typhoon on the Pacific Ocean and a cyclone on the Indian Ocean.

hydrometer: An instrument used to determine the specific gravity of a liquid and hence its strength.

hypothermia: A lowering of the core body temperature due to exposure to cold water or air resulting in a subnormal body temperature that can be dangerous or fatal.

impeller: A rubber, neoprene, or stainless steel device within a water pump that pumps water and circulates it throughout a marine engine, or through the nozzle of a jet drive.

imposing silence: A vessel in distress or the station in control of distress communications may impose silence on any station that interferes by sending "Seelonce Mayday."

inboard engine: An engine toward the center of a ship, inside the hull.

inboard-outboard powered: A propulsion arrangement that places the engine inside the boat against the transom. The driveshaft passes through the transom and into a stern-drive unit that resembles the lower half of an outboard motor and contains the reduction gear and propeller shaft.

inboard-powered: A propulsion arrangement in which the engine and reduction gear are mounted inside the hull, and power is transmitted to the propeller through a driveshaft that penetrates the hull.

induction system: A system in a gasoline-powered internal combustion engine that brings fuel and air together and then mixes them in the proper proportion, vaporizes the mixture, and delivers it to the engine.

international channels: The channels used in foreign countries that in some instances have different frequencies than those used in the United States.

intership safety channel: The internationally defined frequency (VHF Channel 6, 156.300 MHz) for search-and-rescue and salvage operations.

Intracoastal Waterway (ICW): An inland waterway that runs parallel to the Atlantic and Gulf coasts from Manasquan Inlet on the New Jersey shore to Brownsville, Texas.

isolation switch: A switch used to disconnect batteries from the electrical system on a boat.

jam cleat: Similar to a horn cleat, but one of its horns forms a tapered slot into which the line is jammed.

jet drive: A propulsion arrangement in which an inboard engine is used to drive a high-capacity pump that forces water through a nozzle to achieve thrust. Steering is achieved by changing the direction of thrust.

Jet Ski: Trademark name for a personal watercraft that uses a jet drive instead of a propeller.

jet stream: A long narrow current of high-speed winds blowing from a generally westerly direction and often exceeding a speed of 250 mph.

jibsheet: The line, usually paired, that controls the athwartships movement of the jib.

keel: The main structural member of a vessel running fore and aft; the backbone of a vessel.

"king of knots": Another name for the bowline because of its many everyday uses on boats and elsewhere.

knot (kn or kt): A measure of speed equal to 1 nautical mile (6,076 feet) per hour.

knot: A fastening made by interweaving rope to form a stopper, to enclose or bind an object, to form a loop or noose, to tie a small rope to an object, or to tie the ends of two small ropes together.

laid rope: Rope made by twisting fibers together to form yarns.

land station: A radio station on land, such as a Coast Guard station.

latitude: Angular distance north or south of the equator expressed in degrees from 0 to 90, and labeled north or south to indicate the direction of measurement; e.g., Lat. 35°N.

lay: To "lay a mark" is to be able to reach it without tacking. The lay of a line is the direction in which its strands are twisted, usually to the right.

lead line: A weighted line used to measure the depth of the water.

leeward: The direction away from the wind. Opposite of "windward."

liaison channel: Channel 22A, a working channel of the U.S. Coast Guard.

light: The signal emitted by a lighted aid to navigation. The illuminating apparatus used to emit the light signal. A lighted aid to navigation on a fixed structure.

lighthouse: A lighted beacon of major importance that assists the mariner in determining his position or safe course, or warns of obstructions or dangers to navigation.

line of position (LOP): A line of bearing to a known origin or reference, upon which a vessel is assumed to be located. An LOP is determined by observation (visual bearing) or measurement (RDF, loran, radar, etc.). An LOP is assumed to be a straight line for visual bearings, or an arc of a circle (radar range), or part of some other curve such as a hyperbola (loran). LOPs resulting from visual observations (magnetic bearings) are generally converted to true bearings prior to plotting on a chart.

line-of-sight transmission: Communication when one antenna can "see" another. VHF-FM is a line-of-sight system that reaches only a little way beyond the horizon.

lines: A general term for rope used aboard a boat, but especially rope used for a specific function.

line whipping: Treating the end of a line with Dacron or nylon whipping twine to keep it from unraveling temporarily.

list: Permanent leaning of a vessel to one side.

longitude: Distance east or west of the prime meridian expressed in degrees from 0 to 180 east or west; e.g., Long. 123°W.

long splice: A method of joining two ropes without increasing the diameter of the rope. Normally used when line must pass through a block or over a fairlead without jamming.

loran: An acronym of **lo**ng **ra**nge **n**avigation; an electronic navigation system that uses a chain of transmitting stations to allow mariners and aviators with specialized receivers to determine their geographical positions.

lubber's line: An index mark or permanent line on a compass, which is used to read the compass heading of a vessel.

magnetic compass: A compass for indicating any horizontal reference direction relative to the earth's magnetic field and magnetic north. It is equipped with a graduated compass card (which is balanced and is free to turn in a horizontal plane), and a lubber's line, which serves as a reference point for direction indication.

magnetic north: The northerly direction of the earth's magnetic field indicated by the north-seeking pole of a compass needle.

magneto: An alternator with permanent magnets used to generate current for the ignition of an internal combustion engine.

major lights: A light of high intensity and reliability exhibited from a fixed structure or on a marine site (except range lights). Major lights include primary seacoast lights and secondary lights.

MariTEL: Private marine telephone business that once provided ship-to-shore telephone and data services.

maritime control channel: Channel 17, used to talk to ships and coast stations operated by state or local governments. The message must be about regulation and control, boating activities, or assistance to ships.

Maritime Mobile Service Identity (MMSI) number: A unique serial number that identifies an individual vesssel, a group of vessels, or a coast station. Required for use with digital selective calling equipment.

marlinespike: A spike for opening the strands of a rope while splicing. The art of handling and working rope.

Mayday: Spoken international distress signal, repeated three times, given to indicate that a mobile station is threatened by grave and imminent danger and requests immediate assistance.

mean high water (MHW): A tidal datum that is the average of all high water heights observed over a specific 19-year cycle.

mean lower low water (MLLW): A tidal datum that is the average of the lowest low water heights of each tidal day observed over a specific 19-year cycle.

measuring rope: Once done by a rope's circumference, but now usually done by its diameter.

Mercator projection: The projection technique most commonly used in the production of navigational charts. This is a cylindrical projection ingeniously modified by expanding the scale at increasing latitudes to preserve directions and to maintain the correct relationships between the latitude and longitude scales.

meridian (geographic meridian): A great circle of the earth passing through both the geographic poles and any given point on the earth's surface.

minor lights: An automatic unmanned light on a fixed structure usually showing low to moderate intensity. Minor lights are established in harbors, along channels, along rivers, and in isolated locations.

mixed tide: Type of tide with a large inequality in the high or low or both water heights, with two high waters and two low waters usually occurring each tidal day. Actually, all tides are mixed, but the name is usually applied to the tides intermediate to those predominantly semidiurnal and those predominantly diurnal.

mooring: Chain or synthetic line that attaches a floating object to a stationary object (e.g., dock, mooring buoy).

mooring cleat. See *horn cleat*.

mooring line: The line, often made of nylon, used to secure a boat to a mooring buoy or pier.

mushroom anchor: A stockless anchor with a cast-iron bowl at the end of the shank; used principally in large sizes for permanent moorings.

National Ocean Service (NOS): An agency of the National Oceanic and Atmospheric Administration that publishes charts of all U.S. waters other than those used on navigable rivers. It also makes data available showing the times and levels of predicted tides for the Atlantic, Gulf, and Pacific coasts and for tidal rivers.

National Weather Service (NWS): A division of the National Oceanic and Atmospheric Administration that gives accurate weather forecasts.

natural fiber rope: Rope made of natural fibers such as manila, sisal, hemp, jute, cotton, and flax.

nautical chart: Printed or electronic geographic representation of waterways showing positions of aids to navigation and other fixed points and references to guide the mariner.

nautical mile (nm): Length of 1 minute of latitude, approximately 6,076 feet compared to 5,280 feet per a statute mile.

navigable waters: Coastal waters, including bays, sounds, rivers, and lakes, that are navigable from the sea.

navigation: The art and science of locating your position (knowing where you are) and how to get where you want to go (plotting a course).

navigational channel: A bridge-to-bridge radio channel available to all ships; the messages must be about vessel navigation.

Navigation Rules: Regulations governing the movement of vessels in relation to each other, formerly Rules of the Road.

nimbus: A rain cloud or thunderhead.

noncommercial channel: A channel used to send messages about the needs of a vessel, such as fishing reports, rendezvous, repair scheduling, and berthing.

Northill anchor: An anchor with a stock at the crown instead of at the head. The arm is at right angles to the shank and the broad flukes are set at an angle carefully designed to assure a quick bite and penetration of the bottom.

no-wake zone: An area where you must slow your vessel so it does not make either a bow or stern wake; usually this means the vessel is off plane and level in the water.

nylon rope: Rope made of the synthetic fiber nylon does not shrink when wet, stretches more than any other synthetic or natural fiber rope, and resists chafing.

occulting light: A light in which the total duration of light in each period is clearly longer than the total duration of darkness and in which the intervals of darkness (occultations) are all of equal duration. (Commonly used for a single occulting light that exhibits only single occultations, which are repeated at regular intervals.)

operating cycle: The cycle by which a marine engine operates, either two- or four-cycle.

operations message: A message about navigation or the movement or management of vessels.

outboard: Toward or beyond the boat's sides, opposite of inboard. A detachable engine mounted on a boat's stern.

outboard-powered: The engine is mounted outside the hull on the transom.

outdrive: The system of engine gears mounted outside the boat on the transom.

overhand knot: Used as a stopper or to prevent a freshly cut rope from unlaying or unraveling. Tied by making an overhand loop in the standing part of the line, then passing the working end up through the loop and pulling it tight.

painter: A line attached to the bow of a small boat for use in towing or making fast.

Pan-Pan: Spoken urgency signal, repeated three times, used when the safety of a vessel or person is in jeopardy.

parallel of latitude: Any of the imaginary lines parallel to the equator and representing latitude.

parallel rulers: An instrument for transferring a line parallel to itself, used in chartwork for drawing and measuring courses or bearings.

part: To sever or otherwise break apart, as a line.

pay out: To ease out a line, or let it run in a controlled manner.

pendant: A line by which a boat is made fast to a buoy.

pennant: A small flag, most often a signal flag.

personal flotation device (PFD): A life jacket that, when properly used, will support a person in the water. Available in several sizes and types.

personal locator beacon (PLB): A device worn by an individual that emits a continuous radio signal alerting authorities of a distress situation. See *emergency position indicating radio beacon (ERIRB)*.

personal watercraft (PWC): A small motorized vessel powered by a jet-drive engine.

phonetic alphabet: Used when radio signals are weak and reception is poor to express words by saying each letter in a clear and particular way.

phonetic numbers: Used when radio signals are weak and reception is poor to express numbers in a clear and particular way.

pile (piling): A long, heavy timber driven into the seabed or riverbed to serve as a support for an aid to navigation or dock.

piloting: Navigation involving frequent or continuous reference to charted objects and landmarks, ATONs, and depth soundings.

pitchpoling: A boat being thrown end-over-end in rough seas.

pivot point: A point somewhat aft of the bow, somewhere forward of the midpoint. To an observer on board, a vessel appears to turn about its pivot point.

planing: A boat is said to be planing when its displacement decreases, it lifts itself over its bow wave, and it moves on the top of the water at high speeds.

polyconic projection: A map or chart projection in which the earth is projected on a series of cones concentric with the earth's axis and tangent to the sphere of the earth. Charts of the Great Lakes are typically based on the polyconic projection.

polyester rope: A synthetic fiber rope often used for sheets and halyards; aka Dacron, Terylene, etc.

polypropylene rope: The least costly of the common synthetic ropes; major advantage is that it floats.

port: The left side of a boat looking forward. A harbor.

port operations channel: A radio channel used to direct the movement of ships in or near ports, locks, or waterways.

position: On the earth this refers to the actual geographic location of a vessel defined by two parameters called coordinates. Those customarily used are latitude and longitude. Position may also be expressed as a bearing and distance from an object, the position of which is known.

pram: A small utility boat (8 to 10 feet long) with a wide beam relative to its length; used as a tender.

preferred channel mark: An aid to navigation that indicates a channel junction or bifurcation between a main (preferred) and a subordinate channel. Its color scheme and its light characteristics or its shape assist the navigator in identifying the preferred channel.

prime meridian: The meridian passing through Greenwich, England, from which both east and west longitude are measured; i.e., the 0° meridian.

private aid to navigation (PATON): Any aid to navigation that is not established and maintained by the U.S. Coast Guard.

procedure words (prowords): An oral shorthand used to express common words and phrases in radiotelephone communication.

propeller: A device consisting of a central hub with radiating blades forming a helical pattern that when turned in the water creates a discharge that drives a boat.

public correspondence: Ship-to-shore radiotelephone communications through a public coast radio station.

pulpit: A platform built forward of a vessel's bow currently used to assist in raising or lowering an anchor but formerly the place where a harpooner stood.

push-to-talk button: A button on a microphone that you press to begin sending a radio message.

quarter: The sides of a boat aft of amidships.

quick light: A light with more than 50 but less than 80 flashes per minute. (Previously called quick flashing light.)

radar: Self-contained navigation and collision avoidance system consisting of a shipboard transmitter and receiver. The transmitter transmits briefly, then shuts off to permit the receiver to "listen" for the reflected transmission or echo.

radiobeacon: Electronic apparatus that transmits a radio signal for use in providing a mariner a line of position.

radio check: Spoken test call by a boater asking what the strength and clarity of the transmission is; a response indicates one's radio is working.

radio direction finding (RDF): Older short-range radio navigation system consisting of a series of land-based stations broadcasting in the LF/MF band and onboard receivers with directional antennas.

radio language: Special words used to transmit radio messages quickly and clearly.

radio station log: A record of calls made and received by a radio station.

range: The distance in nautical miles that the vessel can travel with the available fuel on board. The range may or may not include an allowance for a fuel reserve. Range is a function of throttle setting and other factors.

ranges: A pair of ATONs placed a suitable distance apart, with the far daymark mounted higher than the near one. When the range marks are in line, the vessel is in the channel. Ranges can also be established by any charted objects.

reciprocal bearing or course: A bearing or course that differs from the original by 180°.

reciprocal direction: Corresponding but reversed direction.

red, right, returning: Saying to remember which aids you should be seeing off the vessel's starboard side when returning from seaward.

red sector: A sector of the circle of visibility of a navigational light in which a red light is exhibited. Such sectors are designated by their limiting bearings, as observed at some point other than the light. Red sectors are often located such that they warn of danger to vessels.

reef knot: A square knot used to secure a reefed sail to a boom.

reformulated gasoline: A cleaner-burning fuel that contains a "chemical oxygen," which is either an alcohol or an ether.

regulatory mark: A white and orange aid to navigation with no lateral significance. Used to indicate a special meaning to the mariner, such as danger, restricted operations, or an exclusion area.

restricted visibility: Any condition in which visibility is restricted by fog, mist, falling snow, heavy rainstorms, sandstorms, or other similar causes.

rigging: The general term for all the lines of a vessel.

rolling hitch: A hitch made by tying one line to the standing part of another; used to tie a line to the working end of a second line.

rope: Cordage made of natural or synthetic fibers; can also be made of steel wire.

rudder: A vertical plate or board that can be pivoted to steer a boat.

runabout: A small, sporty craft intended for general use such as day cruising, waterskiing, and fishing.

running rigging: Sheets, halyards, topping lifts, downhauls, vangs, etc., used for raising and adjusting sails.

sacrificial zincs: Zinc plates or bars used to prevent destruction of metal parts on engines by galvanic action.

safety call: A DSC alert to all stations to warn of hazards to normal waterway use.

safety signal. See Sécurité.

sail stop: A tie used to hold a lowered sail to its boom.

samson post: A single bitt in the bow or stern of a boat, secured to a structural member, usually the keel.

scope: Length of anchor line or chain. The ratio of the length of anchor line deployed to the depth of the water, including the distance from the vessel's bow to the water.

seacock: Valve in the ship's hull through which seawater may pass.

sea trial: A short cruise to test the mechanical and handling characteristics of a boat.

seaworthy: Refers to a boat capable of putting to sea and meeting any usual sea conditions.

secrecy of communication: The Federal Communications Act protects the secrecy of radio communications and requires that a person not communicate the contents of any radio message to anyone other than the addressee or the addressee's agent or attorney unless authorized to do so.

Sécurité: Spoken safety signal, repeated three times, used to warn others of hazards to normal waterway use.

seelonce. See silence.

selectivity: A measure of how well a radio receiver rejects signals from other channels close to the channel you are using.

self-tailing winch: A winch that has a notched channel in the top of its drum that holds the line as it feeds off the drum; the notched channel also acts as a cleat to hold the line.

semidiurnal: Having a period or cycle of approximately half a tidal day. The predominating type of tide throughout the world is semidiurnal, with two high waters and two low waters each tidal day. The tidal current is said to be semidiurnal when there are two flood and two ebb periods each day.

sensitivity: The ability of a radio set to pick up distant signals.

72 COLREGS. See *COLREGS 72.*

shackle: A U-shaped connector with a pin or bolt across the open end.

sheet: The line used to control the forward or athwartships movement of a sail.

sheet bend: A bend used to join two ropes of unequal size. Functionally different from a square knot in that it should be used between lines of different diameters.

ship station license: An FCC license required to operate marine VHF radio equipment aboard a vessel.

shock cord: A multistrand rubber line with a synthetic cover and hooks or eyes on each end.

short splice: A method of permanently joining the ends of two ropes.

shortwave radio: Operates in eight frequency bands and can often reach around the globe.

shroud: The standing rigging that supports the mast at the sides of the boat.

signal strength: The power on which a radio transmits; a VHF-FM set must be able to transmit on a power of 1 watt and may have a maximum power of 25 watts.

silence: The word (pronounced "seelonce") used by a vessel in distress or the station in control of distress communications to impose silence on any radio station that interferes. "Silence distress" is a command to maintain radio silence during a Mayday, issued by other vessels in the vicinity of the rescue.

single-braid rope: One braid of rope made by interweaving individual fibers or by weaving three or four strands of fiber. Used for things such as sailbag ties and flag halyards.

single-sideband radio (SSB): A radio that varies in range depending on the time of day, the season, and the frequency of the channel being used. Covers the marine portion of the medium-frequency band and the international marine channels in the high-frequency band.

skiff: A utility boat, flat-bottomed with either straight or slightly flared sides.

slippery sheet bend: A variation of the sheet bend that is easier to untie. Tie it by forming a bight in the end of the smaller line and tucking this bight under the standing part of the smaller line.

spar: A general term for masts, yards, booms, etc.

speed curve: A curve relating the vessel's speed through the water to the engine's throttle setting expressed in revolutions per minute (rpm).

spinnaker: A large, light-weather headsail used for running or reaching.

splice: A method used to tie two pieces of line together or to form a permanent loop, called an eye, at the end of a line.

spoken emergency call: Any of the three spoken emergency signals—distress, urgency, and safety—initiated on Channel 16.

spring line: A fore-and-aft line used in docking and undocking, or to prevent the boat from moving forward or astern while made fast to a dock.

square knot. See *reef knot.*

squelch: A radio control that suppresses background interference.

standing part: That part of a line that is made fast. The main part of a line as distinguished from the "bight" and the "bitter end."

standing rigging: The system of wires, terminals, and fittings that hold a stayed spar upright.

stand-on vessel: The vessel that continues its course in the same direction at the same speed during a crossing or overtaking situation, unless a collision appears imminent. (Formerly called "the privileged vessel.")

starboard: The right side of a boat when looking forward.

stay: That part of the standing rigging supporting the mast from forward and aft.

steerage: The act or practice of steering. A ship's steering mechanism.

steerageway: The lowest speed at wich a vessel can be steered.

stem: The foremost upright timber of a vessel to which the keel and ends of the planks are attached. The forwardmost part of the bow.

stern: The after part of the boat.

stern drive: An engine that is mounted inside a boat, near its stern.

stopper knot: A knot at the end of a line to keep the line from slipping through a hole or a block.

stratus clouds: Air masses that are lifted gently and evenly form clouds that are even, flat, and layered.

swamp: To fill with water, but not settle to the bottom.

swells: Relatively long wind-generated waves that have traveled out of the generating area. They exhibit more regular and longer periods (distances between swells) and flatter crests.

synthetic rope: Rope made from materials such as nylon, polyester, and polypropylene.

tachometer: An instrument that indicates the speed of the engine measured in revolutions per minute (rpm).

tack: To come about. The lower forward corner of a sail. Sailing with the wind on a given side of the boat, as in starboard or port tack.

tacking: Moving the boat's bow through the wind's eye from close-hauled on one tack to close-hauled on the other tack. Same as coming about.

thimble: A grooved metal loop around which a rope or wire rope may be spliced, thus making the spliced eye more chafe resistant.

through-bolt: A bolt that is used to fasten a fitting to the deck. It goes through the deck and backing plate (located belowdeck).

thwart: A seat or brace running laterally across a boat.

tidal current: Horizontal motion of water caused by the vertical rise and fall of the tide.

tide: Periodic vertical rise and fall of the water resulting from the gravitational interactions between the sun, moon, and earth.

tiller: A bar or handle for turning a boat's rudder or an outboard motor.

transceiver: A radio set such as a VHF-FM set that is both a transmitter and a receiver.

transom: The stern cross section of a square-sterned boat.

trawler: A general term to describe a noncommercial vessel with a displacement or semidisplacement hull designed for long-distance cruising. Trawlers often resemble fishing vessels of the same name.

tunnel drive: A variant of a direct-drive engine; the tunnel is a trough in the bottom of the boat, extending forward from the stern.

turn: A bight, or the middle part of a slack line, that is around an object or the rope itself.

turnbuckle: A threaded fitting to pull two eyes together for adjustment of standing rigging.

twin propellers (screws): A boat equipped with two engines and two propellers.

two half hitches: The same as a clove hitch tied around the standing part of a line.

underway: A vessel not at anchor, made fast to a pier or wharf, or aground.

Uniform State Waterway Marking System (USWMS): A unique waterway marking system for state inland waters and rivers that was phased out in 2003 in favor of using the U.S. Aids to Navigation System.

urgency signal. See *Pan-Pan*.

U.S. Aids to Navigation System: The principal buoyage system used in the United States. Conforms to the Region B standards of the International Association of Lighthouse Authorities (IALA). The U.S. ATON System uses buoys, beacons, and minor lights as marks. These mark obstructions, dangers such as wrecks, the edges of navigable channels, and other things of importance to mariners. The U.S. Coast Guard maintains the marks in the system.

USA-International switch: A two-position switch on a VHF-FM radio used to choose channels in the United States and those in foreign countries.

utility outboard: A boat specifically designed for outboard motors.

variation: The angular difference between the magnetic meridian and the geographic meridian at a particular location.

V-drive inboard: An inboard engine that faces aft, with its crankshaft connected to a gearbox. Its propeller shaft connects to the gearbox, and reverses the direction of the propeller shaft to face the stern.

very high frequency (VHF) radio: A radio system with a frequency of 30 MHz to 300 MHz that is essentially a line-of-sight system limited in range to just beyond the horizon.

vessel traffic service (VTS): A shore-based service to control movements of large ships in harbors.

visual distress signal (VDS): A signal to attract attention and to guide rescuers in a search-and-rescue situation.

wake: Disturbed water astern of a moving vessel.

warm front: An advancing edge of a warm air mass.

wave: A periodic disturbance of the sea surface, most often caused by wind.

wave height: The height from the bottom of a wave's trough to the top of its crest, measured in the vertical, not diagonal.

waypoint: A place established on the globe that represents fixes that boaters want to go to or come from.

weather channel: Any of three radio channels in the United States used to give weather forecasts.

weather hitch: A hitch made by making a figure eight and finishing it off with an underhand loop over one of the horns of a cleat.

weaver's knot. See *sheet bend*.

webbing: A flat line formed by weaving together synthetic fibers.

wharf: A man-made structure bounding the edge of a dock and built along or at an angle to the shoreline, used for loading, unloading, or tying up vessels.

whipping: The act of wrapping the end of a piece of rope to prevent it from fraying.

winch: A device to increase hauling power when raising or trimming sails, adjusting tows, or weighing anchor.

windward: Toward the direction from which the wind is coming.

wire rope: A kind of rope used on boats that is nearly always stainless steel, which provides maximum strength and minimum stretch. The standing or permanent rigging on a sailboat is usually wire rope, and running rigging is often wire rope.

working channel: A radio channel used for voice communications.

working end: The end of a rope opposite the bitter end that can be attached to an anchor or a cleat.

yaw: Rotary oscillation about a vessel's vertical axis in a seaway. Sheering off alternately to port and starboard.

Numbers in **bold** indicate pages with illustrations